国际工程管理系列丛书

国际工程合同管理英语写作手册

A GUIDE TO WRITTEN ENGLISH
FOR CONTRACT MANAGEMENT IN INTERNATIONAL CONSTRUCTION PROJECTS

崔军　崔捷思　著

机械工业出版社

本书结合国际工程合同管理的理论与实践，详细论述了与国际工程合同管理有关的英语写作基本原则、英文信函写作以及与国际工程合同管理中的主要事件相关的英文写作问题。本书不仅是一本有关合同的英文写作书，也是一本有关国际工程项目合同管理的书，有助于中国企业提高国际工程项目的合同管理水平，进而维护合法权益。

本书适用于从事国际工程项目管理和合同管理的人员，也适用于从事国际工程的咨询工程师、顾问，同时可供参与国际工程项目争议解决的律师和仲裁员等人员使用。

图书在版编目（CIP）数据

国际工程合同管理英语写作手册/崔军，崔捷思著. —北京：机械工业出版社，2022.4

（国际工程管理系列丛书）

ISBN 978-7-111-72038-6

Ⅰ.①国⋯ Ⅱ.①崔⋯②崔⋯ Ⅲ.①英语—国际承包工程—经济合同—管理—写作—中国—手册 Ⅳ.①F752.68 – 62

中国版本图书馆 CIP 数据核字（2022）第 215870 号

机械工业出版社（北京市百万庄大街 22 号　邮政编码 100037）
策划编辑：闫云霞　　责任编辑：闫云霞　刘　晨
责任校对：吴海宁　陈　越　刘雅娜
封面设计：鞠　杨　责任印制：刘　媛
盛通（廊坊）出版物印刷有限公司印刷
2023 年 1 月第 1 版第 1 次印刷
184mm×260mm・26 印张・2 插页・640 千字
标准书号：ISBN 978-7-111-72038-6
定价：128.00 元

电话服务　　　　　　　　网络服务
客服电话：010-88361066　　机　工　官　网：www.cmpbook.com
　　　　　010-88379833　　机　工　官　博：weibo.com/cmp1952
　　　　　010-68326294　　金　书　网：www.golden-book.com
封底无防伪标均为盗版　　　机工教育服务网：www.cmpedu.com

作者简介

崔军,北京大学法学学士、北京大学法学硕士、中国国际经济贸易仲裁委员会仲裁员、中国海事仲裁委员会仲裁员、北京仲裁委员会仲裁员、英国特许土木工程测量师学会资深会员。

自1989年起长期在国外从事国际工程承包项目工作,先后在中东、非洲、亚洲、欧洲工作21年。在国外工作期间,主要从事项目索赔、合同管理、驻在国公司的管理和运营、国际BOT/PPP项目开发、出口信贷项目运作等工作,熟谙国际工程承包市场的历史、现状及其运作模式,具有大型工程项目运作和全面管理经验,善于国际工程项目争议解决、国内建设工程仲裁和国际工程仲裁。

主要工作领域:国际工程项目合同起草和谈判、国际工程索赔、BOT/PPP项目、国际工程争议和纠纷解决、国内建设工程和国际工程仲裁。

主要著作:

专著:《FIDIC合同原理与实务》《FIDIC分包合同原理与实务》《国际工程承包市场开发实务》《FIDIC分包合同原理与实务》(第二版)

译著:《FIDIC用户指南:1999年版红皮书和黄皮书实用指南》《施工合同索赔》《工期索赔》

合著:《国际工程承包总论》(第二版)、《国际工程承包实用手册》《中国工程承包企业海外经营风险与实务应对》、*Legal Risks and Opportunities Facing Chinese Engineering Contractors Operating Overseas*

主编:《国际工程总承包项目管理导则》《国际工程总承包项目合同管理导则》

主要论文和文章:

发表论文和文章100多篇,主要涉及中国对外承包工程企业发展模式、国际工程项目融资、FIDIC分包合同、FIDIC合同、国际工程项目索赔、工期索赔、BOT/PPP项目融资等多个领域。

崔捷思,澳大利亚悉尼大学商学院金融学硕士。

前　言

　　本书的写作目的不是为读者提供一个能提高英语水平和进行语法学习的工具，而是让读者运用已经学习和掌握的英语知识和技能来进行国际工程合同管理，写出更好的与国际工程合同管理相关的英文信函和报告，提高从事国际工程合同管理人员的英文写作水平，并根据合同的约定和适用法律，更加清晰地表述自己的观点，据理力争，维护自身的合法权益。

　　在国际工程实践中，特别是在承包商与业主和工程师发生争议时，中国承包商如何运用英语语言能力表达自己的主张和抗辩，在争议早期阶段确定承包商的权利和应得的利益，从而避免最终走向仲裁或诉讼，是考验承包商合同管理和法律管理能力和水平的试金石。更为重要的是，承包商在日常合同管理过程中，通过往来信函、会议纪要、补充协议、变更文件等记录工程中发生的事件或情况，请牢记英国著名学者马克斯·W. 亚伯拉罕森在《工程法和 ICE 合同》一书中指出的"争议的一方当事人，特别是将争议诉诸仲裁时，应汲取下述三个教训（通常为时已晚）：第一是记录的重要性，第二是记录的重要性，第三还是记录的重要性"。记录能够为之后国际工程争议委员会解决争议，或者通过国际仲裁或诉讼最终解决工程施工过程中的争议提供可供采信的证据，为律师和专家顾问介入国际仲裁或诉讼奠定牢固的基础。

　　对于中国承包商而言，运用英语在国际工程合同管理中进行通信交流，是一名合格的国际工程项目管理人员应掌握的一项必不可少的能力。特别是汉语与英语存在巨大的差异，国际工程项目管理人员必须在工程管理过程中逐步掌握交流语言，通过日常的英语学习，熟练运用英语进行口语和文字交流，是提高英语水平的必经之路。而且，英语学习是一个长期的过程，不可畏难，不可半途而废，在工作中学习，在学习中工作，假以时日，必有所成。

　　本书共 15 章，其中第 1~5 章论述了写作基本原则、写作构思、造句和用词选择、写作表述方式、英文信函写作、国际工程项目常用文件格式等内容，帮助读者在国际工程合同管理过程中建立英语写作的思维模式，构建使用英语的基本要求，同时，提出了对英文信函写作、会议纪要等日常英语文书的写作提高有益的建议。第 6~12 章重点阐述了国际工程合同管理过程中常见的事件、问题或争议，包括国际工程合同的拟定、合同条款的编制和写作、其他主要合同文件的编制、工程变更、不可抗力、暂停工程和终止合同以及国际工程索赔报告的编制。通过论述国际工程中遇到问题的合同原理和法律原理，不仅为读者建立了国际工程合同管理的原理和理念，还为读者提供了英语写作的范例。读者可通过学习这些范例，提高英语写作水平，更好地主张承包商的权利，维护承包商的合法利益。第 13 章法律选择和适用，第 14 章争议委员会和第 15 章国际仲裁论述了国际工程争议解决中遇到的法律适用的实体问题，以及如何通过争议委员会或最终通过国际仲裁解决争议。

  在本书的写作过程中，英国其礼律师事务所（Clyde & Co.）Maurice Kenton 先生依靠他多年的法律从业经验和深厚的法律英语文字功底，为本书中的英文内容提供了范例，并对英语语法和用词进行了修正和补充，使得本书中的英语更加准确和生动。

  在本书的写作过程中，作者还得到了机械工业出版社闫云霞编辑及其他编辑的大力帮助，在此一并表示感谢。

2020 年 8 月 23 日于北京

目 录

作者简介
前言
缩略语表

第1章 写作基本原则 ………………… 1
1.1 使用简明英语 ………………… 1
1.2 弄清事实 ……………………… 6
1.3 明确合同约定 ………………… 10
1.4 确定核心争议 ………………… 12
1.5 记录的重要性 ………………… 13
1.6 记录的及时性和充分性 ……… 14
1.7 记录形式及效力 ……………… 17

第2章 写作构思、造句与用词选择
2.1 写作构思 ……………………… 23
2.2 写作造句 ……………………… 34
2.3 用词选择 ……………………… 40

第3章 写作表述方式 ………………… 59
3.1 国际工程合同管理往来信函分析 … 59
3.2 信函写作基本原则 …………… 61
3.3 英文信函写作结构 …………… 67
3.4 英文信函写作的其他表述方式 … 80
3.5 英文信函写作应注意的问题 … 84

第4章 写作常用格式 ………………… 90
4.1 国际工程项目常用文件 ……… 90
4.2 国际工程项目常用文件格式 … 92
4.3 其他常用文件格式 …………… 122

第5章 常用英文通知函写作 ………… 131
5.1 英文通知函 …………………… 131
5.2 国际工程常用英文通知函 …… 133

第6章 国际工程合同拟定 …………… 150
6.1 国际工程合同构成 …………… 150
6.2 国际工程合同中的优先次序 … 152
6.3 《合同协议书》文本格式 …… 155
6.4 《中标函》文本格式 ………… 160
6.5 专用合同条款文本 …………… 162
6.6 国际工程合同完备文件要求 … 169

第7章 合同条款编制和写作 ………… 171
7.1 国际工程合同核心条款及编制 … 171
7.2 国际工程合同主要条款及编制 ………………… 193

第8章 其他主要合同文件编制 ……… 223
8.1 谅解备忘录 …………………… 223
8.2 意向书 ………………………… 229
8.3 联合体协议 …………………… 237
8.4 保障和保证协议 ……………… 241
8.5 保密协议 ……………………… 250

第9章 工程变更 ……………………… 258
9.1 变更定义 ……………………… 258
9.2 变更的司法验证标准 ………… 264
9.3 变更估价原则和公平估价 …… 264

第10章 不可抗力 …………………… 277
10.1 不可抗力定义 ……………… 277
10.2 普通法系和大陆法系中的不可抗力 ………………… 280
10.3 不可抗力条款 ……………… 282

10.4 不可抗力通知 …………………… 290
10.5 FIDIC 合同条款中不可抗力索赔 … 295
10.6 新冠肺炎疫情不可抗力索赔 …… 303

第 11 章 暂停和终止合同 …………… 309
11.1 暂停施工 ……………………… 309
11.2 整改通知 ……………………… 316
11.3 业主终止合同 ………………… 317
11.4 承包商终止合同 ……………… 320

第 12 章 工程索赔报告编制 ………… 328
12.1 索赔通知及索赔时效 ………… 328
12.2 递交索赔报告的信函 ………… 332
12.3 索赔报告的编制 ……………… 334

第 13 章 法律选择和适用 …………… 357
13.1 法律冲突 ……………………… 357
13.2 所有权的法律冲突和物之所在地法原则 …………………… 357
13.3 合同的法律选择和适用 ……… 358
13.4 国际工程合同的法律选择和适用 …………………………… 359
13.5 工程所在地法律对工程合同的影响 ………………………… 359

第 14 章 争议委员会 ………………… 361
14.1 争议委员会成员任命和成立 … 361
14.2 递交争议委员会作出决定通知 … 365
14.3 递交争议委员会作出决定申请书 ………………………… 368
14.4 争议委员会管辖权 …………… 373
14.5 争议裁决申请书的答辩 ……… 376
14.6 争议委员会听证会 …………… 376
14.7 争议委员会决定和不满通知 … 377
14.8 充分利用争议委员会机制解决争议 ………………………… 379

第 15 章 国际仲裁 …………………… 383
15.1 仲裁条款和仲裁协议 ………… 383
15.2 使用 FIDIC 合同条款时常见的仲裁条款问题 ……………… 389
15.3 仲裁机构 ……………………… 394
15.4 仲裁规则 ……………………… 394
15.5 仲裁程序 ……………………… 395

参考文献 ……………………………… 404

缩略语表

BOQ	Bill of Quantity/工程量表
BOT	Built-Operation-Transfer/建造-运营-移交
CIETAC	China International Economic and Trade Arbitration Commission/中国国际经济贸易仲裁委员会
CPM	Critical Path Method/关键线路法
DAAB	Dispute Avoidence/Adjudication Board/争议避免与裁决委员会
DAB	Dispute Adjudication Board/争议裁决委员会
DB	Dispute Board/争议委员会
DNP	Defects Notification Period/缺陷通知期
EOT	Extension of Time/工期延长
EPC	Engineering-Procurement-Construction/设计-采购-施工
FIDIC	Fédération Internationale des Ingénieurs Conseils,法文缩写 FIDIC/国际咨询工程师联合会
FPC	Final Payment Certificate/最终付款证书
HSE	Health,Safety and Environment/健康、安全和环境管理体系
ICC	International Chamber of Commerce/国际商会
ICE	Institute of Civil Engineers/英国土木工程师学会
IPC	Interim Payment Certificate/期中付款证书
JV	Joint Venture/联营体
LCIA	London Court of International Arbitration/伦敦国际仲裁院
NEC	New Engineering Contract/新工程合同条件(英国土木工程学会编制)
NOD	Notice of Dissatisfaction/不满通知

PFI	Private Finance Initiative/私营主动融资,民间主动融资
PPP	Public Private Partnership/公共私营合作,政府和社会资本合作,政企合作
SCL	Society of Construction Law/英国建筑法学会
SIAC	Singapore International Arbitration Centre/新加坡国际仲裁中心
TCC	Technology and Construction Court/英国科技和建筑法庭
TOC	Taking-Over Certificate/接收证书
UNCITRAL	United Nations Commission on International Trade Law/联合国国际贸易法委员会

第1章 写作基本原则

> Brevity is the soul of wit.
>
> 莎士比亚:《哈姆雷特》(*Hamlet 2.2*)

1.1 使用简明英语

1.1.1 法律文件中使用简明英语的趋势

使用简明英语(writing in plain English)是合同和法律英语写作的第一基本原则。无论是合同文件、法律文书写作,还是国际工程合同管理文件,避免使用繁琐的英语写作,是每一位从事英文写作人士应该牢记的要义。

在美国 Chase 诉 Kalber,153 P. 397, 398 (Cal. Ct. App. 1915) 案中,法官在判决中写道:

"And, in the outset, we may as well be frank enough to confess, and, indeed, in view of the seriousness of the consequences which upon fuller reflection we find would inevitably result to municipalities in the matter of street improvements from the conclusion reached and announced in the former opinion, we are pleased to declare that the arguments upon rehearing have convinced us that the decision upon the ultimate question involved here formerly rendered by this court, even if not faulty in its reasoning from the premises announced or wholly erroneous in conclusions as to some of the questions incidentally arising and necessarily legitimate subjects of discussion in the decision of the main proposition, is, at any rate, one which may, under the peculiar circumstances of this case, the more justly and at the same time, upon reasons of equal cogency, be superseded by a conclusion whose effect cannot be to disturb the integrity of the long and well-established system for the improvement of streets in the incorporated cities and towns of California not governed by freeholders' charters. "⊖

译文:并且,我们最初可能也有足够的理由承认的是,实际上,鉴于我们发现的后果的严重性,其可能不可避免地导致市政府在街道改造问题上仍然坚持已得出的结论和先前主张的观点,因此,我们在此高兴地宣布,根据当事人在再次庭审上所主张的理由,使我们信服的是,即使法院判决的主要部分对某些涉及的问题和论证的法律内容所给出的理由是正确

⊖ 153 P. 397,28 Cal. App. 561, at 563 (https://www.courtlistener.com/opinion/3289666/chase-v-kalber/).

的，但无论如何，根据本案的特殊情况，法院对本案所涉及的重大问题作出的判决更为公正，同时，鉴于当事人所述理由具有很强的说服力，在不影响加州城镇街道改造过程中长期形成的整个制度以及不动产所有权宪章的情况下，先前法院的判决应被推翻。

本案是1915年美国法院的判决书，使用了超长的语句表达了一个非常简单的结论，即"We made a mistake last time"。在本案判决书中，法官还使用了许多超长句式，例如：

"The petition alleges that, within thirty days after the final passage of said resolution, and within the time allowed by law, a petition protesting against the passage of said resolution and petitioning for a referendum election thereon, signed by qualified voters of the said town of Rio Vista equal in number to more than ten per cent (to wit: forty-four per cent) of the entire vote cast for all candidates for governor of the state at the last preceding general municipal election held in said town of Rio Vista, and duly verified as prescribed by an act of the legislature entitled 'An act to Provide for direct Legislation by Cities and Towns, including Initiative and Referendum,' approved January 2, 1912 (Stats. (Ex. Sess.) 1911, p. 131), was filed with and presented to the said respondent, as clerk, etc., with the demand upon him that he proceeds within the time required by said law to examine the signatures to said petition and certify as to the sufficiency of said signatures."[注]

如此超长的语句在现代判决书中已经很少见。在某国法院推迟庭审的决定书中，法官裁定如下：

ORDER

"Let the leave petition be posted for hearing in list on 31st October, 2016 and stay, as prayed for, is granted till that date."

法律语言，包括法律英语，是在立法和司法等活动中形成的，具有鲜明法律特征的语言，历来以语句冗长、法律术语繁多、晦涩难懂、大量使用被动句和倒装句、法律措辞堆积为非法律人士所诟病。为顺应现代社会的发展，法律英语正经历由法律措辞（legalese）向简明英语发展，特别是美国提倡法律语言简明化，使得法律英语由"法言律语"变成使用简明英语。英国法院的判决也正在使用简明英语写作判决书，例如英国技术和建筑法院（Technology and Construction Court, TCC）。但在一些原来的英联邦国家，例如印度、孟加拉国等国家，仍在法院判决书等法律文件中使用传统的法律英语。

在Obrascon Huarte Lain SA v Her Majesty's Attorney General For Gibraltar [2014] EWHC 1028 (TCC) 案中，Akenhead法官在判决中写道：

"377 I will not set out each of the issues listed by the parties (for which see Paragraph 24 above) but I will list my answer below:

[注] 153 P. 397, 28 Cal. App. 561, at 564-565 (https://www.courtlistener.com/opinion/3289666/chase-v-kalber/).

1. GOG, the Defendant, lawfully terminated the Contract by notice dated 28 July 2011, alternatively by notice dated 4 August 2011, with the termination occurring 14 days later.

1(a)(i). The Engineer was entitled to issue the Clause 15.1 Notice to Correct on 16 May 2011 in relation to Clause 8 breaches relating to (i) suspending tunnel excavation work on 20 December 2010, (ii) suspending cutting and repairing outer diaphragm walls on 21 January 2011, (iii) failing to start underwater trenching and ducting work for the Western SALS, (iv) failing to provide acceptable details of method which OHL proposed to adopt for tunnel excavation work and (v) failing to proceed with dewatering with due expedition. …"

从摘录的文字可以看出,上述判决书使用了简明英语格式和语言,而未在每一段文字开头使用"THAT"作为开头用语,且使用的语言简明清晰、表达准确,堪称与FIDIC合同1999年第1版《生产设备和设计-施工合同条件》有关的英国技术和建筑法院判决的典型判例。

例如,在国际商会国际仲裁院(International Court of Arbitration, International Chamber of Commence)仲裁的某国际工程分包合同仲裁案中,申请人在仲裁申请书(Request for Arbitration)写道:

"2 That, as per clause 4.4 of the said contract the respondent entered into a subcontract agreement with the claimant dated 31 October 2011 for the execution of the civil construction works of the KWS Project, contract No. KWSP-C-1 as detailed in the subcontract agreement signed on 1 November 2011.

3 That, the claimant was supposed to commence the work as soon as the respondent handed over the possession and the respondent was supposed to hand over the possession free from all encumbrance to the claimant but the respondent failed to deliver possession of the work site to the claimant on time; that, this stalemate condition deferred and caused delay in starting of the subcontract works by up to 5 months; that, the claimant raised this issue by a numbers of letters and e-mails but the respondent maintained meaningful silence."

法律语言有其自身发展规律,法律文本必须严谨,且法律术语的正确使用是法律严肃性和准确性的保证,因此,法律术语不能简化。但是,法律英语中的一些古英语词汇和外来语词汇可以用普通英语单词替代,且可以简化,例如 interalia,可以用 among otherthings 等词语替代。

1.1.2 合同格式中使用简明英语的趋势

在现代合同格式中,例如在国际工程业界广为使用的国际咨询工程师联合会编制的

FIDIC 合同格式，随着时代的进步，在合同条款中逐渐使用更为简明的英语，以便为广大母语非英语的用户，包括政府、业主和外国承包商使用。例如，FIDIC 合同 1987 年第 4 版《土木工程施工合同条件》第 67.1 款 [工程师决定] 规定：

"If a dispute of any kind whatsoever arises between the Employer and the Contractor in connection with, or arising out of, the Contract or the execution of the Works, whether during the execution of the Works or after their completion and whether before or after repudiation or other termination of the Contract, including any dispute as to any opinion, instruction, determination, certificate or valuation of the Engineer, the matter in dispute shall, in the first place, be referred in writing to the Engineer, with a copy to the other party. Such reference shall state that it is made pursuant to this Clause. No later than the eighty-fourth day after the day on which he received such reference the Engineer shall give notice of his decision to the Employer and the Contractor. Such decision shall state that it is made pursuant to this Clause."

对于同样的将争议递交争议裁决委员会（Dispute Adjudication Board，DAB）作出决定，而非递交给工程师作出决定的安排，FIDIC 合同条款 1999 年第 1 版《施工合同条件》第 20.4 款 [取得争议裁决委员会的决定] 规定如下：

"If a dispute (of any kind whatsoever) arises between the Parties in connection with, of arising out of, the Contract or the execution of the Works, including any dispute as to any certificate, determination, instruction, opinion or valuation of the Engineer, then after a DAB has been appointed pursuant to Sub-Clause 20.2 [*Appointment of the DAB*] and 20.3 [*Failure to Agree DAB*] either Party may refer the dispute in writing to the DAB for its decision, with copies to the other Party and the Engineer. Such reference shall state that it is given under this Sub-Clause."

FIDIC 合同条款 1987 年第 4 版《土木工程施工合同条件》第 67.1 款 [工程师决定] 使用了 143 个单词，但在 1999 年第 1 版 FIDIC《施工合同条件》第 20.4 款 [取得争议裁决委员会的决定] 中仅使用了 96 个单词。总体而言，对比 1987 年第 4 版和 1999 年版 FIDIC 合同，不难发现，1999 年第 1 版合同使用了更为简明的合同语言，使得 1999 年第 1 版 FIDIC 合同更为容易地在所有母语非英语的国家或地区推广和使用。

但是，对一个合同条款而言，表述文字的多少和繁复可能给读者产生不同的印象、观点和看法。以承包商责任限额条款为例，FIDIC 合同 1999 年第 1 版《施工合同条件》第 17.6 款 [责任限制] 规定：

"Neither Party shall be liable to theother Party for loss of use of any Works, loss of profit, loss of any contract or for any indirect or consequential loss or damage which may be suffered by the other Party in connection with the Contract, other than under Sub-

Clause 16.4 [*Payment on Termination*] and Sub-Clause 17.1 [*Indemnities*].

The total liability of the Contractor to the Employer, under or in connection with the Contract other than under Sub-Clause 4.19 [*Electricity, Water and Gas*], Sub-Clause 4.20 [*Employer's Equipment and Free-Issue Material*], Sub-Clause 17.1 [*Indemnities*] and Sub-Clause 17.5 [*intellectual and Industrial Property Rights*], shall not exceed the sum stated in the Particular Conditions or (if a sum is not so stated) the Contract Price stated in the Contract Agreement.

This Sub-Clause shall not limit liability in any case of fraud, deliberate default or reckless misconduct by the defaulting Party."

在作者谈判的某国大型工程 EPC 合同中,有关承包商责任限制的条款规定如下:

"9.1 <u>Total Liability Cap</u>. Contractor's total liability to Owner arising under this Contract (individually or in the aggregate, and whether arising before or after termination of this Contract), shall be limited to an amount equal to the Contract Price; provided that such total liability limit shall be exclusive of:

(a) Contractor's obligation to complete the Work;

(b) Contractor's obligations to correct any Defects in the Work;

(c) Contractor's obligations under Section 6.6.3 hereof;

(d) Contractor's obligations under Section 7 hereof;

(e) Contractor's obligations under Section 10 hereof;

(f) Contractor's obligations under Section 11.1 hereof;

(g) Contractor's obligations under Section 11.2.1 hereof;

(h) Contractor's obligations under Section 11.2.5 hereof;

(i) Contractor's obligations under Section 20 hereof;

(j) Contractor's obligations under Section 21 hereof;

(k) Liability arising out of Contractor's Willful Misconduct; and

(l) Any insurance proceeds received by Contractor in respect of Contractor's Insurance.

9.2 <u>Application of Limitations</u>. The releases, limitations of liability, limitations of remedy and benefits of the indemnities expressed in this Contract shall apply regardless of whether the Claim, liability, remedy or subject of indemnity arises out of contract, tort (including negligence) or strict liability, and shall extend to the Affiliates, shareholders, members, partners, other owners thereof, directors, officers, personnel and agents of the relevant Party to the benefit of which such provisions operate, and in the case of Owner, to all Owner Insured Persons. Notwithstanding the foregoing, the releases, limitations of liability, limitations of remedy and benefits of the indemnities expressed in this Contract shall not apply to matters unrelated to this Contract or outside the Scope of Work to be performed hereunder, or to other agreements between or among the Parties or any agreements between or among any of the companies that comprise them or the Affiliates, entities, shareholders, members, partners, other owners thereof, directors, officers, personnel or agents of any of them."

对比 FIDIC 合同条款 1999 年第 1 版《施工合同条件》第 17.6 款［责任限度］和业主聘请的律师编制的 EPC 合同条款第 9.1 款和第 9.2 款，在承包商均承担合同总额的责任限额情况下（除非另有规定），两者存在不同的规定。

第一，除外范围不同。FIDIC 合同条款 1999 年第 1 版第 17.6 款［责任限度］将第 4.19 款［电、水和燃气］、第 4.20 款［雇主设备和免费供应的材料］、第 17.1 款［保障］和第 17.5 款［知识产权和工业产权］除外。上述 EPC 合同将第（a）至（i）项除外。

第二，FIDIC 合同条款 1999 年第 1 版第 17.6 款［责任限度］将承包商的欺诈、故意违约和轻率的不当行为作为例外，即，如果承包商存在欺诈、故意违约和轻率的不当行为时，合同规定的合同总额责任限度将不再适用。而上述 EPC 合同中侵权（包括疏忽）、严格责任等违约行为可以追溯至下属公司、股东、成员、合伙人、董事、职员或承包商代理等，但与合同和工程范围无关的协议，以及下属公司、股东、成员、合伙人、董事、职员、承包商代理签署的其他合同不予适用。

第三，从上述内容可以看出，合同违约时一方当事人可以追溯的主体存在区别。FIDIC 合同条款 1999 年第 1 版《施工合同条件》第 17.6 款［责任限度］没有约定可以向下属公司、股东、成员、合伙人、董事、职员或承包商代理行使追索权，但上述 EPC 合同第 9.2 款规定可向下属公司、股东、成员、合伙人、董事、职员或承包商代理行使追索权。

因此，当遇到不同的合同条款时，读者应仔细分析每一项合同条款的表述和含义，分析是否可以接受合同条款的约定。需要指出的是，不同的合同格式、不同主体编制的合同格式存在不同的考虑，有利有弊。在可谈判的情况下，应据理力争，不应接受那些无法接受的合同条款，应维护自身权益和利益。

1.2 弄清事实

在国际工程项目合同管理中，特别是在争议委员会（Dispute Board）、仲裁和诉讼等争议解决过程中，事实的重要性不言而喻。但这些事实，特别是引起业主和承包商争议的事实，是在国际工程项目日常合同管理过程中发生的，并以往来信函、会议纪要、备忘录、施工日志或协议等方式记录下来予以保存的，在发生争议时当作证据予以出示，证明事实真相并支持各方主张和诉求。在绝大多数情况下，这些事实都是以追溯的方式经事后查明，而在仲裁和诉讼中，还将进行质证，并辅以证人作证，验证曾经发生事实的真伪。因此，这些事实如何以文字的方式予以记录，记录是否准确无误，无疑非常重要。

以 Obrascon Huarte Lain Sa v Her Majesty's Attorney General For Gibraltar ［2014］ EWHC 1028（TCC）案为例，法官以大事记（chronology）为主线叙述了本案事实的发生及其过程，包括工程范围、项目开工、施工期间遇到的地质条件的问题、业主和承包商之间的争议发生以及最终终止合同等事实，摘录部分内容如下：

"Chronology

33. The main area of work which features most in this litigation is the tunnel. Broadly the work to be done involved the following:

(a) The lengths of the new road approaching the tunnel are from the west and curved north and south down ramped sections into the tunnel area; the entrances to the tunnel itself were known as the North and South Portals. Each part of the tunnelled section comprised north and south dual carriageway, divided by a full length wall.

(b) The walls both on the east and west sides as well as the dividing wall were known as "embedded" or "diaphragm", which, put simply were reinforced concrete walls constructed before the rest of the tunnel was constructed. These walls were created first by constructing "guide walls" of limited depth (to define the bentonite slurry trenches and guide the excavation), and secondly by excavating with a large clam shell excavator to a considerable depth and supporting the sides of excavation with impervious bentonite slurry, which has the effect of counterbalancing the (often) hydraulic pressures on the sides of the excavations. Bentonite can also resist groundwater pressures at least up to a certain point. This work is often done (as on this project) in panels some metres long.

(c) Reinforcement cages are then lowered into the excavations and concrete pumped in. Thus the concrete is, so to speak, cast against the excavated earth. The bentonite is displaced out of the excavation and returned to holding tanks.

(d) At some stage after the concrete has cured and set, there are essentially three possible ways of proceeding. The first, initially adopted by OHL here, was to cut down the embedded walls to the height at which the tunnel roof would be located, and then cast the reinforced onto the tops of the three embedded walls (east, west and central) onto a prepared surface on top of the earth remaining in between; thereafter, the earth will be excavated from underneath which will expose the underside of the roof and one side of the east and west and both sides of the central embedded walls. The second is a variant on the first and was adopted in its revised design proposal in the months before termination of the Contract involving the same use of embedded walls but before casting the roof some metres depth of earth would be excavated from the area below. The third way would also involve embedded walls but excavation of the whole of the earth down to road formation level at the bottom of the tunnel would take place before the roof was cast. Whichever method was used, the road base would need to be constructed with drainage.

(e) Provision for drainage would require "attenuation tanks" to which rain or other water would be drained from the road surface within the tunnel; they would be located below the road surface level and outside the line of the outer embedded walls. There would be pumping arrangements so that the collected water could be taken away.

(f) Additionally, arrangements were and would have to be taken to guard against the impacts of exceptional marine impacts such as serious storms and tidal surges which might result in seawater surging into the tunnel. Accordingly, flood walls were constructed above the roof level in places to prevent the entry of such water into the tunnel.

34. The Commencement Date was 1 December 2008. On 4 December 2008 the Development Planning Commission of Gibraltar issued its Environmental Impact Assessment Certificate which contained a schedule of conditions:

"(1) The proposed development will incorporate the mitigation measures proposed in the [ES] namely...

(c) Agree a method statement with the Environmental Agency for the handling, classification and disposal of any contaminated materials and to secure and adhere to the conditions of relevantlicences for their disposal;

(d) Ensure the preparation, submission and adherence to a Construction and Environmental Management Plant ("CEMP") which shall be agreed with the Environment Agency and the Department of the Environment prior to the commencement of work on site;

(e) Ensuring themaximum possible re-use of demolition material and other materials arising from this project so as to ensure minimal offsite disposal".

35. There was a "start-up" meeting on 18 December 2008 attended by GLRC, Gifford and OHL. The meeting covered a large number of mostly administrative and planning topics but the following wasminuted:

"2.3 OHL confirmed that the CEMP is due to be issued on 15-02-09."

"2.7 OHL...consider the Geotechnical report made available by the Employer to be of a very good quality. However as part of its QA they would like to carry out a further 3 boreholes along the line of the proposed tunnel and will prepare the geotechnical report following that additional site investigation".

36. At the next meeting on 21 January 2009, the Health and Safety Plan was promised by OHL for early February 2009 and the minutes record on the second page against a heading "Disposal of material":

"OHL would like to dispose of excavated material in Gibraltar but were informed that there is currently no tip currently open. It was agreed that further discussion with the Chief Technical Officer would be beneficial in order to explore alternatives."

37. On 16 February 2009, OHL submitted its first draft CEMP "Construction Environmental Management Plan" ("CEMP") which was introduced as providing "the necessary management framework for the planning and implementation of engineering and construction activities in accordance with environmental commitments identified within Gibraltar's environmental legislation". It listed various laws which were to be considered, including various Landfill Acts and the Environmental (Waste) Regulations 2007 specifically in relation to land contamination and wastes. It described the tunnel work in some detail, going on in Paragraph 6 to provide for a "Monitoring Plan" to check "the effectiveness of the proposed mitigation measures":

...

41. In June 2009 OHL produced its Health and Safety Plan which amongst other

things identified that forced air ventilation was to be installed for the tunnel excavation and construction. There was little if any specific attention given in this document to the risk of contaminated land being encountered.

42. OHL, sensibly, did not defer starting work on the detailed design of the tunnel (being the most complex part of the design) until the Approval in Principle of the tunnel design. However, OHL fell well behind with this. Approval of the detailed design was programmed for 3 June 2009 but OHL did not begin detailed design work on the tunnel until 15 July 2009, only submitting the first revision of the detailed design to the Engineer on 30 September 2009; this was rejected on 23 October 2009; for instance the design at this stage did not include details of the deep drainage or cladding. In fact, the detailed design of the tunnel and construction drawings (albeit without deep drainage to the North and South tunnel portals and cladding) was not approved until March and May 2010 respectively.

43. Physical work started on site on about 1 October 2009 with some service diversions relating to the fuel farm (for the airport), which involved limited excavation. The trench arisings were reported as being removed to a tip (see Site Diary 19 October 2009).

44. On 6 October 2009, OHL submitted a method statement for the "Open Excavation of the Tunnel (Pre-Excavation)". The proposed work involved the excavation of theexisting runway pavement in the area under which the tunnel was to run and in the approaches to the tunnel and the removal of soil and other material down to a depth of 2 metres. This was scheduled to take 7 weeks. This was not accepted by the Engineer on many grounds listed in a Review Record dated 15 October 2009, amongst which were:

(a) Investigation for ground contaminants was not identified and no clear action was proposed in respect thereof.

(b) Topsoil storage and method of removing soil were not identified and no clear action was proposed in respect thereof.

(c) Questions were raised as to whether the excavated material was intended for re-use and where it would be stored.

It is clear that, although no plans or arrangements had been made by OHL for the disposal of the excavated materials, OHL was planning or at least hoping that the "disposal location" would be somewhere in Gibraltar, as Mr. Doncel wrote in an e-mail dated 12 October 2009 to a Mr. Dunn (engaged by OHL).

45. OHL had not really considered or made arrangements for the disposal of materials until mid-October 2009. Although the EIA certificate referred to "Ensuring themaximum possible re-use of demolition material and other materials arising from this project so as to ensure minimal offsite disposal", the reality was that there was limited availability to re-use the excavated demolition material and soils on the road and tunnel site. There was a need for the tunnel roof eventually to be covered with excavated soil but that would involve only a few thousand cubic metres. However, it was known that there was limited use for any-

thing other than clean sand in Gibraltar, there were limited places to dump materials and there was no place for the deposition of contaminated materials.
..."

在本案中，法官通过大事记的方式，系统地总结性地回顾和概括了本案的基本事实，特别是承包商与业主有争议的地质条件问题，这种回顾和概括性的总结，特别适用于承包商的工期和额外费用索赔报告、提交争议委员会的申请书、仲裁申请书、起诉状以及仲裁裁决书或诉讼判决。

在国际工程项目合同管理过程中，弄清事实，将事实以文字叙述的方式描述清楚和准确，是对业主、工程师和承包商的最基本的要求。只有这样，才能清晰地记录真实发生的情况和事件，为今后的索赔和争议解决打下良好的基础。

1.3 明确合同约定

在国际工程项目合同管理过程中，弄清合同约定的内容是决定某个事件或争议的核心。承包商和业主往往就合同的某一个单词的解释发生争议，或者就合同约定的解释出现歧义，从而产生合同争议，可能需要通过争议委员会或最终通过仲裁或诉讼予以解决。

在下面的案例中，工程师和承包商就变更令中的一个单词"including"发生争议，工程师认为"including"可以理解为"including, but not restricted to"，而承包商认为"including"仅能理解为"including"，不能扩大理解为"but not restricted to"。该项争议涉及了变更令中的单价争议，承包商认为工程师后续的评估和调整价格的范围仅限于"including production, number of personnel and support personnel required"，不能包括该项变更工程涉及的设备和材料，而工程师认为不限于"including production, number of personnel and support personnel required"，还包括变更工程涉及的设备和材料。为此，承包商在根据 FIDIC 合同 1987 年第 4 版第 67.1 款提交工程师作出决定的申请书中写道：

"36. It is worthy to recall that Clause V22-4, Appendix 9 to VO-2 R2 provides a mechanism to adjust TBM Mining Rate in the following terms：

The TBM Mining rates are provisional and will be re-evaluated after one (1) kilometer of TBM Mining by M/sHerrenkencht and TBM Mining for the second kilometer of TBM Mining by the Contractor for both tunnels including production, number of personnel for TBM manning and support personnel required. Any adjustment to the rates will be applied retroactively."

...

38. The overall disputes relating to Clause V22-4, Appendix 9 to VO-2 R2 between the Engineer and the Contractor are focused on the following：

■ The wording："including production, number of personnel for TBM manning and support personnel required."

...

41. *Keating on Construction Contracts*, a recognized and authoritative legal book in common law systems, addresses the doctrines for construction of contracts, in which the law is summarized thus:

"1. *Expressed Intention*
In construing a contract the court applied the rule of law that: ' while it seeks to give effect to the intention of the parties, [it] must give effect to that intention as expressed, that is, it must ascertain the meaning of the words actually used'. For the purpose of construction 'intention' does not mean motive, purpose, desire or a state of mind but intention as expressed, and the common law adopts an objective standard of construction excluding general evidence of actual intention of the parties.
...
If the rule were otherwise,' all certainty would be taken from the words in which the parties have recorded their agreement'.

(a) *Extrinsic Evidence-not normally admissible*
It follows from the principle just stated that, for a written contract, no evidence outside the document itself, i. e. extrinsic evidence, may normally be adduced to contradict, vary, add to or subtract from the written terms.⊖"
...

44. To judge the true meaning of the word "including" being a term of art under the law, *Black Law Dictionary* provides the legal definition of the word "including", quoting unamended as under:

" INCLUDE. (Lat. inclaudere, to shut in, keep within). To confine within, hold as in an inclosure, take in, attain, sut up, contain, inclose, comprise, comprehend, embrace, involve. Including may, according to context, express an enlargement and have the meaning of and or in in addition to, or merely specify a particular thing already included within general words theretofore used. Miller v. Johnston, 173 N. C. 62, 91 S. E. 593. Prairie Oil and Gas Co. v. Motter, D. C. Kan. , 1 F. Supp. 464, 468; Decorated Metal Mfg. Co. v. U. S. , 12 Ct. Cust. App. 140; In re Sheppard's Estate, 179 N. Y. S. 409, 412, 189 App. Div. 370; Rose v. State, 184 S. W. 60, 61, 122 Ark. 509; United States ex rel. Lyons v. Hines, 103 F. 2d 737, 740, 70 App. D. C. 36, 122 A. L. R. 674."
...

45. Based on the doctrine of construction of contract as given in *Keating on Construction Contracts* , such as "*all certainty would be taken from the words in which the parties have recorded their agreement*" and " *for a written contract, no evidence outside the docu-*

⊖ Paras 3-002&003, Keating on Construction Contracts. Sweet & Maxwell. Eighth Edition. 2006. Page 47.

ment itself, i. e. extrinsic evidence, may normally be adduced to contradict, vary, add to or subtract from the written terms", it is concluded that "including" is worded and written in Clause V3-1, Appendix 1 to VO-2 R2, whereas the wording "but was not restricted to" as contended by the Engineer isn't worded and written in Clause V3-1, Appendix 1 to VO-2 R2. Therefore, the wording "but was not restricted to" as contended by the Engineer shall not add to the wording of Clause V3-1, Appendix 1 to VO-2 R2.

46. In the light of the legal definition of "INCLUDE" as given in *Black Law Dictionary*, such as "*Including may, according to context, express an enlargement and have the meaning of and or in in addition to, or merely specify a particular thing already included within general words theretofore used*", it is concluded that the description of "including production, number of personnel for TBM manning and support personnel required" as set out in Clause V22-4, Appendix 9 to VO-022 R2 just means that the scope of review covers production, number of personnel for TBM manning and support personnel required, but does not cover Equipment and Material involved as asserted by the Engineer."

在承包商的上述论证过程中，引用了英国法律权威著作 *Keating on Construction Contracts*，用以论证合同解释的基本原则，即根据本意予以解释，而不能将合同条款中未表述的内容强加给合同条款的原则。*Black Law Dictionary* 对"include"单词进行了法律解释，表明其具有"keep within"等含义，而不能随意扩大解释。对于承包商而言，一个单词的理解可能涉及重大的利益，在上述案例中"including"单词的理解偏差导致业主和承包商之间的争议金额高达两千多万美元。

1.4 确定核心争议

在国际工程项目合同管理过程中，特别是在争议解决阶段，包括争议委员会、仲裁或诉讼阶段，弄清业主和承包商，或者承包商与分包商或供应商之间的核心争议是什么，这点非常重要。当业主或工程师与承包商之间就某一事项发生争议时，确定争议的焦点，有的放矢，依据合同和适用的法律据理力争，才能更好地维护自身权益。

以某国际工程仲裁案件为例，以下是仲裁庭在庭审前总结的申请人和被申请人之间的争议内容：

"Subject to Article 23 of the ICC Rules, the principal issues to be determined shall be those arising from the parties' submissions, including future submissions, which are relevant and necessary for the adjudication of the parties' claims and defence but subject to the limitation imposed by Article 23(4).

The issues may include all or any of the following specific issues:

(a) Is the sub-contractor a nominated sub-contractor?

(b) Is time the essence of this contract?

(c) Is the claimant entitled to extension of time as of right or should time extension be treated as the claimant's legitimate expectation?

(d) Can the respondent allow a time extension prayer of the claimant without approval of the employer?

(e) Has either party committed any fundamental breach of the terms of the contract?

(f) Was the termination of the sub-contract in violation of the terms of the contract?

(g) Was the sub-contract terminated without lawful authority?

(h) Was the termination in breach of the sub-contract terms?

(i) Is the claimant entitled to damages and other ancillary relief as prayed?

Pursuant to Article 23(1)(d) of the ICC Rules, the Arbitral Tribunal deems it inappropriate to set the list of issues to be determined, at this stage. The Arbitral Tribunal will, however, consider with the parties at what stage of the proceedings the Tribunal should address the issue of the identity of the Respondent."

在某国际工程项目争议解决过程中，承包商在根据 FIDIC 合同条款 1987 年第 4 版第 67.1 款递交给工程师作出决定的申请书中，在争议焦点一节中写道：

"31. This raises some issues of law and fact, which involves the general principle of offer and acceptance in common law as well as the governing law of this Contract, the Applicable Law. Thus, the sub-issues arise in eyes of the fact, the law and the Contract, such as:

A. Is it necessary to form an agreement signed by three stakeholders after issuance of variation order?

B. Does the Contractor's letter of 7 April 2014 constitute acceptance or counter-acceptance in terms of law?

C. Did the Employer accept the Contractor's letter of 7 April 2014 when he signed the VO-017 R3 on 28 October 2014?

D. Which version of the VO-017 R3 is required forms a formal agreement?

E. Does the Contractor's letter of 7 April 2014 include VO-017 R3?

F. Is the Contractor's letter of 7 April 2014 still valid to date?"

确定争议焦点后，承包商应紧紧围绕争议焦点展开论证，提供和出示相关支持性文件和证据来证明自己的观点或抗辩。这不仅体现在国际工程项目合同争议解决阶段，还体现在业主或工程师与承包商之间的日常往来函件以及承包商的索赔报告中。承包商应牢记的是，在发生争议后，应确定业主与承包商之间的争论是什么、争议焦点和问题是什么，以便在争议过程中聚焦重点，避免无谓的争议。

1.5 记录的重要性

英国著名学者马克斯·W. 亚伯拉罕森在《工程法和 ICE 合同》（*Engineering Law and*

ICE Contract) 一书中指出："A party to a dispute, particularly if there is arbitration, will learn three lessons (often too late): the importance of records, the importance of records and the importance of records."［争议的一方当事人，特别是将争议诉诸仲裁时，应汲取下述三个教训（通常为时已晚）：第一是记录的重要性，第二是记录的重要性，第三还是记录的重要性。］

承包商与工程师或业主之间的往来信函、会议纪要、备忘录、施工日志、月进度报告或在合同履行过程中达成的协议等，都会在不同程度上对发生的事实进行记录。在国际工程项目管理过程中，中国承包商将国内不注重合同、不注重文件管理的不良习惯带到国外，导致文件记录缺失，在项目索赔过程中无法提供完整的索赔证据，使承包商丧失和无法主张自己的索赔权利，从而无法维护自身合法权益，主要表现如下：

（1）现场记录不完整，无法提供完整的、具有证明力的人工费、机械设备费和材料费的证明文件。

（2）文档管理混乱，文件丢失，无法提供相应的完整证据。

（3）国际工程项目经理部人员更换频繁，未能形成良好的更换交接制度，导致有些文件无法找到。

（4）证明施工机械设备原值的海关进口单据管理不善，导致海关单据无法找到或缺失，无法证明施工机械设备原值。

（5）证明人工费的记录不完整，中方人员工资无法证明。在业主或/（监理）工程师需要个人所得税完税证明用以证明个人工资收入时，中国承包商往往未在工程所在国缴纳个人所得税，或者在中国境内缴纳个人所得税，因此，无法提供完税证明。

（6）在现场发生索赔事件时，对索赔事件所影响的人工、施工机械设备台时和材料损失没有记录或记录不完整，或未及时上报业主/（监理）工程师。

（7）文件原件保管不善，保存不全或丢失。在发生仲裁和诉讼时，无法找到文件原件作为证据使用。

承包商在编制索赔报告时，经常发生的情况是无法找到或无法找到全部支持证据和资料，导致丧失索赔权利或不能完整地证明索赔事件。

1.6 记录的及时性和充分性

工程建设项目时间跨度长，具有少则几个月、多则几年或十多年的建设周期。为了避免事后难以查明事实，现代建设工程合同中均要求承包商负有义务，进行当期记录（contemporary record），否则，如果在事后或者几年或若干年后追溯，则可能无法追溯和查明事件发生时的事实。例如，当发生不可抗力事件时，FIDIC 合同条款 1999 年第 1 版红皮书第 19.2 款［不可抗力的通知］要求，承包商在不可抗力事件发生后的 14 天内递交不可抗力通知。当发生承包商索赔事件时，要求承包商在知道或应当知道索赔事件发生后的 28 天内递交索赔通知，否则丧失工期延长和额外费用的权利。因此，在国际工程项目管理过程中，承包商应及时记录现场发生的情况或事件，通过向业主或工程师递交信函的方式记录事件发生的过程及后果。

以某水电国际工程项目为例，下面的信函记录了厂房基础开挖时遇到地基承载力不能满足合同要求，业主未能确定厂房基础处理方案，且业主未能就厂房机电设备进行招标，造成厂房主体混凝土一直无法施工的情况，承包商在向工程师的第一封信函中写道：

Dear Sir,

We are pleased to inform you that we have already accomplished the Powerhouse excavation works up to its lowest design level (i.e. EL 483.0) by March 08, 2009. With reference to the weekly progress meeting on February 26, 2009, we are waiting for the arrival of your experts for the soil bearing test and their decision regarding the foundation treatment so that we may proceed the concrete work without any delay.

Yours faithfully,

在第二封信函中，承包商向工程师发出通知，告知业主的工程技术专家未能按期到达现场。

Dear Sir,

Powerhouse Foundation Pit has been excavated to EL 483.0m by March 05, 2009 evening and the groundwater level at the pit has been lowered to EL 481.5m. Thus the foundation is ready for carrying out the soil bearing test and the foundation treatment measures, but despite our prior information to you, the above mentioned works have not been decided yet, which led to it being impossible for us to further our successive works thereof. However, the dewatering work in the pit shall be continuously carried out during the time period before the foundation and the bearing test.

We acknowledged you on March 02, 2009 that the Powerhouse excavation would be completed by March 05, 2009, requesting you to inform your relative design personnel to reach the site for inspection and perform the bearing test. But, till afternoon March 07, 2009, no related personnel reached our site for the same work.

At the same time, we would like to inform you that we are maintaining the contemporary recordson the event as required by the Sub-Clause 53.2 of the Conditions of Contract.

Yours Sincerely,

承包商向工程师发出通知，向工程师递交地基施工方案和相应的图纸，如下：

Dear Sir,

With reference to your letter No. AAA dated March 13, 2011, we hereby submit to you the treatment method statement and the corresponding drawings of powerhouse foundation.

The treatment method statement has illustrated our proposal for powerhouse foundation treatment, a copy of which is attached for your approval.

Yours faithfully,

鉴于业主对厂房地基基础处理方案批复的延误，承包商为此向业主发出索赔通知，要求相应的工期延长和因此产生的现场管理费等间接费用。在该事件的发展过程中，承包商共向业主和工程师发出了 18 封函件，详细记录了厂房地基承载力不能满足要求，为工期延长和相应的费用索赔提供了支持文件和证据。

在国际工程项目管理过程中，承包商不仅需要及时记录事件发生的情况，进行当期记录并予以保存和提交给工程师。同时，对于承包商的记录还应有准确性、充分性要求。只有记录准确、充分，承包商才能在事后的索赔和争议解决中提供准确的事实和充分的证据，才能充分证明承包商要求的工期延长、额外费用索赔或损害赔偿。以承包商现场发生当地居民阻工为例，承包商不仅需要记录当地居民阻工的事实，包括时间、地点、发生的情况等，按照合同约定递交索赔通知，还应记录当地居民阻工现场受影响的人员姓名、工种和人数受到阻碍（prevention）的施工机械设备名称、类型和数量，及时递交给业主或工程师。如可能，承包商还应向业主或工程师递交受影响的工期天数以及产生的额外费用，包括直接费用和间接费用。对于承包商而言，对记录的准确性和充分性要求如下：

（1）事件发生的时间、地点（桩号）。
（2）事件的具体描述。
（3）事件发生的原因及分析。
（4）承包商受到阻碍的人员姓名、人数和工种。
（5）承包商受到阻碍的施工机械设备名称、类型和数量。
（6）在事件结束后，应记录事件结束的时间。
（7）当发生较长时间的持续性事件时，应记录持续性事件结束的时间。

对于承包商而言，就上述事件，需要向业主或工程师发出信函的基本要求是：

（1）第一封信函：记录事件发生的时间、地点、具体描述、原因及受影响的人员和施工机械设备情况。

（2）第二封信函：如承包商认为工期受到影响或已产生或将产生额外费用，则应在合同约定的索赔通知期限（索赔时效）内，例如 FIDIC 合同条款 1999 年第 1 版和 2017 年第 2 版系列合同规定的 28 天内，向业主和/或工程师发出索赔通知。

（3）第三封信函：当事件结束时，向业主和/或工程师发出信函，通知事件结束。承包商应牢记，在国际工程项目中，很多工程项目例如征地拆迁，只是记录了事件的开始时间，而没有记录结束时间，导致承包商在索赔工期延长和额外费用时无法界定结束时间，从而无法界定工期延长天数，并且在索赔额外费用的情况下，由于无法界定时间期限，从而无法计算受到事件影响的天数。

（4）第四封函件：在持续性事件中，如承包商索赔工期延长或额外费用，应按照合同约定按月向工程师发出通知，通知事件处于持续之中，承包商保留索赔权利，并且向工程师递交工期延长的具体天数和额外费用发生的累计金额。

（5）第五封信函：当事件或持续性事件结束时，向工程师发出信函，递交承包商的索赔报告以及支持文件和资料。

从上述记录基本要求中可以看出，国际工程项目中信函或文件应当记录事件的开始、发展演变过程，直至最终结束的全过程。一个小事件常常可能需要一封信函或多封信函予以记录，但对于大的事件或对工程项目产生重大影响的事件，可能需要几十封信函甚至几百份信函来完整记录，持续时间可能会是从项目开工直至项目竣工的全过程周期，时间会持续几年或多年。因此，承包商应及时记录事件的发生过程，完整准确充分地记录事件，根据合同约定向业主和/或工程师提交这些记录，并要求业主和/或工程师签认这些记录。

根据笔者从事国际工程项目管理和争议解决的实践，绝大多数中国承包商没有及时、准确和充分地进行记录，而这些记录的缺失无法在事后予以挽回和补救，导致中国承包商无法证明索赔权利的成立，无法准确计算工期延长时间和额外费用金额，造成争议委员会、仲裁庭或法庭因证据不足无法支持承包商的索赔主张，无法支持中国承包商的诉求，导致在国际仲裁和法院诉讼中败诉。

1.7 记录形式及效力

在国际工程项目合同管理的过程中，业主和/或工程师与承包商，承包商与分包商或供应商之间形成的记录多是以文字方式记录的，还包括照片、录像、录音等记录形式。随着信息技术和通信技术的发展和进步，这些记录会通过电子邮件、微信、Whats App 等社交平台在国际工程项目的利害关系方（stakeholder）之间相互传递。这些文字和影像资料等记录方式是否能在争议委员会、仲裁或诉讼中具有证明和证据的法律效力，应视合同的约定和适用法律中证据法的规定而定，但一般而言，这些记录均具有一定意义的法律效力。

1.7.1 合同约定的记录形式

在国际工程合同中，不同合同在其条款中对通信和文件往来方式进行了不同的约定，以某国际工程分包合同为例，对于通信往来的约定如下：

"1.4 通信和文件往来

 1.4.1 通知和文件往来

  1.4.1.1 一方根据分包合同发给另一方的任何通知，包括批准、证明、同意、确定和请求均应采用书面形式。通知可由专人送交或通过信件或快递、数据电文（包括电报、电传、传真、电子数据交换和电子邮件）方式发送。由专人送交时，以对方签收之日为通知的收到日期；通过信件或快递方式发送的，以对方签收之日为通知的收到日期；通过数据电文方式发送的，以该数据电文进入对方指定特定系统的时间为抵达时间；对方未指定特定系统的，以该数据电文进入对方的任何系统的首次时间为抵达时间。

  1.4.1.2 在分包合同中，一方递交给另一方的任何通知、同意、批准、证书、确认或决定，如此类文件中规定了另一方需要予以答复的时间，如另一方未能在规定的时间内给予答复，不能视为另一方默认。

  1.4.1.3 在分包合同中，除会议通知等事务性内容外，任何一方可使用电子邮件传递往来信函、通知、批准、证书、确认或决定，但此类信函、通知、批准、证书、确认或决定必须扫描为 PDF 格式，作为电子邮件的附件传递。在使用电子邮件传递信函、通知、批准、证书、确认或决定时，一方应在 3 天内将正式的、书面形式的信函、通知、批准、证书、确认或决定递交给另一方，并由另一方签收。

  1.4.1.4 在分包合同中，如文件通过电子邮箱往来，则承包商和分包商应各自设立单独的项目专用邮箱，用于收发各类文件。

除非承包商和分包商书面同意，否则，分包合同往来邮件不能通过个人电子邮箱进行。

如承包商和分包商双方同意使用个人电子邮箱，则承包商和分包商必须形成书面文件，确认使用或将使用的个人电子邮箱作为项目文件收发邮箱。

1.4.1.5 如果承包商或分包商没有设立项目专用邮箱，也未指明个人电子邮箱作为通信联络和收发文件的邮箱，则《分包合同协议书》上载明的邮箱地址为双方当事人的收发文件邮箱。如一方当事人改变邮箱地址，则应提前7天书面通知另一方。

1.4.1.6 在分包合同中，如发生紧急情况，一方可先口头陈述或告知另一方，但应在事后24小时内以书面形式予以确认。

1.4.2 签收、公章和签字

1.4.2.1 承包商和分包商应各自准备签收章，在签收章上注明分包商名称及项目名称，并留出签收日期的空白。承包商和分包商还应各自准备项目部公章，注明承包商或分包商名称和项目名称，并注明专用字样。

1.4.2.2 承包商和分包商应在签收分包合同之前将上述签收和项目部公章准备妥当，并在本通用条件附件4［签收章、公章印鉴和代表签字样本］上留存签收章、公章和双方代表签字样本。

1.4.2.3 任何一方递交给另一方的任何通知、同意、批准、证书、确认或决定，另一方应予签收，加盖签收章，注明签收日期，并由签收人签字。在分包合同中，任何一方在文件上的签收仅表明文件的收讫，而并不意味着任何同意、批准或认可。如一方对另一方递交的此类通知、同意、批准、证书、确认或决定持有异议，应书面致函给另一方。

1.4.3 文件效力

1.4.3.1 在分包合同中，任何信函、通知、批准、确认、同意或决定应由承包商或分包商授权代表或授权代表授权的人签字并盖章（本通用条件附件4［签收章、公章印鉴和代表签字样本］留存公章印鉴）方为有效。

1.4.3.2 如为承包商或分包商向另一方发送函件或任何文件，则应加盖承包商或分包商的公章，此时，此类函件或任何文件加盖公章并送达对方后即为有效。

1.4.3.3 在一方发给另一方的函件或任何文件页数为两页或两页以上时，发出函件的一方应在每页上由授权代表签字，或者加盖骑缝章。

1.4.3.4 在分包合同中，承包商和分包商应在双方同意的或者承包商决定的期中付款证书、竣工付款证书和最终付款证书上签字和盖章。

1.4.4 分包商不能与业主和/或工程师文件往来

无论如何，分包商不能与业主和/或工程师进行直接的文件往来。分包商应向承包商致函和递交所有文件，通过承包商与业主和/或工程师进行文件往来。

在有些国际工程合同中，特别是国际金融组织融资的工程项目中，例如世界银行在合同专用条款往往对通信往来方式进行限制，例如禁止通信电子邮件方式进行通信联络，承包商与业主和工程师只能通过纸质文件，通过亲自递交的方式进行联络。例如某国际工程项目中的专用合同条款（Conditions of Particular Application）中对FIDIC合同2010年多边开发银行协调版合同通用条款第1.3款［通信联络］进行了修改，不允许工程师与承包商之间进行电子传输系统的联系，如下：

Particular Conditions—Part A：Contract Data

Conditions	Sub-Clause	Data
Electronic Transmission Systems	1.3	Not allowed.

但有些国际金融组织融资的国际工程项目中，则有条件允许工程师与承包商之间进行电子传输系统的联系。以某国际工程项目为例，专用合同条款（Conditions of Particular Application）中对 FIDIC 2010 年多边开发银行协调版合同通用条款第 1.3 款（通信联络）进行了修改，如下：

Particular Conditions—Part A：Contract Data

Conditions	Sub-Clause	Data
Electronic Transmission Systems	1.3	E-mails shall be allowed for specific documents, as per the instruction of the Engineer.

在有些国际工程项目中，业主和承包商约定设立项目数据中心（data room），业主、工程师、承包商、分包商和供应商等项目利害关系方均可以向数据中心上传工程项目往来文件，各利害关系方可通过授权和认证密码进行相应的数据库读取和下载往来信函和文件，而无须通过亲自递交的方式进行通信联络。

因此，对于承包商而言，承包商应遵守合同约定的记录形式和通信联络方式。只有在遵守合同约定的通信联络方式的情形下，在履约过程中形成的记录才能构成具有法律效力的文件，才能在争议委员会、仲裁或诉讼中作为证据使用，而违反合同约定形成的记录文件，可能会在争议委员会、仲裁或诉讼中受到其是否具有法律效力、能否作为证据使用的挑战。

1.7.2 适用法律的规定

各国对于记录的形式，包括书证、电子数据、E-mail、影像证据等证据形式，在民事诉讼法或特别法中对证据形式、证据效力等都作了具体的规定。承包商在不同的司法管辖地进行国际工程争议的仲裁或诉讼时，需要了解国际工程合同适用法律、涉及的证据法的有关规定，以便提供的证据能够被仲裁庭和法庭所接受和采信。

《中华人民共和国民事诉讼法》第六十四条第一款规定："当事人对自己提出的主张，有责任提供证据。"《最高人民法院关于〈中华人民共和国民事诉讼法〉的解释》第九十条规定："当事人对自己提出的诉讼请求所依据的事实或者反驳对方诉讼请求所依据的事实，应当提供证据加以证明，但法律另有规定的除外。在作出判决前，当事人未能提供证据或者证据不足以证明其事实主张的，由负有举证证明责任的当事人承担不利的后果。"

在大陆法系[一]国家，由于存在任何人不必出示对自己不利证据的文化传统，原则上仅要

[一] 大陆法系（Continental Law System），亦称民法法系（Civil Law System）、罗马法系、成文法系、法典法系。大陆法系是在继承和发展"罗马法"的基础上逐渐形成和完善的，并作为一个体系在 13 世纪出现于西欧，1804 年《法国民法典》和 1900 年《德国民法典》的颁布标志着大陆法系的成熟与完善。属于这个法系的除法国、德国两国外，还有奥地利、比利时、荷兰、意大利、瑞士、西班牙、明治维新后的日本以及亚、非、拉部分法语国家或地区的法律。

求当事人就自己的主张举证。但必须注意，中国企业在英美普通法系⊖的仲裁庭进行国际工程仲裁时，在适用国际律师协会 IBA 证据规则时，在面对仲裁庭的证据出示命令时，隐瞒不利证据，会给仲裁庭留下不诚信的印象，因而受到不利推定的后果。因此，国际工程项目面对不同法律体系、不同国家法律规定、不同争议解决方式时，要了解和查明不同法律的证据形式以及是否予以采信的具体法律制度和规定，避免在仲裁庭或法庭庭审过程中出现证据问题。

1.7.3 电子邮件

电子邮件（electronic mail，简称 E-mail），是一种用电子手段传送信息交换的通信方式，是直接通过计算机网络系统来发送传输接收的文字、图像、声音和视频等信息的总称。随着现代科学技术的发展，电子邮件的广泛运用使其成为一种新型证据。

无论各国法律如何界定其法律形式（属于书证、视听资料，还是单独作为一种新型证据形式），电子邮件作为一种证据，得到了绝大多数国家或地区法律的认可。各国法律要求电子邮件作为证据的要求不尽相同，有的要求通过公证方式提供电子邮件证据，例如中国法院；有的则要求当庭开示的方式证明电子邮件的真实性等。但是，由于电子邮件具有易被破坏、易被伪造和篡改，又不留痕迹等特殊性，其是否可以单独作为认定案件事实的依据，存在不同的法律规定。

为了保证合同当事人在商业交易中的电子邮件在仲裁或诉讼中可以作为证据使用，合同当事人应采取措施，确保电子邮箱通信联络的合法性，如下：

(1) 在合同中明确当事双方可以通过电子邮箱进行通信联络。

(2) 确定合同当事双方通信联系的电子邮箱。需要注意的是，在国际工程项目中，双方当事人应设立公用的电子邮箱，而不能以个人电子邮箱替代公用电子邮箱使用，避免事后的仲裁或诉讼中因使用个人电子邮箱而产生的证据效力争议。合同当事双方可在合同中约定：在分包合同中，如文件通过电子邮箱往来，则承包商和分包商应各自设立单独的项目专用邮箱，用于收发各类文件。除非承包商和分包商书面同意，否则，分包合同往来邮件不能通过个人邮箱收发。如承包商和分包商双方同意使用个人邮箱，则承包商和分包商必须形成书面文件，确认使用或将使用的个人邮箱作为项目文件收发邮箱。

(3) 在合同中约定电子邮箱可以传送的具体文件类型和内容。对于必须书面传递的文件，且需要亲自递交的文件，应避免采用电子邮箱传递。

(4) 合同当事双方应在合同中约定，对于在电子邮件中说明的内容，应补充书面文件递交给对方。

(5) 对于在电子邮件中以附件传送的文件，应要求对方以书面方式进行传递。这是因为附件文件在传递过程中存在容易被修改、替换或删除的可能，造成证据文件效力的争议。

(6) 通过公证机构对电子邮件进行证据保全。需要注意的是，在中国境内进行的交易

⊖ 英美普通法系（Anglo-American Law System），又称普通法系（Common Law System）、判例法系（Case Law System），是英国在中世纪时期在继承和发展日耳曼习惯法的基础上，以诺曼王朝国王法院的判例逐步形成的一种法律制度，之后扩展到美国以及过去的英属殖民地国家和地区，主要国家和地区有英国、美国、加拿大、澳大利亚、新西兰、爱尔兰、马来西亚、新加坡、巴基斯坦、印度、非洲的一些英语国家。

或国内建设工程项目中,当事人可以通过公证处进行电子邮件的证据保全,但对于国际工程项目而言,由于各国对公证或认证等法律规定不同,承包商可能无法对电子邮箱涉及的文件和内容进行公证或认证。因此,对于承包商而言,在合同中约定电子邮箱通信联络规则,对于电子邮件证据的效力认定,显得异常重要。

1.7.4 影像记录

影像记录指人对视觉感知的物质再现,主要表现形式有照片、摄影、录像等。在仲裁或诉讼中影像记录是否能够作为证据使用及其证明力,历来是仲裁或诉讼中当事人对证据效力的争议之一,从不缺席。各国法律对影像记录作为仲裁或诉讼的证据及其效力的规定千差万别。承包商在仲裁或诉讼时,应了解和查明影像记录作为证据的地位及其效力认定的法律规定。

影像记录在国际工程项目管理过程中得到了广泛应用。例如,在承包商遇到洪水等不可抗力事件时,通常都会将照片作为函件的附件,以形象的方式表明洪水对工程项目的影响程度。在工程质量出现问题时,业主或工程师也经常以照片的形式表明结构物的裂缝等情况。随着基于互联网的监控系统和物联网的推广和运用,产生了大量的影像资料。影像记录和电子数据能在国际工程项目管理中发挥强化工程管理、提高承包商工程管理水平的重要作用。

在国际工程项目中,为了保证影像记录的合法性和在仲裁或诉讼中的证据效力,承包商需要关注以下各个环节:

(1) 在国际工程项目管理过程中,提高对影像记录重要性的认识。

(2) 在国际工程项目管理过程中如果要使用影像方式,则应在事前通知业主和工程师,取得业主和工程师的事先书面同意。

(3) 在发生某事件后,为了表明事件的真实性和准确性,承包商应在致函给业主和/或工程师时,以信函等文字方式描述事件的发生及其过程,然后辅之以影像资料,并将这些影像资料作为信函的附件递交给业主和/或工程师。

(4) 承包商在使用影像资料时,切忌单独使用这些影像资料。这是因为影像资料容易被修改和删除,例如电子照片上的日期可以被修改,而影像内容也容易通过计算机软件被修改,导致承包商在仲裁或诉讼中无法通过影像记录证明事件的真实性,对方当事人也会挑战影像记录的真实性,从而否认影像记录证据的法律效力和证明力。

1.7.5 电子数据

电子数据(electronic data),是指基于计算机应用、通信、云计算和现代管理技术等电子化技术手段形成包括文字、图形符号、数字、字母等的客观资料○。《中华人民共和国电子签名法》规定:"数据电文是指以电子、光学、磁或者类似手段生成、发送、接收或者储存的信息。"

电子数据包括但不限于下列信息、电子文件:

(1) 网页、博客、微博客、朋友圈、贴吧、网盘等网络平台发布的信息。

(2) 手机短信、电子邮件、即时通信、通信群组等网络应用服务的通信信息。

○ https://baike.baidu.com/item/电子数据/7559956? fr=aladdin.

（3）用户注册信息、身份认证信息、电子交易记录、通信记录、登录日志等信息。

（4）文档、图片、音视频、数字证书、计算机程序等电子文件。

2019年12月26日，《最高人民法院关于修改〈关于民事诉讼证据的若干规定〉的决定》发布，按照该规定，当事人以视听资料作为证据的，应当提供存储该视听资料的原始载体。当事人以电子数据作为证据的，应当提供原件。

各国法律对电子数据在仲裁或诉讼中的应用的规定不尽相同，承包商在仲裁或诉讼中，应根据适用法律的规定，了解和查明适用法律对于电子数据的取证及其作为证据的规定和要求。

在国际工程项目管理过程中，从仲裁和诉讼案件中可以看出，中国企业在使用电子数据方面出现过很多问题，归纳如下：

（1）在国内工程项目和国际工程项目分包和供货管理过程中使用QQ、微信等即时传输方式作为信息、信函和文件的传输方式。而这些即时传输方式无法很好地保存，导致仲裁或诉讼过程中无法证明证据的来源，使得提交的证据缺乏真实来源。对方当事人挑战证据的真实性和效力，使得仲裁庭或法庭无法采信证据。类似的案例数不胜数。

（2）在国际工程项目中，电子数据多出现在CAD设计程序和进度计划管理程序，例如P3、P6或P8软件程序，业主或工程师使用的工程造价软件程序等。在发生争议后，承包商或业主/工程师往往就这些应用软件程序中的计算数据产生争议，认为这些软件程序的使用者，无论是承包商还是业主或工程师，没有完整解释数据的依据和来源，没有履行适当的披露义务，使得一方当事人无法准确了解数据的构成。在合同争议过程中，双方为此争执不休，导致合同责任无法确定。在有些案件中，承包商向分包商递交的是电子版图纸，在发生争议时，分包商往往挑战电子版图纸的法律效力。

（3）在仲裁和诉讼过程中，当事一方主张已经通过某种即时通信工具或电子邮箱或某种介质向对方发送了文件，而当事另一方认为没有收到，或拒绝承认曾经收到发生争议的文件。

因此，在国际工程项目管理过程中，为了避免电子数据导致的一系列问题，并考虑到电子数据在适用法律中的规定和做法，承包商应做到以下几点。

（1）在合同中界定电子数据的使用方式和方法，界定电子数据的法律效力。

（2）避免在工程项目管理过程中使用QQ、微信等即时传输工具进行通信交流。在不得不使用的情况下，应在合同双方当事人之间明确使用规则，即在即时传输工具发送的同时，通过电子邮件或纸质文件进行正式的递交和签收。

（3）在国际工程项目管理过程中，最为妥善的方式是通过纸质文件亲自递交的方式进行通信交流。在对方拒绝接收文件时，可通过电子邮件方式向对方提交文件。

（4）在国际工程项目管理或国内建设工程管理过程中，承包商需牢记，最原始的方法，即纸质文件亲自递交是通信联络和保证记录文件效力最有效的方式。

第 2 章 写作构思、造句与用词选择

The benefit of a style manual is to ensure consistency by codifying the stylistic choices that reflect the judgement of professional editions.

Bryand A. Garner, The Redbook-A Manual On Legal Style. Third Edition

2.1 写作构思

2.1.1 国际工程合同管理写作的主要类型

在国际工程项目管理过程中,承包商需要写作的文件类型和种类繁多,包括但不限于:
(1) 往来信函。
(2) 施工方法报告。
(3) 进度计划文件。
(4) 质量保证文件。
(5) HSE 保证文件。
(6) 月进度报告。
(7) 工程变更报告。
(8) 工期延长索赔报告和额外费用索赔报告。
(9) 设计文件。
(10) 地质水文调查报告。
(11) 竣工报告。
(12) 运营维护手册。
(13) 工程管理所需的其他文件。

从国际金融组织融资的国际工程项目管理的实践看,以公路项目为例,一名国际工程项目承包商与工程师和业主每年的往来信函数量基本均在 800 份左右。在三年工期的施工过程中,承包商与工程师和业主往来信函基本在 2000~3000 份。在某国的水电站工程项目中,在施工的十年期间,承包商向工程师和业主发函数量达到了 15000 份,而工程师向承包商发函数量达到了 30000 份,每年平均约 4000 份往来信函。

2.1.2 写作构思步骤

"作家以创造力和想象力闻名(Writers are well-known for their powers of invention and imagination)",《夜莺》作者安徒生在该书中写道。

在国际工程项目合同管理过程中，英文信函和文件的写作当然不能像写小说那样充满想象力和天马行空式的头脑风暴，而应当依据合同的约定和适用法律的规定，根据既有的事实、合同要求和技术规范，以通常的文件格式和要求，以适当的文体表述，有条理有次序有依据地写出一份具有说服力的信函或文件，使得业主或工程师能够接受承包商阐述的事实和观点，从而使得业主或工程师接受文件的结论或承包商的主张。

一般而言，在国际工程项目合同管理过程中，一份信函或文件写作的步骤如图 2-1 所示。

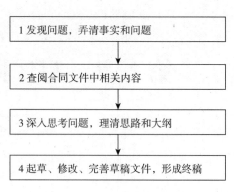

图 2-1　写作步骤示意图

以某国际工程项目标价工程量清单（the Priced Bill of Quantity, BOQ）的算术错误（arithmetic error）为例，签订合同后，承包商在施工过程中发现，标价工程量清单中存在明显的算术错误（obvious arithmetic error）。为此，承包商向工程师和业主致函，要求更正（rectify）标价工程量清单中的算术错误。而业主拒绝承包商的要求，工程师认为更正标价工程量清单中的计算错误将导致增加中标合同金额（Accepted Contract Amount），工程师不是合同当事方，他无权修改中标合同金额，建议承包商与业主直接讨论以寻求解决方案。

承包商在致工程师的函件中写道：

Dear Sir,

We would like to draw your attention for determination of Arithmetic Errors in the Bill of Quantities, which were previously noticed and timely discussed for rectification of the same. During the discussion we were unofficially notrfied that the Contractor might intentionally make errors in order to win the contract during the tender process, which was an absurd and contradicted prediction. However it is stated in the Letter of Tender:

"n) We understand that you are not bound to accept the lowest evaluated Tender or any other Tender that you may receive;"

The Employer will only evaluate and compare the Tenders, which have been determined to be substantially responsive to the requirements of the Tender Documents. Responsive Tenders will first be checked by the Employer for any arithmetic errors in computation and summation, and any errors will be corrected as follows:

(a) The amount entered in the Letter of Tender (as announced when Tenders were opened) may be considered acceptable as the Contract Amount without any of the corrections and adjustments described in these sub-paragraphs. If there is any discrepancy between amounts in figures and in words, the amount in words will take precedence.

(b) If there is any discrepancy between this amount and the equivalent sum computed on the basis of the Bill of Quantities or other Schedules, the Employer may make corrections and/or adjustments (applying the principles described in these sub-paragraphs) and give notice to the tenderer, specifying each error, correction and adjustment. If the tenderer does not accept these notified corrections and adjustments, his Tender may be rejected.

(c) If there is a substantial discrepancy between a stated amount and the correct amount calculated by multiplying the stated unit rate by the quantity, and the rate seems to have been stated in error (inconsistent with the tenderer's likely intentions), the stated unit rate shall be amended and the stated amount will be binding.

According to the statement of GCC *Sub-Clause 1. 8 Care and Supply of Documents*:

" *If a Party becomes aware of an error or defect in a document, which was prepared for use in executing the Works, the Party shall promptly give notice to the other Party of such error or defect.*"

As per the statement of GCC Sub-Clause 12. 2 Method of Measurement, it provides:

" *Except as otherwise stated in the Contract and notwithstanding local practice:*

(a) *measurement shall be made of the net actual quantity of each item of the Permanent Works, and*

(b) *the method of measurement shall be in accordance with the Bill of Quantities or other applicable Schedules.* "

(c) Clarification is provided in the specification as follows:

The measurement preamble addresses that:

(a) The Bill of Quantities shall be read in conjunction with the General Conditions of Contract, Conditions of Particular Application, Technical Specifications, and Drawings Bill of Quantities is provided in the attached excel file and provides the drawings volume as it's currently absent.

(b) The quantities given in the Bill of Quantities are estimated and provisional, and are given to provide a common basis for bidding. *The basis of payment will be the actual quantities of work ordered and carried out, as measured by the Contractor and verified by the Engineer and valued at the rates and prices tendered in the priced Bill of Quantities, where applicable, and otherwise at such rates and prices as the Engineer may fix within the terms of the Contract.*

The Bill of Quantities is based on a preliminary design, and the Contractor will prepare detailed design for approval by the Engineer prior to commencing the works. Payments are to be made according to actual measured quantities, up to the Bill Number budget limits detailed in the Bill of Quantities.

In our case, if we look at the Bill H (sidewalks) section of PK 40 +00 to PK 49 +00 and PK0 +00 to PK12 +00 is where the unit quantity is multiplied by the unit rate, but in the section PK19 +00 to PK40 +00, an arithmetical error occurred because, instead of multiplying the unit quantity to the price they were added, which is negatively reflected in the sum.

John Mullen in Evaluating Contract Claims deals with such errors as well:

"5.2.5 Errors in Rates and Prices

Where contractors erroneously calculate or insert their rates and prices in bills of quantities or other contract documents issues may arise as to what is to be done about such errors. This can lead to various claims including any of the following:

1. That where bills of quantities items have not been priced at all or not extended through to page totals and the contract price, this error should be adjusted in favour of the contractor by an increase in the contract price.
2. That where a rate or price has been erroneously priced high by the contractor' it should be reduced before being applied to variations or additional quantities to the employer's benefit.
3. That where a rate or price has been erroneously priced low by the contractor' it should not be held to that low rate in respect of variations or additional quantities, and the rate or price should be suitably increased."

We kindly request you to consider the above-mentioned statements and take the reasonable decision in order to avoid further litigation of the Contractor and Subcontractors in this aspect.

Sincerely Yours,

在上述函件中，承包商在起草致工程师的函件时，主要经历了如下过程：

（1）发现问题，弄清问题所在。在本例中，承包商在施工过程中发现了标价工程量清单中的算术错误，即本应在 BOQ 中使用数量乘以单价得出总价，但在计算过程中将数量加上单价得出了总价，导致总价结果错误。

（2）承包商查阅了合同中的有关规定，其中招标文件中对投标书中的计算错误规定如下：

(a) The amount entered in the Letter of Tender (as announced when Tenders were opened) may be considered acceptable as the Contract Amount without any of the corrections and adjustments described in these sub-paragraphs. If there is any discrepancy between amounts in figures and in words, the amount in words will take precedence.

(b) If there is any discrepancy between this amount and the equivalent sum computed on the basis of the Bill of Quantities or other Schedules, the Employer may make corrections and/or adjustments (applying the principles described in these sub-paragraphs) and give notice to the tenderer, specifying each error, correction and adjustment. If the tenderer does not accept these notified corrections and adjustments, his Tender may be rejected.

(c) If there is a substantial discrepancy between a stated amount and the correct amount calculated by multiplying the stated unit rate by the quantity, and the rate seems to have been stated in error (inconsistent with the tenderer's likely intentions), the stated unit rate shall be amended and the stated amount will be binding.

（3）承包商还查阅了合同的规定，其中FIDIC合同条款2010年多边开发银行协调版第1.8款［文件的照管和提供］最后一段规定了在施工过程中任何一方当事人发现错误应及时通知另一方，如下：

"*If a Party becomes aware of an error or defect in a document, which was prepared for use in executing the Works, the Party shall promptly give notice to the other Party of such error or defect.*"

（4）FIDIC合同条款2010年多边开发银行协调版第12.2款［计量方法］中规定了计算规则，如下：

"*Except as otherwise stated in the Contract and notwithstanding local practice：*
(a) *measurement shall be made of the net actual quantity of each item of the Permanent Works, and*
(b) *the method of measurement shall be in accordance with the Bill of Quantities or other applicable Schedules.*"

（5）承包商还查阅了计量前言，其中计量前言规定了具体的计量方式，如下：

(a) The Bill of Quantities shall be read in conjunction with the General Conditions of Contract, Conditions of Particular Application, Technical Specifications, and Drawings BOQ is provided in the attached excel file and provide the drawings volume as it's currently absent.
(b) The quantities given in the Bill of Quantities are estimated and provisional, and are given to provide a common basis for bidding. *The basis of payment will be the actual quantities of work ordered and carried out*, as measured by the Contractor and verified by the Engineer and valued at the rates and prices tendered in the priced Bill of Quantities, where applicable, and otherwise at such rates and prices as the Engineer may fix within the terms of the Contract.

（6）承包商查阅了相关文献，认为John Mullen在*Evaluating Contract Claims*一书中支持承包商的观点，即如果BOQ计算错误应予更正。

在回复承包商的函件之前，工程师首先向业主报告了标价的工程量清单中计算错误问题，询问业主的意见，如下：

Dear Sir,

We have already informed you verbally that in some of the approved BOQ items there are mathematical errors which normally should have been corrected during the tender stage.

In some BOQ items, instead of multiplying the unit by the quantity to find the Total Amount, by mistake they added the unit to quantity and wrote it in Total Amount column. And in some of the BOQ items, only numbers are written instead of multiplying the unit with quantity. In Bill item No. 7, there is no any unit and quantity, but there is a Total Amount (USD) shown.

For your convenience, we list the mathematical errors in each BOQ item separately in excel format and the total impact on the Accepted Contract Amount is USD 342,792.35.

We kindly seek your valuable comments and instruction on this issue in order to proceed.

Sincerely Yours,

业主随后回复了工程师的询问函,反对和拒绝更正标价的工程量表中的计算错误和调整合同价格,如下:

Dear Sir,

In response to the letter dated 04.03.2020 ref. No. XXXX, please be informed that after the notice of application acceptance for participation in the tender, which is part of the contract documents, the Contractor has accepted the Accepted Contract Amount of the Contract with all the errors during the signing of the Contract for the construction works, including in BOQ, which was indicated by the Engineer.

Thus, according to Sub-clause 4.11 [*Sufficiency of the Accepted Contract Amount*]:
"It's considered that the Contractor:
Satisfied that the Accepted Contract Amount is correct and sufficient.
Unless specified in the Contract, the Accepted Contract Amount shall cover all of the Contractor's obligations under the Contract (including commitments to Provisional Sum, if applicable) and all necessary for the adequate execution and completion of the facilities and the elimination of all deficiencies."

As for Bill J, if the Contractor has not provided scope, quotation or price, it will be considered that the Contractor will cover this item at the expense of other quotations and prices specified in the BOQ.

Based on this, further payment for these items will be made as follows:
- The Contractor shall be paid for the scope of work in total amount of the Contract, and for the additional scopes the payment shall be made in accordance with the approved Contract price;
- Bill J, the Contractor shall be paid only for the total amount of the Contract for all scope performed work under this item.

We hope that this clarifies the issue.
Sincerely Yours,

在得到业主的回复后,工程师致函承包商,向承包商抄送了业主的回复函件,并表明工程师无权修改中标合同金额(Accepted Contract Amount),建议承包商与业主直接商谈解决 BOQ 清单计算错误的问题。

为此,承包商再次致函工程师并抄送业主,表明 BOQ 中的计算错误为明显的算术错误,根据承包商先前函件中表述的应予更正的理由,并考虑到工程师的建议,承包商建议根据合同条款第 20.5 款 [友好协商] 的规定与业主就此项争议进行友好协商,并建议在友好协商无法达成一致的情况下,根据合同第 20.4 款的规定将争议提交争议委员会(Dispute Board)予以解决,如下:

Dear Sir,

This is in reference to our letter of AAA dated 27 April 2020 and the Engineer's letter BBB with the attached copies of the Engineer's letter CCC dated 04 March 2020 as well as the Employer's letter DDD dated 27 March 2020.

We have learned that by letter of DDD dated 27 March 2020, the Employer takes his position that the Contractor shall be paid for the scope of work in total amount of the Contract, and for the additional scopes the payment shall be made in accordance with approved Contract price. And in respect of Bill J, the Contractor shall be paid only for the total amount of the Contract for all scope performed work under this item.

We have acknowledged as well that by letter of EEE, the Engineer opines that he hasn't authority to approve on his own when determining the costs exceeding the Acceptable Contract Amount and he proposes a discussion between the Contractor and the Employer in seeking solutions on the dispute.

It goes without saying that an obvious arithmetic error appears in Bill H, Sidewalks, lined item 24, 25, 26 and 27 in the Priced Bill of Quantities where the arithmetical error occurred because instead of multiplying the unit quantity by the price they were added, which is negatively reflected in the sum, as illustrated in our letter of AAA, resulting in a price difference in a total sum of USD 203,103.83 (rectified sum USD 389,545.41-priced sum USD 186,441.58).

Further, the FIDIC Contract Conditions contain provisions allowing notification of any error or defect in a document, in which Sub-Clause 1.8 addresses that if a Party becomes aware of an error or defect in a document which was prepared for use in executing the Works, the Party shall promptly give notice to the other Party of such error or defect.

It is obvious that the FIDIC Contract Conditions MDB 2010 Edition which governs and is applied in this Contract is a kind of unit rate contract, rather than lump sum contract. Sub-Clause 12.2 [*Method of Measurement*] of GCC provides the mechanism for measurement and payment for the works performed by the Contractor. More importantly, the Measurement Preamble states that:

"The quantities given in the Bill of Quantities are estimated and provisional, and are given to provide a common basis for bidding. *The basis of payment will be the actual quantities of works ordered and carried out, as measured by the Contractor and verified by the Engineer and valued at the rates and prices tendered in the Priced Bill of Quantities, where applicable, and otherwise at such rates and prices as the Engineer may fix within the terms of the Contract.*"

Thus, when measuring and certifying the related works done, it shall be the actual quantities or works carried out multiplied by the unit rate and prices tendered in the Priced Bill of Quantities.

On the other hand, the Accepted Contract Amount as set out in the Letter of Acceptance shall, according to Clause 14 [*Contract Price and Payment*] of the FIDIC contract Conditions, not be the Contract Price verified and certified by the Engineer, where Sub-Clause 14.1 [*The Contract Price*] provides that the Contract Price shall be agreed or determined under Sub-Clause 12.3 [*Evaluation*] and be subject to adjustments in accordance with the Contract.

In consideration of a dispute arising from the arithmetic error in the Priced Bill of Quantities by the Contractor, the Contractor seeks to find out a solution for obvious arithmetical errors according to Sub-Clause 20.5 [*Amicable Settlement*] in the first place. If the subject of the dispute is not settled amicably between the Employer and the Contractor, we propose to refer to the Dispute Board according to Sub-Clause 20.4 of GCC in seeking a decision from the DB.

We appreciate in advance your understanding and efforts in solving the raised matter.

Sincerely Yours,

承包商在起草致工程师函件的过程中，主要考虑如下问题：
（1）由于承包商与分包商就 BOQ 计算错误问题交换了往来函件，因此，应首先在函件中表明涉及的函件编号和日期。
（2）承包商通过工程师传送的业主回复，而非直接从业主处收到回复，因此，在致函中，承包商应首先了解和知晓了业主立场和工程师观点。
（3）承包商重申 BOQ 计算错误为明显的算术错误，并表明产生结果，即争议的金额。
（4）承包商重申了他认为重要的理由，即计量规则中应使用承包商完成的工程数量乘以单价得出 BOQ 项总价。
（5）承包商考虑到工程师的观点，为此建议与业主就此项争议进行友好协商。
（6）承包商表明，如果友好协商无法达成一致，建议将争议提交争议委员会予以解决。
承包商应深入思考因自己原因导致的 BOQ 计算错误，例如在签订合同后的施工过程中发现明显的算术错误是否能得到更正（rectification），不仅需要从合同规定角度看合同是否规定了此类更正条款，更要从法律视角探究能否为法律所支持。这是承包商在与业主或工程师发生合同争议时必须考量的一个法律问题，即从法律角度考虑承包商的主张是否成立。

关于 BOQ 计算错误（算术错误）问题，毫无疑问，国际工程项目招标文件中的招标须知（Instruction to Tenderer）中均规定了 BOQ 计算错误的更正事宜，例如承包商第一封函件中引述的内容。根据招标须知，在评标过程中，如业主发现投标人的 BOQ 中的计算错误，应根据招标须知规定的更正规则予以更正，以便正确评估投标人的价格和合同总价。但问题是，在签订合同后发现 BOQ 中的计算错误能否予以更正，不仅承包商与业主之间会产生争议，而且在法律界也存在争议。但不得不说，如果承包商在签订合同时没有注意到 BOQ 中的计算错误，而在签订合同后的施工过程中才发现 BOQ 计算错误（算术错误），一般而言，标准格式合同并不允许承包商就 BOQ 中的标价错误获得救济（Standard Form Contracts do not generally allow Contractors relief from pricing errors made in Bill of Quantities⊖）。在 FIDIC 施工合同条款 1999 年第 1 版和 2010 年多边开发银行协调版中，虽然第 1.8 款［文件的照管和提供］规定了任何一方应及时将任何错误通知另一方，但 FIDIC 合同条款并没有明示规定承包商可以就 BOQ 中的计算错误进行更正或获得任何救济。在新加坡的 SIA 合同中，合同规定承包商可以就明显的偶然错误（obvious accidental error）予以更正。

在国际工程法律权威著作 *Keating on Construction Contracts*（《基廷论施工合同》）一书中，针对 BOQ 中的计算错误，该书写道：

"If the employer discovers arithmetical errors operating against the contractor's interest but these errors remain and are incorporated into the contract price, is the contractor entitled to rectification? The answer requires the application of the principles set out above to the facts of each case, but as a guide the following approach is suggested:

(i) If the errors are clearly brought to the attention of the contractor and he decides to keep to his tender price and conditions, there cannot be rectification as there is no mistake.

(ii) If, in addition to the facts in (i) above, the parties agree upon some alteration in the tender price or upon some other alteration in the suggested terms of contract, e. g. as to calculation of the prices for variations, but by mistake the contract does not express these agreed alterations, then upon the agreement being clearly proved there can be rectification.

(iii) If errors are not brought to the attention of the contractor and he, ignorant of them, signs the contract, proof of these facts alone does not, it is submitted, give the contractor grounds for rectification, but if the contractor proves clearly that at the time of entering into the contract he believed the contract price to consist of the true totals of the properly calculated prices in the bills and that the employer at that time knew of the contractor's belief or that he suspected that the contractor so believed then there can be rectification.⊖"

⊖ Para 5-013. Hudson's Building and Engineering Contracts. 14th Edition. Sweet & Maxwell. 2019. P. 609.

⊖ Para 12-026. Keating on Construction Contracts. 11th Edition. Sweet & Maxwell. 2020. P384-385.

在 Keating on Construction Contracts 的上述论述中，可以得出，如果业主发现计算错误影响了承包商的利益，且此类计算错误已经成为合同价格的组成部分，那么承包商是否有权要求予以更正？回答这个问题需要根据每个案件的具体事实，按照上述确定的适用原则进行判断，建议应对指南如下：

（1）如果承包商清楚地注意到了此类错误，并且决定维持其投标价格和条件不变，因不存在承包商认为的错误，则不能予以更正。

（2）除上述（1）的情形外，如果当事人同意对投标价格进行修改，或者同意对建议的合同条款进行某些其他修改，如关于变更价格的计算，但是由于错误，合同没有明确这些已经同意的修改，那么，根据双方达成的一致，如果能清晰地予以证明，则可予以更正。

（3）如果承包商没有注意到此类错误，并且他忽略了此类错误并签订了合同，且事实不能证明承包商有理由更正此类错误，但如果承包商能够清晰地证明在签约时他的确在计算工程量表时进行了适当的计算，且他相信合同价格中的总额是真实的，而且业主在签约时知道承包商的确相信合同总额的真实性，或者他怀疑承包商确信合同总额的真实性，则可对此类错误予以更正。

从国际工程法律的两本权威著作《哈德逊论建筑和工程合同》和《基廷论施工合同》的有关论述可以得出，在一般情形下，承包商很难对签约后的 BOQ 中的计算错误予以更正，但应具体案件具体分析，在某些情形下，例如上述（3）的情形下，承包商还有机会对 BOQ 中的计算错误获得更正的补救措施。需要说明的是，上述两本国际工程法律权威著作，法庭或仲裁庭可以直接引述其中的论述作为裁判案件的依据。

2.1.3　写作构思应考虑的主要内容

在国际工程项目合同管理过程中，不同类型的信函和文件写作需要考虑的主要内容不同，有如下几点。

（1）对于事务性信函，例如办理外籍雇员的签证或工作许可，承包商在写信过程中，无须考虑更多的内容，仅需将需要办理签证或工作许可的外籍雇员的姓名、职务、护照号码、入境日期、办理要求、期限等内容在信函上写明即可。在需要办理外籍雇员人数较多时，承包商可以附人员清单，如需要可附上护照信息页复印件。

（2）对于技术性信函，例如递交设计图纸进行审批，或者递交地质勘探报告或者施工过程中的勘验报告等，承包商在写信过程中无须考虑更多的内容，仅需将设计图纸作为附件递交给工程师审批。在工程师延误审批设计图纸时，承包商需要在信函中指明递交设计图纸日期、工程师尚未批准图纸的事实以及工程师批准的日期。如果工程师审批延误，则承包商应向工程师发出索赔通知，索赔因工程师延误审批图纸导致的工期延长和因此产生的额外费用。如果承包商与工程师或业主就某项技术问题产生争议，则承包商应从合同条款、技术规范、设计要求等多角度进行考量，论证技术的可行性和安全性。此时，承包商应多方面考虑技术问题，与工程师和业主讨论技术问题，得出正确的结论。

（3）对于索赔通知等承包商主张权利的信函，承包商首先需要考虑合同约定的索赔时效（time bar），例如 FIDIC 施工合同条款 1999 年第 1 版、2017 年第 2 版以及多边开发银行协调版 2005 年版、2006 年版和 2010 年版等，均在承包商索赔的合同条款中约定了承包商应在知道和应当知道索赔事件发生的 28 天内提出索赔通知的要求，否则承包商将失去工期延长索赔和额外付款的权利。其次，承包商要考虑索赔事件的性质、类型、事件事实，以便在索赔通知中明确是主张工期延长还是额外费用，或者两者兼而有之。

（4）事实上，对于合同争议性质的往来信函的回复，是对承包商合同管理人员和法律人员关于合同知识、合同理解、法律知识和对法律理解水平的最大考验。以上述第 2.1.2 节承包商与工程师和业主发生的 BOQ 计算错误的往来信函为例，承包商在起草、拟定和回复工程师和业主的观点和意见时，需要从以下方面进行考虑，如图 2-2 所示。

在上述第 2.1.2 节中举例的 BOQ 计算错误中，承包商在施工过程中认识到 BOQ 计算错误对其的不利影响，在给工程师的致函

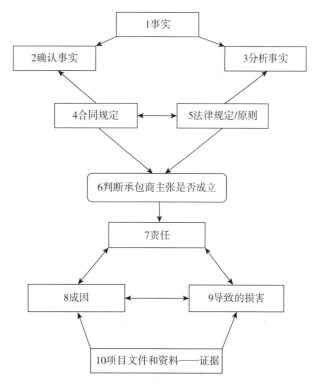

图 2-2　写作构思的主要因素和思维模式

中，考虑了事实、合同约定的规则、测量规则、专家著作的观点等；同时，承包商还从法律角度分析其是否能就 BOQ 计算错误得到予以更正的补救措施，论证了承包商的主张是否成立。

2.1.4　构建思维模式

与小说写作的发散性思维不同，国际工程项目合同管理的写作思维应构建在逻辑、推理和严谨的基础之上，更准确地说，应以法律思维方式，从一个专业律师角度思考国际工程项目合同管理中涉及的写作内容。

如图 2-2 所示，该图清晰地表明了国际工程项目合同管理的思维模式，即从事实出发，确认事实，分析事实，从合同规定或法律规定及原则方面判断承包商的主张是否成立。对于国际工程项目合同管理人员或法律人员而言，还应继续探究下一步的逻辑链条，即确定合同和法律责任，明确成因及其导致的损害，为承包商主张权利确立条件，如图 2-2 所示。

在图 2-2 中，国际工程项目合同管理人员还应首先建立责任、成因、导致的损害和证据的意识和思维。这是因为在合同争议中，特别是在国际仲裁或诉讼过程中，确定责任归属是承包商权利主张的基础。在承包商承担责任的情况下，承包商无法向业主主张赔偿和索赔权利。其次，通过因果分析，确定事件的成因，确定是谁导致了事件的发生。再次，确定事件发生导致的损害结果，从而确定承包商请求（petition）的具体内容和金额，包括损害赔偿金额、实际履行请求、要求支付工程款和利息等。最后，承包商权利主张的基础是证据，是项目文件和资料，能否证明承包商权利主张取决于证据的有效性和证明力。

因此，对于国际工程项目合同管理人员和法律人员而言，建立全过程的写作思维模式，有利于从合同和法律角度出发，以证据为依托，确立责任归属，明确因果关系，确定事件导致的损害，从而以全过程的思维模式主导和贯穿写作过程，这样才能掌握全局，有理有据地主张承包商的权利，而非胡搅蛮缠，没有分寸地主张本不应得到的权利和利益。

2.2 写作造句

与小说叙事和抒情文体不同，从严格意义上说（strict sensu），合同和法律使用的句型（sentence pattern）具有其自身独特的特征。
（1）句型结构完整。
（2）以陈述句为主要句式。
（3）以长句为主。
（4）被动句式的使用。
（5）倒装句的使用。
（6）并列句和平行结构的使用。
（7）避免抒情和情绪化的描述或结论。
（8）禁止使用禁忌语。

2.2.1 句型结构完整

鉴于合同和法律用语的要求严谨，讲求逻辑和准确，因此，为了避免误解、歧义或曲解，合同和法律的句型必须完整，采用主语和谓语都具备的完整主谓句，结构严谨，应尽量不使用省略句。

例1：在某国际工程施工合同条款中，业主关于转让（Assignment）的有关规定如下：

1.7.1 The Employer shall be freely entitled, without the consent of the Contractor, to assign, pledge, charge, declare a trust over or otherwise encumber the whole or any part of the benefit of its interest in this Contract to any Lenders, the Grantor and/or any new concessionaire under the Concession Agreements appointed by the Grantor, including its right to any moneys due, or to become due, under the Contract (and the Lenders may enforce and realize such security by way of sale or otherwise)。

例2：在某国际工程合同中，关于承包商的义务约定如下：

The Contractor shall ensure that emissions, surface discharges and effluent from the Contractor's activities shall not exceed the values indicated in the Employer's Requirements, and shall not exceed the values prescribed by applicable Laws and Authorizations.

例3：在国际商会国际仲裁院（International Court of Arbitration, International Chamber of Commerce, ICC）致函给仲裁当事人的通知中，ICC国际仲裁院写道：

We remind you of your obligations under Article 34(6) of the Rules, which provides: "Every award shall be binding on the parties. By submitting the dispute to arbitration under the Rules, the parties undertake to carry out any award without delay and shall be deemed to have waived their right to any form of recourse insofar as such waiver can validly be made."

例 4：在某国际工程仲裁案件中，仲裁庭在仲裁裁决中对涉案合同写道：
The Main Contract is based on the FIDIC Conditions of Contract for Construction (Multilateral Development Bank Harmonised Ed. Version 1: May 2005). The Subcontract is based on the FIDIC Conditions of Subcontract for Construction (Test Edition, 2009). The Subcontract Agreement is dated 31 October 2011 and was signed on 1 November 2011.

例 5：在英国技术和建设法庭（Technology and Construction Court, TCC）判决的案件中，法官在判决书中写道：
The construction contract is in a pre-printed form entitled "Large Works Contract", and is stated to be intended for use on projects exceeding £5,000 between a private home owner and a builder. There is no evidence as to the source of that pre-printed form, which is not one with I have previously encountered, or as to who proposed its use in this case.[⊖]

2.2.2 陈述句为主要句式

鉴于合同和法律用语和文书的功能是确认合同权利义务和法律关系，特别是在仲裁申请书和诉讼文书中陈述事实和观点，因此，合同和法律用语和文书通常以陈述句为主。而英文合同为了准确、严密、清晰表达，多为复合句式，简单句极少。

例 1：在某国际工程合同中，合同规定了承包商保密义务，如下：
Save as otherwise agreed, the Contractor shall not publish, permit to be published, or disclose any particulars of the Works in any trade or technical paper or elsewhere without the previous agreement of the Employer, and the Contractor shall ensure that each Sub-contract contains provisions similar to those set out in this Clause1.9.

例 2：在某篇评论英国法院判决的文章中，作者写道：
We successfully argued that the Adjudicator should reject this narrow interpretation of the applicability of Sub-Clause 20.1 in our contract. He determined that this Sub-Clause did constitute a condition precedent which applied to all claims relating to matters which the sub-contractor contended constituted Variations, irrespective of whether or not an instruction had been issued by our client.

⊖ Anjali Khurana and Mohit Khurana v. Webster Construction Limited. [2015] EWHC 758 (TCC), at [7].

例3：在英国TCC法院的判决中，法官写道：

At the end of 2013, AUK reached a global settlement with TEP in respect of all of the onshore works, which therefore included the works which AUK had subcontracted to OSR. The settlement involved a payment by TEP to AUK. It therefore appears more likely than not that the AUK offer letter of 13 January 2014 was written following that settlement, in order to try and resolve the remaining claim in respect of the onshore works. The letter was written some three months before these proceedings commenced. ⊖

2.2.3 长句为主

为了准确清晰地表明合同当事人在合同中的权利义务，在法律文书中准确清楚地表述事实和观点，合同和法律用语和文书通常需对某一法律概念成立的条件限定较多，对中心词限定很多，因此，合同用语和法律用语以长句为主，短句为辅。

例1：在某国际工程合同中，业主需要向承包商提供融资安排的证据，合同相应条款约定如下：

The Employer shall submit, within 28 days after receiving any request from the Contractor, reasonable evidence that financial arrangements have been made and are being maintained which will enable the Employer to pay the Contract Price together with applicable value added tax (as estimated at that time) in accordance with Clause13 [*Contract Price and Payment*]. The Employer shall give reasonable advance notice to the Contractor, with detailed particulars, of any material change it intends to make to such financial arrangements.

例2：在某国际工程仲裁案中，仲裁庭在仲裁裁决中写道：

The Claimant, by letter of 13 April 2014, responded to the Termination Notice denying that any ground of termination existed and reiterated the grounds upon which it was entitled to extension of time. The Claimant further asserted that, by the end of March 2014, 33.63% of the work had been completed and that the progress of the work during 2014 had been 5.31%. The Claimant denied that it was in default as regards the delay.

例3：在某个针对英国法院的法律评论中，作者写道：

Our adjudication confirmed that, although the courts may now interpret the FIDIC notice requirements broadly in respect of the trigger for when a notice must be issued, these requirements constitute a condition precedent which applies widely to any claims which a contractor may have for an EOT or additional payment, regardless of the basis of such claims.

⊖ Van OorD UK Limited and Sicim Roadbridge limited v Allseas UK Limited. [2015] EWHC 3385 (TCC).

例4：在英国 TCC 法院判决中，法官写道：

Moreover, it is difficult to see how or why OSR, on receipt of the letter, could have reached any other conclusion. No separate, stand-alone counterclaim had been asserted by AUK at the time of the letter, and no sum was set out in the offer letter (unlike in *AF v BG*) as representing the liquidated amount of any such counterclaim. The most that could be said was that, in the correspondence, AUK were saying that, far from OSR being entitled to further sums, they had actually been overpaid. But the offer was in different terms, because it was expressly accepted that OSR could retain all that they had been paid.[⊖]

2.2.4 被动句式的使用

为了强调合同和法律的客观性，避免产生主观臆断的印象，合同和法律英语通常用被动句进行表述。

例1：在某国际工程的联合体协议中，关于合同修改的条款约定：

This Agreement may not be modified except by amendment in writing and signed by duly authorized representatives of the Parties.

例2：在联合体协议中，合同约定：

In the event that the withdrawal occurs because of the disagreement on the commercial terms of the proposal, a comfort letter will be provided to the Withdrawing Party by the Non-withdrawing Parties upon fulfilment of the Withdrawing Party's share of costs and expenses obligations and liabilities as per Section 3(F)(4)(b) to the effect of releasing the Withdrawing Party from further costs and expenses obligations and liabilities.

例3：在某国际工程合同中，关于非弃权的合同约定如下：

No failure or delay on the part of any Party in the exercise of any right hereunder shall operate as a waiver thereof, nor shall any single or partial exercise of any such right preclude any other or further exercise thereof or of any other right. All rights and remedies under this Agreement are cumulative to, and not exclusive of, any rights or remedies otherwise available.

例4：在某法律评论中，作者关于承包商工期延长或干扰有关的损失和费用问题写道：

Ultimately, claims by contractor for delay or disruption related loss and expense must be proved as a matter of fact.

⊖ Van Oord UK Limited and Sicim Roadbridge limited v Allseas UK Limited. [2015] EWHC 3385 (TCC), at [12]).

2.2.5 倒装句的使用

为了强调或平衡英语句式结构,倒装句广泛应用于合同和法律文书中。倒装句式包括全部倒装和部分倒装。

例1:在某国际工程合同中,关于合同当事人之外第三方利益事宜,合同约定:

Nothing contained herein shall be deemed to create a third-party beneficiary relationship with or upon any other person or entity or confer on any other person or entity any benefit or right to enforce any term of this Agreement whether pursuant to the Contracts (Rights of Third Parties) or any legal instrument or act.

例2:在承包商致函工程师的函件中,承包商写道:

Neither the Contractor nor the Employer denies the existing facts related to the disruption stemming from the local residents in the course of construction.

例3:在某国际工程合同中,合同条款约定:

Save in each case to the extent that any such delay is due to any act, neglect, omission or default of the Contractor, or any person for whom the Contractor is responsible in accordance with this Contract.

2.2.6 并列句和平行结构的使用

为了更好地表述合同条款和法律文书之间的逻辑关系,更为重要的是,合同和法律用语能够涵盖全部的情形或情况,避免遗漏,并列句和平行结构广泛应用于合同和法律英语中。

例1:并列句在合同中的表述如下:

Any such assignment, pledge, charge, declaration or encumbrance shall include the right to make second and subsequent assignments, pledges, charges, declarations or encumbrances and freely to enforce the same by way of sale or otherwise. The Contractor hereby gives its consent for such assignment, pledge, charge, declaration or encumbrance of rights under this Contract in accordance with this Clause1.7. No assignment, pledge, charge, declaration of trust or encumbrance under this Clause 1.7.1 shall be permitted to the extent that it causes the Contractor to be in breach under any applicable Law.

例2:平行结构如下:

Each Party hereby represents and warrants to each of the other Parties as of the Effective Date that:

(i) the Party will cooperate, in order to agree to the terms of the Qualification Application and the Proposal to be submitted to the Project Sponsor. The Party further agrees to (*) abide by all the RFQ and RFP requirements and provisions, and (**) meet and fulfill the obligations and undertakings in the RFQ and RFP;

(ii) it is duly organized, validly existing and in good standing under the laws of the jurisdiction of its organization, and it has all necessary power, authority and legal right to execute and deliver, and perform its obligations under this Agreement;

(iii) the execution, delivery and performance by such Party of this Agreement have been duly authorized;

(iv) the execution, delivery and performance by such Party of this Agreement do not contravene with the constitutive documents of such Party, or any applicable law or regulation, or any order, injunction or decree of any government authority or agency, or any agreement or instrument commitment binding on such Party;

(v) this Agreement has been duly and validly executed and delivered by such Party and constitutes its legal, valid any binding obligation, enforceable against such Party in accordance with its terms; and

(vi) that all representations and statements made and information provided by each Party to the Consortium and to the Project Sponsor in connection with the Qualification Application and the Proposal is accurate and not misleading in any way.

例3：平行结构在合同中的应用如下：

Subject to Clauses 8.4.2 to 8.4.9 (inclusive) and 19.1 [*Contractor's Claims*], the Contractor shall only be entitled to an extension of time to the extent any of the following causes results or will result in the Handover Date being delayed beyond the Time for Handover:

(i) any occurrence of a Force Majeure event, in accordance with Clause 18 [*Force Majeure*];

(ii) any Variation directed by the Employer, in accordance with Clause 12 [*Variations and Adjustments*] (unless an adjustment to the Time for Handover has been agreed under Clause 12.4 [*Variation Procedure*] in respect of such Variation);

(iii) any permitted Statutory Modification, in accordance with Clause 12.6 [*Adjustments for Changes in Legislation*];

(iv) any suspension directed by the Employer, in accordance with Clause 8.7 [*Suspension of Work*], except to the extent that such suspension is caused by an act or omission of the Contractor which is not expressly permitted under this Contract;

(v) The Contractor following the Employer's instructions issued in accordance with Clause 4.23 [*Fossils*]; or

(vi) any delay, impediment or prevention caused by or attributable to the Employer, the Employer's Personnel, the Employer's other contractors on the Site or the Employer's Equipment Suppliers; and

(vii) any delay giving an entitlement under this Contract to an extension to the Time for Handover.

2.2.7 避免抒情和情绪化的描述或结论

在合同和法律文书写作过程中，包括承包商与业主和/或工程师之间的往来信函，无论是承包商还是业主或工程师，应避免使用抒情和情绪化的描述或结论。这些抒情或情绪化的表述方式包括：

（1）在法律文书中使用情绪化的语言指责另一方，例如指责鉴定机构的鉴定水平太低或者不合格。争议双方正确的态度应是指出鉴定机构所做的鉴定意见哪些不符合合同约定或鉴定规范要求等。

（2）在法律文书中指责仲裁庭有失公平。争议双方正确的态度和做法应是指明仲裁庭在庭审中的问题，而非指责。

（3）在给工程师的致函中指责工程师技术水平太低等。

在合同和法律用语中，包括往来信函中，应客观地表述事实和陈述观点，这就是为什么合同和法律文书中具有上述特征的根本原因。承包商需要牢记：

（1）客观的表述比主观的臆断更容易被对方、争议委员会、仲裁庭或法庭接受。

（2）让事实说话，以证据为佐证，是解决争议的决胜之道。

（3）抒情或情绪化表述，并非专业律师应有的素质。作为律师或仲裁或诉讼代理人，客观地对待事实、冷静分析得出可靠的结论，远比情绪化表述更能体现专业素养。

（4）作为律师或仲裁或诉讼代理人，客户需要的是一名客观的、冷静的专业律师，而非情绪化的、易激动的律师。

2.3 用词选择

2.3.1 正确和准确性要求

对于合同用语，特别是对于法律文书而言，选择用词的最基本要求，而最高要求是正确和准确。

（1）正确（correctness）。这不仅体现在英文用词正确，而且需要情景和场景使用正确，能够正确表达作者的真实意图。在国际工程合同过程管理中的信函往来、法律文书，例如提交争议委员会的申请书（dispute referral）、仲裁申请书（request for arbitration）、答辩状（rejoinder）、起诉状（petition）中，承包商项目管理人员更应使用正确的词汇，谨慎选择英文词汇，避免使用错误的词汇，导致出现歧义或误解。承包商需要牢记：恶语伤人六月寒。因为一旦英文用语或词汇使用错误或不当，读者的注意力就会分散，从而忽视了作者要表达的本意。

（2）准确（precision）。这不仅体现在英文用词准确，还体现在作者的真实意图和本意。例如，在某国际工程合同中，对恶劣气候条件的定义如下：

"Adverse Weather Conditions" means weather and climatic conditions which are not foreseeable at the Site, not shown in the Site data or are not a usual occurrence in the Country.

承包商在合同谈判中需要特别注意的是，在 FIDIC 1999 年第 1 版、2017 年第 2 版合同条款中，并没有对恶劣的气候条件给出定义，但这份国际工程合同却对此给出了定义。承包商需要考虑上述恶劣气候条件的定义是否妥当。根据上述定义，恶劣气候条件是指现场无法预见的，且在现场数据中显示或者在工程所在国不是通常发生的天气或气候。在上述定义中，Country 一词为大写，意味着是工程所在国，无法预见的（not foreseeable）是指在签约时一名有经验的承包商无法预见的情形。在合同谈判过程中，承包商还需要了解和查阅工程所在国和现场的气候条件，考虑是否需要在上述定义中界定降雨量。承包商还需要考虑是否在合同中增加一个名为恶劣气候条件的附件，以便全面和准确界定降雨量及其对工程进度的影响程度。

2.3.2 法律英语与简明英语的替换

法律英语具有典型的准确性特征，具有法律赋予的特定含义。一般而言，法律英语在法律词典中，例如英国《牛津法律词典》或者美国 *Black Law Dictionary* 中均能查到英文词汇的解释，从而帮助读者了解和认清法律用语在法律上的确定含义。在现实的法律环境中，并非一定需要用简明英语来替代法律英语特有词汇这是因为在长期的法律实践中法律英语确定了准确的含义，并广泛运用在正式文件中，例如合同、协议、仲裁文书或法院文书中。但在日常往来信函和文件中，为了避免用词累赘或者文牍主义，人们常常使用简明英语替代法律英语，如下：

法律用语	简明英语
as to	about, of, by, in
bring an action against	sue
herein	in this [agreement, etc.]
in as much as	since, because
in the event that	if
not less than	at least
prior to	before
pursuant to	under, by, in accordance with
said	the, this, that
same	it, them
subsequent to	after
such	that, this, those, the
thereafter	later
therein	in it, in them, inside

为了更为清晰和简明地表达作者的意图，避免赘述，可以使用下述常用英语替代复杂短语，如下：

复杂短语	通常用法
an adequate number of	enough
a number of	many, several
a sufficient number of	enough

at the present time	now
at the time when	when
at this point in time	now
during such time as	while
during the course of	during
for the reason that	because
in the event that	if
in the near future	soon
be able to	can
notwithstanding the fact that	although
on a daily basis	daily
on the ground that	because
prior to	before
subsequent to	after
the majority of	most
until such time as	until

为了避免使用累赘用语来表述，也可以使用动词替代复杂短语，使得语言更生动和具有力量，如下：

累赘短语	更佳表述
are in mitigation of	mitigate
conduct an examination of	examine
make accommodation for	accommodate
make adjustments to	adjust
make provision for	provide for
submit an application	apply
take into consideration	consider

但是在正式合同文件或法律文书中，为了更加准确地表达当事人的本意，仍不可避免地广泛使用法律英语或者上述累赘短语，例如，在某国际工程分包合同中，大量使用了法律用语表述，包括拉丁语，如下面例句中加下划线部分：

<u>Notwithstanding</u> anything to the contrary contained in this Subcontract, <u>in the event that</u> Suspension is not revoked within 180 (one hundred and eighty) days from the date of Suspension <u>hereunder</u> or within the extended period, if any, set forth in Clause 22.1, this Subcontract shall, upon expiry of the aforesaid period, be deemed to have been terminated by mutual agreement of the Parties and all the provisions of this Subcontract shall apply, *mutatis mutandis*, to such Termination as if a Termination Notice had been issued by the Main Contractor upon occurrence of a Subcontractor Default but subject always to the Main Contractor exercising its rights under the Project Agreement.

因此，为了在合同和法律用语中使用更正式的语言，需要用正式用词替代一般用法，如下：

法律用语	一般用法
assist	help
advise	tell
render	give
rescind	cancel
commence	begin, start
employ	use
cease to do	stop doing
convene	hold, call
construe	explain, interpret
deem	think, believe
terminate	end
partake in	join
require	ask
surrender	give
conveyance	transfer of real estate
prior to	before
provided that	if
in accordance with	according to
by virtue of	due to, because of
as regards, relating to	about
in effect	in fact
miscellaneous	other matters
pursuant to	according to
said	this, that
aforesaid	previous
forthwith	immediately
henceforth	from now on
herein	in the document
hereinafter	after this
thenceforth	after
thereafter	after that, accordingly
theretofore	up to that time
hitherto	before
whence	from what place, source
whereby	through, in accordance
whilst	during

2.3.3 合同用语常用表述方式

在国际工程项目合同管理过程中,承包商与业主和工程师往来函件、往来文件以及争议解决的法律文书中,通常需要使用一些常用的表述方式,例如"参见你方的来函""根据合同条款第 20.1 款""关于某某事项的争议""合同规定的"或者"技术规范规定的"等表述方式。这些表述方式在往来信函、往来文件和争议解决的法律文书中通常构成固定的用法,在国际标准格式合同,例如 FIDIC 系列合同中亦得到广泛的使用。了解和掌握这些用法,并利用 word 文档编辑中的同义词功能,作者可以变换使用这些固定表述方式,避免文法呆板和用词单一的问题,例如,在下面国际工程合同管理写作中,使用得最为广泛的"根据合同条款第 20.1 款",可以表述为:

(1) "according to Sub-Clause 20.1 of Conditions of Contract",或
(2) "in accordance with Sub-Clause 20.1 of Conditions of Contract",或
(3) "pursuant to Sub-Clause 20.1 of Conditions of Contract",或
(4) "in pursuance of Sub-Clause 20.1 of Conditions of Contract",或
(5) "as per Sub-Clause 20.1 of Conditions of Contract",或
(6) "per Sub-Clause 20.1 of Conditions of Contract",或
(7) "under Sub-Clause 20.1 of Conditions of Contract" 等。

作者通过变换不同的表述方式,使读者可以更有兴趣阅读信函,深入了解作者的本意。

在国际工程项目合同管理过程中,在往来信函、往来文件和法律文书中,承包商使用最多的表述方式汇总如下:

1 表述参考当事一方的来函
(1) referring to
(2) this is in reference to
(3) further to
(4) with reference to
(5) refer to
(6) in reference to

2 根据……,按照……
(1) according to
(2) as per
(3) in accordance with
(4) in pursuance of
(5) in the light of
(6) per
(7) pursuant to
(8) under

3 关于……
(1) about
(2) as to

（3）as regards

（4）be associated with

（5）concerning

（6）in connection with

（7）in relation to

（8）in regard to

（9）in respect of

（10）on the subject of

（11）pertaining to

（12）regarding

（13）relating to

（14）relative to

（15）respecting

（16）with regard to

4　规定的……

（1）as set out

（2）as set forth

（3）as prescribed

（4）as laid out

（5）as described

（6）set out

5　表述通知

（1）notify

（2）notice

（3）inform

（4）advice

6　表述如果

（1）if

（2）in the event that

（3）in the event of

（4）provided that

（5）provided

7　归责于……

（1）be attributable to

（2）culpable

（3）responsible

（4）liable

8　引起……

（1）give rise to

（2）induce

（3）bring about

（4）make

（5）lead to

（6）result in

（7）be the occasion of

（8）cause

9 导致……后果

（1）result in

（2）bring about

（3）lead to

（4）cause

（5）produce

（6）give rise to

10 由于……

（1）as a result of

（2）because of

（3）in consequence of

（4）on account of

（5）due to

（6）owing to

（7）by reason of

（8）attributable to

（9）thanks to

（10）since

（11）as

11 发生的费用……

incurred cost

12 ……引起的

（1）arising out of

（2）arising from

（3）stemming from

13 表示除非合同另有约定

（1）notwithstanding anything to the contrary contained in the contract

（2）unless otherwise stated in the contract

（3）except as otherwise stated in the contract

（4）save as otherwise agreed

（5）except where the context requires otherwise

（6）save and except as otherwise provided in the contract

(7) save to the extent expressly provided otherwise in the contract

(8) save insofar as the provision of Sub-Clause

(9) save where expressly provided otherwise in the contract

(10) save where provided otherwise in the contract

(11) save to the extent that the same are inconsistent with the Output Specifications

(12) notwithstanding anything to the contrary

(13) except insofar as it is otherwise provided under the Contract

14　举例

(1) for instance

(2) for example

(3) as one example

(4) to cite but one example

(5) for one thing

(6) for another thing

(7) likewise

(8) another

15　表明补充一个观点

(1) and

(2) also

(3) in addition

(4) besides

(5) what is more

(6) similarly

(7) nor

(8) along with

(9) likewise

(10) too

(11) moreover

(12) further

16　表示相反的

(1) but

(2) yet

(3) instead

(4) however

(5) on the one hand

(6) on the other hand

(7) still

(8) nevertheless

(9) nonetheless

（10） conversely

（11） on the contrary

（12） whereas

（13） in contrast to

（14） unfortunately

17　表示对比

（1） similarly

（2） likewise

（3） in the same way

18　表示重申

（1） in other words

（2） that is

（3） this means

（4） therefore

（5） accordingly

（6） then

（7） hence

19　表示强调观点

（1） in fact

（2） as a matter of fact

（3） indeed

（4） of course

（5） without exception

（6） still

（7） even so

（8） anyway

（9） the fact remains

（10） assuredly

20　表示时间

（1） that is

（2） then

（3） earlier

（4） previously

（5） meanwhile

（6） simultaneously

（7） now

（8） at once

（9） until now

（10） soon

(11) no sooner

(12) that being so

(13) afterward

(14) later

(15) eventually

(16) in the future

(17) at last

(18) finally

(19) in the end

21　表示总结

(1) to summarize

(2) to sum up

(3) to conclude

(4) in conclusion

(5) in short

(6) in brief

(7) so

(8) and so

(9) consequently

(10) therefore

(11) all in all

(12) for the reasons given above

(13) based on the foregoing

(14) for all those reasons

22　表示顺序

(1) first, second, third, finally

(2) firstly secondly, thirdly, finally

23　表示期满到期和应付款

(1) to be due

(2) to fall due

(3) to become due

24　表明观点

(1) be of the opinion that

(2) opine

(3) allege

(4) aver

(5) contend

(6) assert

(7) avow

（8） claim

（9） declare

（10） state

（11） say

（12） proclaim

（13） emphasize

25　表明立场

（1） take position

（2） take one's position

（3） be of the opinion that

（4） maintain one's position

（5） hold

（6） maintain

26　复合副词的表示方式

（1） hereafter（此后，今后）

（2） hereby（特此，兹）

（3） herein（此中，于此，在本合同中）

（4） hereinafter（以下，此后，在下文）

（5） hereof（于此，在本合同中）

（6） hereto（于此）

（7） hereunder（在下文，据此，根据本合同）

（8） hereunto（于此）

（9） here with（与此一道）

（10） thereafter（此后，后来）

（11） thereby（因此，由此，在那方面）

（12） therefrom（由此，从此）

（13） therein（其中，在其中）

（14） thereinafter（在下文）

（15） thereof（关于，由此，其中）

（16） thereto（此外，附随）

（17） thereunder（在其下，据此，依据）

（18） whereas（然而，鉴于）

（19） whereby（因此，由是，据此）

（20） wherefore（为此，因此）

（21） wherein（在那方面）

（22） whereof（关于那事/人）

27　近义词和成对语

（1） by and between（由）

（2） for and in consideration of（考虑到，鉴于）

(3) for and on behalf of（为了，代表）

(4) save and except（除了）

(5) furnish and provide（提供）

(6) make and enter into（达成）

(7) fulfill or perform（履行）

(8) procure and ensure（保证和确保）

(9) force and effect（效力）

(10) right and interest（权益）

(11) power and authority（权利）

(12) terms and conditions（条款）

(13) goods and chattels（个人动产，有形动产）

(14) losses and damages（损失和损害）

(15) null and void（失效，无效）

(16) sole and exclusive（唯一且排他的）

2.3.4　Shall，May 等情态动词用法

英语中的情态动词本身具有一定的词义，表示说话人对这一动作或状态的看法或主观设想。情态动词不能单独用作谓语，只能与动词原形一起构成谓语。情态动词主要包括：can（could），may（might），must，need，ought to，dare（dared），shall（should），will（would）。

在英语的一般用法（general usage）中，通常使用的是 would，will，can，could，may，should，must，might，shall 等情态动词，但在合同和法律英语中，would，will，can，could，might 使用得较少，而 should，must，may，shall 使用得较多，其中 shall 在合同和法律英语中是使用频率最高的词汇，其次是 may。

在合同和法律英语中使用"shall"时，其所属句子均涉及权利与义务内容，含有"本条款具有法律规定的指令性或强制性"的意义，具有应当或必须遵守的含义。"shall"表示"义务"或"责任"时，通常也表明应当或必须遵守的含义。在将"shall"翻译为中文时，通常被译为"应""应当""须""必须"。例如：FIDIC 合同条款 1999 年第 1 版《施工合同条件》（红皮书）第 4.1 款 [承包商的一般义务] 规定："The Contractor shall design (to the extent specified in the Contract), execute and complete the Works in accordance with the Contract and with the Engineer's instructions, and shall remedy any defects in the Works."（承包商应按照合同及工程师的指示，设计（在合同规定的范围内）、实施和完成工程，并修补工程中的任何缺陷）。在第 4.1 款中，"shall"表示义务，表明承包商应遵守这项义务。

在合同和法律英语中使用"may"时，一是表示"给予许可"或者"给予某人做某事的权利"，这主要体现在法律法规之中；二是表示"也许"或者"可以"，表明涉事当事人具有选择权，可以选择去做某事，也可以选择不去做某事。例如，FIDIC 合同 1999 年第 1 版《施工合同条件》（红皮书）第 15.1 款 [通知改正] 规定："If the Contractor fails to carry out any obligation under the Contract, the Engineer may by notice require the Contractor to make good the failure and to remedy it within a specified reasonable time."（如果承包商未能根据合同

履行任何义务，工程师可通知承包商，要求其在规定的合理时间内，纠正并补救上述违约。）在第15.1款中，"may"表示"可""可以"，即工程师拥有选择权，工程师可以向承包商发出整改通知，工程师也可以选择不发出整改通知。承包商在审查和阅读合同条款时，应特别注意"may"一词的使用。特别是在技术规范、业主要求或技术要求中，使用"may"一词往往意味着业主具有选择权，他可以选择使用某设备，也可以选择使用其他设备。而对于承包商而言，需要在投标阶段或者合同谈判过程中明确使用何种设备，而不能推论出业主就是要使用承包商认为便宜的设备。

为了避免业主和承包商在国际工程合同中对"may"和"shall"的误解和歧义，FIDIC合同条款2017年第2版系列合同第1.2款［解释］中对"may"和"shall"给出了定义，如下：

"(e) 'may' means that the Party or person referred to has the choice of whether to act or not in the matter referred to;

(f) 'shall' means that the Party or person referred to has an obligation under the Contract to perform the duty referred to;"

(e) "may"是指当事人或相关的人员对于述及的事项有权选择是否作为。(f) "shall"是指当事人或相关的人员负有义务履行合同项下的责任。

在法律法规或合同中，有时也会出现情态动词"must"和"should"。"must"表示毫无选择的、最高的强制性和义务性。"should"具有"应当""应该"的含义。但需要注意的是，在合同和法律英语中，"shall"一词可以完全涵盖"must"和"should"的含义，特别是在合同条款中，使用"shall"一词足以表示一方应履行的责任和义务，而应避免使用"must"和"should"。

2.3.5 英文写作中的大小写

英语与中文表述中最大的不同之一是英文区分大小写，而中文没有大小写之分。除了在英文句子第一个单词第一个字母应使用大写，表示人称代词"I"（我）、头衔、国家、国籍、宗教、种族、企业、组织、学校、政府机构名称等之外，英语大写还表示专用术语，特别是在合同文件中，合同约定了这些专用术语的特定含义。例如，FIDIC合同1999年第1版第1.1款［定义］给出了许多专用术语的定义，举例如下：

1.1.1.1 "Contract" means the Contract Agreement, these Conditions, the Employer's Requirement, the Tender, and further document (if any) which are listed in the Contract Agreement.

1.1.1.2 "Contract Agreement" means the contract agreement referred to in Sub-Clause 1.6 [*Contract Agreement*], including any annexed memoranda.

1.1.1.3 "Employer's Requirements" means the document entitled employer's requirements, as included in the Contract, and any additions and modifications to such document in accordance with the Contract. Such document specifies the purpose, scope, and/or design and/or other technical criteria, for the Works.

  这些定义和专用术语在合同中具有特定的、定义中规定的含义。在2017年第2版FIDIC合同条款中，FIDIC继承了1999年第1版合同的优点，按照字母顺序对定义进行排序，可以使得业主和承包商以及其他的合同使用人快速查找相关的定义。

  在合同和法律英语中，英语大写单词或词汇作为专用术语，具有特定的含义。在FIDIC 1999年第1版《EPC交钥匙合同条款》第1.1款［定义］中，在争议解决过程中频繁使用的专用术语如下：

1.1.1.2 "Contract Agreement" means the contract agreement referred to in Sub-Clause 1.6 [*Contract Agreement*], including any annexed memoranda.

1.1.1.3 "Employer's Requirements" means the document entitled employer's requirements, as included in the Contract, and any additions and modifications to such document in accordance with the Contract. Such document specifies the purpose, scope, and/or design and/or other technical criteria, for the Works.

1.1.1.5 "Performance Guarantees" and "Schedule of Payments" mean the documents so named (if any), as included in the Contract.

1.1.2.9 "DAB" means the person or three persons so named in the Contract, or other person(s) appointed under Sub-Clause 20.2 [*Appointment of the Dispute Adjudication Board*] or Sub-Clause 20.3 [*Failure to Agree Dispute Adjudication Board*].

1.1.3.1 "Base Date" means the date 28 days prior to the latest date for submission of the Tender.

1.1.3.2 "Commencement Date" means the date notified under Sub-Clause 8.1 [*Commencement of Works*], unless otherwise defined in the Contract Agreement.

1.1.3.3 "Time for Completion" means the time for completing the Works or a Section (as the case may be) under Sub-Clause 8.2 [*Time for Completion*], as stated in the Particular Conditions (with any extension under Sub-Clause 8.4 [*Execution of Time for Completion*]), calculated from the Commencement Date.

1.1.3.4 "Tests on Completion" means the tests which are specified in the Contract or agreed by both Parties or instructed as a Variation, and which are carried out under Clause 9 [*Tests on Completion*] before the works or a Section (as the case may be) are taken over by the Employer.

1.1.3.5 "Taking Over Certificate" means a certificate issued under Clause 10 [*Employer's Taking Over*].

1.1.3.6 "Defects Notification Period" means the period for notifying defects in the Works or a Section (as the case may be) under Sub-Clause 11.1 [*Completion of Understanding Works and Remedying Defects*], as stated in the Particular Conditions (with any extension under Sub-Clause 11.3 [*Extension of Defects Notification Period*]), calculated from the date on which the Works or Section is competed as certified under Sub-Clause 10.1 [*Taking Over of the Works and Sections*]. If no such period is stated in the Particular Conditions, the period shall be one year.

1.1.4.1 "Contract Price" means the agreed amount stated in the Contract Agreement for the design, execution and completion of the Works and the remedying of any defects, and includes adjustment (if any) in accordance with the contract.

1.1.4.2 "Cost" means all expenditure reasonably incurred (or to be incurred) by the Contractor, whether on or off the Site, including overhead and similar charges, but does not include profit.

1.1.4.4 "Foreign Currency" means a currency in which part (or all) of the Contract Price is payable, but not the Local Currency.

1.1.4.5 "Local Currency" means the currency of the Country.

1.1.4.6 "Provisional Sum" means a sum (if any) which is specified in the Contract as a provisional sum, for the execution of any part of the Works or for the supply of Plant, Material or services under Sub-Clause 13.5 [*Provisional Sums*].

1.1.5.1 "Contractor's Equipment" means all apparatus, machinery, vehicles and other things required for the execution and completion of the Works and remedying of any defects. However, Contractor's Equipment excludes Temporary Works, Employer's Equipment (if any), Plant, Materials and any other things intended to form or forming part of the Permanent Works.

1.1.5.2 "Goods" means Contractor's Equipment, Materials, Plant and Temporary Works, or any of them as appropriate.

1.1.5.3 "Materials" means things of all kinds (other than Plant) intended to form or forming part of the Permanent Works, including the supply-only materials (if any) to be supplied by the Contractor under the Contract.

1.1.5.4 "Permanent Works" means the permanent works to be designed and executed by the Contractor under the Contract.

1.1.5.5 "Plant" means the apparatus, machinery and vehicles intended to form or forming part of the Permanent Works.

1.1.5.6 "Section" means a part of the Works specified in the Particular Conditions as a Section (if any).

1.1.5.7 "Temporary Works" means all temporary works of every kind (other than

Contractor's Equipment) required on Site for the execution and completion of the Permanent Works and the remedying of any defects.

1.1.5.8 "Works" means the Permanent Works and the Temporary Works, or either of them as appropriate.

1.1.6.2 "Country" means the country in which the Site (or most of it) is located, where the Permanent Works are to be executed.

1.1.6.3 "Force Majeure" is defined in Clause 19 [*Fore Majeure*].

1.1.6.5 "Laws" means all national (or state) legislation, statutes, ordinances and other laws, and regulations and by-laws of any legally constituted public authority.

1.1.6.7 "Site" means the places where the Permanent Works are to be executed and to which Plant and Materials are to be delivered, and any other places as may be specified in the Contract as forming part of the Site.

1.1.6.8 "Variation" means any change to the Employer's Requirements or the Works, which is instructed or approved as a variation under Clause 13 [*Variation and Adjustment*].

在国际工程合同管理过程中，承包商应特别注意这些专用术语的特定含义，特别是在合同文件中或往来信函及会议纪要中，正确使用这些专用术语，可避免产生争议。中国企业在合同谈判和合同争议过程中，往往因一个英文大小写而损失巨大，案例如下：

在某国际工程项目中，FIDIC合同条款多边开发银行协调版（2005年版）第14.8款[延误的付款]规定：

"Unless otherwise stated in the Particular Conditions, these financing charges shall be calculated at the annual rate of three percentage points above the discount rate of the central bank in the country of the currency of payment, and shall be paid in such currency."（除非专用条件中另有规定，上述融资费用应以高出支付货币所在国中央银行的贴现率三个百分点的年利率进行计算，并应以同种货币支付。）

合同专用条款规定："14.8 simple interest 1% above the central bank discount rate."

在合同履约过程中，承包商按照工程所在国中央银行的贴现率14%加1%计算业主延迟支付工程款利息。在合同履行即将结束时，业主对此提出异议，认为不应该按照工程所在国中央银行的贴现率加1%计算利息，而应根据美联储的美元利率加1%计算延迟支付工程款利息。业主和承包商为此发生争议，最终将争议提交由独任成员（sole member）组成的争议委员会（Dispute Board）进行裁决。

争议委员会在审查了业主和承包商之间关于延期支付工程款利息的争议，认为相关争议核心焦点是：

（1）在FIDIC合同条款中，第一个字母大写词汇是否具有特殊含义（whether the capitalized words in FIDIC provisions have any special meaning）。

(2) 利息计算的来源是工程所在国中央银行还是美国的中央银行（whether the source of interest rate for calculation of financing charges is the central bank of ···. or the central bank of United States）。

争议委员会在审理中注意到，FIDIC 合同条款第 1.1.6.2 款对"Country"的定义如下："Country means the country in which the Site (or most of it is) is located, where the Permanent Works are to be executed,"而通用合同条款第 14.8 款［延误的付款］规定的是："the central bank in the country of the currency of payment"，这里的 country 为小写，因此，通用合同条款第 14.8 款［延误的付款］中的 country 不应是"Country"，即工程所在国，而是支付货币所在国的中央银行，即美国的中央银行——美联储。争议委员会在审理中还注意到，合同专用条款第 14.8 款［延误的付款］没有指明为工程所在国的中央银行。因此，应按照通用合同条款第 14.8 款［延误的付款］中的"the central bank in the country of the currency of payment"予以解释。争议委员会认为，如果不存在美联储的贴现率，则可使用伦敦银行同业拆借利率 LIBOR 计算延迟支付工程款的利息。

本案对承包商的启示在于：

（1）FIDIC 合同条款中第 14.8 款［延误的付款］第二段计算延迟支付工程款的利率为"支付货币所在国中央银行的贴现率三个百分点的年利率"，这里的 country 是小写，而不是大写的"Country"，即工程所在国。因此，在业主支付外币，例如美元或欧元等货币时，应注意是支付货币所在国中央银行。但是，在业主支付工程所在国的当地货币时，应为工程所在国中央银行的贴现率等。

（2）合同专用条款中的合同数据（Contract Data）规定了"simply interest, 1% above the central bank discount rate"，实质上是对通用合同条件第 14.8 款第二段的修改。承包商在投标或者合同谈判过程中，应注意及时向业主澄清是哪国中央银行的贴现率。承包商可通过投标答疑的方式，或者合同谈判中明确国别的方式确定计算延迟支付工程款利息的来源国。

（3）在合同语言中，英文大写在合同中具有合同赋予的特定含义，承包商应在投标或合同谈判中特别加以注意，检查大小写的差异及适用范围。

2.3.6 常用拉丁语

在合同和法律英语中，有时为了表达确切的含义，通常会使用拉丁语。在西方法律中，与法律有关的拉丁词语的含义在法律界已沿用了多个世纪，其含义已被界定得非常准确，这就是拉丁语词汇依然保留在法律英语中的主要原因。拉丁语在法律语言中始终处于权威性的地位，法律格言往往使用拉丁语表述，例如，"contra bonos mores"，英语为"contrary to good morals"，即"违背公序良俗的"；"accusare nemo se debet"英语为"nobody is bound to incriminate himself"，即"一个人不应被强迫去做出对其不利的证词"。法律英语的拉丁语化是法律英语的最显著特征之一。

在合同和法律英语中，特别是在国际工程合同和争议解决过程中，通常使用的拉丁语词汇如下：

a priori 公理的，自明的

averbis legis non est recedendum 法律文字不容违反

bona fide 在法律术语中指良好的意图/一般表示真诚的和善意的

de facto   事实上的、实际的

gratis dictum   空言,仅仅是主张

jus standi   出庭资格

interalia   除了别的以外;在其他事物中,其中包括

inpari delicto   同样过失、互有过失、同样有罪

inso facto   根据事实[行为]本身,因此

mutatis mutandis   已做必要的修改;准用

per se   本质上,本身

ratione materiae   属事管辖权

ratione personae   属人管辖权

ratine temporis   属时管辖权

stricto sensu   从严格意义上说

verbatim   逐字逐句的/地

vice versa   反之亦然

status quo   现状

在法律英语中,著名的拉丁语法律名句传世久远,中国人比较熟悉的法律名言有:"Ignorantia facti excusat—Ignorantia juris non excusat",英译:Ignorance of fact excuses—ignorance of the law does not excuse。汉译:不知事实可以作为借口,但不知法却不能开脱(罪责)。"Nullus commodum capere potest de injuria sua propria",英译:No man should benefit from his own injustice,汉译:没有人应当从自己的过错中获益。"Res inter alios acta alteri nocere no debet",英译:A transaction between two parties shouldn't operate to the disadvantage of a third party not in their debt,汉译:两方当事人之间的交易不得对利益无涉的第三方不利。

关于合同和法律英语中拉丁语的用法,例句如下:

(1) The provisions of this Subcontract, insofar as they relate to the carrying out, completion, and testing of the Subcontract Works, shall apply *mutatis mutandis* to the works carried out under this Clause 15.4.3.

(2) Any works which are provided under and in accordance with this Clause 15 shall form part of the Sub contract Works and the provisions of this Sub contract shall apply *mutatis mutandis* to such works.

(3) This might be interpreted as a de facto recognition of the republic's independence.

(4) If a crime occurs then there is, inso facto, a guilty party.

(5) Amendments Parties may amend this Agreement having regard, inter alia, to the experience gained in implementation.

(6) Before dealing with the scope of the Price Escalation/Adjustment Clause by looking into the detail of all the terms surrounded the contract in this regard we would like to explain the settled law that parties to the contract must acknowledge that they are obliged by law to adhere to all the terms and conditions of the contract stricto sensu (in its true sense).

2.3.7 禁止使用禁忌语

承包商在与业主或工程师交往过程中无论发生了什么令人义愤填膺的事情，或者无论业主或工程师做出了对承包商如何不利的事情或决定，使承包商火冒三丈、难以容忍，承包商均不应在往来信函和法律文书中使用禁忌语，而应冷静对待，通过合同约定的争议解决方式，例如争议委员会或仲裁方式解决施工过程中发生的争议。

禁止在往来信函和法律文书中使用禁忌语，是承包商应牢记的最为重要的事项之一。

承包商需牢记，如果在往来文件和法律文书中，或在与业主或工程师的会议上使用了禁忌语，承包商的相关工作人员将面临被驱逐出现场的后果。如果业主或工程师认为造成了人身伤害，可能还会采取法律行动。

第3章 写作表述方式

"A party to a dispute, particularly if there is arbitration, will learn three lessons (often too late): the importance of records, the importance of records and the importance of records."

马克斯·W. 亚伯拉罕森:《建筑法和ICE合同》

3.1 国际工程合同管理往来信函分析

在国际工程项目中，除了承包商参与投标或通过合同谈判获得签署工程项目合同文件外，自工程项目开工至履约完毕，承包商与工程师和/或业主之间的通信交流基本上是靠往来信函的书面形式。承包商与工程师和/或业主之间的书面往来文件包括往来信函、会议纪要、补充协议、变更指示及变更协议、各种技术报告，例如地质勘探报告、水文勘探报告、承包商索赔通知和索赔报告，以及业主向承包商提供的各类与施工有关的报告和文件等。在这些施工或者设计、采购和施工过程中的往来文件中，绝大部分是往来信函方式。技术报告、变更协议以及补充协议等文件，也是以一方向另一方发出信函并将这些文件作为附件的方式发送给对方。因此，往来信函是国际工程项目合同管理的最基本方式，也是国际工程合同管理的基本特征之一。

在某国际工程项目中，承包商与工程师自开工至2018年底往来信函总数为1332封，其中承包商发函给工程师函件数量719份，工程师致函承包商的函件数量为613份。这些往来信函涉及的函件类型见表3-1。表3-1所述的承包商与工程师之间往来信函函件类型的占比示意图见图3-1。

表3-1 某国际工程项目2018年往来信函统计

序号	类别	总数	其中：承包商致函工程师	其中：工程师致函承包商
1	合同信息	45	23	22
2	开工通知书	2	1	1
3	工程保险	21	11	10
4	预付款支付	4	3	1
5	许可	1	1	0
6	进度计划	95	44	51
7	基准测量点	35	15	20
8	设计	303	153	150
9	技术问题	338	192	146

（续）

序号	类别	总数	其中：承包商致函工程师	其中：工程师致函承包商
10	结构物	18	7	11
11	管涵	11	5	6
12	实验	291	192	99
13	交通维护	94	44	50
14	计量	6	2	4
15	环保	15	6	9
16	安全	11	3	8
17	索赔	2	1	1
18	争议解决	10	8	2
19	会议安排	17	4	13
20	其他（休假）	13	4	9
合计：		1332	719	613

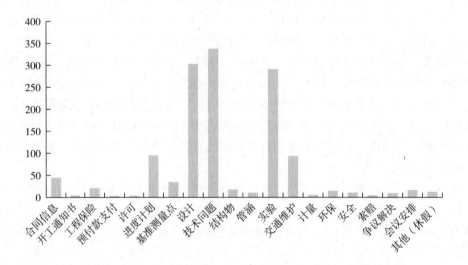

图 3-1　某国际工程项目承包商与工程师 2018 年往来信函统计

从表 3-1 和图 3-1 中信函的数量和类型中可看到如下事项和问题：

（1）承包商与工程师在一年内涉及设计和技术问题的往来信函多达 296 封，说明设计和技术问题是该国际工程项目的主要问题。

（2）与实验有关的往来函件多达 99 封，说明承包商在工程项目前期进行了大量的实验工作，包括道路施工所需的混凝土配合比、沥青混凝土配合比等实验，以及既有道路潜在缺陷（latent defect）等实验等。

（3）与交通维护有关的往来信函为 50 封，说明工程师与承包商之间就交通维护进行讨论和执行工程师的交通维护指示。

（4）与进度计划有关的往来信函为 51 封，说明工程师与承包商之间就进度计划进行讨论和确定基准进度计划等问题。

(5) 与基准测量点有关的往来信函为 20 封，说明承包商要求工程师提供基准测量点，工程师就基准测量点进行了回复。

因此，有经验的国际工程项目管理人员可以从往来信函类型和数量看出工程项目的问题所在，从而制定具有针对性的工程项目管理计划和重点。

3.2 信函写作基本原则

在国际工程项目合同管理过程中，承包商与工程师和/或业主之间往来信函的基本原则可归纳为：

(1)"一事一函"原则。
(2)"一函一回复"原则。
(3)"在合同约定的期限内发出通知或回复"原则。
(4)"向工程师致函而非向业主致函"原则。

3.2.1 "一事一函"原则

"一事一函"原则是英文信函写作的最基本原则之一。具体而言，就是一封信函仅表述一件事情，而不能在一封信函中同时表述两件事情。如果承包商需要向工程师或业主致函，说明两件事情，则应草拟两封信函，分别致函工程师或业主。例如，承包商在同一天或同一时段需要向工程师致函催促尽快批准递交的图纸，同时，承包商也需致函工程师催促工程师批准递交的进度计划。此时，承包商应写两封信函，分别以"批准递交的图纸"和"批准递交的进度计划"为信函的标题（Subject 或 Reference），以不同的函号致函工程师，而不能将催促工程师批准递交的图纸和进度计划都写在一封函件中。

3.2.2 "一函一回复"原则

"一函一回复"原则是英文信函写作的最基本原则之二。也就是说，在工程师或业主向承包商致函，承包商收到函件后，应予以回复。承包商需要注意的是，"一函一回复"原则适用所有信函，但业主或工程师的批准不在回复之列。例如工程师批准承包商某段道路施工，或批准承包商递交的施工图纸等，承包商无须对业主或工程师的批准予以书面回复，没有必要回复说收到了工程师或业主的批准。

在"一函一回复"原则中，承包商在与工程师或业主就某事件发生激烈合同争议时，双方经过 70 多封函件往来后，工程师最后回复说他不能接受承包商的主张，建议依据合同约定的争议解决机制诉诸争议委员会予以解决或者诉诸仲裁予以最终解决，而承包商认为，工程师的最后一封函件表明其不接受承包商的主张，这个结论承包商无法接受。因此，承包商再次致函表明不接受工程师的结论。承包商的观点在于，如果在最后一封函件中工程师或业主表达了其不接受承包商的观点，在此种情况下，如果承包商没有反驳对方的观点，则意味着承包商最后接受了工程师或业主的观点。因此，承包商认为，在涉及合同争议时，无论如何，承包商一定要发出最后一封函件表明他不同意工程师或业主的主张，即使工程师或业主已经在函件中表明双方已经存在合同争议，一再请求承包商不要再致函的情况下，承包商仍要发出最后一封函件。

那么，承包商坚持发出最后一封函件主张自己的观点，否则就视为承包商"同意"了工程师或业主的观点的看法是否成立呢？应当说，承包商的这种观点不能成立，理由有如下几点。

第一，FIDIC 合同条款 1987 年第 4 版《土木工程施工合同条件》（红皮书）第 67.1 款至第 67.4 款规定了争议解决方式、程序以及工程师决定的法律效力。第 67.1 款规定了业主和承包商可将争议提交工程师作出决定：

"如果业主和承包商之间由于或起因于合同或工程施工而产生任何争议，包括对工程师的任何意见、指示、决定、证书或估价方面的任何争议，无论是在工程施工中还是竣工后，也不论是在否认合同有效或合同在其他情况下终止之前还是之后，此类争议事宜应首先以书面形式提交工程师，并将一份副本提交另一方。……"

FIDIC 合同条款 1999 年第 1 版《施工合同条件》第 20 条［索赔、争议和仲裁］规定了争议解决方式和程序。第 20.2 款规定："争议应按第 20.4 款［取得争议裁决委员会的决定］的规定，由争议裁决委员会（DAB）裁决。……"第 20.5 款规定："经 DAB 对之做出的决定（如有）未能成为最终的和有约束力的任何争议，除非已获友好解决，应通过国际仲裁对其作出最终解决。"

第二，英国 1996 年建筑法本身并没有界定"争议"的定义，由此引发了法律适用的问题。在 Edmund Nuttall Ltd. v R. G. Carter Ltd.［2002］EWHC400（TCC）案中，法院认为只有在进入到既定的程序后才会产生争议。英国法院在 Halki Shippiing Corp. v Sopex Oils Ltd.［1998］1 W. L. R. 726 案中对"争议"一词进行了界定，判决认为，"争议"一词应当符合通常的理解（common sense approach）。在 Amec Civil Engineering v Secretary of State for Transport［2004］EWHC 2339（TCC）案中，杰克逊法官确定了界定"争议"的七个标准，最终得以解决"争议"标准的法律难题。杰克逊法官在本案判决中的"争议和分歧"一节中的第 68 段写道：

"通过评估上述权威观点，法官做出了如下主张：

（1）在很多仲裁条款和 1996 年《建筑法》第 108 条中的"争议"一词应具有通常理解的含义。它不具有律师们赋予的某些特定的或者特殊的含义。

（2）尽管"争议"一词含义简单，但多年来，许多诉讼案件都涉及了在特定情况下是否存在争议问题的讨论。关于什么是争议或者什么不是争议，本案并不就此做出任何泾渭分明的法律规则，但是，总结这些判例可以提供有益的指南。

（3）仅仅是当事一方（我称之为"原告"）向当事另一方（我称之为"被告"）通知索赔的事实本身并不能自动或立即产生争议。从语言和法院判决来看，非常明确的是，除非或直至索赔不被认可，才会产生争议。

（4）索赔不被认可的情形多种多样。例如，被对方明确拒绝，或者当事方对此进行讨论，从而推断出对方不接受索赔。被告也可能会搪塞此事，从而推断出他不接受索赔。被告还可能会保持一段时间沉默，从而得出不接受索赔的推论。

（5）被告保持沉默多长时间才能推断出他对索赔持有异议，主要依据案件的事实和合同结构来确定。在索赔要点清晰并存在明显争议时，即使沉默时间很短，也可以作出此类推断。在将索赔通知发给被告，对那些法律义务进行独立评估索赔，相应回复的代理人，此时可能需要更长时间才能推断出沉默是否会导致争议。

(6) 如果原告强行要求被告在最后期限之前对索赔给予回复，那么，最后期限并不具有自动剥夺被告在合理时间内给予回复权利的效力。另一方面，在考虑给予索赔回复合理时间是多长时，法院可能会参考这个声明的最后期限和强行要求被告给予回复的理由。

(7) 如果原告提出的索赔模棱两可，以致被告无法给予明确的回复，为仲裁或管辖权的目的，无论被告沉默还是明确表明不予认可，都不能产生争议。"

在上述 Amec 案中，杰克逊法官的著名论断确定了"争议"的确切含义，这将有助于解决工程合同争议中的管辖权问题。无论是争议裁决委员会（DAB）机制，还是仲裁或者诉讼，作为争议解决方式，在确定管辖权问题时，应探究 DAB、仲裁或诉讼的管辖权起源和基础，即"争议"是 DAB、仲裁或诉讼的管辖权的基础和起源。在此需要指出的是，DAB 和仲裁管辖权是基于合同当事人在合同中的约定，诉讼则是基于成文法，即民事诉讼法的法律规定获得对案件的管辖权。

在 Fastrack Construction Ltd. v Morrison Construction Ltd. ［2000］BLR 168 案中，桑顿法官判决：如果提出的索赔随后被拒绝，则构成争议。桑顿法官在判决第 27~29 节中写道：

"一旦索赔、问题或其他事项的标的引起了对方当事人的注意，且对方当事人有机会考虑、承认、修改或拒绝索赔或明确肯定，则才能产生'争议'。要构成一项争议，提出的索赔必须被拒绝。"

杰克逊法官在上述 Amec 案中写道：

"在 Ellerine Bros[①] 案和 Halki Shipping[②] 案中，出现的问题是根据现有的成文法，一项争议是否能够停止法院诉讼而继续仲裁。在 Ellerine Bros 案中，坦普尔曼法官认为，如果信函写明了要求或请求，而被告没有回复，则构成争议。对于产生的争议而言，被告没有必要回信写明'我不同意'。在 Halki 案中，斯维顿·托马斯法官认为，一旦提出了索赔金额，则构成争议，除非或直至被告承认是应付款。鉴于这两个案件的时间比 Monmouthshire 案更晚，埃肯黑德法官认为，他应受到 Ellerine Bros 和 Halki 这两个判例的约束。由于 ICE 合同第 66 条与通常英语表述意思相同，鉴于 1996 年《住宅许可、建设和重置法》第 108（1）款已应用于许多案件中，由于他推崇这种逻辑推理，因此，他认为交通大臣在 2002 年 12 月 6 日的信函中递交了索赔，且符合一项公认的索赔的要件。而 2002 年 12 月 10 日 Amec 公司的回复不能构成一项认可。关于 Halki 案，在 Amec 案事实上没有认可索赔时，构成一项争议。埃肯黑德法官也得出结论，认为 2002 年 10 月 2 日的信函尽管非常具有原则，但仍构成一项索赔，且其内容构成争议。"

因此，根据上述判例可以得出，合同当事一方的主张何时构成争议，在英国 Amec 案杰克逊法官的著名的七点论述中得到了确切的答案，即合同当事一方的索赔主张本身不构成争议，只有在当事另一方不认可或否决或以沉默方式表达不予认可时，才构成争议。在构成争议的情况下，争议裁决委员会仲裁庭或法院才拥有案件的管辖权，按照约定的程序规则解决实体合同争议。

从上述 FIDIC 和英国法院判例中可以得出，在一方提出主张，另一方表示不同意的情况下，构成争议。无论谁发出最后一封函，都无法改变当事双方之间存在合同争议的事实。因

---

① Ellerine Bros v Kliinger ［1982］1 WLR 1375.
② Halki Shipping Corporation v Sopex Oils ［1998］1 WLR 726.

此,关于承包商认为如果不发出最后一封函表明自己的观点,就意味着自己同意工程师或业主观点,这种情况是不存在的。

3.2.3 "在合同约定的期限内发出通知或回复"原则

"在合同约定的期限内发出通知或回复"的原则是国际工程合同管理中的基本原则之三。在国际工程合同中,特别是国际标准格式合同,例如 FIDIC 合同,均在合同条款中规定了承包商或工程师应"立即(immediately)""尽快(as soon as practicable)""及时(promptly)"和"索赔通知需要在规定的期限内发出,否则失效",即索赔时效(time bar)的四种情况:

(1) FIDIC 合同条款 1999 年第 1 版《设计采购施工(EPC)/交钥匙工程合同条件》规定应"立即"回复的条款包括:

1)第 4.20 款[业主设备和免费供应的材料],使用了"立即"一词,如下:"The Employer shall supply, free of charge, the "free-issue materials" (if any) in accordance with the details stated in the Employer's Requirements. The Employer shall, at his risk and cost, provide these materials at the time and place specified in the Contract. The Contractor shall then visually inspect them, and shall promptly give notice to the Employer of any shortage, defect or default in these materials. Unless otherwise agreed by both Parties, the Employer shall immediately rectify the notified shortage, defect or default."

2)第 5.2 款[承包商文件],该款规定:"(c) if the Contractor wishes to modify any design or document which has previously been submitted for review, the Contractor shall immediately give notice to the Employer. Thereafter, the Contractor shall submit revised documents to the Employer in accordance with the above procedure."

3)第 6.5 款[工作小时],该款规定:"(c) the work is unavoidable, or necessary for the protection of life or property or for the safety of the Works, in which case the Contractor shall immediately advise the Employer."

4)第 14.2 款[预付款],该款规定:"If the advance payment has not been repaid prior to the issue of the Taking-Over Certificate for the Works or prior to termination under Clause 15 [*Termination by Employer*], Clause 16 [*Suspension and Termination by Contractor*] or Clause 19 [*Force Majeure*] (as the case may be), the whole of the balance then outstanding shall immediately become due and payable by the Contractor to the Employer."

5)第 15.2 款[业主终止合同],该款规定:"In any of these events or circumstances, the Employer may, upon giving 14 days' notice to the Contractor, terminate the Contract and expel the Contractor from the Site. However, in the case of sub-paragraph (e) or (f), the Employer may by notice terminate the Contract immediately." 和 "The Contractor shall then leave the Site and deliver any required Goods, all Contractor's Documents, and other design documents made by or for him, to the Engineer. However, the Contractor shall use his best efforts to comply immediately with any reasonable instructions included in the notice (i) for the assignment of any subcontract, and (ii) for the protection of life or property or for the safety of the Works."

6)第 16.2 款[承包商终止合同],该款规定:"In any of these events or circumstances, the Contractor may, upon giving 14 days' notice to the Employer, terminate the Contract. However, in the case of subparagraph (f) or (g), the Contractor may by notice terminate the Contract immediately."

在这些条款中,"立即"应按照该词本身的基本含义,即表示应"马上"采取行动的含义。

(2) FIDIC 合同条款 1999 年第 1 版《设计采购施工(EPC)/交钥匙工程合同条件》规定应"尽快(as soon as practical)"予以通知和回复的条款包括:

1) 第2.5款 [业主的索赔]。
2) 第4.5款 [指定分包商]。
3) 第6.7款 [健康和安全]。
4) 第8.1款 [工程开工]。
5) 第10.3款 [竣工试验的干扰]。
6) 第11.1款 [完成扫尾工作和修补缺陷]。
7) 第12.1款 [竣工后试验的程序]。
8) 第13.3款 [变更程序]。
9) 第15.3款 [终止日的估价]。
10) 第16.1款 [承包商暂停工程的权利]。
11) 第20.1款 [承包商索赔]。

虽然 FIDIC 合同没有给出"尽快 as soon as practicable"的定义,但根据该词的通常理解,应理解为"尽快"的基本含义,但不要求"立即"。

(3) FIDIC 合同条款 1999 年第 1 版《设计采购施工(EPC)/交钥匙工程合同条件》规定应"及时(promptly)"予以通知和回复的条款包括:

1) 第1.8款 [文件的照管和提供]。
2) 第3.3款 [受托人员]。
3) 第4.20款 [业主设备和免费供应的材料]。
4) 第4.24款 [化石]。
5) 第7.3款 [检查]。
6) 第7.5款 [拒收]。
7) 第8.3款 [进度计划]。
8) 第13.1款 [变更权]。
9) 第14.9款 [保留金的支付]。
10) 第15.2款 [业主终止合同]。
11) 第16.3款 [停止工作和承包商设备的撤离]。
12) 第16.4款 [终止时的付款]。
13) 第17.4款 [业主风险的后果]。
14) 第18.1款 [有关保险的一般要求]。
15) 第20.4款 [取得争议裁决委员会的决定]。

虽然 FIDIC 合同条款没有给出"及时"的定义,但根据该词通常意义的理解,"及时"是指在合理的时间内尽快予以书面回复。在国际工程项目合同管理的实践中如何确定"及时",这是一个事实问题(a matter of fact)。一般而言,应在 1~7 天内给予书面回复。

在国际工程实践中，承包商经常问及的问题是：如果承包商未能及时或未能向工程师或业主发出通知或予以回复，是否意味着承包商默认工程师或业主的观点？反之亦然。

可以肯定的是，如果合同没有明示约定默认条款，则合同当事人不能推定另一方未能回复或未能及时回复构成对自己提出观点或事实的默认。如果合同约定了默认条款，则合同一方应仔细检查默认条款适用的情形，只有在默认条款约定的情形发生时，才能予以默认，否则不构成默认。例如，合同约定承包商在递交给工程师的图纸后，如果工程师未能在 7 天内提出意见予以回复，则视为工程师同意承包商递交的图纸，承包商可以依据该图纸进行施工。在此类默认条款中，应确定其适用的范围仅限于承包商递交给工程师审批的图纸，但不能扩大到任何其他事项上，例如承包商递交给工程师签认的工程结算证书。

(4) FIDIC 合同条款 1999 年第 1 版《设计采购施工（EPC）/交钥匙工程合同条件》规定的"索赔通知需要在规定的期限内发出，否则失效"，即索赔时效（time bar）的条款。

FIDIC 合同条款 1999 年第 1 版红皮书、黄皮书和银皮书第 20.1 款［承包商的索赔］规定：

"If the Contractor considers himself to be entitled to any extension of the Time for Completion and/or any additional payment, under any Clause of these Conditions or otherwise in connection with the Contract, the Contractor shall give notice to the Employer, describing the event or circumstance giving rise to the claim. The notice shall be given as soon as practicable, and not later than 28 days after the Contractor became aware, or should have become aware, of the event or circumstance.

If the Contractor fails to give notice of a claim within such period of 28 days, the Time for Completion shall not be extended, the Contractor shall not be entitled to additional payment, and the Employer shall be discharged from all liability in connection with the claim. Otherwise, the following provisions of this Sub-Clause shall apply."

（如果承包商未能在上述 28 天期限内发出索赔通知，则竣工实践不得延长，承包商应无权获得追加付款，而业主应免除有关该索赔的全部责任。否则，应使用本款以下规定。）

FIDIC 合同条款 2017 年第 2 版第 20.2 款［付款和/或工期延长索赔］规定了两个索赔时效的制度，该款不仅规定了承包商未能在知道和应当知道索赔事件发生后 28 天内发出索赔通知，否则承包商丧失索赔工期延长和/或付款的权利，而且规定了承包商未能在知道和应当知道索赔事件发生后 42 天内递交索赔详情，即索赔报告，也丧失索赔工期延长和/或付款的权利的制度。因此，承包商在使用 FIDIC 合同条款 2017 年第 2 版时，应特别注意索赔时效的问题。

根据上述 28 天索赔时效的规定，承包商未能在知道和应当知道索赔事件发生之日 28 天期限内发出索赔通知，则承包商丧失索赔工期延长和额外费用的权利。

承包商需要注意的是，在合同没有明确规定或约定索赔时效的情况下，索赔时效不应予以适用。在合同明确约定索赔时效时，承包商应遵守合同约定的索赔时效，避免索赔权利的丧失。

3.2.4 "向工程师致函而非向业主致函"原则

在国际工程项目中，业主均聘用咨询工程师或监理工程师（在 FIDIC 合同条款中称为

"工程师")代为行使工程项目管理的职责,特别是在国际金融组织融资的项目中,工程师作为业主的代理(agent),行使项目管理责任。因此,在有工程师的情况下,承包商应向工程师致函并抄送业主,而非向业主直接致函抄送工程师。这种情况适用于国际金融组织,例如世界银行、亚洲开发银行、亚洲基础设施投资银行、非洲开发银行、欧洲复兴开发银行等融资的国际工程项目,也适用于某些地区银行、基金等融资的工程项目。

"向工程师致函而非向业主致函的情形一是:如果业主直接管理工程项目,或者业主同时作为工程师,此时,承包商应向业主致函和回复相关函件。

"向工程师致函而非向业主致函的情形二是:如果工程师不是国际金融组织融资工程项目项下的典型意义上的 FIDIC 所称的工程师,而业主聘任的咨询工程师仅负责技术审核时,则承包商应向业主致函和回复函件,而不应向咨询工程师致函和回复函件,除非业主指示承包商可就技术审核事宜与咨询工程师直接进行信函通信往来。

"向工程师致函而非向业主致函的情形三是:如果业主尚未聘任工程师,或者业主聘任的工程师尚未到达现场开始工作,则承包商可以在项目前期向业主致函和回复信函。一旦承包商接到业主通知已经聘任工程师和开始工作的通知,则承包商应直接向工程师致函和回复相关信函,并抄送业主。

需要注意的是,如果业主向承包商致函,则承包商应直接回复业主并抄送工程师。

对于承包商与工程师日常往来的函件,有些业主要求需抄送业主,在这种情况下,承包商在致函工程师时,应同时抄送业主。

3.3 英文信函写作结构

3.3.1 国际工程合同管理使用的信函类型

在国际工程合同管理过程中,按照性质分,承包商使用的函件类型可以分为:

(1) 通知类型函件。例如通知承包商人员和设备到场,因发生引起承包商索赔的事件,承包商发出的通知等。

(2) 递交审批类型函件。例如承包商递交给工程师审批的进度计划、图纸、施工计划、质量保证计划和 HSE 计划等。

(3) 技术交流类型函件。例如承包商与工程师讨论技术方案的可行性等。

(4) 与合同争议有关的函件。例如承包商不同意工程师作出的变更指示,或者对变更的估价存在异议等。

(5) 其他杂项的函件。例如承包商递交的人员签证和工作许可、需要业主出具相关文件、海关清关等函件。

承包商在回复工程师或业主的函件时,函件的类型与上述类型基本相同。

3.3.2 英文信函格式

英文信函,特别是商业性质的英文信函,有相对固定的格式,即信函中应包括:
(1) 信函文号。
(2) 日期。

（3）收件人。
（4）标题或事由（Subject/Reference）。
（5）收信人称呼，例如 Dear Mr. Max 或 Dear Sir/Madam 等。
（6）信函主体内容。
（7）表达此致等客气用语，例如 yours faithfully，sincerely yours 等。
（8）写信人信息和签字，有时需要盖章。
（9）抄送信息。
（10）附件信息。

在国际工程项目中，由于承包商均为公司，因此，应在信函抬头部分使用承包商公司的名称，即中标时的承包商名称，或者为承包商某某项目经理部名称。如承包商为联合体，则应在信函抬头位置标注联合体名称，切忌只标注联合体牵头公司的名称。举例如下：

Letter Head of the Contractor

Ref. No. AAA/DDD/20
Date：05/12/2020

To：Mr. Adis Max
　　Resident Engineer
　　AAA Consulting Co. Ltd.
　　No. BBB，Street ABC，
　　城市名称，国家或地区名称

Subject：XXXXX

Dear Sir,

函件正文部分

Yours Faithfully,

Liang Songhong
Project Manager

抄送 CC.：业主
　　　　姓名
　　　　职务

附件 Encl.：（1）Feasibility Study Report for Geological Conditions
　　　　　　（2）Technical Proposal for Treatment of Site Conditions

为了更好地说明英文信函的结构,举例如下:

Letter Head of the Contractor

Ref. No. AAA/DDD/20
Date: 25/04/2020

To: [insert the name of the Employer]
[insert the address of the Employer]

Subject: Notice of Force Majeure Event under Sub-Clause 19. 2 of Conditions of Contract

Dear Sir or Madam,

We write to inform you that the rapid escalation of COVID-19 has been declared by the World Health Organization (WHO) as a "Pandemic" event on 12 March 2020 after announcement of the outbreak of COVID-19 as a Public Health Emergency of International Concern (PHEIC) on 30th January 2020. WHO has urged countries to continue to implement a containment strategy which accelerates their efforts to control the disease.

On _____ [insert the date], the government of _____ . [insert the name of country or state] has issued further measures, among which are,

[insert the list of local government directions on obviating the impact by COVID-19]

Those measures imposed by the local government have caused the site operations to become impossible, being;

(a) The local government instruction has made the transportation of the workers become impossible;

(b) The social distancing requirement that the workers must keep distance and non-gatherings caused the site operations to be difficult;

(c) The local governmental instructions enforced the contractor to encamp and quarantine the worker for 14 days which was impossible for him to fulfil.

In light of the above measures taken by the local government, the Contractor is left with no choice but to render you a notice under Sub-Clause 19. 2 [*Notice of Force Majeure*] of the Conditions of Contract to suspend the site works commencing from the date of this notice, and the works to be suspended include:

[insert the name of the works to be suspended]

Accordingly, our performance of contractual obligations under the Contract to deliver the project as originally scheduled has substantially been prevented due to the natural catastrophe of COVID-19 and the attendant mitigation measures by the local government.

Apparently, the enumerated event(s) constitute Force Majeure in accordance with Sub-Clause 19. 1 [*Definition of Force Majeure*] of the Conditions of Contract as defined thereofviz. In this Clause, Force Majeure means an exceptional event or circumstance: (a) which is beyond a Party's

Control; (b) which such Party could not reasonably have provided against before entering into the Contract, (c) which, having arisen, such Party could not reasonably have avoided or overcome, and (d) which is not substantially attributable to the other Party.", which spreads its ripple effect to the project onwards. Since the COVID-19 and the attendant measures taken by the local government is beyond the reasonable control of the Contractor, is unavoidable and directly affects the execution of the Works, it thus falls within the definition of Force Majeure set forth in Sub-Clause 19.1 [*Definition of Force Majeure*] of the Conditions of Contract.

The Contractor, pursuant to Sub-Clause 19.2 [*Notice of Force Majeure*] of the Conditions of Contract, notifies you of the above event(s) and/circumstances which prevent us from executing our contractual obligations and complying with the requirement of Time for Completion in particular.

In compliance with Sub-Clause 19.4 [*Consequence of Force Majeure*] and subject to Sub-Clause 20.1 [*Contractor's Claim*] of the conditions of Contract, the Contractor believes that he is contractually entitled to and fully qualified for an extension of time for any such delay and payment of any such cost pursuant to Sub-Clause 8.4 [*Extension of Time for Completion*] of the Conditions of Contract.

As it is an evolving event, the Contractor shall duly update by providing thecontemporaneous records during the pendency of COVID-19, and providing the further particulars once the Force Majeure event ceases to affect the site operations.

Despite the negative influence of the COVID-19 event, the Contractor will exert his best endeavor to cooperate with you to obviate any delay in the performance of the contract in accordance with Sub-Clause 19.3 [*Duty to Minimize Delay*] of the Conditions of Contract.

Yours Faithfully,

Project Manager

CC.:

Encl.:

    需要说明的是，在现代商业信函中，为了提高行文效率，大多使用"齐头式"的行文方式，而不是使用缩进式，即第一行缩进5个字母的方式。当然，在现代英文信函写作中，也不禁止写作人采用缩进式的行文方式，但采用缩进式的行文时，"此致（Yours Faithfully,）"应放置在该行的四分之三的位置。写作人的姓名和签字也需要放置在"此致"的下方，示例如下：

    Despite the negative influence of the COVID-19 event, the Contractor will exert his best endeavor to cooperate with you to obviate any delay in the performance of the contract in accordance with Sub-Clause 19.3 [*Duty to Minimize Delay*] of the Conditions of Contract.

Yours Faithfully,

Project Manager

3.3.3 英文信函内容构成

英文信函，特别是商业信函，其内容可分为三个部分：
（1）开头。
（2）事实和观点陈述部分。
（3）结尾。

国际工程项目合同管理过程中，往来信函也符合上述商业信函内容的构成规律，即开头、叙事或讨论以及结尾。将一封英文信函分为上述三个部分，有利于作者轻松地起草英文信函，使得英文信函符合其基本格式和叙事方法，并有利于函件的读者较好地理解作者的本意、陈述的事实及所持的立场（position）和观点（opinion）。

1. 信函开头部分

在国际工程项目合同管理过程中，一封信函的开头内容取决于承包商发出信函的类型和回复工程师或业主信函的类型。承包商应根据不同情况分别处理，一般原则如下：

（1）对于承包商第一次向工程师和/或业主的致函，如果没有可以引述的往来信函的函号（Reference Number）和日期，则承包商在向工程师和/或业主发函时，可以直接表述如下：

我方兹通知你方，某年某月某日在某地点，发生了当地居民不让承包商施工的阻工事件。

在英文信函中，承包商可以根据已发生的事实或将要发生的事实，采用不同的语气表达英文信函的开头部分，示例如下：

1) We are pleased to inform you that…
2) We have pleasure in informing you that…
3) We would like to inform you that…
4) We take this opportunity to inform you that…
5) We are pleased to have this opportunity to remind you that…
6) We regret to inform you that…

对于一封英文信函的开头部分，此类表述还有很多，上面的例子中使用了"我们"作为主语，在实践中，还可以使用被动语句表达"通知对方"，如下：

1) Please be noted that…
2) Please be informed that…
3) Attention shall be paid to the fact that…

（2）对于承包商收到的工程师或业主的来函，由于工程师或业主的来函均载明了函号和日期，因此，承包商在回复此类函件时，可以使用下述表述方式：

1）承包商在信函的开头，即第一段应表明承包商收到了工程师或业主的函件，英文可参考如下表述：

① We acknowledge receipt of your letter with reference No. AAA dated BBB…

② We have pleasure in acknowledging receipt of your letter No. AAA of 28 December 2019…

③ We are pleased to acknowledge receipt of you letter No. AAA dated BBB…

④ We are in due receipt of your letter No. AAA dated BBB…

⑤ We have duly received your letter No. AAA dated BBB…

⑥ We thank you for your letter No. AAA dated BBB…

⑦ In acknowledging receipt of your letter of 28 December 2019…

⑧ Many thanks for your letter No. AAA dated BBB…

2）或者，承包商在信函的开头，即第一段表明"参考"或"参见"工程师或业主的来函，英文表达方式可参考如下：

① With reference to your letter No. AAA dated BBB…

② Referring to your letter No. AAA dated BBB…

③ This is in reference to your letter No. AAA dated BBB…

④ Reference is made to your letter No. AAA dated BBB…

⑤ We refer to your letter No. AAA dated BBB…

⑥ Further to your letter No. AAA dated BBB…

3）承包商在收到工程师或业主的信函后，在回复信函时可以直接表明"回复……函件"的表述，英文表达方式可参考如下：

① In reply to your letter No. AAA dated BBB…

② In response to your letter of 25 April 2019…

③ Replying to your letter No. AAA dated BBB…

④ In answer to your letter No. AAA dated BBB…

⑤ Answering your letter of 25 April 2019…

需要注意的是，承包商在回复工程师或业主的信函时，必须提及工程师或业主信函的函号和日期。这一方面是为了表明承包商一对一回复了工程师或业主的信函，另一方面也是为了检索信函使用，特别是承包商与工程师或业主就某一事件进行多轮往来信函。例如，有时承包商与工程师为了某一事件往来信函多达50封甚至上百封。为了查明承包商和工程师陈述的事实和观点，梳理往来信函，必须在信函中标明往来信函的函号和日期。

4）承包商在首次发函时，也可以直接表述发生某件事实，而不使用"我方兹通知你方"的表达方式，例如：

① On 25 April 2019, the Contractor, during the construction of excavation works on km 12 +000, encountered disruptions from the local residents…

② The Contractor encountered disruptions from the local residents during the construction of excavations works on km 12 +000…

5）对于递交进度计划或图纸等信函，承包商可以采用各种表述方式，以便工程师在合同约定的期限内进行审批，英文表述方式可参考如下：

① We are pleased to attach the programme herewith…

② Enclosed herewith please find…

③ Attached herewith please find…

④ We enclose herewith…

⑤ We have pleasure in enclosing herewith…

⑥ We are pleased to enclose herewith…

⑦ We take the liberty to enclose herewith…

2. 事实和观点陈述部分

英文信函的中间主体部分是事实和陈述部分,由事实陈述和观点主张两部分组成。为了更好地写作英文信函的主体部分,对于作者而言,非常有必要辨别和区分"事实"和"观点"的不同。

"事实(fact)"是记录的客观存在,是现实或事件的陈述,不以人的意志为转移。事实具有客观性,是能够得到有效证据支持的陈述,在语言陈述中体现出理性。

"观点(opinion)"是思想的主观判断,是对信念或感受的陈述。观点具有主观性,可能是无法得到有效证据支持的陈述,在语言陈述中体现出感性。

人们在生活中有时很难区分事实和观点。与此不同的是,在国际工程项目合同管理过程中,区分事实和观点是相对简单的事情,见表3-2。

表 3-2 事实和观点识别

事实	观点
2019年3月20日,在km15+560处,发生了当地居民阻止承包商施工的事件,承包商停工一周	根据合同条款第2.1款,业主未能履行给予承包商现场占有权和进入权的义务,根据合同条款第20.1款,他有权索赔工期延长和相应的停工费用
某工程的施工图已经完成,递交工程师审核	工程师未能在合同约定的期限内审核图纸,导致承包商停工,承包商有权索赔相应的工期延长和额外费用
在某年某月某日,工程师签发了第×××号变更指示,要求承包商施工额外增加的工程	工程师签发的变更指示,增加了承包商的施工时间,承包商要求相应的工期延长
合同条款第20.6款规定了仲裁作为最终解决双方争议的方式	工程师认为业主和承包商之间的争议无法解决,建议使用第20.6款仲裁的规定解决合同争议
某年某月某日11—12时,现场遭遇暴雨袭击,降雨量为50mm	承包商认为属于极端恶劣的气候条件,根据合同条款第8.4款应给予工期延长

(1)事实陈述

无论是在商业信函还是法律英语中,事实陈述往往采用陈述句式、被动句和无主句表达。这样的表达方式往往给人以客观的印象,例句如下:

1) The trial of the preliminary issues was heard on 17 and 18 November 2015. This judgment sets out my decision and reasons.

2) From the start of Arup's involvement in about 1992, contamination and pollution were recognized as potential problems at the site.

3) Interpretation should be neither uncompromisingly literal nor unswervingly purposive.

承包商在陈述现场发生事实时,可以采用陈述句式描述现场发生的事实,例如:

1) MMT, a process engineering contractor, entered into a contract with ICI for the installation of Steelwork and Tank Works at ICI's new paint processing plant in Ashington, Northumberland. The contract was made on the basis of an amended NEC3 form of contract. The initial contract sum was for just under £2 million. It is not in dispute that during the course of the work MMT was instructed to carry out a great deal of extra work. ⊖

2) On 25 December 2019, the Contractor encountered disruption of site operation that a number of the local residents entered into the site to stop the construction works.

3) In due course disputes arose about the quality of the welding carried out by MMT and as to the value of MMT's work: These resulted in a referral to adjudication in January 2015 by MMT ("Adjudication No 1") in which it claimed about £7,500,000 following service of an Interim Payment Notice on 21 November 2014. The adjudicator decided that ICI had not served a valid Payment Notice with the result that MMT was entitled to the sum claimed. ⊖

4) On 21 November 2015, the Engineer served a letter of AAA on the Contractor upon the benefits of installation of Double Rail Track in TBM tunnels.

5) By letter G-10137 dated 19 January 2016, the Contractor responded to the Engineer's letter of AAA, interalia:

(2) 观点陈述和主张

承包商在英文信函中陈述事实后,还需要陈述观点和主张,例如"根据合同条款第8.4款[竣工时间的延长],承包商认为他有权获得相应的工期延长和/或额外费用"或者"承包商认为工程师的理由不成立,不能接受工程师的决定"等。

需要注意的是,承包商在陈述事实后,为了支持其观点和主张,应在信函中给出观点和主张所依据的理由,而不能在陈述事实后直接给出观点或主张,而不给出支持其观点和主张的任何理由。为了寻找支持其观点和主张的理由,承包商首先应检查合同条款、技术规范、工程量表、图纸等合同文件,从中寻找有利的支持理由。例如:

1) 3.1 During the execution of the Works, events have occurred which have disrupted the Contractor's arrangement and planned programme. Those events have caused the Contractor to incur unavoidable delay, disruption and additional costs. Those delay events can be summarized and classified into the following catalogue, namely:

- Delay in advance payment and IPC's payment to the Contractor by the Employer;
- Delay in approval of route selection;
- Delay due to exceptional adverse climate conditions;
- Delay due to the gun shoot by the locals on site.

2) 3.2 It is generally accepted in construction industry that any activity on the critical

---

⊖ Imperial Chemical Industries Ltd. v Merit Merrel Technology Ltd. [2015] EWHC 2915 (TCC).
⊖ Imperial Chemical Industries Ltd. v Merit Merrel Technology Ltd. [2015] EWHC 2915 (TCC).

path that experiences a delay will consequently delay the project completion date. Conversely, any delay on the non-critical path will not accordingly delay the time for completion of the project.

3)3.3　Thus, an extension of time being claimed by the Contractor is relied on the delayed events and circumstances on the critical path of the Works.

4)3.4　There are terms and conditions within the Contract which define that, should the Contractor suffer certain causes of delay for reasons outside his control, then, after due consultation with the Employer and the Contractor, he shall be granted an appropriated Extension of Time for completion.

5)3.5　Similarly, there are terms which state that, under certain defined circumstances, should the Contractor be caused to incur additional costs, then those shall be reimbursed to him, after due consultation with the Employer and the Contractor.

在陈述事实之后，在观点和主张之前，承包商必须在信函中给出理由。否则，从事实陈述直接到陈述观点，缺乏中间的说理过程，给人以唐突的感觉。信函读者一定会问承包商为什么会陈述如此的观点和主张、原因是什么等问题。举例如下：

Our Ref.：BB/AA/2015
Date：18/10/2015

Mr. AAAA
Director General
CCC Road Authority
No. DDD, Street EEEE
Capital of Country, Country name

Subject：Contractor's Claim due to Delayed Advance Payment

Dear Sir,

As per Contract Agreement and Sub-Clause 14.2 and 14.7 of Particular Conditions of Contract, the last date of advance payment arrived on 22 September 2010, by which the Employer had been required to pay mobilization advance at 15% of the accepted contract amount excluding the specified provisional sums payable in the currencies and proportion in which accepted contract amount was payable, being:

　　Total Advance Payment Amount = TS 9,744,147,064
　　20% Local Currency Payment：= TS 1,793,129,412.87
　　80% Foreign Currency Payment：= USD 5,873,501.45

The Contractor expected to receive total advance payment of TS 9,744,147,064 no later than 22 September 2010 during three months of the mobilization period. The Employer, however, failed to pay the same. The details of advance payment paid by Employer in total six installments are as stated below;

First Installment：…
Second Installment：…
…
Sixth Installment：…
From the above details it is clear that the Employer paid the mobilization advance to the Contractor in stages over a total delayed period of 474 days beyond 22 September 2010.

The Contractor considered himself entitled to a claim on account of delay in payment of mobilization advance, according to Sub-Clause 14.2 and 14.7 as well as Sub-Clause 20.1 of General Conditions of Contract, claiming an extension of time of 296 days and additional cost in a total sum of TS 10,690,305,924.

Yours Faithfully,

Project Manager

在上面的信函中，承包商陈述的事实包括：①合同约定的预付款支付日期和金额；②业主共计六次实际支付预付款的日期和金额。承包商陈述的理由是，根据合同条款第14.2款、第14.7款的规定，业主未能在合同规定的期限内全额支付预付款，因此，业主违约。承包商的观点是根据合同条款第20.1款的规定，提出工期延长和额外付款的补偿，并提出具体的工期延长天数和主张的补偿金额。

承包商可使用下列动词引出他的观点和立场，例如：

① be of the opinion that
② allege
③ aver
④ contend
⑤ assert
⑥ claim
⑦ declare
⑧ state
⑨ emphasize
⑩ maintain one's position
⑪ hold
⑫ maintain

承包商为了表达观点和立场，可采用多种英文句式，灵活多样地表达自己的观点和立场，例句如下：

① The Contractor considered himself entitled to a claim on account of delay in payment of mobilization advance, according to Sub-Clause 14.2 and 14.7 as well as Sub-Clause 20.1 of General Conditions of Contract, claiming an extension of time of 296 days and additional cost in a total sum of TS 10,690,305,924.

② For the foregoing reasons and in light of the above made submissions, the Contractor holds that he is entitled to recover the payment as stated inVO-08 which was to be paid in IPC-91 in March 2017 but deducted in IPC-103 in August 2018, in a sum of USD827,659, since the Employer's refusal to pay such amount is entirely without merit and is unsupported by the terms of the Contract.

③ This referral is put forward without limiting or restricting the Contractor's right to pursue any additional or alternative claims arising from the same or related events.

在英美法院的判决中，法官对于其观点和立场的陈述也采用了多种方式，例句如下：

① From this it must follow that the court is not in a position to formulate an order for delivery up that would fairly reflect the adjudicator's declaration of entitlement, even if it would otherwise be appropriate to do so. Indeed, as I have already mentioned, even if it were possible to draw up such an order-in other words to identify the documents that ICI really needed-I consider that to make such an order would be going further than a mere declaration of entitlement would warrant. ⊖

② In my view, the only way in which the position might be preserved, and effect thereby given to the adjudicator's declaration of entitlement, would be by way of an interim injunction requiring MMT to preserve the documents until further order so that relevant documents, if sufficiently identified, could be the subject of a more focused application for delivery up. However, ICI has not made such an application and so it would not be appropriate to grant relief in that form on this application. ⊜

③ So far as the adjudicator's decision in relation to his fees is concerned, that should plainly be enforced. ICI is therefore entitled to summary judgment for the amount of those fees, plus VAT, together with interest to date. ⊜

④ I therefore conclude that GOG was entitled to, and did, terminate the contract under clause 15.2(b) and 15.2(c)(i) of the Conditions. I reject the fifth and sixth grounds of appeal. ⑭

⑤ In my view, the Judge was correct in all three matters identified in the previous paragraph. Accordingly, if my Lord and my Lady agree, this appeal will be dismissed. ⑮

⑥ In broad terms, GOG was entitled to and did effectively terminate the Contract. ⑯

⑦ For these reasons, RMP is entitled to enforce the award and is entitled to summary judgment in the sum of £318,529.30 (including the Adjudicator's fee and VAT), plus interest of £7,231.15 as of the date of judgment and continuing at the daily rate of £60.26

⊖ Imperial Chemical Industries Ltd. v Merit Merrel Technology Ltd. [2015] EWHC 2915 (TCC), at [67].
⊜ Imperial Chemical Industries Ltd. v Merit Merrel Technology Ltd. [2015] EWHC 2915 (TCC), at [69].
⊜ Imperial Chemical Industries Ltd. v Merit Merrel Technology Ltd. [2015] EWHC 2915 (TCC), at [71].
⑭ Obrascon Huarte Lain SA v Her Majesty's Attorney General for Gibraltar [2015] EWCA Civ 712, at [147].
⑮ Obrascon Huarte Lain SA v Her Majesty's Attorney General for Gibraltar [2015] EWCA Civ 712, at [131].
⑯ Obrascon Huarte Lain SA v Her Majesty's Attorney General for Gibraltar [2014] EWHC 1028 (TCC), at [376].

awarded by the Adjudicator until further order. ⊖

⑧ I would therefore hold that the Adjudicator had jurisdiction because, however the contractual arrangements between the parties are correctly to be described, they mandated the use of the Scheme and he was properly appointed by the Scheme's procedure. ⊜

⑨ In reaching this conclusion, I do not ignore the possible difference in substantive outcome that could arise from identifying the contract correctly. But it seems to me to be consistent with the legal policy and authority that I have summarised above to treat these substantive differences as going not to jurisdiction but to substantive outcome only. Once that approach is adopted, the present case is to be treated as one where the Adjudicator had jurisdiction to resolve the dispute that was referred to him (namely, how much was owing under interim Application Number 8) and addressed the correct question without bias, breach of natural justice or any other vice that would justify overturning his decision. If, which cannot be resolved now, he has made an error of law in referring to the wrong contractual provisions when deciding the substantive question that was referred to him, that falls within the category of errors of procedure, fact or law which the Court of Appeal has repeatedlyemphasized should not prevent enforcement. ⊝

⑩ I consider that the figure of £1.3 million, as against the overall figure of £2.12 million meets that test. That is therefore the amount of the interim payment to be made by OSR on account of AUK's costs. ⑭

➤ I would therefore hold that the Adjudicator had jurisdiction because, however the contractual arrangements between the parties are correctly to be described, they mandated the use of the Scheme and he was properly appointed by the Scheme' procedure. ⑮

⑪ In the circumstances, I am quite satisfied that there is no basis for acceding to the application on this basis. However, I should also consider a wider question, which is what would have been the proper and proportionate response to the events which have occurred, even if I had reached the conclusion that one or the other or both of the experts ought not to have allowed themselves to have been involved in these unilateral and concealed instructions. ⑯

⑫ For completeness, I should say that, even considering all of the separate allegations in the round, I do not consider that they come anywhere near justifying the draconian order sought by the defendant and supported by the other parties. ⑰

⑬ It follows from the above that PBS's claim fails, and Bester's counterclaim suc-

---

⊖ Rmp Construction Services Limited v Chalcroft Limited [2015] EWHC 3737 (TCC), at [54].
⊜ Rmp Construction Services Limited v Chalcroft Limited [2015] EWHC 3737 (TCC), at [52].
⊝ Rmp Construction Services Limited v Chalcroft Limited [2015] EWHC 3737 (TCC), at [53].
⑭ Van Oord UK Limited and Sicim Roadbridge Limited v Allseas UK Limited [2015] EWHC 3385 (TCC), at [46].
⑮ Rmp Construction Services Limited v Chalcroft Limied [2015] EWHC 3737 (TCC), at [52].
⑯ Blackpool Borough Council v Volkerfitzpatrick Limited and others [2020] EWHC 387 (TCC), at [73].
⑰ Blackpool Borough Council v Volkerfitzpatrick Limited and others [2020] EWHC 387 (TCC), at [77].

ceeds. Had PBS's claim succeeded, the issues as to quantum, save as to the degree of progress at the time of termination, would have been resolved in Bester's favour. ⊖

⑭ For the reasons given above, I decide that the sum due from M&M in respect of interim Payment Application No. 70 is £223,597.21 + VAT, payable to Flexidig by no later than Monday 6 January 2020." ⊖

在国际工程项目合同管理过程中，在起草英文信函时，可以从上述表述方式中学到如何使用法律英语表述自己的观点和主张。承包商可以使用下述用语，引导进入观点和主张：

① Based on the foregoing…

② For the reasons given above…

③ For these reasons…

④ In the circumstance…

⑤ In all circumstances…

⑥ In consideration of the submission above…

⑦ In conclusion…

⑧ In a word…

⑨ In brief…

⑩ In summary…

⑪ It is evident from the above tables and, indeed, it is common ground, that…

除上述表述方式外，承包商还可以使用表示结论的英文短语或单词表达自己的观点和主张，也可以使用强调句式，例如 it is concluded that, it is obvious that, it is clear that 等表达结论性的观点和主张。

3. 信函结尾部分

与个人之间往来信函或者外交公函不同，商业信函的结尾较为简单，特别是涉及合同争议和仲裁、诉讼等内容的信函。在陈述完毕事实、理由以及观点和主张后，信函的结尾往往不为读者所重视，可能仅被当作一种客套话，不存在合同或法律上的实质意义。但是，无论如何，一封英文信函需要有结尾部分，以示作者的礼貌、客气和尊重。因此，在国际工程项目合同管理过程中，承包商可以用如下表述作为信函的结尾。

（1）使用 yours faithfully, faithfully yours, yours sincerely, sincerely yours 等表示"此致"含义的用语作为结尾。这种方式最为简单明了，也表明了客气和礼貌，读者对此无可厚非。

（2）在表示期待对方的回复时，可以使用下述句式：

1）We look forward to your reply soon.

2）We are looking forward to hearing from you.

3）We should be obliged by your early reply.

4）We await the pleasure of receiving your reply at an early date.

5）We should appreciate an early reply from you.

6）Your prompt reply would be greatly appreciated.

⊖ PBS Energo A. S v Bester Generaction UK Ltd. and others [2020] EWHC 223 (TCC), at [480].

⊖ Flexdig Ltd. v M&M Contractors (Europe) Ltd. [2020] EWHC 847 (TCC), at page 23.

(3) 在表示感谢时,可以使用下述句式:

1) We thank you for your reply.
2) We are greatly obliged for your decision just received.
3) We are obliged to you for your kind attention on this matter.
4) We are grateful for your cooperation.
5) Thank you for your prompt response.

承包商在写作英文信函时,需要注意,在国际工程项目中,业主、工程师和承包商是平等的主体关系。工程师作为业主聘任的工程项目管理人员,是工程合同的利害关系方(stakeholder),与承包商一样,是平等的主体关系。因此,在写作信函的结尾时,承包商需要特别注意以下问题:

第一,没有必要使用"希望业主或工程师给予照顾""希望业主和工程师手下留情"等用语。

第二,没有必要使用那些非常谦恭的用语,例如 your esteemed office 等,只需表达客气和礼貌就是很好的结尾。

第三,没有必要表示道歉或表达"请宽恕我方的错误(please excuse this clerical error)"或者 we wish to express our regret for the annoyance this mistake has caused you 等。

第四,在承包商承认错误时,请谨慎对待认错的措辞。这是因为如果承包商认错,今后发生合同争议时,无法挽回认错表态,错误已成为承包商承认的事实。

因此,为了使承包商写作信函时更为简明,在结尾时不涉及实体权利的放弃或损害承包商的权利,建议使用最为简明的结尾方式,例如上述给出的 yours faithfully, faithfully yours, yours sincerely, sincerely yours 等用语。

3.4 英文信函写作的其他表述方式

在国际工程项目英文信函写作过程中,承包商、业主和工程师经常引用合同和技术规范等条款内容,用以证明其观点和主张的依据。在英文信函和法律英语中,如何表达所引用合同和技术规范等文件中的约定或规定,特别是在争议委员会、仲裁或诉讼的争议解决过程中,是承包商应掌握的技巧。在工期延长和额外费用索赔报告中,或者争议委员会、仲裁或诉讼中,承包商需要引用大量合同条款或技术规范等规定。因此,需要变换不同的表述方式,避免行文枯燥单一,举例如下:

(1) The Contract, that was signed as a deed on 18 December 2012, set out the documents that formed part of it. They were as follows:

1) *Invitation to the tender letter*.
2) *The instructions totenderers ("ITT")*.
3) *This form of tender*.
4) *The Contract Data Part One (and all Annexes)*
5) *Contract Data part two*.
6) *The form of agreement*.
7) *The Works information*.

8) *The Site information.*

9) *The scope of works, specifications and drawings provided by the Project Manager.*

10) *Agreed technical and commercial queries provided and authorized by the Project Manager.*

(2) Defendants in this matter argue that SFX's performance under the Agreement was excused by the Force Majeure provision, which states, in pertinent part:

(3) Page 3 of the ITT included the following, under the heading "Secondary Option Clauses":

"*This Engineering and Construction Contract conditions of contract are the core clauses, dispute resolution Option W2 and the clauses for Secondary Options X2, X4, X7, X13, X16, Y(UK)2, Y(UK)3, X18 and Z of the NEC3 Engineering and Construction contract June 2005 (with amendments June 2006 and September 2011) as amended by the Additional Conditions of Contract (Option Z).*"

(4) Option W2 is the Dispute Resolution provision in the NEC 3 contract. In its original form it looks like this:

(5) In Schedule 1, which contains the Z clauses, Page 43 is in the following form:

Appendix 2 included the following:

APPENDIX 2

Dispute Resolution Procedure

1. Disputes

Any Dispute shall be resolved in accordance with this Appendix 2.

(6) The Schedule of Amendments to the Contract which, as I have already mentioned, was signed on 11 February 2013, stated that it was to supersede all other provisions contained within the Contract. Under the heading "Dispute Resolution Option" were these words:

"*Option W2—Add new sentence 'Notwithstanding any provisions to the contrary, this contract is deemed to be a construction contract within the meaning of Part II of the Housing Grants, Construction and Regeneration Act 1996 as amended by the Local Democracy, Economic Development and Construction Act 2009'.*"

(7) It provides that in such an eventuality the builder is entitled to be paid for all works and materials on-site at the time of termination, and further provides that:

"*If an agreement cannot be reached as to how much is owed the services of an independent quantity surveyor (who is acceptable to both parties) should be sought and both parties should agree in writing to abide by his figure. Both parties will meet the cost.*"

(8) The letter set out the claimants' position that it was an abuse of process to proceed with a statutory demand in such circumstances, and concluded as follows:

"*If your client considers that it has a genuine claim then it should in accordance with the contract appoint an independent quantity surveyor.*"

(9) That provoked a response from Gorvins dated 30 September 2013 in which, having said they would take instructions on the contents of Blackstone's letter and would not issue bankruptcy petitions in the meantime, they said as follows:

> "In the event ··· that [the] dispute ··· is not capable of resolution by further dialogue, our client is prepared to agree to resolution of the dispute by an independent quantity surveyor subject to certain clarifications to the contractual procedure being agreed."

(10) So far as any actual or apparent conflict between Gorvins' letter of 30 September 2013 and Blackstone's letter of 24 October 2013 is concerned, Chitty [§2-032] says this:

> "A communication may fail to take effect as an acceptance because it attempts to vary the terms of the offer. ··· Nor, generally, can an offer be accepted by a reply which varies one of its other terms (e.g. that specifying the time of performance), or by a reply which introduces an entirely new term. Such a reply is not an acceptance; but it may, on the contrary, be a counter-offer, which the originalofferor can then accept or reject. On the other hand, statements which are not intended to vary the terms of the offer, or to add new terms, do not vitiate the acceptance, even where they do not precisely match the words of the offer. ··· The test in each case is whether the offeror reasonably regarded the purported acceptance as introducing a new term into the bargain and not as a clear acceptance of the offer."

(11) Subject to some amendments, the General Conditions of Contract were the Conditions of Contract for Plant and Design-Build, published by FIDIC, first edition, 1999. This is sometimes known as *the FIDIC Yellow Book*. The Conditions included the following:

> "1.1.6.8 'unforeseeable' means not reasonably foreseeable by an experienced contractor by the date for submission of the Tender."

(12) Paragraphs 8 to 11 of Part 1 of Volume 3 of the Employer's Requirements provided:

> "8 DESIGN DATA
>
> Contractor's Documents to be submitted for review in accordance with theContract shall include, without limitation, the following: ···"

(13) Paragraph 1.2 of Part 2 of Volume 3 of the Employer's Requirements provided:

> "The Contractor shall carry out any further ground investigation necessary to produce an acceptable design for the new works that takes account of the risks indicated by the ground investigation information collated to date. The Contractor shall also carry out such investigation, testing, and research as is necessary to ensure that waste materials are disposed of in the appropriate manner according to local and EU regulations."

(14) Clause 15 is of importance in this case addressing as it does termination:

"15.1 If the Contractor fails to carry out any obligation under the Contract, the Engineer may by notice require the Contractor to make good the failure and to remedy it within a specified reasonable time. "

(15) Clause 8 addressed progress and delays:

"8.1 The Engineer shall give the Contractor not less than 7 days' notice of the Commencement Date. Unless otherwise stated in the Particular Conditions, the Commencement Date shall be within 42 days after the Contractor receives the Letter of Acceptance. "

(16) Clause 4 covered a number of important areas of risk and responsibility on the part of OHL:

"4.1 The Contractor shall design, execute and complete the Works in accordance with theContract, and shall remedy any defects in the Works. When completed, the Works on every element thereof shall be fit for the purposes for which the Works on every element thereof are intended.

The Contractor shall provide the Plant and Contractor's Documents specified in theContract and Contractor's Personnel, Goods, consumables and other things and services, whether of a temporary or permanent nature, required in all this design, execution, completion and remedying of defects. "

(17) Clause 1.3 stated:

"Wherever these Conditions provide for the giving or issuing of consents, determinations, notices and requests, these communications shall be: ..."

(18) Subject to some relatively minor changes, the General Conditions of Contract were those contained in the FIDIC Conditions of Contract for Plant and Design-build (amongst other things) for building and engineering works designed by the Contractor 1st Edition 1999, sometimes known as *the FIDIC Yellow Book*. Relevant definitions in Clause 1 were:

"1.1.3.1 *'Base Date' means the date 28 days prior to the latest date for submission of the Tender.* "

(19) Clause 20.1 which addresses claims and dispute resolution is material:

"20.1 *If the Contractor considers himself to be entitled to any extension of the Time for Completion and/or any additional payment under any Clause of these Conditions or otherwise in connection with the Contract, the Contractor shall give notice to the Engineer, describing the event or circumstance giving rise to the claim. The notice shall be given as soon as practicable, and not later than 28 days after the Contractor became aware, or should have become aware, of the event or circumstance.* "

(20) Sheet 2 of 4 contained further information as set out below:

"*The following information is given from the main contract, and shall apply to this sub-contract which is placed under the general terms and conditions of the*

JCT standard form of sub-contractor (DSC/C) as adjusted or amended by the following：…"

(21) The letter went on to say：

" This letter is intended to have the consequences of a claimant's offer to settle in accordance with Part 36 of the Civil Procedure Rules…"

(22) Clause 6 set out primary obligations of the parties：

" *Operation and Maintenance of Trains*

6.1.1 *The Train Operator shall ensure that the Specified Equipment is maintained and operated to a standard which will permit provision of the Services in accordance with the Working Timetable*…"

(23) There was also Clause 4.12 which provided：

" *Clause* 4.12 *Unforeseeable Difficulties* ［C 2/1/42］"

(24) It reads as follows：

" *A declaration that the adjudicator did not have jurisdiction to reach his decision dated* 29 *December* 2019. *The said decision was given in breach of natural justice or an abuse of process. The decision was wrong in law and should be set aside as a whole.* "

(25) The real battle ground in my view is over the requirements in subparagraphs (3) and (4) of 6.37 as follows：

" (3) *The court will not give permission unless satisfied that England and Wales are the proper places in which to bring the claim.* "

以上为合同条款引用的25种表述方式，承包商可以从中学习如何用英文表述所引用的合同条款或信函内容。当然，引用合同条款的表述方式有很多，承包商可以根据具体行文的要求予以表述。

3.5 英文信函写作应注意的问题

在国际工程项目合同管理过程中，中国企业在英文信函写作时出现过很多问题和瑕疵，这些问题可归纳如下：

1. 关于收件人业主或工程师的称谓

关于业主的称谓，承包商应分清对方的行政级别。在一般情况下，如果业主主管官员为当地政府的部长级（包括副部级）官员，则应在姓名前写明"阁下"的尊称，英文表述为"His Excellency"，或者简称为"H. E."，举例如下：

His Excellency
Mr. AAA BBB
Minister for Public Works
No. CCCC, Street. DDDD
City Name, Country Name

需要注意，承包商在向副部长级以上官员致函时，在收件人处用"His Excellency"，而不能用"Your Excellency"。但在信函正文（body）部分，在作者直接对收件人说话时，则只能用"Your Excellency"，而不能用"His Excellency"。承包商在写作此类函件时千万不要犯错。

如果业主主管官员为局级或以下级别，则只能称呼"先生"或"女士"，而不能以"阁下"称呼，举例如下：

Mr. WWW QQQ
Director General
OOO Road Authority
No. CCCC, Street. DDDD
City Name, Country Name

关于工程师的称谓，由于工程师均是业主聘任负责项目管理的人员，不涉及行政级别，因此只能以"先生"或"女士"称呼，举例如下：

Mr. EEE FFF
Resident Engineer
DDD Consulting Co. Ltd.
No. TTT, Street UUU
City Name, Country Name

如果收件人业主或工程师的称谓仅表明职务，却给出收件人业主的具体姓名时，则应在收件人之后，另起一行表明"Attention：Mr. DDD"，举例如下：

Project Manager
XXX Project Consultancy Co. Ltd.
No. TTT, Street UUU
City Name, Country Name
Attention：Mr. YYY NNN

需要注意的是，在中国公文行文中，不写明具体收件人姓名，而仅写明收件单位名称，例如"XXX 管理局"，这是中国公文行文的习惯做法。但在英文信函中，必须写明收件人姓名，例如 Mr. YYY NNN，而不能仅写明收件公司或机构名称，这是中国公文行文与英文信函的最大不同。为此，承包商在国际工程项目中应遵守英文信函的表述方式。

2. 关于信函标题（Subject）或事宜（Reference）

英文信函的标题或事宜应以名词方式表述，而不应以动词形式表述，举例如下：

Subject：Application for Construction Permit，或者
Reference：Application for Construction Permit。

但不能使用动词形式表述标题或事宜，例如：

Subject：To Apply for Construction Permit。

为了突出信函标题或事宜，在英文信函中，一般应加重字体或加下划线，使得阅读人直接了解信函所要表述或说明的事情或问题，举例如下：

Subject：Application for Construction Permit

在信函的标题或事宜栏中，承包商可以采用上述简明表述方式，也可以在标题或事宜栏中增加项目名称，例如：

Subject: Application for Construction Permit
    Contract No. IBC 2.8
    DDD Area Development Project

信函的标题或事宜栏不宜加载过多的内容，信息过多会干扰阅读人的阅读速度，只要能使阅读人一目了然信函表达的主要内容，就是好的标题名称，例如：

Subject: VO-2 TBM Supplementary Agreement for Additional Herrenknecht Technical Services

作为读者，可以从以上标题中清晰地了解这封函是关于第 22 号变更令项下 TBM 盾构制造商海瑞克公司提供额外技术服务补充协议的问题，此类表述达到了作者使读者清晰了解信函内容的目的。

3. 关于称呼

在英文信函正文的开头，与家人和朋友之间通信的称呼不同，一般在商业信函正文开头使用的称呼有：

(1) Dear Sir
(2) Dear Madam
(3) Dear Sir/Madam
(4) Dear Mr. EEE DDD

需要注意的是，如果作者知道收件人是男性，则只能使用 Dear Sir 的称呼。如果收件人是女性，则只能使用 Dear Madam 的称呼。如果作者不确定或不知道收件人是男性或女性，可以使用 Dear Sir/Madam 的称呼，但在这种情况下，往往作者发出的商业信函是发给不确定的收件人。而在国际工程项目中，承包商知道业主的项目经理或工程师的人员，因此，不能使用 Dear Sir/Madam 的称呼，而只能使用 Dear Sir 或 Dear Madam 的称呼。当然，承包商也可以直接称呼某人姓名，例如 Dear Mr. EEE DDD。但由于承包商写给业主或工程师的信函，业主或工程师需要其他人员处理，因此建议仅使用 Dear Sir 或 Dear Madam 的称呼，礼貌得体，无须直接称呼某人姓名。

4. 关于引述的合同条款、技术规范和其他内容

在英文信函正文部分需要引述合同条款、技术规范或其他内容时，应以斜体文字表述，并以缩进方式表达，举例如下：

In broad terms Paragraph 5 allocates responsibility for Minutes Delay and Cancelled Stops. Paragraph 5.5 states:

  "*Responsibility for Minutes Delay on any day in respect of a Service Group [a 'collection of Services provided by the TOC']" caused by incidents which are unidentified…shall be allocated as follows:*

    (a) if there is any Minutes Delay in respect of the Service Group recorded as being caused by incidents which Network Rail or the Train Operator are allocated responsibility:…"

5. 关于引述内容中表示强调的方式

如果是作者在引用合同条款或其他内容时增加下划线或加粗字体，则应在引述合同条款或其他内容后面注明"（下划线和加粗字体为承包商所注）"，英文表述为"(underlined and bolded by Contractor)"，举例如下：

Mr Lester isminuted as saying that he was：

"…happy to go through the open book with Shoreline as the relationship between the partners is paramount. **_Taking off the current codes and substituting the other codes will incur a lot of work_**. A number of works are not charged for as codes in accordance with the agreement because the cost is included in the £35.85. To work backwards through all of the jobs to ascertain what these should be will be a real problem."(Underlined and Bolded by Contractor)

在信函正文中，作者对某些表述加重或下划线，一方面是为了引起读者注意这些事实、观点和主张，另一方面是为了更为清晰地表述事实、观点和主张。这是在英文信函或法律英语中经常使用的"强调重点"的方式，是一种有力的表达方法。不得不说，作者应恰当使用这种方法来表达事实、观点和主张，但不能滥用。如果通篇都是下划线或加粗字体，不仅使信函显得很乱，而且缺乏重点，失去了强调的意义。

6. 关于信函的签字和/或盖章

与中国公文只能加盖公章不同，对于商业往来信函，特别是在国际工程项目中，在某些国家，例如肯尼亚、乌干达、南非等大多数国家或地区，英文信函作者仅需签字即可，不需要加盖任何公章即有效。但在某些国家，例如印度尼西亚，不仅需要作者签字，而且需要加盖公章，方能有效。对于是否需要作者签字，以及是否需要加盖公章，承包商可以根据该国家的具体情况，根据业主或工程师的要求确定，以便确定有效的英文函件具有当地法律认可的法律效力。

在国际工程项目中，一份毫无争议的、有效递交和送达的函件应具备如下要件：

（1）信函签字和/或盖章，其中签字人具有签字权力或授权。

（2）信函载明日期，从中可以清楚地知晓发函日期。

（3）信函上载明收件人的签收信息，包括"收讫（Received）"、收件日期和收件人签字。

具备上述三个要件的信函，无论是在争议委员会、仲裁或诉讼中，均被认为是业主和承包商之间真实的往来信函。一般情况下，在国际仲裁中，当事双方均对这种信函的真实性不会表示异议。

7. 关于注释

在国际工程项目往来信函中，承包商或工程师及业主往往会引述有关合同条款、技术规范、会议纪要、补充协议以及之前双方往来信函内容等。在法律文件中，还可能会引述适用法律的法律条文和相关判例。为此，为了保证往来信函或法律文件的清洁整齐，英文信函的作者往往在文件中加以注释。例如以脚注的方式说明引用内容的来源，举例如下：

"Though not directly related, the rationale for not allowing an earlier unapproved AP to affect a validly executed variation order principle is grounded in the common law rule of parole evidence which stipulates that '*if there has been a contract which has been reduced to writing, verbal evidence is not allowed to be given… so as to add to or subtract from, or in any manner to vary or qualify the written contract.* 'The rule has been extended to apply and disallow preliminary agreements, drafts or letters of negotiations from affecting the agreement reduced in writing and executed between the parties."

在上例的文字中，承包商引用了判例 Goss v Lord Nugent (1833) 5 B. & Ad. 58, 64 案以及 Chitty on Contracts（《奇蒂论合同》）一书中的论述。为此，作者使用 Word 文件中的脚注编辑功能，在脚注位置注明：

Goss v Lord Nugent (1833) 5 B. & Ad. 58, 64 ⊖

Chitty on Contracts XXIX Edition at paragraph 12-069 ⊖

承包商也可以在文件的末尾利用尾注功能加以注释，但这种情况多用在论文或文章长度不长的情况下。如果承包商编制索赔报告，篇幅较长时，最好使用脚注功能。这样可以从本页脚注上很快得知内容来源，避免读者为了弄清内容来源翻阅到文件末尾。

承包商有时需要大量引述与工程师的往来信函，因此，承包商可以充分利用 Word 文件的脚注编辑功能说明引用内容的来源，而不是在文件的正文上注明其来源，以保持文件的清洁整齐，避免影响读者的阅读体验。

8. 关于抄送

在国际工程项目中，由于工程师是业主的代表，在法律上形成代理关系，工程师在授权范围内代理业主行使项目管理权力。因此，承包商应与工程师事先商定与工程师往来信函是否需要抄送业主，以及哪些函件需要抄送业主。如果工程师认为往来信函不必抄送业主，则承包商只需向工程师发信，如果认为有必要，工程师会将承包商的信函，转送给业主。

如果工程师认为所有往来信函均需抄送业主，则承包商应将其发出的信函抄送业主。需要注意的是，承包商在抄送业主时，应写明抄送给业主的姓名、职务、业主机构名称及其地址信息，切忌只写"业主（the Employer）"，以表示尊重。举例如下：

CC.:Mr. EEE FFF
　　　Project Director
　　　XXX Road Authority
　　　No. DDD, Street WWWWW
　　　City Name, Country Name

9. 关于附件

在国际工程项目中，笔者发现很多项目经理部在发函中附带附件时，只是在附件（Enclosure, Encl.）上注明"附件"，而没有注明附件的具体文件名称。毫无疑问，这样的表述不能准确地表明承包商到底向工程师递交了什么文件。在国际工程的仲裁或诉讼中，承包商和业主，或者承包商与分包商往往各执一词，争论是否收到了承包商递交的文件。

英文信函附件的合格写作标准是：应明确清晰地写明附件的文件名称、份数以及页数，

⊖ Goss v Lord Nugent (1833) 5 B. & Ad. 58, 64.

⊖ Chitty on Contracts XXIX Edition at paragraph 12-069.

举例如下:

　　Encl.:(1) Geological Report on Site Conditions　3 copies　289 pages/copy
　　　　 (2) Technical Proposal on Foundation Treatment　3 copies　120 pages/copy
　　　　 (3) Construction Method Statement　3 copies　256 pages/copy

承包商还需特别注意,在国际工程实践中,很多项目经理部在发出信函后未能及时归档,导致无法找到信函的附件,而信函正文中又无法看出整个事件的内容,完全依赖信函附件进行判断。因此,承包商应加强文档管理工作,及时归档或扫描全部文件,包括附件文件,以便在发生合同争议时可以查阅全部文件。否则,只会给承包商仲裁或诉讼带来不利的后果。

第4章 写作常用格式

> It is a question partly of fact and partly of construction to determine which documents are contractual, but those here briefly referred to are common.
>
> Paras 1-015, *Keating on Construction Contracts*, 11 *Edition* 2020

4.1 国际工程项目常用文件

在国际工程项目合同管理过程中，从投标阶段到签订合同，从工程项目开工直至竣工和缺陷通知期届满，承包商在工程项目管理和施工过程中接触了大量的文件。这些文件依不同项目、不同情况而有所差异，但并非无迹可寻。可以根据项目不同阶段进行划分，将国际工程项目中的文件类型分为：

4.1.1 业主招标文件

一般而言，业主发出的国际工程项目招标文件包括：

1. 第一部分：招标程序（Bidding Procedure）

（1）招标通知（Notice of Tender）。

（2）投标人须知（Instruction to Bidders）。

（3）招标数据清单（Bid Data Sheet）。

（4）评标和资格标准（Evaluation and Qualification Criteria）。

（5）投标表格（Bidding Forms）。

（6）投标资格合格国别（Eligible Countries）。

（7）银行政策：贪腐和欺诈实践（Bank Policy：Corrupt and Fraudulent Practice）。

2. 第二部分：工程描述

（1）工程范围（Scope of Works）。

（2）规范（Specifications）。

（3）图纸（Drawings）。

（4）与工程有关的其他补充信息（Supplement Information that describe the Works to be procured）。

3. 第三部分：合同条款和合同格式（Conditions of Contract and Contract Forms）

（1）通用合同条款（General Conditions of Contract）。

（2）专用合同条款（Particular Conditions of Contract）。

（3）合同格式（Contract Forms）。

需要注意的是，如果业主进行资格预审或资格后审，则业主文件中包括资格预审或资格后审文件。

4.1.2 承包商投标文件

承包商根据业主招标文件要求，在投标截止日期进行投标，承包商的投标文件包括：

（1）投标函（Letter of Tender）。
（2）投标保函（Tender Security）。
（3）填写完毕并签字盖章的业主招标文件中的表格、合同格式等。
（4）承包商的报价清单（Priced Bill of Quantities）。
（5）需要随承包商投标文件一同递交的业主招标文件。
（6）承包商的施工组织方法（Construction Method Statement）。
（7）承包商编制的进度计划（Programme）。
（8）需要承包商递交的其他证明文件或者人员、设备、分包商清单。
（9）承包商需要递交的其他文件。

4.1.3 合同文件

在承包商中标后或通过合同谈判获得合同后，承包商与业主签署的合同文件包括：

（1）合同协议书（Contract Agreement）。
（2）中标函（Letter of Acceptance）。
（3）投标函（Letter of Tender）。
（4）专用合同条款（Particular Conditions of Contract）。
（5）通用合同条款（General Conditions of Contract）。
（6）规范（Specification）。
（7）图纸（Drawings）。
（8）资料表和构成合同组成部分的其他文件（The Schedule and any other documents forming part of the Contract）。

在《合同协议书》中，可能还包括其他合同文件，例如承包商的标价工程量表、付款计划、保险要求、预付款保函、履约保函、保留金保函等合同文件。

4.1.4 工程管理过程形成的文件

承包商在签订工程合同，进入项目履约阶段、竣工、缺陷责任期直至项目清算完毕，形成了大量的工程管理过程文件。这些文件包括：

（1）承包商与业主或工程师往来信函。
（2）承包商递交的进度计划。
（3）承包商递交的施工方法、质量保证计划、HSE 计划。
（4）承包商递交和工程师签认的付款证书。
（5）工程师签发的变更指示。
（6）会议纪要。
（7）备忘录。

（8）补充协议。

（9）竣工文件和资料，以及运营和维护手册。

（10）工程管理过程中形成的其他文件。

在上述文件中，特别是在业主与承包商产生合同争议的情况下，分清什么是合同文件，什么是工程管理文件，即非合同文件，十分重要。在国际工程管理实践中，区分合同文件和非合同文件的标准是：

（1）在合同文件条款中，明确规定或约定为合同文件的文件构成合同文件，例如《合同协议书》和《通用合同条款》或《专用合同条款》中，合同文件条款约定了合同文件。

（2）在工程管理过程中形成的具有合同效力的文件，例如补充协议、双方签署的会议纪要、双方达成协议的备忘录、工程师签署的付款证书、实验记录和现场记录等具有约束当事一方或当事双方权利和义务的文件。

（3）除上述文件之外，在国际工程项目中，施工方法往往不作为合同文件。在绝大多数国际标准格式合同中，有时进度计划也不作为合同文件。另外，国际工程管理文件中，不具有约束当事双方权利义务的文件，不视为构成合同文件。

在国际工程项目中，区分合同文件和非合同文件具有重要的法律意义。特别在国际仲裁或诉讼过程中，合同文件具有法律约束力，当事双方应当遵守，而违约方应承担相应的违约责任。对于非合同文件，并不对当事双方产生法律约束力，违反此类非合同文件，并不产生法律上的违约责任，也不产生相应的法律责任。

在国际工程管理过程中，项目合同管理人员会接触大量的合同文件和非合同文件。因此，了解、熟悉和掌握这些文件的写作、编制和运用，是项目管理人员必备的能力。

4.2　国际工程项目常用文件格式

4.2.1　英文信函格式

承包商在签署工程合同进入施工现场时，承包商需要设计英文信函格式，以便在整个工程项目过程中使用相同的信函格式。完整的英文信函应具有如下内容：

（1）抬头。信函抬头位置写明承包商名称，如果是联合体，则应标明联合体名称。在有联合体情况下，承包商切忌仅标明联合体牵头公司名称，应注明联合体成员。如果联合体成员超过三家公司，无法在信函抬头全部注明时，应给联合体另起一个"某某项目联合体"的称呼。承包商的标识（logo）可以放在承包商名称之前。

（2）函号。承包商自己的函号可用"Our Ref.："，而工程师或业主的函号可用"Your Ref.："表示。承包商在编制函号时，其设计应清晰标明信函编号、项目简称、公司简称和年份，例如"023/ETA01/SHCO/2019"。承包商还需要注意，为了使函件编号更加明确，则应按照数字顺序从小到大进行编号，例如1、2、3……，这样按照数字顺序编号的信函，不会重复编号，易于查询。

（3）日期。在英文中日期的表述有两种方式，一种是"日／月／年"，例如："28/05/2019"，另一种是"月／日／年"，例如"05/28/2019"。承包商可选择其中一种方式。如果承包商选择了其中一种表述方式，则应自第一封至最后一封函件，都使用同一种表述方式，避免使读者困惑。

(4) 收件人。应注意的问题已在本书第 3.5 节中说明。

(5) 标题或事宜。应注意的问题已在本书第 3.5 节中说明。

(6) 信函正文称呼。应注意的问题已在本书第 3.5 节中说明。

(7) 信函正文。应注意的问题已在本书第 3.5 节中说明。

(8) 写信人落款。应注意的问题已在本书第 3.5 节中说明。

(9) 抄送信息。应注意的问题已在本书第 3.5 节中说明。

(10) 附件信息。应注意的问题已在本书第 3.5 节中说明。

为了使读者更好地学习和了解英文信函格式，能够在国际工程实践中使用英文信函格式，举例如下：

Contractor's Letterhead

Ref. No.：[填写信函编号]
Date：【填写发文日期】
To：The Employer's name【填写业主或工程师名称】
　　Add：【填写地址】

Attn：Mr.【填写姓名和职务】

Contract No.：【填写合同编号】
Name of Contract：【填写合同名称】
Subject：[填写事由]
　　　　For your action　　　　until：
　　　　Request for approval　　until：
　　　　Answer Required　　　　until：
　　　　For your Information　　until：
Dear Sir,
[正文内容]

Faithfully yours,

：_____
Name：
Project Manager,

CC：
Encl：

在上例中，承包商在信函中写明了收信人，即业主或工程师是否应采取行动及时间要求。在信函中表述下述内容可以使收信人明确信函的性质，是否需要对方采取行动，或是要求批准，或是要求回复或仅为对方了解，且有时间要求。这样在承包商与业主或工程师之间能够更好地沟通交流，提高工作效率。

For your action　　　　　　　　until:
Request for approval　　　　　　until:
Answer Required　　　　　　　 until:
For your Information　　　　　　until:

承包商也可以使用更为简明的英文信函格式，但无论如何，完整英文信函必备的11项内容不可缺少，举例如下：

Contractor's Letterhead

Ref. No.:［填写信函编号］
Date:【填写发文日期】

To:The Employer's name【填写业主或工程师名称】
　　Add:【填写地址】

Attn:Mr.【填写姓名和职务】

Contract No.:【填写合同编号】
Name of Contract:【填写合同名称】
Subject:［填写事由］
Dear Sir,
［正文内容］

Faithfully yours,

_____

Name:
Project Manager,

CC:
Encl:

如果承包商需要引述以前往来信函，则可在信函的标题或事宜（Subject 或 Reference）之后、在收件人称呼之前增加："References"的内容，例如：

```
Subject: Variation Order No. 9 on Retaining Wall

Reference: (1) Contractor's letter No. SSS dated 24/02/2020;
           (2) Engineer's letter No. POPO dated 29/03/2020.
           …

Dear Sir,
```

承包商可以使用自己公司固定的英文信函格式，采用已印好的英文信函纸张进行通信交流。需要注意的是，英文信函第一页应有发信公司名称，但第二页可以使用 A4 白纸打印信函内容，不必使用带有公司抬头信函纸。

承包商也可以使用计算机设计英文信函抬头，但需要注意的是，英文信函的第一页可以有公司抬头，但第二页可以使用 A4 白纸打印信函内容，不必仍使用带有公司抬头信函纸。

4.2.2 会议纪要格式

在国际工程项目管理过程中，记录了业主和承包商就某项事宜达成一致，或者就某项事宜进行下一步的安排的会议纪要，可能具有重要的意义。这份会议纪要往往构成对双方在签字日期时签订"静态"合同文件进行"动态"修改或更改。因此，此类会议纪要意味着双方权利和义务的变更。在某种程度上，履行过程中对合同文件的修改，属于"合同变更（amendment of contract）"。因此，在合同争议解决过程中，包括争议委员会解决机制、国际仲裁或诉讼，此类会议纪要会起到关键作用。以某国际工程项目为例，合同技术规范规定水电站厂区变压器为 4 台，但双方在项目开工前的技术会议上，经讨论同意将水电站厂区变压器从 4 台改为 2 台，在双方签署的会议纪要中记录了该项协议。在水电站机组安装过程中，工程师又提出将 2 台增加到 4 台。在这种情况下，工程师将 2 台增加到 4 台，属于工程变更。此类变更导致的工期延长和额外费用，应给予承包商补偿。

一份完整的会议纪要应具备如下内容：
(1) 日期。
(2) 地点。
(3) 参加人员。
(4) 会议主题。
(5) 会议达成的事项。
(6) 业主或工程师和承包商的签字。
(7) 参加人员签到表。

需要注意的是，会议纪要不是会议记录。会议纪要仅记录双方各自表达的观点和达成一致的内容，无须记录每个人发言中的每一句话。会议纪要格式如下：

> Project Name
> Minutes of Meeting on [insert the meeting subject]
>
> Dated:
> Venue:
> Participants:
> Employer:
> Engineer:
> Contractor:
> Discussion Issues:
> (1)
> (2)
> (3)
> (4)
> (5)
> …
> Conclusion:
> Signature:
> Employer:
> Engineer:
> Contractor:
> Enclosed: Table of Participant's Signature

  如果一份会议纪要需要具有法律约束力，业主、工程师和承包商参会人代表需在会议纪要上签字和/或盖章。如果参会各方或者任何一方，在会议结束后没有在会议纪要上签字和（或）盖章，则该会议纪要没有法律约束力。在国际工程项目中，如果工程项目进展顺利，业主、工程师和承包商各方能够按照合同约定履约，即在正常履约的情况下，工程项目各方容易在会议纪要中达成一致，并履行签字手续。如果承包商履约异常不顺利，无论是业主或工程师造成的，还是由于承包商自身原因导致履约困难，即在非正常履约情况下，业主、工程师和承包商往往很难达成一致，各方也难以签署会议纪要。不得不说，在履约困难时，承包商可能不可避免地面临业主终止合同的风险。

  在国际工程实践中，会议纪要往往是工程师或者业主在会议之后准备并提交给承包商进行检查后签字。此时，承包商应仔细检查会议纪要的内容，是否是承包商在会议上所述的内容，是否是双方达成一致的内容等。承包商在收到会议纪要草稿后，如果发现与会议上所述内容不一致，应致函予以修改、更正和补充，使会议纪要记录的内容与其在会议上所述一致。

4.2.3 月进度报告格式

在国际工程项目中,承包商除了应按照合同规定递交进度计划,并按月更新进度计划外,还应按月向工程师或业主递交月进度报告(Monthly Progress Report),将承包商上月实际实施的项目进度报告给工程师或业主。以某铁路港口项目为例,合同附件明确规定了月进度报告的内容,如下:

1. Introduction 概况
2. Executive Summary 总结报告
3. General Project Information 一般项目信息
   3.1 Project Description 项目描述
   3.2 Project Design Description 项目设计描述
4. Progress of Works 工程进度
   4.1　General Requirements 一般要求
   4.2　Preparatory Works, Site Installation and Site Yard 准备工程、现场安装和场地
   4.3　Subgrade 基层
   4.4　Pavement and Track Construction 面层和轨道施工
   4.5　Drainage System, Culverts and Underpasses 排水系统、涵洞和地下通道
   4.6　Bridge Works 桥梁工程
   4.7　Railway Markings and Signals 轨道标识和信号
   4.8　Port Construction 港口施工
   4.9　Dredging Works 疏浚工程
   4.10　Auxiliary Constructions 附属工程
   4.11　Environmental EMP Compliance 环境合规
5. Time Schedule 进度计划
   5.1　Work Plan of the Month 当月工程计划
   5.2　Planned and Actual Project Milestone 计划与实际项目里程碑
   5.3　Planned and Actual Delivery Schedule 计划与实际交付进度
6. List of Notices Given under Clause 2.5 [*Employer's Claims*] 第2.5款项下发出的通知(业主索赔)
7. Project Implementation 项目实施
   7.1　Organization Chart of Contractor 承包商组织结构图
   7.2　List of Personnel on Site and History 在场和历史人员清单
   7.3　List of Equipment on Site and History 在场和历史设备清单
8. Subcontractors and Suppliers 分包商和供应商
   8.1　List of Subcontractors 分包商清单
   8.2　List of Suppliers 供应商清单
9. Variations 变更
10　Claims 索赔
11. Quality Assurance 质量保证

12. Environmental Aspects 环境

   12.1 Site Yard 场地

   12.2 Cutting Trees and Bushes 树木砍伐

   12.3 Storage Places of the Cut Bushes and Trees 砍伐树木的存放场所

   12.4 Anti-erosion Measures/Slope Protection 防腐措施/边坡防护

   12.5 Topsoil and Spoil Stripping and Storage and Waste Soil Management 清表和弃土剥离、存放和垃圾土管理

   12.6 Borrow Pits and Quarries 取土场和料场

   12.7 Archeological Problems 考古问题

   12.8 Waste Management on Site 现场垃圾管理

   12.9 Sanitary Conditions 卫生条件

   12.10 Emission and Dust 排放和粉尘

13. Health and Safety 健康和安全

   13.1 Health and Safety Trainings 健康和安全培训

   13.2 Accident on Site 现场发生的事故

   13.3 Health Measures 健康措施

   13.4 Safety Measures 安全措施

   13.5 Traffic Management 交通管理

14. Security 安保

   14.1 Security Accident on Site 现场发生的安保事故

   14.2 Security Management on Site 现场安保管理

   14.3 Security Solutions 安全解决方案

15. Weather Conditions on Site 现场气候条件

   15.1 Daily Temperature 每日气温记录

   15.2 Daily Rainfall Record 每日降雨记录

16. Problems Encountered by the Contractor 承包商遇到的问题

17. Record List for Meetings 会议记录清单

18. Cash Flow Estimation 现金流量估算

19. Appendices 附件

对照上述19项内容，承包商可以根据具体国际工程项目类型，适当调整第4项"工程进度"的内容，将具体的工程项目进行替换，即可形成通用的月进度报告。

上例中所述19项月进度报告的内容，是针对大型和复杂国际工程项目设定的，并经过业主和承包商谈判确定的月进度报告应包括的内容。承包商还可以根据项目的大小、复杂程度，编制简明月进度报告，内容可以简化。但承包商在起草和编制月进度报告时，应事先与工程师或业主进行协商，明确月进度报告的内容，避免被工程师或业主驳回。

以某国际工程项目为例，简明月进度报告的目录如下：

1. Description of the Project 项目概况

   1.1 Construction Progress Report Summary 施工进度报告总结

   1.2 General Description of Works Completed 已完工程概况

1.3 Differences between Works and Works Completed 工程与已完工程对比

1.3.1 S Curve Charts for Scheduled, Completed and Payment 表明计划、完成和付款的 S 曲线图

1.3.2 Status of Work Progress 工程进度状况

2. Payment of This Month 本月付款情况
3. Quality and Safety 质量和安全
4. Existing Problems 现存问题
5. Main Events of This Month 本月发生的主要事件
6. Allocation of Manpower 人力资源分配
7. Allocation of Equipment and Facilities 设备和设施的分配
8. Status of Construction Material 施工材料状况
9. Photos of Construction Site 施工现场照片

上述 19 项内容涵盖了国际工程项目月进度报告应包含的内容。需要注意的是，在国际工程项目中，有时还需要承包商在月进度报告中提供承包商进度"S 曲线（S Curve）"（图 4-1）。通过 S 曲线，工程师或业主可以直观地了解和知晓工程项目的实际进度与进度计划之间的差异。

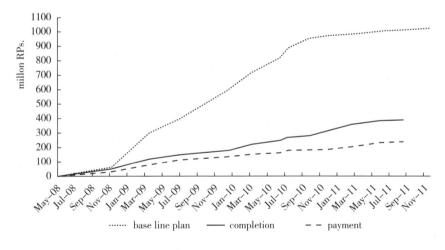

图 4-1 S 曲线示意图

月进度报告是记录承包商施工的重要文件。它记录了当月或先前施工进度、付款情况、会议情况、承包商与工程师或业主之间的往来信函、变更、业主索赔、承包商索赔、承包商在现场遇到的问题，以及现场照片等内容。在国际工程项目的争议解决过程中，月进度报告是证明承包商履约情况最直接的证据之一。通过梳理每月的月进度报告，可以清晰地看到承包商每月施工进度以及遇到的问题等，可以非常直观地得出承包商是否按合同履约以及业主是否存在违约情况的结论。根据月进度计划以及相关事件往来信函，可以清晰地判断某一争议事实、观点和主张是否正确。因此，在国际工程项目中，月进度计划起到了证明承包商和业主是否履约的作用。

4.2.4 进度计划格式

1. FIDIC 合同对进度计划的要求

FIDIC 1999 年第 1 版红皮书第 8.3 款进度计划规定：

"承包商应在收到根据第 8.1 款［工程的开工］规定发出的通知后 28 天内，向工程师提交一份详细的进度计划。当原定进度计划与实际进度或承包商义务不相符时，承包商还应提交一份修订的进度计划。每份进度计划应包括下列内容

（1）承包商计划实施工程的工作顺序，包括设计（如有）、承包商文件、采购、生产设备的制造、运到现场、施工、安装和试验各个阶段的预期时间安排。

（2）由各指定分包商（按第 5 条［指定分包商］定义）从事的以上各个阶段。

（3）合同中规定的各项检验和试验的顺序和时间安排。

（4）一份支持报告，内容包括：在工程实施中各主要阶段和承包商拟采用的方法和各主要阶段一般描述；以及承包商对工程各主要阶段现场所需各级承包商人员和各类承包商设备合理估计数量的详细情况。

除非工程师在收到进度计划后 21 天内向承包商发出通知，指出其中不符合合同要求的部分，承包商即应按照该进度计划，并遵守合同规定的其他义务开展工作。业主人员有权依照该进度计划安排他们的活动。

承包商应及时将未来可能对工作造成不利影响、增加合同价格或延误工程施工的事件或情况，向工程师发出通知。工程师可要求承包商提交此类未来事件或情况预期影响的估计，和/或根据第 13.3 款［变更程序］的规定提出建议。

如果任何时候工程师向承包商发出通知，指出进度计划（在指明的范围内）不符合合同要求，或与实际进度和承包商提出的意见不一致时，承包商应按照本款向工程师提交一份修订进度计划。

FIDIC 1999 年第 1 版黄皮书第 8.3 款［进度计划］对红皮书第（a）和（b）项修改如下：

"（a）承包商计划实施工程的工作顺序，包括每一设计阶段的预计时间、承包商文件、采购、制造、检查、运到现场、施工、安装、试验、试车和试运行。

（b）第 5.2 款［承包商文件］规定的审核期限，以及业主要求规定的任何其他递交、批准和同意。"

根据 FIDIC 1999 年第 1 版红皮书第 8.3 款［进度计划］的规定，承包商提交和修改进度计划的程序和时间要求如图 4-2 所示。

FIDIC 1999 年第 1 版红皮书、黄皮书和银皮书第 8.3 款［进度计划］仅对进度计划的内容作了具体规定，但没有对进度计划的形式，即横道图计划、CPM 网络计划、PERT 图示法等作出明确的规定。承包商在编制进度计划之前，应检查专用条款中的具体要求，查看承包商应递交进度计划的格式。在专用条款没有明确规定的情况下，承包商应致函工程师，询问进度计划的格式，并按照工程师的指示，准备工程师要求的编制进度计划所需软件程序，如微软的项目管理软件或 Primavera 的项目管理软件等。在工程师确定编制计划所需项目管理软件程序后，承包商应使用这个项目管理平台，编制进度计划、监督项目进度，并按照合同

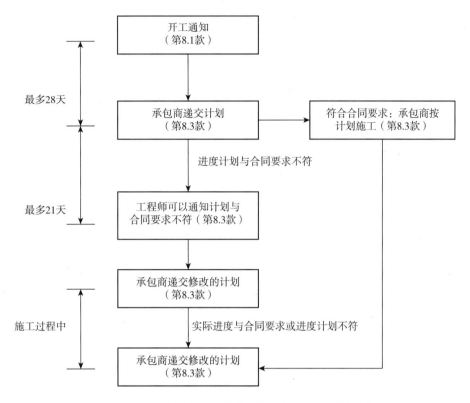

图 4-2 承包商提交和修改进度计划的程序和时间要求

的明确要求,按月向工程师递交进度计划的纸质文件和电子版文件。

2. 更新进度计划

FIDIC 合同条款 1999 年第 1 版红皮书第 8.3 款 [进度计划] 规定:"如果任何时候工程师向承包商发出通知,指出进度计划(在指明的范围内)不符合合同要求,或与实际进度和承包商提出的意见不一致时,承包商应按照本款向工程师提交一份修订进度计划。"

在施工过程中,承包商应在一定的时间期限内,如每周或每月定时更新进度计划,或者按照工程师的要求定期更新进度计划,以便使更新后的进度计划反映项目的实际进度,便于承包商管理和控制项目每一个分项工程或作业的工期,保证项目在合同规定的工期内竣工。

承包商在更新进度计划时,首先要搜集项目实施的进度信息,应根据项目的类型,采用不同的方法采集数据,然后才能对进度计划进行更新。承包商可采用表格的方式,对每一项分项工作或工程进行数据采集,见表 4-1。

表 4-1 工程进度数据

作业		计划进度		实际进度		进度	备注
代码	工作内容	开始日期	结束日期	开始日期	结束日期	%	

(续)

作业		计划进度		实际进度		进度	备注
代码	工作内容	开始日期	结束日期	开始日期	结束日期	%	

3. 进度计划构成合同文件时业主和承包商的义务

在建筑和土木工程项目中，由于不可预见的风险很多，并且建筑和土木工程易受外界因素的影响，设计是否合理、承包商资源是否充足、施工方法是否恰当，这些都会对施工进度计划产生直接的影响。因此，绝大多数标准合同格式都不将进度计划列为合同文件，即进度计划不是合同文件的一个组成部分。在这种情况下，进度计划的作用只是协助工程师监控工程的进度，帮助承包商控制和管理进度。在某些情况下，进度计划还可以成为承包商证明其有权要求工期延长索赔的证据。

对业主和承包商而言，如果进度计划成为合同文件，那将是一把双刃剑。一方面，它可以约束承包商严格按照进度计划要求和安排进行施工；但另一方面，它也要求业主严格按照进度计划要求和安排履行义务。否则，业主的行为将构成违约，将导致承包商提出损失和费用索赔和（或）工期延长的要求。

如果进度计划构成合同文件，则业主和承包商应遵守进度计划中规定双方必须遵守的义务。此时，进度计划应明确界定业主和承包商在进度计划中的义务，明确进度计划的作用和功能。按照合同文件的优先次序，进度计划可以对业主和承包商的义务做出具体规定。另外，进度计划也可以只表明在某个特定竣工日期完工前的施工次序。

如果进度计划中包括了完成某项工程的施工方法，则进度计划中写明的施工方法将构成一种特定的施工方法。如果业主打算改变这种施工方法，则承包商有权将施工方法改变视为一种变更。在 Yorkshire Water Authority 诉 Sir Alfred McAlpine and Son（Northern）Ltd.（1985）32 BLR 114 案中，施工合同使用的是 ICE 第 5 版合同格式，承包商在投标时递交了进度计划。根据 ICE 合同第 14 条的规定，承包商也递交了施工方法的声明。法院判决：只要这种施工方法合法并且切实可行，则承包商负有义务按照递交的施工方法进行施工。此时，这种施工方法就成为一种特定的施工方法。根据 ICE 合同第 13.1 款的规定，如果承包商无法按照这种方法进行施工，则承包商有权要求按照第 51 条的规定进行变更，并有权要求按照合同第 51.2 款和第 52 款付款。

在 Havant Borough Council 诉 South Coast Shipping Company Ltd.［1996］CILL 1146 案中，由于施工噪声对周围环境造成了干扰，承包商无法按照原定的施工方法进行施工。法院判决：由于施工方法构成合同文件的一个组成部分，因此，对施工方法的改变构成变更。在构成变更时，业主应按变更条款的有关规定进行变更估价和付款。

4. 使用什么进度计划软件编制进度计划

除非工程合同明确规定编制进度计划软件的确切名称，否则承包商可以有权选择使用哪种软件编制进度计划。目前，在国际工程项目中，广为使用的进度计划软件有：微软公司的 Project 软件以及甲骨文公司的 Premavera P3、P6 和 P8 软件。承包商可选择其中一个来编制进度计划和更新进度计划。

5. 承包商在编制进度计划时应注意的问题

承包商在编制进度计划时，为了避免给自己挖坑埋雷，而且为了今后工期延长索赔的需要，应注意如下问题：

（1）如果工程合同明确规定了进度计划软件，则应使用合同规定的软件编制进度计划。

（2）如果合同约定了浮时（Float）的归属，无论浮时属于承包商、业主还是项目，承包商均应尽量将浮时计算安排在承包商一方。

（3）如果合同约定了进度计划应显示关键线路（critical path），则承包商应在进度计划中显示关键线路。但是，承包商应该注意，在处理关键线路时，应进行现场考察，特别是线性工程项目，例如公路和铁路等，应明确项目施工困难的桩号和地段，例如存在大量的征地拆迁工作，或者存在桥梁等控制线工程，应将这些施工困难的地段列在关键线路上。

（4）如果合同没有明确规定进度计划应显示关键线路，则承包商应尽量不要在进度计划中表示关键线路。

（5）如果合同没有规定进度计划需要建立逻辑链接，则承包商尽量不要在进度计划中建立各项工作之间的逻辑链接。

（6）承包商应按照合同的规定及时更新进度计划。

（7）在国际工程实践中，有时大部分国际工程项目，工程师或业主都没有同意、批准承包商的进度计划。此时，承包商应根据现场的情况确定一份对自己有利的基准进度计划（baseline programme），并将这份有利的进度计划作为基准进度计划使用。承包商在索赔工期延长时，以基准进度计划为准，通过对比实际进度，得出承包商有权要求工期延长的请求。或者，采用其他工期延误计算方法，例如视窗法、时间影响分析法等计算工期延长天数。

4.2.5 期中付款证书格式

承包商在递交付款申请时需要提交大量的文件资料，这些文件资料可分为：

（1）承包商递交的付款申请书（Statement）。

（2）承包商以 Excel 格式递交的付款计算书，包括汇总表（Summary Sheet）、各单项工程计算表、预付款扣还汇总表、暂定金使用表、索赔汇总表及其杂项表格。

（3）支持文件和资料，包括设计图纸、测量数据、工程师验收单等。

以某国际工程项目为例，合同规定承包商递交付款申请（Payment Statement）格式如下：

ContractorLetterhead

Project name：

Employer:
Contractor:
Month and year:[   ]

To: The Employer
Cc: Lenders' Representative
(Number of copies: [·])
Pursuant to Clause 13.3 [*Application for Interim Payment Certificates*] of the engineering, procurement and construction contract dated [   ] between the Employer and the Contractor (as amended, supplemented or otherwise modified, the "Contract"), the Contractor hereby applies for an Interim Payment Certificate for the items listed below. Capitalised terms used but not defined herein shall have the meanings ascribed to such terms in the Contract.

Description	Amount (US dollar)
The estimated contract value of the Works executed and the Contractor's Documents produced up to the end of the month (including Variations but excluding items described in Clauses 13.3.2(iii) to 13.3.2(vii), inclusive, of the Contract;	
The amount of any applicable value added tax;	
Any amounts to be added and deducted for changes in legislation, in accordance with Clause 12.6 [*Adjustments for Changes in Legislation*] of the Contract;	
Any amounts to be deducted pursuant to Clauses 8.6 [*Consequences of Delay*] or 9.6 [*Failure to Pass Handover Tests*] of the Contract (to the extent not already paid by the Contractor);	
Any amounts to be added and deducted for the Advance Payment and repayments in accordance with Clause 13.2 [*Advance Payment*] of the Contract;	
The deduction of amounts certified in all previous Payment Certificates; and	
Any other additions or deductions which may have become due under the Contract or otherwise, including those under Clause 19 [*Claims, Disputes and Arbitration*] of the Contract.	
Total amount due and payable to the Contractor:	

The following supporting documents are attached to this Statement:
[insert the list of supporting documents]

For and on behalf of the Contractor:
Name:_____
Title:_____
Date:_____
Signature:_____

承包商也可以通过使用往来信函格式，向工程师或业主递交期中付款证书付款申请。此类递交给工程师的往来信函仅需表明付款申请意向，要求工程师在合同约定的期限内签字批准。需要特别注意的是，根据 FIDIC 合同条款的规定，自承包商递交付款申请之日起算，工程师签字批准承包商递交的付款申请期限为 28 天。在国际工程实践中，经常发生的争议是，工程师主张自承包商递交"正确的"付款申请书之日起算 28 天，而非承包商递交"可能含有错误或瑕疵信息"的付款申请之日起算。关于这个问题，根据 FIDIC 合同条款的规定，应自承包商递交付款申请之日起算，承包商可以援引的依据是 FIDIC 前言中"第 14 条中设想的付款事项的典型顺序（Typical Sequence of Payment Events envisaged in Clause 14）"。

承包商除了需要向工程师递交付款申请信函外，还需递交 Excel 格式的付款计算书。付款申请书包括：

(1) 封面（cover）。
(2) 汇总表（Summary of Statement for Payment）。
(3) 各单项工程的工程量和价款计算表。
(4) 在场设备、材料付款汇总表。
(5) 工程变更付款汇总表。
(6) 预付款扣还汇总表。
(7) 暂定金汇总表。
(8) 保留金扣留汇总表。
(9) 价格调整计算表（如有）。
(10) 承包商索赔汇总表（如有）。
(11) 其他增加/减少项汇总。
(12) 争议委员会费用支付汇总表。
(13) 其他项目汇总表。

承包商在付款申请中递交的 Excel 表，可以事先与工程师或业主进行沟通和协商，确定递交付款申请书及其计算表的格式。下面是付款证书的付款汇总表（Summary of Statement for Payment）的格式，承包商可以参考编制付款证书。对于具体各单项工程项目，承包商仅需对照标价工程量单（Priced Bill of Quantities），在每一单项工程中输入对应的价号、单价、完成工程数量，即可设定付款证书格式，见表 4-2。

表 4-2 付款证书汇总

Summary of Statement for Payment

AIPC/Statement No: 32	Submission Date:
Period covering from	
Employer:	Engineer:
Project:	Component:
Contract No:	Contract Amount:
Contract Start Date（NtC）: 21 Apr 2009	Contract Closing Date:
Contractor:	

(续)

S. N.	Works Doscription	Roferoncos	Total to Dato	Prevlous	Current
A	EXCLUDING HYDRAULIC STEEL WORKS				
A1	General Items	Appendix 1	146,008,490.76	144,048,731.14	1,959,759.62
A2	Access to Headworks	Appendix 2			
A3	Head Works	Appendix 3			
A4	ambathan Adit	Appendix 4	24,900,501.33	22,065,449.81	2,35,051.52
A5	Gyalthum Adit	Appendix 5	13,508,312.86	12,839,489.74	668,823.12
A6	Sindhu Audit	Appendix 6	59,239,389.40	53,332,656.10	5,906,733.30
A7	Sundrijal Portal & Upstream Tunnel	Appendix 7	58,266,743.01	54,250,716.03	4,016,026.98
A8	Permanent Camp Works	Appendix 9			
A9	Variations	Appendix 10A	5,105,544.78	5,105,544.78	
A10	Adjustment for Changes in Legislation	Appendix 11A			
A11	Adjustment for Changes in Cost	Appendix 12A	33,655,197.37	18,691,822.22	14,963,375.15
A12	Claims	Appendix 13A	32,828,726.77	32,828,726.77	
A13	Provisional Works	Appendix 14A			
	SUM A (A1 to A13)		373,512,906.28	343,163,136.59	30,349,769.69
B	HYDRAULIC STEEL WORKS				
B1	Hydraulic Steel Works	Appendix 8			
B2	Variations	Appendix 10B			
B3	Adjustment for Changes in Legislation	Appendix 11B			
B4	Adjustment for Changes in Cost	Appendix 12B			
B5	Claims	Appendix 13B			
B6	Provisional Works	Appendix 14B			
	SUM B (B1 to B6)				
C	OTHER CONTRACTUALS				
C1	Plant/Materials Intended for Works (Payment/Repayment)	Appendix 15	42,220,203.04	38,433,846.40	3,786,356.84
C2	Mobilization Advance Payment/Repayment	Appendix 16			
C3	DB Reimbursable Cost	Appendix 17	1,692,000.00	1,488,000.00	204,000.00
C4	Any Other Additions or Deductions	Appendix 18			
	SUM C (C1 to C4)		43,912,203.04	39,921,846.40	3,990,356.64
	Total (A+B+C)		417,425,109.32	383,084,982.99	34,340,126.33
D	DEDUCTIONS				
D1	Retention Money 10 % of A	Appendix 19A	37,351,290.63	34,316,313.66	3,034,976.97
D2	Retention Money 10 % of B	Appendix 20B			
D3	Repayment of Advance 25 % of A	Appendix 20A			
D4	Repayment of Advance 25 % of B	Appendix 20B			

（续）

	Total of D (D1 to D4)		37,351,290.63	34,316,313.66	3,034,976.97
E1	Payable for Excluding Hydraulic Steel Works (A+C-D1-D3) (excl. VAT)		380,073,818.69	348,768,669.33	31,305,149.36
E2	Payable for Hydraulic Steel Works (B-D2-D4) (excl. VAT)				
	Total Payable (E1+E2)		380,073,818.69	348,768,669.33	31,305,149.36

Breakdown the Net Payable Amount in Different Currencies

	Exchange Rate NPR	Excluding Hydraulic Steel Work		Hydraulic Steel Works		Total Payable
		%	Amount	%	Amount	Amount
Payable in NPR	1.00	30	9,391,544.81	16		9,391,544.81
Payable in USD	64.45	45	218,577.46	54		218,577.46
Payable in EUR	100.84	25	77,610.94	30		77,610.94

Note:

Submitted by the Contractor

Project Manager

Date

4.2.6 接收证书格式

雇主/业主或工程师签发的接收证书（Taking-Over Certificate, TOC）并没有固定的格式。但对于接收证书而言，必须表明承包商已经根据合同履行了合同义务并竣工。在竣工的情况下，雇主/业主或工程师向承包商发出接收证书。接收证书格式如下：

FORM OF TAKING-OVER CERTIFICATE

1. The Works under [insert the contract number and name] has been achieved.

2. Each of the Works has been satisfied, namely:

   2.1 [*Note*: Add the relevant Substantial Completion Conditions for each sections or the whole works under the EPC Contract.]

   2.2 [*Note*: add the name of the Works]

3. Attached hereto is a report of the Works completed with sufficient detail to enable the Owner to determine whether the Substantial Completion Conditions for the Relevant Package have been satisfied.

4. The Warranty for the Package is in full force and effect and will remain in full force and effect for the relevant Warranty Period.

5. The Owner's approval and countersignature of this Substantial Completion Certificate (Package) shall not in any way modify or alter Contractor's obligations under the EPC Contract.

IN WITNESS WHEREOF, the Contractor has caused this Taking-Over Certificate to be executed by its duly authorized representative on the date first above written.

 The Contractor：

  By _____
   Name：
   Title：

The Owner hereby (a) accepts the foregoing Taking-Over Certificate for purposes of Section _____ of the EPC Contract, it being understood that such acceptance shall not be deemed an acknowledgement that any of the matters certified above is correct (except that substantial completion has been achieved) and (b) acknowledges that the substantial completion Date for the Relevant Package is _____ .

 The Employer

  By _____
   Name：
   Title：
   Date：

4.2.7 履约证书格式

颁发履约证书意味着承包商已经履行了缺陷责任期的所有义务。为此，在缺陷责任期结束后，业主向承包商出具履约证书，证明承包商完全履行了合同义务。履约证书格式如下：

To：Mr. DDD
  XXX Company Limited
  The Contractor
  Address：

Subject：Performance Certificate

Dear Sir,

The Defects Liability Certificate/Performance Certificate is issued in accordance with the Sub-Clause 11.9 of the General Conditions of Contract as the Contractor [insert the Contractor's name], completed obligations to execute and complete the Works under the Contract [insert the contract name] and remedy defects therein.

Sincerely yours,

Name:
The Engineer

在国际工程实践中,业主或工程师也可以使用最终接收证书表明承包商已经履行了合同义务,最终接收证书格式如下:

FINAL ACCEPTANCE CERTIFICATE

Dated:_____

To: Mr.
XXX Company Limited
the Contractor
ADD:

Attention:_____

Re: Engineering, Procurement and Construction Contract—Final Acceptance

Gentlemen:

Reference is made to the Engineering, Procurement and Construction Contract, dated _____, 20_____, between_____. ("Owner"), a statutory corporation established under the laws of_____. and_____("Contractor") (as amended, restated, supplemented, novated or otherwise modified from time to time, the "EPC Contract"). Capitalized terms used but not otherwise defined herein shall have the meanings ascribed thereto in the EPC Contract.

Contractor hereby certifies as follows:

1. Final Acceptance has been achieved.
2. Each of the Final Acceptance Conditions has been satisfied, namely:
   2.1 [Note: Add the relevant Final Acceptance Conditions under the EPC Contract.]
3. Attached hereto is a report of the Works completed with sufficient detail to enable the Owner to determine whether the Final Acceptance Conditions have been satisfied.
4. The Warranty is in full force and effect and will remain in full force and effect for the Warranty Period.

5. The Owner's approval and countersignature of this Final Acceptance Certificate shall not in any way modify or alter the Contractor's obligations under the EPC Contract.

IN WITNESS WHEREOF, the Contractor has caused this Final Acceptance Certificate to be executed by its duly authorized representative on the date first above written.

The Contractor：

By _____
　Name：
　Title：

The Owner hereby (a) accepts the foregoing Final Acceptance Certificate for purposes of Section _____ of the EPC Contract, it being understood that such acceptance shall not be deemed an acknowledgement that any of the matters certified above is correct (except that Final Acceptance has been achieved) and (b) acknowledges that the Final Acceptance Date is _____.

The Owner：

By _____
　Name：
　Title：
　Date：

4.2.8　银行保函格式

1. 见索即付担保

见索即付担保是指担保人（一般是指银行和其他担保机构）应申请人（一般指承包商）的要求或指示对受益人（一般指业主）承诺下述义务：只要受益人要求付款，担保人应立即支付约定的金额。受益人的付款要求是无条件的，他既不需要证明其付款要求是有根据的，也不需要证明被担保主债务未能履行或主债务人违约。担保人一旦收到受益人付款要求（on first demand），即应向受益人付款。担保人不得以申请人根据基础交易合同所产生的抗辩来对抗受益人。见索即付担保是无条件的担保（unconditional guarantee, unconditional bond），其特征如下：

（1）见索即付担保是非从属性的担保，担保人（银行）所承担的义务独立于基础交易合同的，担保人不能以基础合同所产生的抗辩对抗受益人。从独立于基础交易合同的角度而言，见索即付担保与国际贸易中普遍使用的信用证交易相似。对银行而言，是一种单证业务。

（2）见索即付是无条件的，即担保人仅凭受益人要求即应付款，而不能介入其所担保的主债务是否得到履行。

（3）见索即付担保中，担保人（银行）承担的义务是付款义务，而不是实际履行主债务人本应履行的义务。

见索即付担保与信用证是有区别的，尽管很多美国银行习惯采用备用信用证为客户提供银行担保，但两者区别如下：

（1）备用信用证是一种付款方式，而见索即付担保是一种担保方式。

（2）备用信用证一般是跟单信用证，而见索即付担保不是跟单的，担保银行仅凭受益人的要求即应予以支付。

判断一项担保是否是见索即付担保，应根据担保文件的明示规定进行判断，而不能根据默示推定其是否为见索即付担保。见索即付担保的典型用语如下：

"应委托人请求，我方（银行名称）_____ 在此不可撤销地承诺，在我方收到你方的书面要求和关于（在要求中）下列事项的书面声明后，向你方，受益人/业主，支付总额不超过_____（"保证金额"，即：_____）的任何一笔或几笔款项。"

在担保函中，只要出现 on demand, on first demand, on your first demand, onwritten demand, on your written demand 用语，并且明示规定银行在收到受益人的要求立即付款的内容，或者遵守国际商会 458 号或 758 号出版物《见索即付保函统一规则》，或者载明独立于基础交易时，即可判断这种担保是见索即付担保。

2016 年 12 月 1 日实施的中华人民共和国最高人民法院《关于审理独立保函纠纷案件若干问题的规定》第三条规定：

"保函具有下列情形之一，当事人主张保函性质为独立保函的，人民法院应予支持，但保函为载明据以付款的单价和最高金额的除外：

（一）保函载明见索即付；

（二）保函载明适用国际商会《见索即付保函统一规则》等独立保函交易示范规则；

（三）根据保函文本内容，开立人的付款义务独立于基础交易关系即保函申请法律关系，其仅承担相符交单的付款责任。

当事人以独立保函记载了对应的基础交易为由，主张该保函性质为一般保证或连带保证的，人民法院不予支持。

当事人主张独立保函适用担保法关于一般保证或连带保证规定的，人民法院不予支持。"

目前，在国际工程承包行业，普遍使用的是见索即付担保，其担保文件的名称通常为见索即付保函。

2. 凭单据付款担保

凭单据付款担保是指受益人（一般指业主）在要求担保人（一般指银行）付款时必须向担保人提交担保函内规定的单据，担保人在收到单据并在形式上进行审查认为其符合担保函要求后，才能向受益人支付担保的款项。凭单据付款担保是有条件担保（conditional guarantee）。

凭单据付款担保使用的单据，可分为三种：

（1）凭担保申请人（一般指承包商）与受益人之间的书面协议支付。

（2）凭鉴定人或工程师出具的证明承包商违约事实存在的证书支付。

（3）凭法院判决或仲裁庭裁决支付。

在第（1）种单据中，由于是业主和承包商之间的争议，因此，他们之间达成业主没收保函协议的可能性极低。在实践中不会采用这种单据，因为这对业主而言极为不利，业主无法实现担保项下其应获得的补偿。

第（2）种单据中，如工程师出具证明证实承包商违约，是一种可行的做法，但会使工程师处于非常难堪的地位，也可能面临承包商的诉讼。

第（3）种单据中，毫无疑问，法院的判决或仲裁庭的裁决无疑具有不容置疑的地位，但法院和仲裁庭耗时很长，对受益人实现其付款极为不利。

鉴于以上种种原因，在国际工程承包业中，业主使用的都是见索即付担保，使用凭单据付款担保极为罕见。

3. 国际商会《见索即付保函统一规则》

国际商会《见索即付保函统一规则》（*Uniform Rules for Demand Guarantees*）（简称URDG）是国际商会于1992年4月发行的第458号出版物，是国际上关于独立保函认可度和知名度最高、应用范围最广的国际惯例，对于独立保函在国际上的推广和运用起到了巨大作用。为适用市场的需要，2009年11月国际商会通过了第758号出版物，发布了新版URDG，并于2010年7月1日正式实施。

与第458号出版物相比，第758号出版物借鉴了《跟单信用证统一惯例》（*Uniform Customs and Practice Documentary Credits*）的原则，引入了申请人与被担保人的概念，将保函索赔细化为部分索偿和多次索偿，明确了审单时限即不延期即付款的操作办法，区分了保函转让和款项让渡两种模式。总体而言，第758号出版物对保函各方当事人的权责关系更为明确，内容更加清晰，操作流程更加明确。

第458号URDG共计28条。其中对于见索即付保函，承包商在按照第458号出版物开立独立保函时，应删除第20条第a款第（ii）项的规定，如下：

"本保函适用国际商会《见索即付保函统一规则》第458号出版物，但删除适用第458号出版物第20条第a款第（ii）项。"（This Guarantee is subject to *Uniform Rules for Demand Guarantees*, ICC Publication No. 458. However, the requirement of supporting statement under Article 20（a）（ii）is excluded）

第458号URDG第20条规定：

"a）保函项下的任何付款要求都应当采用书面形式，且（除了保函可能规定的其他单据外）应当辅之以书面声明（或者在付款要求时提出，或者在付款要求随附的单独单据中提出，并在付款要求中提出）；

（i）声明被担保人违反了基础合同项下的义务，或者，如果是投标保函，违反了招标条件；

(ⅱ) 指明被担保人的违约情形。"

因此,删除适用第20条第a款第(2)项意味着排除了"(ⅱ)指明被担保人的违约情形",即排除了"在履约保函索赔时履约保函受益人,需要告知被担保人的违约情形"。因此,根据本款规定,在索赔履约保函时,履约保函受益人,即反担保受益人不需要说明承包商的违约情形。

在适用第758号出版物时,独立保函中应删除适用第15条第(a)项,如下:

"本保函适用国际商会《见索即付保函统一规则》第758号出版物,但删除适用第758号出版物第15条第a款。"(This Guarantee is subject to *Uniform Rules for Demand Guarantees*, ICC Publication No. 758. However, the requirement of supporting statement under Article 15 (a) is excluded)

第758号URDG第15条第a项规定:
"a. 保函项下的索赔,应得到保函指定其他单据支持,并且在任何情况下均应附上受益人声明,说明申请人在哪些方面违反了基础关系项下的义务。该声明可以在索赔书中提出,也可以在单独签署的该索赔书随附的单据中提出,或在单独签署的指明该索赔书的单据中提出。"

上述删除适用第458号第20条第a款第(ⅱ)项和第758号第15条第a项意味着删除了独立保函索赔人提供被担保人违反了基础合同项下义务的责任,也就是说,索赔人仅依靠一份声明,声称被答辩人违约即可索赔独立保函。

4. 承包商常用保函格式

国际工程项目常用的保函格式有:

(1) 投标保函。

Tender Security

Brief description of Contract _____

Name and address of Beneficiary _____(whom the tender documents define as the Employer).

We have been informed that _____(hereinafter called the "Principal") is submitting an offer for such Contract in response to your invitation, and that the conditions of your invitation (the "conditions of invitation", which are set out in a document entitled Instruction to Tenders) require his offer to be supported by a tender security.

At the request of the Principal, we (name of bank) _____ hereby irrevocably undertake to pay you, the Beneficiary/Employer, any sum or sums not exceeding in total the amount of _____ (say: _____) upon receipt by us of your demand in writing and your written statement (in the demand) stating that:

(a) the Principal has, without your agreement, withdrawn his offer after the latest time specified for its submission and before the expiry of its period of validity; or

(b) the Principal has refused to accept the correction of errors in his offer in accordance with such conditions of invitation; or

(c) you awarded the Contract to the Principal and he has failed to comply with Sub-Clause 1.6 of the conditions of the contract; or

(d) you awarded the Contract to the Principal and he has failed to comply with Sub-Clause 4.2 of the conditions of the contract.

Any demand for payment must contain your signature(s) which must be authenticated by your bankers or by a notary public. The authenticated demand and statement must be received by us at this office on or before (the date 35 days after the expiry of the validity of the Letter or Tender) _____, when this guarantee shall expire and shall be returned to us.

This guarantee is subject to the Uniform Rules for Demand Guarantees, published as number 758 by the International Chamber of Commerce, except as stated above.

Date _____ Signature(s) _____

(2) 预付款保函格式。

Advance Payment Guarantee

No. _____

To: _____ (*Beneficiary's full name and address*)

Issuing date: _____

Dear Sirs,

We have been informed that _____ (hereinafter referred to as the "Applicant") has entered into a _____ contract No. _____ dated _____ (hereinafter referred to as the "Underlying Contract") with you, for the supply of _____ (*description of goods and /or services*). Furthermore we understand that, according to the terms of the Underlying Contract, an advance Payment guarantee is required.

At the request of the Applicant, we, the _____ Bank of China, hereby irrevocably undertake to pay you any amount up to _____ (say _____) (hereinafter referred to as the "Guaranteed Amount") upon receipt by us of your complying demand, supported by such other documents as may be listed below and in any event by your statement, indicating in what respect the Applicant is in breach of its obligations under the Underlying Contract.

Your demand for payment must also be accompanied by the following document(s): [*specify document(s), if any*]

_____
_____

Your demand and accompanying documents shall be forwarded to us through your bank for verification of your authorized signature thereon.

This Guarantee shall become effective upon the effectiveness of the Underlying Contract and receipt by the Applicant of Master Letter of Credit specified in the Underlying Contract _____.

The Guaranteed Amount shall be automatically and proportionally reduced according to the progress of the Underlying Contract, which is evidenced by our receipt of the following document(s) from the Applicant:

_____
_____

This Guarantee shall expire after the date of _____ (calendar date) (hereinafter referred to as the "Expiry Date"). Any demand under this Guarantee must be received by us our _____ Branch, with its office at _____, on or before the Expiry Date. After the Expiry Date, this Guarantee shall automatically become null and void and be cancelled whether it is returned to us or not.

This Guarantee is subject to the Uniform Rules for Demand Guarantees (URDG) 2010 Revision, ICC Publication No. 758.

Any dispute or claim arising out of or in relation to this Guarantee shall be submitted to the exclusive jurisdiction of the courts of Beijing, the People's Republic of China.

_____
(Authorized Signature)
For and on Behalf of _____ Bank

对于预付款保函,在业主扣还了部分预付款后,承包商可要求业主减少预付款保函金额，承包商要求减少预付款保函金额的函件举例如下：

ADVANCE PAYMENT GUARANTEE FOR INTERIM PAYMENT STEP DOWN NOTIFICATION

To：

With reference to _____ [insert the contract name] (the "Contract") dated _____ between _____ (the "Employer") and _____ (the "Contractor"):

(a) The Employer hereby provides notification/confirmation to the Contractor that the following works in a sum of USD _____ has been done by the Contractor.

(b) Accordingly the Employer allows the Maximum Sum of the Advance Payment Guarantee for Interim Payment to be reduced by an amount equal to _____% of the value of the relevant works.

We confirm that the Maximum Sum of the Advance Payment Guarantee for Interim Payment No. _____ shall be reduced to USD _____.

This notice shall be interpreted in accordance with the provisions of the Contract.

The Contractor：
By：_____
Name：
Title：
Date：

Counter signed by the Employer：
By：_____
Name：
Title：
Date：

---

(3) 履约保函格式。

Performance Guarantee

No. _____

To：_____(Beneficiary's full name and address)

Issuing date：_____

Dear Sirs，

We have been informed that _____ (hereinafter referred to as the "Applicant") has entered into a _____ contract No. _____ dated _____ (hereinafter referred to as the "Underlying Contract") with you, for the supply of _____ (*description of goods and /or services*). Furthermore we understand that, according to the terms of the Underlying Contract, a performance guarantee is required.

At the request of the Applicant, we, the _____ Bank of China, hereby irrevocably undertake to pay you any amount up to _____ (say _____) (hereinafter referred to as the "Guaranteed Amount") upon receipt by us of your complying demand, supported by such other documents as may be listed below and in any event by your statement, indicating in what respect the Applicant is in breach of its obligations under the Underlying Contract.

Your demand for payment must also be accompanied by the following document(s): [*specify document(s), if any*]

_____
_____

Your demand and accompanying documents shall be forwarded to us through your bank for verification of your authorized signature thereon.

This Guarantee shall become effective upon the effectiveness of the Underlying Contract and receipt by the Applicant of Master Letter of Credit specified in the Underlying Contract _____.

The Guaranteed Amount shall be automatically and proportionally reduced according to the progress of the Underlying Contract, which is evidenced by our receipt of the following document(s) from the Applicant:

_____
_____

This Guarantee shall expire after the date of _____ (calendar date) (hereinafter referred to as the "Expiry Date"). Any demand under this Guarantee must be received by us our _____ Branch, with its office at _____, on or before the Expiry Date. After the Expiry Date, this Guarantee shall automatically become null and void and be cancelled whether it is returned to us or not.

This Guarantee is subject to the Uniform Rules for Demand Guarantees (URDG) 2010 Revision, ICC Publication No. 758.

Any dispute or claim arising out of or in relation to this Guarantee shall be submitted to the exclusive jurisdiction of the courts of Beijing, the People's Republic of China.

                                                  (Authorized Signature)

                              For and on Behalf of _____ Bank

(4) 保留金保函格式。

Retention Money Guarantee

                                                          No. _____

To: _____ (*Beneficiary's full name and address*)

Issuing date: _____

Dear Sirs,

We have been informed that _____ (hereinafter referred to as the "Applicant") has entered into a _____ contract No. _____ dated _____ (hereinafter referred to as the "Underlying Contract") with you, for the supply of _____ (*description of goods and/or services*). Furthermore we understand that, according to the terms of the Underlying Contract, a retentionmouey guarantee is required.

At the request of the Applicant, we, The _____ Bank of China, hereby irrevocably undertake to pay you any amount up to _____ (say _____) (hereinafter referred to as the "Guaranteed Amount") upon receipt by us of your complying demand, supported by such other documents as may be listed below and in any event by your statement, indicating in what respect the Applicant is in breach of its obligations under the Underlying Contract. Your demand for payment must also be accompanied by the following document(s): [*specify document(s), if any*]

_____

_____

_____

Your demand and accompanying documents shall be forwarded to us through your bank for verification of your authorized signature thereon.

This Guarantee shall become effective upon the effectiveness of the Underlying Contract and receipt by the Applicant of Master Letter of Credit specified in the Underlying Contract _____.

The Guaranteed Amount shall be automatically and proportionally reduced according to the progress of the Underlying Contract, which is evidenced by our receipt of the following document(s) from the Applicant:
_____
_____
_____
_____

This Guarantee shall expire after the date of _____ (calendar date) (hereinafter referred to as the "Expiry Date"). Any demand under this Guarantee must be received by us our _____ Branch, with its office at _____, on or before the Expiry Date. After the Expiry Date, this Guarantee shall automatically become null and void and be cancelled whether it is returned to us or not.

This Guarantee is subject to the Uniform Rules for Demand Guarantees (URDG) 2010 Revision, ICC Publication No. 758.

Any dispute or claim arising out of or in relation to this Guarantee shall be submitted to the exclusive jurisdiction of the courts of Beijing, the People's Republic of China.

_____
(Authorized Signature)
For and on Behalf of _____ Bank

5. 分包商常用保函格式

在国际工程项目中，分包商常用的保函格式包括银行保函或保险公司出具的保函，有投标保函、预付款保函、履约保函和保留金保函等。

以分包商出具的预付款保函为例，预付款保函格式如下：

FORM OF ADVANCE PAYMENT GUARANTEE

To:

Subject: Adoauce Payment Guarantee

Dear Sirs,

We have been informed that _____ (hereinaftercalled "the Subcontractor") is the Subcontractor under such Subcontract and wishes to receive an advance payment, for which the Subcontract requires him to obtain a guarantee.

At the request of the Subcontractor, we _____. [insert the name of the issuing bank] at the address _____ [insert the address of the issuing bank] hereby irrevocably undertake to pay you, the General Contractor _____ [insert the name of the General Contractor], any sum or sums not exceeding in total the amount of _____ ("the guaranteed amount", say "_____") upon receipt by us of your demand in writing and your statement stating:

(a) that the Subcontractor has failed to repay the advance payment in accordance with the conditions of the Subcontract; and
(b) the amount which the Subcontractor has failed to repay.

Our obligation and liabilities under this guarantee shall not be discharged by any variation or suspension of the works to be executed under the Subcontract, or by any amendments to the Subcontract which has been done between the Subcontractor and the General Contractor, whether with or without our knowledge or consent.

This guarantee shall expire no later than 28 days from issuance of _____ Any demand for payment under this guarantee must be received by us at this office on or before that date.

This guarantee shall be governed by the laws of _____ and shall be subject to the Uniform Rules for demand Guarantees, published as number 758 by the International Chamber of Commerce.

Date: _____

Signature: _____

以分包商出具的履约保函为例，其格式如下：

FORM OF PERFORMANCE GUARANTEE

To:

Subject: Performance Guarantee

Dear Sirs,

We have been informed that _____ (hereinafter called as "the Subcontractor") has entered into Subcontract for execution of the Subcontract Works for _____ (hereinafter called "the Subcontract").

Furthermore, we understand that, according to the conditions of the Subcontract, a performance guarantee is required.

At the request of the Subcontractor, we _____ [insert the name of the issuing bank] at the address _____ [insert the address of the issuing bank] hereby irrevocably undertake to pay _____ [insert the name of the General Contractor] (hereinafter called as "Principal") any sum or sums not exceeding in total the amount of _____ [insert the figure of currency], such sum being payable in the types and proportions of currencies in which the Subcontract price is payable, upon receipt by us of the Principal's first demand in writing accompanied by a written statement stating that the Subcontractor is in breach of its obligations under the Subcontract, without your needing to prove or to show grounds for your demand or the sum specified therein.

Our obligation and liabilities under this guarantee shall not be discharged by any variation or suspension of the works to be executed under the Subcontract, or by any amendments to the Subcontract which has been done between the Subcontractor and the Principal, whether with or without our knowledge or consent.

This guarantee shall expire no later than 28 days from issuance of _____ Any demand for payment under this guarantee must be received by us at this office on or before that date.

This guarantee shall be governed by the laws of _____ and shall be subject to the Uniform Rules for demand Guarantees, published as number 758 by the International Chamber of Commerce.

Date: _____

Signature: _____

4.3 其他常用文件格式

4.3.1 施工日志格式

施工日志是承包商记录每天施工状态的记录性文件，简明格式和复杂格式见表4-3和表4-4：

表4-3 施工日志简明格式

Dally Report 施工日志											
Dally Report 施工日志				Date 日期						No. 编号	
Contract No. 合同编号												
Project Name 工程名称												
Sections 单位工程名称												
Contractor 承包商								Temperature 温度			
Employer 业主			Engineer 工程师					Weather 天气			
	Foreman 领工	Ord worker 工人	Type of equipment 设备类型	Excavator 挖掘机	Bulldozer 推土机	Grader 平地机	Loader 装载机	Compactor 压路机	Water truck 洒水车	Dumper 自卸车	
Contractor											Working Onsite
Local											
Total											
Bill No.	English Executed Works 工作执行状况										
Report on the work of the engineer represe ntative records site. Given reasonable technical evaluation of the relevant requirements of the contractor 工程师代表人记录工地的工作报告，对承包商的相关要求给出了合理的技术评价						Particular occurrences, Sample Taken, Problems 特殊问题和情况					
Signature of Engineer 工程师签字 Date 日期						Signature of Contractor 承包商签字 Date 日期					

表4-4 施工日志复杂格式

DAILY REPORT

Location：部门名称　　　　　　　　　　　　　　　　　　　　　　　　　　　　　　　Date：日期

Shift S. N.		Shift 1				Shift 2				Shift 3			
Time（Hrs.）													
Weather Condition	Sunshine												
	Cloud												
	Rain（mm）												
	Wind												
	Temperature（℃）	Max.：				Min.：				Relative Humidity（%）：			

Description of Work（Quantity and location of work）：

1.
2.
3.
4.
5.
6.
7.

Delays of any nature（material supply, equipment, instructions, weather, etc.）：

Reason of interruption of work, if any：

Tests carried out/result：

Accident Reported：

Supplied/Prepared Material：

Plant & Equipment	Type	Model	Capacity	Unit/No.	Work-Hr.	Idle-Hr.	Repair-Hr.
Sovel loader				1			
Excavator				1			
Blower fan				1			
Welding machine				2			
Grinding machine				2			
Wet Shotcrete machine				1			
Batching plant				1			
Air compressure				1			
Air leg driller				2			
Genrator				3			
Pickup				1			
Tripper				3			
Local dump truck				3			
Lumesha Percussion machine				1			
GL-6000 Geological drilling ma				1			
Electronic grout pump machin				1			

(续)

Activities \ Time (Hrs.)		Shift 1						Shift 2						Shift 3					
1.	Security of material/equipment																		
2.	Electrical work																		
3.	Security of material/equipment																		
4.	Casting concrete																		
5.																			
5.																			
6.																			

Manpower:

Category	Work-No.	Work-Hr	Idle-No.	Idle-Hr	Remarks
Supervisor					
Foreman					
Skilled Labour					
Electrician					
Surveyor					
Semi-skilled Labour					
Operator					
Driver					
Mechanical technician					
Cook					
Engineer					
Lab assistant					
Geologist					
Mechanics					
Communinity health assistant					
Driller					

Reason of idling of equipment/labour:

Vsitors on site:

REF No. of any correspondence issued:　　SI/_____　　RFI/_____　　CVI/_____
　　　　　　　　　　　　　　　　　　　　CN/_____　　VO/_____　　RFP/_____
　　　　　　　　　　　　　　　　　　　　NCN/_____

Prepared by (the Contractor)	Checked and Submitted by (the Contractor)	Verified by (the Engineer)
Signature _____ Print Name: _____ Date:	Signature _____ Print Name: _____ Date:	Engineer's Comment: Signature _____ Print Name: _____ Date:

SI = site instruction　　　　　　RFI = request for instruction　　　CVI = confirmation of verbal instruction
CN = Constractor Notification　　VO = Variation Order　　　　　　RFP = Request for proposal
NCN = Non Conformance Notice

需要说明的是，在国际工程项目中，承包商最为常见的错误是自己私下记录施工日志，而不是递交给工程师并由工程师签字。不得不说，承包商自己私下记录的施工日志，在争议解决过程中没有任何证明效力，也不具有法律效力，承包商无法拿出自己记录的施工日志证明其施工活动或事件。因此，要想让施工日志具有证明力和法律效力，必须由工程师或业主签字确认。

在国际工程项目中，工程师在施工日志上签字时的表现形式有三种状态，第一是签字，不加任何批注；第二是签字，但加上批注或注释；第三是工程师拒绝签字。准确记录施工日志，不弄虚作假，是对承包商最基本的要求。如果工程师签字时加上批注，则会减弱施工日志作为证据的证明力和法律效力。而当工程师拒绝签字时，在保证记录真实性和准确性的前提下，承包商应积极与工程师沟通，保证工程师在施工日志上签字确认。

4.3.2 检查申请格式

在施工现场施工时，承包商应根据合同规定及时向工程师递交已完工程检查申请（Inspection Request），要求工程师检查已完工程，特别是隐蔽工程等，以便在工程师检查完毕并签字确认后开始下一道工序的施工。

在国际工程项目中，承包商递交检查申请并没有固定的格式可循。可根据工程项目的具体情况，设计和编制检查申请格式，并事先与工程师或业主沟通，获得工程师或业主的同意或认可，以便在施工过程中使用这些检查申请格式。

下面是检查申请格式样例，可供承包商在国际工程项目中使用。

INSPECTION REQUEST

Description of requested inspection: _____

_____

_____

_____

Field contact name and mobile number: _____

Address of the field: _____

Date & time inspection requested: _____

Note: Normal inspection hours are Monday through Saturday from 7:00 to 12:00 and from 13:00 to 18:00

REMAINDER OF FORM TO BE FILLED OUT BY INSPECTOR

Work as described above has NOT been accepted. Explanation: _____ _____ _____ _____ Re-inspection required prior to proceeding with work Yes ☐　No ☐　N/A ☐	Inspector's Initial/Date

	(续)
Work as described above has been inspected and accepted.	Inspector's Initial/Date Not accepted unless initialed and dated by Inspector

4.3.3 现场规则格式

在某些国际工程项目中，特别是在项目公司（Project Company）进行项目融资（project finance）时，项目公司作为业主往往会要求承包商遵守现场规则（site rules），即明确约定哪些行为承包商可以去做，哪些行为承包商不能做或禁止承包商去做。以某国际工程项目为例，业主和承包商通过谈判确定的现场规则如下：

Site Rules

The SITE RULES are a condition of employment and must be followed at all times.

➤ The rules apply to everybody: Employees, contractors, service suppliers and visitors.

➤ Where you consider a task cannot be carried out safely——do not commence and do not continue to perform the task.

RULE 1——THE FUNDAMENTALS(LIFE-SAVING RULES)

✓ Do not carry out a task unless you are trained and authorized to do it.

✓ Make sure you assess the risks involved and guard against them.

✓ Always wear your personal protective equipment ("PPE") and obtain a permit where required.

❖ Be competent and authorized to perform the task;

❖ Be fit for work and unaffected by drugs and alcohol;

❖ Have assessed the risk associated with the task;

❖ Have the right tools and equipment and ensure that these are in good conditions;

❖ Wear and use PPE that is appropriate for the task and in good conditions;

❖ Understand whether a Permit to work is required before commencing the task; in doubt ask your supervisor;

❖ Know what to do in an emergency.

IF THE TASK OR CIRCUMSTANCES IN WHICH YOU ARE WORKING CHANGE

❖ Stop what you are doing and re-assess the risk.

RULE 2——MOBILE EQUIPMENT AND LIGHT VEHICLE(LIFE-SAVING RULES)

✓ Always follow the traffic rules, wear your seat belt, keep within speed limits, and do not use phones while driving.

✓ Pedestrians must always stand clear of mobile equipment.

VEHICLES AND EQUIPMENT

❖ Perform all required pre-operation inspections and checks on equipment and

ensone it is safe to operate;
- Adhere to site traffic rules and speed limits, 60kph (gravel roads) and 90kph other roads;
- Ensure all occupants wear seat belts fitted;
- Only travel in vehicles that are specifically approved for transport of people;
- Take appropriate steps to ensure the equipment cannot be operated by unauthorized persons;
- Ensure persons and unsecured material and equipment are separated.

PEDESTRIANS
- Pedestrians must give way and stand clear of mobile equipment;
- Alert mobile equipment operators of your presence and do not approach without their approval.

NEVER
- Overload a vehicle or equipment;
- Use hand held phones when driving.

RULE 3——JOURNEY MANAGEMENT PLAN(LIFE-SAVING RULES)
✓ Follow the prescribed Safe Journey Management Plan.
- Ensure journey is necessary and obtain permission from authorized persons where required;
- Ensure the validity of theROPs, driving license and driving permit where required and that the driver is physically and mentally fit to drive;
- Ensure that the driver has completed the daily checks of the vehicle and that defects have been repaired, if any;
- Confirm completion of inspection (checklist-loading and lashing of equipment) by the line supervisor for transportation of heavy equipment and materials;
- Brief the driver about hazards involved, road conditions, route and necessary steps for adhering to the Safe Journey Plan, destination and any problem pertaining to the journey and steps to be taken in the event of an accident or an emergency;
- Ensure issue of a Safe Journey Plan if required and explain contents.

NO ISSUE OF SAFE JOURNEY PLAN
- Driver not in posession of a valid driver's license and permit;
- Driver is not physically and mentally fit to drive;
- Driver is not equipped with the correct PPE for the task concerned;
- Driver has not inspected the vehicle and load or ensured its roadworthiness.

RULE 4——CONFINED SPACES(LIFE-SAVING RULES)
✓ Do not enter a confined space without understanding and following your site's confined space procedure.
- Only work in a confined space only when all other ways of performing the task

has been ruled out;
- ❋ Ensure there is a person who can instigate an emergency response should you encounter difficulty;
- ❋ Understand and work strictly in accordance with the site's confined space procedure and be in possession of a valid special work permit;
- ❋ Understand the entry and safe work requirements for the confined space you are going to work in.

RULE 5——WORKING AT HEIGHTS(LIFE-SAVING RULES)
- ✓ Always use fall protection safety equipment when working at heights.
  - ❋ Never work at any height where there is a risk of injury from falling and in any case above 1.8 metres, unless you have fall prevention or protective measures in place;
  - ❋ Ensure there is a person who can instigate an emergency response should you encounter difficulties;
  - ❋ Ensure platforms, scaffolds and other temporary structures are only constructed by competent and authorized persons;
  - ❋ Prevent items falling and causing injury to other persons.

RULE 6——ENERGY AND MACHINERY ISOLATION(LIFE-SAVING RULES)
- ✓ Always follow your site's isolation procedure.
- ✓ Make sure all energy sources have been safely isolated and energy released before working on the piece of equipment. Release Energy, Lock, Tag & Test.
  - ❋ Identify all energy sources including electrical, mechanical, potential (e.g. gravity), kinetic etc.
  - ❋ Ensure that all energy sources that could cause you harm have been properly isolated at source using your personal lock and tags and energy released;
  - ❋ Check and test the right equipment and energy released;
  - ❋ Ensure that any stored energy has been released;
  - ❋ Ensure that all guards and safety systems are put back when the work is completed.

RULE 7——LIFTING AND MECHANICAL ENERGY AND MACHINERY ISOLATION HANDLING(LIFE-SAVING RULES)
- ✓ Make sure the lifting device is capable of lifting the load. Never allow anyone to be in the drop zone of the load.
- ✓ Do not walk under a crane or suspended load.

DO NOT OPERATE OR USE ANY LIFTING EQUIPMENT UNLESS
- ❋ The load and reach does not exceed the capacity of the lifting equipment;
- ❋ All safety devices are working;
- ❋ You ensure you or other persons are never positioned underneath or in the drop zone of a suspended load.

RULE 8——CHEMICALS & HAZARDOUS SUBSTANCES(LIFE-SAVING RULES)
- ✓ Make sure you know how to handle, store and dispose of any chemicals or hazardous substances you are working with.
- ✓ Do not light up cigarettes, cigars or pipes in no-smoking areas.
  - ❖ Always obtain, read, understand and follow instructions on the Material Safety Data Sheet for the hazardous substance that you will be handling;
  - ❖ Never handle or use chemicals or hazardous substances if you have not been trained and authorized in their use, handling, storage and disposal.

RULE 9——DRUGS AND ALCOHOL SUBSTANCES(LIFE-SAVING RULES)
- ✓ Do not drive or work under the effect of drugs or alcohol.

MUST NOT
- ❖ Use, sell, purchase, transfer, receive or possess alcohol, illegal drugs or controlled substances on any project site or work location;
- ❖ The introduction of any illegal drugs or controlled substances on any project site or work location is prohibited and any person who violates this policy is subject to disciplinary action up and including dismissal.

ALCOHOL AND DRUG TESTING
- ❖ A ZERO TOLERANCE approach will be considered in the affected person by all illegal drugs or controlled substances on any project site or work location;
- ❖ Alcohol testing is compulsory for every person entering, exiting or working on any project site or work location and in the case of refusal, it is supposed that the worker is under the influence of alcohol;
- ❖ Alcohol testing will be performed randomly or intentionally at all project sites or work locations;
- ❖ Compulsory alcohol testing will be conducted on all drivers at all project sites or work locations by Security or Health and Safety Officers at the discretion of management;
- ❖ Persons who are taking medication must notify the Camp Doctor.

RULE 10——WORK PERMITS(LIFE-SAVING RULES)
- ✓ Obtain a valid permit to work whenever required for the task at hand.

MUST NOT
- ❖ Conduct any task if you do not have a valid permit to work;
- ❖ Conduct any task if an effective, TRIC and toolbox talk has not been done by the Permit Applicant to ensure that all workers understand the conditions of the permit;
- ❖ Conduct any task if the proper controls and procedures are not in place or followed.

WORK PERMIT MANAGEMENT
- ❖ Permit to Work Applicant must visit the worksite when planning the task;

- ❖ Permit to Work Approver must also visit the worksite when required by the Permit to Work Procedure;
- ❖ Through site visits, supervisors and department heads shall verify Permit to Work process is adhered to and Job Safety Plans are being followed.

第5章 常用英文通知函写作

> If you don't understand what it is you are trying to achieve, the chances of ultimate success are slim.
>
> William Rose：*Pleadings Without Tears*

5.1 英文通知函

对于变更、不同地质条件（differing Site Conditions）、额外工程（extra work）或可能影响承包商履约工期和成本的任何其他事件，大多数国际工程合同都要求发出通知。承包商发出通知（giving notice）的行为非常重要，它是启动承包商根据合同寻求额外工期和成本，或者保留相关追索权利的一把钥匙。不得不说，如果承包商未能根据合同规定递交或在合同规定的期限内递交通知，则可能对承包商的权利产生影响。例如 FIDIC 合同条款第 20.1 款[承包商索赔]中规定了 28 天索赔时效。如果承包商未能在知道或应当知道索赔事件发生起的 28 天内发出索赔通知，则意味着承包商放弃索赔工期延长和/或额外费用的权利。

英国咨询工程师布赖恩·托特蒂尔在《FIDIC 用户指南》一书对 FIDIC 1999 年第 1 版红皮书涉及的各种通知进行了总结，如下：

（1）合同当事一方向合同当事另一方发出的通知，应抄送给工程师：

1）第 1.8 款规定的文件中的错误或缺陷。
2）第 17.5 款规定的侵犯知识或工业产权。
3）第 19.2 款规定的不可抗力事件和情况。
4）第 19.3 款规定的不可抗力停止影响情形。
5）第 19.6 款规定的因不可抗力引起的终止合同。
6）第 20.4 款规定的不满争议裁决委员会的决定。

（2）业主向承包商发出的通知，应抄送给工程师：

1）根据第 2.4 款对其融资安排的变更。
2）第 2.5 款项下的索赔细节。
3）第 3.4 款规定的更换工程师细节。
4）第 11.1 款规定的缺陷通知期限内的缺陷。
5）第 11.2 款规定的非承包商自费负责的缺陷。
6）第 11.4 款规定的未能修复缺陷的日期。
7）第 15.2 款规定的业主终止合同。
8）根据 15.2 款在终止后撤走设备。
9）第 15.5 款规定的方便性终止。

(3) 承包商向业主发出的通知，应抄送给工程师：
1) 第 16.1 款规定的暂停或减少工程量。
2) 第 16.2 款规定的终止。
3) 第 18.2 款规定的停止保险。
(4) 工程师向承包商和业主发出的通知：
第 3.5 款规定的协议书或工程师的决定。
(5) 工程师向承包商发出的通知，应抄送给业主：
1) 第 7.3 款规定的不要求检查。
2) 第 7.4 款规定的参加验收的意愿。
3) 第 7.5 款规定的拒收。
4) 第 8.1 款规定的开工日期。
5) 第 8.3 款规定的计划与合同不符。
6) 第 8.3 款规定的计划与实际进度不符。
7) 第 9.2 款规定的延迟试验的指示。
8) 第 10.3 款规定的因业主原因延迟的竣工试验。
9) 第 11.5 款规定的进一步试验。
10) 第 12.1 款规定的需测量的工程。
11) 第 14.8 款规定的拖延付款。
12) 第 15.1 款规定的履行改正错误的义务。
(6) 承包商向工程师发出的通知：
1) 第 1.9、4.12、4.24、16.1、17.4、19.4 款规定的索赔。
2) 第 1.9 款规定的延误的图纸或指示。
3) 第 4.4 款规定的分包商工程开工日期。
4) 第 4.16 款规定的设备和其他主要物品交付到现场。
5) 第 4.20 款规定的免费材料的短缺或缺陷。
6) 第 5.2 款（红皮书）和第 4.5 款（黄皮书）规定的拒绝指定分包商。
7) 第 7.3 款规定的覆盖前的检查。
8) 第 8.3 款规定的可能引起负面影响的情况。
9) 第 8.11 款规定的拖长的暂停。
10) 第 9.1 款规定的延误竣工验收的日期。
11) 第 9.2 款规定的延误的竣工验收。
12) 第 10.1 款规定的接收证书的申请。
13) 第 12.1 款规定的不准确记录。
14) 第 17.4 款规定的因业主风险造成的损害。
(7) 合同当事双方向争议裁决委员会每名成员发出的通知：
1) 根据附录第 2 项争议裁决协议书生效。
2) 根据附录第 7 项争议裁决协议书终止。
(8) 争议裁决委员会成员向当事双方发出的通知：
1) 附录第 2 项规定的辞职。

2）根据附录第 7 项规定的争议裁决协议书的终止。

3）附件第 5 项下的决定通知。

4）附件第 7 项下的听证通知。

在 FIDIC 1999 年第 1 版黄皮书中，需要补充 FIDIC 1999 年第 1 版红皮书中内容的是第 5 条 "设计" 的规定。按照第 5 条的规定，工程师应通知承包商第 5.1 款［设计义务的一般要求］、第 5.2 款［承包商文件］、第 5.4 款［技术标准和法规］、第 5.5 款［培训］、第 5.6 款［竣工文件］、第 5.7 款［操作和维修手册］和第 5.8 款［设计错误］涉及的有关问题。

在大多数国际工程合同格式中，通知应具备的要素包括：

（1）通知应为书面文件。

（2）书面通知应送达到某个特定的当事人。

（3）发出通知的当事方（the notifying party），应在知晓影响事件或情况发生后，尽快发出通知。

（4）通知应在规定的时间内（within a defined time period）发出。

（5）如果产生了工期和额外费用影响，则应对工期和额外费用同时发出通知。

（6）如可行，实际或预期影响后果的详情。

（7）受影响的工期和成本估算。

（8）在规定的期限内递交支持文件（supporting documentation）。

（9）受到影响的具体计划和活动。

（10）因果关系。

5.2 国际工程常用英文通知函

5.2.1 现场进入权和提供现场延误通知

在国际工程项目中，承包商遭遇阻碍现场施工的最大障碍是业主未能履行征地拆迁义务，未能及时向承包商提供现场进入权（access to site）和现场占有权（possession of site）。当承包商遇到现场进入权和现场占有权问题时，应在合同规定的期限内向工程师或业主发出通知，告知其无法进入现场的遭遇，业主未能履约提供现场占有权义务及其导致工期延长或额外费用的后果，承包商应在函件中保留索赔工期延长和额外费用的权利。

以某国际工程项目为例，承包商向工程师发出通知，要求业主完成路权（Right of Way, ROW）范围内的征地拆迁工作，如下：

```
Ref.: No. DDD AAA
Date: 28 Jan. 2019

To: the Engineer
Attn: Mr. AAA
     Team Leader
```

Subject: Resettlement of Existing Building at the Structure 208A

Our Ref.: (1)…
(2)…
Your Ref.: (1)…

Dear Sir,

We would like to express our serious concerns regarding long-term delay of resettlement process against the existing buildings at km2 + 185. As we have provided construction of Overpass 208A and Retaining wall 234A in this area, we have to conduct major works on substructures of the Overpass 208A up to the date. Unfortunately, we are not able to continue works on the Overpass 208A and to begin works for Retaining wall 234A because of unavailability of possession of site.

Furthermore, according to the Project Design, new utility lines should be located on the territory of existing civil buildings. Prior to relocation of utility lines, all existing buildings must be resettled and removed. However, these buildings are not resettled and are still existing there till now.

It should be noted that this fact entails impossibility of Utilities relocation and further construction works for Overpass 208A and Retaining wall 234A. In addition, we note again that further protraction of Resettlement process entails delays of Project schedule and causes large costs for the Contractor.

Based on the above, we kindly ask you to resolve the issues of resettlement of existing buildings and provide the Contractor with access to the above areas in the shortest time so as to speed up the construction works. Should any delay and/or additional costs occur, we reserve our right to claim any extension of time under Sub-Clause 8.4 of the Conditions of Contract and this letter shall be taken as the notice to claim under Sub-Clause 20.1 of the Conditions of Contract.

Your cooperation in minimizing this impact will be appreciated.

Sincerely yours,

Name of Project Manager

在国际工程项目中，承包商通常还会遇到当地居民阻工事件。为此，承包商应及时向工程师发出通知，告知当地居民阻工的详情，并要求索赔工期延长和额外费用，举例如下：

Ref.：No. DDD AAA
Date：RRR

To：The Engineer

Attn：Mr. AAA
　　　Team Leader

Subject：Main Gate Blockade by Locals

Dear Sir,

It is to kindly notify you about the incident that happened in our camp at VVV as follows：

A group of local people gathered in front of our main entrance at our VVV camp at 6:30 A. M. on November 21, 2018 and blocked the gate preventing our manpower and vehicles from going out/coming in through the gate. Shortly thereafter we tried to contact the Engineer via telephone, but we could not get through, and afterward we reported the incident to the Project Director of the Employer by phone.

The disruption or condition, which in our opinion, could not have been reasonably foreseen by an experienced contractor, forad to stop all our work and it fully affected our work progress. Furthermore, all equipment and manpower have been remaining idle from the time. However, we should resume our work once we receive your further instruction.

We will keep contemporary records as set out by Clause 53.2 as we believe necessary, or may be required by you, to substantiate the reimbursement of our additional costs and to support our request for a time extension pursuant to Clause 44 and this, where applicable, is to be taken as the notification required under Sub-Clause 44.2 and 53.1 of the Conditions of Contract.

Meantime, we submit the list of idle manpower and equipment for your record.

Sincerely,

Name of Project Manager

　　在国际工程项目中，根据笔者参与中国承包商工程索赔实践，对于业主延迟提供现场进入权和现场占有权，中国承包商发出通知信函时应注意如下问题：

（1）在信函中应写明业主未能提供现场进入权或现场占有权的具体位置。
（2）承包商应在信函中说明哪些工作受到了影响。
（3）承包商应在信函中说明其工期受到了影响，和/或产生了额外费用。
（4）承包商应在信函中保留索赔工期延长和/或额外费用的权利。
（5）业主完成拆迁工作的日期。需要特别注意的是，在业主完成拆迁工作，承包商进入施工现场施工时，很多中国承包商都未能记录业主完成拆迁的日期，导致在计算工期延长时无法找到相应的证据。

5.2.2　业主未能按期支付工程款通知函

支付或承诺支付是国际工程项目中业主的最重要的义务。在施工合同中，施工合同的对价是承包商实施工程项目，而业主为此支付工程价款。施工合同的性质不同，支付方式也有所不同。1987年第4版红皮书和1999年第1版红皮书属于单价合同，业主按月向承包商支付工程款。1999年第1版黄皮书和银皮书属于总价合同，业主按付款计划中确定的里程碑支付工程价款。

业主未能按期支付承包商的工程款，承包商享有的权利包括：
（1）依据合同延迟付款利息的规定，要求业主支付延期支付工程款利息。如合同没有规定延迟付款利息，承包商可以查询工程所在地的法律规定，确定延迟付款利息计算标准。如果工程所在地法律也没有规定延迟付款利息，则承包商可要求业主支付合理的利息。
（2）降低施工速度（reduce the rate of progress）。
（3）暂停施工（suspension of the works）。
（4）终止合同（termination of contract）。

以某国际工程项目为例，承包商向工程师递交业主延迟付款通知函，并抄送业主，如下：

To: the Engineer
　　Address of the Engineer

CC. XXX Roads Authority
　　Address of the Employer

Sub: Delayed Payment against Advance Payments and IPC Payments
Dear Sirs,
In accordance with Sub-Clause 13.7 of GCC and Particular Application Conditions, "*the Employer shall pay the amount certified in each Interim within 42 days from the date on which the Employer's Representative received the Contractor's statement and supporting documents*"; it is noticed that from the commencement of the project to date, all the advance payment and certain Interim payment have been delayed by the Employer. Please refer to the attachment for detailed information, which shows the delayed days and amount for advance payments and IPC payments respectively.

As a result of the delayed payment by the Employer, the Contractor is always in shortage of cash flow to arrange site construction as the planned progress. Meanwhile, extra cost has occurred to the Contractor due to the delayed payment.

Sub-Clause 16.1 of GCC provides that:

"*If the Contractor suffers delay and/or incurs Cost as a result of suspending work or reducing the rate of work in accordance with this Sub-Clause, the Contractor shall give notice to the Employer's Representative. After receipt of such notice, the Employer's Representative shall proceed in accordance with Sub-Clause 3.5 to agree or determine:*

(a) any extension of time to which the Contractor is entitled under Sub-Clause 8.3, and
(b) the amount of such Cost plus reasonable profit, which shall be added to the Contract Price, and shall notify the Contractor accordingly."

According to the above Sub-Clause, we reserve the right to claim for the extension of time and additional cost caused by the Employer's late payment.

Attachments—Summary of the Payment Release Schedule

Yours truly,
Name of Project Manager

业主延迟支付工程款是国际工程项目争议中最大的一项争议。根据2017年英国技术和建设法院（TCC）的统计，承包商与业主之间最大的争议是付款争议，达到21%。而根据中国最高人民法院2019年建设工程案件统计，国内建设工程项目涉及付款争议高达50%。不得不说，业主延迟支付工程款是业主严重违约。因此，在业主延迟支付工程款时，承包商可以向业主发出更为严厉的信函，举例如下：

To: the Engineer
　　　Address of the Engineer

CC. XXX Roads Authority
　　　Address of the Employer

Sub: Notice of Non-Payment

Dear Sir,

This is to notify you that, as of the date of this letter, we have not received USD [insert amount] representing payment due for previous progress payment(s)[insert progress payment and invoice number or IPC number] approved and certified by the Engineer. This failure to make payment constitutes a material breach of the contract. If within seven days from this letter, we do not receive payment of the sums due and owing to us, we will exercise our rights under the contract, which may include termination for material breach.

Nothing contained herein shall constitute a waiver of our claims for interest on past-due amount or for interest on past-due amount or for other damages that may result from this breach or the exercise of our right to terminate the contract.

Sincerely,

Name of Project Manager

由于业主延迟支付工程款,承包商可以向业主发出降低施工速度的通知,举例如下:

To: the Engineer
  Address of the Engineer

CC. XXX Roads Authority
  Address of the Employer

Subject: Notice of Intention to Reduce Work Rate due to Delayed Payment under IPC No. 7

Dear Sir,

In accordance with Sub-Clause 13.7 of Particular Application of Conditions, it provides that "the Employer shall pay the amount certified in each Interim within 42 days from the date on which the Employer's Representative received the Contractor's statement and supporting documents". We hereby inform you that the captioned payment hasn't been received by us, up to now exceeding 12 days from due date on March 11, 2016.

Unfortunately, the delayed payment has caused the regular progress to slow down. We thus reserve the right to reduce the progress of the works pursuant to Sub-Clause 16.1 of General Conditions of Contract.

Yours truly,

Name of Project Manager

Encl.: Summary of the Payment Release Schedule

因业主延迟支付工程款，承包商也可以向业主发出暂停施工的通知，举例如下：

Mr. CCC
Director General
FFF National Roads Agency
Address of Employer

Subject: Notice to Suspend the Works within 21 days
　　Sub-Clause 16.1: Contractor's Entitlement to Suspend Work

We refer to the Site Meeting No. 10 held on 13 June, 2016, in which we made it clear that the Employer had failed to adhere to the Financial Arrangement issued on 30 June 2015 and that the ongoing delayed payment of the overdue amounts was causing serious financial constraints and if not solved forthwith, the Contractor would be left with no option other than to suspend the Work.

To date, the situation is still persisting and no payment has been made. The cumulative overdue amounts from Interim Payment Certificates No. 3 to 9 are in sum of Euro10,250,976.47 and Shellings 7,688,528,877.00.

Consequently, we write to notify you that we shall suspend the Work at the expiry of 21 days if the overdue amounts are not received within this period pursuant to Sub-Clause 16.1 [*Contractor's Entitlement to Suspend Work*] of the Conditions of Contract. Subsequently, a claim for reimbursement of the additional costs arising from the suspension will follow shortly in the range of Shellings 80 million each day.

Yours faithfully,
Name of Project Manager
Name of the Contractor

5.2.3　更换工程师通知函

虽然FIDIC 1987年第4版红皮书没有明确规定业主更换工程师的内容，但业主和工程师之间的咨询设计服务合同通常会对协议终止、工程师更换作出明确规定。即使咨询设计服务合同没有明确规定合同终止和替换工程师条款，但一般法律原则也允许当事一方违约时，当事另一方也可以终止合同。

FIDIC 1999年第1版红皮书第3.4款［工程师的替换］规定如下：

"如果业主拟替换工程师，业主应在拟替换日期42天前通知承包商，告知拟替换工程师的姓名、地址和相关经验。如果承包商通知业主，对某人提出合理的反对意见，并附有详细的依据，业主就不应用该人替换工程师。"

根据该款的规定，业主必须在拟更换日期 42 天前通知承包商。如果对拟替换的工程师提出合理的反对意见，并提供了详细的依据时，业主不得使用该人替换原工程师。

业主有权在任何时候替换工程师，并且业主没有义务向承包商提供替换的理由。本款规定的关键问题在于承包商的反对意见。如果承包商对拟替换的工程师提出反对意见，他必须提供详细的依据。否则，业主有权作出自己的决定。

承包商计划向业主发出更换工程师通知时，应依据合同规定程序发出通知书，且应在通知书中给出充分的理由，否则，业主不会同意更换工程师。举例如下：

TO：Mr. XXX
　　Director General
　　AAA Roads Athority
　　Address of the Employer

Subject：*Replacement of the Resident Engineer*

Dear Sir,

With reference to the Contractor's former letter Ref. No. EEE dated on November 2nd 2018 requesting the Employer's clarification on the Engineer's role on site but no response received to date, we, as a Party of the Contract signed with the Employer, report to the Employer that the Engineer is not suitable and incapable of performing his duties on site and thus request the Engineer's Replacement immediately by the following concerns：

1. The Engineer is not compliant with the Contract especially FIDIC in terms of Engineer's duty；
　　（1）Drawing review delay；
　　（2）Self-contradictory comments；
　　（3）No weekly meeting even after the Contractor's requirement；
　　（4）No interest in Site Diary；
　　（5）Lacking in care diligence and duty lacking；
　　（6）Silent or negative behavior on the key contract events or issues；
　　（7）Failure to certify the first Interim Payment in time；
　　（8）Ambiguous judgement on maintenance and repairing works；
2. The Engineer is not familiar with the Project；
3. The Engineer doesn't know EIA and Environment Practice of Ukraine；
4. Negative behavior of contractual events；
5. Discrimination and reputation slandering.

By reference to the Sub-Clause 3.1 of GCC, which provides：

> 3.1 *Engineer's Duties and Authority*
>
> *The Employer shall appoint the Engineer who shall carry out the duties assigned to him in the Contract. The Engineer's staff shall include suitably qualified engineers and other professionals who are competent to carry out these duties.*
>
> *The Engineer shall have no authority to amend the Contract.*
>
> *The Engineer may exercise the authority attributable to the Engineer as specified in or necessarily to be implied from the Contract. If the Engineer is required to obtain the approval of the Employer before exercising a specified authority, the requirements shall be as stated in the Particular Conditions. The Employer shall promptly inform the Contractor of any change to the authority attributed to the Engineer.*
>
> *However, whenever the Engineer exercises a specified authority for which the Employer's approval is required, then (for the purpose of the Contract) the Employer shall be deemed to have given approval.*
>
> Based on the performance of the Resident Engineer, we maintain that he is not capable of being the Engineer under the Contract.
>
> The Engineer's behavior contributed to the Current Status and shall be responsible to certain extent for the possible Huge Trouble of Suspension and Termination Consequence which will definitely not onlyhurt the Contractor but also damage the Employer in terms of reputation and financial loss finally. It's hereby noticed that the Engineer should be subject to the legal prosecution, if necessary.
>
> By all the above mentioned, we, as a Party of the Signed Contract, for sake of both parties' benefit, hereby report to the Employer that the Engineer was not competent on site and request the Engineer's Replacement immediately.
>
> Sincerely,
>
> Name of Project Manager

5.2.4 指令赶工通知函

承包商收到业主或工程师的赶工指示后，应及时回复业主或工程师，表明其遵守赶工指示，但需要业主考虑相应的工期延长和产生的额外费用，举例如下：

Employer Name
Address of Employer

Attn: Mr. GGG

Re: Notice of Directed Acceleration

On 25 April 2019, you directed that we add manpower, work extra shift, and work overtime to achieve completion of milestone(s) [number of activity] on or before [date]. This is [number of days, weeks, months] prior to the scheduled completion of this milestone [or activity], adjusted for excusable delays for which we are entitled a time extension.

This directive constitutes a directed acceleration of our work because …

We will attempt to comply with this directive by increasing the manpower and equipment as necessary. However, we request additional compensation for all direct and indirect costs of this acceleration effort including, but not limited to, any resulting inefficiencies from disruption, rescheduling, overmanning, stacking of trades, overtime, dilution of supervision, and any other impacts. We assure you that we will do everything we can to minimize those costs.

As soon as we are able to quantify the costs of the accelerated effort, we will prepare a change order request.

Sincerely,

Name of Project Manager

5.2.5 延迟提供和审批设计图纸通知函

在业主负责设计、承包商负责施工的承包模式中，业主有义务及时提供设计图纸。在承包商负责设计和施工的承包模式中，或者在EPC和交钥匙承包模式中，业主有义务在合同约定的期限内审批图纸。

业主未能及时提供图纸时，承包商应及时向业主或工程师发出书面通知，告知现场正在等待图纸施工，请求业主尽快提供施工图纸，举例如下：

Mr. SSS
Resident Engineer
Name of Engineer's company

Address of Engineer

Subject: Delayed Delivery of Construction Drawings

We write to inform you that the retaining wall at km 23 +000 LHS has been completed on 24 May 2016, and regarding the next retaining wall at km 24 +350 RHS, the works are scheduled to commence in early June 2016 accordingly.

Unfortunately, we have not received any construction drawings as to the retaining wall at km24 + 350 RHS, which may prevent us from preparing the works, such as allocation of construction equipment, forms, scaffolds and materials as necessary. To this effect, we kindly request you to provide us with the construction drawings before the end of May 2016.

If applicable, this particular letter will be taken as the notice required under Sub-Clause 20.1 [*Contractor's Claims*], which entitles the Contractor to claim a time extension and/or additional costs such as idle manpower and equipment on site due to delayed provision of construction drawings in question.

Your prompt cooperation will be appreciated.

Sincerely,

Name of Project Manager
Name of the Contractor

在承包商承担设计时，业主和工程师有义务在合同规定的期限内审查和批准承包商递交的施工图纸。如果业主和工程师未能在合同规定的期限内审查和批准图纸，则承包商应致函业主和工程师，要求在规定的期限内完成审批，举例如下：

Mr. SSS
Resident Engineer
Name of Engineer's company
Address of Engineer

Subject: Approval of Construction Drawings

It is to notify you that the construction drawing in relation to Section B of the Works have not been approved by you, and it may prevent us from executing the related works as per the schedule of 18 June 2017.

Attention shall be drawn that Sub-Clause 5.2 [*Contractor's Documents*] provides:

"*Unless otherwise stated in the Employer's Requirements, each review period shall not exceed 21 days, calculated from the date on which the Employer receives a Contractor's Document and the Contractor's notice.*"

It is recorded by letter of XXX that we served the notice as required under Sub-Clause 5.2 of the Condition of Contract on 25 July 2018. Since this letter was served, we have not received any reply from you regarding the captioned drawings, which has already exceeded 40 days. To this effect, we kindly request you to review the same and the reply with your comments soon.

Sincerely,

Name of Project Manager
Name of the Contractor

5.2.6 与技术问题有关通知函

在国际工程施工过程中，承包商往往与工程师和业主就技术问题产生争议。这些技术问题涵盖了工程项目的方方面面，从技术规范的理解、执行到技术可行性、技术方案和设计问题等。承包商与工程师和业主之间关于技术问题的往来信函占绝大部分，见表3-1。

以某国际工程为例，在施工过程中，承包商与工程师就土石方鉴别问题发生争议，承包商认为应为石方，而工程师认定开挖为土方，承包商因此向工程师致函，表明其观点和立场，如下：

Dear Sir,

Deliberations on the classification of material excavation from km42 + 550 to km45 + 000 have been jointly organized by the parties and have not achieved any agreement.

The argument between us is how to unify and clarify the standard and methodology for classifying rock excavation rather than the chainage and extension. It is better to confirm which is the same or similar with rock excavation on site.

Obviously, Table 6113/1 ROCK CLASSIFICATION in SERIES 6000 STRUCTURES of *Standard Specification* is a reference specified for classifying the rock classes (Class as R1, R2, R3, R4, R5 and R6 respectively) which have been confirmed as rock according to its Unconfined Compressive Strength instead of a criterion for judging Rock Excavation or Common Excavation. Table 6113/1 is as follows:

Table 6113/1
CLASSFICATION OF ROCK HARDNESS

Class	Description	Field Indicator Tests	Unconfined Compression Strength (Mpa)
	Description of Hardness		
R1	Very soft rock	Material crumbles under firm (moderate) blows with the sharp end of geological pick and can be peeled off with a knife; it is too hard to cut a triaxial sample by hand. SPT refusal.	1 to 3
R2	Soft rock	Can just be scraped and peeled with a knife, firm blows of the pick point leave indentations 2mm to 4mm in specimens.	3 to 10
R3	Medium hard rock	Cannot be scraped or peeled with a knife; hand-held specimen can be broken with the hammer end of a geological pick with a single firm blow.	10 to 25
R4	Hard rock	Point load tests shall be conducted for distinguishing these categories. These results may be verified by means of uniaxial compressive strength tests.	25 to 70
R5	Very hard rock		70 to 200
R6	Extremely hard rock		>200

Classification on Rock Excavation and Common Excavation should be referred to the criteria setting in Table 3603/1 of Standard Specification and Sub-Clause 3603(a)(iv) Boulders

Table 3603/1
CLASSIFICATION OF MATERIALS FROM CUT EXCAVATIONS

Classification	Description
Rock excavation	Rock excavation shall be excavation in material which requires drilling and blasting or the use of hydraulic or pneumatic jackhammers to be loosened and to be loaded for transportation.
Common excavation	Common excavation shall be excavation in all materials other than rock as defined above, whether the materials are suitable for use in the Works, or to be spoiled and paid for as Common Excavation to Spoil. The classification includes excavation in earthworks or any pavement layers of an existing pavement not covered by a separate item in the Bill of Quantities regardless of the nature of the material excavated, other than rock excavation.

"Individual boulders greater than one cubic meter in volume shall be classified as rock when their nature and size are such that, in the opinion of the Engineer, they cannot be removed without recourse to one of the methods described under rock excavation in TABLE 3603/1. where a portion of excavation contains 50% or more by volume of boulders of this order, such portion shall be considered as rock excavation throughout."

It is clearly noted that in accordance with what has been described above, the difficulty or ease of excavation construction is the main base to classify Rock Excavation and Common Excavation. As stipulated in Clause (iv) Section 3603 of Specification "where a portion of excavation contains 50% or more by volume of boulders of this order, such portion shall be considered as rock excavation throughout". *This classification does not take into consideration the strength of the boulders and does not deduct the volume of the remainder material, showing that the difficulty or ease of site workings is the main basis for classifying Rock Excavation and Common Excavation.*

Sub-section 3603(a)(iii) of the Standard Specification state that "In the event of a disagreement between the Contractors shall at his own cost, make available such mechanical plant as required by the Engineer in order to determine whether or not the material can reasonably be removed."

Our mechanical plant brand and power provided in accordance with the Bidding is as follows: Hitachi 350, 207.3KW; Case 360, 207.3 KW; Shantui SD 32, 235 KW and Shantui SD 175 KW.

If the Engineer considers the power of existing mechanical plant for excavation is lower, it is also acceptable if the Engineer could base on the concerned Standard & Specification to request us to rent appropriate and capable equipment from other Constructors to test.

Note that the statement in the above Specification "Whether or not the materials can reasonably be removed" shows the fairness and reasonableness of Standard Specification. The mechanical plant made of steel, of which the strength is stronger than any rocks, is easy to clear any rocks with its mechanical power. Classification on Reasonable Clearance and Unreasonable Clearance should be referred to the Working Efficiency, that is to say, the workload per unit time. Therefore, we advise that Engineer should nominate appropriate and capable equipment, appoint operators and decide the same time, starting the excavation work, recording their workload completed. After comparing efficiency, we can classify whether the rock materials of this section is removed or not.

As per the instruction of the Engineer, you have seen drilling and blasting have been opted for rocks by us at the mentioned section from K42 + 500 to K45 + 000 since we removed the surface and the soft stuff to loosen for excavating, loading, transporting and unloading. The exposing rocks in slopes are the proofs of the fact of theexistence of rocks in this section.

It is the contract obligation for the Contractor to complete the excavation work of the section from K42 + 550 to K45 + 000 and for the Engineer to classify excavation materials of this section fairly and reasonably pursuant to Standard Specification.

Please kindly take all into consideration on the views we state above and make a fair and reasonable judgement in line with the Standard Specification.

Your promptly approval will be appreciated.

Yours faithfully,

Name of Project Manager

5.2.7 变更指示通知函

在国际工程项目中,承包商收到工程师或业主签发的变更指示(Variation Order,或 Change Directive/Change Order)后,应根据合同规定的变更程序及其他规定,向工程师或业主发出函件,通知收到变更指示。对于工程师或业主发出的变更指示,承包商如存在不同意见,则致函给工程师或业主,表明其意见和观点,举例如下:

Re: Your Change Directive (Variation Order) No. 9

Dear Sir,

We were given instructions by you on 23 August 2019 to execute the captioned changes including the addition of a new retaining wall at km12 + 240 and its ancillary works.

This change directive for work is not within the scope of our present contract, and we, therefore, request a written modification to cover the added [material, labor, equipment, and so forth] required to perform the work as ordered.

Our proposal for the added cost resulting from this change directive is being prepared and will be submitted for your approval as soon as possible. We cannot determine at this time the effect on the contract completion date, or other work under the contract. We assure you that we will do everything we can to minimize those costs and the necessary contract time extension, and will advise when a full analysis has been made.

Sincerely,

Name of Project Manager
Name of the Contractor

5.2.8 进度计划通知函

在施工过程中，对于进度计划的提交、工程师审核批准、更新，承包商应根据合同要求进行。在进度计划的编制、提交和更新过程中，承包商与工程师之间的交流和往来信函的难点主要集中在关键线路的确定上。为了使读者了解在写作过程中如何与工程师交流工程项目的关键线路，以某国际工程项目为例，如下：

Mr. SSS
Resident Engineer
Name of Engineer's company
Address of Engineer

Re: Scheduling Data

Dear Sir,

We would appreciate you providing us with the following scheduling data so that we can together determine the delays to the project and the exact schedule to complete the project based on the new extended time of performance:

➢ As-planned and approved CPM logic diagram for all activities on the project;

➢ An approved As-planned Schedule Activity report listing all the activities in ascending order including activity numbers, descriptions, progress status, area code, early and late start, early and late finish and total float;

➢ Predecessor/successor logic report in ascending and numeric order showing all activities in the approved As-planned Schedule;

➢ An approved As-planned Schedule report sorted by total float;

➢ List of all time extensions to the project and where they are referenced in the CPM Update for which they were incorporated;

➢ All CPM updated (including activity, total float, predecessor/successor reports for each update); and

➢ A copy of all scheduling computer disk files that comprise the approved as-planned CPM schedule and all statused schedule updates to date.

Once we have both had the opportunity to review the information, we believe we can reasonably discuss the delays to the project that have been incurred and the impacts related thereto. We would also be in a better position to discuss how we can work together to complete this project.

Sincerely,

Name of Project Manager

5.2.9　不合格通知函

在施工过程中，承包商可向分包商发出工程不合格通知函（Non-Compliance Notice），书面通知分包商施工的工程不合格，并要求分包商根据合同要求予以更正，举例如下：

Date:＿＿＿＿＿＿＿＿＿＿　　　　Date:＿＿＿＿＿＿＿＿＿＿＿＿＿＿＿＿＿＿＿

Time:＿＿＿＿＿＿＿＿＿ am　　　To:＿＿＿＿＿＿＿＿＿＿＿＿＿＿＿＿＿＿＿＿

　　　＿＿＿＿＿＿＿＿＿ pm　　　Project Name:＿＿＿＿＿＿＿＿＿＿＿＿＿＿＿

Inspector:＿＿＿＿＿＿＿＿＿　　　Subcontractor:＿＿＿＿＿＿＿＿＿＿＿＿＿＿

Affected Contract No. ＿＿＿＿＿＿＿＿＿＿＿＿＿＿＿＿

You are hereby notified that ☐ tests ☐ inspections indicate that the
＿＿＿

does not conform to the specification requirements. The specification violated is

Section ＿＿＿＿＿＿＿　Article/Paragraph ＿＿＿＿＿＿＿＿＿＿＿＿

Under the provisions of the contract specifications, the requirements are ＿＿＿＿＿＿＿＿＿
＿＿＿

Non-complying works shall be required to be removed and replaced at your cost.

It shall be your responsibility to determine the corrective action necessary, and to determine whether you wish to discontinue operations until additional investigations confirm or refute the initial findings.

Your response is required by:＿＿＿＿＿＿＿＿＿＿＿＿＿＿＿＿＿＿＿＿＿＿＿＿＿＿＿＿

Sincerely,

Name of Project Manager
Name of the Contractor

第6章 国际工程合同拟定

> Many of the problems likely to arise under a construction contract are concerned with the meaning to be given to words in a written contract.
>
> Paras 3-001, *Keating on Construction*

6.1 国际工程合同构成

根据 FIDIC 施工合同条款（红皮书）1987 年第 4 版第 5.2 款和 1999 年第 1 版第 1.5 款［文件优先次序］的规定，施工合同的文件通常包括：

(1) 合同协议书（the Contract Agreement）。

(2) 中标函（the Letter of Acceptance）。

(3) 投标书（the Tender，1987 年第 4 版）或者投标函（the Letter of Tender，1999 年第 1 版）。

(4) 合同条款（Conditions of Contract）；在 FIDIC 合同中，合同条款分为通用条款（General Conditions）和专用条款（the Particular Conditions）两个部分。

(5) 规范（the Specification）。

(6) 图纸（the Drawings）。

(7) 标价的工程量表（the Priced Bill of Quantity，1987 年第 4 版）或者清单（the Schedules，1999 年第 1 版）。

(8) 构成合同组成部分的任何其他文件（any other documents forming part of the Contract）。

6.1.1 合同协议书

FIDIC 施工合同条款（红皮书）1987 年第 4 版第 1.(b)(vii) 款规定："合同协议书指第 9.1 款所述的合同协议书（如有）"。第 9.1 款［合同协议书］规定："在被邀请签约时，承包商应同意签订并履行合同协议书，本协议书有业主根据本合同条款所附格式拟订，如必要，可对其进行修改"。

FIDIC 1999 年第 1 版红皮书第 1.1.1.3 款将合同协议书定义为："合同协议书指根据第 1.6 款［合同协议书］所述的合同协议书（如有）"。第 1.6 款规定："除非另有协议，双方应在承包商收到中标通知书后的 28 天内签订合同协议书。合同协议书应以专用条款所附格式为依据。为签订合同协议书，业主应承担依法征收的印花税和类似费用（如有）"。

在英美法系国家，合同的成立应具备要约、承诺和对价三项要素。在施工合同中，只要有承包商的要约（投标书）、业主的承诺（中标通知书）即可构成具有法律约束力的合同。但在有些大陆法系国家，当事方需要签订一份名为"合同协议书"的文件，合同才得以成立。

根据英国法，合同协议书构成一项声明（statement），表明当事双方达成的所有重要事项，如日期、当事方、工程项目名称、合同金额和对价。FIDIC合同条款所附合同协议书的格式符合这些要求。除上述重要事项外，合同协议书还可能规定建筑师或工程师以及验工测量师的名称等内容。

6.1.2 中标函

FIDIC红皮书1987年第4版第1.(b)(vi)款规定："中标通知书指业主对投标书的接受"。

FIDIC红皮书1999年第1版规定："中标函系指业主签署的正式接受投标函的信件，包括其所附的含有双方间签署的协议的任何备忘录。如无此类中标函，则中标函一词系指合同协议书，发出或收到中标函的日期系指签署合同协议书的日期"。

中标函构成一项业主的承诺。根据英美法，一旦业主作出承诺，合同即告成立。如中标函附有条件，只有在条件成就时合同才能成立。

6.1.3 投标书

FIDIC 1987年第4版红皮书第1.(b)(v)款规定："投标书指承包商根据合同的各项规定，为了工程实施、完成和修补任何缺陷，向业主提出的并被中标通知书接受的报价书"。

FIDIC红皮书1999年第1版弃用了"投标书"一词，而改为"投标函"。根据其规定和解释，"投标书"和"投标函"具有相同的含义。第1.1.1.4款规定："投标函系指由承包商填写的题为投标函的文件，包括其签署的向业主的工程报价"。

投标书构成承包商的要约。无论是英美法系还是大陆法系，均要求要约符合招标文件的规定，否则，构成反要约。

6.1.4 合同条款

合同条款主要规定了合同当事双方应遵守的主要权利和义务、违约和补救措施、争议解决等内容。根据FIDIC合同条款，合同条款可分为《通用条款》和《专用条款》，但在ICE、JCT合同中，没有《专用条款》这份文件。

6.1.5 规范

FIDIC红皮书1987年第4版第1.(b)(ii)款规定："规范指合同中包括的工程规范，以及第51条规定的或由承包商提出并经工程师批准的对规范的任何修改或补充"。

FIDIC红皮书1999年第1版规定："规范指合同中题为规范的文件，以及按照合同对规范所作的任何补偿或修改。此类文件规定了对工程的要求"。

规范是一个比"工程量表"含义更为不确切的术语，通常是指工程如何实施和材料标准的文件。业主有权挑选使用任何规范性的标准，如英国规范、德国规范或者美国规范等，但因工程项目的不同，建筑师或工程师在编制合同文件时需要重新制定、补充和修改相关标准，构成工程项目使用的规范。

6.1.6 图纸

FIDIC 红皮书 1987 年第 4 版第 1.(b)(iii) 款规定："'图纸'指工程师根据合同规定向承包商提供的所有图纸、计算书和类似性质的技术资料，以及由承包商提供并经工程师批准的所有图纸、计算书、样品、图样、模型、操作和维修手册和类似性质的其他技术资料"。

FIDIC 红皮书 1999 年第 1 版第 1.1.1.6 款规定："'图纸'系指包含在合同中的工程图纸，以及由业主（或其代表）按照合同发出的任何补充和修改的图纸"。

图纸和规范构成了工程项目物化过程（从构想到实现过程）中最为重要的两份工程技术性质的文件。

6.1.7 标价工程量表/清单

FIDIC 红皮书 1987 年第 4 版第 1.(b)(iv) 款规定："'工程量'表指构成投标书一部分的已标价的以及完成的工程量表"。

FIDIC 红皮书 1999 年第 1 版第 1.1.1.10 款规定："'工程量表'和'计日工作计划表'系指包含在清单中的如此命名的文件（如有）"。

第 1.1.1.7 款对清单作了规定："清单指合同中名为各种表的文件，由承包商填写并随投标函一起递交。此类文件包括工程量表、数据、表册、费率和（或）价格"。

FIDIC 1987 年第 4 版红皮书规定的工程量表和 FIDIC 1999 年第 1 版红皮书规定的清单的文件范围大不相同，FIDIC 1999 红皮书规定的清单包括工程量表。

工程量表不是必然构成合同文件的一份文件。在单价合同中，工程量表是构成合同的一份文件。但在总价合同、成本加酬金合同中，工程量表可以不是合同的一个文件。一般而言，如果工程量表构成合同文件的一部分，应在合同中予以明确规定。

在 FIDIC 1987 年红皮书和 1999 年红皮书中，工程量表都是一份重要的合同文件。

6.1.8 构成合同组成部分的任何其他文件

投标邀请、承包商在签约谈判期间签订的会议纪要、往来信函、估价等可能会构成合同文件的一部分。这些文件会对合同文件的优先次序以及解释带来很大麻烦。因此，当事双方在签署这些文件时应在文件中明确其地位和优先性，如构成了对合同协议书、中标通知书、规范、图纸、工程量表等文件的修改或补充，应明确规定修改或补充的内容及其效力。

6.2 国际工程合同中的优先次序

6.2.1 合同文件优先次序

由于组成工程合同的文件多种多样，因此，需要明确构成合同文件的优先次序，避免业主、建筑师/工程师、承包商以及分包商等在对文件理解不一致导致的无所适从、莫衷一是。

FIDIC 红皮书 1987 年第 4 版第 5.2 款［合同文件的优先次序］规定如下：
(1) 合同协议书（如果已签）。
(2) 中标函。
(3) 投标书。
(4) 本合同条款第二部分（专用条款）。
(5) 本合同条款第一部分（通用条款）。
(6) 构成合同一部分的任何其他文件。

FIDIC 红皮书 1999 年第 1 版第 1.5 款规定的文件优先次序是：
(1) 合同协议书（如果有）。
(2) 中标函。
(3) 投标函。
(4) 专用条款。
(5) 本通用条款。
(6) 规范。
(7) 图纸。
(8) 清单和构成合同组成部分的任何其他文件。

FIDIC 黄皮书 1999 年第 1 版中，"业主要求"代替了红皮书中的"规范"，"承包商建议书"代替了红皮书中的"清单"。

FIDIC 银皮书 1999 年第 1 版中，合同文件的优先次序是：
(1) 合同协议书。
(2) 专用条款。
(3) 本通用条款。
(4) 业主要求。
(5) 投标书和构成合同组成部分的其他文件。

根据 FIDIC 1999 年第 1 版红皮书、红皮书、黄皮书和银皮书的规定，构成合同的这些文件是可以相互说明的。虽然 FIDIC 作了如此规定，但当合同文件出现不一致时，应使用优先文件在先的原则进行解释。

在工程合同谈判过程或在施工过程中，如果业主和承包商达成了任何其他协议、会议纪要或备忘录等，除非在这些其他协议、会议纪要或备忘录明确规定了文件的优先性，否则，应按照合同通用条款或专用条款规定的优先次序判定其他协议、会议纪要或备忘录的效力。当这些文件内容出现相互矛盾时，应按照文件的优先次序进行解释，即优先次序在前的文件具有法律效力，而优先次序在后的文件的法律效力被优先次在前的合同文件所替代。

6.2.2 编制合同文件优先次序应遵循的原则

承包商在投标前检查业主提供的合同文件优先次序条款时，或者承包商在合同谈判过程中以及在编制分包合同时，应遵循如下原则：

(1) 特殊规定优先于一般规定原则，在法律上，称为"特殊法优先于一般法"。例如，合同专用条款优先于通用合同条款，特殊技术规范优于通用技术规范。因此，在合同文件排序中，常见的合同次序是：专用合同条款在前，通用合同条款在后；特殊技术规范在前，通用技术规范在后。

（2）在国际工程实践中，《合同协议书》往往附相关附件，例如标价工程量表（Priced Bill of Quantity）、付款条件（Payment Terms）、进度计划（Programme）、银行保函格式等。这些附件构成合同文件的一个组成部分，其法律效力优先于其他合同文件。

（3）在概括性列举时，例如"清单和构成合同组成部分的任何其他文件"，如果承包商能在合同谈判和编制分包合同时清楚地明确这些概括性文件，则应一一列明这些文件，而不用所谓的概括性列举方式表示。在国际工程合同争议中，承包商与业主往往会就某个文件是否构成合同文件争执不休，莫衷一是。因此，如果合同可以清晰界定，则应予以明确的规定。

6.2.3　合同文件优先次序条款格式

承包商在投标或合同谈判中，可参照 FIDIC 合同条款中第 1.5 款 [合同优先次序] 的规定。在合同谈判或编制分包合同时，承包商可与业主就合同文件优先次序进行谈判，确定适合于具体项目的合同文件组成和优先次序，举例如下：

1.5　Priority of Documents

1.5.1　The documents forming this Contract are to be taken as mutually explanatory of one another. For the purposes of interpretation, the priority of the documents shall be in accordance with the following sequence：

(a) this Contract, other than the Schedules；

(b) the Employer's Requirements；

(c) allAppendices to the Employer's Requirements and all Schedules other than the main body of Schedule 1 [*Employer's Requirements*]；and

(d) any other documents forming part of this Contract.

1.5.2　Each Party shall, acting in good faith, notify the other Party any inconsistencies, errors, omissions, ambiguities, discrepancies, inadequacies, conflicts or other defects in or between any documents forming part of this Contract, as soon as they come to that Party's attention.

1.5.3　Without prejudice to Sub-Clause1.5.1, any ambiguity or discrepancy in the documents forming part of this Contract shall be promptly clarified by the Employer in accordance with, and subject to the terms of, Sub-Clause 3.4[*Instructions*].

以某国际工程项目为例，合同文件的组成和优先次序如下：

Article 1. Contract Documents	1.1　Contract Documents [Reference General Conditions ("GC") Clause 2] The following documents shall constitute the Contract between the Employer and the Contractor, and each shall be read and construed as an integral part of the Contract：

(a) This Deed of Agreement and the Appendices hereto; (b) Power of Attorney issued by Contractor for signing the Contract; (c) Negotiated Price Schedules including arithmetic correction; (d) Performance Security; (e) Vetting from relevant departments and if any other correspondences; (f) Minutes of Contract Negotiation Meeting(s); (g) Special Conditions of Contract; (h) General Conditions of Contract; (i) Specifications; (j) Technical Proposal; (k) Employer's requirement. 1.2　Order of Precedence (Reference GC Clause 2) 　　In the event of any ambiguity or conflict between the Contract Documents listed above, the order of precedence shall be the order in which the Contract Documents are listed in Article 1.1 [Contract Documents] above. 1.3　Definitions (Reference GC Clause 1) 　　Capitalized words and phrases used herein shall have the same meanings as are ascribed to them in the General Conditions.

承包商可以根据具体项目的实际情况，确定不同合同文件的组成和优先次序。但需要注意的是，一旦文件成为合同文件，则对承包商和业主产生法律效力。因此，在确定哪些文件构成合同文件时，承包商需要予以认真考虑和权衡。

6.3　《合同协议书》文本格式

合同协议书构成一项声明（statement），表明当事双方达成所有重要事项，如日期、当事方、工程项目名称、合同金额和对价。在 FIDIC 合同条款 1999 年第 1 版和 2017 年第 2 版附录中，FIDIC 提供了《合同协议书》的格式。承包商通过合同谈判或编制分包合同时，可以根据具体项目编制《合同协议书》，举例如下：

Contract Agreement THIS AGREEMENT was made at _____. on the _____. day of _____,20×× 　　　　　　　　　　　　　　　BETWEEN M/S. _____, having its principal place at _____. represented

by its _____ Mr. _____, hereinafter referred to as the "Employer" (which expression shall unless excluded by or repugnant to the context, mean and include its legal representatives, successors-in-interests, administrators, and assignees of the FIRST PARTY).

AND

M/S. _____, a company limited duly incorporated under the relevant laws of _____ and having its registered office at _____ represented by its authorized representative Mr. _____, Passport No.: _____, Nationality: _____, hereinafter referred to as the "Contractor" (which expression shall unless excluded by or repugnant to the context, mean and include its legal representatives, successors-in-interests, administrators, and assignees of the SECOND PARTY).

WHEREAS the Employer desires to engage the Contractor for construction of _____ (hereinafter called "the Project"), and the Contractor has agreed to such engagement upon and subject to the terms and conditions hereinafter appearing.

NOW IT IS HEREBY AGREED as follows:

Article 1. Contract Documents

1.1 Contract Documents [Reference General Conditions ("GC") Clause 1.5]

The following documents shall constitute the Contract between the Employer and the Contractor, and each shall be read and construed as an integral part of the Contract:

(a) This Deed of Agreement and the Appendices hereto;
(b) Power of Attorney issued by the Contractor for signing the Contract;
(c) Price Schedules;
(d) Minutes of Contract Negotiation Meetings (if any);
(e) Particular Conditions of Contract;
(f) General Conditions of Contract;
(g) Specifications;
(h) Technical Proposals;
(i) Employer's requirement (if any).

1.2 Order of Precedence (Reference GC Clause 1.5)

In the event of any ambiguity or conflict between the Contract Documents listed above, the order of precedence shall be the order in which the Contract Documents are listed in Article 1.1 (Contract Documents) above.

	1.3 <u>Definitions</u>(Reference GC Clause 1)
	Capitalized words and phrases used herein shall have the same meanings as are ascribed to them in the General Conditions.
Article 2. Contract Price and Terms of Payment	2.1 <u>Contract Price</u>(Reference GC Clause 11)
	The Employer hereby agrees to pay the Contractor the Contract Price in consideration of the performance by the Contractor of its obligations hereunder. The Contract Price shall be the aggregate of: _____(*insert amount(s) in foreign currency/Currencies in words and figures*), excluding (or including, as the case may be) all and any import duties, value added tax, withholding tax, income taxes and other taxes and levies of any kind whatsoever, or such other sums as may be determined in accordance with the terms and conditions of the Contract.
	2.2 <u>Terms of Payment</u>(Reference GC Clause 12) The Contract Price shall be paid by the Employer to the Contractor at the times, in the manner, and in accordance with the provisions of Appendix 1 (Terms and Procedures of Payment) hereto.
Article 3. Effective Date	3.1 <u>Effective Date</u>(Reference GC Clause 1)
	The Effective Date is the date when all of the following conditions have been fulfilled:
	(a) This Agreement has been duly executed for and on behalf of the Employer and the Contractor;
	(b) The Contract Document has been duly signed for and on behalf of the Employer and the Contractor;
	(c) The Loan Agreement has been signed by the Government of _____ and the relevant bank/banks from _____ pursuant to the mutual agreement/understanding between the Government of _____ and the Government of _____ and has come into force and effect;
	(d) The Contractor has submitted to the Employer the performance security and the advance payment guarantees in accordance with the format as attached in this Contract Agreement within 30 days after the effectiveness of the Loan Agreement between the Government of _____ and the Government of _____;
	(e) The Advance Payment from the Employer has been received by the Contractor.

Article 4. Communications	4.1	The address of the Employer for notice purposes, pursuant to GC Clause 1.3 is:_____
	4.2	The address of the Contractor for notice purposes, pursuant to GC Clause 1.3 is:_____
Article 5. Appendices	5.1	The Appendices listed in the attached List of Appendices shall be deemed to form an integral part of this Deed of Agreement.
	5.2	Reference in the Contract to any Appendix shall mean the Appendices attached hereto, and the Contract shall be read and construed accordingly.

IN WITNESS WHEREOF the Employer and the Contractor have caused this Agreement to be duly executed by their duly authorized representatives the day and year first above written.

Signed by:
For and on behalf of the Employer

Mr. _____

Signed by:
For and on behalf of the Contractor

Mr. _____

承包商在编制分包合同时,在采用《分包合同协议书》体系时,可根据主合同的《合同协议书》编制,举例如下:

SUBCONTRACT AGREEMENT

THIS SUBCONTRACT AGREEMENT was made the _____ day of _____ [insert month], _____ [insert year]:

Between

_____, a company duly established under and by virtue of the laws of _____, having its principal office at _____, which expression shall unless excluded by or repugnant to the context, mean and include its successors, executors, administrators, representatives and assignees, represented by Mr. _____ in his capacity as General Director, (hereinafter referred to as the "General Contractor") on the one hand, and

And

_____ [insert name of the Subcontractor], a company duly established under and by virtue of the laws of _____, having its principal office at _____, which expression shall unless excluded by or repugnant to the context, mean and include its successors, executors, administrators, representatives and assignees, represent by Mr. _____ in his capacity as _____, (hereinafter referred to as "the Subcontractor") on the other hand.

Whereas the General Contractor is desirous that certain Subcontract Works should be executed by the Subcontractor and has accepted a Subcontractor's offer for the execution and completion of such Subcontract Works and the remedying of any defects therein.

Now this Subcontract Agreementwitnesseth as follows:

1. In this Subcontract Agreement words and expressions shall have the same meanings as are respectively assigned to them in the Conditions of Subcontract hereinafter referred to.

2. The following documents shall be deemed to form and be read and constructed as part of this Subcontract Agreement, viz:

    (a) Subcontract Agreement;
    (b) The General Contractor's Letter of Acceptance;
    (c) The Subcontractor's Offer;
    (d) Conditions of Particular Application;
    (e) Conditions of Subcontract;
    (f) The Subcontract Data;
    (g) The Subcontract Deliverable;
    (h) The Scope of Subcontract Works;
    (i) The Construction Schedule;
    (j) The Specifications and Code;
    (k) The Drawings.

3. In consideration of the payments to be made by the General Contractor to the Subcontractor as hereinafter mentioned the Subcontractor hereby covenants with the General Contractor to execute and complete the Subcontract Works and remedy and defects therein in conformity in all respects with the provisions of the Subcontract and the Commercial Contract signed between the Owner and the General Contractor.

4. The General Contractor hereby covenants to pay the Subcontractor in consideration of the execution and completion of the Subcontract Works and the remedying of any defects therein the

Subcontract Price or such other sum as may become payable under the provisions of the Subcontract at the times and in the manner prescribed by the Subcontract.

In Witness Whereof the parties hereto have caused this Subcontract Agreement to be executed the day and year first before written in accordance with their respective laws.

Signed and sealed by
The General Contractor

_____
Name:
Title :

Signed and sealed by
The Subcontractor

6.4　《中标函》文本格式

中标函是雇主向承包商发出的接受其报价及其合同条款的函件，或者是承包商向分包商发出的接受分包商报价及其合同条款的函件，举例如下：

LETTER OF ACCEPTANCE

Name of Contract: _____
To: _____

We acknowledge receipt of your Offer dated _____ for the execution and completion of the Works comprising the above-named contract and remedying defects in conformity with the Conditions of Subcontract, the Subcontract Specification, the Drawings and related documents attached herewith.

We accept your offer of : _____ [insert currency and amount in figures and words] (the "Accepted Subcontract Amount"), which includes Value Added Tax (VAT), withholding tax and all taxes under the contract.

In consideration of your properly performing the contract, we agree to pay you the Accepted Contract Amount or such other sum to which you may become entitled under the Contract, at such times as prescribed by the contract.

> We acknowledge that this Letter of Acceptance creates a binding contract between us, and we undertake tofulfill all our obligations and duties in accordance with this Subcontract.
>
> Signed by: _____
> In the capacity of _____

承包商需要特别注意的是，根据英美普通法，一旦业主作出承诺，合同即告成立。如中标函附有条件，只有在条件成就时合同才能成立。因此，承包商在收到业主发出的中标函时，应仔细检查中标通知书的内容，例如，有的中标通知书中增加了如下内容：

> "In accordance with Article 46.2 of Proclamation No. 649/2009; the Contract between yourselves and the Employer will be formed upon signature of the Contract Agreement. The issuance of this Letter of Acceptance will not constitute the formation of the Contract between yourselves and the Employer."

在中标函有上述内容时，则中标函本身不具有约束当事双方的法律效力，只能在当事双方签订书面的《合同协议书》后，当事双方签署的合同才具有法律约束力。

在业主发出的中标函中，有的还表明："Subject to Contract（以合同为准）"。在中标函中存在"Subject to Contract"时，则不应将中标函视为法律上的"承诺（acceptance）"，而应视为要约邀请。所谓要约邀请（Invitation for offer, invitation to treat）是指发出此项邀请人邀请他人向他提出要约，要约邀请不是要约。如国际工程招标，业主向承包商发出邀请，邀请承包商投标即是要约邀请，而承包商的投标行为是要约，如业主接受，才能构成有法律约束力的协议。有些公司寄出的报价单、价目表和商品目录、商店的橱窗展品等不是要约，而是要约邀请，其目的是请对方向自己提出具有要约性质的订单。其他典型要约邀请还包括拍卖、招标、土地售卖、公交车时间表、以合同为准（subject to contract）等。在"以合同为准"式的要约邀请中，根据英国法，应将 subject to contract 明显注在信头。在外贸实务中，标有保留性或限制性条件的，如"价格随时调整，恕不通知"，或"仅供参考""须经我方最后确认""以我方货物售出为准"等亦构成要约邀请。

中国承包商更应注意的是，在国际工程合同争议中，经常发生的争议是业主发出的中标函是否构成具有法律约束力的承诺（acceptance）。如果认为中标函构成承诺，则当事方之间的合同成立，无论是否签署书面的《合同协议书》。因此，承包商应仔细检查业主发出的中标函的内容，或者在承包商向分包商发出中标函时，谨慎使用措辞。建议采用谨慎的做法，即在中标函中明示表明当事双方应签署合同协议书，以当事双方签署的合同协议书为准。

在国际金融组织融资的国际工程项目中，业主发出中标函时往往注明如下内容：

> "You are therefore required to present Performance Security in the amount equal to Ten Percent (10%) of the Accepted Contract Amount boforo signing of the Contract Agreement."

根据上述要求，承包商应在签订合同协议书时向业主递交履约保函。如果承包商未能在签订合同之前递交履约保函，则业主将不会签署合同协议书。有时，业主将承包商未能在签订合同之前递交履约保函视为承包商放弃合同签约，放弃合同，业主因而会没收承包商的投标保函。

6.5 专用合同条款文本

6.5.1 合同数据

在 FIDIC 合同体系中，专用合同条款（Particular Conditions of Contract）包括第一部分合同数据（Contract Data）和第二部分专用条款。合同数据的作用是使得合同用户能够从列表中清晰地看到合同的主要信息和条款内容，避免从冗长的合同条款中去寻找相应的条款，然后再得出相关的数据。以国际金融组织融资的某国际工程项目为例，在使用 FIDIC 合同条款时，合同数据汇总如下：

The following Particular Conditions shall supplement the GC. Whenever there is a conflict, the provisions herein shall prevail over those in the GC.

Part A—Contract Data

Conditions	Sub-Clause	Data
Employer's Name and Address	1.1.2.2 & 1.3	SSS Water Resources Authority Add：
Engineer's Name and Address	1.1.2.4 & 1.3	NNN Consultants Co., Ltd. Japan Add：
Bank's Name	1.1.2.11	XXX Bank Limited
Borrower's Name	1.1.2.12	Government of RRR
Time for Completion	1.1.3.3	900 days
Defects Notification Period	1.1.3.7	365 days
Electronic Transmission Systems	1.3	E-mails shall be allowed for specific documents, as per the instruction of the Engineer.
Governing Law	1.4	EEE country
Ruling Language	1.4	English
Language for Communications	1.4	English
Time for Access to the Site	2.1	15 days after Commencement Date
Engineer's Duties and Authority	3.1(b)(ii)	Variations resulting in an increase of the Accepted Contract Amount in excess of 10% shall require approval of the Employer
Performance Security	4.2	The performance security will be in the form of a bank guarantee and/or performance bond in the amount(s) of 10% percent of the Accepted Contract Amount (excluding contingency amount) and in the same Currency/Currencies of the Accepted Contract Amount.

(续)

Conditions	Sub-Clause	Data
Normal Working Hours	6.5	Eight (8) hours. The locally recognized days of rest/special day shall be Friday, Ramadan, National Holidays, and other special holidays declared by the Government of ＿＿＿, unless otherwise agreed between the Contractor and his staff and labor.
Delay Damages for the Works	8.7 & 14.15(b)	0.1% of the Contract Price per day.
Maximum Amount of Delay Damages	8.7	10% of the final Contract Price, excluding contingency amount.
Provisional Sums	13.5.(b)(ii)	Shall be integrated in the BOQ in all relevant cases.
Adjustments for Changes in Cost	13.8	Period "n" applicable to the adjustment multiplier "Pn": not applicable
Total Advance Payment	14.2	15% of the Accepted Contract Amount (excluding contingencies) payable in the currencies and proportions in which the Accepted Contract Amount is payable.
Repayment amortization rate of Advance Payment	14.2(b)	30% of the amount of the Monthly Interim Payment Certificates
Percentage of Retention	14.3	10% of Interim Payment Certificates
Limit of Retention Money	14.3	5% of the Accepted Contract Amount excluding contingency amount
Plant and Materials	14.5(b)(i)	If Sub-Clause 14.5 applies: Plant and Materials for payment Free on Board Not applicable
	14.5(c)(i)	Plant and Materials for payment when delivered to the Site: BOQ Part 2 Pipelines Sections 2 to 8 except Subsection 3.1.1 Water bridge BOQ Part3 Optical Fibre Cable
Minimum Amount of Interim Payment Certificates	14.6	BT Ten Million (Tk 10,000,000.00)
Limitation of Liability	17.6	The product of one times the Accepted Contract Amount.
Periods for submission of insurance:	18.1	
a. evidence of insurance		14 days
b. relevant policies		14 days
Maximum amount of deductibles for insurance of the Employer's risks	18.2(d)	5% of total contract amount, per occurrence
Minimum amount of third party insurance	18.3	Tk 2,000,000 per occurrence

163

(续)

Conditions	Sub-Clause	Data
Date by which the DB shall be appointed	20.2	28 days after the Commencement date
The DB shall be comprised of	20.2	Three Members
Appointment (if not agreed) to be made by	20.3	The President of FIDIC or a person appointed by such President

6.5.2 专用条款

在 FIDIC 合同体系中，合同专用条款第二部分——专用条款（Specific Provisions）是业主对 FIDIC 通用合同条款的修改和补充。但不得不说，一方面，国际工程合同格式中的专用合同条款扩大了合同格式的使用范围，但另一方面，也给业主利用专用合同条款修改通用合同条款中的公平条款提供了条件，使得合同条款更为苛刻，增加了承包商的风险，是不争的事实，并为工程业界所诟病。无论是业主还是承包商，在编制合同条款时，应根据具体项目的具体情况修改通用合同条款。以某国际金融组织融资的工程项目为例，专用条款对 FIDIC 合同 2005 年多边开发银行协调版修改如下：

Part B—Specific Provisions

1.1.1 Sub-Clause 1.5 Priority of Contract Documents

Replace with:

"The documents forming the Contract are taken as mutually explanatory of one another. For the purposes of interpretation, the priority of the documents shall be in accordance with the following sequence:

(a) the Contract Agreement (if completed);
(b) the Letter of Acceptance;
(c) the Letter of Technical Bid;
(d) the Letter of Price Bid;
(e) the Addenda Nos. [insert addenda numbers, if any];
(f) the Instructions to Bidders;
(g) the Bid Data Sheet;
(h) the Particular Conditions-Part A;
(i) the Particular Conditions-Part B;
(j) the General Conditions;
(k) the Particular Specifications;
(l) the Standard Specifications;
(m) the Drawings;
(n) the Priced Bill of Quantities.

1.1.2 Sub-Clause 4.3 Contractor's Representative

Variation orders, and approved revisions to Drawings and Specifications shall take precedence over these. Detailed plans shall take precedence over general plans."

Delete the last paragraph and replace it with:

" The Contractor's authorized representative shall be fluent in speaking, reading and writing English. If the Contractor's authorized representative is not, in the opinion of the Engineer, fluent in the English language, the Contractor shall replace his authorized representative within 42 days after the request of the Engineer. The Contractor shall make an arrangement within 10 days after the request of the Engineer to have available on site at all times a competent interpreter to ensure the proper transmission of instructions and information during the period of said arrangement for replacement. Required cost for such replacement and interpreter are payable by the Contractor. "

1.1.3 Sub-Clause 4.18
1.1.4 Protection of the Environment

The final paragraph to be added to after the second paragraph:

" The Contractor shall, throughout the execution and completion of the Works and the remedying of any defects therein, comply with all provisions in the Loan Agreement between the Bank and the Borrower with respect to the protection of the environment, which are as follows:

All provisions with the Project EIA report, and all that is necessary for the compliance of *the Environmental Act* and other relevant laws and regulations prevailing in _____ "

1.1.5 Sub-Clause 6.6 Facilities for Staff and Labour

Add to the end:

" On completion of the contract, the temporary camps/housing provided by the Contractor shall be removed and the site reinstated to its original condition, all to the approval of the Engineer. "

1.1.6 Sub-Clause 6.7 Health and Safety

Add to the end:

" In the event of any outbreak of illness of an epidemic nature, the Contractor shall comply with and carry out such regulations, orders and requirements as may be made by the Government, or the local medical and sanitary authorities, for the purpose of dealing with and overcoming the same. "

1.1.7 Sub-Clause 6.8 Contractor's Superintendence

Add to the end:

" In case Contractor's superintendence is not fluent in English, the Contractor should have available at all times a sufficient number of competent interpreters to ensure the proper transmission of instructions and information. "

1.1.8 Sub-Clause 6.9 Contractor's Personnel

Add to the end:

" The Contractor shall be responsible for the return to the place where they were recruited or to their domicile of all such persons as he recruited and employed for the purpose of or in connection with the Contract and shall maintain such persons as are to be so returned in a suitable manner until they shall have left the Site. "

1.1.9 Sub-Clause 6.12 Foreign Personnel

Add to the end of the second sentence:

" … and shall bear all costs related to obtaining these documents. "

1.1.10 Sub-Clause 7.8 Royalties

Add to the end:

" (c) The Contractor shall also be liable for all payments or compensation, if any, levied in relation to the dumping of part or all of any such materials. "

1.1.11 Sub-Clause 10.2 Taking Over of Parts of the Works

Add to the second paragraph:

" (d) If by reason of any default by the Contractor, a Taking-Over Certificate has not been issued, the Contractor shall be afforded reasonable opportunity for taking such steps as may be necessary to permit the issue of a Taking-Over Certificate.

(e) Not less than seven days before the Employer makes use of the part of the works and for which a Taking-Over Certificate has been withheld, the Engineer shall give the Contractor written notice of the Employer's intention to make use of the same. "

1.1.12 Sub-Clause 13.8 Adjustments for Changes in Cost

Replace with the following:

" The amounts payable to the Contractor shall be adjusted for rises or falls in the cost of labour, Goods and other inputs to the Works, by the addition or deduction of the amounts determined by the formulae prescribed in this Sub-Clause. To the extent that full compensation for any rise or fall in Costs is not covered by the provisions of this or other Clauses, the Accepted Contract Amount shall be deemed to have included amounts to cover the contingency of other rises and falls in costs.

The adjustment to be applied to the amount otherwise payable to the Contractor, as valued in accordance with the appropriate Schedule and certified in Payment Certificates, shall be determined from formulae for each of the currencies in which the Contract Price is payable. No adjustment is to be applied to work valued on the basis of Cost or current prices. The formulae shall be of the following general type:

$$P_n = a + b(L_{L_n}/L_{L_o}) + c(F_{L_n}/F_{L_o}) + d(F_{U_n}/F_{U_o}) + \cdots$$

where:

"P_n" is the adjustment multiplier to be applied to the estimated contract value in the relevant currency of the work carried out in period "n", this period being a month unless otherwise stated in the Contract Data;

"a" is a fixed coefficient, stated in the relevant table of adjustment data, representing the non-adjustable portion in contractual payments;

"b" "c" "d" ··· are coefficients representing the estimated proportion of each cost element related to the execution of the Works, as stated in the relevant table of adjustment data; such tabulated cost elements may be indicative of resources such as labour, equipment and materials;

"L_{L_n}" "F_{L_n}" "F_{U_n}" ··· are the current cost indices or reference prices for period "n", expressed in the relevant currency of payment, each of which is applicable to the relevant tabulated cost element on the date 49 days prior to the last day of the period (to which the particular Payment Certificate relates); and

"L_{L_o}" "F_{L_o}" "F_{U_o}" ··· are the base cost indices or reference prices, expressed in the relevant currency of payment, each of which is applicable to the relevant tabulated cost element on the Base Date.

The cost indices or reference prices stated in the table of adjustment data shall be used. If their source is in doubt, it shall be determined by the Engineer. For this purpose, reference shall be made to the values of the indices at stated dates (quoted in the fourth and fifth columns respectively of the table) for the purposes of clarification of the source; although these dates (andthus these values) may not correspond to the base cost indices.

In cases where the " currency of index" (stated in the table) is not the relevant currency of payment, each index shall be converted into the relevant currency of payment at the selling rate, established by the central bank of the Country, of this relevant currency on the above date for which the index is required to be applicable.

Until such time as each current cost index is available, the Engineer shall determine a provisional index for the issue of Interim Payment Certificates. When a current cost index is available, the adjustment shall be recalculated accordingly.

If the Contractor fails to complete the Works within the Time for Completion, adjustment of prices thereafter shall be made using either (i) each index or price applicable on the date 49 days prior to the expiry of the Time for Completion of the Works, or (ii) the current index or price: whichever is more favourable to the Employer.

The weightings (coefficients) for each of the factors of cost stated in the table (s) of adjustment data shall only be adjusted if they have been rendered unreasonable, unbalanced or inapplicable, as a result of Variations. "

Sub-Clause 13.9 Payment for Road Reinstatement

Add Sub Clause 13.9 as following:

" Regarding cost for permanent reinstatement of the public roads under the responsibility of the Roads and Highways Department (RHD), Chittagong Development Authority (CDA), and Chittagong City Corporation (CCC), or any other authority, the Contractor shall be paid by the Employer based on the rates he has entered against the relevant items in the BOQ for the permanent pavement and/or reinstatement work completed by the Contractor only on completion of work in each road and upon successful final handover of the said road to the relevant authority.

	If the relevant authority opts to carry out any repair of the reinstated work completed by the Contractor within the defects liability period of the Contract, and claim the repair cost from the Employer, the said amount will be recovered from the retention money of the Contractor.
	If the relevant authority request to pay charges on damage of the road instead of implementation of the permanent reinstatement work by the Contractor, the Contractor shall pay those charges which will be reimbursed by the Employer. In such case, the volume of the work shall be fixed as the one shown in the BOQ in the Contract and the rates shall be those agreed between the Employer and relevant road authority."
Sub-Clause 13.10 Bank Charges and Commissions Required for the Contract	Add Sub Clause 13.10 as follows: "All bank charges and commissions including those for opening and negotiation of Letter of Credits required for the Contract shall be at the Contractor's expense. Those costs shall be deemed to be included in the contract price."
Sub-Clause 14.8 Delayed Payment	Financing charges shall be as follows: "3% per annum for payment inLocal currency. For other currencies, prime rate of commercial interest for daily borrowing in origin countries, plus 1 percent per annum."

需要注意的是，在上述工程项目施工过程中，承包商与业主之间就上述第1条至14条没有发生争议。但在分包工程中，承包商发现的主要问题是合同第20.6款［仲裁］的规定不清，导致承包商与分包商在发生争议时就管辖权产生分歧，最终只能通过当地法院予以解决。

6.6 国际工程合同完备文件要求

国际工程合同具有不同的合同体系，以FIDIC合同、法语工程合同和日本工程促进协会ENAA为代表的国际工程合同格式，其合同文件构成如下：
(1) 合同协议书。
(2) 中标函。
(3) 投标函。
(4) 专用条款。
(5) 通用条款。
(6) 规范。

（7）图纸。

（8）清单和构成合同组成部分的任何其他文件。

在某些国际工程项目中，特别是涉及项目融资的项目公司作为业主的工程项目，项目公司往往倾向于编制自己的国际工程合同文本，其合同文件体系构成如下：

（1）合同条件。

（2）附件，包括。

1）工程范围。

2）付款条件。

3）业主需求（技术规范）。

4）工期安排和计划。

5）物价调整（如有）。

6）预付款保函、履约保函和保留金保函格式。

7）保险要求。

8）分包商和供货商名录（如有）。

9）标价工程量表或价格表。

10）招标文件。

11）可行性研究报告（如有）。

12）地质和水文勘察报告（如有）。

13）图纸（如有）。

14）验收标准。

15）质量保证计划。

16）HSE 计划。

17）月进度报告。

18）许可手续。

19）安保计划。

在上述附件中，工程范围、付款调价、业主需求、工期安排和计划和标价工程量表或价格表是合同的要件，必不可少。其他附件可以根据具体项目需要进行编制或通过谈判确定。

国际工程合同是最为复杂的合同类型之一。因此，大部分国际工程合同都在几百页左右，有些则多达几千页。同时，国际工程合同的完备性也要求国际工程合同具备上述合同文件的组成。无论是以 FIDIC 合同为主导的通用合同条款加专用合同条款模式，还是某些国际工程项目的合同条款加附件模式，只要能够清晰地界定业主和承包商之间的权利和义务，就能够确定该合同具有完备性特征。而对于合同条款而言，合同条款的完备性更为重要。

国际工程的实践表明，简单合同或合同条款不完备的合同，对于工程合同中相对弱势的一方更为不利。在国际工程合同中，承包商就是相对弱势的一方。因此，完备的合同文件和合同条款对承包商至关重要。

第7章 合同条款编制和写作

> Assuming that a contract has been validly created, it is necessary to consider the extent of the obligations imposed on the parties by the contract.
>
> Paras 13-01, *Chitty on Contracts*

7.1 国际工程合同核心条款及编制

7.1.1 核心条款

国际工程合同的核心条款,亦称合同要件,是指工程范围、合同价格、工期以及业主需要达到的技术标准等。在国际工程仲裁中,仲裁庭也常常将上述合同要件进行法律验证,判定上述条款是否构成合同要件(the essence of the contract)。除了上述合同要件外,国际工程合同的核心条款还涉及工程合同的关键事项,这些核心条款可包括:

(1) 合同生效条件。
(2) 工程范围。
(3) 标价工程量表或价格表。
(4) 支付条款。
(5) 合同货币和汇率。
(6) 价格调整公式。
(7) 工期和进度计划。
(8) 技术规范或业主要求。

7.1.2 合同生效条件

合同生效前提条件是指合同当事方设定一定的条件,并将条件满足作为决定合同效力发生或消灭的根据。为合同是否生效设定前提条件(conditions precedent)的合同,称为附条件合同。附条件合同的条件须符合如下要求:

(1) 条件必须是将来发生的事实。
(2) 条件是合同当事方设定而非法定的。
(3) 条件必须是合法的。
(4) 条件不得与合同的主要内容相矛盾。

附条件合同的种类包括:
(1) 生效条件,亦称延缓条件,是指当事方约定某一条件或全部的条件满足时合同才能生效的条件,或者当事方明示放弃某一条件时其他合同条件满足,合同予以生效的条件。附条件合同虽已成立,但其效力并不立即发生,直到条件满足时合同才生效。

(2) 解除条件,亦称消灭条件,是指合同中所确定的权利和义务在附条件满足时失去法律效力的条件。在此类合同中,合同确定的权利义务已发生法律效力,但在条件满足时,则合同效力消灭,如合同所附解除条件不满足,则合同继续有效。

各国法律对附条件合同进行了法律限制,即当事方为自己的利益不正当地阻止条件满足的视为条件已满足;不正当地促成条件满足的,视为条件不满足。

在国际工程合同中,可能同时存在生效条件和解除条件,例如合同终止条款规定的一方严重违约或实质性违约时,另一方有权终止合同,即可视为是合同解除条件。一般而言,在国际金融组织融资或工程所在国当地政府预算资金的项目中,由于资金已经落实,工程所在国通过公开招标的方式进行工程招标,在确定承包商后,业主和承包商即可签署工程合同。此时,合同不设定生效前提条件,在签署时即可产生法律效力。在资金尚需落实的工程项目中,例如涉及项目融资的工程项目、投资项目或者某些银行提供信贷融资,但尚需得到政府批准和银行贷款协议生效的项目,由于融资尚未完全确定,则合同当事方需要在工程合同中约定合同生效条件,避免因资金最终没有落实时产生的商务和法律问题。

承包商在与业主谈判合同生效条件或者承包商在编制分包合同时,应根据具体项目的情况确定合同生效条件。在确定合同生效条件时,应遵守如下原则:

(1) 在需要落实银行融资时,应在合同中约定银行贷款协议生效为生效条件,或者约定银行贷款协议生效,并且在第一次提款后合同生效。

(2) 在工程项目中,应将资金落实、政府批准、项目许可获得等主要条件作为合同生效条件,而不宜设定过多的合同生效条件,或者将完全由当事一方行为影响的条件列入生效条件。

(3) 在工程项目中,如需落实资金,则应将承包商获得预付款作为合同生效条件。

(4) 在BOT/PPP投资项目中,投资人应与东道国政府通过谈判确定特许经营权协议(concession agreement)或者实施协议(implementation agreement)的合同生效条件,详细列明每一个生效条件。

(5) 在通过议标而非公开投标方式获得国际工程项目时,尽可能在前期合理规避工程所在国法律要求的招标要求,通过合同生效条件豁免/合法规避公开招标程序,使获得的工程合同符合工程所在国法律要求。

(6) 合同当事方应认真评估每一项合同生效条件是否可以满足、存在的困难和障碍、能否满足以及满足所需的时间。

以某国际工程项目为例,合同生效条件如下:

---

3. Effectiveness of the Contract Documents
3.1 The above mentioned agreements (hereinafter referred to as the "Contract Documents") shall come into full force and effect on the date when all the following conditions precedent have been satisfied:

This Contract has been signed by the parties hereto;

> The loan agreement between the Employer and the financing banks/institutions have been executed.
>
> 3.2 The date on which all these conditions including (a) and (b) above have been satisfied shall be the Effective Date of Contract. Both Parties shall confirm the date of effectiveness in writing accordingly.

以某国际工程项目为例，在需要中国金融机构融资时，合同生效条件如下：

> 3.1 Effective Date (Reference GC Clause 1)
>
> The Effective Date is the date when all of the following conditions have been fulfilled：
>
> (a) This Deed of Agreement has been duly executed for and on behalf of the Employer and the Contractor;
> (b) The Contract Document has been duly signed for and on behalf of the Employer and the Contractor;
> (c) The Loan Agreement has been signed by the Government of _____ and relevant bank/banks pursuant to the mutual agreement/understanding between the Government of _____ and the Government of _____ and has come into force and effect;
> (d) The Contractor has submitted to the Employer the performance security and the advance payment guarantees in accordance with the format as attached in the this Contract Agreement within 30 days after the effectiveness of the Loan Agreement between the Government of _____ and the Government of _____ /Bank;
> (e) Exemption of the Public Procurement Act-2006 and/or the Public Procurement Rules-2008 with all amendments of _____ for the procurement under this Project; and
> (f) The Advance Payment from the Employer has been received by the Contractor.

以某特许经营投资项目为例，特许经营权协议的生效条件规定如下：

> 5. Condition Precedent
>
> The effectiveness of this Concession Contract is subject, under the legal rules for monitoring public expenditure, to the issuance of the "Visa" by the Administrative Court confirming the effectiveness of this Concession Contract and that it is in accordance with the Applicable Laws and Regulations.

7.1.3 工程范围

在国际工程合同中，工程范围（scope of works）一般采用合同条款概括性描述加附件的方式。合同条款中的工程范围，以日本工程促进协会 ENAA 格式合同中《制炼厂国际合同标准格式》(*the Model Form of International Contract for Process Plant Construction*) 第7条［工程范围］规定如下：

"7.1 Unless otherwise expressly limited in the Employer's Requirements, the Contractor's obligations cover the provision of all Plant and the performance of all Installation Services required for the design, the manufacture (including procurement, quality assurance, construction, installation, associated civil works, Precommissioning and delivery) of the Plant and the installation, completion and commissioning of the Facilities in accordance with the plans, procedures, specifications, drawings, codes and any other documents as specified in the Section, Employer's Requirements. Such specifications include, but are not limited to, the provision of supervision and engineering services; the supply of labor, materials, equipment, spare parts (as specified in GCC Sub-Clause 7.3 below) and accessories; Contractor's Equipment; construction utilities and supplies; temporary materials, structures and facilities; transportation (including, without limitation, unloading and hauling to, from and at the Site); and storage, except for those supplies, works and services that will be provided or performed by the Employer, as set forth in the Appendix (Scope of Works and Supply by the Employer) to the Contract Agreement.

7.2 The Contractor shall, unless specifically excluded in the Contract, perform all such work and/or supply all such items and materials not specifically mentioned in the Contract but that can be reasonably inferred from the Contract as being required for attaining Completion of the Facilities as if such work and/or items and materials were expressly mentioned in the Contract.

7.3 In addition to the supply of Mandatory Spare Parts included in the Contract, the Contractor agrees to supply spare parts required for the operation and maintenance of the Facilities for the period specified in the SCC and the provisions, if any, specified in the SCC. However, the identity, specifications and quantities of such spare parts and the terms and conditions relating to the supply thereof are to be agreed between the Employer and the Contractor, and the price of such spare parts shall be that given in Price Schedule No. 6, which shall be added to the Contract Price. The price of such spare parts shall include the purchase price therefore and other costs and expenses (including the Contractor's fees) relating to the supply of spare parts."

根据上述第7条，承包商的义务不仅包括设计、设备供货和施工，还包括备件配件的供应等义务。在使用 ENAA 合同格式时，除了合同条款规定的一般性描述工程范围外，还需要对具体的工程范围制定专门的附件，对工程范围作出特殊的规定。工程范围附件并没有标准格式，但对于承包商而言,需要考虑工程范围是否能够准确地界定具体项目范围,不仅包括物理上的位置、范围、规模、长度等,还包括业主想实现的预期目的以及性能考核指标等内容。

对于工程范围的准确描述,一般而言,仅靠合同条款的一般规定和工程范围附件的规定往往还不能准确界定具体项目的工程范围,还应用其他合同文件,例如标价工程量表、图纸和技术规范或业主要求等文件准确界定。对于设备供货以及备品配件供货的范围,应在工程合同中编制单独的设备供货和备品配件范围,包括品名、规格、数量等内容。

在国际工程项目中,特别是设计施工或 EPC/交钥匙合同,工程范围往往是业主和承包商之间经常争议的问题。因此,在合同中严格界定具体项目的工程范围,是一件十分重要的事情。

7.1.4 标价工程量表或价格明细表

标价工程量表（Priced Bill of Quantity）或价格明细表（Price Schedule）是承包商向业主报价后,由业主经投标审核后接受的或通过谈判接受的承包商的报价,是 FIDIC 合同所称的中标合同价格（Accepted Contract Amount）,也是在合同履行期间业主向承包商支付工程价款的基础。

1. 工程量表前言

无论业主通过公开招标还是议标方式采购工程项目,或者承包商向分包商分包的工程项目,工程量表不仅体现了各单项或分项工程项目名称、工程数量、单价和总价,也体现了合同界定的工程范围。由于工程量表不可能包罗万象,在承包商阅读和理解工程量表时,应与招标文件、技术规范和图纸等文件一同阅读,切忌只就工程量表上表述的内容片面理解工程量表。由于工程量表不可能包括每一项工程或工作的所有的细节,有必要在工程量表的前言部分予以说明,并要求承包商根据技术规范理解工程量表。

工程量表中所载明的内容,包括各个单项或分项工程的名称、单位、单价和总价,往往是承包商与业主发生争议的焦点。因此,明确表明工程量表的含义,是业主编制招标文件或承包商编制投标文件的一项非常重要的内容。完备的工程量表前言示例如下:

A. Preamble

1. The Bill of Quantities shall be read in conjunction with the Instructions to Bidders, General and Special Conditions of Contract, Technical Specifications, and Drawings. The item number and Specification number refer to the relevant sections of the Standard and/or Special Specifications.

2. The quantities given in the Bill of Quantities are estimated and provisional, and are given to provide a common basis for bidding. The basis of payment will be the actual quantities of work ordered and carried out, as measured by the Contractor and verified by the Engineer and valued at the rates and prices bid in the priced Bill of Quantities, where applicable, and otherwise at such rates and prices as the Engineer may fix within the terms of the Contract.

3. The rates and prices bid in the priced Bill of Quantities shall, except insofar as it is otherwise provided under the Contract, include all Constructional Plant, labour, supervision, materials, erection, maintenance, insurance, profit, taxes, and duties, to-

gether with all general risks, liabilities, and obligations set out or implied in the Contract.

4. A rate or price shall be entered against each item in the priced Bill of Quantities, whether quantities are stated or not. The cost of Items against which the Contractor has failed to enter a rate or price shall be deemed to be covered by other rates and prices entered in the Bill of Quantities.

5. The whole cost of complying with the provisions of the Contract shall be included in the Items provided in the priced Bill of Quantities, and where no Items are provided, the cost shall be deemed to be distributed among the rates and prices entered for the related Items of Work.

6. Without affecting the generality of the foregoing provisions, the rates and prices entered by the Contractor in the Bill of Quantities shall include the cost and expense of the following:

   i) The provision, storage, transport, use and maintenance of all materials, equipment, machinery and tools;

   ii) The provision, transport, use and maintenance of all staff and labour and their accommodation, transport etc, and the supply of all immigration permits and other requirements;

   iii) Setting out, measuring, inspection, supervision and topographical survey and drawing necessary for the execution or measurement of the work;

   iv) The provision, transport, use and maintenance of all consumable stores, fuel, water, drainage, electricity and telephones;

   v) Sampling, testing and trials, including checking information given by the Engineer;

   vi) Injury caused to the works under construction, equipment, materials andconsuable stores by weather conditions;

   vii) The provision, erection and removal of all Contractor's offices, equipment yard, stores and temporary works, including fencing and all site restrictions;

   viii) Restoration of services disrupted during implementation of the works;

   ix) Repairs to the Works during the Defects Liability Period.

7. General directions and descriptions of work and materials are not necessarily repeated nor summarized in the Bill of Quantities. References to the relevant sections of the Contract documentation shall be made before entering prices against each item in the priced Bill of Quantities.

8. Any arithmetic errors in computation or summation will be corrected by the Employer as follows:

   (a) Where there is discrepancy between amounts in figures and in words, the amount in words will govern; and

   (b) Where there is a discrepancy between the unit rate and the total amount derived from the multiplication of the unit price and the quantity, the unit rate as quoted will govern, unless in the opinion of the Employer, there is an obviously gross misplacement of the decimal point in the unit price, in which event the total amount as quoted will govern and the unit rate will be corrected.

9. Rock is defined as all materials that, in the opinion of the Engineer, require blasting, or the use of metal wedges and sledgehammers, or the use of compressed air drilling for their removal, and that cannot be extracted by ripping with a tractor of at least 150 brake hp with a single, rear-mounted, heavy-duty ripper.

10. Bidders shall price the Bill of Quantities in local currency only and shall indicate in the Appendix to Bid the percentage expected for payment in foreign currency.

在上述工程量表前言中，业主对工程量表进行了界定，主要是：①工程量表中数量是预估的和暂时的，工程量以承包商实际完成工程量为计量标准，这是单价合同的典型表述。②承包商的价格应包括的内容，采用了列举法。在国际工程项目中，所有单价和价格都包括了临时工程和工程措施费用，不能将单价和价格理解为不包含临时工程和措施费用，除非工程量表明确给出了工程措施单独计量的价号。③承包商没有在工程量表中填写价格的项目，视为已经包含在其他项目的价格之中。④对于工程量表计算错误，业主给出了更正规则。为了更全面地体现承包商价格包括了所有的工程内容，可以在该项中更详细地列举包含的项目，举例如下：

RATES AND PRICES TO BE FULLY INCLUSIVE

In pricing the items of the Bill of Quantities, the Contractor shall cover himself and will be deemed to have covered himself for:

(a) All work, services and materials which according to the true intent and meaning of the Contract may be reasonably inferred as necessary for completion of the Works described in the Specifications and Bill whether expressly mentioned therein or not.

(b) All duties, obligations, liabilities and responsibilities which the Contract places upon the Contractor in connection with or in relation to the Contract. More particularly, the Contractor shall include, but not by way of limitation in his bid prices, unless itemized separately, for:

i) All costs of design, where applicable, e.g. layout of RE's houses, royalties and supply to the Engineer of all necessary drawings and technical documents;

ii) All profits and charges for the supply and delivery of the relevant items;

iii) All costs arising out of inspection and testing at manufacturer's works, including inspection to satisfy Government import regulations;

iv) All fittings, bolts, nuts, fixings, wiring, etc., not specifically itemized but essential for the proper installation and operation of the Works;

v) All costs of packing as specified for export overseas and storage under tropical conditions;

vi) All loading and off-loading charges;

vii) All costs and insurances of delivering the Equipment, Plant and Materials to site;

viii) All costs of handling, moving into position, erecting and fixing including supervision, tools, special appliances, scaffolding, tackle, consumable items, etc. ;

ix) All costs for testing, disinfecting, setting to work and putting into service;

x) Making good defects or damage to the Works in accordance with the Contract;

xi) All insurances as required by the Conditions of Contract;

xii) All costs arising out of connecting into and extending existing facilities, including any investigations required to ensure that the works are compatible with the existing environment;

xiii) All costs associated with working along the operational canal and adjacent to and in conjunction with the Employer's operating staff;

xiv) The cost of preparing and submitting all designs, drawings, details, manuals and progress reports required under the terms of the Contract;

xv) All costs associated with training the Employer's personnel in the safe and efficient operation of the Works;

xvi) Supply and delivery of the specified spare parts.

Prices shall be entered against each item in the Bill of Quantities. The cost of items against which the Contractor has failed to enter a price shall be deemed to be covered by other prices entered in the priced Bill of Quantities.

需要注意的是，在设计施工以及 EPC/交钥匙合同中，需要特别关注工程量表的表述，即应在合同工程量表中注明工程量风险的分担方式。

2. 工程量表正文

工程量表正文是由一系列表格组成的，每个工程价号（item）表明每个单项或分项工程的名称、单位、数量、单价和总价构成的，应由承包商在投标或报价时填具单价和总价的表格。工程量表的法律性质为承包商的报价，一经业主接受，即成为合同价格。各个国家和地区编制工程量表的格式大同小异，其组成如下：

（1）汇总表，表明每个单项工程的价格，汇总后加上增值税和预提税（如有），即构成合同总价。

（2）每个单项工程的分项报价单，包括总则项（General）和各分项工程构成及其价格。

需要注意的是，各个国家和地区的价号体系不一，但与其技术规范的规定相对应，自成体系。因此，各个国家和地区的各项工程价号不同，测量和付款（measurement and payment）规则不同，承包商在投标时或合同谈判时需要特别予以注意。

承包商还需要注意，在工程量表汇总表中，增值税是应该单独列项的一个价号。见表7-1，工程量表应在各个分项工程合计金额后，单独列明增值税项，承包商在计算增值税时，应以各个分项工程小计金额加上暂定金额（provisional sum）并乘以增值税税率，得出增值税金额，然后计算合同总价，即各分项工程小计金额加上暂定金额加上增值税构成整个合同总价。在国际工程实践中，在投标报价时，承包商经常在计算增值税时出错，即应为各个分项工程小计金额加上暂定金额（provisional sum）并乘以增值税税率，但有人理解成应为除以增值税税率（1+16%），导致增值税计算错误，从而合同总价出现错误。因此，在投标报价时或合同谈判时，承包商应按照工程量表的规定进行计算，而不能根据自己的片面或错误理解计算工程量表。除非在业主评标阶段发现明显的算术错误，并按照投标须知中更正规则予以更正外。如果在签订合同后发现计算错误，则承包商没有机会予以更正，只能按照承包商填写的工程量表予以计量和付款。如果工程量表中没有单独列明增值税，则承包商应在投标阶段答疑时提出增值税的问题。如果视为已经包含增值税，则承包商应在计算价格时增加增值税。但无论如何，增值税应在工程量表的汇总表中单独列项，这是各个国家和地区税法明确规定，而不能采用含增值税的方式报价。在实践中会产生法律争议，承包商认为其报价不包含增值税。在一定程度上，承包商的这种主张会得到仲裁庭的支持，中国承包商在某些项目的仲裁得到了仲裁庭的支持。

表 7-1 工程量表汇总

Gov + A1：D22emment of KKK			Phase 1
DDD Water Services Board			Part 1-Bidding Procedures
Water and Sanittion Service Improvement Project Additional Financing			Bill of Quantifies
		EXECUTVE SUMMARY	
Bill No.	Bill ltem	Amount (with Aternative Technical Solution 1：Conventional Methods) (currency)	Amount (with Aternative Technical Solution 2：TBM Method) (currency)
0	General		
1	AAA Irtake		
2	BBB Intake		
3	CCC lrtake		
4a	Main Tunnel-AlternativeTechnical Solution 1		
4b	Main Tunnel-AlternativeTechnical Solution 2		
5	AAA Adit		
6	AAA Shaft and Adit		
7	DDD Adit		
8	BBB Outfall		
9	Sub-total excluding Day Works and contingencies		
10	Daywork		
11	Base cost (9 + 10)		
12	Allow 10% Pravisional Sum for Cortingercies (10% ×11)		
13	Sub-total (11 + 12)		
14	Add 16% VAT (16% ×13)		
Total-Bid Price (13 + 14)			
	SIGNATURE OF BIDDER'S AUTHORISED REPRESENTATNE：		
		COMPANY STAMP·	
		DATE：	

表 7-2 为某个分项工程的工程量表。

表 7-2　分项工程的工程量表

Government of DDD				Plase1
XXX Water Services Board				Part 1-Bddirg Procedures
Water and sanitation Service lmprovement Prgjcct Additonal Financing				Bill of Quantitles
Bill No.1：MARAGUA IHTAKE				
SECTON S3：OPEN-CUTEEAVATOH AND EARTHWORKS				
Work No.	Work ltem	Unit	Quantity (a)	Unit Price (Ksh.) (b)	Amount (Ksh.) (c) = (b) × (a)
	CLASS D：DEMOLITION AND SITE CLEARANCE				
D1	General clearance	ha	0.300		
D2	Trees				
D2.1	Trees, girth 500 mm to 1 m	nr	10		
D2.2	Ditto but girth 1 to 2m	nr	2		
D3.1	Stumps, diarneter 150-500 mm	nr	20		
D3.2	Ditto but diameter 500 mm to 1 m	nr	10		
D3.3	Ditto but diameter 1 m to 2m	nr	2		
	CLSS E：ERRTHORKS				
E2.1.1	Exacavation for cuttings in common soil	m^3	1812		
E2.2.3	Ditto but in weathered rock	m^3	7246		
E2.3.4	Ditto but in rock	m^3	12317		
E3.1.1	Excavation for foundations in common soil	m^3	251		
E3.2.3	Ditto but in weathered rock	m^3	1001		
E3.3.4	Ditto but in rock	m^3	2393		
	Excavation ancillianes：				
E5.1.3	Trimming of excavated rock surfaces	m^2	6119		
E5.2.3	Preparation of excavated rock sufaces to receive concrete	m^2	6119		
E5.3.1	Disposal of excavated material, cammon soil	m^3	2063		
E5.3.2	Ditto but weathered rock	m^3	1811		
E5.3.3	Ditto but rock	m^3	6158		
E5.4	Double handing of excavated material	m^3	14987		
E5.5	Dredging to remove silt	m^3	130		
E5.6	Excavation of material below the Final Surface and re-placement with backfill concrete	m^3	242		
E6.1.3	Random backfill behind structures with excavated material other than common soil or rock	m^3	125		
E6.2.4	Embankment fill with selected excavated material other than topsoil or rock	m^3	200		
E6.2.5	Ditto with imported natural material other than topsoil or rock	m^3	1000		
	Total for Section 1.S3 camied to Summary				

7.1.5 支付条款

在国际工程项目中，完整的支付条款应包括以下内容：

（1）支付方式。在单价合同中按月支付，在总价合同中按照约定的里程碑或时间节点或其他方式支付。

（2）支付期限及其计算起点。以承包商递交付款申请之日起算，FIDIC 合同条款中规定为 42 天，其中工程师应在收到承包商递交付款申请之日起 28 天签字批准工程付款证书，业主应在签认付款证书后 14 天予以支付，支付期限适用于单价合同和总价合同。

需要注意的是，承包商应特别注意支付期限的计算起点，切忌"以工程师签字批准付款证书之日起 14 天内支付"这种条款签订合同，这意味着合同没有约定支付期限计算起点，工程师可以拖延签字批准付款证书。

（3）预付款金额、支付期限及其偿还方式。

（4）支付货币。合同中应明确约定支付货币及其占比，例如美元为 70%，工程所在国当地货币 30%等。

（5）汇率。合同中应明确约定支付货币之间的汇率，如美元或欧元等货币与工程所在国当地货币之间的汇率，避免汇率损失。

（6）业主延迟付款利息。应在合同中明确业主延迟付款利息，明确计算标准，避免模糊性的规定。需要注意的是：

1）在以美元、欧元等货币计算业主延迟付款利息时，应明确具体利息，如 3%、4%、5%等，或者以 12 个月 LIBOR 利率加 1%、2%、3%等为计算利息的利率。

2）在以 LIBOR 利率计算利息时，应明确是 6 个月利率还是 12 个月利率。一般而言，应以 12 个月年利率为准。

3）FIDIC 合同条款 1999 年第 1 版第 14.8 款 [延误的付款] 规定的延误付款利息条款暗藏玄机，即"Unless otherwise stated in the Particular Conditions, these financing charges shall be calculated at the annual rate of three percentage point above the discount rate of the central bank in the country of the currency of payment, and shall be paid in such currency."中的"the central bank in the country of the currency of payment"，其中"country"为小写，而不是大写。在小写的情况下是指"支付货币所在国"，这意味着支付货币为美元时是指美联储，支付货币为欧元时是指欧洲中央银行，支付货币为日元时是指日本中央银行，而不是工程所在国的中央银行。因此，承包商应仔细核查专用合同条件第 14.8 款的表述。

4）在业主延误付款时承包商的补救措施。在 FIDIC 合同条款 1999 年第 1 版和其他版本中，合同赋予承包商的补救措施包括要求支付延误付款利息、减缓施工速度、停工和终止合同。

5）有些业主主张承包商已经要求支付延误付款利息，则承包商就丧失了主张减慢施工速度、停工和终止合同的权利。不得不说，这是业主对付款条款的片面理解，在业主延迟付款的情况下，承包商享有上述补救措施的权利，且并不因为主张其中一项补救措施就丧失了主张其他补救措施的权利。

（7）保留金金额及其偿还方式。一般而言，保留金的合理范围应在 5%～10%内。在业主颁发接收证书后应退还 50%，剩余的 50%应在业主颁发履约证书时退还。或者，承包商向业主提交保留金保函,业主在颁发接收证书时将全部保留金退还给承包商。

(8)承包商递交付款支持文件的种类和名称。合同中应详细列明承包商应递交的文件种类和名称。

以某国际工程项目为例,通过合同谈判确定了付款条款,其中对于设计、设备、土建工程及其安装工程等付款规定如下:

Terms and Procedures of Payment

In accordance with the provisions of GC Clause 12[Terms of Payment], the Employer shall pay the Contractor in the following manner and at the following times, on the basis of the price breakdown given in the Price Schedules. Applications for payment in respect of partial deliveries may be made by the Contractor as work proceeds.

PROCEDURE OF PAYMENT:

Since this Contract is financed by the Loan of China _____ Bank, the agreement of which is entered into by and between the related government authority of _____ and _____ Bank. All the payments in connection with this Contract shall be made by _____ Bank against the receipt of the Notice of Drawdown attached with all other necessary documents required by the _____ Bank (hereinafter collectively called as "Notice of Drawdown"), which shall be issued by the related government authority of _____ and accepted by _____ Bank. Therefore, the issuance of the above Notice of Drawdown is deemed as the payment by the Employer to the Contractor.

TERMS OF PAYMENT

1. Advance Payment

    Twenty percent (20%) of the total Contract Price shall be paid in one (1) installment as advance payment by the Employer within forty-five (45) days from the date of presentation of the following documents by the Contractor:

    (a) Application for Payment in three (3) originals;

    (b) CompleteProforma Invoice in three (3) originals and three (3) copies;

    (c) Advance Payment Guarantee for the same amount in favor of the Employer and in the same currency issued by China _____ Bank substantially in the form attached to the Contract Agreement.

2. Interim Payments

2.1 Payment for Plant, Equipment and Material supplied from abroad

    In respect of plant, equipment and material supplied from abroad, the following payments shall be made:

    (1) Fifty percent (50%) of Contract Price for Plant, Equipment and Material shall be paid at each shipment against and within forty-five (45) days from the date of presentation of the following documents by the Contractor:

(a) Application for Payment in three (3) originals;

(b) Full set of clean on-board bill of lading (B/L) or airway bill marked "freight prepaid", notifying the Employer;

(c) Complete Commercial Invoice in three (3) originals and three (3) copies;

(d) Packing list in three (3) originals and three (3) copies.

(2) Twenty percent (20%) of Contract Price for Plant, Equipment and Material shall be paid upon delivery to site for each shipment against and within forty-five (45) days from the date of presentation of the following documents by the Contractor:

(a) Application for Payment in three (3) originals;

(b) Complete Commercial Invoice in three (3) originals and three (3) copies;

(c) Post Landing Inspection Report in one (1) original and one (1) copy.

(d) Packing list in three (3) originals and three (3) copies.

(3) Fivepercent (5%) of Contract Price for Plant, Equipment and Material shall be paid, upon issue of the Completion (Take-over) Certificate on section/lot basis, within forty-five (45) days from the date of presentation of the following documents by the Contractor:

(a) Application for Payment in three (3) originals;

(b) Complete Commercial Invoice in three (3) originals and three (3) copies;

(c) Completion Certificate on section/lot-wise basis in one (1) original and one (1) copy;

(4) Fivepercent (5%) of Contract Price for Plant, Equipment and Material shall be paid, upon issue of the Operational Acceptance Certificate on section/lot basis, within forty-five (45) days from the date of presentation of the following documents by the Contractor:

(a) Application for Payment inthree (3) originals;

(b) Complete Commercial Invoice in three (3) originals and three (3) copies;

(c) Operational Acceptance Certificate on section/lot-wise basis in one (1) original and one (1) copy;

However, this five percent (5%) payment may be paidafter receipt of invoice and an irrevocable bank guarantee for the equivalent amount made out in favor of the Employer. The bank guarantee will be released at the end of defect liability period.

2.2 Payment for Survey, Design and Testing

Eighty percent (80%) of the total or pro rata survey & design services amount upon approval of design and acceptanceof test reports of the relevant equipment/materials by the Project Manager or authorized person by the Employer within forty-five (45) days from the date of presentation of the following documents by the Contractor:

(a) Application for Payment in three (3) originals;

(b) Complete Commercial Invoice in three (3) originals and three (3) copies;

(c) Approval letter or acceptance letter of the relevant drawing or documents or design as applicable by the Project Manager or authorized person by the Employer.

2.3 Payment for Civiland Installation Works, Training and other services

(1) Seventy percent (70%) of the Contract Price for Civil Works and Installation Works performed by the Contractor on section/lot basis, as identified in the Interim Payment Certificate issued by the Employer, during the preceding month' will be made within forty-five (45) days from the date of presentation of the following documents by the Contractor:

(a) Application for Payment in three (3) originals;

(b) Complete Commercial Invoice in three (3) originals and three (3) copies;

(2) Five percent (5%) of Contract Price for Civil and Installation Works, Training and other services shall be paid, upon issue of the Completion (Take-Over) Certificate on section/lot basis, within forty-five (45) days from the date of presentation of the following documents by the Contractor:

(a) Application for Payment in three (3) originals;

(b) Complete Commercial Invoice in three (3) originals and three (3) copies;

(c) Completion Certificate on section/lot-wise basis in one (1) original and one (1) copy;

(3) Fivepercent (5%) of Contract Price for Civil and Installation Works, Training and other services shall be paid, upon issue of the Operational Acceptance Certificate on section/lot basis, within forty-five (45) days from the date of presentation of the following documents by the Contractor:

(a) Application for Payment inthree (3) originals;

(b) Complete Commercial Invoice in three (3) originals and three (3) copies;

(c) Operational Acceptance Certificate on section/lot-wise basis in one (1) original and one (1) copy;

However, this five percent (5%) payment may be paidafter receipt of invoice and an irrevocable bank guarantee (a copy will be attached for each payment) for the equivalent amount made out in favor of the Employer. The bank guarantee will be released at the end of defect liability period.

对于合同规定的付款条款，承包商可参考 FIDIC 合同条款 1999 年第 1 版规定的付款条款进行对比。

7.1.6 合同货币和汇率

1. 外汇风险

由于国际工程项目具有跨越国界的特征，必然产生国际资金转移或本国货币与其他货币之间的兑换，并相应产生外汇风险。承包商在工程过程中，至少需要使用以下多种货币：

（1）承包商本国货币。用以支付在承包商国内购置的设备、材料，以及支付派出人员的国内工资、本国运输、税收、保险和各种日常开支费用。

(2) 工程所在国的当地货币。用以支付当地购买材料、设备、工具等，支付当地雇员和工人的工资、当地的运输、税收、保险和各种日常开支费用。

(3) 第三国货币，用以支付从不同国家进口材料、设备和支付第三国雇员部分工资和补偿费用等。

由于工程承包工期长，上述多种货币在国际市场上汇率不断变化，使承包商收入和支出货币价值总是处于浮动变化之中。稍有失误，就会造成损失。这也就是人们常说的汇率风险。

在国际工程项目中，因项目性质不同、项目资金来源不同、项目所在国不同、项目所在国的外汇政策不同、业主态度不同等因素，合同中支付外币的条款会有所差别。有些项目招标文件对支付货币有明确规定，也有些招标文件则要求投标人提出自己的意见，并在确定合同之前讨论确定。为此，承包商应事先调查有关情况，包括：

(1) 项目所在国的外汇管制政策和程度，包括是否允许外汇汇出、手续是否复杂等。

(2) 调查项目所在国货币历年来与世界主要自由外汇汇率变化情况、变化幅度及金融专家的预测趋势。

(3) 认真计算该项目所需进口物资及其他各项所需外汇总金额与合同金额比例。

忽视外汇风险会给承包商带来灾难性损失。例如，我国某一大型国际承包公司在某国承包了一项大型水利工程项目，签约时美元对该国货币汇率为1美元兑4.81当地币。开工后直到工程完工的4年间，工程所在国的货币不断贬值，到完工时汇率为1美元兑25当地币，平均每年贬值近70%。而我方由于某种原因未重视汇率可能发生的变化，造成该项目亏损严重。近些年来，部分发展中国家货币贬值现象严重，这种情况在国际工程承包项目中并不鲜见。

2. 货币种类

在投标和合同谈判过程中，承包商应确定如下问题：是否支付外汇、是否限定外币币种、是否限定外汇币种数量、是否限定外汇比例（金额）限额、外汇是按浮动汇率还是固定汇率和汇率如何确定等。

国际承包工程投标报价，在选择货币方面，常见以当地货币支付或当地货币加外汇（多币种报价）两种方式。例如，世界银行在其推荐的合同范本中，关于货币支付方法，在其投标人须知第15条中提出了两种可供业主选择的方式：

"方案A：投标人全部使用当地币报价

15.2 投标人应用招标数据表和合同专用条款中规定的业主所在国货币填报所有单价和价格，对于因业主所在国以外的工程投入需支付的其他货币开支（简称为'外币需求'），投标人应在投标书中说明支付此类货币需占填报总价（扣除暂定金额）的百分比，支付币种不得超过世界银行成员国任何3种货币。就本条而言，欧洲货币单位应认为是合格货币。

15.3 投标人应在投标书中明确其计算当地货币等值金额所采用的汇率以及第15.2款提到的百分比。此汇率应适用于合同项下的全部支付。因此，中标人将不承担任何汇率风险。

15.4 投标人应在投标书附件中说明预计的外汇需求。

15.5 业主可要求投标人澄清其内外币需求，并证明其单价和价格中以及投标书附件中列明的金额是合理的，且符合第15.2款的规定。投标人应提供外币需求的详细分解。

15.6 在工程过程中，合同价格中未付余额的外币部分可根据业主和承包商之间的协议，按照合同专用条款第72.4款的规定进行调整，以反映外币需求变化。此类任何调整应通过投标书中填报的百分比，与工程已用金额和承包商将来进口需求的比较而得出。

方案B：投标人使用工程所在国货币和外币报价

15.2 投标人应按下列货币分部填写报价单和价格：

（a）投标人预期将从业主所在国内供应的工程投入费用，以招标数据表和合同专用条款指明的所在国货币报价；

（b）投标人预期将从业主所在国国外供应的工程投入费用（简称外币需求）可采用世界银行成员国最多3种任何货币。就本条而言，欧洲货币单位应认为是合格货币。

（第15.3~15.6款与方案A相同，从略。）"

方案A属于当地币报价按比例和承包商自定的（不超过3种）外汇种类和固定汇率向承包商支付，方案B则是多币种报价，并固定汇率。对于这两种方案，如果业主不对其进行实质性改变，无论选择哪一种都是可以接受的。

FIDIC通用合同条款中货币支付方式建议与世界银行的基本相同，但没有世界银行范本那样明确，有些具体规定要在第二部分专用合同条款中作补充说明。因此，在使用FIDIC合同的工程项目中，承包商还应注意专用合同条件中有关支付的补充条款可否支付外汇，外汇种类和金额或比例有无限制等。如果专用合同条款未对通用合同条款具体实施作出进一步规定，则承包商应在投标报价中提出自己的具体建议或声明，以此奠定在合同谈判时提请业主讨论的基础。

3. 货币选择原则

承包商选择投标报价或签订合同货币时应遵循如下原则：

（1）如果招标文件或业主允许承包商可以选择货币，则承包商应选择硬通货币，例如美元、欧元等作为支付货币。

（2）根据预计发生的需要来选择币种和比例。如预计在欧洲采购设备和材料时，则应选择欧元，如预计在日本采购设备和材料，则可选用日元，尽量避免货币之间的兑换。

（3）在外汇管制严格、货币贬值较快的国家，在尽可能的条件下应少收当地币，争取多收外币。

（4）尽量选用在合同工期内有升值潜力的货币。除非必须使用，尽量回避汇率波动较大的币种。

（5）如在多个货币之间无从选择，可采取选择美元或欧元的策略。

（6）在中国政府与工程所在国签署货币互换协议的国家，可选择人民币作为支付货币。

随着全球一体化态势的加强，世界经济变化莫测，没有人能够预测项目所在国货币与承包商本国货币及其第三国货币之间的汇率变化的长期趋势。因此，完全规避外汇风险是不可能的事情。除在签订合同时应认真分析考虑和确定货币币种外，承包商还应树立外汇风险的防范意识，采用在银行进行外汇套期保值的措施，尽可能规避外汇风险。

需要注意的是，对于一般由业主出资招标项目或国际金融组织的国际招标项目，除非业主给出选择余地，否则，承包商应避免在投标书中提出自己的货币支付条件。如果招标文件规定了货币支付币种的条款，承包商应遵守，不能在投标文件中提出自己的条件，否则会被业主判定为"有条件的报价"，而使该投标被评为"废标"。但在买方信贷、卖方信贷等带资投标、BOT 或 PPP 项目中，承包商有机会与业主协商支付条件和支付币种。这时，承包商应利用机会争取有利于自己的支付条件。

4. 选择货币合同条款

承包商投标或合同谈判确定的合同货币，可以在多个文件中表明合同货币的种类和比例，例如在中标通知书中则会体现合同货币，如下：

Notification of Award
[on letterhead of the Employer]

Date：_____
To：[insert name and address of the Contractor]
Subject：Notification of Award Contract No _____

This is to notify you that your Bid dated _____（date）_____ for execution of the _____（name of the contract and identification number, as given in the Appendix to Bid） _____ for the Accepted Contract Amount of the equivalent of _____（amount in numbers and words and name of currency）_____ as corrected and modified in accordance with the Instruction to Bidders is hereby accepted by our Authority.

You are requested to furnish the Performance Security within 28 days in accordance with the Conditions of Contract, using for that purpose the Performance Security Form included in Section IX [Contract Forms] of the Bidding Documents.

Authorized Signature：
Name and Title of Signatory：
Name of Authority：

如果存在两个或以上合同货币币种时，应在合同协议书（Contract Amount）中增加条款表明货币种类和比例，如下：

With respect to payment disbursements, the designated foreign currency, payment distribution (i. e. local and foreign portion) and the rate of exchange or currency conversion purposes are as indicated below：

Payment	Designated Currency	% of Total Payment	Amount	Rate of Exchange
Foreign Currency Component	(Foreign Currency)			
Local Currency Component	(Local Currency)			

7.1.7 价格调整

1. 概述

由于大多数国际工程项目的工期超过一年，施工期间的价格浮动，或称物价上涨，成为业主和承包商关注的一个焦点。在 FIDIC 红皮书、ICE 合同等这种单价合同中，物价上涨、价格浮动的风险是由业主承担的，承包商有权根据合同条款规定的价格浮动条款进行调价，弥补承包商因物价上涨、通货膨胀造成的损失。在总价合同中，如果合同规定承包商无权因物价上涨而调价，则承包商承担了物价上涨和通货膨胀的风险。承包商应在投标报价过程中考虑物价上涨因素，根据通货膨胀率计算物价上涨因素，并将其计算在合同价格之中。

2. FIDIC 合同中的物价调整公式

在国际工程项目中，物价调整公式多种多样，调差项、调差系数和权重等安排也不尽相同。FIDIC 施工合同 1987 年第 4 版在第 70.1 款［成本上涨和下降］的替代条款中规定了价格浮动的机制和公式，推荐使用基本价格调整和物价指数调整两种方式，但在 FIDIC 施工合同（红皮书）1999 年第 1 版第 13.8 款［因成本改变的调整］中，明确规定了物价指数调整的方式。

在本款中，"调整数据表"系指投标附录中填好的调整数据表。如果没有此类调整数据表，本款应不适用。

如本款适用，可付给承包商的款项，应就工程所用的劳动力、货物和其他投入的成本的涨落，按本款规定的公式确定增减金额进行调整。在本条或其他条规定对成本的任何涨落不能完全补偿的情况下，中标合同金额应被视为已包括其他成本涨落的应急费用。

根据有关清单，并在付款证书中确认的、付给承包商的其他应付款要做的调整，应按合同价格应付每种货币的公式确定。对于根据成本或现行价格进行估价的工作，不予调整。所用公式应采用以下一般形式：

$$P_n = a + b\frac{L_n}{L_o} + c\frac{E_n}{E_o} + d\frac{M_n}{M_o} + \cdots$$

式中   "P_n"——用于在"n"期间所完成的工作以相应货币的估计合同价值的调整乘数，除非投标附录另有说明，此项期间单位为一个月；

"a"——在相关调整数据表中规定的固定系数，表示合同付款中的不予调整的部分；

"b""c""d"…——代表相关调整数据表中列出的，与工程施工有关各成本要素的估计比例系数；表列此项成本要素，可表示劳动力、设备和材料等资源；

"L_n""E_n""M_n"…——适用于（与特定付款证书有关的）"n"期间最后一天前第 49 天的相关成本要素的现行成本指数或参考价格，用相应支付货币表示；

"L_o""E_o""M_o"…——适用于基准日期时表列相关成本要素的基准成本指数或参考价格，用相应支付货币表示。

应使用调整数据表中列明的成本指数或参考价格。如对其来源有疑问，应由工程师确定。为此目的，应参考所述日期的指数值（分别在该表第 4 列和第 5 列），以澄清来源；尽管这些日期（因而还有这些数值）可能与基准成本指数不相对应。

在"指数对应的货币"（表中所列）不是相应支付货币时，每个指数应按工程所在国中央银行规定的此相应支付货币在上述要使用该指数的日期的卖出汇率，换算成相应支付货币。

在获得每种现行成本指数前，工程师应确定一个临时指数，用以签发临时付款证书。当取得现行成本指数时，应根据该指数重新计算调整。

如承包商未能在竣工时间内完成工程，其后应利用（i）适用于工程竣工时间期满前第 49 天的各项指数或价格，或（ii）现行指数或价格；取两者中对业主更有利的，对价格做出调整。

只有当由于变更使调整数据表中所列的各项成本要素的权重（系数）变得不合理、不平衡或不适用时，才应对其进行调整。"

3. 其他类型的物价调整公式

除 FIDIC 施工合同（红皮书）1999 年第 1 版第 13.8 款［因成本改变的调整］规定的物价调整公式外，国际工程项目中还可以约定其他类型的物价调整公式。以某国际工程项目为例，采用 FIDIC 施工合同 1987 年第 4 版价格调整的计算方法和过程如下：

（1）物价调整公式

1）当地币部分按照某国统计局发布的表 1.15 第 3 条目公路桥梁港口公共建设工程材料价格综合指数。

2）外币部分按照进口材料出口国承包商指定的合适单项指数。

3）每月完成产值减去不适合调价的进场、退场、承包商临时工程、暂定金、日工和技术科研费乘以权重再乘以现行指数减去基础指数差与基础指数的比进行调整，即：

$$价格调整金额 = [(V - N) \times W \times (C - B) \div B]$$

式中　V——当月完成产值；

N——当月完成进场、退场、承包商临时工程、暂定金、日工和技术科研费；

W——价格调整权重；

C——现行指数（完成工程当月指数）；

B——基本指数（投标书截止日期前 28 天价格指数）。

（2）基础数据来源

根据合同条款第 70.3 款，价格指数及权重来源于标书附件（表 7-3、表 7-4、表 7-5）。

表 7-3　标书附件中价格指数及权重

价格调整系数公式		
指数编号	指数描述	权重（%）
A	表 1.15 第 3 条目公路桥梁港口（合同当地币部分）	80
B	中国经济景气监测中心	80

表 7-4　当地币部分价格指数及权重

指数编号	指数描述	指数来源	投标人建议权重	投标人相关货币金额
A	表 1.15 第 3 条目公路桥梁港口公共建设工程	某国 Badan Pusat Statistik 发布的材料价格综合指数	80%	合同价当地币部分

表 7-5　外币部分价格指数及权重　　　　　　　　　　（单位：美元）

指数编号	指数描述	指数来源	基础值及日期	投标人相关货币金额	转换为FCI	投标人建议权重
B	人工输出	见上表	126.2（07 04）			20%
	机械设备		102.8（07 04）			20%
	钢筋		122.4（07 04）			30%
	钢板		125.8（07 04）			10%

根据合同条款第70.4款：基本价格（指数）指在递交投标书截止日期以前28天当日通行的价格（指数）。

由于递交投标书的截止日期为2004年8月16日，故基本价格（指数）采用2004年7月14日当天通行的价格（指数），即：当地币基本价格指数为147.56，外币的基本价格指数为：人工工资126.2，机械设备102.8，钢筋122.4，钢板125.8。

现行价格（指数）指临时支付证书截止日期前28天当日通行的价格（指数）。

4. 物价调整结果

在国际工程项目中，物价调整的结果往往是出现正调差和负调差两种情况。前者是工程所在国物价上涨和物价指数上涨时产生正调差，后者是物价下降或指数下降时产生负调差。无论是正调差和负调差，均应根据合同的规定对合同价格予以调整。

5. 物价调整公式范例

以某国际工程项目为例，业主和承包商通过谈判达成的物价调整公式如下：

Price Adjustment Formula

Prices payable to the Contractor, in accordance with the Contract, shall be subjected to adjustment to reflect changes in the cost of labor and material components, in accordance with the following formula：

The formula for calculating the price adjustment to be applied to the Contract Price component of civil works carried out in AAA is as follows：-

$$P_1 = P_0 \times \left\{ a + b\frac{L_1}{L_0} + c\frac{M_{11}}{M_{01}} + \left(d\frac{M_{12}}{M_{02}} \times \frac{T_1}{T_0}\right) + e\frac{M_{13}}{M_{03}} + f\frac{M_{14}}{M_{04}} \right\} - P_0$$

Where,

P_1——Price Adjustment amount of civil works carried out in XXX, payable to the Contractor

P_0——Contract Price (base price)

a——percentage of fixed element in Contract Price ($a = 15\%$)

b——percentage of DDD Expatriate component in Contract Price ($b = 5\%$)

c——percentage of Chinese expatriate component in Contract Price ($c = 5\%$)

d——percentage of materials (diesel) component in Contract Price ($d = 35\%$)

e——percentage of materials (Steel) component in Contract Price ($e = 30\%$)

f——percentage of materials (Cement) component in Contract Price ($f = 10\%$)

T_0——Exchange Rate between US Dollar and XXX currency on the date of 5 August 2016 (Base Date)

T_1——Current Exchange Rate between US Dollar and XXX currency on the date of IPC application in the course of the works

L_0, L_1——DDD expatriate indices applicable to the appropriate industry in the country of origin of the base date and the date for adjustment, respectively, published by DDD bureau of statistics.

M_{01}, M_{11}——Chinese expatriate indices applicable to the appropriate industry in the country of origin of the base date and the date for adjustment, respectively, published by China bureau of statistics or Hong Kong bureau of statistics.

M_{02}, M_{12}——Material (Diesel) indices applicable to the appropriate industry in the country of origin of the base date and the date for adjustment, respectively, published by XXX Bureau of Statistics.

M_{03}, M_{13}——Material (Steel) indices applicable to the appropriate industry in the country of origin of the base date and the date for adjustment, respectively.

M_{04}, M_{14}——Material (Cement) indices applicable to the appropriate industry in the country of origin of the base date and the date for adjustment, respectively, published by XXX Bureau of Statistics.

CONDITIONS APPLICABLE TO PRICE ADJUSTMENT

The Contractor shall indicate the source of index applicable to the Contract and the base date indices in the Contract.

Item	Country of Origin	Source of Indices	Base Date
DDD expatriate	DDD	Statistical Bulletin published by DDD Statistics	5 August 2016
Chinese expatriate	China	Statistical Bulletin published by China Bureau of Statistics or by Hong Kong Statistics	5 August 2016
Materials (Diesel)	XXX	Statistical Bulletin published by XXX Bureau of Statistics	5 August 2016
Materials (Steel)		Statistical Bulletin published by the country of origin	5 August 2016
Materials (Cement)	XXX	Statistical Bulletin published by XXX Bureau of Statistics	5 August 2016

The following conditions shall apply:

(a) TheBase Date shall be the date of 5 August 2016.

(b) Price adjustment shall be applied to the period of Time for Completion including any Time of Extension for Completion.

(c) No price adjustment shall be payable on the portion of the Contract price paid to the Contractor as an advance payment.

(d) The above payment implication due to the Price Adjustment shall be input and settled for every and each interim payment application in accordance with the Contract.

6. 承包商在投标和合同谈判时对于物价调整公式需要考虑的因素

承包商在投标时应分析业主招标文件中对于调价公式的几个主要因素：

（1）调差公式类型和方式，即按照劳动力、材料和设备调差，还是按照工程所在国的物价指数进行调差。

（2）指数来源，即中国统计局指数和外国统计局指数，包括工程所在国及其劳务、材料、设备来源国指数。

（3）基期，即以哪个日期作为调价公式计算的起点。在通常情况下，一般以投标截止日期之前28天为基期。在通过合同谈判签订工程合同时，可以签订日期为基期。

（4）权重系数 a、b、c……其中不可调整权重系数为 a。一般而言，不可调整权重系数越高，则意味着承包商获得调差的金额越少。例如，如不可调整权重系数为10%，则意味着承包商可就其他90%部分进行调差；如果不可调整权重系数为50%，则意味着承包商仅能就剩余的50%部分进行调差。因此，不可调整权重系数越低，对于承包商越有利；反之，则对承包商不利。

（5）权重项。承包商考虑权重系数分配应主要从工程项目所使用的劳务、材料和设备的比例方面考虑权重系数，并考虑在工程所在国劳务、材料和设备指数的历史数据。

（6）权重系数比例分配，这是承包商能够实现价格调整的关键因素，上述权重系数合计应为1或100%。例如不可调整权重系数为0.1（10%）、中国劳务为0.2（20%）、本地劳务为0.05（5%）、水泥0.3（30%）、钢筋0.2（20%）、油料0.15（15%），上述权重系数合计为1或100%。

在投标项目中，如招标文件已有此类规定，承包商应遵守招标文件确定的基期、指数来源和权重系数等。在招标文件要求承包商填写指数来源、权重系数时，承包商应填写完整全部的空白表格，以便能在施工过程中进行价格调整，避免调差公式无效或视为承包商放弃调差。在通过合同谈判方式签订合同时，应针对工程项目的具体情况，与业主谈判确定基期、指数来源、权重项和权重系数。

7. 物价调整公式中汇率调整系数

在某些国际工程合同中，业主为了考虑工程所在国汇率变化给承包商带来的影响，在物价调整系数中增加了汇率调整系数，举例如下：

$$P_n = \left(a + b\frac{L_n}{L_0} + c\frac{E_n}{E_0} + d\frac{M_n}{M_0} + \cdots \right) \times \frac{E_1}{E_0}$$

在上式中，$\frac{E_1}{E_0}$ 是汇率调整系数（Foreign Exchange Correction Factor），其中 E_0 是工程所在国与美元或欧元等货币的基期汇率，E_1 为当期期中付款证书汇率。

承包商在遇到调价公式中存在汇率调整系数时，应充分考虑工程所在国汇率的变化趋势，并考虑汇率调整给承包商结算金额带来的影响。在上式中，如果工程所在国汇率持续贬值，则汇率调整为正值，例如 $\frac{E_1}{E_0} = \frac{110}{100} = 1.10$，此时，适用的调差金额应乘以1.10系数，为汇率正调差。如果工程所在国汇率持续升值，例如 $\frac{E_1}{E_0} = \frac{100}{110} = 0.90$，则适用的调差金额应乘以0.90系数，汇率调整为负值。

7.1.8 工期和进度计划

承包商应按照招标文件的要求编制工期和进度计划，响应业主招标文件的要求，是承包商中标的前提条件。

除工期应响应业主要求外,承包商应按照招标文件的要求编制进度计划。在投标阶段,承包商不必编制过于详尽的进度计划。

7.1.9 技术规范或业主需求

在国际工程合同中,技术规范或业主需求可用以下两种方式表示:

(1) 招标文件或工程合同列明使用的技术规范或业主需求的目录,由承包商自己查阅相关的技术规范。

(2) 业主编制专用技术规范,在合同中列明专用技术规范和通用技术规范或业主需求,供承包商设计和施工使用。

技术规范门类庞杂,业主只能根据工程项目的性质和类型选择适用的技术规范和业主需求。

7.2 国际工程合同主要条款及编制

7.2.1 国际工程合同主要条款

国际工程合同涉及的主要合同条款可以定义为涉及业主和承包商主要义务的条款,这些条款包括:

(1) 银行保函条款。
(2) 工程开工。
(3) 竣工验收。
(4) 保险。
(5) 现场移交计划。
(6) 许可。
(7) 工期延长。
(8) 工期延误违约金。
(9) 不可抗力条款。
(10) 风险分担条款。
(11) 违约责任及其上限。
(12) 合同终止条款。
(13) 索赔条款。
(14) 税务条款。
(15) 适用法律条款。
(16) 争议解决机制:争议委员会。
(17) 仲裁条款。

鉴于本书将用专门章节阐述不可抗力、索赔、合同终止、适用法律、争议解决机制和仲裁内容,因此,本章将阐述除不可抗力、索赔、合同终止、适用法律、争议解决机制和仲裁之外的合同主要条款。

7.2.2　银行保函条款

1. 预付款保函

在国际工程合同中，完备的预付款条款应包括如下内容：
（1）预付款保函格式。
（2）预付款保函金额和货币种类。
（3）预付款保函期间。
（4）开证行。
（5）预付款减额。
（6）预付款保函延期。
（7）预付款保函索赔条件。

除第（5）项预付款减额外，上述内容同样适用于履约保函、保留金保函或者维修保函（如有）。以某国际工程项目为例，预付款及其预付款保函条款如下：

14.3　Advance Payment

14.3.1　The Employer shall pay the Advance Payment in accordance with Schedule 2 [*Payment Schedule*].

14.3.2　The face value of the Advance Payment Bond shall, following each payment in accordance with Schedule 2 [*Payment Schedule*], be reduced in accordance with Schedule 2 [*Payment Schedule*]. The Contractor shall ensure that the Advance Payment Bond is valid and enforceable until the amount of the Advance Payment Bond has been reduced to zero.

14.3.3　If the Advance Payment has not been repaid prior to the issue of the Handover Certificate or prior to termination under Clause 14 [*Termination by Employer*], Clause 15 [*Suspension and Termination by Contractor*] or Clause 18 [*Force Majeure*] (as the case may be), the whole of the balance then outstanding shall immediately become due and payable by the Contractor to the Employer which, if not paid, shall entitle the Employer to claim the whole of the balance of the Advance Payment Bond then outstanding.

日本工程促进协会 ENAA 版 *The Model Form of International Contract for Process Plant Construction* 第 13.2 款规定的预付款保函条款如下：

13.2　Advance Payment Security

13.2.1　The Contractor shall, within twenty-eight (28) days of the notification of contract award, provide a security in an amount equal to the advance payment calculated in accordance with the Appendix [Terms and Procedures of Payment] to the Contract Agreement, and in the same currency or currencies.

> 13.2.2 The security shall be in the form provided in the bidding documents or in another form acceptable to the Employer. The amount of the security shall be reduced in proportion to the value of the Facilities executed by and paid to the Contractor from time to time, and shall automatically become null and void when the full amount of the advance payment has been recovered by the Employer. The security shall be returned to the Contractor immediately after its expiration.

2. 履约保函

日本工程促进协会 ENAA 版 *The Model Form of International Contract for Process Plant Construction* 第 13.3 款履约保函规定如下：

> 13.3 Performance Security
>
> 13.3.1 The Contractor shall, within twenty-eight (28) days of the notification of contract award, provide a security for the due performance of the Contract in the amount specified in the SCC.
>
> 13.3.2 The security shall be denominated in the currency or currencies of the Contract, or in a freely convertible currency acceptable to the Employer, and shall be in one of the forms *of bank guarantees* provided in the bidding documents, as stipulated by the Employer in the SCC, or in another form acceptable to the Employer.
>
> 13.3.3 Unless otherwise specified in the SCC, the security shall be reduced by half on the date of the Operational Acceptance. The Security shall become null and void, or shall be reduced pro rata to the Contract Price of a part of the Facilities for which a separate Time for Completion is provided, fivehundred and forty (540) days after Completion of the Facilities or three hundred and sixty five (365) days after Operational Acceptance of the Facilities, whichever occurs first; provided, however, that if the Defects Liability Period has been extended on any part of the Facilities pursuant to GCC Sub-Clause 27.8 hereof, the Contractor shall issue an additional security in an amount proportionate to the Contract Price of that part. The security shall be returned to the Contractor immediately after its expiration, provided, however, that if the Contractor, pursuant to GCC Sub-Clause 27.10, is liable for an extended defect liability obligation, the performance security shall be extended for the period and up to the amount specified in the SCC.

以某国际工程合同为例，本合同条款对履约保函作了严格的规定，其中第（c）项包括限制总承包商对于业主 WDP 索赔履约保函时诉权的限制，如下：

12　PERFORMANCE SECURITY

12.1　Performance Bond

(a) The General Contractor shall, within fourteen (14) Days from the date of the Letter of Acceptance, provide the WDP with an on-demand bond from a First Tier Bank and in a sum equal to the amount specified in Appendix 1 and in the form appearing in Appendix 3, for the due observance and performance of the Contract by the General Contractor (the "Performance Bond"). The General Contractor shall be responsible for obtaining and maintaining the Performance Bond at its own costs and expense and shall be deemed to have included such costs and expense in the Contract Sum.

(b) After the issuance of the Certificate of Practical Completion, the Performance Bond shall be reduced to five percent (5%) of the Contract Sum. The Performance Bond shall be effective from the date of issuance until five (5) years after the date of Practical Completion.

(c) The General Contractor agrees that the WDP shall be free to make any demand on, or to apply the proceeds of any demand upon the Performance Bond in any way as it may in its absolute discretion deem fit, without any interference by the General Contractor or any attempt by it to prevent, prohibit or restrict the making of any such demand or application, and accordingly the General Contractor undertakes not to interfere or to prevent, prohibit or restrict the making of any such demand, or to attempt to do so.

(d) Notwithstanding anything contained in the Contract, if the General Contractor fails to perform any of its obligations, the WDP shall at its absolute discretion be entitled to call upon the Performance Bond, wholly or partially.

(e) Upon a payment being made to the WDP pursuant to any claim under the Performance Bond, the General Contractor shall issue to the WDP further security by way of additional performance bond or bonds in the form appearing in Appendix 3 for an amount not less than the amount so paid to the WDP on or prior to the date of such payment so that the total sum of the Performance Bond shall be maintained at all times at the value specified in Clause 12.1(a).

(f) Notwithstanding the above, in the event that the Contract is terminated under Clauses 64.1 or 65 the said Performance Bond or any balance thereof shall be called upon orencashed by the WDP.

(g) If the terms of the Performance Bond specify an expiry date and the Date for Completion is extended in accordance with the Contract, the General Contractor shall at its own costs and expense extend the validity period of the Performance Bond until the Works have been completed and any defects have been remedied in accordance with the Contract.

　　在履约保函中是否需要限制承包商对业主索赔保函的诉权，即通过诉讼方式阻止业主索赔保函，一般而言，限制承包商诉权的规定可视为不公平合同条款，大多数国际工程合同格式，例如 FIDIC 等均无此项规定。但在普通法系国家或者工程合同适用普通法时，如果合同约定了此类限制性条款，只要不违反不公平合同条款的法律规定，则应视为合法有效。

7.2.3 工程开工

在国际工程合同中，工程开工是否设置前提条件，应视项目的具体情形。在国际金融组织融资的并经公开招标的工程项目中，一般是以业主或工程师发出开工通知（Notice to Proceed/Notice of Commencement）为准，有些合同给予承包商1至3个月的动员期（mobilization period），有些则没有动员期，承包商应在收到业主或工程师发出的开工通知后立即开工。对于中国金融机构提供融资的项目，例如买方信贷项目和卖方信贷项目，因为需要双方政府的批准和贷款协议的生效，应在合同条款中设置工程开工前提条件，举例如下：

The Contractor shall commence the work on the Facilities section/lot-wise within 28 days upon his receipt of Notice of Commencement for each section/lot. The date for starting calculating the Time for Completion shall be the date when the Contractor receives the Notice of Commencement.

The Notice of Commencement shall be issued by the Employer on the section/lot-wise basis, and detailed as the following scenarios:

1. For substations with auxiliary buildings: the issue date of Notice of Commencement shall be the day when all of the following conditions have been fulfilled:
   A. The Contract has come into effect in accordance with Article 3 of Contract Agreement, and
   B. The Employer has handed over the Site and necessary permissions to the Contractor.
2. For substations without auxiliary buildings: the issue date of Notice of Commencement shall be the day when all of the following conditions have been fulfilled:
   A. The Contract has come into effect in accordance with Article 3 of Contract Agreement, and
   B. The Employer has handed over the Site to the Contractor.
3. For power transmission lines (including overhead lines and underground lines): the issue date of Notice of Commencement shall be the date 28 days after the Contract Effective Date.

需要注意的是，上述合同生效是以贷款协议签订并生效为条件，因此，工程开工应是在合同生效之后。

在融资的项目中，工程开工的前提条件应严格规定，且应规定在无法获得融资支持时承包商报价在多长期限内有效，以及如何处理承包商报价等问题，举例如下：

8.1　Commencement of Works

　　8.1.1　At any time after the date of this Contract, the Employer may, subject to Clause 8.1.2, issue to the Contractor the Notice to Proceed. The Employer shall give the Contractor no less than five Business Days' notice of the anticipated date on which the Notice to Proceed will be issued.

　　8.1.2　The Employer may not issue the Notice to Proceed until each of the following conditions precedent has been satisfied or (x) in the case of Clauses 8.1.2(i), 8.1.2(iii), 8.1.2(iv), 8.1.2(v), 8.1.2(vii), 8.1.2(ix) and 8.1.2(xii), waived by the Employer, and (y) in the case of Clauses 8.1.2(ii), 8.1.2(vi), 8.1.2(viii), and 8.1.2(xi), waived by the Contractor:

8.1.2.1 The Government of AAA and the Employer have entered into an addendum to each of the Concession Agreements on terms acceptable to the Employer, as confirmed in writing by the Employer;

8.1.2.2 The Employer having obtained all Employer's Authorisations necessary for the commencement of the Works on the Site before issuing the Notice to Proceed;

8.1.2.3 The Employer has received from the Contractor a certificate in respect of each of the member of the Contractor, signed by a duly authorised officer of such entity and attaching the following documents:

8.1.2.3.1 A copy of the entity's constitutional documents;

8.1.2.3.2 A true copy of a resolution of the applicable board of directors:

8.1.2.3.2.1 Approving the terms of, and the transactions contemplated by the Contract and resolving that it execute such documents;

8.1.2.3.2.2 Authorising a specified person or persons to execute the documents on its behalf; and

8.1.2.3.2.3 Authorising a specified person or persons, on its behalf, to sign and/or despatch all documents and notices to be signed and/ordespatched by it under or in connection with such documents; and

8.1.2.3.3 A specimen signature of each person authorised by the resolutions referred to in Paragraph(b) above;

8.1.2.4 The Employer has received from the Contractor:

8.1.2.4.1 Duly executed and delivered on-demand Advance Payment Bonds;

8.1.2.4.2 Duly executed and delivered on-demand Performance Bonds as required under this Contract; and

8.1.2.4.3 Legal opinions confirming the capacity and dueauthorisation of the Contractor to enter into the Contract, in form and substance satisfactory to the Employer, such Bonds to be in full force and effect (other than in respect of any condition that requires the Commencement Date to have occurred or the Advance Payment to have been made);

8.1.2.5 The Employer has received from the Contractor the Direct Agreement duly executed and delivered by all parties other than the Employer and the Lenders;

8.1.2.6 The Employer has submitted to the Contractor, reasonable evidence that financial arrangements have been made and are being maintained which will enable the Employer to pay the Contract Price (as estimated at that time) in accordance with Clause13 [*Contract Price and Payment*];

8.1.2.7 The Contractor has provided the Employer with evidence that it has procured the Contractor's Insurances in accordance with the provisions of Clause17[*Insurance*], as are required to be in effect on the date that The Notice to Proceed is issued;

8.1.2.8　The Employer has provided the Contractor with evidence that it has procured the Project Insurances in accordance with the provisions of Clause17 [*Insurance*], as are required to be in effect on the date that The Notice to Proceed is issued;

8.1.2.9　The Employer has received written confirmation from the Contractor that such of the Contractor's Authorisations as are required as a pre-condition to the commencement of the Works have been obtained;

8.1.2.10　That Financial Close has occurred and the Employer has given irrevocable instructions to the Lenders to make the Advance Payment in accordance with Schedule 2 [*Payment Schedule*];

8.1.2.11　The Employer has given the Contractor access to and possession of the Site in accordance with, and to the extent required by, Clause2.1.1; and

8.1.2.12　The Contractor has provided the Employer with a statement that there are noexisting claims for an extension of the Time for Handover or additional costs under the Contract prior to the Commencement Date, and each Party shall use reasonable endeavours to satisfy or procure the satisfaction of such conditions precedent as soon as practicable after the Contract Date. The condition in Clause 8.1.2 (x) may only be waived by the mutual written agreement of the Employer and the Contractor.

8.1.3　On and from the later of the date of issue of the Notice to Proceed and the receipt in cleared funds of the Advance Payment by the Contractor (the "Commencement Date"), the Contractor shall commence carrying out the Works and thereafter proceed with the Works with diligence, due expedition and without delay in accordance with the Contract.

8.1.4　Each Party shall, promptly upon the satisfaction (or waiver by the Party or Parties for whose benefit the conditionexists) of a condition precedent, give the other Party written notice that such condition precedent has been so satisfied (or waived).

8.1.5　If the Employer requires the Contractor to perform limited portions of the Works prior to the issue of the Notice to Proceed, the Employer may issue a notice ("Limited Notice to Proceed") to proceed in respect of only the portion of the Works to be undertaken (the "Limited Works"). The Limited Notice to Proceed will set out the scope, price and timetable for the Limited Works, each of which shall be required to be agreed between the Parties prior to the issue of the Limited Notice to Proceed. The Employer will not be required to give a Limited Notice to Proceed before giving a Notice to Proceed.

8.1.6　If the Commencement Date has not occurred on or before the date falling 12 months after the Contract Date, then the Parties shall discuss in good faith the impact (if any) of such delay on the Contract Price and the Time for Handover.

8.1.7 If the Commencement Date has not occurred on or before the date falling 18 months after the Contract Date:

8.1.7.1 Either Party may terminate this Contract by notice to the other Party and upon the provision of such notice this Contract shall terminate;

8.1.7.2 No compensation shall be due from either Party to the other in respect of the termination of this Contract;

8.1.7.3 The Employer shall immediately return the bid bonds procured by them; and

8.1.7.4 Neither Party shall have any claim against the other for breach or loss of Contract, consequential, indirect or special damages, loss of profit, loss of expectation or other loss arising out of any failure by the Employer to issue the Notice to Proceed or as a result of either Party issuing notice under this Clause 8.1.7.

8.1.8 Notwithstanding the foregoing, the Contractor shall not start any stage of the Works, unless and until all permissions, Contractor's Authorisations, authorisations, consents or other Documents which are required by Law to have been obtained prior to the commencement of that stage of the Works have been obtained.

7.2.4 竣工验收

国际工程项目的验收标准根据不同类型的工程项目而定，各个工程项目的验收标准不同。对于土木工程项目，例如公路、铁路和民用建筑，验收标准较为单一，但在发电厂和制造工厂类的项目中，涉及性能指标考核（performance test）和性能担保（functional guarantee）问题。以日本工程促进协会 ENAA 版合同第 28 条 [性能担保]（Functional Guarantee）条款为例，规定如下：

28.1 The Contractor guarantees that during the Guarantee Test, the Facilities and all parts thereof shall attain the Functional Guarantees specified in the Appendix [Functional Guarantees] to the Contract Agreement, subject to and upon the conditions therein specified.

28.2 If, for reasons attributable to the Contractor, the minimum level of the Functional Guarantees specified in the Appendix [Functional Guarantees] to the Contract Agreement are not met either in whole or in part, the Contractor shall at its cost and expense make such changes, modifications and/or additions to the Plant or any part thereof as may be necessary to meet at least the minimum level of such Guarantees. The Contractor shall notify the Employer upon completion of the necessary changes, modifications and/or additions, and shall request the Employer to repeat the Guarantee Test until the minimum level of the Guarantees has been met. If the Contractor eventually fails to meet the minimum level of Functional Guarantees, the Employer may consider termination of the Contract, pursuant to GCC Sub-Clause 42.2.2.

28.3　If, for reasons attributable to the Contractor, the Functional Guarantees specified in the Appendix [Functional Guarantees] to the Contract Agreement are not attained either in whole or in part, but the minimum level of the Functional Guarantees specified in the said Appendix to the Contract Agreement is met, the Contractor shall, at the Contractor's option, either

(a) make such changes, modifications and/or additions to the Facilities or any part thereof that are necessary to attain the Functional Guarantees at its cost and expense, and shall request the Employer to repeat the Guarantee Test or

(b) pay liquidated damages to the Employer in respect of the failure to meet the Functional Guarantees in accordance with the provisions in the Appendix [Functional Guarantees] to the Contract Agreement.

28.4　The payment of liquidated damages under GCC Sub-Clause 28.3, up to the limitation of liability specified in the Appendix [Functional Guarantees] to the Contract Agreement, shall completely satisfy the Contractor's guarantees under GCC Sub-Clause 28.3, and the Contractor shall have no further liability whatsoever to the Employer in respect thereof. Upon the payment of such liquidated damages by the Contractor, the Project Manager shall issue the Operational Acceptance Certificate for the Facilities or any part thereof in respect of which the liquidated damages have been so paid.

对于太阳能项目而言，试运行试验和性能考核值（performance ratio，PR）试验更为复杂，合同当事方需要在合同中加以特殊约定，举例如下：

COMMISSIONING TESTS AND PR TESTS

Testing of PV Plant：

It will be the EPC contractor's responsibility for arranging all the consumables, instrumentation, material and human resources as required for complete commissioning, start-up tests and performance ratio calculation.

Developer/Developer's independent engineer shall witness all the tests, which shall be conducted prior and post commissioning of the PV plant. Developer/Developer's/Lender's representative shall independently validate all the subsequent test results with the contractually agreed acceptance criteria and shall be in compliance to the agreed acceptance criteria. Key milestones and test procedures are as follows：

Start-up Tests：

The start-up tests shall be the first step for provisional acceptance of plant. These tests shall essentially include：

– Establish peak power (Wp): Prior to conducting any tests, the EPC contractor must establish the total installed peak power of the plant. Peak power measurement shall be carried out at string level for the entire plant using an industry accepted PV analyser. Peak power obtained during test conditions shall be extrapolated to STC conditions to arrive at the plant installed capacity. Accepted deviation in extrapolated peak power and module nameplate power should always be in the range of ±5%. For negative deviations each module in the string shall be checked and any damaged module shall be replaced.

- Open circuit voltage (Voc): This test verifies that strings are properly connected (module and string polarity) and that all modules are producing the expected voltage according to the module data sheet. To measure Voc, the following procedure must be used: (i) Array junction box is opened. (ii) Array Junction box fuses leading to the sub main junction box are removed. (iii) The voltage is measured with a calibrated, industry accepted instrument from the negative bus bar to the module side of the string diode, for each string.

The start-up test shall be carried out immediately after 7 days of physical completion of plant. (Scheduled Completion date)

Provisional Acceptance Test (PAT):

Provisional Acceptance Test shall commence immediately after all issues arising from the start-up test have been rectified. Visual inspection shall be carried out for the entire plant to ensure all installations are in-line with manufacturer recommendations and client's technical specifications. All PV module installations, electrical connections and civil construction will be checked and if found satisfactory, a physical completion certificate will be issued.

The Performance Test at Provisional Acceptance will determine the Actual Corrected Performance Ratio of the Plant.

The facilitiespyranometers must be cleaned before the test commences and then visually inspected for cleanliness during the tests.

The data for the Performance Test report will be collected during a rolling 30 (thirty) Days duration, between sunrise and sunset. In the event the Plant is not fully available for some time during the test period. The respective daily dataset will be skipped and the test period will be extended in order to obtain a full set of data for an equivalent 30 days period with 100% availability. The test should be repeated in case more than 5 days have been skipped, except days that were skipped due to circumstances that are beyond the Contractor's control (e. g. weather or grid faults, etc.). All data collected during PAT shall be shared with the Developer/Developer's representatives. PAT will incorporate the following:

- Availability test: This test verifies the plant availability during operating hours. The test shall be conducted for fifteen days during Provisional Acceptance and for a year for Final Acceptance of the plant. Plant availability will be checked by comparing the energy exported to the grid with corresponding irradiation measured at a time-step of 15 minutes for the test duration. Plant availability shall not, for any given period fall below 99% (as calculated as per the annexure on availability).

- Performance ratio test: The performance ratio (PR) is a measure of the quality of the design and the components of the PV Plant. It is the relationship between the actual produced Energy measured at the Plant's energy meter and Energy theoretically produced by the PV modules. For PR calculation, the plantauxiliary consumption shall be deducted from the energy measured.

The Performance Test Procedure shall determine:
- The Actual Corrected Performance Ratio of the Plant at the time of Provisional Acceptance, to be compared to the Guaranteed Performance Ratio. This is referred to as the Provisional Acceptance Test (PAT).
- The performance test shall be carried out to compare the guaranteed PR and measured PR. Performance Ratio during the acceptance test shall be calculated using the following formula.

$$PR_{PA} = \frac{\sum_j E_{meas,j}}{\sum_j \left[P_{nom} \times (I_{nel}/I_{stc}) \left(1 - \frac{\beta}{100} \times (T_{mod,n} - T_{meas,j})\right)\right]}$$

$E_{meas,j}$ ——Net of energy generation over a period of "j". The net generation is the difference between the Energy exported and the Energy imported recorded at the SCADA integrated ABT meter at the 33kV outgoing feeders located within the plant premises.

P_{nom} ——DC installed capacity (in MWp)

I_{nel} ——Difference of the solar insolation (I_{inc}) on collector plane and Solar Insolation lost (I_{lost}).

I_{stc} ——Insolation at Standard Test Conditions (1000W/m²)

β ——Temperature coefficient from the module data sheet.

$T_{mod,n}$ ——expected average monthly module temperature extracted from PVsyst simulation;

$T_{meas,j}$ ——the average module temperature measured during each Metering Interval j (in ℃).

The PR test shall be conducted as specified below:
- The PR measured on-site shall be compared with the guaranteed performance levels provided by EPC contractor for the specified time period.
- Measuring instruments to record on-site data shall include a calibrated pyranometer with an accuracy of more than or equal to 98%, temperature sensor, data logging systems and operator approved grid meters.
- Contractor shall be responsible for conducting the first PR test (as a part of PAT) only after achieving physical/mechanical completion, synchronizing the plant with the grid, commissioning of fully functional SCADA system and by complying with all relevant requirements from utility and other statutory agencies as per local regulations and policies. Following the acceptance of this PR value, the Developer shall issue a certificate of the operational approval of the Solar PV plant.

- The PR values shall be computed based on actual energy exported to the grid at 33kV side of the substation transformer after deducting theauxiliary consumption of the plant.
- If the Contractor fails to achieve the guaranteed performance levels, the Contractor shall at its own cost rectify all the defects identified during the test and take necessary steps/efforts to pass the PR test within the stipulated time span. Subsequent to rectification the PR shall be re-tested.

Annual PR Measurements:

The duration of the annual PR measurement shall be the 12 month period after the plant acceptance by the Developers.

The procedure for establishing PR will match the procedure described above but will be extended to cover a full 12 month period.

The Performance Test Procedure shall determine:
- The Actual Annual Performance Ratio of the Plant over the full 12 months period following the date of Provisional Acceptance, to be compared to the Guaranteed Annual Performance Ratio.
- The performance test shall be carried out to compare the guaranteed PR and measured PR. Performance Ratio during the acceptance test shall be calculated using the following formula.

$$PR = \frac{\{Energy\ Produced\ (kW \cdot h) - Auxiliary\ Consumption(kW \cdot h)\} \times Irradiance\ at\ STC\left(\frac{kW}{m^2}\right)}{Total\ installed\ capacity(kW \cdot p) \times Irradiation\ on\ inclinded\ plane\left(\frac{kW \cdot h}{m^2}\right)}$$

The plant PLF shall also be computed as part of the annual performance assessment, which will however not be guaranteed by the contractor.

The PLF of a PV power plant (usually expressed as a percentage) is the ratio of the actual output over the period of a year and its output if it had operated at nominal power the entire year, as described in the formula. The plant PLF will be computed using the following formula:

$$PLF = \frac{Energygneraleper\ aum\ (kW \cdot h) - Aullaray\ Consumption(kW \cdot h)}{8760(hours/annum) \times Installed\ Capacity(kW \cdot p)}$$

对于土木工程项目,例如公路项目,竣工验收不涉及机械竣工(mechanical completion),但在发电站和工厂类的工程项目中,则涉及机械竣工及其机械竣工证书的颁发。

[Contractor Letterhead]

MECHANICAL COMPLETION CERTIFICATE (Package)

Dated: _____

Employer's name
Address of Employer
Attention: _____

Re: Engineering, Procurement and Construction Contract-Mechanical Completion (Package)

Gentlemen:

Reference is made to the Engineering, Procurement and Construction Contract, dated _____,20_____, between _____ ("Employer"), a statutory corporation established under the laws of _____ and _____ ("Contractor") (as amended, restated, supplemented, novated or otherwise modified from time to time, the "EPC Contract"). Capitalized terms used but not otherwise defined herein shall have the meanings ascribed thereto in the EPC Contract.

Contractor hereby certifies as follows:

Mechanical Completion of [SPECIFY PACKAGE] (the "Relevant Package") has been achieved.
Each of the Mechanical Completion Conditions for the Relevant Package has been satisfied, namely:

[Note: Add the relevant Mechanical Completion Conditions from the EPC Contract.]

Attached hereto is a report of the Work completed with sufficient detail to enable the Employer to determine whether Mechanical Completion of the Relevant Package has been achieved.

Employer's approval and countersignature of this Mechanical Completion Certificate (Package) shall not in any way modify or alter Contractor's obligations under the EPC Contract.

IN WITNESS WHEREOF, Contractor has caused this Mechanical Completion Certificate (Package) to be executed by its duly authorized representative on the date first above written.

The Contractor:

By _____
  Name:
  Title:

Employer hereby (a) accepts the foregoing Mechanical Completion Certificate (Package) for purposes of Section _____ of the EPC Contract, it being understood that such acceptance shall not be deemed an acknowledgement that any of the matters certified above are correct [except that Mechanical Completion (Package) has been achieved] and (b) acknowledges that the Mechanical Completion Date of the Relevant Package is _____.

The Employer:

By _____
 Name:
 Title:
 Date:

7.2.5 保险

1. 保险种类和要求

世界上绝大多数国家对于保险都有法定要求，如：保险种类、强制保险种类、保险税/费、对出单公司的要求、对再保险公司评级的要求等。承包商或者分包商在项目初期就需要了解项目所在国的保险法定要求，或委托专门机构，例如国际保险经纪公司提供专业分析报告。

涉及当地相关法律保险要求主要有四个方面：

（1）强制保险要求。例如机动车辆第三方责任保险是典型的强制保险。此险种无论在承包工程合同中是否体现，都是承包商或分包商必须购买的保险。

（2）当地法律是否承认非当地注册保险公司（一般为境外保险公司）签发的为当地项目提供保险保障的保单。一般而言，大多数第三世界国家都要求必须是当地注册的保险公司才能为当地项目提供保险保障，境外保险公司提供的保险单不合法，且将来在工程完工后，税收扣减也可能发生问题，但有些国家另有规定的除外。

（3）有些国家为保护本国保险市场，对于当地保险市场承担风险的份额有强制要求，即：当地保险市场必须承担不低于一定比例的份额。

（4）对再保险公司的评级。需要注意的是，很多国家对再保险公司有最低评级要求，通常为不低于标准普尔 A - 或其他国际评级公司（穆迪、惠誉或 A. M. Best）相当于标准普尔 A - 的评级。

国际工程承包合同一般都规定了业主对保险的要求，包括：

（1）保险范围：保险应该包括对工程、材料、生产设备和承包商设备、第三方责任、除工程外承包商对业主财产损失的赔偿责任等，保险单的适用范围，如司法管辖范围、保单地域范围要求等。

（2）险种：建设期的建筑工程一切险、安装工程一切险、第三方责任险、施工机具保险（大部分国家采用单独保单承保）、工伤/劳工赔偿保险、货运险、机动车辆第三方责任险、职业责任保险，和运营期的财产一切保险和公众责任保险等。

（3）险种适用情况。

1）建筑工程一切险：主要用于土木工程为主的工程项目，例如公路、铁路、隧道、桥梁和码头等。

2）安装工程一切险：主要用于涉及大型成套设备安装的承包工程项目，例如燃煤电厂、燃气电厂、大型水电站、水泥厂、炼油厂、化工厂和化肥厂等。

建筑工程一切险与安装工程一切险保险条款略有不同。

3）第三方责任保险/综合责任保险：主要针对工程第三方责任的保险。

4）施工机具保险：主要承保承包商施工机具，大部分国家采用单独保单承保。

5）工伤/劳工赔偿保险：需要根据项目所在国法定要求以及当地市场惯例，并参考国内法规要求办理。

6）货运保险：承保大型设备、工程材料以及承包商施工机具在运输过程中发生的自然灾害和意外事故损失。特别需要注意的是货物在东道国内陆运输的风险，建议在货运保险项下妥善安排。

7）机动车辆第三方保险：通常为当地强制保险，需要注意的是，承包商在当地租用车辆时，需要租赁公司或车主提供上述保单，否则承包商须自行购买，以满足当地法规要求。

8）职业责任保险（professional indemnity insurance）：有些国家的项目可能会要求投保以该国司法管辖或第三国司法管辖为基础的职业责任保险，保险期间从工期加质保期至十几年不等。上述险种投保比较复杂，承包商应在正式投标前向专业的国际保险经纪公司咨询。在欧洲和美洲地区，如承包商负责设计，工程合同均规定承包商需要为其设计投保职业责任保险。因此，承包商应向保险公司投保该险种，并向业主递交有关保险证明和交纳保费的收据。

9）财产一切险：部分项目完工后需要承包商运营一段时间，因此需要投保财产一切险，承包商可根据合同要求咨询专业的国际保险经纪公司。

10）十年民事责任险：在法语区国家，在工程合同中一般会要求承包商投保十年民事责任险，以保障建筑物建成后出现的潜在缺陷（latent defects）及其造成的损失。

（4）保险公司：有些项目业主在工程合同中指定了当地保险公司。

（5）再保险：有些项目业主在工程合同中指定了再保险公司（一般为国家再保险公司），如需安排再保险，需要优先考虑当地再保险公司、区域性再保险公司，同时，还需要对再保险公司规模、再保险公司国际评级等设定要求。

（6）保险经纪公司：对于保险经纪公司在当地开展业务，尤其是协助客户在当地招标选定保险公司，有些国家要求保险经纪公司必须持有当地合法的保险经纪牌照，在选择保险经纪公司协助其投保业务时，承包商需要了解该公司在当地是否持有合法牌照。

（7）保险生效：一般而言，在土木工程中，业主签发开工令前就需要承包商提供保险证明文件，但部分项目由于前期工作时间较短，无法按期完成保险安排。这时承包商可以在当地保险经纪公司的协助下，与当地保险公司协商先出具保险凭证，以保证工程顺利开工。另外，有些险种可能在当地保险市场难以购买，因此，需要承包商或保险经纪公司在合同谈判时就向业主说明，与业主协商由业主购买相关保险，或在承包合同中取消上述保险要求，或请保险经纪公司到国际保险市场上购买。

业主在施工合同中可能要求承包商购买某些特殊险种，如十年期民事责任保险、缺陷责任保险和职业责任保险等。如合同要求承包商投保此类保险，承包商应咨询保险公司或保险经纪公司。

除上述国际工程合同中明确规定的保险外,承包商还可以投保货物运输险、社会福利险、战争险、投资险或其他政治风险保险。

承包商在办理与工程项目有关的保险时,应注意如下问题:

(1) 保险公司的赔付能力。

(2) 保险公司的信誉。

(3) 是否可选择国内保险公司投保。

承包商在投保时,应如实填报保险公司的调查表格,认真审核保险条款,包括保险范围、除外责任、保险期间、保险金额、免赔额、赔偿限额、保险费、被保险人的义务、索赔、赔款、争议和仲裁等。承包商在签订保险合同时应与保险公司逐条修改或补充,取得共同一致的意见,注意保护自身的权益。通常,对于国际工程项目,特别是大中型或复杂的项目,国际上通行的做法是聘请专业的、国际保险经纪公司协助办理各类保险。

2. 保险要求

在投标和合同谈判过程中,承包商需要了解工程项目的保险要求。为此,需要在合同条款的基础上确定具体的险种、保险金额、免赔额等。最好的方法是在合同中以附件的形式明确保险要求,以某国际工程项目为例,如下:

Schedule XX-Insurance Requirements

Insurances to be Taken Out by the Contractor:

In accordance with the provisions of Clause 18, the Contractor shall at its expense take out and maintain in effect, or cause to be taken out and maintained in effect, during the performance of the Contract, the insurances set forth below in the sums and with the deductibles and other conditions specified. The identity of the insurers and the form of the policies shall be subject to the approval of the Employer, such approval not to be unreasonably withheld.

(a) Cargo Insurance

Covering loss or damage occurring, while in transit from the supplier's or manufacturer's works or stores until arrival at the Site, and to the construction equipment to be provided by the Contractor or its Subcontractors.

Amount	Deductible Limits	Parties Insured	From	To
[in currency/currencies]	[in currency/currencies]	[name]	[place]	[place]
110% of the Contract Price	—	The Employer	Supplier's or manufacturer's works or stores	The Project Site in the Country

(b) Installation All Risks Insurance

Covering physical loss or damage to the Project at the Site, occurring prior to Final Acceptance Certificate, with an extended maintenance coverage for the Contractor's liability in respect of any loss or damage occurring during the defect liability period while the Contractor is on the Site for the purpose of performing its obligations during the defect liability period.

Amount	Deductible Limits	Parties Insured
[in currency/currencies]	[in currency/currencies]	[names]
100% of the Contract Price		The Employer and Contractor/Subcontractors

(c) Third Party Liability Insurance

Covering bodily injury or death suffered by third parties (including the Employer's Personnel) and loss of or damage to property (including the Employer's property and any parts of the Facilities that have been accepted by the Employer) occurring in connection with the supply and installation of the Facilities.

Amount	Deductible Limits	Parties Insured
[in currency/currencies]	[in currency/currencies]	[names]
USD 1.0 million	—	The Employer

(d) Automobile Liability Insurance

Covering use of all vehicles used by the Contractor or its Subcontractors (whether or not owned by them) in connection with the supply and installation of the Facilities. Comprehensive insurance is in accordance with statutory requirements.

(e) Workers' Compensation Insurance

Be in accordance with the statutory requirements applicable in any country where the Facilities or any part thereof is executed.

(f) Employer's Liability Insurance

Be in accordance with the statutory requirements applicable in any country where the Facilities or any part thereof is executed.

(g) Other Insurances

The Contractor is also required to take out and maintain at its own cost the following insurances:

Details:

Amount	Deductible Limits	Parties Insured
[in currency/currencies]	[in currency/currencies]	[names]

The Employer shall be named as the co-insured under all insurance policies taken out by the Contractor pursuant to Clause 18, except for the Workers' Compensation and Employer's Liability Insurances, and the Contractor's Subcontractors shall be named as co-insureds under all insurance policies taken out by the Contractor pursuant to Clause 18, except for the Cargo, Workers' Compensation and Employer's Liability Insurances. All insurer's rights of subrogation against such co-insureds for losses or claims arising out of the performance of the Contract shall be waived under such policies.

7.2.6 现场移交计划

在国际工程项目中,合同通常规定业主应移交现场给承包商,即在开工通知发出前给予承包商现场进入权和现场占有权,例如 FIDIC 合同条款 1999 年第 1 版第 2.1 款 [现场进入权] 的规定。如果业主未能在开工日期之前给予承包商现场进入权和现场占有权,承包商有权根据合同规定要求工期延长和/或额外费用。如果合同没有类似现场进入权的规定,则合同中也包括一项默示条款,即业主也应在签订合同后的合理时间内向承包商移交现场占有权。《哈德逊论建筑和工程合同》写道:

"Since a sufficient degree of possession of the site is clearly a necessary preconditions of the Contractor's performance, there must be an implied term that the site will be handed over to the Contractor within a reasonable time of signing the contract[⊖]."

大型国际工程项目,特别是线性工程项目,例如公路、铁路等以及占地面积大的工程项目,在业主无法同时将现场进入权和现场占有权移交给承包商的情况下,应在合同中拟定现场移交计划(Site Hand-Over Plan),规定在一定期限内或某个具体日期之前移交现场给承包商,例如:

Km0-Km50: within 3 months from the Commencement Date;
Km50-Km100: within 6 months from the Commencement Date;
Km100-Km200: within 6 months from the Commencement Date;
All other sections: within 3 months from the Commencement Date.

7.2.7 许可

在国际工程合同中,特别是涉及项目融资的国际工程项目,业主和承包商应明确办理许可的义务,如在合同中以附件形式规定哪些许可由业主办理,哪些许可由承包商办理。由于许可是项目开工的前提条件,应由谁办理许可为避免业主和承包商之间发生争议,有必要在合同中以附件形式约定许可办理的要求,举例如下:

Schedule XX: Permits

The Employer shall assist the Contractor for all permits, approvals and/or licenses from all local, state or national government authorities or public service undertakings in the Country, as follows:

(1) the Employer shall acquire and pay for the following permits, licenses and approvals or any other documents of same nature obtained or to be obtained by the Employer:

(a) land utilization permits for the area of the Works;

(b) environmental licenses;

(c) any permits, licenses and approvals to be obtained by the Employer as set forth in the Concession Agreements.

[⊖] Para 3-089, page 456, Hudson's Building and Engineering Contracts. 14th Ed. Sweet & Maxwell. 2019.

> (2) upon receiving the Contractor's requests, the Employer shall assist the Contractor to acquire the permits, licenses and approvals or any other documents which are required to proceed with the Works.
>
> The Contractor shall acquire and pay for all permits, approvals and/or licenses from all local, state or national government authorities or public service undertakings in the Country, as follows:
>
> (1) Permits, licenses and approvals or any other documents of same nature obtained by the Contractor:
>
>   (a) All Building Contractor and Consultancy Services licenses, as foreseen in Decree 94/2013 dated 31 December 2013 and Ministerial Diplomas 77/2015 and 76/2015 dated 22 May 2015 and remaining applicable legislation in force, required to execute all the Contract Works, as agreed by the Parties;
>
>   (b) quarry permits;
>
>   (c) design approval for overpass of the existing railway;
>
>   (d) explosive utilization permits;
>
>   (e) transportation permits to pass through the existing bridge; and
>
>   (f) any permits, licenses and approvals to be obtained by the Contractor to perform its activities in Mozambique.

在上例中，业主需要办理土地使用许可、环境许可和需要业主办理的其他许可。承包商办理工程所在国法律要求的所有建筑承包商和咨询服务许可、料场开采许可、跨越现有铁路跨线桥设计批准、炸药使用许可、通过现有桥梁的运输许可以及承包商应取得的其他许可等。

有些国际工程项目还需要承包商办理施工许可，承包商应根据所在国的法律规定办理工程的施工许可。在分包工程项目中，可根据分包合同义务的划分，由承包商办理施工许可和环境许可，以便分包商进行施工。不得不说，在某些国家或地区，办理环境许可是一件非常麻烦的事情，因此，业主应负责办理环境许可，承包商负责提供其工程范围内可以提供的资料给业主，或者，在承包商负责办理环境许可的情况下，承包商应聘请当地的工程设计咨询公司完善工程设计和环境保护要求，使得设计和施工符合当地的环境保护要求，保证取得环境许可。

7.2.8 工期延长条款

在国际工程合同中，一般均会规定竣工时间延长(Extension of Time for Completion)条款，约定在哪些情况下承包商可以获得竣工时间的延长，即工期延长(Extension Of Time，EOT)。一般而言，承包商可以有权获得工期延长的因素如下：

(1) 工程变更。

(2) 工程数量的实质性变化。

(3) 合同条款中规定的可以要求工期延长的延误事件。

(4) 极端恶劣的气候条件(exceptional adverse climate conditions)。

(5) 由于传染病或政府行为导致的人员或货物的不可预见的短缺。

(6) 因业主原因导致的任何延误、妨碍或阻碍。

由于上述原因造成的工期延长，承包商有权索赔工期延长，在FIDIC合同中，承包商还有权索赔相应的额外费用。例如，FIDIC 合同条款 1999 年第 1 版红皮书和黄皮书第 8.4 款［竣工时间延长］规定：

"8.4 Extension of Time for Completion

The Contractor shall be entitled subject to Sub-Clause 20.1 [*Contractor's Claims*] to an extension of the Time for Completion if and to the extent that completion for the purposes of Sub-Clause 10.1 [*Taking Over of the Works and Sections*] is or will be delayed by any of the following causes:

(a) a Variation (unless an adjustment to the Time for Completion has been agreed under Sub-Clause 13.3 [*Variation Procedure*]) or other substantial change in the quantity of an item of work included in the Contract;

(b) a cause of delay giving an entitlement to extension of time under a Sub-Clause of these Conditions;

(c) exceptionally adverse climatic conditions;

(d) Unforeseeable shortages in the availability of personnel or Goods caused by epidemic or governmental actions; or

(e) any delay, impediment or prevention caused by or attributable to the Employer, the Employer's Personnel, or the Employer's other contractors on the Site.

If the Contractor considers himself to be entitled to an extension of the Time for Completion, the Contractor shall give notice to the Engineer in accordance with Sub-Clause 20.1 [*Contractor's Claims*]. When determining each extension of time under Sub-Clause 20.1, the Engineer shall review previous determinations and may increase, but shall not decrease, the total extension of time."

除了 FIDIC 合同条款 1999 年第 1 版红皮书和黄皮书第 8.4 款［竣工时间的延长］规定的承包商可以获得工期延长的事件外，在 FIDIC 合同条款 1999 年第 1 版银皮书第 14 款中，承包商有权获得的工期延长事件只有 3 项：

（1）工程变更。

（2）根据本条款某款，有权获得延长期的原因。

（3）由业主、业主人员、或在现场的业主的其他承包商造成或引起。

与 FIDIC 合同条款 1999 年第 11 版红皮书和黄皮书第 8.4 款相比，在银皮书第 8.4 款中，承包商有权获得工期延长的原因少了工程数量的实质变化、极端恶劣的气候条件以及由于传染病或政府行为导致的人员或货物不可预见的短缺。因此，承包商在使用 FIDIC 合同 1999 年第 1 版银皮书时应特别予以注意。

在日本工程促进协会 ENAA 版合同中，第 40 条［竣工时间延长］对于承包商有权获得工期延长的原因做了更多的规定，包括：

（1）不可抗力。

（2）业主发出的暂停施工指示。

（3）法律变更。

(4) 分包商延误，但分包商的延误可归于承包商有权索赔工期延长的原因。

日本工程促进协会 ENAA 版合同中，第 40 条 [竣工时间延长] 规定如下：

"40.1 The Time(s) for Completion specified in the SCC shall be extended if the Contractor is delayed or impeded in the performance of any of its obligations under the Contract by reason of any of the following:

(a) any Change in the Facilities as provided in GCC Clause 39;

(b) any occurrence of Force Majeure as provided in GCC Clause 37, unforeseen conditions as provided in GCC Clause 35, or other occurrence of any of the matters specified or referred to in paragraphs (a), (b) and (c) of GCC Sub-Clause 32.2;

(c) any suspension order given by the Employer under GCC Clause 41 hereof or reduction in the rate of progress pursuant to GCC Sub-Clause 41.2; or

(d) any changes in laws and regulations as provided in GCC Clause 36; or

(e) any default or breach of the Contract by the Employer, or any activity, act or omission of the Employer, or the Project Manager, or any other contractors employed by the Employer; or

(f) any other matter specifically mentioned in the Contract;

(g) any delay on the part of a sub-contractor, provided such delay is due to a cause for which the Contractor himself would have been entitled to an extension of time under this Sub-Clause by such period as shall be fair and reasonable in all the circumstances and as shall fairly reflect the delay or impediment sustained by the Contractor.

40.2 Except where otherwise specifically provided in the Contract, the Contractor shall submit to the Project Manager a notice of a claim for an extension of the Time for Completion, together with particulars of the event or circumstance justifying such extension as soon as reasonably practicable after the commencement of such event or circumstance. As soon as reasonably practicable after receipt of such notice and supporting particulars of the claim, the Employer and the Contractor shall agree upon the period of such extension. In the event that the Contractor does not accept the Employer's estimate of a fair and reasonable time extension, the Contractor shall be entitled to refer the matter to a Dispute Board, pursuant to GCC Sub-Clause 45.3.

40.3 The Contractor shall at all times use its reasonable efforts to minimize any delay in the performance of its obligations under the Contract.

In all cases where the Contractor has given a notice of a claim for an extension of time under GCC 40.2, the Contractor shall consult with the Project Manager in order to determine the steps (if any) which can be taken to overcome or minimize the actual or anticipated delay. The Contractor shall there after comply with all reasonable instructions which the Project Manager shall give in order to minimize such delay. If compliance with such instructions shall cause the Contractor to incur extra costs and the Contractor is entitled to an extension of time under GCC 40.1, the amount of such extra costs shall be added to the Contract Price."

需要注意的是，日本工程促进协会 ENAA 版合同规定了承包负有减轻延误影响的义务。虽然 FIDIC 1999 年第 1 版合同条款第 8.4 款［竣工时间的延长］没有规定承包商负有减轻延误影响的义务，但在很多法律和判例中，承包商负有减轻延误影响的义务。

在国际工程实践中，对于承包商遇到合同条款中列明的工期延误原因，承包商的权利并非像 FIDIC 1999 年第 1 版合同条款第 8.4 款［竣工时间的延长］约定的那样可以索赔工期延长和额外费用。在某些业主修改的专用合同条款或者涉及项目融资的工程项目中，承包商只有索赔工期延长的权利，但没有索赔额外费用的权利，举例如下：

8.4 Extension of Time

8.4.1 Subject to Clauses 8.4.2 to 8.4.9 (inclusive) and 19.1 [Contractor's Claims], the Contractor shall only be entitled to an extension of time to the extent any of the following causes results or will result in the Handover Date being delayed beyond the Time for Handover：

(i) any occurrence of a Force Majeure event, in accordance with Clause 18 [*Force Majeure*]；

(ii) any Variation directed by the Employer, in accordance with Clause 12 [*Variations and Adjustments*] (unless an adjustment to the Time for Handover has been agreed under Clause 12.4 [*Variation Procedure*] in respect of such Variation)；

(iii) any permitted Statutory Modification, in accordance with Clause 12.6 [*Adjustments for Changes in Legislation*]；

(iv) any suspension directed by the Employer, in accordance with Clause 8.7 [*Suspension of Work*], except to the extent that such suspension is caused by an act or omission of the Contractor which is not expressly permitted under this Contract；

(v) the Contractor following the Employer's instructions issued in accordance with Clause 4.23 [*Fossils*]; or

(vi) any delay, impediment or prevention caused by or attributable to the Employer, the Employer's Personnel, the Employer's other contractors on the Site or the Employer's Equipment Suppliers; and

(vii) any delay giving an entitlement under this Contract to an extension to the Time for Handover；

save in each case to the extent that any such delay is due to any act, neglect, omission or default of the Contractor, or any person for whom the Contractor is responsible in accordance with this Contract.

8.4.2 If the Contractor considers that it is entitled to an extension of the Time for Handover, the Contractor shall give notice to the Employer in accordance with Clause 19.1 [*Contractor's Claims*].

8.4.3 In determining any extension of time, the Employer may consider any omission of any work permitted or instructed under this Contract and, in the event of an extension of time relating to Adverse Weather Conditions, work that could continue at locations other than the part of the Site affected by the Adverse Weather Conditions.

8.4.4 The Contractor shall not be entitled to an extension to the Time for Handover to the extent that the applicable delay is caused by the Contractor failing to comply with its obligations under Clause 4.5[*Interfaces*] or to the extent that the applicable delay is occurring concurrently with any delay caused by the Contractor or for which it is responsible under the Contract which results or will result in the Handover Date being delayed beyond the Time for Handover.

8.4.5 The Employer may at any time review all relevant circumstances and revise or confirm by notification to the Contractor any previous decision given by it in relation to any claim by the Contractor for an extension of time and/or elect to grant an extension of the Time for Handover, notwithstanding that the Contractor has failed to comply with the requirements as to the giving of notices and provision of information under this Clause 8.4.

8.4.6 If the Employer declines to grant an extension of time and fix a revised Time for Handover or if the Contractor considers that a different Time for Handover should be fixed, then either Party shall be entitled to refer the matter for determination in accordance with the procedures set out in Clause 19[*Claims, Disputes and Arbitration*].

8.4.7 The Contractor shall be entitled to be paid its Costs that are necessarily incurred together with Reasonable Profit where the Contractor has been granted an extension of time for the events specified in Clause 8.4.1 (iv) or (vi). The Contractor shall not be entitled to be paid its Costs in the event of an extension of time relating to the other events or circumstances specified in Clause 8.4.1, unless the relevant Clause entitling the Contractor to make such claim expressly states that the Contractor may also claim its Costs, and, if specified, Reasonable Profit.

8.4.8 The Contractor shall use all reasonable endeavours and act in accordance with Good Engineering and Construction Practices to eliminate or minimise any delay in achieving the Handover Date beyond the Time for Handover.

8.4.9 The Contractor shall have no claim for any extension of time or in respect of delay save as and to the extent set out in this Clause 8.4.

7.2.9 工期延误违约金/误期损害赔偿金条款

在国际工程合同中,工期延误违约金上限通常为合同金额5%~15%,视工程项目规模而定。对于规模和投资中小型项目,承包商可接受的范围一般是10%~15%;在国际金融组织融资的工程项目中通常为10%,大型或特大型国际工程项目,例如合同金额超过5亿美元时,则应降低工期延误违约金的比例,以5%~10%为上限。

除工期延误违约金上限外,国际工程合同还约定承包商工期每延误一天、一周或一个月的百分比或具体金额,例如每天 0.05% 或者 10 万美元等。以 FIDIC 施工合同(红皮书)1999 年第 1 版为例,工期延误违约金规定如下:

"8.7 Delay Damages

If the Contractor fails to comply with Sub-Clause 8.2 [*Time for Completion*], the Contractor shall subject to Sub-Clause 2.5 [*Employer's Claims*] pay delay damages to the Employer for this default. These delay damages shall be the sum stated in the Appendix to Tender, which shall be paid for every day which shall elapse between the relevant Time for Completion and the date stated in the Taking-Over Certificate. However, the total amount due under this Sub-Clause shall not exceed the maximum amount of delay damages (if any) stated in the Appendix to Tender.

These delay damages shall be the only damages due from the Contractor for such default, other than in the event of termination under Sub-Clause 15.2 [*Termination by Employer*] prior to completion of the Works. These damages shall not relieve the Contractor from his obligation to complete the works, or from any other duties, obligations or responsibilities which he may have under the Contract."

由于 FIDIC 合同条款 1999 年第 1 版系列第 8.7 款[误期损失赔偿金]没有规定具体的赔偿金比例或金额,而在专用合同条款中规定了具体比例或金额,举例如下:

Part A-Contract Data

Conditions	Sub-Clause	Data
Delay Damages for the Works	8.7 & 14.15 (b)	0.1% of the Contract Price per day.

上述误期损害赔偿金,第 8.7 款规定为每天合同价格的 0.1%。不得不说,该比例适用于合同金额较小的项目,例如 3000 万美元以下的项目,但对于合同金额较大的项目,每天为合同金额的 0.1%,则明显过高。承包商如何判断工期延误违约金的高低,应在投标或合同谈判中根据合同金额具体判断,即业主给出的每天或每周的工期延误违约金百分比乘以合同金额得出每天或每周的违约金金额,然后计算出延误多少天达到合同规定的工期延误违约金责任上限,例如 10%,如果 100 天即达到工期延误违约金上限,则可以判断工期延误违约金占合同金额的百分比或者合同约定的每天的工期延误违约金金额过高。一般而言,工期延误违约金达到违约金上限 10%,应大致在 6 个月左右,即 180 天左右视为合理范围。如果 360 天后才能达到 10% 上限,则可能工期延误违约金占合同金额百分比过低,或者每天工期延误违约金金额过低,无法对承包商起到按期履约的作用。

在某些涉及项目融资的国际工程合同中,合同约定的工期延误违约金条款如下:

> 8.6.2 The Contractor shall, subject to prior notification by the Employer pursuant to Clause 8.6.1, be liable for and shall pay or allow on demand, without set-off or counterclaim, to the Employer liquidated damages in the amount of US $750,000 ("Delay Liquidated

Damages") for each day or part day for the period commencing on the day immediately following the Time for Handover and expiring on the Handover Date.

8.6.3 The amounts due in respect of Delay Liquidated Damages shall be subject to the applicable limitation of liability pursuant to Clause 16.6[*Limitation of Liability*].

8.6.4 Any Delay Liquidated Damages paid or allowed pursuant to Clause 8.6.1 shall be repaid to the Contractor to the extent that the Contractor receives any extension of time in accordance with Clause 8.4[*Extension of Time*] in respect of the period to which such Delay Liquidated Damages relate.

承包商支付的工期延误违约金应受合同规定的承包商责任上限（limitation of liability）的限制，即不能超过合同规定的责任上限金额。同时，如果承包商获得了工期延长，则业主应将已扣除的工期延误违约金按照其同意的工期延长期限相对应的金额返还给承包商，即使合同中没有如此规定，例如 FIDIC 系列合同条款，则法律和相关判例也要求业主返还其扣留的应予返还的工期延误违约金。

7.2.10 风险分担条款

对于国际工程项目中的风险分担，以 FIDIC 合同条款为代表的国际工程合同格式给出了具体的答案，即 FIDIC 合同 1999 年第 1 版红皮书第 17.3 款 [业主风险] 中列明的风险，这些风险包括：

（1）战争、敌对行动（不论宣战与否）、入侵、外敌行动。

（2）工程所在国内的叛乱、恐怖主义、革命、暴动、军事政变或篡夺政权，以及内战。

（3）承包商人员及承包商和分包商的其他雇员以外的人员，在工程所在国内的骚动、喧闹或混乱。

（4）工程所在国内的战争军火、爆炸物资、电离辐射或放射性引起的污染，但可能由承包商使用此类军火、炸药、辐射或放射性引起的除外。

（5）由音速或超音速飞行的飞机或飞行装置所产生的压力波。

（6）除合同规定以外业主使用或占有的永久工程的任何部分。

（7）由业主人员或业主对其负责的其他人员所做的工程任何部分的设计。

（8）不可预见的或不能合理预期的、一个有经验的承包商已采取适宜预防措施的任何自然力的作用。

FIDIC 1999 年第 1 版红皮书对于业主风险的列举，实际上界定了业主风险的范围，一般而言，在业主风险范围之外以及合同规定应由业主履行义务之外的风险应由承包商承担。

对于业主风险的后果，FIDIC 红皮书第 17.4 款 [业主风险后果] 规定承包商有权索赔相应的工期延长和额外费用。FIDIC 红皮书第 17.3 款 [业主的风险] 和第 17.4 款 [业主风险的后果] 规定如下：

"17.3 Employer's Risks

The risks referred to in Sub-Clause 17.4 below are:

(a) war, hostilities (whether war be declared or not), invasion, act of foreign enemies;
(b) rebellion, terrorism, revolution, insurrection, military or usurped power or civil war, within the Country;
(c) riot, commotion or disorder within the Country by persons other than the Contractor's Personnel and other employees of the Contractor and Subcontractors;
(d) munitions of war, explosive materials, ionising radiation or contamination by radio-activity, within the Country, except as may be attributable to the Contractor's use of such munitions, explosives, radiation or radio-activity, and
(e) pressure waves caused by aircraft or other aerial devices traveling at sonic or supersonic speeds;
(f) use or occupation by the Employer of any part of the Permanent Works, except as may be specified in the Contract;
(g) design of any part of the Works by the Employer's personnel or by others for whom the Employer is responsible, and
(h) any operation of the forces of nature which is Unforeseeable or against which an experienced contractor could not reasonably have been expected to have taken adequate preventative precautions.

17.4 Consequence of Employer's Risks

If and to the extent that any of the risks listed in Sub-Clause 17.3 above results in loss or damage to the Works, Goods or Contractor's Documents, the Contractor shall promptly give notice to the Engineer and shall rectify this loss or damage to the extent required by the Engineer.

If the Contractor suffers delay and/or incurs Cost from rectifying this loss or damage, the Contractor shall give a further notice to the Engineer and shall be entitled subject to Sub-Clause 20.1 [*Contractor's Claims*] to:

(a) an extension of time for any such delay, if completion is or will be delayed, under Sub-Clause 8.4 [*Extension of Time for Completion*], and
(b) payment of any such Cost, which shall be added to the Contract Price. In the case of sub-paragraphs;
(f) and (g) of Sub-Clause 17.3 [*Employer's Risks*], reasonable profit on the Cost shall also be included.

After receiving this further notice, the Engineer shall proceed in accordance with Sub-Clause 3.5 [*Determinations*] to agree or determine these matters."

7.2.11 违约责任上限

在国际工程合同中，承包商违约责任上限是一个非常重要的条款。如果承包商违约，则承包商承担的损害赔偿金额将不能超过违约责任上限，通常只包括直接损失，但欺诈

（fraud）、故意违约（deliberate default）和轻率不当行为（reckless misconduct）除外。上述除外条款意味着当事一方可以向对方索赔违约责任以上的损害赔偿金额。

以 FIDIC 合同条款为代表的国际工程合同格式规定了责任限额，即承包商对业主的全部责任不应超过专用条款规定的总额，或者如果专用条款没有规定总额，则为中标合同金额。FIDIC 合同条款1999年第1版红皮书第17.6款［责任限度］规定：

"17.6 Limitation of Liability

Neither Party shall be liable to the other Party for loss of use of any Works, loss of profit, loss of any contract or for any indirect or consequential loss or damage which may be suffered by the other Party in connection with the Contract, other than under Sub-Clause 16.4 [*Payment on Termination*] and Sub-Clause 17.1 [*Indemnities*].

The total liability of the Contractor to the Employer, under or in connection with the Contract other than under Sub-Clause 4.19 [*Electricity, Water and Gas*], Sub-Clause 4.20 [*Employer's Equipment and Free-Issue Material*], Sub-Clause 17.1 [*Indemnities*] and Sub-Clause 17.5 [*Intellectual and Industrial Property Rights*], shall not exceed the sum stated in the Particular Conditions or (if a sum is not so stated) the Accepted Contract Amount.

This Sub-Clause shall not limit liability in any case of fraud, deliberate default or reckless misconduct by the defaulting Party."

日本工程促进协会 ENAA 版合同第30条［责任限额］规定：

30. Limitation of Liability
30.1 Except in cases of criminal negligence or willful misconduct,
   (a) the Contractor shall not be liable to the Employer, whether in contract, tort, or otherwise, for any indirect or consequential loss or damage, loss of use, loss of production, or loss of profits or interest costs, provided that this exclusion shall not apply to any obligation of the Contractor to pay liquidated damages to the Employer and;
   (b) the aggregate liability of the Contractor to the Employer, whether under the Contract, in tort or otherwise, shall not exceed a multiple of the Contract Price specified in the SCC or, if a multiple is not so specified, the total Contract Price, provided that this limitation shall not apply to the cost of repairing or replacing defective equipment, or to any obligation of the Contractor to indemnify the Employer with respect to patent infringement.

日本 ENAA 版合同第30条［责任限额］规定承包商对于业主的全部责任应为专用合同条款中规定的合同价格的百分比，例如100%、50%或者任何一个百分比，如果没有规定此百分比，则应为合同总额（total Contract Price）。

承包商是否可以接受高于中标合同价格的责任上限，在国际工程实践中，由于业主公开招标的合同条款规定如此，承包商在投标时只能响应招标要求，接受招标文件中规定的责任上限。但是，一般而言，承包商不应接受违约责任高于中标合同价格的上限，承包商应在投标答疑中或合同谈判中明确指出违约责任上限问题，力争低于中标合同金额的违约责任上限。

7.2.12 税务条款

无论是承包商还是分包商，应对税务问题给予极大的关注。在国际工程项目中，承包商面临的主要税务问题包括：

(1) 进口永久性货物和设备的关税及其关税上的进口增值税。
(2) 进口承包商的施工设备和配件的关税及其关税上的进口增值税。
(3) 增值税。
(4) 预提税。
(5) 个人所得税。
(6) 企业所得税。

在处理分包合同增值税时，承包商和分包商应明确以下思路。

(1) 业主免承包商增值税，但承包商必须向分包商支付增值税，并由分包商出具增值税票，承包商的进项增值税和销项增值税相抵，处理在税务上的增值税事宜。参见上述印度尼西亚案例。此外，在上案中，如果印度尼西亚政府不免除承包商向分包商支付增值税，则承包商需要向分包商支付增值税。在这种情况下，承包商受到的影响是：

1) 因承包商需要向分包商支付增值税，而承包商从业主处无法获得增值税的支付，因此导致承包商现金流增加。承包商需要先行向分包商支付增值税，然后才能从税务机关进行增值税进项和销项税抵扣。

2) 可能导致承包商遭受损失。在某些国家，增值税退税需要支付一定费用，因此，承包商可能损失这笔费用。

(2) 根据有些国家法律的规定，例如孟加拉税法第52条规定，增值税采用代扣代缴制。工程师在签发期中付款证书时扣除增值税和预提所得税8.5%，然后承包商在分包商的期中付款证书中扣除相应的8.5%增值税和所得税。在这种情况下，承包商应履行税法规定的代扣代缴义务，并向税务局支付相应的增值税和所得税。

(3) 在采用机打发票的国家，例如中国、埃塞俄比亚等国，分包商在向承包商开具发票时，税控系统按照增值税税率自动计算增值税，然后税务局从分包商的账户中划拨相应的增值税金额，完成纳税义务。

在一些不发达国家，特别是非洲国家，承包商可向税务局或当地财政部申请免除增值税，以避免承包商现金流负担和退税损失风险。

承包商和分包商应关注的第二个税务问题是分包合同价格是否应包括增值税及其所有税和费的问题。一般而言，分包合同应包括增值税及其所有税和费。但是，在承包商获得税务减免的情况下，例如关税，则承包商应给予分包商同样的关税减免待遇。

承包商需要牢记的是，如合同中规定给予承包商免税待遇，但承包商不能将其理解为业主免除了个人所得税和企业所得税。对于增值税，也需要在合同谈判时确实落实增值税的减免规定，而不是简单理解为免除。这不仅会造成合同价格中缺少增值税金额，造成价格缺陷，而且还会导致承包商在履约过程中支付增值税，导致承包商损失。

日本工程促进协会 ENAA 版合同第 14 条对税务和关税规定如下：

14. Taxes and Duties

14.1　Except as otherwise specifically provided in the Contract, the Contractor shall bear and pay all taxes, duties, levies and charges assessed on the Contractor, its Subcontractors or their employees by all municipal, state or national government authorities in connection with the Facilities in and outside of the country where the Site is located.

14.2　Notwithstanding GCC Sub-Clause 14.1 above, the Employer shall bear and promptly pay all customs and import duties as well as other local taxes like, e.g., a value added tax (VAT), imposed by the law of the country where the Site is located on the Plant specified in Price Schedule No.1 and that are to be incorporated into the Facilities.

14.3　If any tax exemptions, reductions, allowances or privileges may be available to the Contractor in the country where the Site is located, the Employer shall use its best endeavors to enable the Contractor to benefit from any such tax savings to the maximum allowable extent.

14.4　For the purpose of the Contract, it is agreed that the Contract Price specified in Article 2 (Contract Price and Terms of Payment) of the Contract Agreement is based on the taxes, duties, levies and charges prevailing at the date twenty-eight (28) days prior to the date of bid submission in the country where the Site is located (hereinafter called "Tax" in this GCC Sub-Clause 14.4). If any rates of Tax are increased or decreased, a new Tax is introduced, an existing Tax is abolished, or any change in interpretation or application of any Tax occurs in the course of the performance of Contract, which was or will be assessed on the Contractor, Subcontractors or their employees in connection with performance of the Contract, an equitable adjustment of the Contract Price shall be made to fully take into account any such change by addition to the Contract Price or deduction therefrom, as the case may be, in accordance with GCC Clause 36 hereof.

在以上第 14 条中，承包商实际上承担了与工程项目有关的所有税费，也就是说，该款项下的国际工程项目不是免税的，举例如下：

12.1　Taxes and Duties Paid by the Contractor
All the customs duties, value added taxes (VAT), income tax (IT), levies, corporate

tax and all other taxes and charges of any nature, at present and in future, arising from or incurred outside the Country for implementation of this project, shall be borne by the Contractor if not specifically mentioned in the Contract.

如果工程项目需要免税，或对税费进行特殊约定，则应在合同条款中规定，举例如下：

Sub-Clause 14.1 is replaced as below:
(a) Income Tax, surcharge and all taxes of similar nature and VAT levied on the Contractor which is deductible on payment of bill as Tax Deducted at Source (TDS) in the Country of _____ in connection with the execution of this Contract, shall be paid by the Employer. The Contractor will deduct income tax as per law from salary or remuneration paid to expatriate and local personnel as well as payment to sub-contractors and deposit to the government ex-chequer within the stipulated time as per rule.

To facilitate payment of such taxes by the Employer, the Contractor shall submit to the income tax authorities through the Employer all statutory statements and returns with necessary documents and information well before the dates fixed for submission of such returns and the Contractor shall also comply with all requirements in the course of the proceedings before the tax authorities. If, for the Contractor's failure to submit such statement/returns in time, any interest, penalty or any other levy is imposed by the tax authorities, the Employer shall not be liable to pay such amount, which will be the liability of the Contractor. The Employer will not be liable for payment of tax, VAT etc., if an arbitrary assessment is made for the failure of submission of proper documents by the Contractor.

(b) The Contractor's final payment shall not be released until full compliance of this provision of the Contract by the Contractor.

在以上第14.1款专用条款中，合同规定根据工程所在国税法应代扣代缴的所得税（Income Tax，IT）和增值税（VAT）等应由业主支付。同时，承包商应在支付分包商或供货商时，履行工程所在国税法规定的代扣代缴所得税和增值税的义务。

第 8 章　其他主要合同文件编制

> The negotiations for complex contracts are often long drawn out, and the parties draw up documents which are stated to be subject to contract, or subject to other conditions, such as the approval of a third party.
>
> Paras 1-015, *Hudson's Building and Engineering Contracts*

8.1　谅解备忘录

谅解备忘录（Memorandum of Understanding，MOU 或 MoU）是两个或两个以上当事方之间经协商谈判，达成一致后，用文字方式记录的共识。谅解备忘录通常可用于国家间的外交安排或国际条约谈判达成的共识。在商业交易中，谅解备忘录通常被视为是商业交易谈判的起点，用以记录当事方业已达成一致的内容。例如，当事方通过签署谅解备忘录建立正式的合作关系，双方可以根据谅解备忘录的安排开展下一步的工作或程序，以便为将来签署正式合同奠定基础。

一般而言，在商业交易中，谅解备忘录不具有法律约束力（legally binding）。但谅解备忘录是否具有法律效力，不应只看谅解备忘录的标题，还要看谅解备忘录载明的内容，即是否具有约束当事方权利义务的内容。判断谅解备忘录是否具有法律约束力，可参考下节意向书的法律效力判断。

谅解备忘录可根据当事方之间达成的内容和共识而定，并无固定格式，也无繁简之说，只要能够准确记录和载明当事人之间达成的共识，就应视为一份合格的谅解备忘录。

完整的谅解备忘录条款应包括：

（1）当事方名称和地址信息。

（2）前言。

（3）条文正文，包括目的、共识内容、合作方式、双方当事人的义务、进一步安排、通信、保密、终止、反腐败、修改、语言等条款。

（4）当事人签字。

以在某国开展 PPP 项目合作为例，双方签署谅解备忘录示例如下：

```
                    Dated:_____
         _____（insert name of Owner）
                            and
                  TTT Co., Ltd. P. R. China
```

# MEMORANDUM OF UNDERSTANDING
# FOR
_____(insert name of project)
# IN _____

THIS MEMORANDUM OF UNDERSTANDING (hereinafter referred to as the "MOU") is executed to be effective as of (·) (the "Effective Date"), by and between:

1. _____, a government authority of _____ duly established and existing under and by virtue of the laws of _____ with its principal office at _____, which expression shall unless excluded by or repugnant to the context, mean and include its successors, executors, administrators, representatives and assignees, represented by Mr. _____ in his capacity as _____, (hereinafter referred to as "BBB") of one party, and

2. TTT Co., Ltd., a stock listing company duly established and existing under and by virtue of the laws of the People's Republic of China with its principal office at _____, which expression shall unless excluded by or repugnant to the context, mean and include its successors, executors, administrators, representatives and assignees, represented by Mr. _____ in his capacity as _____, (hereinafter referred to as "TTT") of the other party.

BBB and TTT shall be referred to as "Parties" when acting collectively and as "Party" when acting individually.

BEING parties that Memorandum of Understanding for development of _____ in _____ is intended to development of the captioned project between the Parties in the light of the legislation under Public Private Partnership ("PPP") scheme.

RECOGNIZING that the feasibility study, the technical proposal, environmental impact assessment, cost estimate, financing arrangement and financing analysis are, for the purpose of realizing the development in the form of PPP model for the captioned project, will be prepared properly by TTT to meet the necessary requirements as set out in MOU.

WHEREAS the Parties agree that the successful implementation of the captioned project shall relay on the application, approval and a series of negotiations in accordance with the procedures as set forth in the laws of _____.

NOW THEREFORE, on the basis of the foregoing recitals and in consideration of the mutual promises and covenants entered into this Memorandum of Understanding, the Parties, intending to be legally bound, hereby covenant and agree as follows:

Article 1　Interpretation

1. In this Memorandum of Understanding:
    a) clause headings are for convenience only and are not to be used in its interpretation;
    b) an expression which denotes:
        i. any gender includes the other genders;

ii. a natural person includes a juristic person and vice versa; and

iii. the singular includes the plural and vice versa.

2. In this MOU, unless the context indicates a contrary intention, the following words and expressions bear the meanings assigned to them and cognate expressions bear corresponding meanings:

a) "BBB" means _____ .

b) "Confidential Information" means confidential information as defined in the Article below.

c) "TTT" means TTT Co., Ltd. .

d) "Concession Agreement" means the concession agreement to be executed by the BBB and TTT on a mutual agreement under the applicable laws of People's Republic of _____

e) "Concession Term Sheet" means the major terms of concession agreement which is to be proposed by TTT and finalized by BBB and TTT in the process of negotiation.

f) "Parties" means the BBB and TTT.

g) "Signature date" means the date of signature of this MOU by the Party last signing.

h) "The Project" means _____ .

3. Words and expressions defined in any clause shall, unless the application of any such word or expression is specifically limited to that clause, bear the meaning assigned to such word or expression throughout this MOU.

4. Reference to "days" shall be construed as calendar days unless qualified by the word "business", in which instance a "business day" shall be any day other than a Saturday, Sunday or public holiday as gazette by the government of _____ from time to time. Any reference to "business day" shall be construed as being the hours between 07h30 (seven hours and thirty minutes) and 15h30 (fifteen hours and thirty minutes) on any business day. Any reference to time shall be based upon _____ Standard Time.

5. Where figures are referred to in numerals and in words, and there is any conflict between the two, the words shall prevail, unless the context indicates a contrary intention.

Article 2　　Objective

1. This MOU shall facilitate an application to develop _____ in the form of PPP model for the captioned project as set forth in the following articles under the laws.

2. The Parties hereby agree to initiate negotiation of concession term sheet, concession agreement, power purchase agreement based on the feasibility study report, environment impact assessment, the technical proposal, the cost estimate to be submitted by TTT with the time prescribed in this MOU, in a PPP model, on an exclusive authorized to TTT basis.

3. Except otherwise provided in this MOU, the Parties hereby agree to cooperate each other to initiate the financing and insurance arrangement to satisfy the requirements of financing institute and insurance agency in a good endeavor manner.

Article 3　　Name and Scope of the Project

1. The Parties agree hereby that the name of _____ shall be defined as _____ ,

locate at _____ .
2. The capacity and main technical parameters of _____ shall be ascertained as:

   (1) _____ ;
   (2) _____ ;
   (3) _____ .

Article 4   BBB's Responsibilities

1. BBB is, within 15 days from the date of submission of feasibility study, environment impact assessment, the technical proposal, cost estimate, concession term sheet, obliged to appoint a committee to initiate the process of negotiation of concession agreement.
2. BBB is obliged to verify the feasibility study, the technical propel, environment impact assessment, cost estimate, concession term sheet of the project as proposed by TTT upon delivery of such submittal by TTT.
3. BBB is obliged to coordinate the relevant governmental departments, local municipal authorities and public organizations in _____ to acquire and obtain the approvals, permits, licenses, consents of the Project hereof.
4. Nevertheless the above, BBB is also obliged to coordinate with the relevant governmental departments to approve the feasibility study report, environment impact assessment, cost estimates, concession agreement, power purchase agreement as well as technical specifications thereunder.
5. BBB shall coordinate with the relevant governmental departments to fulfill all and any obligations, the documents, procedures, approvals, consents, permits, guarantees of any kind, whether the administrative or legal nature, in connection with, arising from, related to the financing arrangements from China's bank(s) or financing institutions.
6. BBB shall provide any and all assistance to TTT in obtaining the visas, working permits for his employees, staff of the Project.
7. BBB shall not use the feasibility study report, environment impact assessment, cost estimates, concession agreement, power purchase agreement prepared and submitted by TTT or disclose any of its contents to a third party or for the benefit of any other party other than BBB and TTT. BBB shall not use the feasibility study report, environment impact assessment, cost estimates, concession agreement, and investment agreement prepared and submitted by TTT to call for a tender or bid for the Project at any time.

Article 5   TTT's Responsibilities

1. TTT is obliged to submit the feasibility study report, environment impact assessment, cost estimates, concession term sheet, concession agreement, and investment agreement within 6 months from date of execution of this MOU.

2. TTT is, within 30 days from date of execution of this MOU, obliged to form a technical and commercial team to prepare the feasibility study, technical proposal and then proceed negotiation of concession agreement, power purchase agreement and investment agreement.
3. TTT is obliged to coordinate with BBB, the governmental departments, the local municipal authorities and public organizations of _____ to proceed negotiation of concession agreement, and investment agreement.
4. TTT is obliged to design, construct, complete, operate and maintain the Project as set forth in the concession agreement to be agreed upon by the Parties.
5. TTT is obliged to coordinate with the banks from China or financing institute(s) to finalize and realize the financing supports and arrangements for the Project.
6. TTT shall provide assistance in obtaining the visas for the employees and staff of BBB to China.

Article 6　Further Arrangements

The Parties, for the purpose of proceeding the preparation and negotiation of concession agreement, power purchase agreement and investment agreement, agree to fulfill the following schedule:
(i) BBB and TTT shall, within 30 days from the date of execution of this MOU, appoint a joint committee to proceed preparation and negotiation of concession agreement, and investment agreement.
(ii) Upon delivery of suchsubmittals by TTT, BBB and TTT shall hold a kick-off meeting to finalize the schedules to negotiate concession agreement, investment agreement and financing arrangements.
(iii) To satisfy the requirements of financing, insurance and construction, BBB and TTT shall exert their own endeavors to reach an agreement for the Project within the legal framework of the laws of _____.

Article 7　Communications

Any and all communications shall be sent to the following contact person for each side:
If sent to _____:
Address: _____
Fax: _____
Email: _____
Attention: _____
If sent to _____:
Address: _____
Fax: _____
Email _____
Attention: _____

Article 8　Confidentiality and Non-Disclosure

The Parties hereby shall keep confidential and take all reasonable steps to keep confidential, and neither disclose to any third person, nor make use of otherwise than for the benefit of the other party, any information, or proprietary information including but not limited to the terms and conditions of this MOU, theexistence of the discussions and negotiations between the Parties, information regarding documents, written or coded information, oral information, abstracts or summaries thereof, computer records, specifications, formulas, evaluations, methods, processes, technical descriptions, business plans, market analysis, trade secrets, product concepts and plans, product designs, product costs, product prices, finances, marketing plans, ideals, research and development reports and other data, records, drawings, personnel, research and development activities, know-how and pre release products and information relating or referring to, concerning, created by, commissioned by, provided to, arising from or acquired by either party.

Article 9　Exceptions to Confidentiality

The Parties understand and acknowledge that the receiving party may disclose confidential information:
(i) In response to a valid order issued by any government agency requesting such information in accordance with any law.
(ii) To any court acting in pursuance of its powers or in connection with any proceedings before a court.
(iii) If the financing conditions have not come effective according to the terms of this MOU.

Article 10　Anti-corruption

The Parties compromise not to offer, direct or indirectly, advantages to any third parties, even promise or accept for own benefits or from others; offers to obtain advantages relating to the services contained in this MOU, under penalty of law.

Article 11　Amendment

1. This MOU may be amended mutually in writing and signed by both Parties.
2. This MOU shall be subject to the further review by the Parties, if such reviews are deemed necessary.

Article 12　Termination

The Parties agree that this MOU shall be terminated in the event of any failure of negotiation of concession agreement within two year from the effective date of this MOU.

Article 13　Disputes Settlement

Any disputes between the Parties arising out of the interpretation or implementation of this MOU shall be settled amicably through consultation or negotiation between the Parties.

> Article 14　Language
>
> 1. This MOU is written in English.
> 2. All notes, approvals or demands arising from this MOU shall be written in English. In any case of translating any words from English into other language needed, the Parties agree that English edition is prior. All notes, approvals or demands stated above shall be validly given by hand, electronic mail, telegram, and fax to the addresses provided below or other address stated by one party in writing.
>
> In witness whereof the Parties set their hands and with or without seals on the date first written above,
>
> BBB
>
> _____
>
> Name：
>
> Position：
>
> TTT Co., Ltd.
>
> _____
>
> Name：
>
> Position：

8.2　意　向　书

关于意向书概念的描述，在 Turriff Construction Ltd. 诉 Regalia Knitting Mills Ltd. 案中，法官 Fay 解释道：

"意向书只是一方当事人以书面形式提出将在未来某一天签订合同的意向。除特殊情况外，它没有约束力[一]。"

在不同的情况下使用意向书会产生不同的效果：

（1）在某些融资项目中，应业主要求，在签署正式合同之前，业主与承包商签署意向书，要求承包商开始工程的施工。

（2）承包商在起草与分包商签订的正式合同时，由于某种原因，要求分包商开始工作

[一] Turriff Construction Ltd. v Regalia Knitting Mills Ltd (1971) 222 E. G. 169, at page 29.

时，分包合同文本没有准备妥当。这时，承包商就会向分包商发出意向书，详细规定将包括在协议中的所有文件。可能会也或许不会要求分包商签收意向书回执以表示同意规定条款。虽然这份文件是暂时性的，但它仍具有与双方达成的协议的同等效力，除了按照有关规定需要盖章才能成为契据的合同外。

（3）意向书是开始工作或开始准备工作并承诺给付的请求，如果工程没有开始或该分包商还没有开始工作也许只支付分包商实际成本。

（4）意向书是承包商通知分包商对其报价感兴趣，但是还没有或不想成为约束双方的合同。

在第（1）和（2）种情况下，由于没有新建议或对合同条款进行修改，意向书构成了一种承诺，当承包商将意向书送达给分包商时，双方之间就存在有约束力的合同了。

在第（3）种情况下，承包商的意向书只是一项要约，分包商可以接受也可以提出反要约。一旦分包商签字或以其他方式签收，当事人就应遵守该协议，但仅限于要约规定。例如，如果意向书中要求分包商开始设计工作，则分包商没有义务去做除设计工作之外的其他工作；如果意向书要求达到一定的预定金额，一旦完成预定金额，协议就应终止，分包商就不应继续执行意向书。根据英国法院的判例，如 Monk Construction 诉 Norwich Union 案[1]，如果意向书中规定了封顶价格（capped price）或预定金额（set price），履约当事方就没有权利主张超出该封顶价格的任何金额，即使履约当事方可证明他已支付超出封顶价格的费用。

在第（4）种情况下，意向书没有法律约束力，意向书只是一种意向性声明而已。

在实践中，如何判断意向书是否具有法律约束力，是合同当事方不得不面对的法律难题。法官 Anthony Thornton 在 A C Controls Ltd. 诉 British Broadcasting Corporation，Queen's Bench Division，（2002）89 Con LR 52；[2002] EWHC 3132 案中总结了有关判断原则：

"1）经分析，当事方称为或视为意向书的文件可以构成有约束力的合同，如果在客观解释时当事方的语言确有如此效果。

2）通过对其条款的客观解释，该份文件可以构成一种"如果"性质的合同，即当事一方向当事另一方发出标准要约，如果他履行已界定的服务，那么他将为此得到报酬。然而，他们之间没有形成履行义务，而且要约中的明示或默示条款也限制了获得给付的相互义务。

3）如果已完全履行交易，并且已在合同谈判时和履行过程中合同成立的所有障碍消除了，那么，即使没有完成正式合同的签字和履行手续，合同也是可能存在的。

4）在解释意向书的语言效力时，有必要考虑产生意向书的实际背景。"[2]

法官 Humphrey Lloyd 在 Durabella Ltd. 诉 J. Jarvis & Sons Ltd. （2001）83 Con LR 145 案中解释道：

"另一方面，除非通过客观判断，非常清楚的是，当事双方事实上同意他们认为必要的以及构成合同所必需的所有事项，否则合同不成立。"[3]

---

[1] Monk Construction v Norwich Union Life Insurance Society 62 B. L. R. 107.

[2] [2002] EWHC 3132, at [35].

[3] (2001) 83 Con. L. R. 145, at [7].

从英国法院的判例,包括 British Steel 诉 Cleveland Bridge 案、Mitsui Babcock Engergy Ltd. 诉 John Brown Engineering Ltd. (1996) 51 Con LR 129 案和附录 7.2、7.3 等,可以清楚地看出,如果意向书想要具备合同约束力,必须满足如下条件:

(1) 当事人必须声明他们有签订合同的意愿,无论是通过意向书内容还是其行为。

(2) 当事人必须就一些必要条款达成一致,如当事人、工程内容、价格和时间,并应具备充分确定性以使合同能够在商业上运作。

(3) 对要约的承诺必须清楚,无论是在文字上还是在行为上。

判断意向书是否具备合同效力,还应考虑意向书中规定的条件是否具备充分确定性,以使合同能够成立,以及意向书中哪些事项还需要解决。

判断意向书的效力,如同安慰信一样,不能简单地从信函的字面意思来解释其效力。不能认为只要是意向书,就没有约束力,而应该具体问题具体分析,仔细甄别意向书的背景、内容、是否产生权利和相互义务关系,依据有关判例和其他有关判例来解读意向书的含义,判断是否产生合同效力,是否对当事方具有法律约束力。

意向书的内容取决于当事方想要或当事方之间达成一致的内容,并无固定格式,也无繁简要求。一项意向书的范例如下:

Name of Recipient
Title
Company Name
Address
City, Country Name

Dear [Name of Recipient]

Indicate you are submitting this letter with the intent to do a specific action and this intent is based on the following conditions:

　　Considerations-propose what we are willing to provide as compensation or other as considerations for the specifics listed above.

Indicate that this letter is not an official offer and that all details would need to be negotiated and executed through a formal purchase agreement.

Indicate your expected timing for the transaction to take place assuming you were selected.

Sincerely,

Name and Title

事实上,也可将上述第 8.1 节中的谅解备忘录标题修改为意向书,作为当事方合作进行

某工程项目的意向性协议。以某开发独立燃气电站意向书为例，如下：

LETTER of INTENT
On Independent Power Provider of Gas Power Station in _____

The present letter of intent (hereinafter referred to as "Letter of Intent") was concluded on _____ in _____ by and between:

_____ of the _____, incorporated under the laws of _____, having its registered office at _____ (hereafter referred to as "First Party") which expression shall unless excluded by or repugnant to the context, mean and include its successors, executors, administrators, representatives and assignees, *represented by* _____, _____ (insert the title of the person)

and

_____ (hereafter referred to as "Second Party"), a corporation incorporated under the laws of People's Republic of China, and having its principal place of business at _____ which expression shall unless excluded by or repugnant to the context, mean and include its successors, executors, administrators, representatives and assignees, represented by _____;

The First Party and the Second Party shall be jointly referred to hereinafter as the "Parties" or separately-the "Party".

RECITAL

A. The First Party is desirous of purchasing electricity supplied by the Second Party as an independent power supplier, together with a combined service of investment, building, and operation of the Gas Turbine Combined Cycle Power Plant in _____ for the First Party and _____ (hereinafter referred to as "Project") provided by the Second Party.

B. The Second Party has the expertise and experience in performing specialist works associated with the design, construction and operation of gas power stations.

NOW THEREFORE, the Parties have agreed upon the following terms and conditions:

Article 1 Objective

1. The objective of this Letter of Intent is to establish the formal cooperation relationship between the Parties in connection with power supply to the First Party and _____ and providing a combined service including investment, building and operation of the Gas Turbine Combined Cycle Power Plant in _____ by the Second Party as an independent power provider.

2. The Project shall be developed in separate stage as agreed upon by the Parties thereto, in which the first phase shall be _____ with _____ capacity. The further development shall, upon the successful implementation of the Project, be arranged by the Parties thereto.

Article 2　Nature of Cooperation

The nature of cooperation in relation with the Project shall, for the purpose of preparation of technical proposal and relevant documents as well as the financing arrangement by the Second Party, be exclusive and sole relationship between the Parties.

Article 3　Ways of Cooperation

The Parties commit to cooperate in the manner of following ways:

(1) Upon the First Party's request, the Second Party will use his best endeavor to obtain financing support from the financial institutes in the form of _____ or others that is applicable, and shall accept the engagement from First Party to supply electricity to the First Party and _____ as an independent power provider while providing a combined service including investment, building and operation of the gas power plant as set forth in Article 1 [Objective] in this Letter of Intent hereof.

(2) In the event of availability of financial support, the Parties agree to cooperate that, on the basis of equitability and mutual benefit, the Second Party shall invest, build, operate and supply electricity to the National Grid and the First Party as the independent power supplier as specified in Article 1 [Objective] in this Letter of Intent hereof.

Article 4　Financing Arrangement

1. The Parties shall, upon the agreement between the Parties, cooperate with each other and use their best endeavors to obtain financing support in the form of supplier's credit or others that is applicable for the project as set forth in Article 1 [Objective] in this Letter of Intent hereof.

2. For the purpose of financing arrangement for the Project, the First Party shall provide therelevent documents as required by the Second Party and relevant financing institute in China within the time to be required.

3. The First Party understands and undertakes to arrange the sufficient financing guarantee as requested by the financial institute and the Second Party.

4. The Parties shall comply with the regulation and procedure inconnetion with the supplier's credit facility.

Article 5　Technical Proposal and Further Issues

1. The Second Party has, for the purpose ofpromption of the Project with financing arragement, prepared the technical proposal at his own cost for the First Party. The First Party has received the technical proposal dated _____ submitted by the Second Party, and is generally satisfied with the technical proposal. On the basis of Second Party's proposal, both Parties agree to further discussions on the details, and eventually form a consensus.

2. The technical standards and specifications specified by the designer which are valid in _____ will apply in the Project, unless otherwise stated in the construction contract.

Article 6　The First Party's Principal Responsibility

1. The First Party shall provide the land for the construction and operation of the project, obtain and acquire all permits, approvals and/orlicences from all local, state or national government authorities for development of the named Project in _____ .

2. The First Party shall purchase the electricity monthly at a negotiated price for 25 years monthly since the power station is ready to operate normally according to the power supply agreement that will be signed between the Parties as set forth in Article 9 [Further Arrangements] in this Letter of Intent hereof.

3. The First Party shall use his best endeavors to achieve the connection between the power plant and national grid of _____, so that to guarantee that the power plant can operate with full capacity during its life time. The First Party shall use his best endeavors to arrange and obtain the connection permit of national grid of _____ . In the event of availability of signing the grid-connection agreement, the First Party shall sign the agreement as Witness as set forth in Article 9 [Further Arrangements] in this Letter of Intent hereof.

4. The First Party shall, for the purpose of reducing the risk of gas supply and the price influctuations, supply gas for the Project at the price of USD _____ per cubic meters. The agreement of gas supply will be signed as set forth in Article 9 [Further Arrangements] in this Letter of Intent hereof.

5. The First Party shall, for the purpose of financing arrangement, obtain and acquire sufficient guarantee for the Second Party.

6. The First Party shall, during the negotiation and construction of the named Project, assist the Second Party to obtain the necessary visa, working permits as well as residential permits in _____ .

7. If requested by the Second Party, the First Party shall use his best endeavors to assist the Second Party in obtaining in a timely andexpeditous manner all necessary permits, approvals and/or licences necessary for the execution of the Work from all local, state or national government authorities or public service in _____ .

8. It is also understood and agreed that First Party has, during their visit to China (if any), to follow local rules and regulations including labor and immigration laws of the Government of _____ .

Article 7　The Second Party's Principal Responsibility

1. The Second Party shall prepare the technical proposal, feasibility study report as well as the design documents necessary for thepromption of the Project with loan facility support.

2. In the event that the three principle agreements including power supply agreement, grid-connection agreement and gas supply agreement, have been finally reached, the Second Party shall, upon the terms and conditions of the agreements, invest, build and operate the Project within the time which the Parties agreed.

3. For the financing purpose, the Second Party shall use his best endeavors to promote the Project and settle the financing support issues in relation to the development of the Project.

4. It is also understood and agreed that Second Party has, during negotiation and construction of the Project, to follow local rules and regulations including labor and immigration laws of _____.

Article 8 Joint Efforts

The Parties shall take advantage of their resources to promote and develop the named projects with the concerted efforts in aspects of acquiring the approval in both government departments, financing solutions and commencement of construction works.

Article 9 Further Arrangements

It is understood and undertaken by both Parties that the further arrangement shall be done in the following manner:

(1) To prepare gas supply agreement and grid connection agreement and negotiate on the detailed terms, and the Second Party to provide the offer for price negotiation of power supply within one month since the date that this Letter of Intent is signed by the Parties.

(2) To enter into a power supply agreement and negotiate with each other in two months since the date that this Letter of Intent is signed by the Parties.

(3) To reach the gas supply agreement and grid connection agreement under the condition that the power supply agreement will be finally concluded within three months since the date that this Letter of Intent is signed by the Parties.

(4) To conclude the power supply agreement within four months since the date that this Letter of Intent is signed by the Parties.

(5) Upon the relevant guarantee being provided by the First Party, the Second Party shall take over the land for the project and relevant permits, approvals or licences and commence the construction of the project.

Article 10 Explanation

Neither the First Party nor the Second Party shall recognize the signature of this Preliminary Agreement as permanent establishment of a legal entity, and/or a legal joint venture, and/or consortium contracted by the Parties unless the Parties sign individual agreement for the project in particular.

Article 11 Confidential Information

1. The First Party and the Second Party shall keep confidential and shall not, without the written consent of the other party hereto, divulge to any third party any documents, data or other information furnished directly or indirectly by the other party hereto in connection with the Agreement whether such information has been furnished prior to, during or following termination of the Agreement. Notwithstanding the above, the Parties may furnish to its financial institutes and consultant (if any) such documents, data and other information it receives from the other party to the extent required for the financial institutes or consultants to perform its works under the Agreement, in which event the Parties shall obtain from such institute or person an undertaking of confidentiality.

2. The First Party shall not use such documents, data and other information received from the Second Party for any purpose other than the development and construction of the Project. Similarly, the Second Party shall not use such documents, data and other information received from the First Party for any purpose other than the development and construction of such project under the Agreement.

Article 12 Entry into Force, Duration and Termination

1. This Letter of Intent shall come into force on the date of signing thereof and shall remain in force for a period of 2 (two) years unless otherwise mutually extended by the Parties in writing at least 3 (three) months prior to its expiration of this Letter of Intent.

2. This Letter of Intent shall become void unless otherwise mutually extended by the Parties in writing at least 3 (three) months prior to its expiration of this Agreement.

IN WITNESS THEREOF this Letter of intent is signed by the respective authorized representatives of the Parties on the day and the year first here above written.

Done in duplicate in the English language.

The First Party

_____

 Name:
 Title:

The Second Party

_____

 Name:
 Title:

8.3 联合体协议

在国际工程项目中,联合体协议通常用于承包商组成联合体,以紧密型或非紧密型联合体方式,作为承包商实施和完成工程项目。以承包商之间组成紧密型的联合施工联合体为例,承包商双方签订的联合体协议如下:

Joint Venture Agreement

THIS JOINT VENTURE AGREEMENT is hereby made and entered into by and between:

_____(hereinafter referred to as AAA), a company incorporated under the laws of _____, and having a place of business at _____.

and

_____(hereinafter referred to as BBB), a company incorporated under the laws of _____, and having a place of business at _____.

PREAMBLE

WHEREAS AAA and BBB (hereinafter referred to as the "Parties") have formed a Joint Venture in order to submit a tender to _____(hereinafter referred to as the "Client") for the construction of _____(hereinafter referred to as the "Works").

NOW THEREFORE, IT IS AGREED AS FOLLOWS:

1. FORMATION OF JOINT VENTURE

    1.1 The Parties hereby associate themselves into and as a Joint Venture in accordance with the provisions of this Joint Venture Agreement under the style or firm name of AAA and BBB Joint Venture (hereinafter referred to as the "JV"), which is an unincorporated joint venture.

    1.2 The Parties hereto agree and undertake that they will not disclose the contents of this Joint Venture Agreement to persons with whom they may have any dealings directly or indirectly arising from the conclusion of this Joint Venture Agreement and the operation and establishment of the Works.

    1.3 Notwithstanding that the Parties may be jointly and severally bound to the Client, should the JV awarded the contract by the Client of the Works, nothing herein contained shall be interpreted as giving rise to a general partnership between the Parties or limiting the rights or powers of either party to carry on its separate business for its sole benefit.

2. OBJECT AND MOTIVATION

The sole object for which this JV is established and the sole business of the JV is to submit a tender, negotiate for and conclude a contract for the execution of the Works and to carry out such Works to finality, all in accordance with the terms of this Joint Venture Agreement.

3. PROFIT AND LOSSES

3.1 The profits and losses of the JV shall be borne by AAA and BBB in the proportions 70% and 30% respectively (hereinafter referred to as "the Specified Proportions").

3.2 The Parties agree that AAA shall be the lead member of the JV.

3.3 In addition to any other provisions contained in this Joint Venture Agreement, the functions, duties, obligations and responsibilities of AAA and BBB under this Joint Venture Agreement and in the execution of the Works will be to provide all bridging finance, working capital, guarantees and resources necessary to successfully carry out the Works in proportion to the Specified Proportions, in which proportions all profits, losses, costs, liabilities and assets and any other responsibilities, whether pecuniary or otherwise, shall be proportional to the Specified Proportions.

4. DURATION

4.1 The operation of this Joint Venture Agreement shall be deemed to have commenced on the date of signature of this agreement and shall terminate, except insofar as the provisions of Clause 5 and 6 apply, upon the happening of any of the following events, whichever shall be earlier.

4.2 The Contract is not awarded by the Client, or

4.3 In the case of contract award to the JV, at the time the contract is terminated and all rights and obligations of the Parties in connection with such contract and in connection with this Joint Venture Agreement have ceased, but in no case before the conclusion of any maintenance period in the contract and the cancellation and/or refund of all guarantees and bonds. The JV's existence shall also be deemed to continue insofar as the JV is responsible for latent defects under the contract.

4.4 The Parties unanimously agree to terminate it subject to the terms then agreed between the Parties.

5. EXCLUSIVITY

The Parties agree and undertake in favour of each other that neither of them shall, except in accordance with the intention expressed in this Joint Venture Agreement, be associated in any manner, either directly or indirectly, with any investigation, negotiation, tender or proposal for the performance or incidental to the execution of the Works and including any variation by way of addition or omission from the scope of the Works or the extension to the Works, nor invest in any company, enterprise or partnership in any manner related thereto, either as previously agreed by the Management Committee of the JV in writing.

6. PRE-CONTRACT COSTS

   6.1 All costs incurred by the Parties prior to the date of contract award of the Works shall be for their own account.

   6.2 Costs incurred by the Parties after the date of contract award of the Works and approved by the Management Committee of the JV, shall be borne by the Parties in the Specified Proportions.

7. MANAGEMENT COMMITTEE

   (to be decided by the JV after winning of the Contract)

8. POWER OF THE MANAGEMENT COMMITTEE AND DIRECTION OF THE PROJECT MANAGER

   (to be decided by the JV after winning of the Contract)

9. PERSONNEL

   9.1 The Project Manager shall be appointed as provided in Clause 8 hereof.

   9.2 The person nominated to the office of Project Manager shall be subject to removal from such office by decision of the Management Committee.

   9.3 All the remuneration and emoluments of employment of the Project Manager shall be an expense of and paid by the JV, provided that a party shall be entitled by notice in writing delivered to the other Parties to elect that the person to be nominated by it to fill the offices of Project Manager shall be seconded to the JV in which event the remuneration and emoluments which would otherwise have been paid to such persons while filing such offices shall be paid to the member responsible for the nomination or otherwise as such member shall direct and subject to such payment being duly and promptly paid to the member or its nominee, the member will hold harmless and keep indemnified the JV and the other members from all actions, proceedings, claims and demands by such persons or otherwise howsoever in respect of such remuneration and emoluments. The remuneration and emoluments to be paid and allowed by the JV to the Project Manager shall be determined from time to time by the Management Committee and borne by the Parties hereto in the Specified Proportions.

   9.4 The members of the Management Committee and their proxies and alternates shall not be the employees of the JV and shall not be entitled to claim any salary or remuneration from the JV by virtue of such appointments unless the Management Committee shall otherwise decide in writing.

   9.5 AAA shall nominate a person or firm to be appointed as Secretaries to the JV. Save for matters pertaining to the Works and the Contract, such Secretaries shall be consulted on all matters of an administrative and financial nature arising in connection with the business of the JV where their particular experience, knowledge, facilities and skills in matters of this nature shall be considered to be of benefit to the JV.

10. FINANCING

   (to be decided by the JV after winning of the Contract)

11. ACCOUNTS

   (to be decided by the JV after winning of the Contract)

12. WINDING UP

   Upon the determination of the JV in accordance with the provisions of this Joint Venture Agreement, a full and general account shall be taken of the assets and liabilities of the JV and of the transactions and dealings thereof, and with all convenient speed, such assets shall be sold and realized and the proceeds applied in paying and discharging such liabilities and the expenses of and incidental to the winding-up of the JV affairs and thereafter in paying to each JV member its share of such proceeds in the Specified Proportions. The JV members respectively undertake to do all such things as may be necessary so as to give effect to the above.

13. BREACH

   If any Party breaches any material provision or term of this Joint Venture Agreement (other than those which contain their own remedies or limit the remedies in the event of a breach thereof) and fails to remedy such breach within 7 (seven) days of receipt of written notice requiring it to do so [or if it is not reasonably possible to remedy the breach within 7 (seven) days], within such further period as may be reasonable in the circumstances (the onus of demonstrating such reasonableness being on the Party in breach) provided that the Party in breach also furnishes evidence within the period of 7 (seven) days, reasonably satisfactory to the other Party, that it has taken whatever steps available to it, to commence remedying the breach, then the aggrieved Party shall be entitled without notice, in addition to any other remedy available to it in accordance with law or under this Agreement, including obtaining an interdict, to cancel this Agreement or to claim specific performance of any obligation whether or not the due date for performance has arrived, in either event without prejudice to the aggrieved Party's right to claim damages.

14. DISPUTES

   14.1 Having regard to the high degree of good faith which must exist between the Parties, the Parties agree to do their utmost to ensure that the disputes between them are settled equitably and amicably and where possible without resort to arbitration.

   14.2 In the event of any differences or dispute of whatever nature arising from this Joint Venture Agreement (which shall include any failure to agree on any matter which requires the Parties agreement for the purposes of implementation of this Joint Venture Agreement) or any other matter related thereto which cannot be settled by direct negotiation between the Parties, the differences or dispute shall be referred to arbitration in terms of Clause 15 hereof.

> 15. ARBITRATION
>
>   15.1 Save as hereinafter provided, any dispute at any time between any of the Parties hereto in regard to any matter arising out of this Joint Venture Agreement or its interpretation or rectification shall be submitted to and decided by arbitration, _____, according to its existing Arbitration Rules.
>
>   15.2 The place of arbitration shall be _____.
>
>   15.3 The language of arbitration shall be English.
>
>   15.4 The Parties irrevocably agree that the decision in those arbitration proceedings (a) shall be binding on them, (b) shall be carried into effect and (c) can be made an order of any court of competent jurisdiction.
>
> This shall be done and signed at _____ on this _____ day of _____.
>
> For and on behalf of AAA：
>
> For and on behalf of BBB：

8.4 保障和保证协议

保障和保证免受损害条款（Indemnity and Hold Harmless Clause）或称免责条款，是指当事双方在合同中事先约定的，旨在限制或者免除其未来责任的条款。保障和保证协议是当事方事先约定的旨在限制或免除其未来责任的协议。

免责条款广泛应用于各类合同文本中，如贷款协议、施工合同、分包合同、保险合同等，以及各种格式合同中。为避免合同一方滥用免责条款逃避合同责任，各国法律对免责条款均有一定的限制性规定。

免责条款的成立或有效，应不违反下述原则：

(1) 不得违反法律或公共利益。

(2) 不得免除故意或者重大过失。

(3) 不得免除合同当事方的基本义务。

(4) 不得违反公平原则。

(5) 不得免除人身伤害责任。

在国际工程实务中，承包商或分包商也会经常遇到保障和保证免受损害条款，如 FIDIC 施工合同 1987 年第 4 版第 22 条、FIDIC 施工分包合同 1994 年第 1 版第 13 条、ICE 合同第 22 条、AIA 分包合同格式以及 AGC 分包合同格式等。

以某国际工程项目为例，承包商要求分包商出具担保和保障协议如下：

FORM OF SUBCONTRACTOR'S WARRANTY AND INDEMNITY

THIS AGREEMENT is made given the _____ day of _____,20XX

between

_____, a company duly established under and by virtue of the laws of _____, having its principal office at _____, which expression shall unless excluded by or repugnant to the context, mean and include its successors, executors, administrators, representatives and assignees, represented by Mr _____ in his capacity as General Director, (hereinafter referred to as the "General Contractor") on the one hand,

and

_____ [insert the name of Subcontractor], a company duly established under and by virtue of the laws of _____, having its principal office at _____, which expression shall unless excluded by or repugnant to the context, mean and include its successors, executors, administrators, representatives and assignees, represented by Mr _____ in his capacity as _____, (hereinafter referred to as "Subcontractor") on the other hand.

The General Contractor and the Subcontractor shall be called collectively the "Parties" hereunder.

WHEREAS

(a) By the Contract dated _____ made between the General Contractor and the Subcontractor, the Subcontractor has agreed to execute the Subcontract Works as described in and upon the terms and conditions contained in the Contract.

(b) The Subcontractor has had an opportunity of examining the provisions of the Contract and each of the documents forming part of the Contract (other than its financial provisions).

(c) Pursuant to the Contract, the Subcontractor wishes to enter into the Subcontract for the Subcontractor to carry out the Subcontract Works more particularly described in the Subcontract.

(d) It is acknowledged that in consenting to the appointment of the Subcontractor, the General Contractor is relying upon the skill, judgment and expertise of the Subcontractor to carry out the Subcontract Works.

NOW IT IS HEREBY AGREED as follows:

1 DEFINATIONS AND INTERPRETATION
2 Definitions

In this Agreement, the following words and expressions shall have the meanings hereby assigned to them, except where the context otherwise requires:

"Agreement" means this agreement entered into by the parties hereto setting out the Subcontractor's warranties and indemnities pursuant to the Subcontract.

"Contract" means the agreement between the Owner and the General Contractor for completion of the works as defined in the Contract.

"Design Service Contract" means the agreement between the General Contractor and the Subcontractor for completion of Subcontract Works as defined in the Subcontract.

"Design Service" means any and all services to be provided by the Subcontractor as setting out in the Subcontract.

"Documents" means plans, calculations, records, drawings, documents, computer software, materials, knowhow, information and/or other documents (including information technology material and computer assisted material) prepared by or on behalf of the Subcontractor in relation to the Works and/or the Project and all revisions and additions (whether inexistence or to be made).

"Project" means Implementation of _____ .

3 Interpretation

(a) Words importing persons or parties shall include firms and corporation and any organization having legal capacity including its successors in title and/or permitted assigns.

(b) Words importing the singular shall also include the plural and vice versa.

(c) References to Clauses and Appendices in this Agreement and the Appendices thereto shall, unless otherwise specified, be Clauses and Appendices of this Agreement.

(d) References to any enactment, statute, ordinance, by-law or regulation (or any provision thereof) shall mean such enactment, statute, ordinance, by-law or regulations (or any provision thereof) as may be amended or replaced from time to time.

(e) The *contra proferentem* rule shall not apply to the interpretation of this Agreement.

(f) The headings and marginal notes in this Agreement shall not be taken into consideration in the interpretation or construction thereof or of the Agreement.

4 Notices, Consents, etc. to be in writing

Wherever in this Agreement provision is made for the making, giving or issue of any acceptance, account, acknowledgement, application, approval, certificate, communication, confirmation, consent, demand, determination, direction, estimate, instruction, notice, order, proposal, requirement or request by any person, unless otherwise specified shall be in writing and the words "accept" "account" "acknowledge" "apply" "approve" "certify" "communicate" "confirm" "consent" "demand" "determine" "direct" "estimate" "instruct" "notify" "order" "propose" "require" or "request" (and cognate expressions for each of these) shall be construed accordingly.

5 CARE, SKILL AND RELIANCE

6 In consideration of the Owner consenting to the Subcontractor being appointed by the General Contractor to perform the Subcontract Works, the Subcontractor warrants and undertakes:

(a) in and about the performance of the Subcontract, the Subcontractor has exercised and will exercise all the skill, care and diligence to be expected of a properly qualified and competent subcontractor experienced in carrying out work of a similar size, scope and complexity to the Subcontract Works; and

(b) it has complied and will continue to comply with the terms of and fulfill its obligations set out in the Subcontract.

7 If the Subcontractor is undertaking and/or carrying out any design under or in connection with the Subcontract, the Subcontractor will not specify or permit the use of substances generally known at the time of design to be deleterious to health or safety during construction or during the design life of the Subcontract Works nor other substances generally known at the time of design to be likely to adversely affect the functioning or design life of the Subcontract Works or the health and safety of persons using the same.

8 The Subcontractor acknowledges and accepts that the General Contractor has been and shall be deemed to have relied upon the Subcontractor's skill, expertise and judgment in respect of those matters which are related to the Subcontractor's obligations pursuant to the Subcontract, and the management and coordination thereof.

9 INDEMNITY

The Subcontractor undertakes to indemnify the General Contractor from and against:

(a) all claims, damages, expenses and/or losses which the General Contractor may have incurred, or may in its reasonable opinion incur, and/or

(b) each and every liability that the General Contractor may have to any person whatsoever and from and against any claims, demands, proceedings, damages, costs, losses and/or expenses that may be sustained, incurred or payable by the General Contractor insofar as and to the extent that the same has arisen by reason of any act, omission, negligence and/or default by the Subcontractor, its servants, employees and/or agents of the Subcontractor in connection with the Subcontract or this Agreement and/or any mistake, deficiency and/or inadequacy of any Subcontract Works provided pursuant to the Subcontract or any part thereof undertaken by the Subcontractor, its servants or agents. For the avoidance of doubt, the Subcontractor's liability to indemnify shall not exceed the liability of the General Contractor under the Contract.

10 KNOWLEDGE OF AND FORBEARANCE BY THE GENERAL CONTRACTOR

The obligations of the Subcontractor under this Agreement shall not be diminished, discharged or released or in any other way lessened or affected by any independent enquiry into any relevant matter that may be carried out by the Owner, or any knowledge of the Owner, or by any allowance of time by the Owner hereunder of by the General Contractor under the Subcontract, or by any forbearance or forgiveness in respect of any matter or thing concerning this Agreement or the Subcontract on the part of the Owner or the General Contractor, nor by any act, omission, negligence and/or default attributable to the Owner or the General Contractor.

11　NOVATION

12　In the event that the Contract is terminated or the employment of the General Contractor under the Contract is determined for any reason whatsoever, the Subcontractor, if so requested by the Owner, shall carry out and complete its obligations under this Agreement. The Subcontractor shall, within such period as the Owner may specify, enter into a novation agreement with the Owner or its nominee and the General Contractor in which the Subcontractor will undertake, interalia, to perform the Subcontract Works and be bound by the terms and conditions of the Subcontract as if the Owner had originally been named as a contracting party in place of the General Contractor. The said novation agreement will be in such form as the Owner may reasonably require.

13　In the event that the Owner does not require the Subcontractor to enter into a novation agreement as required by Clause 5.1, the Subcontractor shall have no claim whatsoever against the Owner for any damage, loss or expense howsoever arising out of or in connection with this Agreement.

14　AMBIGUITY AND CONFLICT

14.1　In the event of any ambiguity or conflict between the terms of the Subcontract and this Agreement, the terms of this Agreement shall prevail.

14.2　The provisions of this Agreement shall be without prejudice and shall not be deemed or construed so as to limit or exclude any rights or remedies which the General Contractor may have against the Subcontractor whatsoever.

15　COPYRIGHT

15.1　In so far as the copyright or other intellectual property rights, in any Documents relating to the Subcontract Works, the Works and/or the project shall be vested in the Subcontractor, the Subcontractor shall at its own cost, and within such period as the General Contractor may specify or if no period is specified, within a reasonable period after execution of this Agreement, take all necessary or desirable steps to assign or transfer the said copyright or other intellectual property right in any Documents to the General Contractor. The Subcontractor shall not be liable for any use by the General Contractor of any Documents for any purpose other than that for which the same were prepared and/or provided by the Subcontractor. To the extent that the beneficial ownership of any such copyright or other intellectual property right is vested in anyone other than the Subcontractor the Subcontractor shall use its best endeavors to procure that the beneficial owner thereof shall assign or transfer such right to the General Contractor.

15.2　The Subcontractor shall, upon written request, provide to the General Contractor, immediately upon payment of the reasonable cost of producing the same:

(a) copies of and extracts from the Documents; and

(b) such other information in relation to the Project and/or the Works and/or Subcontract Works as the Subcontractor can reasonably supply.

16 NOTICES

All notices or communications to be served arising out of or in connection with this Agreement shall be served:

17 to the General Contractor, at:

[insert address and the contact person]

18 to the Subcontractor, at:

[insert address and the contact person]

19 Any notice to be served pursuant to this Agreement shall be in writing and may be served by personally delivering the same by hand, by sending the same by telex, facsimile transmission or other means of telecommunication in permanent written form or by recorded delivery post. The addresses for service of the General Contractor and, the Subcontractor are those stated in this Agreement or such other address as the party to be served may have previously notified in writing to the other party. A notice sent by registered post shall be deemed to have been served on the date of receipt by the addressee as confirmed by the postal authorities.

20 Copies of all notices required by this Agreement shall be given to either the Subcontractor or the General Contractor and shall be sent simultaneously to the other party or parties in this Agreement by the party giving the notice.

21 GOVERNING LAW

This Agreement shall be governed by and construed according to the laws for the time being in force in _____.

22 DESIGN CONSULTANT's WARRANTY AND INDEMNITY

For the avoidance of doubt, the warranty and indemnity provided by the Subcontractor herein, shall continue to be valid and in force for the entire duration of this Agreement and for further period of _____ years set out in the Contract.

IN WITNESS whereof the parties hereto have hereunto set their respective hands the day and year first above written.

Signed by:

For and on behalf of the General Contractor:

In the presence of :

Signed by:

For and on behalf of the Subcontractor:

In the presence of :

在国际工程融资项目中,分包商还应签署更换协议(Novation agreement),约定在分包商未能履约或不能履约时应将有关权利转让给业主，以保护业主的权利和利益。以某国际工程项目为例，分包商应出具的更换协议如下：

[Subcontractor's Letterhead]
Form of Subcontractor Conditional Novation

[DATE]

[Name and address of Contractor]
Attention:

Dear Sirs:
This Subcontractor Acknowledgment and Consent (this "Acknowledgment and Consent") is delivered pursuant to Clause 4.4.5 of the engineering, procurement and construction contract, dated [_____] (as amended, supplemented or otherwise modified, the "Contract"), between [_____] ("Employer") and [_____] ("Contractor"). Reference is also made to the subcontract, dated [_____] (as amended, supplemented or otherwise modified, the "Subcontract"), between Contractor and [_____] ("Subcontractor") for the execution of certain work in connection with the Works. Capitalised terms used but not defined herein shall have the meanings ascribed to such terms in the Contract.

Subcontractor hereby acknowledges, consents and agrees that:

(a) the Subcontract may be assigned by Contractor to Employer and the Lenders (or any security agent on behalf of the Lenders) without further consent of Subcontractor;

(b) upon notification (the "Notice") to Subcontractor from Employer or the Lenders (or any security agent on behalf of the Lenders) that (i) the Contract has been terminated and/or Contractor's right to proceed with the Work under the Contract has been terminated and (ii) Employer or the Lenders will be assuming Contractor's future obligations under the Subcontract, the Subcontract will be novated pursuant to a deed of novation in the form of Attachment 1 hereto, and Subcontractor agrees (a) to execute such deed of novation, (b) to perform Subcontractor's responsibilities under the Subcontract for the benefit of Employer or the Lenders and (c) to recognise Employer or the Lenders (or any security agent on behalf of the Lenders) as being vested with all the rights (including rights with respect to Subcontractor warranties and guarantees under the Subcontract) and responsibilities of Contractor under the Subcontract; provided that Contractor shall maintain all rights and claims against Subcontractor for the portion of work previously performed; and

(c) notwithstanding the foregoing, it is specifically understood and agreed that Subcontractor shall have no right to look to Employer or any Lender for the performance of Contractor's obligations under the Subcontract unless and until Subcontractor has received the Notice and then only with respect to future obligations arising under the Subcontract.

Yours faithfully,

[SUBCONTRACTOR]
By
Name:
Title:

ATTACHMENT 1 TO THE SUBCONTRACTOR ACKNOWLEDGMENT AND CONSENT
Deed of Novation

THIS DEED OF NOVATION is made and entered into on [_____] by and among:
(1) [NAME OF CONTRACTOR], a _____ ("Transferor");
(2) [NAME OF SUBCONTRACTOR], a _____ ("Subcontractor"); and
(3) [NAME OF EMPLOYER/DESIGNEE], a _____ ("Transferee"),
together, the "Parties", and each, a "Party".

RECITALS:

WHEREAS, Transferor and Employer are party to the engineering, procurement and construction contract, dated [_____] (as amended, supplemented or otherwise modified, the "Contract");

WHEREAS, Subcontractor and Transferor are parties to the [Name of Subcontract], dated as of [_____] (as amended, supplemented or otherwise modified, the "Subcontract");

WHEREAS, Subcontractor executed and delivered to Transferor the Subcontractor Acknowledgment and Consent, dated [_____] (as amended, supplemented or otherwise modified, the "Subcontractor Acknowledgment and Consent"); and

WHEREAS, pursuant to Clause 4.4 [*Subcontractors*] of the Contract and the Subcontractor Acknowledgment and Consent, (a) Transferor may novate the Subcontract to Transferee and (b) in such case, the Parties shall execute and deliver a deed of novation in respect thereof.

It is hereby agreed as follows:

1 Definitions; Interpretation

   The provisions of Clauses [·] and [·] of the Subcontract are incorporated herein by reference and shall apply hereto unless the context of this Deed of Novation otherwise requires.

2 Novation of the Subcontract

2.1 Novation. The Parties hereby agree that, with effect from the date first written above:

   2.1.1 Transferor shall cease to be a party to the Subcontract and Transferee is hereby substituted in place of Transferor as a party to the Subcontract;

   2.1.2 All of Transferor's rights, title and interest in and to the Subcontract are hereby transferred to and vested in Transferee as if Transferee had at all times been a party to the Subcontract in place of Transferor, and Transferee shall enjoy and exercise all of Transferor's rights thereunder in full substitution of Transferor;

   2.1.3 Transferor's obligations under the Subcontract shall be transferred to and assumed by Transferee, which hereby assumes and undertakes to be bound by all the terms and conditions of the Subcontract, to perform all of Transferor's obligations under the Subcontract and to assume responsibility for all claims and liabilities under the Subcontract from the date first written above;

2.1.4 Transferor shall arrange, within a reasonable period of time, transfer or assignment to Transferee of any bank guarantees and/or other means of securities Transferor has received from Subcontractor as agreed upon under the Subcontract; and

2.1.5 Transferor is hereby released and forever discharged from all manner of actions, causes of action, suits, debts, dues, sums of money, accounts, bonds, bills, controversies, promises, damages, judgments, executions, claims, liabilities and demands whatsoever in law, admiralty, and/or equity, whether known or unknown, that Subcontractor or its heirs, executors, administrators, successors, or assigns have against Transferor under the Subcontract, from the date of this Deed of Novation for, upon or by reason of any matter, cause or thing whatsoever, and Subcontractor shall have no further recourse to Transferor under the Subcontract after the date of this Deed of Novation.

3 Miscellaneous

3.1 Effect on the Subcontract. Except as expressly provided in this Deed of Novation, all provisions of the Subcontract shall remain in full force and effect and binding on the parties thereto, insofar as the same are in force and effect and binding on such parties immediately prior to the date of this Deed of Novation.

3.2 Dispute Resolution. Any claim, dispute or difference of any kind whatsoever under or in connection with this Deed of Novation between or among any or all of the Parties shall be resolved in accordance with Clause 19.2.2 [*Arbitration*] and Clause 19.2.3 [*Consolidation of Arbitrations*] of the Contract; provided that for purposes of appointing the arbitrators under Clause 19.2.2 [*Arbitration*] of the Contract, each Party shall appoint one arbitrator.

3.3 Governing Law. The validity, construction and interpretation of this Deed of Novation shall be governed by the laws of England and Wales, excluding any choice of law rules that would refer the validity, construction or interpretation of this Deed of Novation to the laws of another jurisdiction.

3.4 Contracts (Rights of Third Parties) Act 1999. It is not intended that a third party should have the right to enforce a provision of this Deed of Novation pursuant to the Contracts (Rights of Third Parties) Act 1999.

3.5 Notices. Transferee's address for notices pursuant to the Subcontract shall be changed to the following:

[Name of Transferee]

[Address of Transferee]

3.6 Counterparts; Facsimile Delivery. This Deed of Novation may be executed in one or more counterparts, each of which shall be an original but all of which, taken together, shall constitute only one legal instrument. It shall not be necessary in making proof of this Deed of Novation to produce or account for more than one counterpart. The delivery of an executed counterpart of this Deed of Novation by facsimile shall be deemed to be valid delivery thereof.

IN WITNESS WHEREOF, this Deed of Novation has been executed and delivered as a deed on behalf of the Parties by their duly authorised representatives the day and year first above written.

SIGNED as a DEED by
[   ] acting by [a director and its secretary]
Director

Director/Secretary

SIGNED asa DEED by
acting by [a director and its secretary]
Director

Director/Secretary

8.5 保密协议

保密协议是当事方之间约定的不得向任何第三方披露一方提供给另一方或者双方拥有的信息的协议。负有保密义务的当事方若违反协议，将保密信息披露给第三方，将承担相应的责任。

保密协议可就一方提供给另一方的信息不得披露给第三方进行约定，此时该协议为单方保密协议。当事人也可以约定双方拥有的信息不得披露给第三方，此时该协议为双方保密协议。

适用于各种情况的一般性保密协议内容如下：

Non-Disclosure Agreement No _____
This non-disclosure agreement (hereinafter——the "Agreement") dated _____, 2020 is entered into by and between:

_____, a legal entity incorporated in _____, represented by its Director _____, acting on the basis of the Charter, (hereinafter——"PARTY 1"); and

_____, a legal entity duly incorporated under the laws of _____, identification code _____, represented by its Director _____, acting on the basis of the Charter, (hereinafter——"PARTY 2").

("PARTY 1" and "PARTY 2" are jointly referred to as the "Parties".)

THE PARTIES hereby agree as follows:

1. In connection with discussions that PARTY 1 is having with PARTY 2 regarding a Possible Transaction (as defined herein) between PARTY 1 or an Affiliate (or any other related entity on behalf of whom PARTY 1 is authorized to act) and PARTY 2, the Parties hereto have agreed to provide each other with certain information, regarding PARTY 2 and PARTY 1 and the Possible Transaction (collectively, the "Confidential Information"). The term "Confidential Information" also includes the Parties' analyses and other work product based on the Confidential Information received from the other Party. The term "Possible Transaction" means a conclusion of any probable agreement (agreement, preliminary agreement, etc.) between PARTY 2 and PARTY 1, or between affiliated entities and individuals.

2. Throughout this Agreement, the Party providing the Confidential Information is referred to as the "Disclosing Party", and the Party receiving the Confidential Information is referred to as the "Receiving Party". For the avoidance of doubt, the Receiving Party shall not be limited in any way with respect to its own Confidential Information. Each Party will provide the Confidential Information to the other Party on the condition that such other Party agrees and will instruct its Representatives (as defined herein) to maintain it in strict confidence and use it solely in connection with its initial and ongoing evaluation of the Possible Transaction. The Receiving Party hereby recognizes and acknowledges the confidential nature of the Confidential Information and the damage that could result to the Disclosing Party if the Confidential Information is disclosed to any third party and agrees to treat the Confidential Information in accordance with the provisions hereof.

3. The subject-matter of this Agreement is the protection of the Confidential Information of the Disclosing Party which is transferred to the Receiving Party upon the terms and conditions set out in this Agreement.

   The Receiving Party agrees to keep the Confidential Information confidential and use solely for the purpose of evaluating or otherwise pursuing the Possible Transaction. The Receiving Party further agrees not to disclose any of the Confidential Information to any third party without the Disclosing Party's prior written consent.

4. The Confidential Information does not include information which, (i) was or becomes generally available to the public other than as a result of a disclosure by the Receiving Party or its Representatives in breach of this Agreement, (ii) becomes available to the Receiving Party or its Representatives from a source not known by the Receiving Party to be bound by an obligation of confidentiality to the Disclosing Party with respect to such information, or (iii) was or is independently developed by the Receiving Party without reliance upon the Confidential Information.

5. Upon the Disclosing Party's written request, the Receiving Party will promptly redeliver to the Disclosing Party all written Confidential Information or destroy (to the extent technically possible) any other written Confidential Information in the Receiving Party's possession. Notwithstanding the foregoing, the Receiving Party may retain copies of the Confidential Information to the extent necessary to comply with its recordkeeping policies and/or applicable law, court or regulatory agency or authority although all such retained Confidential Information shall remain subject to the terms of this Agreement.

6. Although the Receiving Party understands that the Disclosing Party will endeavor to include in the Confidential Information all information known to it that it believes to be relevant for purposes of the Receiving Party's evaluation of the Possible Transaction, the Receiving Party further understands that neither the Disclosing Party nor any of its representatives makes any representation or warranty, express or implied, as to the accuracy or completeness of the Confidential Information, except to the extent such representation or warranty is given in any agreement superseding this Agreement.

7. In the event that the Receiving Party and its Representatives are requested or required in any legal, judicial or regulatory proceeding or investigation to disclose any Confidential Information, the Receiving Party will, to the extent reasonably practicable and permitted by law, judicial or regulatory authority, give the Disclosing Party as soon as reasonably practicable notice of such request, and the Receiving Party may disclose such information without liability hereunder, but may only disclose that portion of the Confidential Information that is required to be disclosed.

8. This Agreement contains a complete statement of all of the arrangements between the Parties hereto with respect to its subject matter and supersedes all previous agreements between them concerning this subject matter. It is hereby also acknowledged that this Agreement contains all essential terms, including, without limitation, those which have to be agreed by the Parties pursuant to the requirements of the applicable law.

9. This Agreement enters into force from the moment of its execution. This Agreement shall terminate on the first to occur of the following: (a) the date that is two (2) years from the date hereof or (b) the date that any definitive agreements relating to the Possible Transaction are executed and delivered.

10. If due to the Receiving Party's disclosure of the Confidential Information in breach of the terms of this Agreement the Disclosing Party incurs damages, the Receiving Party shall be held liable and recover all the documented damages in accordance with applicable laws.

11. This Agreement is governed by and shall be construed in accordance with _____ law.

12. Any dispute, controversy or claim arising out of or relating to this Agreement, or the execution, breach, termination or invalidity thereof (a "Dispute"), shall be settled by the courts of _____ in accordance with the applicable _____ legislation.

13. This Agreement may not be amended, modified or assigned without the express written consent of each of the Parties hereto.
14. This Agreement is executed in two copies (one copy for each of the Parties) in English language. Each copy shall have equal legal force.

IN WITNESS WHEREOF, the Parties have signed and entered into this Agreement on the day and year first above written.

PARTY 1
Address:
_____
Director

PARTY 2
Address:
_____
Director

在保密协议中，当事方需要约定以下主要条款：

（1）保密内容。

（2）责任主体。

（3）保密期限；一般而言，保密期限不宜过长，以交易完成的 2 年或 3 年为限。

（4）保密义务；当事一方或当事双方负有保密义务时，应明确约定信息披露的例外情形，如根据法律或上市公司要求予以披露的除外。此外，还应约定向第三方披露时，应得到另一方的书面同意

（5）违约责任。

在当事方之间签订保密协议中，当事方也可以采用一方签署当事另一方同意并接受的方式签署保密协议，举例如下：

NON-DISCLOSURE AGREEMENT

(Private and Confidential)

_____
_____
_____

Dear Sir,

In connection with the interest of your company _____ (hereinafter referred to as "Recipient") in a possible acquisition of certain interests in _____ (the "Transaction"), _____ ("AAA") may furnish to Recipient, or may procure that Recipient is furnished with, certain information relating to AAA, which AAA, at its sole discretion, may decide or agree to disclose to Recipient. Any such furnishing or disclosure of information by AAA or anyone on its behalf shall be strictly and expressly conditional upon Recipient undertaking and complying with the obligations set out hereinbelow and solely for the purpose of the evaluation of the Transaction by Recipient.

Therefore in consideration of AAA's willingness to disclose or furnish such information as AAA may deem fit to disclose or furnish, Recipient hereby agrees and undertakes to AAA as follows:

1. For the purposes of this Agreement the term "Information" shall include:

    1.1 Information of whatsoever nature relating to AAA, which shall be made available to Recipient or anyone on its behalf in writing, electronically, orally or in any other manner or medium by AAA, its officers, employees, shareholders, representatives or advisers, or any other person or entity on their behalf during the validity period of this Agreement;

    1.2 Notes, analyses, data, compilations, forecasts, studies and other documents or details arrived at or prepared by Recipient, its officers, employees or advisers or any other person or entity on its behalf, which record, cite, summarize, analyse, contain, or otherwise reflect or embody Information referred to in paragraphs above.

2. Recipient's obligations contained herein shall not apply to Information that Recipient can prove by written records:

    2.1 was known to Recipient on a non-confidential basis or was public knowledge at the time of its disclosure by AAA or anyone on AAA's behalf; or

    2.2 has subsequent to such disclosure become public knowledge other than a result of a breach of this Agreement by Recipient or as a result of disclosure by anyone who receives the Information or access thereto from Recipient or anyone on its behalf; or

    2.3 was rightfully disclosed to Recipient on a non-confidential basis, subsequent to disclosure by AAA, by a third party unrelated to AAA and such disclosure was not in breach of any obligation of confidentiality obligations owed by that third party; or

    2.4 was independently developed by Recipient without reference to or use of the Information.

3. Recipient shall not be deemed to be in breach of its obligations contained herein as a result of disclosure of Information that does not exceed the extent absolutely necessary, which Recipient can prove by written records:

    3.1 Recipient was obligated to disclose to any official authority under any compelling statutory law or regulation; or

    3.2 Recipient was obligated to disclose pursuant to a court order issued by a competent court of law, provided that prior to disclosure Recipient had given written notice of the said court order to AAA in order to allow AAA to apply to the court for revoking or limiting such order.

4. Recipient shall hold the Information in the strictest confidence and shall not disclose or divulge any part of the Information to any person or entity (other than as permitted in clauses below), whether or not the Transaction materializes, without the prior written consent of AAA which may be withheld or given upon such terms and conditions as AAA may consider appropriate, at its absolute discretion.
5. Recipient shall not make any use whatsoever of the Information, all of which shall remain the property of AAA, except for the purpose of evaluating the Transaction.
6. Recipient may disclose the Information only to such of its affiliates, officers, employees and professional advisors (collectively: "Authorised Persons") who strictly need to have such Information for the purpose of evaluating the Transaction and are committed, in law or under a signed written undertaking substantially in the form of this NDA to keep the Information in strict confidence and refrain from using the Information for any purpose other than the evaluation of the Transaction. Recipient shall ensure that each of such Authorized Persons are made aware of and adhere to the terms of this Non-Disclosure Agreement as if they were parties hereto.
7. Recipient shall be liable to AAA for any disclosure or use of the Information by its Authorized Persons or by any other person or entity who had received the Information from Recipient or its Authorized Persons, which if made by Recipient, would have constituted a breach of this Agreement.
8. Neither Recipient nor its Authorized Persons shall initiate or engage directly or indirectly in any contacts of any kind in connection with the Transaction or the Information with any of AAA's officers, employees, customers, suppliers or creditors without the prior express written consent of AAA. Unless otherwise notified by AAA in writing, AAA's contacts for the purpose of any and all communications related to the Transaction or the Information are the following persons only:

    _____

    _____

9. Recipient shall not copy or reproduce or part with possession of any of the Information except with the prior express written consent of AAA and then only to the extent it is strictly necessary for the purpose of evaluating the Transaction and as is consistent with its obligations under this Agreement.
10. Recipient hereby represents and agrees as follows:
    10.1 Recipient is acting in this matter as principal and not as agent, or broker, for or on behalf of, any other person or entity;
    10.2 Recipient realizes, confirms and agrees that no representation, warranty or undertaking is made or given by AAA, or by anyone who may disclose or furnish to Recipient information on AAA's behalf, as to the correctness, accuracy, completeness or fitness for purpose of the Information and Recipient hereby waives any claim or complaint based on or relating to the above matters;

10.3 Recipient realizes, confirms and agrees that this Agreement does not commit or obligate AAA to disclose or furnish to Recipient any information whatsoever;

10.4 Recipient realizes, confirms and agrees that neither AAA or any shareholder thereof is not committed or obligated to accept any offer or proposal which may be made by Recipient or on its behalf in the course of any negotiations.

11. Forthwith upon AAA's first request Recipient shall:

11.1 Return to AAA all Information referred to in Clause [1] without retaining any copy or summary or synopsis thereof;

11.2 Destroy and/or cause to be destroyed all Information referred to in Clause [1] in its possession or in the possession of anyone on its behalf and provide AAA with a written confirmation that all copies of such Information have been destroyed.

12. Recipient shall notify AAA of any unauthorized disclosure or use of the Information by anyone on its behalf promptly after becoming aware of such disclosure or use and cooperate with AAA in stopping and/or remedying the effects of such disclosure or use.

13. Neither Recipient nor anyone on its behalf shall, directly or indirectly, propose employment or engagement to any person whom Recipient knows is an employee of AAA for a period until 2 (two) years shall have elapsed as of the latest disclosure of Information by AAA or anyone on its behalf.

14. Recipient hereby represents and undertakes that to the best of its knowledge its compliance with the terms of this Agreement shall not violate and contradict any law, regulation, statutory duty applicable to Recipient, any applicable corporate regulation, by-law, duty or limitation or any other statutory, corporate, or contractual obligation owed by Recipient.

15. AAA and Recipient hereby agree that nothing in this Agreement shall obligate either of them to enter into any agreement or make or accept any offer in relation to the Transaction or pursue the Transaction. Each of AAA and Recipient shall be entitled to discontinue the disclosure of Information and/or the evaluation of the Transaction and/or any negotiation with view to realizing the Transaction at any time without having to reason its decision.

16. Unless a binding agreement in writing explicitly to the contrary is executed by AAA and its shareholders and Recipient, AAA and/or its shareholders shall not be precluded from offering rights, interests or shares in AAA to others or from discussing, negotiating or entering into any agreement with any third party in relation to the acquisition of rights, interests or shares in AAA by others, regardless of whether or not any discussions, communications or negotiations between AAA and/or or its shareholders are or will be taking place at the same time.

17. Neither Recipient nor AAA shall publicize or make or solicit any announcement of (i) either party's interest in the Transaction or (ii) the existence or the cessation of discussions and/or negotiations in relation to the Transaction (iii) any detail concerning the Transaction, or its proposed terms and conditions, (iv) this Agreement and the parties' entry into this Agreement. Notwithstanding the foregoing, to the extent either party or its affiliate is obligated under

any applicable law or regulation, under any applicable stock exchange rules, or by any competent official authority having jurisdiction to report details relating to the Transaction, such party or affiliate shall be entitled to make such report, provided that notice of such report shall be given to the other party.

18. The invalidity for any reason whatsoever of any provision of this Agreement shall in no way affect any other provisions hereof, and all such other provisions shall in all respects remain valid and enforceable. If any provision or restriction is held to be invalid, AAA shall be entitled to modify or adjust the same so as to render it valid, in which event such adjusted or modified provision or restriction shall replace the initial provision or restriction and shall be deemed part of this Agreement.
19. This undertaking shall benefit AAA and its shareholders.
20. Any forbearance or failure by AAA to exercise any right hereunder in any instance or with regard to any matter shall not constitute a waiver of that right and shall not prevent it from exercising that right in any other instance or with regard to any other matter.
21. Recipient irrevocably agrees and acknowledges that the breach or anticipated breach of any of its above obligations is likely to cause AAA irreparable damage and/or such damage which cannot be adequately remedied solely by monetary relief, and therefore AAA shall have the right to seek and obtain restrictive injunctions (temporary or permanent) to enjoin or discontinue any breach or anticipated breach without prejudice to any other remedies which may be available to it.
22. This Agreement shall be governed and construed under the laws of _____ . The Courts of _____ shall have exclusive jurisdiction over any dispute, claim or action relating to the validity, performance, interpretation, termination or breach of this undertaking. However, AAA shall be entitled to instigate proceedings for the enforcement of this undertaking in any court having jurisdiction in any other territory.
23. This Agreement shall enter into force on the date of its signature thereon and shall remain in force for until 5 (five) years shall have elapsed following the latest disclosure of any Information by AAA or anyone on its behalf.
24. If Recipient is in agreement with the foregoing, please sign and return to us the enclosed duplicate of this letter.

Yours sincerely,

AAA:

Agreed and accepted on _____

For Recipient:_____
Name: Position:

第 9 章　工程变更

> The general rule is that a contractor who has been requested to do work which is in fact a variation will be able to recover payment for it if the employer has expressly or impliedly requested the work knowing it to be such.
>
> Paras 5-025, *Hudson's Building and Engineering Contracts*

9.1　变更定义

现代工程合同赋予了业主广泛的变更权利。FIDIC 施工合同（红皮书）1999 年第 1 版第 13.1 款［变更权］规定的变更定义是：

"每项变更可包括：

（1）合同中包括的任何工作内容的数量的改变（但此类改变不一定构成变更）。

（2）任何工作内容的质量或其他特性的改变。

（3）任何部分工程的标高、位置和（或）尺寸的改变。

（4）任何工作的删减，但要交他人实施的工作除外。

（5）永久工程所需的任何附加工作、生产设备、材料或服务，包括任何有关的竣工试验、钻孔和其他试验和勘探工作。

（6）实施工程的顺序或时间的改变。"

以某国际工程项目为例，在施工过程中，承包商与业主就路基底基层材料发生争议，承包商认为使用机轧碎石和天然料 1:2 掺拌材料构成了工程变更，增加了工程成本，因此要求业主给予补偿。承包商在论述掺拌料是否构成变更时，论述了工程量表中支付价号是否包括掺拌材料等问题，示例如下：

5.4　Contractor's Entitlement and Central Issues

5.4.1　To establish the Contractor's entitlement to the blended Subbase material, the following central issues that arose from this particular claim shall be examined carefully and fully pursuant to the provision of ERA 2002 and the Contract provisions:

- Issue 1: Do Clause 5102 of Particular Technical Specification and Clause 5103 of ERA 2002 prevent the Contractor from getting compensation for the 2:1 (natural to crushed) blended subbase material?
- Issue 2: Does the Priced BOQ include the pay items of the blended subbase material pursuant to Clause 5113 of ERA 2002?

- Issue 3: Does the Contractor perform his obligations to investigate borrow pits in the project area with due diligence?
- Issue 4: Does the blended subbase material requirement from the Engineer constitute a variation under Sub-Clause 13.1?
- Issue 5: Can the Contractor claim additional cost on the blended subbase material even though it does not constitute a variation?
- Issue 6: Does the Engineer deny the Contractor entitlement for the blended subbase material during the ascertaining process of the subbase material?
- Issue 7: Does the Contractor submit the unit price quotation and breakdown on the blended subbase material pursuant to the requirement of Sub-Clause 12.3?

5.4.2 Answers to Central Issues:
- Issue 1: Do Clause 5102 of Particular Technical Specification and Clause 5103 of ERA 2002 prevent the Contractor from getting compensation for the 2:1 (natural to crushed) blended subbase material?

The Contractor's Answer: NO

5.4.3 Clause 5102 of Particular Technical Specification provides:

Quote:

Specification 5102

Subbase material shall be obtained from sources located by the Contractor and approved by the Engineer or from existing pavement layers. The Contractor is required to obtain suitable sources, which are closest to the area where subbase is being placed.

Specification 5103 Material Sources for Subbase

The materials used for the construction of subbase layers shall be either:

1. *Natural gravel;*
2. *Crushed gravel;*
3. *Crushed rock or crushed boulders.*

Unquote.

5.4.4 What do Clause 5102 of Particular Technical Specification and Clause 5103 of ERA 2002 express actually? It is plain that both Clause 5102 and Clause 5103 as set forth above explain the sources of subbase material. The subtitle of Clause 5103 says expressly that material sources for subbases can come from either natural gravel, crushed gravel, crushed rock or crushed boulders. It is concluded that Clause 5102 and Clause 5103 do-not include the pay items in BOQ, i.e. the measurement and payment items. That is to say, the source of subbase material and measurement and payment for subbase material are utterly different things in the construction contract.

5.4.5 Therefore, both Clause 5102 and Clause 5103 cannot prevent the Contractor from getting compensation on the blended subbase material.

- Issue 2: Does the Priced BOQ include the pay item of the blended subbase material pursuant to Clause 5113 of ERA 2002?

The Contractor's Answer: NO

5.4.6 As contended in the Contractor letter C-507 dated 14 January 2013, the Contractor alleged further that the material used for the construction of subbase layers shall be natural gravel, crushed gravel or crushed rock/boulders specified in Clause 5103. This is just a general description for subbase material, which means all the three materials above can be used as subbase material if they satisfy the specification. However, as for the measurement and payment of subbase, it shall be in accordance with different pay items and different unit rates, just as specified in Clause 5113 of ERA 2002. In Clause 5113 of ERA 2002, there are two pay items for subbase: one is 51.01 (a) [gravel subbase] which means natural subbase material, the second is 51.01(c) [crushed stone]. It is clearly indicated in the Priced BOQ of the Contract that the subbase material is natural subbase as specified in pay item 51.01(a), which is the Contractor's bidding basis for this item during the tender period.

5.4.7 Because no suitable natural subbase material can be found in the project area, the Engineer, after consultation with the Employer, thus approved the blended subbase material at the ratio of 2:1 (natural to crushed) to substitute the specified subbase material, i.e. natural subbase material in 51.01(a) in the Price BOQ of the Contract.

5.4.8 It can be easily concluded from the Priced BOQ of the Contract that only pay item 51.01(a) [natural gravel] is available. There is no any pay item in the Price BOQ to regulate the blended subbase material.

- Issue 3: Does the Contractor perform his obligations to investigate borrow pits in the project area with due diligence?

The Contractor's Answer: YES

5.4.9 In the previous letter from the Engineer, he alleged that the Contractor didn't exert his best endeavors to investigate the borrow pit in the project area, so the Contractor has to be responsible for the non-availability of suitable subbase material.

5.4.10 The Contractor disagreed with the Engineer that 20 borrow pits in the project area had been investigated by himself and jointly with the Engineer, which are:

(1) K60 +100 RHS 100m;
(2) K72 +400 LHS 3.5km;
(3) K99 +700 LHS 1km;
(4) K107 +000 LHS;
(5) K53 +400 RHS;
(6) K71 +600;
(7) K84 +400 LHS 15km;
(8) K116 +500 RHS 15 km;
(9) K53 +400;
(10) K60 +100 RHS;

(11) K67 +800 RHS;
(12) K70 +940 LHS;
(13) K72 +400 RHS 3.5km;
(14) K73 +600 RHS 100m;
(15) K73 +800 RHS;
(16) K84 +400 LHS 15km;
(17) K92 +600 RHS 14km;
(18) K99 +700 LHS 1km;
(19) K107 +000 LHS;
(20) K116 +500 RHS 15km.

5.4.11 The Engineer, in the letter to the Employer dated 10 July 2012 under reference R-120, concluded that joint assessment and continuous check on possible natural subbase had continued since the commencement of the project. However, all the borrow pits investigated to date show deficiency mainly on PI, gradation and PP (plasticity product).

5.4.12 Consequently, it can be concluded from the foregoing fact and findings that the Contractor has performed his obligations under the Contract with due diligence. Non-availability of natural subbase material in the project area is an objective situation which the Contractor shall not be responsible for.

- Issue 4: Does the blended subbase material requirement from the Engineer constitute a variation under Sub-Clause 13.1?

The Contractor's Answer: YES

5.4.13 The Engineer alleged in letter RI/MDRUP-2/C/310 dated 8 January 2013 that themixing of the natural gravel and crushed rock material which are both specified in Clause 5103 of Contract Specifications for subbase to meet specified material requirements does not therefore constitute a variation.

5.4.14 Sub-Clause 13.1 of GCC states:
Quote:
Each variation may include:
(b) Changes to the quality and other characteristics of any item of work.
Unquote.

5.4.15 The Contractor holds that the Engineer issued the letter to approve the blended subbase material at the proportion ratio 2:1 (natural to crushed) to constitute a variation under Sub-Clause 13.1 of GCC since the nature, characteristics of the subbase as specified in the Contract has been changed by way of blending crushed stone.

5.4.16 In Sub-Clause 13.1 (b), the FIDIC Contract does not give the definition of "other characteristics". However, it can be understood from the common sense approach. Changes of characteristics may include physical or chemical or any other changes. In this particular case, themixing natural subbase material and crushed stone can be defined as change in physical characteristics. Accordingly, the event of any changes in characteristics by way of mixing natural subbase material and crushed stone, as described herein, clearly falls under the provision of "Changes to the quality and other characteristics of any item of work" under Sub-Clause 13.1 (b). Consequently, the Engineer's letter RI/C/290 dated 20 December 2012 under the subject of Approval of Contractor's Proposal for Blending Natural Gravel and Crushed Stone Subbase Material Constitute a Variation under Sub-Clause 13.1 of GCC.

- Issue 5: Can the Contractor claim additional cost on the blended subbase material even though it does not constitute a variation?

The Contractor's Answer: YES

5.4.17 Whether the blended subbase material constitutes a variation is a disputed issue between the Contractor and the Engineer. Even though it cannot be treated as a variation, can the Contractor have the right to get cost compensation from the Employer?

5.4.18 Does the requirement for blending subbase material constitute a constructive variation? At this stage and in this particular submission, the Contractor does not intend to discuss the issue. However, the Contractor reserves his right to do so.

5.4.19 YES. The pay item of 51.01(a)[natural grave] is available in the Priced BOQ of the Contract, but there is no any other pay item, such as 51.01(c), in the Priced BOQ.

5.4.20 As described in Contractor's answer to Issue No.2 above, it is a common knowledge, as a matter of fact, that natural gravel and blended subbase material is a different matter utterly, and the cost for those two things is ranged differently as well.

5.4.21 Accordingly, the Employer cannot pay for the blended subbase material under pay item 51.01(a)[natural gravel]. If and to the extent that there is no pay item in the Priced BOQ, under the common practice of FIDIC Contract, the Engineer should issue a variation order, or, if there is no rate in the Contract, the Engineer shall have the right pursuant to Sub-Clause 12.3 and 3.5 to decide a new rate. Unfortunately, the Engineer fails to perform his obligations as assigned to him by FIDIC Contract.

5.4.22 In terms of legal action, such action of the Employer by paying the blended subbase with natural gravel pay item constitutes unjust enrichment, or unjustified benefit under the applicable law.

- Issue 6: Does the Engineer, _____ and Others, deny the Contractor entitlement for the blended subbase material during the ascertaining process of the subbase material?

The Contractor's Answer: NO

5.4.23 When scrutinizing the Engineer's letter as attached herewith, it can be found that the Engineer does not deny the Contractor's entitlement to the blended subbase material. The disputed issues between the Engineer and the Contractor inchorological manner are:

> (1) finding the suitable borrow pits for the subbase material;
>
> (2) concluding on non-availability of suitable material;
>
> (3) understanding Clause 5102 and 5103 of ERA 2002;
>
> (4) whether it constitutes a variation.
>
> 5.4.24 The Engineer has never denied the Contractor's entitlement to the blended subbase material. And on the contrary, the Engineer asked the Contractor to put forward the new rate for the blended subbase material.
>
> - Issue 7: Does the Contractor submit the unit price quotation and breakdown on the blended subbase material pursuant to the requirement of Sub-Clause 12.3?
>
> <u>The Contractor's Answer: YES</u>
>
> 5.4.25 The Contractor, vide letter C-524 dated 21 January 2013, put forward the unit rate of the blended subbase material at ETB 516.64 and the unit breakdown in the attached Annex I accordingly.

对于承包商的上述主张,争议委员会在决定中写道:

"65. This conclusion however does not automatically mean that the additional cost of executing the blended solution is not recoverable by the Contractor as an item of the Permanent Works executed by the Contractor. Under a remeasurement contract such as the FIDIC Conditions of Contract for Construction, MDB Harmonised Edition [2005], this issue is governed by Sub-Clauses 12.2 [*Method of Measurement*] and 12.3 [*Evaluation*] and in this case the language of the Preamble of the BOQ and Particular Technical Specification §1212-Measurement: General, (b) Bill of Quantities. This point is discussed in section (b) below.

80. While the DB is satisfied that its Decision above interprets the letter of the Contract correctly, it has asked itself if the Parties truly intended for the contractual provisions to operate in this manner under these particular circumstances when they signed the Contract, however in the absence of any evidence pertaining to the Parties' intent, the DB is obliged to find as it has done herein. Nevertheless, it may not have been obvious to the Contractor that the risk of the unavailability of natural granular materials lay with him and the Employer may have chosen not to include a unit price for crushed stone subbase on the optimistic belief that the identified borrow pits would produce compliant materials. Therefore, there may not have been an entirely conscious transfer of the risk to the Contractor, nor an absolute understanding of the size of the risk. In the period following the publication of the DB Decision, the Parties may wish to take into consideration the foregoing in any amicable discussions, but are of course under no obligation to do so."

9.2　变更的司法验证标准

由于工程变更是引起承包商与业主发生争议和引起承包商索赔的主要原因之一，在英美多年的司法实践中，对变更的定义和验证标准作出了司法解释，进一步完善了标准格式合同中变更的概念。最著名的典型案例是 Watson Lumber Company 诉 Guennewig，226 NE 2d 270（1967）案。在此案中，确定的变更和承包商有权获得变更付款的定义和验证标准是：

（1）工程应在原始合同的范围之外。
（2）应由业主或其代理人发出变更指示。
（3）业主通过言语或行为同意支付额外工作。
（4）额外工作不是承包商自愿完成的。
（5）额外工作不是因承包商过错而必须实施的。
（6）如适用，业主已经放弃承包商未能遵守合同要求的程序或格式的规定。

在考虑是否应该支付变更的额外费用时，应满足上述六项标准。

上述六项验证标准在英联邦国家和美国的司法实践中得到了广泛的运用。英美法院在处理有关变更的案件时通常采用上述标准进行验证，以判断是否构成变更、承包商是否有权得到额外工程的付款。

针对上述原则，Hudson's Building and Engineering Contracts 第 5-019 节总结如下：

In concise form, the general principles entitling a Contractor to receive payment for a change or variation have been admirably summarized in a leading case in the US, in terms which are applicable equally in England and the Commonwealth, as being:

(1) that the work should be outside the narrower "agreed scope" of the contract, that is, outside the Contractor's express or implied obligations in regard to the works described in the original contract;

(2) that it should have been ordered by or on behalf of the Employer;

(3) that the Employer should, either by words or conduct, have agreed to pay for it;

(4) that any extra work has not been furnished voluntarily by the Contractor;

(5) that the work should not have been rendered necessary by the fault of the Contractor; and

(6) where applicable, that any failure of the Contractor to comply with contract requirements as to procedure or form should have been waived by the Employer.○

9.3　变更估价原则和公平估价

FIDIC 施工合同 1987 年第 4 版红皮书、1999 年第 1 版红皮书、多边开发银行协调版 2005 年版、2006 年版和 2010 年版粉皮书均规定变更估价的一般原则，如下：

○ Hudson's Building and Engineering Contracts. 14th Ed. 2019. Para 5-019.

(1) 如合同中规定了有关的费率和价格，应根据合同规定的费率和价格进行估价。即，如果合同中有工程量表，则估价必须根据准备工程量表的相同指导原则进行估价。

(2) 如与工程量表中标价的工程性质类似，并且在类似条件下工作，如适用，应根据工程量表中规定的费率或价格进行估价。

(3) 如果工程性质不同，或不是类似条件下工作或在缺陷更正期限内发出变更指示，工程量表中的费率或价格应用作合理估价的基础，并应公正合理。

(4) 如合同中没有适用于该变更的费率或价格，则应在合理的范围内使用合同中的费率或价格作为估价的基础。

(5) 如第 (1) ~ (4) 项的内容不存在，则工程师和承包商应对变更估价进行协商，由工程师和承包商协商一致合适的费率或价格。

(6) 如工程师和承包商不能就适当的费率或价格达成一致，可由（监理）工程师决定暂定的费率或价格，以便在临时付款证书中支付变更工程款项。

(7) 如承包商不满工程师对变更估价的决定，可根据合同条款，如 FIDIC 合同 1999 年第 1 版第 20 条［索赔、争议和仲裁］提出索赔，进入 FIDIC 规定的索赔程序。

在施工合同中，影响变更估价的因素主要有：

(1) 条件或情况的变化。与投标阶段相比，由于变更使工程性质发生了根本性的改变，承包商需在完全不同的情况下实施变更的工程项目。例如，在某个工程项目施工中，承包商原定使用铲土机进行开挖工程，并将废土堆放到毗邻的临时废坑中，留待以后处理。但变更令要求承包商在临时废坑处开挖一条排水明渠，为遵守变更指示，承包商不得不将开挖后的废土装上自卸车运到别处堆放。按照修改后的施工方法，承包商花费了很长时间才完成这项工程。由于是在雨季施工，还导致了承包商费用的增加，但没有对工程造成任何延误，也没有发生干扰事件。业主应根据合同规定的变更估价条款，对这项变更予以估价。

(2) 数量变化。有时，即使工程的性质和施工方法没有发生任何改变，但有些工程数量的变化将会严重影响承包商的施工成本。例如，在浇筑混凝土数量大幅增加时，为了按时完成楼板的浇筑工作，不影响随后计划中的关键工程，承包商不得不加班工作。再例如，工程数量的增加还会推迟有些工程的施工时间。如果砌砖工程数量增加了 20%，在施工使用的资源不变时，这将会造成施工时间的拖长（但其他活动或者整个合同期限没有拖长），并导致承包商支付劳务费用的增加，而劳务费用的增加又导致了额外成本的增加，所有这些都会在估价价值中有所反映（假定是固定单价合同）。

(3) 时间变化。业主可能在不同时间对合同规定的类似性质工程作出变更，在这种情况下，与原合同相比，不同时间内的材料和劳动力成本是不同的。

(4) 工程数量的少量变化。在变更涉及的工程数量很少时，承包商可能无法获得订货折扣，也会因此增加应付给分包商的工程价款。

(5) 与时间有关的成本变化。在可将延误期间从部分或全部工程分离出来并构成一项单独变更（或一组变更）时，应在变更估价时考虑与时间有关的成本。例如，对第一层地板结构变更可能会导致第二层楼板施工延误，延误时间为 1 周。除在变更估价中考虑包括混凝土、钢结构、木工的成本外，还应考虑混凝土拌和、混凝土泵、自卸车、塔式起重机、管理和其他预备费成本。由于需要对工程量表以外的工程进行计量，因此，也需要额外时间进行有关测量工作。

因变更工程的估价发生争议,是业主和承包商发生争议的主要原因之一。在变更估价过程中,承包商与业主的争议主要体现在承包商和业主或工程师不能就价格或费率达成一致,承包商往往要价高,而业主或工程师往往压低价格或费率,这正是承包商和业主发生争议的主要原因。

在大多数变更估价的合同规定中,可经常看到的是工程师应"公平"地进行变更工程的估价。但何谓"公平估价(fair valuation)",每个案例中所体现的判断标准和原则不尽相同,这是一个主观的判断标准。根据有关判例,"公平"可依如下标准予以确定:

(1)合同的明示规定。如 FIDIC 施工合同 1999 年第 1 版第 12.3 款 [估价] 规定,如果工程师按照合同中该项规定确定变更的费率和价格,则应认为工程师是公平的。

(2)根据变更估价原则进行估价。

(3)在缺乏上述规定的情况下,由工程师作出"公平的"决定,或在仲裁和诉讼中由仲裁员或法官作出"公平的"判断。

(4)在不同的工程项目中,公平价格都有不同的标准。一般而言,法官会根据这个费率或价格在具体项目发生的和与价格有关的情况下作出裁断。

(5)公平的费率和价格是否包括利润,应根据合同条款的具体规定进行判断。如合同条款明确规定包括费用和利润,则公平的费率和价格应将利润计算在内。如果合同条款只规定承包商有权索偿费用,并不包括利润,则公平的费率和价格不应包括利润。如果合同条款没有对利润做出明确的规定,根据相关判例和专家意见,则应包括利润在内。

在"公平地"决定变更的估价时,可参考同行的成本、承包商的实际成本等作出决定。

以某国际工程为例,关于第 7 号变更令,承包商陈述意见涉及了事实概述、第 7 号变更令的调整、禁反言等内容,示例如下:

"Variation Order 7

i. Factual Overview

At the time of execution of the Contract, the main source of electricity was the grid. However, due to shortage of electricity from the grid, the Contractor had to procure to electricity from two other sources; 1) use of generators owned by the Contractor and 2) use of High Furnace Oil Generators ("HFO Generators").

Since the Employer was required to supply electric power to the Contractor as per the terms of the Contract, the Employer authorized the supply of High Furnace Oil Generators fromWartsila and the O&M from Fatima Engineering Company as subcontractor.

Prior to the move to an alternative source of electricity, the Contractor was being paid/paying for the electricity at grid tariff which had not been specified as a separate item in the BOQ and formed part of the concrete cost quoted in the BOQ. But after the switch, we understand that it became expensive for the Contractor to produce electricity from HFO Generators at the same rate as the grid electricity since the O&M of the HFO Generator wasapproximately PKR 15.82 per kilo watt in 2006. The rate was accepted by the Employer in Board of Directors Meeting No. 8 and it was decided that it would be paid to the Contractor based on the units consumed.

Consequently, the Engineer determined the cost of grid electricity included in the rate of concrete as per the _____ . Schedule of Electricity Tariffs effective from 1st July 2005 at PKR 5.09 per kilo watt and deducted that amount from the HFO Generator cost quoted by the Contractor. The difference between the two amounts was calculated as PKR 10.73 per kilo watt net payable to the Contractor for LOT C1, C2 and C3.

Following the determination, the Engineer issued an Appropriation Request ("AP-7") (revised through subsequent AP-7 Revision-1) which was approved by the Employer vide letter dated 10th December, 2010 in the following terms:

"Approval of the competent authority to the final/revised proposal submitted by the Contractor M/s _____ vide letter at Srn No. (i) for the procurement/supply, installation and operation of 3 ×4 MW WARTSILA (Finland) Diesel Generators Operable on HSFO (including HSFO storage, testing and commissioning etc.) at the three sites of _____ at total price of US $ 18,672,987 along with O&M of these generator sets as Rs. 15.82 per kilo watt hours inclusive of administrative, fuel and repair/maintenance of the equipment."

Following the AP-7 Rev. 1, the Parties executed VO 7 which was signed by the Employer on 19-08-2015.

ii. Adjustment to VO 7

We understand that the Engineer has alleged a duplication of payment for electricity between VO 6 and VO 7 and through Letter No. P-252 dated 14 June 2018 ("P-26932"), the Engineer has proposed to remove the measurement of electricity from HFO Generators at PKR 10.73 per Kilo Watt rate from VO 7 that has been countered in VO 26 concrete price already. The Engineer has treated the measurement as an "oversight" and suggested a deduction of excess cost of PKR 9.91 per Kilo Watt from VO 7.

In light of the documents provided, the Contract and the laws of Pakistan, it appears that the Engineer cannot unilaterally amend VO 7 and the terms agreed between the parties without express consent of the Contractor.

(i) Amendment and Novation

As discussed in the Part II Sub-Part A of this opinion, any variation to the Contract is governed by Clause 51.1 of the Contract which authorizes the Engineer to make any variation of form, quality or quantity of the works for *increasing or decreasing the quantity of any work, omitting any such work, changing the character or quality or kind of any such work, changing the levels, lines, position and dimensions of any part of the Works, executing additional work of any kind necessary for the completion of the Works, or changing any specified sequence or timing of construction of any part of the Works.*

The Contract does not specifically define the term "Variations", however, in terms of the other modifications of FIDIC Contracts, a Variation has been defined as "any change of the Works, which is instructed or approved as a variation…" or "any change to the Employer's Requirements or Works, which is instructed or approved as a variation "

In view of the definition of variation and Clause 51.1, two distinct lines of arguments can be taken to prevent the Engineer from back charging the Contractor and unilaterally amending the VO 7. The alternative arguments depend on the source of the authority of the Employer and Engineer to alter the Contract respectively.

In the first instance, it can be argued that VO 7 is not a variation but an amendment to the Contract which is beyond the authority of the Engineer.

The language of Clause 51.1 suggests the Engineer only has the authority to vary the "form, quality or quantity of the works", of the Contract, however, to the extent of the tariff fixed in VO 7, a change in the source of electric power and a subsequent increase in the cost is, arguably, not related to the Works directly, it does not relate to any of the items listed in Clause 51.1; nor does it fit neatly within the definition of a variation explained in versions of the FIDIC Contracts.

Even if, for some reason, the O&M of HFO Generators can be categorized as works, it is a settled rule of interpretation of construction contracts that carrying out "additional" work not mentioned in the contract is not a variation in terms of the contract (i.e. it falls outside the purview of Clause 51.1).

Since the "variation" does not fit within the purview of the variation permitted under the contract through a variation order, it can be categorized as an amendment to the Contract.

Under the law, a variation has been expressly distinguished from an amendment.[1] A variation to a contract only addresses the changes the works to be carried out and does not in any way "vitiate or invalidate the Contract", whereas, an amendment has the effect of altering the contract to the extent of the amendment.

Amendment to any agreement is covered by Section 62 of the Contract Act 1872 which reads as:

> "Effect of novation, rescission and alteration of contract. If the parties to a contract agree to substitute a new contract for it, or to rescind or alter it, the original contract need not be performed."

The Courts in Pakistan have recognized an additional obligation or amendment to a contract as novation covered by Section 62 of the Contract Act 1872. In Messrs Industrial Development Bank of Pakistan vs Agha Saiyed Khursheed Alam Shah[2] the court held:

> "Novation is an act of either replacing an obligation to perform with another obligation; or adding an obligation to perform; or replacing a party to an agreement with a new party so in our view retaining the

---

[1] FIDIC Contracts: Law And Practice, by Ellis Baker, Ben Mellors, Scott Chalmers and Anthony Lavers 2009, pg. 118.
[2] 2017 P L C (C.S.) Note 85.

respondents for further period through separate letters to continue seems to have been added obligations to perform over and above the cutoff date."

The primary purpose of the section and subsequent case law is to crystallize the common law principles applicable to alterations to a contract which allow the parties to modify the terms of their contract by mutual agreement[①] and once the agreement has been altered, the original terms to that extent are extinguished and are replaced by the altered right and obligations. [②]

An amendment in writing, in whatever form, is an explicit agreement between the parties to the agreement to by bound by the amended or additional terms and the additional term forms part of the contract in the same way as the original terms of the Contract.

What lends weight to this argument is the fact that the VO 7 has been signed by the Employer as well as the Contractor i. e. the only parties to the Contract and both parties have mutually agreed to fix the "Tariff per kw" at "(15. 82 − 5. 09 = 10. 73 Rs)" for the "Operation and Maintenance Cost of (3) Gen Sets (Including fuel, Lube oil & Operating staff cost)".

As a consequence of the agreement between the parties to pay the Contractor PKR 10. 73 per kilo Watt for the O&M of Generator sets, the parties have voluntarily committed themselves to the rate for electricity produced as a result of HFO Generators till such time that the parties to the Contract i. e. the Employer and Contractor negotiate to change or alter the rate.

This view is recognized under the laws of contract in Pakistan. Section 37 of the Contract Act and the jurisprudence developed by the High Courts of Pakistan recognizes and upholds the sanctities of contracts entered into by parties out of their own free will.

Section 37 of the Contract Act is reproduced below for reference:

"*Obligation of parties to contracts. The parties to a contract must either perform, or offer to perform, their respective promises, unless such performance is dispensed with or excused under the provisions of this Act, or of any other law.*

Promises bind the representatives of thepromisors in case of the death of such promisors before performance, unless a contrary intention appears from the contract. "

---

① Robinson v Page (1826) 3 Russ. 114.
② PLD 2011 Kar. 24.

In a judgment authored by Mr. Justice Wajihuddin Ahmed, the Karachi High Court held that:

> "We would like to re-emphasize the sanctity of contracts. Where parties have, lawfully, entered into mutual commitments, with open eyes and free volition, maturing into contractual obligations, such cannot easily be allowed a unilateral and wilful disclaimer."①

The effect of categorizing VO 7 as an amendment has three consequences: 1) it binds the parties to the rate for the use of HFO Generators for the production of electricity for all subsequent works and VOs unless agreed otherwise including VO 6 since VO 7 was signed later in time, and 2) it cannot be changed by the Engineer through a variation order under Clause 51.1 specifically because the Engineer is not a party to the Contract to authorize an amendment in any case, and 3) it cannot be amended unilaterally.①

(ii) Estoppel

In the alternate, if it is argued that VO 7, signed by the Employer, Engineer and Contractor, is a variation pursuant to Clause 51.1 instead of an amendment since, though it relates to the Tariff per kw, it indirectly authorizes "additional works" for "Supply, installation, testing commissioning and operating and managing HFO Generator Sets", which the Engineer has the authority to issue, the Engineer can still not amend it.

The Engineer determined the Tariff per kilo Watt after due consideration and in accordance with the methodology specified in Clause 52.1 of the GCC as amended by Part II A and Part II B.

It is interesting to note that the language of Clause 51.1 does not require the Engineer to consult the Contractor to issue a variation order i.e. the Engineer has the authority to unilaterally instruct the Contractor to give effect to the variation proposed. However, Clause 52.1 specifically requires the Engineer to consult the Contractor to determine the rate. The Contractor had made a detailed proposal to the Engineer as well as Employer vide its letter referenced G-1429 dated 14th July 2010, for the O&M cost of the HFO Generator at Rs. 15.82 per kW · h. There are enough documents available on record to suggest that the rate agreed was endorsed by the Engineer as reasonable and justified. The rate was also categorically accepted by the Employer after due consultation with the Engineer.

Consequently, once the rate had already been set and accepted by all three parties, the Engineer lost its discretion to set the rate or to unilaterally amend the rate and any such amendment would be a breach of the Contract, entitling the Contractor to damages.

The rationale for the restriction on the Engineer from unilaterally amending the rate is

---

① Hafeezullah Khan v. Al-Haj Chaudhri Barkat Ali (PLD 1998 Kar. 274).

grounded in the equitable principles of estoppel. Estoppel has been defined in the Black's Law Dictionary IX Edition as:

> "*A bar that prevents one from asserting a claim or right that contradicts what has been said or done before or what has been legally established as true.*"

The Honorable Supreme Court of Pakistan has also developed the doctrine specifically in the context of promissory estoppel. The Court in Para 23 of Pakistan v. Fecto Belarus Tractors Limited[①] recognized and elucidated on the doctrine in the following way:

> *It will be necessary to Coach the true concept of the doctrine of promissory estoppel. Before proceeding further this doctrine has been variously called " promissory estoppel "" requisite estoppel "" quasi estoppel" and "new estoppel". It is a principle evolved by equity to avoid injustice and though commonly named 'promissory estoppel'. It is neither in the realm of contract nor in the realm of estoppel. The true principle of promissory estoppel seems to be that where one party has by his words or conduct made to the other a clear and unequivocal promise which is intended to create legal relations or effect a legal relationship to arise in the future, knowing or intending that it would be acted upon by the other party to whom the promise is made and it is in fact so acted upon by the other party, the promise would be binding on the party making it and he would not be entitled to go back upon it, if it would be inequitable to allow him to do so having regard to the dealings which have taken place between the parties and this would be so irrespective of whether there is anypreexisting relationship between the parties or not. The doctrine of promissory estoppel need not be inhibited by the same limitation as estoppel in the strict sense of the term. It is an equitable principle evolved by the Courts for doing justice and there is no reason why it should be given only a limited application by way of defence. There is no reason in logic or principle why promissory estoppel should also not be available as a cause of action.*

The Supreme Court of India in M. P. Sugar Mills v. State of UP (1979 AIR 621) went further to lower the standards of detriment needed to invoke the doctrine against the

---

① 2011 P L C (C. S.) 1579.
② PLD 2002 Supreme Court 208.

promisor e. g. the Engineer is prejudiced to the interests of the promisee. The relevant excerpt is copied below for reference:

> "*That it is not necessary in order to attract the applicability of the doctrine of promissory estoppel, that the promisee, acting in reliance on the promise should suffer any detriment. What is necessary is only that the promisee should have altered his position in reliance on the promise. But if by detriment we mean injustice to the promisee which would result if the promisor were to resile from his promise, then detriment would certainly come in as a necessary ingredient. The detriment in such a case is not some prejudice suffered by the promisee by acting on the promise, but the prejudice which would be caused to the promisee if the promisor were allowed to go back on the promise*"

Despite the fact that the VO 7 may potentially be categorized as a variation instead of an amendment, the doctrine established by the Courts of Pakistan precludes the Engineer from unilaterally changing the rate of electricity agreed between the parties especially since the Contractor has already rendered performance based on the rates decided in VO 7 and entered into agreements with the Sub-Contractor, Fatima Engineering (Pvt.) Ltd. for O&M of HFO Generators.

(iii) Amendment through an Interim Payment Certificate

Additionally, it appears that the Engineer desires to correct or modify its oversight with respect to the unit rate of the alternate power source fixed via VO 7 through an Interim Payment Certificate ("IPC"). The unit rates specified in VO 7 were determined as per Clause 52.1 of the GCC as amended by Part II A and Part II B of the Contract. The relevant parts of the amended clauses are reproduced below:

> "*52.1 All variations referred to in Clause 51 and any additions to the Contract Price which are required to be determined in accordance with Clause 52 (for the purposes of this Clause referred to as 'varied work'), shall be valued at the rates and prices set out in the Contract if, in the opinion of the Engineer, the same shall be applicable. If the Contract does not contain any rates or prices applicable to the varied work, the rates and prices in the Contract shall be used as the basis for valuation so far as may be reasonable, failing which, after due consultation by the Engineer with the Employer and the Contractor, suitable rates or prices shall be agreed upon between the Engineer and the Contractor. In the event of disagreement the Engineer shall fix such rates or prices as are, in his opinion appropriate and shall notify the Contractor accordingly,*

with a copy to the Employer. Until such time as rates or prices are agreed or fixed, the Engineer shall determine provisional rates or prices to enable on-account payments to be included in certificates issued in accordance with Clause 60."

The aforesaid clause empowers the Engineer to value the varied works in consultation with the Employer and the Contractor and in case no agreement is reached between the two, then the Engineer is at liberty to fix such or prices as he deems appropriate. However, an agreement was reached between the Employer and the Contractor subsequent to which the tariff per kW·h (15.82 −5.09) = 10.73 Rs/kW·h was fixed.

It should be noted that Clause 52.1 does not empower or stipulate deviation from or authorize a subsequent change in a fixed rate or price. Once a rate has been fixed in a VO, the Employer, the Engineer or the Contractor cannot unilaterally change the same even if it is alleged that the rate was fixed due to an oversight on part of the Engineer.

The only authority that the Engineer does have under the Contract for modification or correction is through the execution of the IPC. Clause 60.4 of the GCC empowers the Engineer to correct or modify any previously issued IPC. Clause 60.4 reads as follows:

"The Engineer may by any Interim Payment Certificate make any correction or modification in any previous Interim Payment Certificate which shall have been issued by him and shall have authority, if any work is not being carried out to his satisfaction, to omit or reduce the value of such work in any Interim Payment Certificate."

We understand that the Engineer vide P-252 dated 14th June 2018, desires to invoke Clause 60.4 and adjust the alleged overpayment in previous IPC's through IPC 101. It is critical at this point to understand the scope of adjustment and extent of adjustments to an IPC. Keating on Construction Contract at Page 147, whilst examining the approach of the courts in the cases of *Secretary of State for Transport v Birse-Farr Joint Venture* (1993) 62 B.L.R. 36 and *Henry Boot Construction Ltd. v Alstom Combined Cycles Ltd.* [2005] 1 W.L.R. 3850, *CA*, to IPC's concluded that Interim certificates are approximate estimates, made in some instances for the purpose of determining whether the Employer is safe in making a payment in advance of the contract sum.

In almost every case where an adjustment is upheld in a subsequent IPC, the decision is based on an estimated amount of the measurement of works done or materials used as stated in the IPC. Thus, such approximate estimates pertain to the total measurement of works that were completed and the quantity of materials used in completion of those works. It is pertinent to mention here that the instant matter the IPC's issued pursuant to VO 7 was based on the tariff for alternate power supply determined by due deliberations of both the Engineer and the Employer.

The precedent case law that supports or protects the right of the Engineer to make adjustments or modifications in IPC's is based on the fact that a previous IPC stated an estimated amount formeasurement of works or materials, which was paid to the Contractor so as to avoid any sort of delay and keep the Contractor financially afloat for carrying out its obligations. However, it needs to be noted that such an estimated amount is adjusted via subsequent IPC's depending on the amount of works completed and material used, which means that if a lesser amount of work is completed than was estimated, the Engineer would adjust the overpayment through an IPC.

In this case the Engineer is not adjusting the IPC amount based on the completed works or materials used, but unilaterally changing the fixed tariff that was worked out as per the cost breakdown provided in VO 7 and agreed between all three Parties. Since, a fixed tariff or rate cannot be changed by making adjustments in a subsequent IPC, if the Engineer makes any sort of amendments or modifications in IPC 101 to affect the tariff duly approved and executed under VO 7, he will be exceeding his authority under the Contract and would be liable for the same.

As a corollary of the above it can be concluded that the Engineer seeks to amend the VO under the guise of an adjustment to the IPC, which is not permissible under the law since it is an accepted principle of law that what cannot be done directly, is not permitted to be done indirectly.

承包商需要牢记的是，在变更的情况下，承包商不受 FIDIC 1999 年第 1 版合同条款第 20.1 款[承包商的索赔]规定的 28 天索赔时效的限制。以某国际工程为例，承包商认为该项工程属于变更，工程师签发了第 3 号变更指示，而变更不受合同规定的 28 天索赔时效的限制。争议委员会支持了承包商的意见，在争议委员会决定中作出如下决定：

"THE EMPLOYER AND THE CONTRACTOR's POSITIONS ON TIME BAR AND DB DISCUSSION

21. The Employer contends that when the Engineer issued Variation Order No. 3 on 9 January 2014 by letter ref. 001, if the Contractor considered himself entitled to additional payment as a result of the Variation, he was required to submit a notice of claim under Sub-Clause 20.1 [*Contractor's Claims*] to the Engineer within 28 days, describing the event or circumstances giving rise to the claim. Nonetheless the Contractor has failed to issue such notice until 30 March 2014 and 28 February 2015.

22. As the Contractor's letter dated 30 March 2014 was sent more than 28 days after the Variation dated 9 January 2014, the Employer should be discharged from all liabilities in connection with the claim pursuant to the second paragraph of Sub-Clause 20.1 which states: "*if the Contractor fails to give notice of a claim within*

such period of 28 days, the Time for Completion shall not be extended, the Contractor shall not be entitled to additional payment, and the Employer shall be discharged from all liabilities in connection with the claim."

23. The Contractor considers that because the disagreement is related to a Variation instruction, the dispute is over the valuation of the Variation and as such the issue at hand is simply a matter of applying the contractual procedures for resolving differences over valuations and that these procedures in the case of a Variation instruction are independent of Sub-Clause 20.1 and not subject to the time bar provisions cited above.

24. The Contractor considers the Employer is in breach of his obligation to evaluate the additional works incurred following the issuance of Variation Order No. 3, which was to be evaluated according to Sub-Clause 12.2 [*Method of Measurement*]. The Contactor contends that disputes over the evaluation of a Variation are to be treated under Clause 12 [*Measurement and Evaluation*] and Clause 13 [*Variations and djustment*] rather than as a claim under Sub-Clause 20.1. In terms of construction contracts, a claim is not an assessment of the evaluation of a Variation, which is a commonly misused interpretation.

25. Therefore, the nature of this dispute is not a claim, but rather a difference over the Variation evaluation and the time bar which might be applicable to claims under Sub-Clause 20.1 is not applicable in these circumstances. The Contractor affirms that if he did issue a notice of claim at some point in regard to this dispute, it was only out of precaution due to the Employer's persistence on the use of notices.

DB's Decision on time bar

26. The DB concurs with the Contractor that cases involving disputes over the valuation of a Variation, including the Engineer's determinations in regard to new unit rates, are not to be treated as a claim in the sense of Sub-Clause 20.1, because the mechanisms in Clauses 12 and 13 and Sub-Clause 20.4 [*Obtaining Dispute Board's Decision*] prevail in such cases.

27. For the reasons explained in the following section of this decision, the DB finds that Variation Order No. 3 was issued as a normal Variation instruction. During the extended period between 28 May 2012, when the Contractor first made a value engineering proposal, and 9 January 2014 when the Variation Order No. 3 was issued, the change in design lost its character as a value engineering matter through the actions of the Parties.

28. As a normal Variation instruction, the Engineer has fixed the unit rates for the two types of ditch covers at the original BOQ rates without any adjustment in Variation Order No. 3. Given that the Contractor had applied for a rate adjustment before and after the issue of the Variation instruction, the Engineer's finding that no increase was due must be considered to be his determination of the matter.

Likewise when he issued ICP certificates going forward, when the works were being executed between December 2014 and December 2016, each certificate represents his determination of the unit rates.

29. Under the contractual mechanisms described in the Contract, there are no provisions requiring the Contractor to issue a notice of claim or dissatisfaction with the determinations of the Engineer which he issues to the Contractor by way of his evaluations of ICPs and Variations.

30. On the contrary, the first paragraph of Sub-Clause 20.4 gives the Parties the right to refer any dispute in connection with any certificate, instruction or valuation of the Engineer directly to the DB without any mention of a prior notice of claim. In effect, the dispute is not over a claim for "additional payment" *per se*, but rather it is a dispute over payment of an amount which is in fact due to the Contractor by application of the Contract provisions under Clauses 12 and 13.

31. It is in fact the Engineer and Employer who have denied payment of an amount due to the Contractor following the issue of a Variation instruction, not the Contractor who is claiming for an "additional payment". The Contractor in effect is only claiming for an amount due, which flows naturally from the issue of a Variation instruction. The issue of Variation instructions is a contractually planned for event, not a contingency, for which Clauses 12 and 13 guide the Parties how to calculate the amounts then due. Failure of the Engineer and the Employer to accept the correct amount due is therefore not the same as a claim for additional payment.

32. In light of the foregoing, the DB finds that the time bar provisions of Sub-Clause 20.1 cannot be applied in these circumstances and the Contractor's claim is not time barred."

第 10 章　不可抗力

> The expression "force majeure clause" is normally used to described a contractual term by which one (or both) of the parties is entitled to cancel the contract or is excused from performance of the contract, in whole or in part, or is entitled to suspend performance or to claim an extension of time for performance, upon the happening of a specified event or events beyond his control.
>
> Paras 15-152, Chitty on Contracts. 33rd Edition

10.1　不可抗力定义

10.1.1　FIDIC 合同条款 1987 年第 4 版特殊风险定义

FIDIC 在不同时期发布的系列合同条款中对不可抗力条款作出了不同的约定。1987 年第 4 版 FIDIC 施工合同在第 20.4 款 [业主风险] 对业主风险作出了定义，并采用了列举的方式列明了业主风险的范围，第 65 条 [特殊风险]（Special Risks）规定了发生特殊风险时合同要求和救济措施。1999 年第 1 版 FIDIC 系列合同条款在第 19 条 [不可抗力]（Force Majeure）中规定了不可抗力定义、不可抗力事件、通知、承包商减轻义务、解除合同的期限及其解除后的安排等。2017 年第 2 版 FIDIC 系列合同条款在第 18 条 [例外事件]（Exceptional Events）规定了与 1999 年第 1 版第 19 条基本相同的内容。国际金融组织使用的多边开发银行协调版《施工合同条件》2005 年、2006 年和 2010 年版合同在第 19 条 [不可抗力] 规定了不可抗力条款，内容与 1999 年第 1 版系列合同相同。

FIDIC 合同 1987 年第 4 版第 65.2 款 [特殊风险] 规定如下：

"65.2　The special risks are：
(a) the risks defined under paragraphs (a),(c),(d) and (e) of Sub-Clause 20.4, and
(b) the risks defined under paragraph (b) of Sub-Clause 20.4 insofar as these relate to the country in which the Works are to be executed."

FIDIC 施工合同 1987 年第 4 版第 20.4 款 [业主风险] 规定了业主承担的风险，如下：

"20.4　the Employer's risks are：

(a) war, hostilities (whether war be declared or not), invasion, act of foreign enemies;

(b) rebellion, revolution, insurrection, or military or usurped power, or civil war;

(c) ionizing radiations, or contamination by radio-activity from any nuclear fuel, or from any nuclear waste from the combustion of nuclear fuel, radio-active toxic explosive or other hazardous properties of any explosive nuclear assembly or nuclear component thereof;

(d) pressure waves caused by aircraft or other aerial devices travelling at sonic or supersonic speeds;

(e) riot, commotion or disorder, unless solely restricted to employees of the Contractor or of his Subcontractors and arising from the conduct of the Works;

(f) loss or damage due to the use or occupation by the Employer of any Section or part of the Permanent Works, except as may be provided for in the Contract;

(g) loss or damage to the extent that it is due to the design of the Works, other than any part of the design provided by the Contractor or for which the Contractor is responsible, and

(h) any operation of the forces of nature against which an experienced contractor could not reasonably have been expected to take precautions."

10.1.2　FIDIC 合同条款 1999 第 1 版不可抗力定义

FIDIC 合同条款 1999 年第 1 版红皮书、黄皮书和银皮书合同条款第 19.1 款［不可抗力定义］将不可抗力风险定义如下：

"19.1 Definition of Force Majeure

In this Clause, "Force Majeure" means an exceptional event or circumstance:

(a) Which is beyond a Party's control;

(b) Which such Party could not reasonably have provided against before entering into the Contract;

(c) which, having arisen, such Party could not reasonably have avoided or overcome, and

(d) Which is not substantially attributable to the other Party.

Force Majeure may include, but is not limited to, exceptional events or circumstances of the kind listed below, so long as conditions (a) to (d) above are satisfied:

(i) war, hostilities (whether war be declared or not), invasion, act of foreign enemies;

(ii) rebellion, terrorism, revolution, insurrection, military or usurped power, or civil war;

(iii) riot, commotion, disorder, strike or lockout by persons other than the Contractor's Personnel and other employees of the Contractor and Subcontractors;

(iv) munitions of war, explosive materials, ionising radiation or contamination by radio-activity, except as may be attributable to the Contractor's use of such munitions, explosives, radiation or radio-activity, and

(ⅴ) natural catastrophes such as earthquake, hurricane, typhoon or volcanic activity. "

10.1.3　FIDIC 合同条款 2017 年第 2 版例外事件定义

FIDIC 合同条款 2017 年第 2 版第 18.1 款［例外事件］将例外风险定义为：

"18.1　Exceptional Events
'Exceptional Event' means an event or circumstance which:
(ⅰ) is beyond a Party's Control;
(ⅱ) the Party could not reasonably have provided against before entering into the Contract;
(ⅲ) having arisen, such Party could not reasonably have avoided or overcome; and
(ⅳ) is not substantially attributable to the other Party.

An Exceptional Event may comprise but is not limited to any of the following events or circumstances provided that the conditions (ⅰ) to (ⅳ) above satisfied:

(a) war, hostilities (whether war be declared or not), invasion, act of foreign enemies;
(b) rebellion, terrorism, revolution, insurrection, military or usurped power, or civil war;
(c) riot, commotion or disorder by persons other than the Contractor's Personnel and other employees of the Contractor and Subcontractors;
(d) strike or lockout not solely involving the Contractor's Personnel and other employees of the Contractor and Subcontractors;
(e) encountering munitions of war, explosive materials, ionising radiation or contamination by radio-activity, except as may be attributable to the Contractor's use of such munitions, explosives, radiation or radio-activity; or
(f) natural catastrophes such as earthquake, tsunami, volcanic activity, hurricane or typhoon. "

2017 年第 2 版 FIDIC 系列合同条款第 18 条将 1999 年第 1 版系列合同条款中第 19 条［不可抗力］的称谓更换为［例外事件］，充满争议。在大陆法系国家，不可抗力作为法律明文规定的法律概念，得到了大陆法系各国的普遍认可。而例外事件不是法律用语，这将在实践中产生困惑，即发生了例外事件时，例外事件与不可抗力是否不同，是否属于大陆法系法律界定的不可抗力，存在诸多疑问。一般而言，在 FIDIC 合同条款下，从定义和罗列的事件看，无论是称为特殊风险，还是称为不可抗力或是例外事件，三者具有基本相同的含义，属于大陆法系中不可抗力的法律范畴。

10.2 普通法系和大陆法系中的不可抗力

10.2.1 普通法系相关规定

在普通法系中，不可抗力不仅不是一个既定的法律概念，而且不是一个法律专有术语（a term of art），而且其法律和判例对此仍不甚明晰，因此，当事方如果想适用不可抗力及其法律救济，则应在合同中明确约定不可抗力的定义及其相关的补救措施，例如不可抗力通知、减轻义务、不可抗力导致的合同终止、不可抗力的法律救济措施等。如果合同中没有约定此类具体的合同条款，则不能默示其已包含在合同中，当事方需要在合同中明确约定此类具体的合同条款。在合同中没有此类约定时，当事方可能无法主张与之相关的法律救济措施，但当事方可以从普通法中的合同落空（frustration of contract）、履约不能（impossibility of performance）或无法履约（impracticability of performance）寻求法律救济。显而易见的是，合同落空、履约不能或无法履约的法律验证标准要比不可抗力更加严格。

在普通法中，构成合同受阻需要符合如下法律验证标准（test）：

（1）合同受阻等于是把合同杀死，必须尽量限制其使用。

（2）合同一旦受阻，合同立即终止，不需要当事双方一致同意，也不需要当事一方做出宣告。

（3）合同受阻成立后，双方没有相互赔偿责任。

（4）合同受阻必须是外来因素导致合同责任的变化，而不是合同当事方的行为导致。

（5）依赖合同受阻的当事一方必须对合同受阻情况没有过失或责任。

适用于巴基斯坦、印度和孟加拉国的《1872年合同法》第56条规定了履约不能的情形。为了证明合同受阻或称落空，应满足如下验证标准：

（1）当事方之间必须存在有效的和尚在存续的合同。

（2）必须还有部分合同需要履行。

（3）尚需履行的部分合同应变成不可能履约或非法；和

（4）不能履约应是缔约方无法避免的原因导致的。

在普通法中，合同当事方一旦签约，当事双方负有严格履行合同义务的责任，如果当事一方不能履行合同，违约的当事方需要承担赔偿责任。需要注意的是，在英国普通法中，合同受阻或称合同落空的法律验证标准采用严格责任制，认为如果给予当事方太多的法定免责，则合同就丧失了约束力，使得合同履行丧失了可能性。

因此，在国际工程项目合同适用普通法时，承包商应首先根据合同约定的不可抗力条款进行抗辩，依合同约定的不可抗力定义或列入的特殊风险或不可抗力事件主张权利。在合同没有约定特殊风险或不可抗力事件时，可引用适用法律中的合同落空或称合同受阻，主张履约不能。必须看到，国际工程合同中，对于特殊风险和不可抗力均约定了给予承包商工期延长和/或额外费用的权利，即延迟履行和损害赔偿的法律救济，这与国际贸易等其他类型的合同存在明显的不同。承包商可利用特殊风险或不可抗力条款，主张工期延长和/或额外费用的法律救济，向业主提出索赔。

10.2.2 大陆法系中的不可抗力

不可抗力（Force Majeure）概念来源于法国民法典，通常在大陆法系国家的民法典中均有明确的法律规定。在大陆法系中，在合同没有明确约定不可抗力条款时，可以默认为其已经包含在合同中，合同当事人可以依据法律的明文规定进行主张或抗辩。

2016年10月1日生效的新的法国《民法典》第1218条明确对不可抗力作了定义："不可抗力是指债务人因无法控制的情况不能履行其合同义务，同时该情况在合同订立时无法被合理预料到，且其后果是无法通过适当措施加以避免的。如果履行障碍仅仅是暂时的，债务人可暂时中止其债务的履行，除非由此导致的迟延使债权人有权解除合同。如果该障碍是永久性的，则合同自动解除，双方当事人依照第1351条和第1351-1条规定的条件不再承担合同义务。"

法国法院认为构成不可抗力的事件必须具备"外在性""不可预见性""无法克服性"三个特征。

（1）外在性表明导致合同不能履行的情况须是合同履行一方无法控制的。法国司法判例采纳的"不可控制"标准意味着即使是债务人内部的原因，例如自身疾病或罢工，也可能构成不可抗力。

（2）可预见性是指合同当事双方无法在订立合同时合理地预见到该事件。如果在当事方的预见能力和预防能力之内，当事方如尽最大的努力可防止其发生，该事件应不属于不可抗力。

（3）无法克服性是指外在原因导致当事人无法履行合同，且没有任何其他替代方案。合同履行的障碍必须是无法克服的，如果可以以更昂贵的成本履行合同，则不能构成不可抗力。

同时，不可抗力事件和合同的无法履行须有直接的因果关系。如果债务的不能履行归责于债务人的过失，则不可适用不可抗力。

10.2.3 不可抗力后果

根据一般法律原则和各国法律规定和普通法中的判例，不可抗力是合同不能履行的法定免责事由，其法律后果如下：

（1）如果合同履行的障碍是暂时的，当事方暂时中止履行合同义务，直到事件结束，再行继续履行合同。延迟履行的一方无须缴纳任何赔偿金。如果当事人认为合同的延期履行造成严重的、无法弥补的损失，可有权要求解除合同。

（2）合同履行的障碍是最终的，合同自动被解除，合同当事方恢复合同订立签订的状况。除非双方约定，合同因不可抗力解除的后果应遵循如下原则：未提供商品或服务时，不必支付合同款项。如已支付押金或部分合同款项，当事另一方应退还。因不构成违约，合同当事另一方无权请求支付违约金或损害赔偿。

（3）如果合同属于分阶段履行，并且解约前合同当事双方已经履行各自的合同义务，无法返还原状，解约效力仅针对后续的合同履行。

10.3　不可抗力条款

在国际工程合同中，完整的不可抗力条款应包括如下内容：

（1）不可抗力定义。

（2）不可抗力事件列举。

（3）不可抗力通知。

（4）减轻义务。

（5）不可抗力后果。

（6）不可抗力影响分包商。

（7）合同终止和付款。

（8）解除合同。

FIDIC 合同条款 1999 年第 1 版红皮书、黄皮书和银皮书第 19 条［不可抗力］的规定堪称国际工程合同不可抗力条款的范本。承包商在合同谈判和起草编制合同中可参考第 19 条的内容，或对照第 19 条的内容审阅不可抗力条款。

FIDIC 合同条款 1999 年第 1 版第 19 条［不可抗力］条款规定如下：

19. Force Majeure	
19.1　Definition of Force Majeure	In this Clause," Force Majeure " means an exceptional event or circumstance： （a）which is beyond a Party's control； （b）which such Party could not reasonably have provided against before entering into the Contract； （c）which, having arisen, such Party could not reasonably have avoided or overcome, and （d）which is not substantially attributable to the other Party. Force Majeure may include, but is not limited to, exceptional events or circumstances of the kind listed below, so long as conditions（a）to（d）above are satisfied： 　（i）war, hostilities（whether war be declared or not）, invasion, act of foreign enemies； 　（ii）rebellion, terrorism, revolution, insurrection, military or usurped power, or civil war； 　（iii）riot, commotion, disorder, strike or lockout by persons other than the Contractor's Personnel, and other employees of the Contractor and Subcontractors. 　（iv）munitions of war, explosive materials, ionising radiation or contamination by radio-activity, except as may be attributable

(续)

	to the Contractor's use of such munitions, explosives, radiation or radio-activity, and (v) natural catastrophes such as earthquake, hurricane, typhoon or volcanic activity.
19.2　Notice of Force Majeure	If a Party is or will be prevented from performing any its obligations under the Contract by Force Majeure, then it shall give notice to the other Party of the event or circumstances constituting the Force Majeure and shall specify the obligations, the performance of which is or will be prevented. The notice shall be given within 14 days after the Party became aware, or should have become aware, of the relevant event or circumstance constituting Force Majeure. The Party shall, having given notice, be excused performance of such obligations for so long as such Force Majeure prevents it from performing them. Notwithstanding any other provision of this Clause, Force Majeure shall not apply to obligations of either Party to make payments to the other Party under the Contract.
19.3　Duty to Minimise Delay	Each Party shall at all times use all reasonable endeavours to minimise any delay in the performance of the Contract as a result of Force Majeure. A Party shall give notice to the other Party when it ceases to be affected by the Force Majeure.
19.4　Consequences of Force Majeure	If the Contractor is prevented from performing any of his obligations under the Contract by Force Majeure of which notice has been given under Sub-Clause 19.2 [*Notice of Force Majeure*], and suffers delay and/or incurs Cost by reason of such Force Majeure, the Contractor shall be entitled subject to Sub-Clause 20.1 [*Contractor's Claims*] to: (a) an extension of time for any such delay, if completion is or will be delayed, under Sub-Clause 8.4 [*Extension of Time for Completion*], and (b) if the event or circumstance is of the kind described in sub-paragraphs (i) to (iv) of Sub-Clause 19.1 [*Definition of Force Majeure*] and, in the case of sub-paragraphs (ii) to (iv), occurs in the Country, payment of any such Cost. After receiving this notice, the Engineer shall proceed in accordance with Sub-Clause 3.5 [*Determinations*] to agree or determine these matters.

(续)

19.5 Force Majeure Affecting Subcontractor	If any Subcontractor is entitled under any contract or agreement relating to the Works to relief from force majeure on terms additional to or broader than those specified in this Clause, such additional or broader force majeure events or circumstances shall not excuse the Contractor's non-performance or entitle him to relief under this Clause.
19.6 Optional Termination, Payment and Release	If the execution of substantially all the Works in progress is prevented for a continuous period of 84 days by reason of Force Majeure of which notice has been given under Sub-Clause 19.2 [*Notice of Force Majeure*], or for multiple periods which total more than 140 days due to the same notified Force Majeure, then either Party may give to the other Party a notice of termination of the Contract. In this event, the termination shall take effect 7 days after the notice is given, and the Contractor shall proceed in accordance with Sub-Clause 16.3 [*Cessation of Work and Removal of Contractor's Equipment*]. Upon such termination, the Engineer shall determine the value of the work done and issue a Payment Certificate which shall include: (a) the amounts payable for any work carried out for which a price is stated in the Contract; (b) the Cost of Plant and Materials ordered for the Works which have been delivered to the Contractor, or of which the Contractor is liable to accept delivery: this Plant and Materials shall become the property of (and be at the risk of) the Employer when paid for by the Employer, and the Contractor shall place the same at the Employer's disposal; (c) any other Costs or liabilities which in the circumstances was reasonably incurred by the Contractor in the expectation of completing the Works; (d) the Cost of removal of Temporary Works and Contractor's Equipment from the Site and the return of these items to the Contractor's works in his country (or to any other destination at no greater cost); and (e) the Cost of repatriation of the Contractor's staff and labour employed wholly in connection with the Works at the date of termination.
19.7 Release from Performance under the Law	Notwithstanding any other provision of this Clause, if any event or circumstance outside the control of the Parties (including, but not limited to, Force Majeure) arises which makes it impossible or unlawful for either or both Parties to fulfil its or their contractual obligations or which, under

(续)

	the law governing the Contract, entitles the Parties to be released from further performance of the Contract, then upon notice by either Party to the other Party of such event or circumstance: (a) the Parties shall be discharged from further performance, without prejudice to the rights of either Party in respect of any previous breach of the Contract, and (b) the sum payable by the Employer to the Contractor shall be the same as would have been payable under Sub-Clause 19.6 [*Optional Termination, Payment and Release*] if the Contract had been terminated under Sub-Clause 19.6.

除了 FIDIC 合同条款 1999 年第 1 版第 19 条 [不可抗力] 的规定外，日本工程促进协会 ENAA 版合同第 37 条不可抗力和第 38 条战争风险条款的规定也是国际工程合同中可圈可点的范本，其中第 37 条不可抗力条款是引用法国工程合同文本的相关规定，广泛被国际工程业界所接受。第 37 条不可抗力和第 38 条战争风险规定如下：

37. Force Majeure	37.1 "Force Majeure" shall mean any event beyond the reasonable control of the Employer or of the Contractor, as the case may be, and which is unavoidable notwithstanding the reasonable care of the party affected, and shall include, without limitation, the following: (a) war, hostilities or warlike operations whether a state of war be declared or not, invasion, act of foreign enemy and civil war; (b) rebellion, revolution, insurrection, mutiny, usurpation of civil or military government, conspiracy, riot, civil commotion and terrorist acts; (c) confiscation, nationalization, mobilization, commandeering or requisition by or under the order of any government or de jure or de facto authority or ruler or any other act or failure to act of any local state or national government authority; (d) strike, sabotage, lockout, embargo, import restriction, port congestion, lack of usual means of public transportation and communication, industrial dispute, shipwreck, shortage or restriction of power supply, epidemics, quarantine and plague; (e) earthquake, landslide, volcanic activity, fire, flood or inundation, tidal wave, typhoon or cyclone, hurricane, storm, lightning, or other inclement weather condition, nuclear and pressure waves or other natural or physical disaster;

(续)

	(f) shortage of labor, materials or utilities where caused by circumstances that are themselves Force Majeure. 37.2 If either party is prevented, hindered or delayed from or in performing any of its obligations under the Contract by an event of Force Majeure, then it shall notify the other in writing of the occurrence of such event and the circumstances thereof within fourteen (14) days after the occurrence of such event. 37.3 The party who has given such notice shall be excused from the performance or punctual performance of its obligations under the Contract for so long as the relevant event of Force Majeure continues and to the extent that such party's performance is prevented, hindered or delayed. The Time for Completion shall be extended in accordance with GCC Clause 40. 37.4 The party or parties affected by the event of Force Majeure shall use reasonable efforts to mitigate the effect thereof upon its or their performance of the Contract and to fulfill its or their obligations under the Contract, but without prejudice to either party's right to terminate the Contract under GCC Sub-Clauses 37.6 and 38.5. 37.5 No delay or nonperformance by either party hereto caused by the occurrence of any event of Force Majeure shall: (a) constitute a default or breach of the Contract, or (b) give rise to any claim for damages or additional cost or expense occasioned thereby, subject to GCC Sub-Clauses 32.2, 38.3 and 38.4 if and to the extent that such delay or nonperformance is caused by the occurrence of an event of Force Majeure. 37.6 If the performance of the Contract is substantially prevented, hindered or delayed for a single period of more than sixty (60) days or an aggregate period of more than one hundred and twenty (120) days on account of one or more events of Force Majeure during the currency of the Contract, the parties will attempt to develop a mutually satisfactory solution, failing which either party may terminate the Contract by giving a notice to the other, but without prejudice to either party's right to terminate the Contract under GCC Sub-Clause 38.5.

（续）

	37.7 In the event of termination pursuant to GCC Sub-Clause 37.6, the rights and obligations of the Employer and the Contractor shall be as specified in GCC Sub-Clauses 42.1.2 and 42.1.3. 37.8 Notwithstanding GCC Sub-Clause 37.5, Force Majeure shall not apply to any obligation of the Employer to make payments to the Contractor herein.
38. War Risks	38.1 "War Risks" shall mean any event specified in paragraphs (a) and (b) of GCC Sub-Clause 37.1 and any explosion or impact of any mine, bomb, shell, grenade or other projectile, missile, munitions or explosive of war, occurring or existing in or near the country (or countries) where the Site is located. 38.2 Notwithstanding anything contained in the Contract, the Contractor shall have no liability whatsoever for or with respect to: (a) destruction of or damage to Facilities, Plant, or any part thereof; (b) destruction of or damage to property of the Employer or any third party; or (c) injury or loss of life. if such destruction, damage, injury or loss of life is caused by any War Risks, and the Employer shall indemnify and hold the Contractor harmless from and against any and all claims, liabilities, actions, lawsuits, damages, costs, charges or expenses arising in consequence of or in connection with the same. 38.3 If the Facilities or any Plant or Contractor's Equipment or any other property of the Contractor used or intended to be used for the purposes of the Facilities shall sustain destruction or damage by reason of any War Risks, the Employer shall pay the Contractor for: (a) any part of the Facilities or the Plant so destroyed or damaged to the extent not already paid for by the Employer and so far as may be required by the Employer, and as may be necessary for completion of the Facilities; (b) replacing or making good any Contractor's Equipment or other property of the Contractor so destroyed or damaged; (c) replacing or making good any such destruction or damage to the Facilities or the Plant or any part thereof.

(续)

	If the Employer does not require the Contractor to replace or make good any such destruction or damage to the Facilities, the Employer shall either request a change in accordance with GCC Clause 39, excluding the performance of that part of the Facilities thereby destroyed or damaged or, where the loss, destruction or damage affects a substantial part of the Facilities, shall terminate the Contract, pursuant to GCC Sub-Clause 42.1.
	If the Employer requires the Contractor to replace or make good on any such destruction or damage to the Facilities, the Time for Completion shall be extended in accordance with GCC 40.
38.4	Notwithstanding anything contained in the Contract, the Employer shall pay the Contractor for any increased costs or incidentals to the execution of the Contract that are in any way attributable to, consequent on, resulting from, or in any way connected with any War Risks, provided that the Contractor shall as soon as practicable notify the Employer in writing of any such increased cost.
38.5	If during the performance of the Contract any War Risks shall occur that financially or otherwise materially affect the execution of the Contract by the Contractor, the Contractor shall use its reasonable efforts to execute the Contract with due and proper consideration given to the safety of its and its Subcontractors' personnel engaged in the work on the Facilities, provided, however, that if the execution of the work on the Facilities becomes impossible or is substantially prevented for a single period of more than sixty (60) days or an aggregate period of more than one hundred and twenty (120) days on account of any War Risks, the parties will attempt to develop a mutually satisfactory solution, failing which either party may terminate the Contract by giving a notice to the other.
38.6	In the event of termination pursuant to GCC Sub-Clauses 38.3 or 38.5, the rights and obligations of the Employer and the Contractor shall be specified in GCC Sub-Clauses 42.1.2 and 42.1.3.

为了更好地界定不可抗力事件,在有些国际工程合同中还列举了不属于不可抗力事件的情形,如下:

Provided that Force Majeure shall not include the following events or circumstances (or any combination of them and any other events or circumstances):

(a) mechanical or electrical breakdown or failure of equipment, machinery or items of Plant or the performance of Plant;

(b) economic hardship or a lack of money or inability to use money or available funds for any reason whatsoever and/or insufficiency of capital to perform the Works;

(c) subject to the operation of Clause 13.1.6, price fluctuations (including a result of currency fluctuations) with respect to materials;

(d) weather and climatic conditions other than Adverse Weather Conditions or conditions set out in Clause 18.1.2(v);

(e) any riot, commotion, disorder, boycott, strike or industrial dispute, picketing, blockade, labour dispute or lockout affecting only or caused by the affected Party or the affected Party's personnel or Subcontractors or personnel of such Subcontractors;

(f) any delay in or shortage of labour, materials, equipment or other resources except to the extent such unavailability results from Force Majeure; and

(g) delays attributable to the realisation of any risks which have been expressly assumed by the affected Party.

关于不可抗力通知，为了避免误解和歧义，在有些国际工程合同中明确约定了更为详尽的要求，如下：

1.1.1 If a Party is or will be prevented from performing any of its obligations under this Contract by Force Majeure (the "Affected Party"), then it shall give notice to the other Party of the event or circumstances constituting the Force Majeure and shall specify the obligations, of which the performance is or will be prevented. The notice shall be given as soon as practicable and in any event within seven days after the Affected Party became aware, or should have become aware, of the relevant event or circumstance constituting Force Majeure. The Affected Party shall give the other Party a second notice, describing the event constituting the Force Majeure in reasonable detail and, to the extent that can be reasonably determined at the time of the second notice, providing:

(i) a preliminary evaluation of the obligations affected;

(ii) a preliminary estimate of the period of time that the Affected Party will be unable to perform the obligations; and

(iii) other relevant matters;

promptly and as soon as reasonably practicable after the initial notice of the occurrence of Force Majeure is given by the Affected Party.

1.1.2 When appropriate or when reasonably requested to do so by the other Party, the Affected Party shall provide further notices to the other Party more fully describing the event of Force Majeure and its causes and providing or updating information relating to the efforts of the Affected Party to avoid or to mitigate the effect thereof and estimates, to the extent practicable, of the time that the Affected Party reasonably expects it will be prevented from carrying out any of its affected obligations due to Force Majeure.

1.1.3 The Affected Party shall, having given notice, be excused from performance of such obligations for so long as such Force Majeure prevents it from performing them.

10.4 不可抗力通知

在发生不可抗力事件时，承包商负有义务向业主发出不可抗力通知。根据1999年第1版FIDIC合同条款第19.2款［不可抗力通知］和2017年第2版第18.2款［例外事件的通知］的规定，在发生不可抗力事件后，受影响的一方应在知道或应当知道不可抗力事件发生后的14天内向业主发出通知，通知中应说明阻碍履行的各项义务。受影响的一方应在收到通知后免于履行受到阻碍的合同义务，且仅限于免除受到阻碍的合同义务。需要特别注意的是，在起草不可抗力通知时，由于合同规定受影响的一方免于履行通知中指明的合同义务，因此，应特别注意其所描述的受阻碍的合同义务的内容。以新冠肺炎疫情COVID-19为例，承包商向业主发出的不可抗力通知示例如下：

Letter Head of the Contractor

To: [insert name of the Employer]
　　[insert address of the Employer]

Subject: Notice of Force Majeure Event under Sub-Clause 19.2 of Conditions of Contract

Dear Sir or Madam,

We write to inform you that the rapid escalation of COVID-19 was declared by the World Health Organization (WHO) as a "Pandemic" event on 12 March 2020 after announcement of the outbreak of COVID-19 as a Public Health Emergency of International Concern (PHEIC) on 30th January 2020. WHO has urged countries to continue to implement a containment strategy while accelerating their efforts to control the disease.

On _____ [insert the date], the government of _____ [insert the name of country or state] has issued further measures, among which are,
　　[insert the list of local government directions on obviating the impact of COVID-19]

Those measures imposed by the local government have caused the site operations to become impossible, being:

(a) The local government instruction has made the transportation of the workers become impossible.

(b) The social distancing requirement that the workers should keep distance and avoid gatherings has caused the site operations to be difficult.

(c) The local governmental instructions requiring the Contractor to encamp and quarantine the workers for 14 days have become impossible for him to fulfil.

In light of the above measures taken by the local government, the Contractoris is left with no choice but render you a notice under Sub-Clause 19.2 [*Notice of Force Majeure*] of the Conditions of Contract to suspend the site works commencing from the date of this notice and the works to be suspended include:

[insert the name of the works to be suspended]

Accordingly, our performance of contractual obligations under the Contract to deliver the project as originally scheduled has substantially been prevented due to the natural catastrophe of COVID-19 and the attendant mitigation measures by the local government.

Apparently, the enumerated event(s) constitute Force Majeure in accordance with Sub-Clause 19.1 [*Definition of Force Majeure*] of the Conditions of Contract as defined thereof viz. "In this Clause, Force Majeure means an exceptional event or circumstance: (a) which is beyond a Party's Control; (b) which such Party could not reasonably have provided against before entering into the Contract, (c) which, having arisen, such Party could not reasonably have avoided or overcome, and (d) which is not substantially attributable to the other Party.", which spread its ripple effect to the project onwards. Since the COVID-19 and the attendant measures taken by the local government are beyond the reasonable control of the Contractor, are unavoidable and directly affect the execution of the Works, they thus fall within the definition of force majeure set forth in Sub-Clause 19.1 [*Definition of Force Majeure*] of the Conditions of Contract.

The Contractor, pursuant to Sub-Clause 19.2 [*Notice of Force Majeure*] of the Conditions of Contract, notifies you of the above event(s) and/circumstances which prevent us from executing our contractual obligations and complying with the requirement of Time for Completion in particular.

In compliance with Sub-Clause 19.4 [*Consequence of Force Majeure*] and subject to Sub-Clause 20.1 [*Contractor's Claim*] of the Conditions of Contract, the Contractor believes that he is contractually entitled to and fully qualified for an extension of time for any such delay and payment of any such cost pursuant to Sub-Clause 8.4 [*Extension of Time for Completion*] of the Conditions of Contract.

As it is an evolving event, the Contractor shall duly update by providing the contemporaneous records during the pendency of COVID-19, and providing the further particulars once the Force Majeure event ceases to affect the site operations.

Despite the negative influence of the COVID-19 event, the Contractor will exert his best endeavor to cooperate with you to obviate any delay in the performance of the Contract in accordance with Sub-Clause 19.3 [*Duty to Minimize Delay*] of the Conditions of Contract.

Sincerely,

在国际工程项目中，发生不可抗力事件后，承包商均应在不可抗力事件发生当天或第二天向业主发出不可抗力通知。以某国际工程为例，在承包商受到恐怖分子袭击后，承包商立即向业主发出不可抗力通知，如下：

Dear Sir,

This is to inform you that a terrorism attack happened on 8 March 2018 against the Contractor's site and camp, of which the detail is described as follows:

1. At the time of 01:00 am, a group of 25 to 30 armed terrorists invaded the Contractor's site management office, robbing the Contractor's camp and burning the houses and construction machinery and equipment on site.
2. In the night of the said date, the armed terrorists robbed all of the properties belonging to the Chinese employees, site engineers and translator on site, including the mobile phones, computers, TVs and burned a number of pickups, a number of truck cranes, a number of generators, houses and materials.
3. At about 3:30 am, the armed terrorists called all of the Contractor's employees to threaten them to stop the construction activities on site fully, and that if found not stopped, they would make more attacks against the Contractor.

The Contractor holds that the said terrorism attack has constituted a force majeure event which falls in the provisions of Sub-Clause 19.1 (ii) of Conditions of Contract. Thus, the Contractor renders this particular notice to claim that such force majeure event has prevented him from executing the works. Furthermore, the Contractor maintains his contestations as below:

(a) Suspend the construction works on site promptly and withdraw all Contractor's employees, unless the Employer can take necessary measures to protect the Contractor personnel's life and property;
(b) Hand over all material, equipment, and plant on site to the Employer whereas the material, equipment and plant shall be paid fully to the Contractor;
(c) Appoint the site to store the material, equipment and plant which are on the way to the site. Upon arrival, all material, equipment, and plant shall be handed over to the Employer, whereas the Employer shall pay it to the Contractor as per the Contract;
(d) Compensate the loss of burned properties of the Contractor;
(e) Compensate the robbed properties of the Contractor;
(f) Pay the costs arising from the withdrawing of the Contractor's personnel;
(g) Compensate the costs incurred on the anti-terrorism team.

To give effect to it, the Contractor shall, in accordance with Sub-Clause 19.4 [*Consequences of Force Majeure*] and Sub-Clause 20.1 [*Contractor's Claim*] of Conditions of Contract, claim both extension of time and additional costs due to the terrorism attack.

The Contractor reserves his right to terminate the Contract if and to the extent he is prevented from executing the works in accordance with Sub-Clause 19.6 of Conditions of Contract.

Sincerely,

在起草不可抗力通知时，由于合同规定受影响的当事一方免于履行通知中指明的合同义务，应需要特别注意所描述受阻碍合同义务的内容。另外，FIDIC 合同条款 1999 年第 1 版第 19.2 款［不可抗力的通知］没有规定延迟发出通知的后果，但 FIDIC 合同条款 2017 年第 2 版第 18.2 款［例外事件的通知］规定，如果未能在 14 天内发出通知，则受影响的当事一方仅应免于当事另一方收到通知后受到阻碍的合同义务。需要注意的是，如果合同条款明确规定未能在规定期限内发出不可抗力通知则丧失索赔权利，那么，法院将会尊重合同条款的内容，支持任何当事方的主张和抗辩。在 Zhoushan Jinhaiwan Shipyard Co., Ltd, v Golden Exquisite Inc. ［2014］EWHC 4050（Comm）案中，英国法院判定原告未能履行合同明确约定的不可抗力通知义务，因此丧失索赔权利。

FIDIC 合同条款 1999 年第 1 版第 19.2 款［不可抗力的通知］（FIDIC 合同条款 2017 年第 2 版第 18.2 款［例外事件的通知］）规定的不可抗力（例外事件）通知与第 20.1 款［承包商的索赔］（FIDIC 合同条款 2017 年第 2 版第 20.2.1 款［索赔通知］）因不可抗力（例外事件）提出的工期延长和/或额外费用的索赔通知属于两种不同性质通知。前者表明不可抗力（例外事件）的发生，而后者表明在发生不可抗力（例外事件）后受到的工期和费用影响以及承包商依据合同约定可以主张的权利。因此，承包商除了需要遵守不可抗力（例外事件）通知的规定外，还应遵守合同规定在知道和应当知道索赔事件发生后 28 天内发出索赔通知的要求，在索赔时效期限内发出索赔通知。否则，承包商丧失任何工期延长和/或额外付款索赔的权利，而业主可以免责。因此，根据 FIDIC 合同条款 1999 年第 1 版第 20.1 款［承包商的索赔］和 2017 年第 2 版第 20.2.1 款［索赔通知］的规定，28 天的书面索赔通知是索赔成立的必要前提条件。

在某国际工程项目中，在发生飓风不可抗力事件后，承包商向业主发出不可抗力通知，内容如下：

Subject: Notice of Claim for Force Majeure Event

Dear Sir,

We would like to report to you that a typhoon of 12 degree occurred on the Works during the period between 19:00-20:00 on 25 August 2016 which fell in the provision of Sub-Clause 19.1 (v) natural catastrophes such as earthquakes, hurricane, typhoon or volcanic activity.

We hereby submit this Notice of Claim for Force Majeure event in accordance with Sub-Clause 19.2 in the Conditions of Contract to you.

The assessment for the impact on the time and cost of the Works is being prepared and will be put forward in due course.

工程师在收到承包商不可抗力通知后，否决了承包商的索赔要求，工程师的回复如下：

Dear Sir,

We refer to your letter of AAA dated 26 August 2016 regarding the Notice of Claim for Force Majeure Event on 25 August 2016.

We note that you have given notice pursuant to Conditions of Contract Sub-Clause 19.2 for the happening of the Force Majeure event on 25 August within 14 days as required. However, you have not given notice pursuant to Sub-Clause 20.1, which is a mandatory requirement for any remedy, within 7 days as specified in the Conditions of Contract.

Please note that Paragraph 3 in Sub-Clause 20.1 of the Conditions of Contract is quoted as below:

"If the Contractor fails to give notice of claim within such period of seven (7) days[⊖], the Time for Completion shall not be extended, the Contractor shall not be entitled to additional payment, and the Employer shall be discharged from all liability in connection with the claim."

In conclusion, there will be no EOT nor additional payment under the Contract.

  在本案中，工程师否决承包商提出工期延长索赔的理由是承包商未能根据第20.1款［承包商的索赔］提出索赔通知，承包商在索赔通知中仅根据第19.2款［不可抗力的通知］。因此，根据合同规定，承包商没有权利索赔工期延长。必须指出，本案中承包商发出的索赔函中已标明了不可抗力索赔通知，且在函中写明索赔工期延长和额外付款，但不得不说，承包商没有注明是根据第20.1款［承包商的索赔］提出索赔工期延长。但判断承包商是否提出索赔，不在于承包商是否引述了第20.1款［承包商的索赔］，而在于承包商是否提出索赔的意向。

  需要说明的是，英国法对于FIDIC合同条款1987年第4版和［FIDIC合同条款］1999年第1版合同中的索赔时效的法律判断不尽相同。对于FIDIC合同条款1987年第4版第53.1款［索赔通知］的规定，英国法中存在两种解释，一是此类规定不能构成索赔的前提条件，即使承包商未能在索赔事件发生后的28天内提交书面索赔通知，也不能因此否决承包商的索赔权利；二是此类规定构成索赔的前提条件，即承包商未能在索赔事件发生后的28天内提出书面索赔通知，则丧失索赔权利。在著名的Obrascon Huarte Lain SA v Attorney General for Gibraltar ［2015］EWCA Civ 712案中，英国法院判定承包商未能在FIDIC 1999年第1版《生产设备设计—施工合同条件》第20.1款［承包商的索赔］规定的28天内发出索赔通知，因此丧失索赔权利。但不得不说，英国法院并非百分之百支持FIDIC合同条款1999年第1版系列合同条款第20.1款［承包商的索赔］规定的28天索赔时效。承包商还应特别注意的是，在FIDIC合同条款2017年第2版系列合同中，第20.2.1款［索赔通知］和第20.2.4款［完整详细的索赔］中规定了28天索赔通知时效和42天递交索赔详情的时

⊖ FIDIC合同条款1999年第1版和2017年第2版，均规定28天内。

效，承包商未能遵守上述任一时效将导致索赔权利的丧失。

10.5 FIDIC 合同条款中不可抗力索赔

10.5.1 不可抗力索赔案例分析

中国承包商从事国际承包工程项目的国家主要集中于亚洲和非洲地区。这些国家或地区经济社会发展不平衡，政治动荡、战争、内乱、骚乱、罢工频发，恐怖主义蔓延，地缘政治冲突加剧，以及在施工过程中遭遇的地震、洪水、滑坡等自然不可抗力事件，中国承包商不可避免地依据合同约定和适用法律的规定对遭遇的不可抗力事件向业主提出索赔。据不完全统计，不可抗力事件是引发中国承包商与业主发生争议的主要原因之一，约占承包商向业主提出索赔事件的4%。中国承包商的不可抗力主张和索赔，受到业主的各种挑战和质疑，索赔之路充满艰辛，结果喜忧参半。

从笔者从事国际工程索赔的实践来看，在非洲和亚洲地区的国际工程索赔中，不可抗力事件索赔占据承包商索赔中一定比例，在某些国家索赔概率更高，例如马里等高风险国家。虽然笔者在表 10-1 中的列项并非中国承包商不可抗力索赔的全部，但其反映的问题和业主抗辩具有一定代表性，反映了中国承包商在不可抗力事件索赔中遇到的多数合同和法律问题。

表 10-1　中国承包商不可抗力索赔汇总

序号	国家	项目类型	不可抗力事件	工期延长	额外费用	是否获准
1	马里	水电站	2012年3月21日至同年5月政变	40天	172万欧元	是
2	马里	水电站	法国人质事件和马里北部动乱	0	155万欧元	是
3	马里	水电站	洪水导致下游围堰垮塌	45天	21万欧元	是
4	马里	水电站	2013年特大暴雨	15天	40万欧元	是
5	马里	桥梁	2018年3月8日恐怖袭击	不适用	停工损失66万美元	解除合同
6	马里	水电站	马里安全局势无法通过安全评估	不适用	不适用	签约未开工，解除合同
7	乍得	公路	洪水	120天	0	是
8	孟加拉	铁路	2013年大选罢工	29天	0	是，业主主张应可预见罢工的发生，应从承包商索赔的77天中扣减48天
9	孟加拉	给水	有组织罢工（hartal）	80天	0	是
10	孟加拉	电力	2019年新冠疫情	持续性事件，进行中	不适用	业主否决新冠疫情为不可抗力，但合同约定可索赔工期
11	巴基斯坦	水电站	2019年10月印度枪击巴基斯坦事件	60天	0	复工与新冠疫情重叠，复工时间存在争议

(续)

序号	国家	项目类型	不可抗力事件	工期延长	额外费用	是否获准
12	巴基斯坦	水电站	2019年新冠疫情	持续性事件，进行中	持续性事件，进行中	业主主张不构成不可抗力
13	俄罗斯	铁矿	洪水		业主认为没有权威机构出具不可抗力证明，承包商可选择其他铁路线路运输，未证明关键线路上工程的延误	否
14	埃塞俄比亚	公路	骚乱，部落枪击		业主否认枪击事件为不可抗力	否
15	埃塞俄比亚	公路	大面积，多地点山体滑坡	业主给予工期延长	业主否决承包商费用索赔	业主给予工期延长，但否决费用索赔
16	菲律宾	电力	2017年台风	不适用	承包商索赔修补费用	业主否决，要求通过保险理赔
17	菲律宾	燃煤电厂	2018年台风	15天		是
18	尼泊尔	水电站	骚乱	15天	承包商索赔停工费用	争议评审委员会给予1618万卢比费用补偿
19	尼泊尔	引水隧道	全国性罢工	业主要求提供支持性证据		否
20	尼泊尔	引水隧道	泥石流	9天	业主否决	是
21	利比亚	所有项目	战争，内乱		2011年2月，利比亚发生骚乱，中国承包商通过中国政府寻求战争补偿，但无结果。某些承包商投保战争保险的，从中国出口信用保险公司获得了部分赔偿	
22	塔吉克斯坦	公路	2019年新冠疫情		承包商发出人员返回受阻的工期延长索赔通知，进行中	

从表10-1可以看出，业主否认承包商不可抗力事件索赔的抗辩理由具有多样性，从不可抗力定义中某个用语的含义，例如从骚乱（riot）的解释（埃塞骚乱案例）到如何理解1999年第1版第19.1款［不可抗力的定义］及其事件列举两者之间的关系（孟加拉铁路项目）、如何构成合同约定的不可抗力事件、合同条款没有列举的事件能否构成不可抗力（巴基斯坦水电站项目和孟加拉电力项目）、不可抗力的证明、承包商减轻义务的履行（俄罗斯铁矿项目）、额外费用补偿途径（菲律宾电力项目）、承包商举证责任，直至解除合同（马里桥梁和水电站项目），涉及了不可抗力事件索赔主张的各个方面。以俄罗斯某项目为例，在2013年8月发生中俄边境洪水事件时，承包商提出了以不可抗力为由要求工期延长的索赔，但索赔遭到了业主的否认。在上述案例中，业主与承包商的争执焦点在于：

（1）证明不可抗力的机构问题。虽然FIDIC合同条款规定了不可抗力的定义并列举了不可抗力事件，但在索赔过程中，业主提出需要中国工商机构出具文件，由权威机构证明发生了不可抗力事件。承包商主张，FIDIC合同条款并未规定在发生不可抗力时应该由某个机构出具书面证明的内容。承包商认为，由中国边境海关出具的证明足以证明不可抗力事件的发生事实，且中国工商部门没有职责出具此类证明文件，中国也没有规定哪一个机构可以出具此类证明文件。

(2) 承包商是否采取了减轻不可抗力影响的措施。业主认为承包商没有采取合同规定的合理措施，将不可抗力的影响减至最低，并举例证明在某个边境口岸发生洪水时，承包商可以选择其他线路运输货物。而承包商认为已经采取措施减轻不可抗力的影响。

(3) 受到不可抗力影响的货物证明。业主要求承包商举证，证明哪些位于关键线路工程的货物运输因不可抗力受到了影响，从而导致关键线路上的工程受到了延误。承包商无法完全举证证明哪些货物因洪水受到了影响，哪些货物位于边境口岸，哪些货物位于运输途中，哪些货物已经制造完毕处于运输状态。在无法完全举证的情况下，承包商的索赔主张受到了质疑并遭到业主否决。

在2013年8月洪水不可抗力事件中，业主在回信中回复道：

"We draw your attention to the fact that the flood itself did not cause occurrence of the insuperable force circumstance which influenced the fulfillment of obligations under the Contract on the part of the Contractor, provided by Clause 19.4 [*Consequences of Force Majeure*] of General Conditions under the Contract, it is necessary for you to submit complete detailed information as proof of the flood influence on the Contractor's fulfillment of its obligations under the Contract as regards equipment and materials which were suspended on the above-mentioned border crossing check points, namely: specify the exact names of materials and equipment, volume, cost, delay time and also how this material and equipment delay influenced the progress of the construction and installation activities under the Contract.

Along with that in accordance with Clause 19.3 [*Duty to Minimize Delay*] of General Conditions of the Contract, the Contractor must take all reasonably necessary actions to minimize nonobservance of his obligations stipulated in the Contract caused by Force Majeure which the Contractor failed to do.

The Contractor also failed to submit any proof why he could not use alternative variant and deliver materials and equipment by vehicular transport through the border crossing check points and by rail transport through the border crossing check points or by marine transport through the sea.

Aside from the specified and in conflict with Clause 19.2 [*Notice of Force Majeure*] of General Conditions of Contract, the Contractor failed to submit notification about occurrence of insuperable force circumstances in due order and with reference to the obligations under the Contractor following which is or will be impossible.

Along with that in spite of the Employer's instruction, the Contractor did not submit documents to inform the competent authorities on the start and the end of the flood which was the reason of closure of the number of the river ports on the river in the zone of border crossing for the purpose of defining the exact duration of insuperable force circumstance."

10.5.2 FIDIC合同项下不可抗力救济措施

在FIDIC合同条款下，承包商可在发生不可抗力事件后，依据1987年第4版第44.1款

［竣工期限的延长］、第65.3款［特殊风险造成的工程损失］和第65.5款［特殊风险引起的费用增加］，或1999年第1版8.4款［竣工时间的延长］、第19.4款［不可抗力的后果］，或2017年第2版第8.5款［竣工时间的延长］和第18.4款［不可抗力的后果］，有权主张如下救济措施：

（1）竣工时间的延长，和/或。

（2）合同规定范围内的额外费用，例如1999年第1版第19.1款［不可抗力的定义］约定的第（b）~（e）项，2017年第2版第18.4款［例外事件的后果］约定的第（ii）~（iv）项。在发生战争、敌对行动、入侵、外敌行为和自然灾害时，承包商无权索赔额外费用。

（3）在不可抗力通知发出后，基本上全部进展中的工程实施受到阻碍已连续84天，或者因同一通知的不可抗力连续阻碍几个期间累计超过140天，任何一方可发出终止合同通知。在该通知发出7天后，合同终止。

10.5.3 不可抗力事件索赔涉及的合同和适用法律问题

在1999年第1版FIDIC系列合同条款下进行不可抗力事件索赔，中国承包商遇到的主要的合同和法律问题涉及了大陆法系国家和普通法系等国家，不同法系的国家对不可抗力事件存在不同的法律规定或判例，给承包商索赔不可抗力事件带来了不可预测的风险。

1. 关于FIDIC合同条款1999年第1版第19.1款［不可抗力定义］中的定义

FIDIC系列合同条款中关于特殊风险（例外风险）或不可抗力进行了定义，但对于其后的列举的事件并未给出具体的定义，如什么是战争、敌对行为、内乱、骚乱，以及什么是洪水、泥石流等。而在实践中，承包商和业主首先在不可抗力事件索赔中，包括在仲裁和诉讼过程中对此纠缠不休。例如，在表10-1第14项埃塞某公路项目中，承包商就当地部落人员枪击中方人员造成当地工人死亡、中方人员受重伤以不可抗力事件中的骚乱为由进行索赔工期延长和停工费用，业主主张因实施枪击的人员仅为1人，而骚乱是群体事件，否决了承包商提出的不可抗力事件索赔。承包商认为，FIDIC合同中不可抗力条款未规定这些事件的确切定义，但根据美国《布莱克法律词典》（第四版）骚乱（riot）的定义，"骚乱是指公共干扰事件，包括由一人或三人或三个以上人员聚集一起实施的一项或多项暴力行为，其行为对他人财产或人身构成了明显的威胁。"因此，枪击事件属于不可抗力中的骚乱。但承包商需要注意的是，国际上著名的法律词典，例如美国《布莱克法律词典》和英国《牛津法律词典》对骚乱的定义不尽相同。《牛津法律词典》对骚乱的定义仅对三人及其以上人员的聚集，且对他人财产或人身实施构成了明显威胁的行为确定为骚乱，但没有涉及一个人的危害行为。因此，承包商在遇到不可抗力事件定义中列举事件的争议时，可从美国《布莱克法律词典》和英国《牛津法律词典》中寻找有利于自己的主张。承包商在回复给工程师的信函中写道：

> "In Sub-Clause 17.3, the definition and understanding of "riot" "commotion" and "disorder" is the central issue in deciding whether or not this particular Sub-Clause 17.3 shall apply on the gunshot incident by the local tribe.

"Black Law Dictionary" provides the definition of riot, inter alia:

"Riot. the term 'riot' means a public disturbance involving (1) an act or acts of violence by one or more persons part of an assemblage of three or more persons, which act or acts shall constitute a clear and present danger of, or shall result in, damage or injury to the property of any other person or to the person of any other individual or (2) a threat or threats of the commission of an act or acts of violence by one or more persons part of an assemblage of three or more persons having, individually or collectively, the ability of immediate execution of such threat or threats, where the performance of the threatened acts or acts of violence would constitute a clear and present danger of, or would result in, damage or injury to the property of any other person or to the person of any other individual."

In terms of the definition of commotion, Black Law Dictionary provides:

"Commotion. A condition of turmoil, civil unrest or insurrection. A civil commotion is an uprising among a mass of people which occasions a serious and prolonged disturbance and infraction of civil order not attaining the status of war of an armed insurrection; it is a wild and irregular action of many persons assembled together."

In respect of the definition of disorder, Black Law Dictionary provides:

"Disorder. Turbulent or riotous behavior, immoral or indecent conduct. The breach of the public decorum and morality. See also Breach of peace; Civil disobedience; Civil disorder, Riot; Unlawful assembly."

It can be concluded from the above definitions prescribed in Black Law Dictionary that (1) both riot and commotion can be defined as a public disturbance involving more persons but not an individual act; (2) disorder can be both a public disturbance and an individual act which may result in turbulent or riotous behavior, immoral or indecent conduct. In this particular case, the gunshot by the local tribe has resulted in the decedent and injury to a person of the Contractor's employees. Consequently, the act of the gunshot by the local can constitute and be treated as a behavior of decedent conduct.

Therefore, the event of the gunshot by the local from tribe that the Contractor encountered as described herein clearly falls in the provision of Sub-Clause 17.3 of General Conditions of Contract which entitles the Contractor to claim both extension of time and additional cost incurred if suspension of the Works happens.

There is a significant overlap between the Employer's risks set out in Sub-Clause 17.3 and the definition of force majeure given in Cl. 19.1 of General Condition of Contract. These are events which the Contractor, although in control of the site, would be powerless to protect itself against. In fact, these are risks which are beyond the control of both Contractor and Employer.

Under Sub-Clause 19.4, the Contractor can claim additional payment for the costs incurred as a result of the events listed in Sub-Clause 19.1, sub-paras (i) to (iv). These four categories of events are exactly the same as those listed under Sub-Clause 17.3, sub-paras (a) to (d) for which the Contractor can also claim additional payment under Sub-Clause 17.4. Consequently, Sub-Clauses 19.1 and 19.4 shall apply to this particular gunshot event as well."

除此之外，在不可抗力事件索赔中，还涉及其他定义的量化问题，例如表10-1第4项马里水电站项目特大暴雨，承包商需要证明在24h内降雨达到了300mm，超过了该地区正常的降雨量。在表10-1第16项台风，承包商需要证明台风风力达到了225km/h，超过了正常台风风力175km/h数值。

2. FIDIC合同条款1999年第1版第19.1款［不可抗力的定义］中的定义与事件举例两者之间的法律关系

应当说，第19.1款［不可抗力的定义］对此给出了清晰的规定。1999年第1版和2017年第2版FIDIC合同条款以及多边开发银行协调版合同条款在特殊风险、不可抗力和例外风险条款中均列明了一项非穷尽事件清单（non-exhaustive list），即"不可抗力可以包括但不限于（Force Majeure may include, but is not limited to）"的表述，列明了从战争到自然灾害等不可抗力事件。虽然FIDIC在不同的合同条款中不可抗力事件清单略有差异，但这些事件仅应视为具体规定的事件举例，决定某项事件是否构成不可抗力仍需满足不可抗力定义中的各项条件。例如1999年第1版第19.1款［不可抗力的定义］中表述的"只要满足上述（a）至（d）项条件（so long as conditions (a) to (d) above are satisfied）"，即（a）一方无法控制的，（b）该方在签订合同前，不能对之进行合理准备的，（c）发生后，该方不能合理避免或克服的，（d）不能主要归因于他方的。

需要注意的是，1999年第1版［不可抗力的定义］和2017年第2版第19.1款第18.1款［例外事件］中均没有规定不可抗力（例外事件）应是不可预见的例外的事件。在表10-1第8项孟加拉某铁路项目中，业主认为罢工在孟加拉是一项可以预见的事件，从而主张某学者总结的孟加拉每年发生48天罢工的结论，从承包商索赔的77天工期延长中扣除48天，仅给予承包商29天工期延长。但从第19.1款［不可抗力的定义］看，在FIDIC合同中，并不要求不可抗力事件是不可预见的事件。在ICC19299/MCP仲裁案中，仲裁庭裁决印度古吉拉特邦石油公司在也门的骚乱和暴动（riot and insurrection）期间阻碍了其履行合同义务，符合合同约定的不可抗力的定义，而不可预见性（unforeseeable）和不可能性（impossibility）并未在当事人明确考虑的范围内，本案不予适用。

还应关注的是，第19.1款［不可抗力的定义］中没有将不可预见的作为构成不可抗力的要件，这可能会与某些大陆法系国家的法律规定相矛盾，导致合同约定与法律规定相矛盾。而且，第19.1款［不可抗力的定义］扩大了不可抗力的含义和范围，无疑将会引起合同当事方的争议。

3. FIDIC合同条款下某事件是否构成不可抗力事件的判断

鉴于FIDIC系列合同条款对不可抗力定义和事件列举做了明确的规定，因此，在FIDIC合同条款下应以定义中规定的四项条件，即满足1999年第1版第19.1款［不可抗力的定义］或2017年第2版第18.1款［例外事件］中的四个条件为准。在大陆法系国家，承包商更应按照合同规定的条件予以解释。同时，还应查阅适用法律中不可抗力法律规定，从法律层面解决某项事件是否构成适用法律项下的不可抗力事件。

对于FIDIC合同条款下约定的不可抗力的解释，朗莫尔法官在著名的Great Elephant Corp, v Trafigura Becheer BV ［2013］EWCA Civ 905案中写道：

"毋庸赘言，不可抗力条款必须按其自身的内容加以解释。无须强调的是：（a）此为例外条款,其任何模糊之处必须依据当事方对其依赖的程度予以解决;并且(b)鉴于原告公司通常会采取措施控制其自身的经营,因此,'一方不能控制的'的概念明确了一项较高的验证标准……总之,应依据具体的合同约定予以解释。"

因此,在普通法国家,特别是在英国法中,对于不可抗力条款应依照合同解释的基本原则予以解释。

在FIDIC合同条款下,为了判断某项事件是否构成不可抗力,综合普通法判例和国际商会(ICC)仲裁裁决,承包商需要确定:

(1)不可抗力事件是否符合第19.1款[不可抗力的定义]中规定的四个条件,即(a)一方无法控制的,(b)该方在签订合同前,不能对之进行合理准备的,(c)发生后,该方不能合理避免或克服的,(d)不能主要归因于他方的。

(2)不可抗力事件阻碍(prevented)了承包商履行合同义务,使得承包商履行实际上或法律上全部或部分合同义务成为不可能,而不是更加困难或无法获取利润。除了阻碍承包商履行全部或部分合同义务外,更低的门槛可能是妨碍(hindered)或延误(delayed)了承包商履行全部或部分合同义务。

关于阻碍、妨碍和延误的含义,在Fairclough Dodd & Jones Ltd. v J. H. Vantol Ltd.○案中,法院判决"阻碍(prevented)"是指只有在合同期限结束前不可能履行运输义务时,合同约定的救济措施才得以成立。在Tennants (Lancashire Ltd. v G. S. Wilson & Co Ltd.○案中,法院判决"阻碍交货(preventing delivery)是指……交货成为不可能;而妨碍(hindering delivery)是指比阻碍要轻一些,即交货变得有些困难,但并非不可能。"而"延误(delayed)"是指在合同约定履约可以延期的情况下,如果是当事一方不能控制的情况导致履约延误,因此没有必要将"延误"等同于"阻碍(prevented)",而仅仅是妨碍(hindered)履约的情况,即可视为符合合同约定○。

(3)不可抗力事件与阻碍承包商履约之间存在因果关系。

(4)没有可采取避免事件发生的合理措施。

在Thames Valley Power Limited v Total Gas & Power Limited○案中,被告道达尔石油公司以天然气市场价格暴涨为由主张其遭遇不可抗力,使得合同履行变得不经济(uneconomic)而停止向原告供应天然气。法官克里斯多弗在判决中写道:

"不可抗力事件应导致道达尔不能履行合同义务,而事实上道达尔的理由是因价格上涨,甚至涨得特别高,但这不意味着道达尔不能履行合同义务。"○

鉴此,法院判决道达尔石油公司的主张不能构成合同约定的不可抗力事件。

在Classic Maritime Inc. v. Limbungan Makmur SDN BHD & another [2019]○案中,被告以巴西大坝溃堤封道为不可抗力为由,导致其无法履行2015年11月至2016年6月期间的运输工作。法院查明,溃堤事件确实使得被告无法履行最后5期的运输工作,同时还查明,即

○ [2013] EWCA Civ 905, at [25].
○ [1917] A. C. 495.
○ Paras 15-159. Chitty on Contracts. 33rd Edition. P1232.
四 [2005] EWHC 2208 (Comm).
五 [2005] EWHC 2208 (Comm), at [50].
六 [2019] EWCA Civ 1102.

使没有溃堤事件，被告也倾向于不会履行合同约定的运输义务。因此，法官运用了若无验证标准（but for test），认为溃堤事件与不履行合同之间的关联不存在因果关系，不可抗力事件的发生不能免除被告的合同义务。

4. 承包商要求工期延长和/或额外费用的主张

1999年第1版FIDIC合同条款第19.4款［不可抗力的后果］规定承包商有权因不可抗力事件要求工期延长和/或额外损失，承包商除需要遵守第19.2款［不可抗力的通知］、第20.1款［承包商的索赔］中索赔通知外，还需进一步证明不可抗力事件对工程进度计划的影响，受不可抗力影响的工作或活动，且受不可抗力事件影响的工作或活动处于工程项目的关键线路上。此外，承包商还应量化工期延长索赔的天数。对于额外费用，由于不可抗力不属于合同任何一方的过错，承包商仅能索赔第19.4款［不可抗力的后果］规定的有权索赔的费用，即直接费用和间接费用，但不包括利润以及间接损失。因战争、敌对行为、入侵、外敌行为和自然灾害事件，承包商无权索赔额外费用。实际上，在发生不可抗力事件后，承包商经常提出的索赔为停工索赔，承包商应提供停工时间、停工期间的承包商设备折旧费、一定期限内的人工工资，以及除利润外的间接费用。

5. 解除合同

1999年第1版FIDIC合同条款第19.6款［自主选择终止、付款和解除］规定了当事方因不可抗力解除合同的权利，自发出不可抗力通知，基本上使全部进展中的工程实施受到阻碍已连续84天，或由于同一通知的不可抗力连续阻碍几个期间累计超过140天的情况下，任何一方均有权解除合同。在国际工程项目中，经常发生的是解除受影响的某个部分合同。在表10-1第5项中，因项目现场发生恐怖袭击，恐怖分子威胁中方人员如继续施工将全部杀光，且当地分包商没有施工能力建造桥梁，因此终止合同。在表10-1第6项中，因项目位于马里北部靠近撒哈拉沙漠地区，是恐怖组织的主要活动区域，经聘请法国著名安保公司评估安全情况，即使马里政府派出军队，也无法在漫长的交通线上和大范围的施工现场保障人身和财产安全，因此解除已签约但尚未开工的施工合同。

6. 承包商的举证责任

根据"谁主张，谁举证"的法律原则，承包商对不可抗力事件负有举证责任，包括不可抗力事件本身的证据，也包括承包商因此主张的工期延长或额外费用等证据。除非合同不可抗力条款明确约定由权威机构出具证明文件对不可抗力事件的证明效力是最终的，否则该证明文件在国际诉讼和仲裁中并不重要。FIDIC系列合同条款没有规定当事方在发生不可抗力事件时负有提供权威机构证明的义务，因此，合同没有明确约定发生特殊风险或不可抗力事件后需要承包商出具权威机构的证明文件时，承包商没有义务向业主递交某些机构出具的不可抗力证明。但另一方面，承包商绝对不能简单地以某些机构出具的不可抗力证明概括性地主张不可抗力事件对其工程项目的影响，以替代承包商在合同和适用法律项下负有的举证责任和义务。

法律不保护躺在权利上睡觉的人。幸运的是，实践表明，绝大部分中国承包商都能够在发生不可抗力事件后立即或迅速向业主发出不可抗力通知和索赔通知，主张合同赋予的工期延长和/或额外费用的权利。在履行通知义务后，承包商还应履行减轻损失义务，积极主张合同约定的救济措施，履行举证责任，维护自身合法权益。

10.6 新冠肺炎疫情不可抗力索赔

10.6.1 新冠肺炎疫情爆发

2020年3月，世界卫生组织将新冠肺炎疫情宣布为全球大流行。新冠肺炎疫情在欧洲地区和美国的集中爆发，以及在其他国家和地区的迅速蔓延，使得许多国家和地区纷纷出台了更为严格的居家、社交距离、出行限制、封城和取消国际航班等限制措施。这些国家和地区发布的抗疫措施不可避免地对中国承包商在当地的工程项目造成了直接影响，导致在建工程项目无法正常施工，工效降低或者直接导致停工。如果说新冠肺炎疫情在中国爆发对于中国承包商的国际工程项目产生了一定程度的间接影响，那么工程所在国或地区采取的抗疫措施则对这些在建国际工程项目产生了直接的影响。对于中国承包商而言，运用合同和法律手段应对新冠肺炎疫情刻不容缓。

10.6.2 承包商与业主分歧

2020年1月，某南亚地区的国际工程项目的承包商向业主发出新型冠状病毒疫情为不可抗力的通知函，提出承包商大多数项目管理人员和工人受交通管制的影响无法按期在春节后返回项目现场，承包商无法在节后按期复工，且由于疫情是承包商无法预见和控制的，属于不可抗力，要求依据 FIDIC 合同条款 1987 年第 4 版第 20.4 款 [业主风险] 和第 65 条 [特殊风险] 索赔工期延长和因此发生的额外费用。承包商同时指出，根据合同第 34.5 款 [健康和安全] 和第 34.6 款 [传染病] 的要求，承包商已自负费用采取相应的预防措施和遵守政府或当地医疗卫生部门有关传染病控制的规定、条例和要求。

业主随后回复称，惊悉新型冠状病毒疫情对中国境内的影响会对位于境外国家的工程项目产生延误的问题，承包商引用的合同第 34.6 款 [传染病] 与位于中国境外的工程项目没有直接关联。根据专用合同条款第 20.4 款和通用合同条款第 65 条 [特殊风险] 的约定，传染病没有列入特殊风险，因此，业主无法接受在境外国家发生传染病引起的业主责任。根据通用合同条款第 8.1 款 [承包商的一般义务] 的约定，承包商负有义务安排其人员履行合同约定的义务。此外，在其他项目上，中资承包商仍然在继续工作，没有因为疫情而暂停任何工作。因此，业主认为承包商发出的新型冠状病毒疫情为不可抗力的通知缺乏理由，不能免除承包商按照合同约定完成剩余工程项目的义务。

承包商在回复业主时主张，2020 年 1 月 30 日世界卫生组织（WHO）已将新型冠状病毒疫情认定为国际关注的突发公共卫生事件（PHEIC），称其为急性呼吸道传染病。承包商再次提醒业主注意一个主要事实是其大部分项目管理人员和工人居住在疫情高发地区湖北省，由于交通管制，这些人员无法按期返回项目现场进行剩余工程的施工。虽然专用合同条款第 20.4 款 [业主风险] 没有将传染病列入业主承担的特殊风险之中，但新型冠状病毒疫情符合第 20.4 款约定的承包商在签订合同时无法预见、无法避免且无法控制的情形，应属特殊风险事件。而且，即使合同没有约定传染病作为特殊风险事件，但根据合同适用的法律，即《1872 年合同法》（Contract Act 1872）第 56 条认可由于当事人无法预见和无法避免的事件为合同目的的落空（frustration of contract），受影响的当事人有权解除和免除合同项下的履约义务。为证明新型冠状病毒疫情对本项目的影响，承包商将尽快向工程师提供受影响的人员名单、居住地点和在本项目中的岗位以及人员费用等。

上述境外项目业主的回复具有一定意义的典型性，主要涉及了（1）在他国境内发生的新型冠状病毒疫情对国际工程项目的影响；（2）1987年第四版FIDIC合同条款以及1999年第1版FIDIC合同系列、多边开发银行协调版FIDIC合同条款和2017年第2版系列合同条款没有将传染病列入特殊风险或不可抗力事件，在合同未将传染病列入合同或合同中将传染病排除在特殊风险或不可抗力事件之外，承包商是否有权主张传染病为特殊风险或不可抗力事件；（3）承包商的举证责任以及如何在国际工程项目中证明疫情的影响；（4）其他境外项目的正常履约是否构成业主对受到疫情影响项目的合理抗辩理由。

承包商在回复业主的函件中答复如下：

Dear Sir,

We write in continuation to our earlier Notification G-608 dated 27th January, 2020 (Notification) on the above subject.

The Employer has responded to the Notification without considering the facts and circumstances which are preventing the Contractor and its staff from full resumption of work in wake of Chinese New Year holidays and contemporaneous occurrence and outbreak of Coronavirus. Nevertheless, the contents of the Employer's response are replied as below:

(ⅰ) Pursuant to Clause 34.5 of the Contract, the Contractor is obligated to take due precautions at his own cost, to ensure the safety of his staff and labour at all times throughout the period of the Contract. The Contractor shall further ensure that suitable arrangements are made for the prevention of epidemics and for all necessary welfare and hygiene requirements. Accordingly the Contractor has advised the workers to follow the instructions of the Government of Pakistan, Government of China and World Health Organization (WHO) in the instant matter as it poses serious risk to the lives which has recommended the quarantine of the affected people, prohibition of evacuation and restriction on travel from and to China.

(ⅱ) Furthermore, Clause 34.6 of the Contract stipulates that in the event of any outbreak of illness of an epidemic nature, the Contractor shall comply with and carry out such regulations, orders and requirements as may be made by the government, or the local medical or sanitary authorities, for purpose of dealing with and overcoming the same. The Government of Pakistan has suspended all air travel and flight operations between Pakistan and China to obviate the threat posed by the outbreak of Coronavirus in Pakistan and has further cautioned to place Chinese workers in Pakistan under strict surveillance, screening and scrutiny.

(ⅲ) It is worthy to reiterate in the Notification letter of 27 January 2020 that most of the workforce from the Contractor are residents of Hubei Province, China where the epicenter of this serious epidemic called 2019-nCoV is just located in Wuhan City, Hu Bei Province, China, and the Government of China has imposed traffic ban in Wuhan City as well as Hu Bei Province, China. Accordingly the Contractor notified the Engineer and the Employer that full work force cannot be deployed at the Project, to prevent spread of the epidemic, due to the prevalence of unforeseeable conditions which are beyond the reasonable control of the Contractor. Thus work will be carried out and completed at reduced speed as a result of lesser availability of workforce.

(iv) The WHO in its latest statement on 31st January, 2020 (30 January 2020 Geneva time) declared the outbreak of Coronavirus (identified as 2019-nCoV by WHO) as a Public Health Emergency of International Concern (PHEIC), which emergency is applicable to Pakistan being a member state of WHO.

(v) The national newspapers of Pakistan including the DAWN, Business Recorder and the NEWS have widely reported the press conference of Health Ministry of Pakistan officials whereby the Coronavirus has been recognized as an emergent threat for which full preventive and precautionary measures are to be taken in Pakistan especially by the Chinese companies operating in Pakistan.

(vi) Special Guidelines have been issued by the Embassy of China in Pakistan to the Chinese companies operating in Pakistan to deal with this international and national emergency.

(vii) The Employer's Risks as such do not illustrate epidemics, however these are illustrative and inclusive events and are not sole or exclusive events. The outbreak of 2019-nCoV is an event which is beyond the reasonable control of the Contractor, was unforeseeable and directly affects the execution of works in Pakistan and hence falls within the definition of force majeure events and thus the Contractor is entitled to relief in time during the pendency of this special event.

(viii) The Contract between the Contractor and the Employer is governed by the laws of Pakistan and hence Contract Act 1872 is applicable to the rights and obligations of the parties under the Contract.

(ix) Pursuant to Section 56 of the Contact Act 1872, Frustration of the Contract is recognized due to occurrence of an event which was not foreseeable and couldn't have been prevented and the affected party is therefore entitled to relief and excuse from performance of its obligations under the Contract.

(x) Even otherwise it will not be in the interest of the general health conditions prevailing in Pakistan that workers should return to the Project anytime soon with the danger of carriage of contagious disease whose source and treatment is yet unknown and which can cause outbreak in Pakistan and this stance has been endorsed by the WHO, Government of Pakistan and Government of China.

> Accordingly, the Contractor rejects the unreasonable, unjustifiable and bookish approach of the Employer and reiterates the contents of the Notification as further expounded hereinabove.
> Furthermore, we shall update by providing a Detailed Labor Report for current manpower on the site including names, passports, positions at site and labor rates. We shall further identify those staff members that are directly or indirectly affected by 2019-nCoV including date of leave from Pakistan, planned date of return, copies of passports, positions and labor rates.
> As it is an evolving event, we shall duly notify and update information as soon as we receive further updates.
> Yours truly,

1. 因新型冠状病毒疫情对国际工程项目的影响

新型冠状病毒疫情是否对位于境外的国际工程项目产生影响,并从而构成合同约定的或适用法律规定的特殊风险或不可抗力事件,应视位于境外国际工程项目的具体情况而定,不能一概而论,且不能进行概括性陈述或主张,盲目地主张特殊风险或不可抗力事件的发生,进而提出工期延长和额外费用的索赔主张,而是应该依据合同约定和适用法律的规定证明新型冠状病毒疫情对具体国际工程项目的影响及其影响程度。

在大多数国际工程项目中,由于中资承包商均会安排春节期间,包括项目管理人员和劳务人员继续在现场施工,因此,2019 新型冠状病毒疫情对国际工程项目履约的影响相对有限,不具有普遍适用的意义。在承包商属地化管理和劳务为当地熟练和非熟练劳务时,承包商不能以某些项目管理或劳务人员未能按期返回现场为由,主张疫情为特殊风险和不可抗力事件,应视项目中方管理和劳务人员的重要性确定。在上述项目中,承包商大部分项目管理人员和劳务人员由于交通管制措施从而无法节后返回复工,承包商主张疫情为特殊风险事件具有事实依据。

为了证明新型冠状病毒疫情对位于境外国际工程项目的影响,承包商应负有举证义务,证明两者之间存在因果关系以及影响的程度。

2. 承包商是否有权主张传染病为特殊风险或不可抗力事件

在中国企业普遍使用的 FIDIC 合同条款中,尽管 1987 年第 4 版、1999 年第 1 版 FIDIC 合同系列、多边开发银行协调版合同系列和 2017 年第 2 版 FIDIC 合同系列没有将传染病列为特殊风险或不可抗力事件,但上述合同条款均约定了相同的特殊风险或不可抗力的定义,系指某种异常事件或情况:①一方无法控制的;②该方在签订合同前,不能对之进行合理准备的;③发生后,该方不能合理避免或克服的;④不能主要归因于他方的。因此,即使合同中没有把传染病列为特殊风险或不可抗力事件,承包商也可以从上述定义中证明新型冠状病毒疫情为特殊风险或不可抗力事件。另一方面,即使合同没有约定传染病为特殊风险或不可抗力事件,各国合同法或判例中均有特殊风险或不可抗力的法律规定,承包商可以引用适用法律中的特殊风险或不可抗力的法律规定主张新型冠状病毒疫情为特殊风险或不可抗力事件。

需要提醒的是,如果合同约定了传染病为特殊风险或不可抗力,除按合同约定主张特殊风险或不可抗力外,承包商更应从适用法律的角度评估新型冠状病毒疫情是否在适用法律下构成特殊风险或不可抗力,以及适用法律规定的法律验证标准。切莫一概而论,盲目主张不可抗力或履约不能,甚至主张解除合同。

3. 承包商如何在国际工程项目中证明疫情的影响

由于某些国家或地区航班的限制措施,导致中资承包商无法按期派出项目管理和劳务人员,导致项目管理和劳务人员出现短缺。由于国内某些地区出行限制措施和节后推迟上班,可能导致负责国际工程项目的设计部门无法按计划进行设计工作,也可能导致设备或材料交货延迟,从而导致项目工期延误和/或发生额外费用。对于从事国际工程项目的承包商来说,如果在建国际工程项目受到了新型冠状病毒疫情的影响,应按照合同的约定,在合同约定的期限内发出不可抗力通知,同时向业主递交索赔通知,并承担相应的举证义务,证明疫情对在建项目的影响及其程度。对于工期延误和/或额外费用的影响,承包商有义务提供证据证明如下事项:

(1) 新型冠状病毒疫情对承包商正在实施的国际工程项目存在影响。

(2) 在项目管理或劳务人员无法按期节后返回现场时,应提供上述人员的名单、身份信息、职务、国内居住地址,并应证明上述人员是否受到交通限制如航班限制的影响,以及这些人的职务和岗位对工程施工的确切影响,是否具有可替代性安排。

(3) 若对设备和材料供货产生延误,需要证明设备和货物如何受到延误,以及是否具有可替代性安排。

(4) 疫情对工程进度计划的影响。

(5) 受疫情影响的工作或活动。

(6) 受疫情影响的工作或活动是否处于项目的关键线路上。

(7) 受影响的天数的计算。可通过更新进度计划的方式,或者利用项目进度管理软件计算受影响的天数。

(8) 受疫情影响产生的实际发生的费用。

(9) 受疫情影响产生的额外费用,包括现场管理费和总部管理费,但不包括利润。

需要注意的是,承包商应在合同约定的期限内发出索赔通知,例如 FIDIC 合同条款 1999 年第 1 版第 20.1 款 [承包商的索赔] 约定的 28 天内发出索赔通知,并应在合同约定的期限内提出索赔报告,包括索赔依据、主要事实、事实与结果之间的因果关系、索赔天数的计算、发生的额外费用计算以及证明上述索赔权利的证据。

另一方面,承包商绝对不能简单地用某些机构出具的不可抗力证明概括地主张新型冠状病毒疫情构成特殊风险或不可抗力及其对其国际工程项目的影响,而替代承包商在合同和适用法律项下负有的举证责任和义务,更不能盲目主张不可抗力或履约不能,甚至主张解除合同。

4. 其他境外项目的正常履约是否构成业主对受到疫情影响项目的合理抗辩理由

上述项目中,承包商主张受影响的因素是其大多数项目管理和劳务人员均居住在湖北省,受交通限制影响节后无法返回现场,而其他项目上的大多数承包商人员并非来自湖北省。因此,业主的上述主张明显与承包商所指的项目无关,业主主张其他境外项目正常履约,包括同一承包商在该国的其他项目的正常履约,均不能构成对受疫情影响项目的合理抗辩理由。

需要指出的是，新型冠状病毒疫情可能但不必然构成特殊风险或不可抗力事件，应视具体国际工程项目是否受到疫情影响，以及受到疫情影响的程度而定。对于国际工程项目而言，新型冠状病毒疫情不具有普遍适用性。承包商在向业主主张新型冠状病毒疫情为特殊风险或不可抗力事件时，应三思而行，切忌盲目主张并向业主索赔工期延长以及额外费用。在国际工程项目确实受到新型冠状病毒疫情影响时，应依据合同约定提出特殊风险或不可抗力通知，履行减轻损失义务，并应根据合同在约定的期限内发出索赔通知，依据合同约定索赔新型冠状病毒疫情构成特殊风险或不可抗力事件时的工期延长和/或实际发生的额外费用。

第 11 章 暂停和终止合同

> This will be by operation of law, and will occur where the guilty party has committed a repudiatory breach and the innocent party has then by word or action elected to accept the repudiation and terminate the contract.
>
> Paras 8-002, *Hudson's Building and Engineering Contracts*. 14th Edition

11.1 暂停施工

11.1.1 业主暂停的权利

在建筑和土木工程施工合同中,业主拥有暂停承包商施工的权利。1999 年第 1 版 FIDIC 合同条款红皮书、黄皮书和银皮书第 8.8 款 [暂时停工]、第 8.9 款 [暂停的后果]、第 8.10 款 [暂停时对生产设备和材料的付款] 和第 8.11 款 [拖长的暂停] 规定了工程师暂停承包商施工的内容。

以某国际工程项目为例,工程师因某部分工程质量缺陷要求承包商停工,示例如下:

> Dear Sir,
>
> This is to inform you that you shall suspend all construction activities relating to section _____ of the works since we are convinced that the quality of such section is not in accordance with the special specification requirements.
>
> Please be noted that unless those defects of such sections are fixed and remedied to meet the specification requirements in the Contract, you are not allowed to continue any construction works on site.
>
> The costs to be incurred arising out of the remedy of any defects in such sections shall be borne by the Contractor.
>
> Sincerely,

11.1.2 承包商暂停的权利

1999 年第 1 版 FIDIC 合同条款红皮书、黄皮书和银皮书第 16.1 款 [承包商暂停工作的

权利]规定了承包商有权暂停施工。根据第16.1款的规定,承包商有权放慢施工速度或暂停工程,如果:

(1) 业主未能提供有关第2.4款[业主的资金安排]规定的资金安排的信息;或者

(2) 工程师未能按照第14.6款[期中付款证书的颁发]签发期中付款证书;或者

(3) 业主未能向承包商支付第14.7款[付款]项下到期的款项。

如果因按照本款暂停工作(或放慢工作速度),使承包商遭受延误和/或导致增加费用,承包商应向工程师发出通知,有权根据第20.1款[承包商的索赔]的规定,要求:

(1) 根据第8.4款[竣工时间的延长]的规定,若竣工已经或将受到延误,对任何此类延误给予延长期;以及

(2) 对任何此类费用加合理利润应计入合同价格,给予支付。

工程师收到此通知后,应按照第3.5款[确定]的规定,对这些事项进行商定或确定。

承包商采取行动放慢施工速度或暂停工程后,不可避免地会发生额外费用和延误,并可能延误竣工时间。承包商应根据第16.1款[承包商暂停工作的权利]在不少于21天发出通知,并遵守第8.4款[竣工时间的延长]和第20.1款[承包商的索赔]规定的程序。工程师可根据第3.5款[确定]的规定尽力达成一致或作出确定。承包商的费用应包括复工费用和有权得到的这些费用产生的利润。

以某国际工程项目为例,由于业主未能按期支付工程进度款,在承包商已经提前21天发出通知的情况下,承包商向业主发出暂停工程施工函通知业主自本函发出之日暂停施工,并要求业主赔偿承包商因此遭受的所有损失,如下:

Subject: Suspension of Works

Dear Sir,

We write further to our letter referenced _____ dated 2 August 2011, in which we gave the Employer the due notice that Interim Payment Certificates No. 3 to 9 were overdue for payment and that unless these certificates were paid within 21 days from the date thereof, we shall be left with no option other than to suspend work pursuant to Sub-Clause 16.1 [*Contractor's Entitlement to Suspend Work*] of the Conditions of Contract.

The cumulative overdue amounts were in the sum of Euro _____ and TS _____. To date no payment has been received despite repeated undertaking by the Employer in the recent past.

Consequently, we give you the requisite notice that in accordance with the provisions of Sub-Clause 20.1 [*Contractor's Claim*], we shall implement suspension of the Works with effect from the date of this letter, 23 August 2011.

We further advise that this event should initially commence with reduced rate of work to enable us to protect the advanced pavement layers and mitigate the additional costs on the part of the Employer. The ongoing works shall comprise the listed works:

(1) Protection of previously stabilized upper subbase with application of curing membrane;
(2) Protection of the underlaying layer of base course with prime coat;
(3) Protection of asphalt wearing with surfacing dressing to carriageway and shoulders;
(4) Maintenance of deviations and care of the works including protection of slopes.

During this period of the delay and disruption of progress, some expatriates and local staff and labour will be sent home (if entitled to leave) unless otherwise required for the above mentioned works pending resumption of the work during which period they will be paid basic salaries and wages.

The plant and equipment will be parked on site unless otherwise required to carry out the above mentioned works. The Contractor shall submit contemporary records of stand-by plant, equipment and personnel on a weekly basis.

Pursuant to the provisions of Sub-Clause 16.1 [*Contractor's Entitlement to Suspend Work*] and Sub-Clause 8.4 [*Extension of Time for Completion*], we shall be claiming for reimbursement of all additional costs incurred and extension of time for completion as a result of the suspension. Such costs shall include, but not limited to:

(a) Additional off-site and on-site overheads cost;
(b) Standby cost of site running costs;
(c) Standby cost of local staff and labour costs;
(d) Standby cost of expatriate staff cost;
(e) Standby cost of plant and equipment depreciation cost;
(f) Demobilization and remobilization;
(g) Remedial work in the event of damages;
(h) Loss of profit earning cost.

For budget purpose, we advise that the said cost should be in the range of TS _____ Each way.

We are available at any time to discuss any aspect of this suspension.
Sincerely,

在某国际工程项目中，承包商向业主发函，考虑到现场发生枪击事件，导致承包商无法施工，被迫暂停施工，如下：

Dear Sir,

It is a sorrow to notify you again that on 1st March 2017, 6 gunmen attacked our camp at No. 1 Quarry located 8km from the main camp, as a consequence of the attack one of our employees _____ (25 years old) was killed when he was talking on the phone at the dining hall.

Since the beginning of the works, we have encountered 9 times of gun shooting on 18 Apr 2015, 15 Jan 2016, 14 Feb 2016, 27 Dec 2016, 30 Dec 2016, 8 Feb 2017, 26 Feb 2017 and 1 March 2017 respectively, which caused deaths of 5 local employees, injury of 2 Chinese and injury of 2 local employees. It is also noticed that the gunmen also frequently attacked local people and vehicles surrounding the project area and nearby sugar plant project. More importantly, the gunmen attacked our camp on 1 March 2017, instead of the attacks on our employees on road operation, which means the attacks are escalating and the nature of attacks is changing materially.

It can be observed from the frequent incidents in the recent days that the security situation becomes worse and worse, and the conflicts between the local government and the tribes in that region has intensified. It is obvious that either the gun shooting incidents or the attacks on our camp conducted by the tribe that, their intention is to stop all works along the stretch of the road.

Despite the occurrence of gun shooting since April 2015 to the date of this letter, and even four times within one month this year, there is no substantial improvement on the security situation and no effective measures taken by both the local government and the Employer. The Contractor has no choice other than suspension of all site works since we cannot take any more risk on our employee's life and personal safety. Meanwhile, the Contractor is really in a dilemma over how to continue the works in the future.

Therefore, this is to notify you that the Contractor is forced to suspend all project activities on site from 2nd March, 2017. During the suspension, we will repatriate our Chinese staff and local employees, but retain certain security persons to take care of equipment and materials on site, at the same time the subcontractor for rented machines will be given notice to departure from site and our own construction equipment will be taken back to camp. In addition, we would like to inform you that this is considered notice to claim in accordance with 20.1 of the GCC.

根据 FIDIC 1999 年第 1 版合同条款第 16.1 款 [承包商暂停工作的权利] 的规定,如果承包商暂停施工或降低施工速度,则承包商有权索赔进一步的工期延长和额外费用。以某国际工程为例,承包商在未按期收到业主应支付的预付款和工程进度款的情况下,致函业主要求索赔工期延长和额外费用,如下:

Dear Sirs,

In accordance with Sub-Clause 13.7 of GCC and Particular Application Conditions, "*the Employer shall pay the amount certified in each Interim within 42 days from the date on which the Employer's Representative received the Contractor's statement and supporting documents*"; it is noticed that from the commencement of the project to date, all the advance payments and certain Interim payments

> have been delayed by the Employer. Please refer to the attachment for detailed information, which shows the delayed days and amount for advance payments and IPC payments respectively.
>
> As a result of the delayed payment by the Employer, the Contractor is always in shortage of cash flow to arrange site construction as per the planned progress. Meanwhile, extra cost has been incurred to the Contractor due to the delayed payment.
>
> Sub-Clause 16.1 of GCC provides that:
>
> "If the Contractor suffers delay and/or incurs Cost as a result of suspending work or reducing the rate of work in accordance with this Sub-Clause, the Contractor shall give notice to the Employer's Representative. After receipt of such notice, the Employer's Representative shall proceed in accordance with Sub-Clause 3.5 to agree or determine:
>
> (a) any extension of time to which the Contractor is entitled under Sub-Clause 8.3, and
>
> (b) the amount of such Cost plus reasonable profit, which shall be added to the Contract Price, and shall notify the Contractor accordingly."
>
> According to the above Sub-Clauses, we reserve the right to claim for the extension of time and additional cost caused by the Employer's late payment.

11.1.3 复工

FIDIC 合同条款 1999 年第 1 版第 8.12 款 [复工] 规定，在发出继续施工的许可或指示后，承包商和工程师应联合对受暂停影响的工程、生产设备和材料进行检查。承包商应负责修复在暂停期间发生的在工程、生产设备或材料中的任何变质、缺陷或损失。

在国际工程实践中，复工问题并没有像 FIDIC 合同条款 1999 年第 1 版第 8.12 款 [复工] 那么简单，复工需要满足一定的条件。在下述情形中，承包商是否复工需要考量：

（1）如果承包商以业主未能支付工程款项为由暂停施工，则承包商需要在获得业主付款后才能复工。

（2）如果承包商以业主未能支付工程款项为由暂停施工，且暂停施工后业主仍未在一定期限内付款，承包商为此向业主发出终止合同通知，此时：

1）如果在终止合同通知尚未生效之前业主支付了工程款项，承包商应予复工。

2）如果承包商发出终止合同通知，在终止合同通知生效后，业主支付了工程款项，则终止合同通知生效，合同解除。如果业主以已向承包商支付了工程款项为由要求复工，则承包商可不予复工，主张合同已被终止，合同应予解除。

（3）在存在安全和安保问题时，则业主应采取措施保证现场施工的人员和财产的安全的前提下，承包商才能复工。

(4) 在因不可抗力事件暂停施工时，应在不可抗力事件结束后复工。在国际工程实践中，承包商与业主往往就不可抗力事件是否结束、何时复工产生争议。例如在巴基斯坦某水电站炮击事件发生后，业主与承包商就复工是否存在安全隐患存在争议，对复工日期争执不下。

以某国际工程项目为例，承包商在接到业主要求复工的要求后致函业主表明现场安全无法保障，无法复工，如下：

Dear Sirs,

We acknowledge the receipt of Employer's Representative letter Ref. No _____ dated 1st April 2017 through which we have been notified to resume the work.

The matter reference is also to be made in the Employer's letter _____ dated 7 April 2017 which was addressed to you and copied to us. Both the Employer and the Employer's Representative have stated that the site is safe at this time.

In his letter referred to above, the Employer's Representative said that the Contractor has a right to claim if any further problem arose. Yes of course, we know that we have a right to claim additional cost and/or additional time *but not for additional life*. Here it is to be noted that the matter is about the life of our staff, which is non-substitutable not only about time and/or cost.

In addition, it is mentioned in the Employer's Representative letter that "armed local bodies have been forced to hand over their weapons". But as to our actual observation around the project site, still armed tribes are seen around the site just the same as before.

Furthermore, it is stated that the Local Government will be responsible if incidents happened in the future. But it shall be clear that the Contractor shall not tolerate any similar problem and thus the Contractor will take any measures in response depending on the severity of the issue, including withdrawing from the site, if such incident happened in the future. For that the Employer shall be responsible for any consequential loss including taking care of all properties to be left on the project site.

The Employer's Representative mentioned that no gun shooting has happened since 2nd March 2017, which is proof for restoration of safe working condition. However, non-occurrence of gun shooting incident since 2nd March 2017 to date could not be considered as an indication of restoration of safe working environment. It is apparent that all project activities are already suspended and such non-occurrence could be associated with the absence of significant movement. What if the project activities were as usual? Obviously, no one could give a correct answer regarding the occurrence of other gun shooting incidents. So, it is very hard to conclude that safe working condition is restored on the project site. Instead, we believe that it is better to understand the actual situation by analyzing the previous problems and taking the general behavior of local society in to consideration.

As we have learned from the previous experiences it is very difficult to evaluate the safety of the project site within such a short period. This is because all incidents happened without indication of any violence or questions raised by local people. The existence of the problem becomes visible just whenever gun shooting happens. Therefore, we still have reservations on the safety condition of the project area.

As to our stance, it is very important to understand the actual situation and implement appropriate remedial measures so as to secure safe working condition. We also believe that the matter cloud not be managed with the contract provisions alone, for instance working with assistance of soldiers is not stated in the condition of Contract. Thus, we insist that the Employer devise an appropriate management scheme for the specific problem. Otherwise extra sacrifice of life is very intolerable to us, as an international Contractor and the issue will be highly complicated.

Keeping our stand-point as mentioned above, if both the Employer and the Employer's Representative request us to resume the work at this time with the current situation, we will start to resume the work in the coming days so long as the following conditions have to be met in parallel:

- We need escorting security force to ensure safety of our staff at living camps, construction site, quarries, crushing plant and water source area. Living camps and crusher sites need arrangement of stationary security force while for the working sites moveable escort is required. Management of the force, arrangement of vehicles, shelter and other materials for the purpose of security forces shall be the responsibility of the Employer because it is not the Contractor's duty.
- We only start at sections covered by security forces and expand our site activity from time to time based on the safety condition and our workers' arrival on site. Reasonable improvements of safety condition need to be observed so as to convince our staff.
- 3 months of trial resumption needs to be allowed for the Contractor to prove the efficiency of the security system and to convince the majority of our local workers and Chinese staff etc. to come and work. Normal working period needs to be counted after the trial period upon evaluation of safety condition on site and restoration of normal work progress.

In addition, the Chinese Security Authority asked us to let them know about the court decision on those illegal persons who committed murder on our project staff. Thus, we want to request the Employer's Representative to communicate with the relevant government bodies and give us copies of court decisions and the incident investigation report if possible so as to report the matter accordingly. At the same time, such information will help us to convince our staff regarding measures taken and attentions given by the government.

> Therefore, please be notified that we will resume some section of the work and extend the working site from time to time based on the conditions described above.
>
> Finally, we would like to remind both parties that the Contractor's right is reserved to be compensated for the time lost and cost incurred in accordance with Sub-Clause 17.4 and 20.1 of the GCC.

11.2 整改通知

FIDIC 合同条款 1999 年第 1 版第 15.1 款通知改正（或称整改通知）规定，如果承包商未能根据合同履行任何义务，工程师可通知承包商，要求其在规定的合理时间内，纠正并补救上述违约。第 15.1 款的英文表述为："If the Contractor fails to carry out any obligation under the Contract, the Engineer may by notice require the Contractor to make good the failure and to remedy it within a specified reasonable time."

从 FIDIC 合同条款 1999 第 1 版第 15.1 款 [通知改正] 的规定可以得出，工程师代表业主向承包商发出整改通知的范围极为广泛，即承包商未能根据合同履行任何义务的事件均在本款规定的范围之内。但在国际工程实践中，工程师代表业主向承包商发出整改通知，一般情况下是较为严重的事件，工程师不宜对任何琐碎的或不重要的合同违约（trivial contractual failure）发出整改通知，这主要是因为工程师发出整改通知，如果承包商未能遵守，则可能导致业主行使终止合同的权利。但必须指出，在国际工程项目中，任何一方终止合同应基于另一方的根本性违约或实质性违约（fundamental breach or substantial breach）。在承包商未能遵守第 15.1 款 [通知改正] 的情况下，不必然导致业主有权终止合同，应视承包商违约的性质以及是否构成根本性违约或实质性违约而定。在 Obrascon Huarte Lain SA v Her Majesty's Attorney General for Gibraltar[①] 案件中，法官论述道：

"第 15.1 款 [通知改正] 仅与较为明显的承包商违约存在关联。此类违约可能是健康或安全违约、不良工程、严重的工期延误等。需要确定的是违约应符合合同的规定。有时可能尚未构成违约，例如，运抵现场的水泥类型错误，但在尚未使用或打算使用之前，可能不构成违约。"[②]

法官接着阐述道：

"在解释合同第 15.1 款 [通知改正] 和第 15.2 款 [由雇主终止] 时，需要遵循商业为先的解释原则。合同当事方不可能（主观地）设想一件不重要的合同违约自身将导致合同终止……即使承包商未能遵守第 15.1 款 [通知改正] 的通知。至于什么是不重要的、什么是重要的或严重的违约取决于具体事实。"[③]

因此，在国际工程实践中，一个理性的、有经验的工程师或业主不会就不重要的合同违

---

① [2014] EWHC 1028 (TCC).
② [2014] EWHC 1028 (TCC), at [318].
③ [2014] EWHC 1028 (TCC), at [321].

约发出整改通知,但不可避免的是,一个总想终止承包商合同的业主或工程师可能会如此行为。

工程师或业主发出的整改通知示例如下:

> Dear Sir,
>
> We refer to the letters of the Engineer in reference to requesting that the Contractor establish additional survey benchmarks in order to have a healthy geodesic grid.
>
> Despite several previous verbal warnings regarding this concerned delay, the required geodesic grid could be established in none of the contract sections.
>
> Therefore, you are hereby being served with Notice to Correct under Sub-Clause 15.1 of GCC to remedy this shortcoming until the end of _____ in order not to be faced with further Contractual measures.

11.3 业主终止合同

在合同当事一方未能履行其义务、未能完成其义务或妨碍另一方履行义务等事项发生时,当事人的行为即构成分包合同项下的违约。1999年第1版FIDIC施工合同(红皮书)第15条[由雇主终止]规定了业主终止合同的程序、业主终止合同的原因以及补救措施。

无论是因承包商违约导致业主采取终止合同的行为,还是业主因方便而终止合同,终止合同的行为都是一件非常严肃的事情。对业主和承包商来说,都需要事前进行认真讨论和谈判,在双方缺少沟通的情况下采取终止合同的措施,对任何一方都会产生严重的后果和问题。

根据1999年第1版FIDIC合同条款第15.2款[由雇主终止]的规定,在下述情形下,业主有权终止合同:

(1) 未能遵守第4.2款[履约担保]的规定,或根据第15.1款[通知改正]的规定发出通知的要求。

(2) 放弃工程,或明确表现出不愿意继续按照合同履行其义务的意向。

(3) 无合理解释,未能:

1) 按照第8条[开工、延误和暂停]的规定进行工程;或

2) 在收到按照第7.5款[拒收]或第7.6款[修补工作]的规定发出通知后28天内,遵守通知要求。

(4) 未经必要的许可,将整个工程分包出去或将合同转让给他人。

(5) 破产或无力偿债,停业清算,已有对其财产的接管令或管理令,与债权人达成和解,或为其债权人的利益在财产接管人、受托人或管理人的监督下营业,或采取了任何行动或发生任何事件(根据有关适用法律)具有与前述行动或事件相似的效果;或

(6) (直接或间接)向任何人付给或企图付给任何贿赂、礼品、赏金、回扣或其他贵重

物品，以引诱或报偿他人。

1）采取或不采取有关合同的任何行动；或

2）对与合同有关的任何人做出或不做有利或不利的表示，或任何承包商人员、代理人或分包商（直接或间接）向任何人付给或企图付给本款第（6）项所述的任何此类引诱物或报偿。但对给予承包商人员的合法奖励和奖偿无权终止。"

业主有权因本款列明的承包商违约或第15.5款［雇主终止的权利］规定的业主认为方便的时候终止合同。第19.6款［自主选择终止、付款和解除］也规定，如果不可抗力事件持续84天并对全部工程的进度造成实际影响，任何一方均可终止合同的规定。这项规定非常宽泛，也包括业主不知情或未经同意的分包商的行为。在这些情况下，要求承包商终止分包合同比终止合同更为适合。

第（1）~（4）项规定了根据合同具体条款承包商未能履行义务的情形，包括未能履行轻微义务（trivial obligation）的情形，而对这些轻微的违约，可能需要采取非常严厉的补救措施。其他条款，如第11.4款［未能修补缺陷］（3）规定的承包商未能修补缺陷的行为，业主也有权终止全部或部分合同。当这些情况发生时，业主也应遵守第15条［由雇主终止］规定的程序以及有关具体条款的要求。

与工程师不同，这些程序要求业主应向承包商发出一份14天的终止通知。这项规定给承包商履行相关义务或与工程师或直接与业主讨论的最后一次机会。

第（5）、（6）项规定了业主有权立即终止合同的承包商破产和行贿的行为。如果业主打算根据这些规定终止合同，他必须十分小心以确保掌握法律能够接受的证据。同时，业主应能够证明第（5）款规定的承包商破产或类似情形，以及要被刑事起诉的行贿行为。如果承包商予以否认并且法庭能够接受的独立证据不能支持这些指控，即使承包商认罪也是不充分的。

终止通知内容应包括有关安全的指示和分包合同的转让，并且可以包括承包商撤离现场的其他任何指示以及工程的价值。在援用本款之前，应核实有关合同适用法律中有关终止的规定。

业主向承包商发出终止合同通知的内容与承包商向业主发出终止合同通知的内容基本相同，即相互指责对方违约，列明承包商违反第15.2款［由雇主终止］中或者业主违反第16.2款［由承包商终止］中的义务内容。以业主向承包商发出终止合同通知为例，如下：

Subject: Notice of Contract Termination under Sub-Clause 15.2 of General Conditions of Contract

Dear Sir,

Despite many warnings by the Employer and the Engineer, it is observed that the Contractor fails to perform his obligations under the Contract.

As of today, after _____ Days elapsed from the Commencement date, there is no significant physical progress on site and no significant evidence of any improvement towards the Works by the Contractor.

Considering that the contract duration is _____ Months and the Contractor has already lost more than 6 moths, there is no possibility to complete the Works within the time frame remaining until the Time for Completion.

The actual progress of contract implementation does not allow the Employer to hold back or delay with making drastic management decisions related to the future of the concerned contract. In point of fact, the Employer has no expectations of the Contractor to remedy the situation prevailing on the Contract. Further delay in the Employer's management decisions clearly provided for by the contract conditions and justified in this case will only escalate the critical situation of the contract implementation.

Based on the above-mentioned, we hereby furnish you with this 14 days' notice, at the end of which our Notice of Termination shall be effective in accordance to Sub-Clause 15. 2 [*Termination by Employer*], named items (a) and (c)(i).

This notice of 14 days shall expire at midnight of the day in which the 14 days calendar period falls due, counting from the date and time of the signed receipt of this notice delivered to the address of the Contractor.

The reasons for serving you with this 14 days' notice before the Termination date are in relation to the Sub-Clause already mentioned above, and which are intended to be effective for purposes of Termination collectively or independently of each other, namely,

(1) Sub-Clause 15. 2 (a) – The Contractor fails to comply with a notice under Sub-Clause 15. 1 [*Notice to Correct*]. According to this Sub-Clause, if the Contractor fails to carry out any obligation under the contract, the Engineer may by notice require the Contractor to make good the failure and to remedy it within a specified reasonable time. The Employer shall be entitled to terminate the Contract if the Contractor fails to comply with such a notice.

(2) Sub-Clause 15. 2 (c)(i) – The Contractor without reasonable excuse fails to proceed with the Works in accordance with Clause 8 [*Commencement, Delays and Suspension*]. According to the provisions of Sub-Clause 8. 1 the Contractor shall commence the execution of the Works and shall then proceed with the Works with due expedition and without delay. The Employer shall be entitled to terminate the Contract if the Contractor fails to comply with the provisions of this Sub-Clause.

Each and all of the above listed circumstances indicate Contractor's non-compliance with the requirements of Clause 8 [*Commencement, Delays and Suspension*], and failure to execute the Works for a protracted period of the time after the Commencement Date, which entitles the Employer to terminate the Contract.

> Following the above, pursuant to Sub-Clause 15.2 of the General Conditions of Contract, we hereby notify that at the end of this 14 days' notice period, termination of the Contract will be effective and until end of this period the Contractor shall leave the site.
>
> Further be advised that the Employer reserve its right to take the privilege envisaged by Sub-Clause 15.2 of the General Conditions of Contract and other available provisions as far as termination of the Contract is concerned.
>
> Sincerely,

11.4 承包商终止合同

1999年第1版FIDIC系列合同条款红皮书、黄皮书和银皮书第16.2款[由承包商终止]规定了承包商终止合同的事项。按照第16.2款[由承包商终止]的规定，如出现下列情况，承包商应有权终止合同：

(1) 承包商在根据第16.1款[承包商暂停工作的权利]的规定，就未能遵循第2.4款[业主的资金安排]规定的事项发出通知后42天内，仍未收到合理的证据。

(2) 工程师未能在收到报表和证明文件后56天内发出有关的付款证书。

(3) 在第14.7款[付款]规定的付款时间到期后42天内，承包商仍未收到根据期中付款证书的应付款额（按照第2.5款[业主的索赔]规定的扣减部分除外）。

(4) 业主实质上未能根据合同规定履行其义务。

(5) 业主未遵守第1.6款[合同协议书]或第1.7款[权益转让]的规定。

(6) 第8.11款[拖长的暂停]所述的拖长的停工影响了整个工程；或

(7) 业主破产或无力偿债，停业清算，已有对其财产的接管令或管理令，与债权人达成和解，或为其债权人的利益在财产接管人、受托人或管理人的监督下营业，或采取了任何行动或发生任何事件（根据有关适用法律）具有与前述行动或事件相似的效果。

在上述任何事件或情况下，承包商可通知业主，14天后终止合同。但在第（6）或第（7）项情况下，承包商可发出通知立即终止合同。

承包商做出终止合同的选择，不应影响其根据合同或其他规定所享有的其他任何权利。

第16.2款[由承包商终止]列明了承包商有权终止合同的理由，包括未能遵守第16.1款[承包商暂停工作的权利]规定的要求。除非承包商在第8.11款[拖长的暂停]规定的拖延的暂停发生时可立即终止合同、业主破产或者发生了本款第（7）项列明的问题，否则承包商必须在终止合同之前发出14天的通知。在发生了第19.6款[自主选择中止、付款和解除]规定的不可抗力事件拖延时，承包商也可以终止合同。

在采取行动之前，承包商必须确保有法律接受的证据，即业主未能履行有关义务。在业主未能付款的例子中，很容易确定有关证据。但是，在第（4）项的"业主实质上未能根据合同规定履行其义务"的情况下，如果业主不同意终止合同，则很难确定有关能够使争议裁决委员会或仲裁庭满意的证据。业主方面的任何重大违约一般都可能成为往来函件的主题,并可能已经导致承包商根据合同其他条款提出索赔。

以某国际工程项目为例,在业主延迟付款达到一定期限时或者达到一定金额,美国判例显示达到三个月的付款金额时,则承包商可以向业主发出终止合同通知,示例如下:

To: The Engineer
    Address of the Engineer

CC. XXX Roads Authority
    Address of the Employer

Subject: Termination of Contract Due to Employer's Failure to Pay IPCs

Dear Sir,

AAA Roads Authority ("the Employer") contracted with BBB ("the Contractor") to construct a road titled "CCC" on 23 January 2013. The Contractor, in the course of the Works, has encountered and suffered extreme difficulties, such as rainy weather of the rainfall days amounting to 9 months annually and has been left with only 3 months of dry season to work which leads to more than 4 to 5 times construction of earth works over again in road section, Employer's failure to give possession of site, landslides in more than 100 locations for which no effective solution has been given by the Employer to date, of the natural and man-made nature, which prevent him from carrying out the Works in a regular progress of the Works.

From the outset of the Works, most of the IPCs payments have failed to be paid to the Contractor within 42 days pursuant to Sub-Clause 60.8 of the Contract, a copy of which is attached herewith for your review, causing serious financial constrains for the Contractor. The ongoing overdue payment, consolidating with continuous delayed payments, will result in the Contractor being left with no option other than to terminate the Contract in pursuance of Sub-Clause 69.1 (a) of the Contract.

Sub-Clause 69.1 [*Default of Employer*] addresses that "in the event of the Employer: (a) failing to pay to the Contractor the amount due under any certificate of the Engineer within 28 days after the expiry of the time stated in Sub-Clause 60.10 within which payment is to be made, subject to any deduction that the Employer is entitled to make under the Contract, ··· the Contractor shall be entitled to terminate his employment under the Contract by giving notice to the Employer with a copy to the Engineer. " This Notice of Termination is thus issued by the Contractor to the Employer as set forth in Sub-Clause 69.1(a) herein.

The Employer's long-term and continuous breach of Contract has accumulated huge and far-reaching adverse effect on the execution of the Contract, including without limitation severe negative impact to the Contractor's cash flow, disruption to the Contractor's working programme, delay to the implementation of the Works, and, what's more problematic, fundamental damage to the Contractor's trust of and confidence in the Employer to perform as stipulated in the Contract.

Given all the above, the Contractor hereby gives his notice to the Employer to terminate the Contract as a whole. This notice is served in accordance with Sub-Clause 69.1 of the General Conditions of Contract as amended in Conditions of Particular Application of the Contract.

The Contractor's decision to terminate, instead of acting otherwise like suspension or reducing the rate of work, has been made after giving due consideration of all particulars of the events and circumstances.

Sub-Clause 69.1 states as well that such termination shall take effect 14 days after the giving of the notice.

Notwithstanding the foregoing, the Contractor hereby reserves all of its rights and remedies under Sub-Clause 69.2 [*Removal of Contractor's Equipment*], Sub-Clause 69.3 [*Payment on Termination*] and other clauses of the Contract and the ⋯ Civil Code for further action.

Yours faithfully,

Name of Project Manager
Name of the Contractor

以某国际工程项目为例，承包商以业主未能按时支付工程款和其他违约为由向业主发出终止合同通知，如下：

Dear Sir,

The Agreement to construct _____ [name of the contract] was signed between the Employer and the Contractor on _____ [date of execution of the contract]. The intended Date for Completion of the Contract had been determined as _____ [date of initial completer date].

The Engineer is _____ [name of the Engineer].

The Project works consisted of _____ [scope of works].

A large number of facts show that, during the execution of the works, the Employer's actions and inactions have violated not only the express terms of the Contract, but also constituted fundamental breach under the Applicable Law.

1. The Employer failed to pay the Contractor part of the amount as certified in Interim Payment Certificate No. (_____).

    Vide its letter ref. No. _____ dated _____, the Engineer instructed the Contractor to carry out necessary diversion works in the River, build temporary river crossings so that heavy equipment could cross the river to the power house site and start excavation works. It is clearly stated in the Engineer's instruction that the works shall be paid on daywork basis.

Vide its letter ref. No _____ dated _____, the Engineer instructed the Contractor to construct a temporary road from the highway to the right bank of the River and this work shall be paid on daywork basis.

Accordingly the Contractor completed the works and incorporated the daywork in the Monthly Statement No. _____ though the Contractor's letter No. _____ dated _____ The Contractor revised and resubmitted the Monthly Statement No. _____ on _____, and the Engineer issued Interim Payment Certificate No. _____ (hereinafter referred to as "IPC _____") on _____ But the Employer has withheld part of the certified amount and has not paid to the Contractor until today.

Detail of the IPC is as follows:
- Amount applied by the Contractor in the Monthly Statement No. _____ : _____ Currency
- Amount Certified by the Engineer in IPC No. _____ : _____
- Time due for payment: _____
- Amount Paid by the Employer: _____
- Amount withheld by the Employer: _____ (mainly consist of dayworks)
- Overdue time: 688 days by _____

Despite our repeated request to the Employer to release the withheld money, the amount still has not been paid by the Employer after about two years have elapsed. This action at the very preliminary stage of the contract performance demonstrated the Employer's non-cooperation with the Contractor in performing the Contract. This has been a clear violation of the Contract by the Employer and the Engineer has failed to perform its duty to effect such payments, as envisaged by the Contract.

2. The Employer interferes with the Engineer's Certification and Issue of Interim Certificates

It is noticed that the Engineer has issued two Interim Payment Certificates No. XX with the same date but with two different certified amounts, i.e. firstly with the amount of _____ (signed and sealed by the Engineer only), and later on secondly with the amount of _____ (signed by both the Employer and the Engineer). According to the Engineer's clarification through its letter ref. No. _____ dated _____, the reason for the reduced certified amount is "Employer has objected that the payment of BOQ Items related to a.m. test cannot be made till the required test report are submitted with satisfactory results."

Because of the Employer's above interferences, _____ [Currency and amount] has been deducted by the Engineer from its previously certified amount. Due payment of the works performed and entitlement of the Contractor as prescribed being essentials of the Contract, this action of the Employer clearly shows that the Employer has interfered with the Engineer's role to perform independently in such essential aspect of the Contract and the Engineer has failed to perform its part of the obligation requiring the Engineer to stand by its certification. The Contract has thus lost its sanctity.

3. The Engineer did not abide by the method of Measurement and Payment in the Contract and unilaterally and deliberately undervalued the IPC.

   When the Engineer was certifying IPC No. _____, _____ and _____, although the quantity of works executed in the billing period had been jointly checked and agreed, the Engineer unilaterally decided the quantity to be less than that actually executed and under valued the works executed in the IPCs.

   The total amount of the above under-certified IPCs has exceeded the total of the amount certified by the Engineer. Such unilateral move of the Engineer has resulted a mistrust and abuse of its power granted by the Contract, and the cooperation as envisaged by the Contract from the Engineer (as an independent body) is missing in its performance.

4. The Engineer did not implement its obligation under Contract Sub-Clause 52.1 to valuate the varied works and failed to fix the provisional rate for payment

   The work items tabulated below are the works agreed by the Engineer and instructed to the Contractor to carry out but the rates of which are not available in the BOQ. The Contractor proposed rates for payment for the Engineer's approval. But the Engineer just ignored and did not respond to the Contractor's requests. Nonresponse in itself is a violation of the intent of the Contract whereby either party was required to facilitate the other party to perform the other party's obligation.

   The Contractor, in accordance with the rates he proposed, prepared the monthly statement for payment but the Engineer rejected the payment. The Engineer, on one hand, did not valuate the rates proposed by the Contractor and on the other hand, he did not determine provisional rates for on-account payment as per the provision made in the Contract.

   Even after the Engineer issued Variation Order No. 3 on 5 October 2010, whose work item and rates are similar with and applicable to the following work items, the Engineer still did not allow the Contractor to incorporate the completed works in the Monthly Statement, and refused to certify the works if the Contractor incorporated them in the Monthly Statement.

5. The Employer's Breach of Contract and non-performance

   The progress of works has been seriously delayed. So far, 95% of the contract period has elapsed, but progress of the works has only achieved about 30%. The major reason for the delay was caused by the Employer's breach of Contract and non-performance.

   5.1 Delay in providing the Contractor possession of Site and access thereto

   One of the Employer's primary obligations under the Contract is to provide the Contractor with possession of the Site and access thereto based on the approved construction program. But during the contract period, the Employer has failed to properly and timely carry out such obligations and as such the progress of the works has been seriously delayed.

   Among the various work front, the connecting tunnel lies on the critical path of the approved Baseline Program. Their start date of the access road was planned on 28 April 2008. But because the Employer could not acquire the land for the access road to the connecting tunnel, the connecting tunnel was finally varied to Audit No. 2 only on 5 October 2010. As a result, the Time for Completion of the whole works has been seriously delayed. The whole of the delay was attributable to the Employer.

5.2 Failure to provide Drawings for Power House causing Abandonment of Excavated Power House Foundation

The works of Power House and Tailrace areas excavation were scheduled to start from July 1, 2008 and be completed by February 28, 2009 as per approved construction program. The foundation of Power House was completed on 5 March 2009. Since 6 March 2009, the work at Power House has hitherto come to a standstill/suspension for want of inputs and drawings of the electromechanical suppliers and erection contractor. The Employer/Engineer has not been able to provide these details to the Contractor to date, without which there is no possibility for the Contractor to continue to perform.

5.3 Misrepresentation in the Tender Document

In the Employer's Tender Document, the class of rock mass and method of rock support were clearly described. But from the exposed rock mass in the tunnel, as it is jointly mapped by the Engineer and the Employer's geologist, the actual classes of rock mass are obviously much poorer than that given in the Tender Document.

5.4 The Employer did not provide proper compensation to the land owners.

Because the Employer did not provide proper compensation to the land owners whose land was acquired or affected by the Project, the local residents frequently called lockout, disrupted and stopped the Contractor's work.

5.5 The Employer did not obtain the necessary permit from the government for the Project.

For example, the Permit from the Forest Authority to cut down the trees on the access road to Audit 2 was obtained by the Employer as late as 1 February 2011, only after that could the Contractor continue the construction of access road to Audit No. 2, and only from 6 of June 2011 could the Contractor start the tunneling work in Audit 2.

5.6 The Electricity supplied by the Employer was not qualified.

According to the second para of General Specification Clause G5.6, the Contractor can receive the electricity power from the delivery point at the construction site. The power will be supplied from 11 kV transmission lines extended to the project site from the integrated power system of _____. But the voltage of the power from the integrated power system was low and not stable. As a result, the ventilation equipment could not work continuously and the progress of work has been continuously delayed.

6. The Engineer failed to act impartially and exercise its authority and carry out its duties in the Contract.

6.1 The Engineer failed to carry out its duties under Contract Clause 52.

The Engineer instructed varied works, but despite the Contractor's repeated request, the Engineer refused to carry out its duties under Clause 52 to evaluate the varied works and did not determine provisional rates for payment. Thus the Contractor could not incorporate the executed works into its monthly statement, despite the fact that the works were executed and costs incurred to the Contractor.

6.2 The Engineer ignored the Contractor's claim for EOT and additional cost.

During the execution of the works, the Contractor has raised various claims for Extension of Time and additional cost incurred due to the Employer's Risk events. But the Engineer ignored and did not respond to the Contractor's claim. The Engineer failed to exercise its authority in the Contract to assess and make determination on the Contractor's claim, as a prudent independent Engineer.

6.3 The Engineer failed to carry out its duties to administer the Contract.

Despite the Contractor's repeated request, the Engineer has called for only 12 monthly progress meetings from the commencement of the Contract until now. Progress meetings are a crucial activity in the construction contract to enable the Contractor to perform its obligations, and the Employer and Engineer failed to provide and facilitate such opportunity.

6.4 The Engineer went on strike.

As is recorded by the Employer's letter dated 29 August 2011, the Engineer went on strike from 3rd to 11th September 2011.

The above-mentioned items 1 to 4 have constituted the default of Employer under Conditions of Contract Sub-Clause 69.1(a) and (b); the above mentioned items 5 to 6 have constituted Fundamental Breach of Contract by the Employer/Engineer under Section 73.(3), Clause 74, and Section 75.(2),(4) of the Contract Act. Those actions of the Employer and also non-performance of the Engineer further violate other clauses of the contract and the governing Act in composite manner, on which we reserve our right to elaborate in due course whensoever needed and if such situation arises.

The Employer's long-term and continuous breach of Contract has accumulated huge and far-reaching adverse effect on the execution of the Contract, not only fundamentally damaged the contractor's cash flow causing the Contractor to be unable to complete the works as scheduled and within the original contract time, and suffering huge economic losses, but more seriously resulted in the Contractor being unable to perform the Contract fundamentally and substantially as well.

As of today, only _____ days are left before the original contract time for completion. The Employer has failed to demonstrate its cooperative intention to perform in accordance with the prescribed procedure of the Contract Conditions and the Contract Act of _____ and positively effect the progress of works in a responsible manner, rejected all the Contractor's entitlement for EOT and additional cost, and fully refused to abide by the DRB recommendations on the Contractor's entitlement to EOT and additional cost, which are clear violation of the motive and intent of the Contract. As a

> result, the Employer has created an impossible situation for the Contractor to continue with and execute the contract and achieve the intended subject matter of the Contract.
> We therefore hereby serve a Notice under Conditions of Contract Sub-Clause 69.1.
>
> Yours faithfully,

需要注意的是，承包商在发出终止合同通知时，应给予 14 天的提前通知，终止合同通知因此在 14 天后生效。承包商在列举业主违约事实时，应对照合同条款规定的承包商可以终止合同条款中的列项，在终止合同通知中一一列明。在引用"业主实质上未能根据合同规定履行其义务"时，承包商应在终止合同通知中列明业主实质上违约的内容。在国际工程终止合同争议中，最具争议性的是"业主实质上未能根据合同规定履行其义务"的内容。

终止合同并非一件简单容易的事情，它会产生一系列法律后果，会给业主和承包商带来极大的麻烦、仲裁甚至诉讼，也会给业主和承包商带来经济利益的损失。一般而言，为了减轻终止合同所带来的后果，大多数标准格式合同中均规定终止后的估价和付款等内容，以便减少业主和承包商之间因终止合同而带来的法律纠纷。

第 12 章　工程索赔报告编制

> Claims are becoming commonplace on many construction projects,
> especially in contract for multi-million amount. In fact,
> it has been stated that a construction claim has become as much
> a part of a contract project as is the pouring of the concrete.
>
> James J. Adrian. *Construction Claims*

12.1　索赔通知及索赔时效

12.1.1　FIDIC 合同索赔通知时效

FIDIC 合同条款 1999 年第 1 版红皮书、黄皮书、银皮书、多边开发银行协调版 2005 年版、2006 年版和 2010 年版合同通用条款第 20.1 款［承包商的索赔］规定：

如果承包商认为，根据本条件任何条款或与合同有关的其他文件，他有权得到竣工时间的任何延长期和/或任何额外付款，承包商应向工程师发出通知，说明引起索赔的事件或情况。该项通知应尽快在承包商知道或应当知道该事件或情况后的 28 天内发出。

如果承包商未能在上述 28 天期限内发出索赔通知，则竣工时间不得延长，承包商应无权获得额外付款，而业主应免除有关该索赔的全部责任。否则，应适用本款的以下规定。"

按照 FIDIC 合同条款第 20.1 款［承包商的索赔］的明确规定，承包商提出索赔的时效为 28 天，即自承包商知道或应当知道引起索赔事件后的 28 天内发出，否则，承包商丧失任何工期延长索赔和/或额外付款的权利，而业主可以免责。因此，根据第 20.1 款［承包商的索赔］的规定，28 天的书面索赔通知是索赔成立的必要前提条件。

在使用 FIDIC 施工合同 1987 年第 4 版的情况下，第 53.1 款［索赔通知］规定：

"尽管本合同有任何其他规定，如承包商根据本条款的任何条款或其他有关规定索偿任何额外付款，他应在引起索赔的事件第一次发生之后的 28 天内，将索赔意向通知工程师，并将一份副本递交给业主"。

对于 FIDIC 施工合同 1987 年第 4 版第 53.1 款［索赔通知］的规定，英国普通法中存在两种解释，一是此类规定不能构成索赔的前提条件，即使承包商未能在索赔事件发生后的 28 天内提交书面索赔通知，也不能因此否决承包商的索赔权利；二是此类规定构成索赔的前提条件，即承包商未能在索赔事件发生后的 28 天内提出书面索赔通知，则丧失索赔权利。在实践中，工程师或业主对此项规定存在上述两种截然不同的做法。

在国际工程实践中，在使用 1987 年第 4 版 FIDIC 施工合同时，有些工程师和业主没有将 28 天视为索赔时效。但在笔者索赔的也门公路项目中，在使用类似的 FIDIC 施工合同 1977 年第 3 版时，工程师认为承包商未能在索赔事件发生后的 28 天内发出书面索赔通知，因此丧失索赔权利。在使用 FIDIC 合同条款 1999 年第 1 版、多边开发银行协调版权 2005 年、2006 年和 2010 年版的情况下，工程师和业主均将 28 天视为承包商索赔的索赔时效，并要求承包商出示证明 28 天内提出书面索赔通知的证据，用以证明承包商在 28 天内发出书面索赔通知，从而有权索赔工期延长和/或额外费用。

FIDIC 合同条款 2017 年第 2 版第 20.2.1 款［索赔通知］和第 20.2.4 款［详细索赔］规定了"双索赔时效"制度，即承包商应在知道或应当知道引起索赔的事件发生后不超过 28 天内发出索赔通知，如果承包商未能发出索赔通知，则承包商丧失索赔工期延长和额外费用的权利。并且，承包商还应在应当知道引起索赔的事件发生之日起 84 天内提交详细索赔，否则承包商在此前发出的索赔通知将无效。同时，如果承包商未能在应当知道引起索赔的事件发生之日起 84 天提交详细索赔时，承包商同样丧失索赔工期延长和/或额外费用的权利。因此，承包商在使用 FIDIC 合同 2017 年第 2 版时，应特别关注索赔时效，承包商应在合同约定的期限内递交索赔通知详细和索赔。

12.1.2 索赔通知的成立

FIDIC 合同 1999 年第 1 版第 20.1 款［承包商的索赔］规定承包商发出书面索赔通知，说明引起索赔的事件或情况，但 FIDIC 合同并未明确规定索赔通知的格式，或者什么样的通知才能构成一份合格的索赔通知。在国际工程实践中，经常发生的情况是，承包商认为其提交的信函构成了一份合格的索赔通知，但业主和工程师认为承包商提交的信函不能构成索赔通知，因此否决承包商的索赔权利。

承包商发出索赔通知涉及的事件或情况非常广泛。在国际工程实践中，承包商发出索赔通知的事件或情况主要包括：

（1）业主未能按期支付预付款。
（2）业主未能按期支付工程进度款。
（3）业主未能提供现场进入权或现场占有权。
（4）业主的工程变更导致的工期延长索赔。
（5）不可预见的物质条件，包括地质条件、人为障碍等。
（6）不可预见的气象条件。
（7）不可抗力事件，包括政治不可抗力和自然不可抗力事件。
（8）因工程数量增加导致的工期延长事件。
（9）业主违约行为。
（10）合同规定的承包商可以获得工期延长和/或额外费用的事件。
（11）适用法律规定的承包商可以获得的赔偿。

关于承包商发出索赔通知信函示例，以某国际工程项目中承包商遭受的不可预见的降雨为例，如下：

Sub: Notice of Intention to Claim for Extension of Time due to the Rainfall Days

Dear Sir,

 It is recalled that we have alreadied notified you for the high intensity rainfall days throughout the project on site date March 22, 2016 by letter of _____ .

Now, we have also reached to give similar notice because of the catastrophic rainfall that had continued since April 15, 2016 and as a result on the date of April 28, 2016, three access Slab & Pipe Culverts were damaged which are located at _____ and the communication between the main camp and stationary camps disconnected and we couldn't access the Site until we maintained it. And the base course crusher plant also became inaccessible for many days because of ponding water. Due to this effect, the project progress became highly affected and caused delay on the cumulative project progress.

Therefore, we hereby give the notice of intention to claim Extension of Time due to the rainfall days on site according to the Sub-Clauses 8.4 and 20.1 of GCC. We are also keeping the contemporary records for the mentioned issue, and will submit the interim claim report at the appropriate time.

如承包商遭受不可预见的气候条件，承包商发出索赔通知的模板如下：

Subject: Notice of Intention to Claim

Dear Sir,

In accordance with [cite contract reference] which forms the General Conditions of the above referenced contract, we advise you that we have encountered unforeseeable, unusually severe weather which has delayed our performance of the work. This delay is beyond our control, and without fault or negligence on our part.

The delay has lasted for a period of _____ days, from _____ through _____

The enclosed charts of weather conditions, provided for us by the _____ Weather Bureau, indicate that the [rainfall, snow] experienced was excessive and of an extremely unusual nature.

We therefore by this letter request a time extension of _____ Days under the terms and provisions of the above referenced contract.

Sincerely,

如业主未能按期支付工程预付款，承包商可向业主发出索赔通知，示例如下：

第 12 章 工程索赔报告编制

> Subject: Notice of Claim under Sub-Clause 20.1 of General Conditions of the Contract
>
> Dear Sir,
>
> We write to serve the notice of claim under Sub-Clause 20.1 of General Conditions of Contract (GCC) to claim an extension of completion and/or additional costs to be incurred due to the failure of the Employer to pay the advance payment [or the IPC payment] which became due on _____ [insert the due date].
>
> Without prejudice to the incurred interest set forth Sub-Clause 14.8 [*Delayed Payment*] of General Condition of the Contract, the Contractor shall, in accordance with Sub-Clause 16.1 of GCC, reduce the rate of progress accordingly.
>
> The Contractor shall keep and maintain the contemporary records in this particular regard, and shall furnish the claim details within the period set forth in the Contract once the event giving rise to the claim ceased.
>
> Sincerely,

一项有效的索赔通知（valid notice）是 FIDIC 合同条款 2017 年第 1 版索赔条款提出概念。根据 FIDIC 合同条款的规定，下述情况构成合同索赔通知：

(1) 信函标题标明"索赔通知"或"索赔意向通知"等含有索赔的文字。

(2) 信函标题没有标明"索赔通知"或"索赔意向通知"文字，但信函内容中写有"承包商保留索赔权利"，或"该函件将视为第 20.1 款项下的索赔通知"，或"索赔不可避免"等文字。

(3) 信函中只要某处写有"索赔"或"要求补偿或赔偿"之类文字，哪怕仅有一处此类文字。

如果信函内容仅说明事件或情况，而承包商没有在信函中写上"索赔"文字，则此函是否构成索赔通知可能会出现争议。一般而言，如果承包商仅仅描述事件或情况，而没有明确提出索赔要求，则应认为此函不构成索赔通知。

建议中国承包商规范国际工程项目合同管理，在发生索赔事件后，以索赔通知为标题发出索赔通知，避免出现是否构成索赔通知的争议。根据 FIDIC 合同条款规定，承包商不能采取防御性的措施，在项目开工时，在索赔事件尚未发生之前，向业主或工程师发出一份声明，主张无论何时发生索赔事件，本声明均构成索赔通知。

需要注意的是，在某些国际工程项目中，业主对承包商索赔时效进行了修改，将 28 天内发出通知修改为 14 天或 7 天，此时，承包商应按照合同约定的 14 天或 7 天发出索赔通知，避免承包商丧失索赔权利。

12.1.3 索赔时效对承包商索赔权利的影响

在国际工程实践中，由于中国承包商普通存在没有在 28 天内发出索赔通知，从而导致丧失索赔权利的现象，FIDIC 合同条款第 20.1 款［承包商的索赔］中的索赔时效对中国承包商具有一定程度的影响。这种影响主要体现在中国承包商在项目建设初期不关注或不知道索赔时效的规定，未能在索赔事件发生后 28 天内发出索赔通知，造成在项目建设中后期无法按时竣工，导致巨额工期罚款或工期延误违约金，而再想起索赔权利时，由于索赔时效条款的限制，承包商已丧失了索赔权利。

在国际工程实践中，索赔时效规定还将产生更为深远的影响。引起承包商索赔的索赔事件可分为两类：

（1）显性事件，是指承包商容易判断的引起索赔的事件或情况，例如当地居民的干扰、业主延迟支付工程进度款、爆炸、战争或恐怖活动等。

（2）隐性事件，是指在事件或情况发生时，承包商不易察觉的事件或情况，例如工效损失索赔、施工方法改变、某些技术问题可能导致的索赔、变更导致的索赔等。

中国承包商对于显性事件，例如当地居民的干扰，均能够在事件发生当日或次日向业主或工程师发出索赔通知。但对于隐性事件，例如工效损失、施工方法改变、变更导致的索赔或图纸改变等，均未能在 28 天内发出索赔通知，从而导致承包商丧失索赔权利。对于隐性事件，如果承包商未能根据 FIDIC 合同条款第 20.1 款［承包商的索赔］的规定在 28 天内发出索赔通知，那么承包商就丧失索赔权利。

12.2　递交索赔报告的信函

承包商编制索赔报告后，应向业主和/或工程师递交索赔报告，此时应递交首封信函，表明承包商根据合同条款递交索赔报告，此类信函的法律意义如下：

（1）表明索赔报告是根据合同条款在规定的期限内容提交，例如 FIDIC 合同 1999 年第 1 版规定的在知道或应当知道引起索赔事件发生后 28 天内，或工程师另行同意的其他期限内提交索赔报告。

（2）表明承包商有权索赔的工期延长时间和/或额外费用金额。

（3）概括性地总结承包商的立场。

承包商在撰写递交索赔报告的首封信函时，应注意如下问题：

（1）不要仅表明"附件为承包商的工期延长和/或额外费用索赔报告，请审阅"（Enclosed herewith please find the Contractor's claim report on EOT and/or additional costs for your review），而应表明承包商索赔的合同依据和法律依据，以及要求工期延长的时间和/或额外费用的金额，使得读者可以从首封函中获知承包商要求工期延长和/或额外费用索赔的合同和法律依据、工期延长时间和额外费用金额等。

（2）承包商的立场，例如承包商要求索赔的总体立场。

以某国际工程项目索赔为例，承包商递交索赔报告的信函示例如下：

Dear Sir,

Re: ABC Stores and Depot, ××× Road, ×××, ×××city

Further to our letter of 22 August 2000 requesting a review of extensions of time, our letter of 12

September 2000 giving particulars of loss and/or expense and our letter of 11 February 2001 requesting a copy of the draft final account, to which we have had no response, we enclose herewith our claim for extensions of time, reimbursement of loss and/or expense and damages.

Please note that the contents of this submission do not contain any particulars (with the exception of rates for finance charges for the period after 12 September 2000) which have not been submitted to you previously in correspondence referred to therein. It is our understanding that you have all information necessary for the preparation of the final account and we can see no reason why it should not have been issued prior to this letter.

Our claim is for further extensions of time of two weeks for section A and the works (up to the dates of practical completion) and for reimbursement of loss and/or expense and/or damages for the amount of £90,637.42 (including finance charges on liquidated damages). We are also requesting the issuance of a certificate of making good defects, a statement pursuant to Clause 30.6.1 of the Contract (including all adjustments mentioned in the submission), release of retention of £21,010.00, release of liquidated damages amounting to £63,000.00 and a final certificate pursuant to Clause 30.8 of the Contract.

Your early response would be appreciated.

Yours faithfully

For and on behalf of ×××.

以某国际工程项目为例,承包商递交工期延长索赔的首封函示例如下:

Dear Sir,

Subject: Submission of Extension of Time Claim Report

We herewith submit our extension of time claim report entitled "Contractor's Statement of Claim on Extension of Time" in three (3) copies. This particular EOT claim arises out of the requirements of the Contract Conditions as well as your requirement of substantiating the EOT claim from your counterpart. Furthermore, this EOT Claim is a contractual matter and thus is directed to the Employer, in accordance with the Letter of Acceptance of the Contract Agreement.

In our EOT Claim Report herewith, it provides the facts and findings, the grounds of claim, cause and effect analysis, and quantum of the amount of extension of time using as-planned v. as-built approach and windows method with substantiation. A total amount of 645 days EOT is thus claimed due to (a) the unforeseeable geological conditions of the foundation of Saddle Dam No. 1 and (b) variation of three generating units to four units initiated by the Employer at the outset of the Works. These delay events have driven the critical paths of the Works to be lagged and delayed further than anticipated and planned, and as such we believe that the Contractor is entitled to a claim to a claim under the provisions of the Contract.

Vide your letter ref. M-3001 dated 6 April 2016, you accepted the overall project schedule which ascertains the date of completion as on 31 May 2017. However, you emphasized as well that the acceptance of this program does not constitute the acceptance of the contract delay. In your letter above, it is alleged expressly and impliedly that the delays of the Works are attributable to the Contractor.

In response to your above allegation via our letter 16427 on 7 April 2016, we hold that your stance is, in any way whatsoever, not acceptable by the Contractor. Especially, your acceptance of the programmed date of completion in the Overall Project Schedule, in terms of contractual and legal respects, is meaningless to us.

Consequently, we truly hope that upon our submission of the EOT Claim Report herewith, an official letter for extension of time for the Works can be issued before the expired date of the original contractual completion date of 22 July 2016. Please note, on the one hand, that the completion date may initiate and become time-at-large in the event of failure of issuing the EOT letter before the expired date. On the other hand, failure of issuing the EOT letter may prevent the Contractor from proceeding (a) the working permit for Chinese expatriates on site; (b) the import of goods of the project; (c) the due payment.

In addition, the claimed EOT days in this submission herewith shall prevail in the event of any difference with the previous EOT claims submitted by us.

In this particular regard, we are looking forward to receiving your reply soon.

Yours faithfully,

12.3 索赔报告的编制

12.3.1 索赔报告体例

承包商如何陈述索赔的依据、事实、记录、工期计算和费用计算，并没有固定书面格式，索赔报告的编写也没有固定格式，但总体而言，承包商的索赔文件可分为：

（1）索赔意向通知书。

（2）索赔详情和支持文件。

（3）期中索赔报告和支持文件。

（4）最终索赔报告和支持文件。

索赔意向通知书是承包商在遭遇合同条款规定的索赔事件，如不利的物质条件、不可抗力、干扰、工程师延误签发图纸等时，根据合同向工程师发出的一封索赔意向的信函。这封信函的内容只是通知工程师，承包商遇到了合同规定的延误和造成费用发生的事件，不需要提供索赔金额和工期，也不需要提供详细计算和支持文件。根据 FIDIC 合同条款 1987 年第 4 版和 1999 年第 1 版的规定，承包商应在知道或应该知道索赔事件发生之日起 28 天内向工程师发出通知，否则丧失索赔权利。

索赔详情和支持文件是在承包商向工程师发出索赔意向通知后，在合同条款规定的时间内向工程师报告索赔详情，并随附支持文件。这份文件要求承包商需要递交详细的索赔内容，包括但并不限于索赔依据的合同条款、索赔事件发生的事实、承包商所遭受的延误或干扰的时间及计算依据、承包商所遭受的直接的损失或费用以及计算依据等。支持文件包括合同条款、同期记录、工程师的指示、图纸、计划、进度、劳务、设备资料等，只要是承包商认为这些文件、资料或数据可以支持所提出的工期延长和费用索赔即可。

期中索赔报告和支持文件是工程进展到一定进度时，承包商将零星提出的或分散提出的工期延长和费用索赔进行分类归纳总结，提出的一份具有对一个阶段索赔事件进行汇总的索赔报告。这份报告的基本要求是叙述完整，对索赔事件进行定性和定量分析，明确提出承包商工期延长和费用索赔主张，具有系统性和完整性，这也是该份索赔报告与索赔详情的区别所在。

最终索赔报告和支持文件是工程竣工时，承包商将所有施工过程中发生的索赔事件、工期延长和费用索赔进行最终分类总结，按照事件的性质归类所提出的一份最终的完整的索赔报告。最终索赔报告的要求与期中索赔报告相同。

以下是某个工程项目索赔的目录，承包商可参考这份索赔报告的体例编写索赔报告。

封面

1.0 导言（Introduction）

1.1 当事人各方（the Parties）

1.2 工程（the Works）

1.3 投标和合同价格（the Tender and the Contract Sum）

1.4 合同（the Contract）

1.5 计划（the Programme）

2.0 事实总结（Summary of Facts）

2.1 现场占有权：工程的开工和竣工（Possession of Site: Commencement and Completion of the Works）

2.2 延误和工期延长（Delay and Extension of Time）

2.3 未完工证书（Certificate of Non-completion）

2.4 直接损失和/或费用（Direct Loss and/or Expense）

2.5 支付和最终账单（Payment and Final Account）

2.6 缺陷（Defects）

3.0 索赔的基础（Basis of Claim）

4.0 索赔细节（Details of Claim）

4.1 导言（Introduction）

4.2 异常的气候条件-延误（Exceptionally Adverse Weather Conditions-Delay（D1））

4.3 第一号建筑师指示-延误（D2）（Architect's Instruction No.1-Delay（D2））

4.4 附加工程-延误（D3）（Additional Works-Delay（D3））

4.5 对直接成本金额的延迟指示-延误（D4）（Late Instruction for Expenditure of PC sum-Delay（D4））

4.6 总结（Summary）

5.0 损失和费用的评估（Evaluation of Loss and/or Expense）

5.1 直接损失和/或费用索赔（Direct Loss and/or Expense Claim）

5.1.1 延期（Prolongation）

5.1.2 干扰（Disruption）

5.1.3 损失和费用的融资成本（Finance Charges on Loss and Expense）

5.1.4 编制索赔报告的成本（Costs for Preparing the Claim）

5.2 损失和/或费用和/或损害赔偿费总结（Summary of Loss and/or Expense and/or Damages）

6.0 索赔声明（Statement of Claim）

6.1 工期延长（Extension of Time）

6.2 损失和费用和/或损害赔偿费（Loss and Expense and/or Damages）

6.3 保留金（Retention）

6.4 合同价格的调整（Adjustments to the Contract Sum）

6.5 误期损害赔偿费（Liquidated Damages）

6.6 孳生的融资成本（Finance Charges Accruing）

承包商索赔报告的主要内容及其要求如下：

1 Introduction/background/executive summary
   ✓ Brief contract particulars relevant to the claim;
   ✓ Brief description of the situation leading to the claim;
   ✓ Reference of the relevant correspondences/notices.

2 Ground of claim
   ✓ Related clauses and alignment of entitlement (reference to relevant contract clauses which entitle the claimant to the claim and where the contract clauses do not provide any remedy; reference to the applicable law where the claim can be legally justified and admissible);
   ✓ Cause and effect analysis and subsequent action.

3 Substantiation of claim-All claims
   ✓ Statement of claim/nature of claim;

- ✓ History of events;
- ✓ Narrative on program and delay analysis with impact on activities as applicable;
- ✓ Summary of time and/or compensation remedy sought;
- ✓ Mitigation measures taken and possible future mitigation measures if applicable;
- ✓ Analysis of baseline schedule versus progress.

3.1 In addition to points under 3.1 for variation
- ✓ Copy of an instruction for variation validly issued and acted upon;
- ✓ The date of issuance and receipt of instruction;
- ✓ Brief nature of the variation;
- ✓ The time to carry out the works pursuant to the variation instruction;
- ✓ Interface of the variation and the original program;
- ✓ Justification of how the variation affected the progress;
- ✓ Supporting particulars and proof of direct loss and/or expenses suffered or incurred;
- ✓ Proof of timely application to the Engineer in respect of direct loss and/or expense;
- ✓ Whether or not the variation order is within the designated limit of the Engineer.

以某国际工程项目工期延长索赔报告为例，作者编制的索赔报告目录如下：

TABLE OF CONTENTS

Forward

Executive Summary

1　Purpose of this Report

2　Documents Considered

3　Summary of Facts

4　Summary of Quantum

5　Contractor's Statement of Claim as to Extension of Time

　　Annex 0: Summary of Contractor's EOT Claim

1　Introduction

　1.1　The Parties

　1.2　Salient Features of the Contract

　1.3　Commencement of the Works and Intended Completion Date

　1.4　Contract Documents

　1.5　EOT Claim History

　1.6　Narrative of the Claimed Statement

　　　Appendix 1: Substantiation with Supporting Documents

2　EOT Claim 1: Claim for Delay in Advance Payment and IPC's Payment

　2.1　Introduction

　2.2　Statement of Claim

  2.3 Facts in Outline
  2.4 Basis of Entitlement
  2.5 Cause and Effect Analysis
  2.6 Evaluation of Extension of Time-Delay Analysis
    Appendix 2：Substantiation with Supporting Documents
3 EOT Claim 2：Claim for Delay in Approval of Route Selection
  3.1 Introduction
  3.2 Statement of Claim
  3.3 Facts in Outline
  3.4 Basis of Entitlement
  3.5 Cause and Effect Analysis
  3.6 Evaluation of Extension of Time-Delay Analysis
    Appendix 3：Substantiation with Supporting Documents
4 EOT Claim 3：Claim for Delay due to Exceptional Adverse Climate Conditions
  4.1 Introduction
  4.2 Statement of Claim
  4.3 Facts in Outline
  4.4 Basis of Entitlement
  4.5 Cause and Effect Analysis
  4.6 Evaluation of Extension of Time-Delay Analysis
    Appendix 4：Substantiation with Supporting Documents
5 EOT Claim 4：Claim for Delay due to Gun Shooting by the Locals
  5.1 Introduction
  5.2 Statement of Claim
  5.3 Facts in Outline
  5.4 Basis of Entitlement
  5.5 Cause and Effect Analysis
  5.6 Evaluation of Extension of Time-Delay Analysis
    Appendix 5：Substantiation with Supporting Documents
6 Conclusion
Appendix：Substantiation with Supporting Documents

  在上述作者编制的索赔中，对于每一索赔项（claim heading），均需要在索赔报告中阐述如下内容：
  （1）概述。
  （2）索赔声明。
  （3）事实简述。
  （4）承包商索赔基础。

(5)因果关系。
(6)索赔量化：延误分析。
(7)支持性文件和证据。

12.3.2 索赔概述

在承包商编制索赔报告时，承包商应提供项目基本信息，例如：
(1)当事人信息，包括工程师信息，如名称、地址和联系方式。
(2)合同签署信息，包括合同签署日期、合同金额、合同工期等。
(3)合同主要数据信息，例如在专用合同条件中"合同数据"中载明的主要信息。
(4)工程范围。
(5)主要大事件。
(6)承包商索赔历史概述。

在笔者编制的某国际工程项目索赔报告中，项目概述示例如下：

1　INTRUDUCTION

1.1　The Parties

1.1.1　The Employer：

1.1.2　The Contractor：

1.1.3　The Engineer：

1.2　Salient Features of the Contract

1.2.1　The salient features of the Contract as set forth in the Contract Documents are summarized herein, inter alia：

- Contract Name：
- Project Name：
- Contract No. ：
- Contract Execution Date：
- Bank Name：
- Contract Form：
- Applicable Law：　　　　　　The Laws of _____
- Initial Contract Price：　　　USD _____ excl. taxes, levies and duties in _____
- Time for Completion：　　　912 days
- Defects Notification Period：　365 days
- Performance Security：　　　5% of the Initial Contract Price
- Commencement Date：　　　28 working days from the effective date of the Contract
- Effective clauses of Contract：　i. The loan agreement between the Chinese bank and the Employer guaranteed by the Government of _____ . is duly signed and effective to finance the Works including its additional scope in _____

	ii. The vesting of the land on the Employer is complete by the _____ .
	Iii. Local presence of the Contractor registered as a branch office.
	iv. Submission of the acceptable advance payment bank guarantee and performance bank guarantee.
	v. Receipt of the advanced payment by the Contractor.
• Delay Damages:	0.05% of the initial contract price, per day
• Maximum Amount of the Delay Damages:	10% of the initial contract price
• Total Advance Payment:	15% of the initial contract price
• Retention Money:	10% of each payment and the limit of retention money shall be 5% of initial contract price
• Minimum Amount of IPC:	1% of Initial Contract Price
• Third Party Insurance:	USD 46,000.00 per occurrence
• Professional Indemnity Insurance:	USD 5,000,000.00
• Appointing Entity for Appointing the Adjudicator:	_____ .
• Arbitration Rule:	_____
• Arbitration Venue:	_____

1.3 Chronology

1.3.1 The Contract entitled "Contract for _____ Project" with Contract No. _____ was executed by _____ of _____ and _____ on 3 January 2012.

1.3.2 The Accepted Contract Price, i.e. the Initial Contract Price, Vide the Contractor Offer, is USD _____ excluding taxes, levies and duty within the territory in _____ or such other sum as may be ascertained in accordance with the Contract Conditions.

1.3.3 On 17 September 2012, the _____ Bank ("Lender") and _____ ("Borrower") signed the agreement entitled "Buyer Credit Loan Agreement" under Contract No. _____ in _____ .

1.3.4 An advance payment was made by the Employer to the Contractor on 9 October 2012, of which the Contractor was informed such payment vide the letter with reference number _____ .

1.3.5 On 14 December 2012, the Employer, vide the letter with reference number _____, issued Notice to Commencement to the Contractor. In this letter, the Employer emphasized that Clauses 5(ii), 5(iii), 5(iv) and 5(v) of the Contract Agreement have been fulfilled even though Clause 5(i) has not been yet satisfied. Thus the Employer instructed the Contractor to commence the Works as on 16 November 2012.

Under this letter it was demonstrated that the date of Site Handing-Over was 1 August 2012.

1.3.6　On 27 June 2013, a letter reference _____ was addressed from Department of _____, Ministry of Finance and Planning, _____ to the Employer, confirming effectiveness of loan.

1.3.7　On 21 January 2013, the piling work was commenced by the Contractor and such works were completed on 5 June 2013.

1.3.8　On 9 June 2013, the tower base structure construction was on track and such works were completed on 15 January 2014.

1.3.9　The base works including tower base structure and tower body structure were completed at the level of ±0.000m on 13 November 2013.

1.3.10　The level of +115m was completed on 26 September 2014 at actual average progress of 20 meters per month.

1.3.11　Until 31 December 2014, the level of +185m was completed by the Contractor.

1.3.12　The level of +210m was completed by the Contractor as on the date of 28 February 2015 consequently.

1.4　EOT Claim History

1.4.1　Several letters pertaining to EOT claims and additional cost claims were put forward to the Employer and/or the Engineer in a piecemeal manner in the course of the Works pursuant to the terms and provisions of the Contract.

1.4.2　No EOT claim report with particular details has been submitted to the Employer and/or the Engineer for requesting an extension of time for completion during the execution of the Works.

1.5　Employer's Granted Extension of Time for Completion

1.5.1　On 7 January 2014, Memorandum of Understanding for Project Progress Review & Planning Session, _____ Project was signed by the Employer and the Contractor.

1.5.2　This Memorandum of Understanding quoted:

"_____ has recommended _____, subsequent to detailed review of construction difficulties submitted by the Contractor due to site conditions during the period 15th November 2012-1st November 2013, to consider granting a time extension until 15th June 2015 excluding cost extension on preliminaries corresponding to the time extension for the completion of Colombo Lotus Tower Project.

<u>The Employer agreed to grant the project duration extension up to 15th June 2015.</u>

Therefore both parties confirmed that, the Project will be completed by June 15, 2015 for the declared opening and the observation period of fifteen days from 16th June 2015 to 30th June 2015 to resolve all teething issues."

1.5.3 Consequently, it can be concluded that an extension of time up to 15 June 2015 was granted by the Employer on 7 January 2014.

1.6 Narrative of the Claimed Statement

1.6.1 For the purpose of proving the Contractor's entitlement to an extension of time for completion, this submission is thus compiled and covered in the following logical order in each claimed statement:
1) Statement of Claim;
2) Narrative-Factual Matrix;
3) Basis of Entitlement;
4) Cause and Effect Analysis;
5) Evaluation of an Extension of Time-Delay Analysis;
6) Appendix: Substantiation with Supporting Documents

12.3.3 索赔项简介

在承包商递交每一个索赔项（claim heads）中，为了使读者了解和建立对承包商索赔项的整体概念、事实和观点，承包商有必要在每一项索赔项中进行索赔简要概述。以某国际工程项目为例，承包商为了索赔当地居民的骚乱（disorder）导致工期延误和额外费用，特此在该索赔项中进行概要介绍，如下：

INTRODUCTION

Within the period of execution of the Contract, the regular progress of the works had been materially affected by reason of the Contractor's main camp lockout by the local people demanding proper compensation for their land and recruitment of them in the works. Further there were time and again various strikes, lockouts, restriction on vehicle movements called by various parties, which resulted in suspension of the whole site activities and incurred extra cost and time to the Contractor.

There were mainly three kinds of strikes:
1. The strike by local people demanding land compensation and job;
2. The strike by local Employees demanding various unwarranted demands; and
3. The strike by various political parties of _____.

There were lots of occasions wherein local people prevented the Contractor from working at various sites and locked out the main gate of the Contractor's camp demanding the jobs and land compensation. The Employer should be responsible for providing the Contractor with a hindrance free site.

Further there were lots of occasions wherein local Employees and local people locked out the main gate of the Contractor's camp making all the works on site at a standstill. Regarding the local employees' strike the Contractor strongly believe that any dispute which arises between Employer and Employee shall be solved in accordance with the prevailing laws of the country, but unfortunately what has happened is just a case of lawlessness or civil disobedience. As per the Labor law of _____ there should be pre-information of the demand and ultimatum if any employees are dissatisfied with the management, so the Contractor is of the strong opinion that this incident is due to lawless duress which occurred during the regular progress of execution of the Contract.

As mentioned above there were lots of occasions wherein the various political parties of _____ have made strikes preventing the Contractor from conducting day to day activities on site.

Due to the above mentioned facts, the Contractor was not in position to carry out the work on site incurring additional time and costs.

12.3.4 索赔声明

在承包商递交的索赔报告中，除了每一项索赔的简介外，承包商应表明立场和观点，即通过索赔声明（statement of claim）明确表示承包商根据合同条款有权索赔工期延长和额外费用，示例如下：

2.0 Statement of Claims

2.01 The underlying principle of this claim is the necessity for the Contractor to invoke the Notification of the Contractors Suspension of the Work (or reducing the rate of work) in compliance with General Condition of Contract (GCC) Sub-Clause 16.1 [*Contractors Entitlement to Suspend Work*] in his letter dated 18th October, 2010. This, in turn, was the culmination of several letters sent by the Contractor expressing concern with the default of the Employer in respect of delayed payments to the Contractor in respect of GCC Sub-Clause 14.7.

Having given due notice under GCC 16.1 of his intention to Suspend Work (or reduce the rate of work) to the Engineer, the Contractor is entitled, subject to GCC Sub-Clause 20.1 [*Contractor's Claims*], to claim for an extension of time and payment of costs plus profit in accordance with GCC 16.1 (a) and (b).

The Contractor has chosen to reduce the rate of work which, due to financial constraints, has been limited to a level of activity required to meet essential obligations and preparation for potential recommencement of works. These activities are as follows:

- Essential maintenance of deviation and existing roads;
- Provisions of the Engineer's facilities;
- Safety and security of the site;
- Crushing Operations;
- Excavation of water pits.

2.02 In compliance with the Contractor's letter dated 2nd November, 2010 and pursuant to GCC Sub-Clause 20.1 [*Contractor's Claims*], the Contractor shall keep such contemporary records as may be necessary to substantiate any claim. These contemporary records were submitted under cover of the Contractor's letter dated 2nd November, 2010 for review and comments by the Engineer. Further contemporary records have been submitted weekly together with a detailed claim for additional payment and an extension of time monthly since 8th November, 2010 as per the attached reference letters. Therefore the Contractor now requests consideration of his claims for an extension of time for completion of the contract together with additional costs arising.

2.03 The claim for an extension of time for completion is presented in accordance with GCC Sub-Clause 8.4 [*Extension of Time for Completion*] and Sub-Clause 20.1 [*Contractor's Claims*]. The Contractor is now requesting an extension of time equivalent to 144 days as at 31st March, 2011.

In due course, cognizance may have to be taken to the effect, if any, of the prevailing weather conditions that may arise during any extension of time and the effect on weather-sensitive activities.

2.04 Given that the conditions prevailing up to 31st March, 2011 in respect of the Contractor's reasons for invoking the Suspension of the Works still remain valid, this claim has a continuing effect. Therefore, the claim can only be considered as interim at this time and the Contractor shall submit further claims at monthly intervals.

The Contractor will resume normal working as soon as is reasonably practicable and when the Contractor subsequently receives full payment of the monies outstanding that gave rise to Suspension of the Works.

2.05 This claim is presented in respect of the additional costs that the Contractor has incurred in respect of the following:

- plant, and equipment depreciation costs;
- on-site and off-site indirect costs;
- maintenance of existing roads;
- financing charges (not included in this claim);
- loss of profit.

The details of the foregoing additional costs will be provided under Section 5.0 of the claim: Assessment on Additional Costs together with the determination of the quantum evaluation.

12.3.5 事实陈述

在承包商的索赔报告中,应对每一项索赔的事实进行陈述,阐明事实的发生及其过程。在陈述事实过程中,承包商需要牢记的是:

(1) 承包商陈述的事实应是真实发生的事实,承包商不能杜撰或编造虚假的事实。
(2) 承包商陈述的事实应有证据支持,例如信函、会议纪要、技术报告等。
(3) 在事实历经长久或事实本身复杂时,应采用概括性的总结手法陈述事实。
(4) 在陈述事实时,应避免主张观点,即承包商仅陈述事实,不在事实陈述中提出主张观点,除非有关事实中承包商或业主/工程师表明了观点或立场。

以某国际工程项目为例,索赔报告的事实部分示例如下:

4.1.2　Facts in Outline

4.1.2.1　The relevant activities of piling works in tower foundation works as illustrated in the Contractor's Foundation Construction Schedule dated 26 December 2012 which was treated as Baseline Schedule at the time for which the piling works was executed, include two activities:
- Engineering Piling works for the tower body (main structure);
- Slope protec tion piling works circling the tower base.

4.1.2.2　As demonstrated in the Contractor's Foundation Construction Schedule—the Baseline Schedule herewith, the original intention for the piling of waterproofing curtain of the tower base and waterproofing curtain of the tower body was to commence on 9 December 2012, and to complete it on 16 February 2013, with a total duration of 70 days. The original intention for engineering piles, slope protection piles, anchor piles and tower crane foundation piles was to commence on 20 January 2013, and to complete on 28 February 2013, with a total duration of 39 days. The duration for both engineering piling works and slope protection piling works can thus be shown in Table 4-1:

Table 4-1 As-planned Programme for Piling Works

No.	Description of Works	Planned Commencement Date	Duration	
1	Slope protection pilling works	20/01/213	28/02/2013	39 days

4.1.2.3 In and around the middle of October 2012, before commencement of piling works, the Contractor and the Employer and the Engineer confirmed for the first time the design drawings as to piling works construction. Upon request from the structure team of the Employer and the Engineer, the Parties asserted that norm of the rock socketing depth shall be RQD > 50%, and reached an agreement on the rock socketing depth for each of the different pile diameter.

4.1.2.4 On the basis of the agreement reached in and around the middle of October 2012, the Contractor and the Engineer signed the agreement, asserting the rock socketing depth and estimated termination level of the 17 engineering piles.

4.1.2.5 On 19 January 2013, the Contractor commenced the first pile construction works, and the first pile works were completed on 20 January 2013 accordingly.

4.1.2.6 Included in Exhibit 3 of Appendix 3 are the Site Records of piling works for each pile including all essential data such as the pile number, the construction date, pile diameter, the bottom level and suchlike. It should be noted that the important data is also being illustrated in the Site Records, i.e. the rock level and the hard rock level which are disputed between the Contractor and the Employer.

4.1.2.7 On 29 January 2013, the piling works Subcontractor – addressed to the Contractor with the letter reference N231-05 to complaint and claim therefore that:

- Increase in depth of rock socket, by saying that rock drilling should be attended to a depth of one pile diameter only pursuant to the Contract, however, the actual rock drilling quantity exceeds more than this anticipated depth.
- The drilling data forth completed 10 piles was summarized in Table 4-2:

Table 4-2 The Drilling Data forth Completed 10 Piles
(extracted from the Subcontractor's letter)

Pile No.	Pile Diameter/mm	BOQ Socketing Depth/m	Actual Rock Socketing Attended/m	Difference
ZH1 – P38	1500	1.5	1.5	0
ZH2 – P14	1500	1.5	3.05	1.55
ZH1 – P20	1500	1.5	2.25	0.75
ZH1 – P40	1500	1.5	2	0.5
ZH2 – P16	1500	1.5	1.6	0.1
ZH1 – P1	1500	1.5	2.2	0.7
ZH3 – P18	900	0.9	2.2	1.3
ZH2 – P6	1500	1.5	1.45	–0.05
ZH3 – P12	900	0.9	3.85	2.95
ZH3 – P3	900	0.9	1.9	1

4.1.2.8 The letter reference N231-05 is also quoted as the reason for construction time consumption, namely:

(a) Hardness of rock increases with the depth—sometimes frequent repair and maintenance cost of machine increases and consumables.

(b) When rock depth increases, plant and equipment input is more, and plant efficiency reduces, so it takes more time than originally anticipated.

(c) Depreciation period of machinery get reduces compared to that was originally forecasted.

4.1.2.9 The reason for increases of rock socketing depth arose from the different opinion on the definition of RQD > 50% between the Contractor and the Employer. In light of this thorny issue, the Contractor is of the opinion that the bottom level of the pile can be fulfilled on the rock level, rather than the hard rock level that the Employer considers to be so.

4.1.2.10 On 30 January 2013, taking into account of the Employer's stance on this thorny issue, the Contractor issued an estimated rock socketing depth and bottom level to meet the requirements of site operation for the piling works.

4.1.2.11 The Employer's requirement that the bottom level of the pile should be seated on the hard rock level, without doubt, increased the difficulties of the construction works, and consequently resulted in more time consumption on each of the piling works due to the increase of rock hardness. In actual practice on the site operation of piling works, the Contactor may complete a pile with time consumption of at least 24 hours. Obviously, this impeded the construction progress of the piling works partly and wholly.

4.1.2.12 On 5 February 2013, the Contractor and the Subcontractor, _____, reached an agreement witnessed by the Engineer, to compensate the Subcontractor arising out of the increase of the rock socketing depth and road hardness.

4.1.2.13 It should be noted that the Contractor's reference to the Subcontractor here is only to exemplify the facts and findings of the increase of rock socketing depth and rock hardness. The Contractor understands fully that the Subcontractor is hired by the Contractor, and thus the Subcontractor has nothing to do with the Employer in line with the contractual relationship.

4.1.2.14 By a letter reference E0227-2 dated 27 February 2013, the Contractor put forward the Design and Construction Method of Contiguous Piles and Dewatering Works.

4.1.2.15 On 16 March 2013, all of engineering piles were completed, and the slope protection piling works were completed on 10 April 2013 accordingly.

12.3.6 承包商索赔依据

承包商索赔依据是指合同依据和法律依据。承包商在索赔时，使用较多的是合同条款依据，包括通用合同条款、专用合同条款、投标文件、技术规范、图纸、标价工程量表等有关文件。承包商在编制索赔报告时，可在索赔报告中独立为一章，避免在每个索赔项中都叙述同样的合同条款，避免索赔报告内容重复。

承包商在索赔报告中引述合同条款时，应注意如下问题：

（1）应全文引述相关的合同某一条款，避免仅引述部分内容。

（2）对于承包商不利的条款内容，如果对其不利的内容在承包商引用的合同条款之中，则应全文引用，承包商此时应检查和核实条款的具体和确切含义，确定承包商是否有权索赔。例如，合同某一条款规定承包商有权索赔工期延长，但不能索赔额外费用，此时，承包商应确定其仅有权索赔工期延长，而不能索赔额外费用。

（3）在引述完合同某一条款时，应说明引起承包商索赔的事件属于哪一合同条款规定的范围。例如，承包商遭遇的业主未能提供现场占有权时，承包商应指明该此类事件属于 FIDIC 合同条款 1999 年第 1 版第 2.1 款 ［现场进入权］ 规定的范围，承包商因此有权要求工期延长和额外费用。

以某国际工程项目为例，承包商在索赔报告中索赔依据（basis of claim）中写道：

Basis

Sub-Clause 6.4 of the FIDIC Standard Conditions of Contract unamended by the Conditions of Particular Application that states：

If, by reason of any failure or inability of the Engineer to issue, within a time reasonable in all the circumstances, any drawing or instruction for which notice has been given by the Contractor in accordance with Sub-Clause 6.3, the Contractor suffers delay and/or incurs costs then the Engineer shall, after due consultation with the Employer and the Contractor, determine：

(a) <u>any extension of time</u> to which the Contractor is entitled under Clause 44, and

(b) <u>the amount of such costs</u>, which shall be added to the Contract Price,

and shall notify the Contractor accordingly, with a copy to the Employer.

Sub-Clause 12.2 of the FIDIC Standard Conditions of Contract unamended by the Conditions of Particular Application that states：

If, however, during the execution of the Works the Contractor encounters <u>physical obstructions or physical conditions</u>, other than climatic conditions on Site, which obstructions or conditions were, in his opinion, not foreseeable by an experienced contractor, the Contractor shall forthwith give notice thereof to the Engineer, with a copy to the Employer. On receipt of such notice, the Engineer shall, if in his opinion such obstructions or conditions could not have been reasonably foreseen by an experienced contractor, after due consultation with the Employer and the Contractor, determine：

(a) <u>any extension of time</u> to which the Contractor is entitled under Clause 44, and

> (b) <u>the amount of any costs</u> which may have been incurred by the Contractor by reason of such obstructions or conditions having been encountered, which shall be added to the Contract Price, and shall notify the Contractor accordingly, with a copy to the Employer. Such determination shall take account of any instruction which the Engineer may issue to the Contractor in connection therewith, and any proper and reasonable measures acceptable to the Engineer which the Contractor may take in the absence of specific instructions from the Engineer.
>
> Sub-Clause 20.4 (a)(v) of the FIDIC Standard Conditions of Contract amended by the Conditions of Particular Application that states:
>
> *The Employer's risks are:*
>
> *Insofar as they directly affect the execution of the Works in Nepal:*
>
> (i) ……
>
> (ii) ……
>
> (iii) ……
>
> (iv) ……
>
> (v) <u>*riot, commotion or disorder*</u>, *unless solely restricted to the employees of the Contractor or of his Subcontractors and arising from the conduct of the Works;*
>
> Sub-Clause 42.2 of the FIDIC Standard Conditions of Contract unamended by the Conditions of Particular Application that states:
>
> *<u>If the Contractor suffers delay and/or incurs costs</u> from failure on the part of the Employer to give possession in accordance with the terms of Sub-Clause 42.1, the Engineer shall, after due consultation with the Employer and the Contractor, determine:*
>
> (a) <u>*any extension of time*</u> *to which the Contractor is entitled under Clause 44, and*
>
> (b) <u>*the amount of such costs*</u>, *which shall be added to the Contract Price,*
>
> *and shall notify the Contractor accordingly, with a copy to the Employer.*
>
> (Underline added for emphasis by Contractor)
>
> Hence as per the condition of contract and above-mentioned facts, in general the Contractor is liable to be reimbursed following but not limited to:
>
> (i) EXTENSION OF TIME (EOT), and
>
> (ii) Idle cost of equipment and manpower.

12.3.7 因果关系

法律上的因果关系（causality, causation）是指一个事件（原因）和第二事件（后果）之间的作用关系（the relationship between cause and effect），其中后一个事件被认为是前一个事件的结果。

因果关系具有如下法律特征：

（1）因果关系的事件连续性表现为原因在前、结果在后，前一现象是原因，后一（或后几个）现象是结果。

（2）因果关系是客观存在的，不以人的意志为转移，因果关系不建立在主观臆断基础之上，而是建立在客观事实基础之上，反映客观事实。

（3）因果关系表现具有多样性，受包括当事人行为在内诸多因素影响。

承包商在编制索赔报告时，在因果关系分析（cause and effect analysis）时需注意如下问题：

（1）在索赔报告中不能仅仅表明"业主的违约造成或导致了承包商的工期延误和/或额外费用"，而应根据事件的发展轨迹具体分析原因与结果之间的因果逻辑关系。

（2）承包商未能在原因和结果之间建立逻辑关系，即原因导致后果之间没有清晰的因果关系。

（3）承包商未能明确事件与后果之间的证据链。

承包商在编制索赔报告时如何叙述因果关系，以某国际工程项目为例，承包商提出桩基础索赔，其在索赔报告中写道：

4.1 Cause and Effect Analysis

4.1.1 The concentration of the issue in dispute between the Employer and the Contractor in the course of the piling works, that is to say, the first reason to cause slower progress than anticipated, was:
- rock socketing depth;
- cognizance of the value of RQD > 50%.

4.1.2 The Contractor was of the opinion that the rock socketing depth, i.e. the bottom level of the pile should be seated in the rock level pursuant to the norm of Chinese specification in question. Conversely, the Employer and the Engineer took a view that the bottom level of the pile should be seated on the hard rock level.

4.1.3 As to the norm of rock level and hard rock level in this case, the Employer and the Contractor recognized that the value of RQD > 50% shall be applied.

4.1.4 However, the value of RQD > 50% was always in dispute between the Contractor and the Employer/the Engineer since no test results can be obtained to verify such value in an objective manner.

4.1.5 Consequently, the discussion time as to whether or not the value of RQD > 50% is achieved elapsed in the course of the piling works, and accordingly, the time consumption caused the progress of the piling works to be slower than anticipated in the Construction Method Statement submitted by the Contractor.

4.1.6 The second reason for slower progress than anticipated was the Employer's/the Engineer's requirement that the bottom level of the pile should be seated on the hard rock level. If so, the Contractor had to take more time to drill the hard rock to satisfy such requirement. The rock hardness was greater than the Contractor had anticipated, as complained by the piling works Subcontractor in the Subcontractor's letter herewith. The evidences in the Site Records presented and the Subcontractor's letter herewith prove such events and circumstances occurred in the course of the piling works.

> 4.1.7 Pursuant to the Contractor's Construction Method Statement, there are 120 slope protection piles in total, and 39 days for construction, thus 4 piles should be completed per day. In respect of the Engineering piles, 2-3 piles should be completed a day. However, in actual practice, 1 pile can be completed per day as illustrated in Site Records for piling works due to the unforeseeable physical conditions.
>
> 4.1.8 Obviously and therefore, the effect of unforeseeable physical conditions was to delay the progress of the piling works, as demonstrated above.

12.3.8 工期延误分析

每个施工索赔都是独一无二的（each construction claim is unique），因此，在特定项目进行工期延误分析时，使用工期延误分析的方法存在不同。除非当事方在施工合同中明确约定了具体的工期延误分析方法（但这种情况非常少见），否则，承包商可以选择适合的工期延误分析方法评估工期延误时间。

当发生了承包商有权进行索赔的事件后，例如工程师未能在承包商要求的时间内提供工程图纸或承包商遇到了其不能控制的自然条件或人为障碍等情况，如何合理或正确地估测造成延误事件对工程进度和工期的影响以及索赔时间的长短，是一个十分复杂的问题，而更难判断的是几个事件或更多事件对工程进度和工期的综合影响及其程度。可以说延误工期的计算是工期索赔的难点，也是承包商提出工期索赔是否合理的关键。

在处理承包商提出的工期延长索赔时，可使用关键线路法等时标网络技术，对于因干扰等因素导致的工期延误，一般可采用如下评估技术进行分析：

（1）计划影响分析法（as planned impacted）。
（2）时间影响分析法（time impact analysis）。
（3）实际与计划工期对比法（as planned v. as built）。
（4）影响事件剔除法（collapsed as built）。
（5）里程碑分析法（milestone analysis）。
（6）视窗分析法（windows analysis）。
（7）滚动计划分析法（rolling programme analysis）。
（8）净影响法（net impact）。
（9）其他分析技术。

在上述分析工期延误的方法中，最常用的是第（1）至（4）种方法，其中计划影响分析法和时间影响分析法是在施工过程中对发生的工期延误进行过程分析，而实际与计划工期对比法和影响事件剔除法是在工程结束后对工期延误的追溯分析。

对于上述工期延误分析方法，读者可参阅《FIDIC 合同原理与实务》一书中的相关章节。

12.3.9 费用索赔评估

1. 直接损失或费用

在大多数标准合同格式中，合同条款均规定，如果承包商遭受干扰或延误，承包商有权就"直接损失和费用"要求额外付款。如 FIDIC 合同条款1999年第1版第4.7款[放线]规定：

"如果承包商在实施工程中由于这几项基准中的某项错误必然遭受延误和/或招致增加费用，而有经验的承包商不能合理发现此类错误，并避免此延误和/或增加费用，承包商应通知工程师，根据第20.1款[承包商的索赔]的规定，有权要求：

（1）根据第8.4款[竣工时间的延长]的规定，如竣工已经或即将受到延误，对任何此类延误给予延长期。

（2）任何此类费用和合理利润，应计入合同价格给予支付。

在1999年第1版合同条款中，根据第1.1.4.3款，将合同条款中的成本（费用）（cost）定义为："系指承包商在现场内外发生的（或将发生的）所有合理开支，包括管理费用及类似支出，但不包括利润"。从这项规定中，可以得出 FIDIC 合同条款中的成本（费用）（cost）是指直接损失或费用。但根据 FIDIC 合同条款规定，承包商也可以就某些干扰或延误事件索赔费用和利润。承包商在有些事件发生时只能索赔费用，在有时事件发生时可以索赔费用和利润。

在某些标准合同格式中，有时使用"直接损失和/或损害"（direct loss and/or damage）或者"直接损失和/或费用"（direct loss and/or expense），这两种用法没有区别，含义相同。

2. 费用和利润

在 FIDIC 合同条款中，在承包商遭受干扰或延误时，承包商可以根据合同条款规定对直接损失或费用进行索赔，但是否可以对利润进行索赔，则应根据合同条款的规定。在 FIDIC 合同条款1987第4版和1999第1版中，承包商是否可以索赔利润的条款有所不同。

FIDIC 合同条款1987年第4版承包商可以索赔利润的条款见表12-1。

表12-1　FIDIC 合同条款1987年第4版承包商可索赔利润条款

合同条款编号	合同条款标题	是否包括利润
1.1（g）(i)	费用（成本）	否
1.5	通知、同意、批准、证明和确定	视具体情况
2	工程师和工程师代表	是
5.2	合同文件的优先次序	否
6.4	图纸延误和延误的费用	否
12.2	不可预见的自然障碍或条件	否
13.1	应遵照合同工作	否
14.1	应提交的计划	否
17.1（c）	放线	否
18.1	钻孔和勘探开挖	是
20.3 和 20.4	修复因业主风险造成的损失或损害、业主的风险	否
26.1	遵守法律法规	否
27.1	化石	是
31.2	为其他承包商提供方便	是
36.2, 36.4, 36.5	样品费用、未规定的检验费用、工程师关于未规定的检验的确定	否
38.2	剥露和开孔	是

(续)

合同条款编号	合同条款标题	是否包括利润
40.1	暂时停工	否
40.3	暂时停工持续84天以上	是
41	开工和延误	否
42.2	未能提供占有权	是
44.1	竣工期限的延长	否
49.3	修补缺陷的费用	是
50.1	承包商进行调查	否
51.1	工程变更	是
52.1、52.2	变更的估价、工程师确定费率的权力	是
52.3	变更超过15%	—
53	索赔程序	视具体情况
59.4	对指定分包商的付款	否
60	证书和付款	否
65	特殊风险	是
66	解除履约	见65.8
69	业主的违约	见65.8
70.1	费用的增加或减少	否
70.2	后续的法规	否
71	货币和汇率	—

FIDIC合同条款1999年第1版承包商可以索赔利润的条款见12-2。

表12-2 FIDIC合同条款1999年第1版承包商可索赔利润的条款

合同条款编号	合同条款标题	是否包括费用、利润
1.9	延误的图纸或指示	费用加上合理利润
2.1	现场进入权	费用加上合理利润
4.7	放线	费用加上合理利润
4.12	不可预见的自然条件	费用,不能加上利润
4.24	化石	费用,不能加上利润
7.4	试验	费用加上合理利润
8.5	当局造成的延误	只能延长工期
8.9	暂停的后果	费用,不能加上利润
10.3	对竣工验收的干扰	费用加上合理利润
13	变更和调整	见8.4(a)
13.7	因法律改变的调整	费用,不能加上利润
16.1	承包商暂停工作的权利	费用加上合理利润
17.4	业主风险的后果	费用,不能加上利润
19.4	不可抗力的后果	费用,但不能加上利润

因此，根据表 12-1，表 12-2，在某些条款下，承包商可以在索赔费用（成本）的基础上加上利润，并将其计入业主应付的款项中；但在某些条款下，承包商只能索赔费用（成本），不能索赔利润。

3. 现场管理费

现场管理费（site overheads）包括与实施工程没有直接关联的所有现场费用。一般而言，现场管理费包括：

（1）非生产人员的工资，包括代理、现场工程师、验工测量师、秘书、一般领班、流动性领班、设备装配工、仓库保管员、测量员、清洁工和茶水工等。

（2）办公室安置、租赁等其他费用，包括照明、供暖、卫生、电话租费、电话费用、文具费用和邮递费用等。

（3）保安：保安监控和照明。

（4）仓库、车间、厕所等的安置、租用、拆除、照明、供暖和清洁费用。

（5）现场便道的施工、维护和拆除费用。

（6）设备运到现场和离开现场的费用。

（7）项目的保险和保函费用。

（8）小型工具的提供和维护。

（9）生活和旅行成本和补贴。

在上述费用中，有些是与时间有关的费用（time-related），有些是以一次性的总价方式出现的。承包商在计算现场管理费用时可按照实际支出进行计算，设备部分应按照工程师承认的折旧进行分期摊销，并计算出索赔期间内应发生的实际费用。以总价方式出现的物品，应按项目工期按月或按周进行摊销，从而计算出索赔期间内应发生的实际费用。

4. 总部管理费

承包商的总部管理费用（head office overheads）是现场以外（off-site）发生的费用，按照西方著名学者的解释和有关判例的诠释，目前，世界上公认的总部管理费计算公式主要有哈得逊公式（Hudson Formula）、艾姆顿公式（Emden Formula）和爱其利公式（Eichleay Formula）。

（1）哈得逊公式

$$总部管理费 = 总部管理费和利润百分比 \times 合同金额 \times \frac{拖延工期}{合同工期}$$

西方建筑和工程业界和法学界对哈得逊公式的批评甚多，并且认为"合同总额"（contract sum）应为"合同总额减去利润和管理费用"，这样表述更为准确。

哈得逊公式是建立在一定的假设基础之上的，主要是：

1）在延误期间，承包商总部仍可从其他地方获得利润和管理费用。

2）利润和管理费百分比是一个合理的比例。

3）在延误期间，存在同等利润水平或管理费补偿的补偿工作。

在加拿大 Ellis-Don Ltd. 诉 The Parking Authority of Toronto（1978）案⊖中，法官奥利瑞

⊖ （1985）28 BLR 98.

接受了哈得逊公式作为计算承包商总部管理费的公式。在该案中，承包商主张合同总额3.87%作为总部的管理费用和利润。但如果根据合同条款，承包商无权索赔相关直接损失或费用的利润时，例如 ICE 小型工程合同条款的规定，如果按照哈得逊公式计算就有可能夸大了承包商的总部管理费用。

（2）艾姆顿公式

在《艾姆顿论建筑合同和实务》第 8 版[一]中，作者提出了计算总部管理费的变通公式，如下：

$$\frac{h}{100} \times \frac{c}{cp} \times pd$$

式中　h——承包商的总部管理费和利润总额除以总营业额而得出的总部管理费比例；
　　　c——合同总额；
　　　cp——合同工期；
　　　pd——延误期限。

在艾姆顿公式中，承包商总部管理费的百分比是根据承包商整个机构管理费得出的，因此，这个数据更为真实。但使用该公式时应给予充分的注意。有的学者认为，在 ICE 合同中，特别是 ICE 小型工程项目合同，由于承包商不能索赔利润，合同总额中应扣除利润。

艾姆顿公式在 Whittall Builders 诉 Chesterle-Street DC（1987）40 BLR 82 案中得到了认可和应用，但在 Alfred McAlpine 诉 Property and Land（1995）76 BLR 59 案中被法官拒绝。因为在本案中，被告在当时只承担了这一个工程项目。在 Norwest Holest 诉 Co-op Wholesale Society（1997/1998）案中，法官多顿写道："艾姆顿公式是可以成立的，并可在确定承包商有权索赔损失和/或费用的下列情况基础上使用这个公式：

1）已证明了实际发生了有关损失。

2）已证明了有关延误造成了承包商不能从事现有的另外一项工程项目，导致承包商无法获得管理费补偿的机会。

3）延误必须与营业额的增加和管理费的补偿没有关联。

4）在承包商不能获得营业额以便支付有关费用的情况下，管理费不能是在任何情况下可能发生的管理费用。

5）在其他地方赚取利润的因素并没有在市场上发生变化，并存在可替代的市场[二]。

（3）爱其利公式

在承包商计算总部管理费时，在实践中使用最为广泛的是爱其利公式。该公式源于美国法院在爱其利公司一案。目前，在实践中广泛使用的是两个版本，第一种版本用于延误索赔，第二种版本用于工程范围的索赔。

1）延误索赔（delay claims）。在承包商因延误索赔而主张总部管理费时，其计算公式分为三步：

① 合同延误期间所占总部的管理费份额 = $\frac{合同签认金额}{合同期间内合同总额}$ × 合同期间公司管理费总额

[一] Emden's Building Contracts & Practice, 8th edition, volume 2, at page N/46.
[二] Norwest Holst Construction Ltd v Co-Operative Wholesale Society Ltd. [1998] EWHC Technology 339, His Honour Judge Thornton Q. C. at [350].

② 每日合同管理费 = $\dfrac{\text{合同延误期间所占总部的管理费份额}}{\text{施工天数}}$

③ 可索赔的公司管理费总额 = 日合同管理费 × 延误天数

2）在承包商进行工程范围索赔时，可以使用爱其利公式：

① 合同延误期间所占总部的管理费份额 = $\dfrac{\text{原合同直接成本}}{\text{合同期间工程直接成本总额}}$ × 原合同期间管理费总额

② 工程直接成本中每一美元成本的公司管理费 = $\dfrac{\text{合同延误期间所占总部的管理费份额}}{\text{合同期间工程直接成本总额原合同直接成本}}$

③ 可索赔的公司管理费金额 = 工程直接成本中每一美元成本的公司管理费 × 工程范围的金额

　　哈得逊公式、艾姆顿公式和爱其利公式各有各的优势，但都存在一定的局限性。承包商在使用这些公式计算总部管理费时应予以注意，使用公式的目的只是提供一种量化的方法和手段，不同的公式也会带来不同的结果。另外，承包商还承担着举证的责任，需要提供相应的文件，如总部的资产负债表、年营业额、管理费总额等文件支持总部管理费的索赔。如合同文件中承包商提供了总部管理费的百分比，则承包商可以使用该百分比作为计算依据，但如果合同中不能体现这个数据，则如何确定一个合理的比例，如百分比是2%，还是5%或者10%，是承包商需要认真考虑和准备有关证据的严肃问题。

第 13 章　法律选择和适用

Each country's legal system reflects its society's values. As a result, national laws and the structure of domestic judicial systems vary considerably from country to country. Cases of conflict of laws arise from differences between legal systems.

Max Rheinstein, *Conflict of Laws*

13.1　法律冲突

在涉外民事法律关系中，由于涉及两个或两个以上国家或地区的法律，而不同国家或地区的法律制度和规定各不相同，在处理同一问题时，会产生不同的结果，这就是所谓的法律冲突（conflict of laws）。

法律冲突的产生，主要有如下几方面的原因：

（1）内国赋予外国人、外国企业民事权利。在现代社会，随着全球化趋势的演进和跨国公司的发展，外国人、外国企业在一国均享有民事权利和参与商业活动的权利。在现实中，含有涉外民事法律关系可能会导致发生法律冲突。

（2）各国法律规定的不同，使法律冲突成为可能。由于各国的政治、经济、法律的规定存在差异，对同一案件处理时，同一当事人，适用不同国家的法律会导致不同的结果。

（3）内国在一定条件下承认外国法的域外效力。

13.2　所有权的法律冲突和物之所在地法原则

所有权，根据我国《民法典》的规定，是指国家、集体和个人对属于各自所有的财产的占有、使用、收益和处分的权利。在国际私法中，所有权是指具有涉外因素的所有权，其涉及的主要问题有因各国法律规定不同产生的所有权法律冲突问题；当国家作为所有权主体时，国家财产的豁免权问题；在采取国有化手段将私人财产转变为国家所有时，国有化法令的域外效力及补偿问题。

目前，为解决所有权的法律冲突，各国普遍适用的是物之所在地法这个基本原则。

物之所在地法（lex rei sitae; lex situs）是指作为法律关系客体的物所在地国家或地区的法律，主要用于解决如下问题：

（1）动产与不动产的划分由物之所在地法决定。

（2）所有权客体的范围以及所有权的内容与行使，由物之所在地法决定。

（3）所有权的取得、转移、变更和消灭的方式及条件，一般应由物之所在地法决定。

（4）所有权的保护方法由物之所在地法决定。

物之所在地法在国际私法中得到了广泛的承认和运用，但在下述两种情况下不适用：

（1）运输途中的物品。由于运输途中的物品随时都在发生移动，有时还会处于公海或公海上的空间，不属于任何国家管辖，因此，不能完全适用物之所在地法，而国际上普遍承认的地是目的地法作为准据法，但如果运输中的物品长期滞留于某地，或被保管在某地的仓库中，如发生货物的买卖和抵押行为，可适用物之所在地法。如所有权随运输单证的移交而转移，也可依单证所在地法、交易所在地法作为准据法。

（2）船舶、飞机、汽车和其他运输机械。由于这些运输工具处于不断移动中，因此，如果以物之所在地法作为处理纠纷的准据法是不恰当和现实的。世界上普遍主张以其所属国法律——旗国法或登记地法作为解决运输工具所有权的准据法。

13.3 合同的法律选择和适用

法律选择（choice of law）是指在存在跨国或涉外法律关系时当事方选择合同适用哪国或哪个地区的法律。法律适用是指涉外民事法律关系应适用哪国法律。承包商需要注意的是，当存在不同司法管辖地时或者当事方是不同司法管辖地的主体时，例如，业主是外国政府部门或法人实体，而承包商是中国企业，或者承包商是中国企业，而分包商是外国法人实体时，当事方可以选择合同适用的法律。根据中国现行法律，在合同当事方均为中国法人实体时，则合同当事方没有选择合同适用法律的权利，合同应适用中国法律。

合同的法律适用（application of law），是指在涉外民事法律关系中合同当事各方发生合同争议时，法院或仲裁机构以哪国的实体法作为处理争议所依据的法律。国际上普遍认为，应采用当事方意思自治原则，并辅之以最密切联系的原则。

意思自治原则（autonomy of will）是指合同中允许当事双方缔结合同时自行约定合同的某国的法律，法律也承认当事方有选择法律的自主权，如果当事方之间产生争议，受案法院或仲裁机构应当以当事方选择的法律作为合同准据法（Governing Law，Applicable Law），以确定当事方之间的权利义务。

最密切联系原则（the doctrine of the most significant relationship）是指当事方没有明确约定解决合同争议所适用的法律，受理合同争议的法院和仲裁机构确定处理合同争议所适用的法律时确定的原则。最密切联系原则选择法律可以采取：

（1）缔约地法。即当事双方签署合同所在地的法律。

（2）履行地法。如有时履行地存在两个或两个以上时，可适用主要履行地法，或以特种履行地为合同履行地。

（3）法院地法或仲裁地法。当事方如未约定应适用的法律，但在合同中规定了一旦发生争议，交由某国法院或仲裁机关管辖时，一般均可据此推定当事方意图适用该国的法律。

（4）物之所在地法。

（5）船旗国法。

（6）当事方或者债务人的居所地、住所地或营业地法。

（7）当事方的共同本国法。

（8）在一合同与其他合同有某种从属关系时，只要无相反的规定，可推定适用原始合同的准据法。

(9) 根据"与其使之无效,不如使之有效"的解释合同的原则确定准据法。如果当事方未选择法律时,而所涉及的数国法律相互抵触,如果依某国法律合同有效,而依他国法律合同无效,则应推定适用使合同有效的那一国家的法律。

13.4 国际工程合同的法律选择和适用

在国际工程项目中,合同的法律选择的基本原则有以下几项。

(1) 在涉及实体工程实施、完成、维护和运行的工程合同中,合同的法律应适用工程所在国的法律。

FIDIC 合同条款 1999 年第 1 版第 1.4 款 [法律和语言] 规定:

"The Contract shall be governed by the law of the country (or other jurisdiction) stated in the Appendix to Tender."

按照上述规定,国际工程合同到底适用哪一个国家或司法管辖地的法律必须查看投标附录 (Appendix to Tender) 的规定。一般而言,投标书附录或合同数据表 (Contract Data) 均规定法律应适用工程所在国的法律。

在国际工程合同中,合同适用法律条款的标准文字为:

"The Contract shall be governed and construed in accordance with the laws of…. [insert the name of the country/territory]."

在不同国籍的承包商之间组成的联合体协议中,联合体协议的法律可以适用国际工程合同的法律,表述如下:

"This Consortium Agreement shall be governed by and construed the laws which governs the Contract."

(2) 在不涉及实体工程的实施、完成、维护和运行的合同中,例如,联合体协议 (Consortium Agreement) 或联营协议 (Joint Venture Agreement) 或合作协议 (Cooperation Agreement) 等,则可选择非工程所在地国家的法律,例如英格兰和威尔士法或其他国家和地区的法律,而不必一定要选择工程所在国的法律。

(3) 在 PPP/BOT 投资项目中,股东协议 (Shareholders Agreement)、贷款协议 (Loan Agreement)、包销协议等不涉及实体工程实施、完成、维护和运行的合同,则可依当事方的合意确定合同适用的法律。而实施协议 (Implementation Agreement)、特许经营协议 (Concession Agreement)、购电协议 (Power Purchase Agreement) 或者购买协议 (Purchase Agreement) 等合同,由于涉及实体工程的实施、完成、维护和运行,则应选择工程所在地国的法律为第一选择。

(4) 在 PPP/BOT 投资项目中,项目公司 (Project Company) 或特殊目的公司 SPV (Special Purpose Vehicle) 应选择适用注册地国家或地区的法律。

13.5 工程所在地法律对工程合同的影响

在中东从事建设项目的承包商经常会忘记或者忽略的风险之一就是工程所在地——当地

法律的影响,这种当地法律通常称为合同的适用法律。对于那些习惯了在普通法管辖国家或地区工作的承包商而言,他们会想当然地认为合同已经充分地描述了项目风险,但出乎意外的是,一旦项目开始实施,当地法律就会强加更多繁琐的责任条款,或者附加一些具有当地官僚主义色彩的解释。

例如,承包商在履行一份明确规定了违约赔偿金的合同时,承包商会理所当然地认定这些损害赔偿条款明确规定了工期延误的责任范围。然而,许多中东国家的民事法典会给予法官自由裁量权,上下调整损害赔偿金额以反映实际损失金额。在合同约定的损害赔偿金额大幅度超过业主的实际损失时,这也许会有利于承包商。但是,在一些大型商业项目上,如果出现这种不确定性因素,将会改变承包商所承担的项目风险。

在施工合同中,对间接损失规定的限定性责任条款是一种经常的和强制性的做法。相反,对于所有的建设施工项目,中东大部分地区的民法典会强制要求承包商承担十年期责任。在项目竣工后,承包商对未来十年可能发生的施工建筑全部或者部分倒塌,以及出现任何影响建筑稳定性的缺陷负有责任。即使承包商能够证明他们拥有合理程度的技能和谨慎,但这种严格责任不能用契约约定加以限制或排除其应用。在阿联酋,即使合同适用法律不是国家法律,但十年期民事责任亦应予以适用。对于未能考虑这种非契约性责任的承包商,可能存在巨大损失的风险。

在实践层面上,当地法律对承包商的日常工作具有重大影响。至少,在中东国家,当地招标投标法规定参与政府合同的承包商在接收变更款项之前,需要同意变更所产生的时间和成本之间的关联。这与标准惯例背道而驰,即一旦工程师确定变更费用,那么不管同意与否,工程师均应按照临时估价计入付款项中予以支付。这就意味着,在承包商使用合同规定的争议解决程序对工程师的变更评估提出异议时,并不是要否决对变更的某些支付要求。如果在付款之前要求承包商同意工程师的变更评估,则可能导致延迟付款,从而对承包商的现金流产生负面影响。此外,通过削弱自由裁量权来为承包商所完成的工程进行付款,这破坏了合同中所表现出来的传统意义上的工程师的权威。面对这样一种局面,承包商陷入进退两难的尴尬境地:尽管承包商一直声称要享有更多的权利,但为了维持现金流,是要承认工程变更,还是为坚持合同权利而导致现金流的减少呢?

对于变更估价,当地法律强加一些限定性条款是常见的事情。政府部门业主批准变更金额,但政府部门业主却不会从招标投标委员会寻求进一步的批准。作为一个旨在控制政府部门支出的措施,这完全是明智之举,但这通常会导致过度官僚的审批过程,如果业主不能有效管理的话,会直接影响到承包商的进度计划和现金流。

当地法律强加给承包商上述义务,虽然会被承包商视作异常繁重的义务,但把缔约双方之其中一方的诚信义务纳入民事法典,此举有积极的一面,它也许能使承包商免于承担业主强加的更加苛刻的责任条款。尽管此处的诚信是不明确的法律概念,在普通法管辖区通常是不被承认的,但是当地法院已在以前的合同关系中曾支持过这一概念。

从上述讨论可以得知,在中东实施大型项目的承包商若不考虑当地法律的影响,那其将可能会承担巨大的风险,并可能会遭遇重大的项目进度问题,甚至血本无归。因此,当地法律不可忽视,承包商在中东实施项目,应针对这些当地法律影响不断寻求法律建议。为了识别和应对当地法律强加于承包商的风险,这些法律建议很可能有助于项目的具体管理。

第 14 章　争议委员会

> A dispute Board is a creature of contract; the parties establish and empower a dispute board with certain jurisdiction and to investigate in an inquisitorial fashion the basis for the dispute/claim involved and to hear and either advise on the resolution of disputes or to make decisions on the disputes presented-hence the difference between a dispute review board and a dispute adjudication board.
>
> Cyril Chern. *Chern on Dispute Boards.* page 5. *Fourth Edition*

14.1　争议委员会成员任命和成立

争议委员会（Dispute Board），包括争议裁决委员会（Dispute Adjudication Board，DAB）、争议评审委员会（Dispute Review Board，DRB）、争议评审专家（Dispute Review Expert，DRE）以及国际商会倡导的综合争议委员会（Combined Dispute Board，CDB）是近年来国际承包工程项目中普遍采用的一种替代性争议解决方式。与英国的法定裁决制度不同，在中国企业从事的国际承包工程项目中，业主和承包商之间的争议均通过合同约定（协议约定）的方式予以解决。在分包合同中，承包商和分包商也可以通过分包合同约定争议裁决的解决方式。

为了保证能够公正地处理国际工程争议，一般而言，国际工程项目的争议委员会均由三名成员组成。在某些国际工程项目中，采用独任裁决员（sole member 或 sole adjudicator）制度。

争议委员会可分为常设争议委员会和临时争议委员会。

（1）常设争议委员会（standing dispute board），即根据合同的约定，在开工之日起 28 天业主和承包商同意选定争议委员会成员，或者合同已经指定的独任争议委员会成员时，争议委员会自工程开工至合同结束时提供争议裁决服务，例如 FIDIC 合同条款 1999 年第 1 版红皮书规定为常设争议裁决委员会。

（2）临时争议委员会（ad hoc dispute board），即在发生争议时，业主和承包商任命争议委员会成员，组成争议委员会对争议作出决定，例如 FIDIC 合同条款 1999 年第 1 版银皮书规定为临时争议裁决委员会。

争议裁决委员会应由具有适当资格的成员组成，成员的数目可为一名或三名（"成员"），具体情况按投标函附录中的规定。如果投标函附录中没有注明成员的数目，且合同双方没有其他的协议，则争议裁决委员会应包含三名成员。

如果争议裁决委员会由三名成员组成，则合同每一方应提名一位成员，由对方批准。合同当事双方应与这两名成员协商，并应商定第三位成员作为主席。

但是，如果合同中包含了意向性成员的名单，则成员应从该名单中选出，除非名单中的成员不能或不愿接受争议裁决委员会的任命。

在独任裁决员的情况下，有些业主会在招标文件中或者合同数据中写明独任裁决员的姓名。此时，承包商只能接受这名独任裁决员，除非在合同谈判中提出异议或反对意见。在响应投标时，承包商没有机会对独任裁决员提出异议或反对意见。

在合同中没有给出独任裁决员的情况下，必须指出，在实践中，随着当事双方争议的升级，当事双方，例如承包商与业主，或者主包商与分包商往往很难就独任裁决员的任命达成一致，此时，需要根据FIDIC合同条款第20.3款［对争议裁决委员会未能取得一致］的规定，请求指定机构任命一名独任裁决员。幸运的是，FIDIC合同条款第20.3款的规定非常全面，包括了所有不能达成协议的情况。

争议当事一方在上述任一情形发生时，均可向指定机构致函，要求指定机构，例如国际商会ICC国际仲裁院（目前由ICC替代性争议解决中心负责）指定裁决员。

需要注意的是，在向指定机构致函要求任命裁决员时，请求任命函应写明以下几项。

（1）函件标题应写明要求指定机构任命裁决员。

（2）背景（Background）。

（3）关于指定机构的合同规定（Contract Provisions relating to Request）。

（4）未能达成一致的事实（Facts concerning Failure to Agree on DAB Member）。

（5）争议事项（Disputes Involved）。

（6）要求任命DAB成员（Request for Appointment of DAB member）。

（7）指定机构任命DAB成员的费用（Fees arising of request）。

（8）联系方式（Communication）。

以某国际工程项目为例，承包商与业主在长达一年多的时间内未能就独任DB成员达成一致，为此，承包商向合同专用条款指定的机构国际商会（International Chamber of Commerce, ICC）发出信函，要求根据合同第20.3款［对争议裁决委员会未能取得一致］的规定，由国际商会任命独任DB成员，示例如下：

To: Chairman

International Court of Arbitration

International Chamber of Commerce (ICC)

33-34 Avenue e President Wilson

75116, Paris, France

By Email: arb@iccwbo.org

Subject: REQUEST FOR APPOINTMENT OF SOLE DISPUTE BOARD MEMBER

for _____ Project

_____ (the "Contractor") is hereby writing to Chairman, International Court of Arbitration, International Chamber of Commerce (ICC) to request appointment of Sole Dispute Board

Member for the project titled "_____" located in _____ ("Request") which the Employer is _____ (the "Employer").

BACKGROUND

1. The Contractor and the Employer had contracted for a _____ project in _____, namely Construction of _____ ("Project"). That Contract was dated on 3 June 2011. The Employer is _____ and the Contractor is _____ The project was financed by World Bank and _____ government jointly. The Contract is based upon <u>FIDIC MDB edition 2005</u> with amended Particular Conditions of Contract.

2. The letter of commencement of the works was issued by the Employer on 6 October 2011. The Taking Over Certificate was issued by the Employer to the Contractor on 15 December 2015 and accordingly the expiry of Defects Notification Period is intended on 15 December 2016.

CONTRACT PROVISIONS RELATING TO REQUEST

3. The several contract provisions of General Conditions of Contract ("GCC") and Particular Conditions ("PC") are concerned with the Request, inter alia:

   (1) Sub-Clause 20.2 of GCC [*Appointment of the Dispute Board*].
   (2) Sub-Clause 20.3 of GCC [*Failure to Agree on the Composition of the Dispute Board*].
   (3) Sub-Clause 20.4 of GCC [*Obtaining Dispute Board's Decision*].
   (4) Sub-Clause 20.7 of GCC [*Failure to Comply with Dispute Board's Decision*].
   (5) Sub-Clause 20.8 of GCC [*Expiry of Dispute Board's Appointment*].
   (6) Sub-Clause 20.2 of PC [*List of Potential DB Sole Members*].
   (7) Sub-Clause 20.3 of PC [*Appointment (if not agreed) to be made by*].

4. Sub-Clause 20.3 [*Failure to Agree on the Composition of the Dispute Board*] addresses that:
   "*If any of the following conditions applies, namely:*
   (a) *the Parties fail to agree upon the appointment of the sole member of the DB by the date stated in the first paragraph of Sub-Clause 20.2, [Appointment of the Dispute Board],*
   (b) *either Party fails to nominate a member (for approval by the other Party), or fails to approve a member nominated by the other Party, of a DB of three persons by such date,*
   (c) *the Parties fail to agree upon the appointment of the third member (to act as chairman) of the DB by such date, or*
   (d) *the Parties fail to agree upon the appointment of a replacement person within 42 days after the date on which the sole member or one of the three members declines to act or is unable to act as a result of death, disability, resignation or termination of appointment,*
   then the appointing entity or official named in the Contract Data shall, upon the request of either or both of the Parties and after due consultation with both Parties, appoint this member of the DB. This appointment shall be final and conclusive. Each Party shall be responsible for paying one-half of the remuneration of the appointing entity or official.*"

5 Sub-Clause 20.3 of PC provides that:

Appointment (if not agreed) to be made by	20.3	The Chairman of the International Court of Arbitration of the International Chamber of Commerce, Paris

FACTS CONCERNING FAILURE TO AGREE ON SOLE DISPUTE BOARD MEMBER

6 On 22 July 2015, the Contractor addressed to the Employer to apply for appointment of Sole Dispute Board Member ("SDBM"), proposing
Mr _____, _____ to be SDBM.

7 On 26 January 2016, the Employer proposed _____ as the candidate of SDBM. However, both Contractor and Employer failed to reach agreement on appointment of SDBM for Mr. _____.

8 Subsequently, both Contractor and Employer failed to appoint SDBM for the following candidates proposed by the Employer from January 2016 to October 2016, namely:
   (1)…
   (2)…
   (3)…
   (4)…

9 These correspondences communicated between Contractor and Employer conclude that both of them have failed to appoint the Sole Dispute Board Member from the outset of the Project up to now. Therefore, Sub-Clause 20.3 (a) is applied.

DISPUTES INVOLVED

10 For the purpose of selection of SDBM, the disputes involved between the Contractor and ERA are concerned with the additional cost claims which the contract provisions entitle him to claim so, including prolongation cost claim, Value Added Tax claim, … claim etc.

11 No extension of time claim arises between Contractor and Employer in this particular project.

REQUIREMENTS FOR APPOINTMENT OF SDBM

12 For avoidance of conflict of interest and fair judgment on the disputes between Contractor and Employer in this particular project, the Contractor proposes that the candidate who never deals with the dispute for the Employer should be the proper candidate.

13 The candidates already disapproved by Contractor and Employer cannot be selected as the Sole Dispute Board Member.

FEES ARISING OUT OF REQUEST

14 If any fees arise out of the Request, please inform Contractor accordingly.

COMMUNICATION WITH THE SECRETARIAT

15 The address, telephone/fax number and email address are provided for communications between the Secretariat of ICC Arbitration Court and Contractor and Employer:
   (1)…
   (2)…

Should you require any further information, please don't hesitate to contact us.

Sincerely,

在任命三名 DAB 成员或者独任裁决员后，业主、承包商和 DAB 成员三方之间应签署争议裁决协议书。FIDIC 合同通用条款后面附有争议裁决协议书格式，但当事方可以根据工程争议的实际情况进行适当修改。例如在合同竣工后解决争议，此时，如果不需要 DAB 成员赴现场考察，则应删除现场考察的有关规定。自三方签署之日，争议裁决协议书生效，争议当事方可以将争议正式提交 DAB 作出决定。

对于中国承包商而言，由于对于 DAB 制度或者国际仲裁制度不了解或所知不深，必须指出，DAB 成员的人选关乎案件的结果，承包商应详细了解 DAB 成员情况，然后作出 DAB 成员的选择决定。由于国际工程 DAB 成员大都是西方国家的律师或工程专家，承包商需要判断其能力、人品和对中国是否存在偏见等问题。特别是歧视或偏见，无法从履历中看出，需要从中国承包商已经从事的国际工程 DAB 的案例中了解情况。在使用 FIDIC 合同的情况下，由于 FIDIC 合同源自英国的法律实践，因此，从英国选择工程专家或律师可能是好的选项。在选择独任裁决员时，应尽量避免选择已在业主的工程上担任了多年 DAB 成员的人，可能存在的问题是这位成员可能会存在偏向业主的倾向。另外，对于中国承包商而言，在国际工程项目存在的三名 DAB 成员时，选择中国籍的 DAB 成员是一项可以考虑的选项。

14.2 递交争议委员会作出决定通知

争议当事方计划将争议提交 DAB/DB 时，是否需要事先书面通知（Notice of Intention to Refer Dispute to DAB/DB）或者裁决通知（Notice of Adjudication），虽然 FIDIC 合同条款没有明确规定，但一般而言，争议当事方需要向 DAB/DB 发出一份通知，并抄送给当事另一方，计划将争议以书面方式提交给 DAB。

裁决通知的目的在于向当事另一方发出通知，告知对方他计划将争议提交给 DAB 作出决定，并启动与 DAB 裁决有关的所有程序，包括递交争议裁决申请书、当事对方答辩、准备证据、听证会和 DAB 作出的决定。如果争议的当事任何一方不满 DAB 作出的决定，还有可能会导致当事一方提起仲裁程序，进入仲裁的最终解决方式。或者，如合同约定诉讼方式，可能意味着争议当事一方起诉，进入诉讼程序解决争议。

承包商要求将争议提交争议委员会作出决定的通知范例如下：

<u>Notice of Adjudication</u>

IN THE MATTER OF A PROPOSED ADJUDICATION
BETWEEN

[● NAME]

Referring Party

AND

[● NAME]

Responding Party

NOTICE OF INTENTION TO REFER A DISPUTE TO ADJUDICATION

To: The Responding Party,

TAKE NOTICE that the Referring Party intends, pursuant to Sub-Clause 20. 4 of General Conditions of Contract under FIDIC MDB 2005 Edition and in accordance with Adjudication Procedure, to refer to Adjudication the dispute of which particulars are set out in this Notice of Intention to Refer a Dispute to Adjudication.

The Parties

1. The Referring Party, [• NAME], is a [• TYPE OF BUSINESS].
2. The Responding Party, [• NAME], is a [• TYPE OF BUSINESS].

The Contract

3. The Contract was made on [• DATE] and is in the terms of [• IDENTIFY CONTRACT CONDITIONS AND CONTRUACTUAL DOCUMENTS] (the "Contract").
4. The Contract is a construction contract for the purposes of [• SUBJECT MATTER OF THE CONTRACT]. The Referring Party is entitled to refer the dispute referred to below to Adjudication in accordance with the Sub-Clause 20. 4 of General Conditions of Contract under FIDIC MDB 2005 Edition.
5. The parties are engaged in a project for [• DESCRIBE PROJECT].
6. The Referring Party's role in the project was as [• IDENTIFY REFERRING PARTY's ROLE IN PROJECT]. The Responding Party is required under the Contract to [• IDENTIFY RESONDING PARTY's ROLE IN PROJECT].

The Dispute

7. A dispute has arisen between the Referring Party and the Responding Party, details of which are set out below.
8. Issues have arisen in respect of [• OUTLINE ISSUES FORMING PART OF THE DISPUTE].
9. As a result, there is a dispute as to [• IDENTIFY THE EXACT SCOPE OF THE DISPUTE (WHICH MAY NOT BE ALL THE DISPUTED ISSUES BETWEEN THE PARTIES) AND ANY CONTRACTUAL PROCEDURES WHICH ARE RELEVANT TO THE FORMATION OF A DISPUTE].
10. The location where the dispute arose is [• IDENTIFY LOCATION].

The Redress Sought by the Referring Party

11. The Referring Party seeks redress of the following nature: [• IDENTIFY NATURE OF

REDRESS SOUGHT] e. g. payment of the sum of USD [● FIGURES] plus interest in respect of the loss and damage incurred by the Referring Party as a result of the breaches of contract referred to.

12. The Referring Party seeks a redress in the form of a decision of the Adjudicator that [● IDENTIFY DETAILS OF REDRESS SOUGHTI]. for example:
    ➢ Payment by the Responding Party by [● DATE] of USD [● FIGURES], or such other sum as the Adjudicator sees fit; and
    ➢ Interest at such rate and in such amount as the Adjudicator thinks fit; and
    ➢ Any declaratory relief sought e. g. if a specified event is or is not a relevant event, or a declaration that the Responding Party is in breach of the contract, or a declaration as to the meaning of a clause in the contract.
    ➢ The Referring Party is awarded an extension of time to the Date for Completion until [● DATE]; and
    ➢ The Referring Party is awarded damage of [● AMOUNT], or such other sum as the Adjudicator sees fit; and
    ➢ The Adjudicator orders the Responding Party to pay the Adjudicator's fees and expenses [and to reimburse the Referring Party for the cost, to the Referring Party, of securing the Adjudicator's appointment].

Crystallization of the Dispute

13. By letter dated [● DATE], the Referring Party wrote to the Responding Party seeking [● SET OUT PECUNIARY OR DECLARATORY CLAIM].
14. By letter of response dated [● DATE], the Responding Party expressly rejected the Referring Party's claim. The reasons for rejecting the claim are [● CONSIDER SUMMARISING THE DEFENCES].
15. The Responding Party has since refused to engage with the Referring Party on the question of [● DETAILS].

Appointment of Adjudicator

16. The Referring Party will apply to the [● NAME OF NOMINATING BODY] for the appointment of an Adjudicator OR [● ADJUDICATOR NAMED IN THE CONTRACT] to act as the Adjudicator in this dispute.

Relevant Address

17. The names and addresses of the parties and the addresses which the parties have specified for the giving of notices to the Contract are set out below:

Referring Party
    [● FULL COMPANY DETAILS]

Responding Party
    [● FULL COMPANY DETAILS]

18. The names and addresses of the parties' representatives:

Referring Party　　　　　　　　Responding Party
[●FULL COMPANY DETAILS]　　[●FULL COMPANY DETAILS]

Dated [●DATE]

[●REFERRING PARTY OR ITS REPRESENTATIVE]

14.3　递交争议委员会作出决定申请书

在国际工程项目中，业主或承包商、主包商或分包商将争议提交 DAB 作出决定的前提是双方的不同主张必须构成"争议"，而确定争议的标准将根据合同规定判断，或者在合同没有约定的情况下，根据法律，包括判例作出判断。

在 FIDIC 合同条款中，业主和承包商之间的分歧应构成"争议"，例如承包商递交索赔不构成争议，只有业主或工程师拒绝了承包商提出的索赔，才能构成争议。在 2017 年第 2 版 FIDIC 合同条款中，第 1 条规定了争议的定义，只有承包商递交索赔，工程师拒绝索赔才能构成争议，或者承包商对工程师作出的决定发出不满通知（Notice of Dissatisfaction, NOD）时，才能构成争议。因此，承包商在使用 FIDIC 合同条款 2017 年第 2 版时，应特别注意"争议"的定义，它需要业主、工程师和承包商之间的书面文件证明存在争议，否则，如果承包商将所谓的"争议"提交 DAB，可能导致 DAB 没有管辖权。

承包商在递交争议裁决申请书时，应按照一定的格式编制争议裁决申请书，基本要求是应具有逻辑性和说服力：

（1）简介，应说明合同基本情况，争议因何而起，DAB 具有管辖权。
（2）合同争议的细节及其合同依据。
（3）争议当事一方提出的任何法律或判例。
（4）每一项争议的详情，如为索赔，索赔权利的确权、合同依据、量化和证据。
（5）要求 DAB 作出决定的事项，即请求项。

具体而言，一份争议裁决申请书的主要章节如下：

（1）封面，表明申请人（Referring Party）和被申请人（Responding Party）。
（2）当事人。
（3）概述，阐明争议或者索赔。
（4）合同，论证申请依据的合同条款或者索赔依据的合同条款。
（5）提交裁决申请函。
（6）事实。
（7）专家证据。
（8）证人证据。
（9）救济措施，即申请书请求 DAB 作出决定的具体请求。
（10）附件。

作为承包商,将争议提交 DAB 作出决定应该不像提交仲裁那样难以决策。在与业主和/或工程师就某项争议难以达成解决方案的情况下,可以将争议递交 DAB 作出决定。对于中国承包商而言,应克服害怕得罪业主和商业关系的考虑,采用国际上均可接受的方法解决争议。

承包商提交争议委员会作出决定申请书范例封面如下:

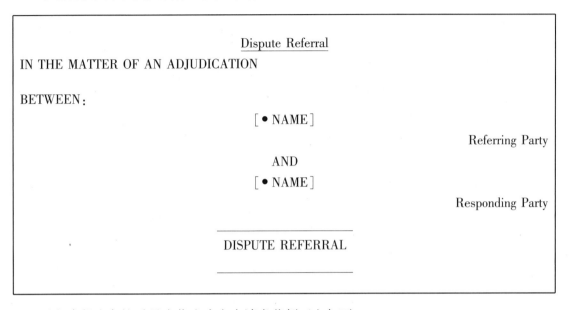

承包商提交争议委员会作出决定申请书范例正文如下:

The Parties

1. The Referring Party,[●NAME],is a [●TYPE OF BUSINESS].
2. The Responding Party,[●NAME],is a [●TYPE OF BUSINESS].

Introduction

3. [●SUMMARISE DISPUTE AND CLAIM].
4. The Referring Party claims from the Responding Party the sum of USD [●FIGURES], plus VAT for [●BRIEF DETAILS OF CLAIM],or such other amounts as the Adjudicator shall decide.
5. These monies are due under the terms of the engagement of the Referring Party as [●ROLE] for [●WORKS OR SERVICES],full particulars of which are set out below.
6. The Referring Party also claims interest on the monies due pursuant to [●NUMBER] of the contract].
7. The Referring Party seeks a declaration from the Adjudicator that [●IDENTIFY NATURE OF DECLARATORY RELIEF SOUGHT e. g. if a specified event is or is not a relevant event].
8. Where the context admits,capitalized terms in the contract have the same meaning in this Referral.

The Contract

9. The contract was made on [• DATE] and is in the terms of [• IDENTIFY CONTRACT CONDITIONS AND CONTRUACTUAL DOCUMENTS](the "Contract").
10. A copy of the Contract is at Appendix 1. [If the Adjudicator requires a complete copy of the contract, this can be provided by the Referring Party].
11. The Contract is a construction contract for the purpose of [• IDENTIFY CONTRACT CONDITIONS AND CONTRUACTUAL DOCUMENTS]. The Referring Party is entitled to refer the dispute referred to below to Adjudication in accordance with Sub-Clause 20.4 of General Conditions of Contract under FIDIC WDB 2005 Edition [• INSERT THE CONTRACT FORM EDITION, IF DIFFERENT].
12. The Referring Party relies on the whole of the terms of the Contract for its true meaning, intent and effect.
13. The following provisions are relevant to this dispute [• INSERT AND EXPLAIN RELEVANT CLAUSES].
14. In summary, the Contractual position is as follows [• SUMMARISE THE CONTRACTUAL POSITION].

Application and Relevant Notices

15. [• SET OUT RELEVANT PAYMENT DETAILS. IN FULL IF APPROPRIATE, WHERE THE CONTRACT DOES NOT COMPLY WITH THE TERMS THAT ARE CONSEQUENTED EXPRESSED BY THE CONTRACT].

The Facts

16. [• SET OUT FACTS AND, WHEN COMPLETING THIS SECTION, CONSIDER:

    For unpaid valuation claims:
    - Has the payment become due?
    - Has the final date for payment passed?
    - Has the Employer issued a Notice of Payment?
    - Has the Employer issued a Notice to Withhold Payment?
    - Does the Notice to Withhold Payment comply with the requirement of the Contract?
    - Is the Employer arguing against set-off or abatement?
    - Have the monies been certified for payment?

    For variation payment claims:
    - What is the scope of the contract works?
    - What was the nature of the change that was requested?
    - Is there a contractual mechanism for dealing with variations?

- Was the request made in accordance with the terms of the Contract?
- Was the change a sufficient departure from the original scope of works or was the change simply the Contractor's way of doing the work?
- How have the variations been measured?

For extension of time claims:
- Are there conditions precedent in the Contract and have they been satisfied?
- What was the Contractor's original planned progress?
- What events are alleged to have caused delay?
- Precisely what effect did those events have on the Contractor's planned progress?
- What does the as-built programme show?
- What methodology has been used to calculate any extension of time?
- How has any concurrent delay been dealt with?
- Has the Employer attempted to apply liquidated damages?
- What evidence is available to support the allegations made?
- Has the Contractor considered the practice set out in the Society of Construction Law "Protocol for Determining Extension of Time and Compensation for Delay and Disruption"?

For loss and expense claims:
- Will the claim for loss and expense be a claim under the Contract (have any conditions precedent in the Contract been satisfied?) or will it be a common law claim for damages for breach of the Contract?
- Has the Contractor considered the practice of the Society of Construction Law "Protocol for Determining Extension of Time and Compensation for Delay and Disruption"?
- Consider the recognized categories of loss and expense: prolongation costs, delay and disruption, head office overheads, loss of profit and finance charges—does the Contractor have claims under every head?
- Can a full cause and effect analysis be produced?]

Expert Evidence

17. Expert(s) were instructed on [• DATE]. The expert(s) produced an expert report on [• DATE], which is attached at [• APPENDIX X].
18. The Expert(s) were instructed to provide an opinion on [• INSERT].
19. In his/her opinion [• SUMMARISE FINDINGS AND CONCLUSION].

Witness Evidence

20. The following witnesses have prepared statement(s) setting out the facts and matters within their own knowledge, or where not within their own knowledge, true to the best of their knowledge and belief. The witnesses are [• LIST NAMES OF WITNESSSES AND ROLES].

21. [● NAME] addresses the following issues: [● LIST ISSUES].
22. In particular, [● NAME] records the following:
    ➢ set out key points;
23. The claim by the Referring Party comprises the following issues [● SUMMARISE IN A LIST EACH OF THE ISSUES. THIS SHOULD, WHERE POSSIBLE, ALIGN WITH HEADS OF RELIEF].
24. [● IN RESPECT OF EACH ISSUE, EXPLAIN HOW THE APPLICATION OF THE CONTRACT TO THESE FACTS SUPPORT THE RELIEF BEING SOUGHT].

The Redress Sought by the Referring Party

25. The Referring Party seeks redress of the following nature: [● IDENTIFY NATURE OF THE REDRESS SOUGHT e.g. payment of the sum of USD [FIGURE] plus interest in respect of the loss and damage incurred by the Referring Party as a result of the breaches of the Contract referred to].
26. The Referring Party seeks redress in the form of a decision of the Adjudication that [● IDENTIFY DETAILS OF REDRESS SOUGHT] e.g.
    ➢ payment by the Responding Party by [● DATE] of USD [● FIGURE];
    ➢ a declaration from the Adjudication that [● DETAILS OF DECLARATORY RELIEF SOUGHT]; and
    ➢ interest at such rate and in such amount as the Adjudication thinks fit; and
    ➢ the Referring Party is awarded an extension of time to the Date for Completion until [● DATE]; and
    ➢ the Adjudicator orders the Responding Party to pay the Adjudicator's fees and expenses].

Severed this [● DATE] by [● NAME OF REFERRING PARTY OR ITS REPRESENTATIVE].

[● REFERRING PARTY OR ITS REPRESENTATIVE]

APPENDICES

[● INSERT APPROPRIATE APPENDICES, INCLUDING:
APPENDIX A: CONTRACT OR RELEVANT EXTRACTS AND
APPENDICES THAT SET OUT KEY INFORMATION SUCH AS:
➢ measured account details, including variations
➢ contractual notices
➢ correspondence (including emails, attendance notes, letters, faxes)
APPENDICES THAT SET OUT ANY EXPERT REPORTS

14.4　争议委员会管辖权

无论是在仲裁、诉讼还是 DAB 争议解决机制中，法庭、仲裁庭或者 DAB 的管辖权均是争议当事方首先面对和解决的问题。管辖权是争议当事方必须力争的事项，是兵家必争之地，其对案件的结果可能产生影响。除非 DAB 对争议具有管辖权，否则 DAB 无权处理国际工程项目中的争议。但是，如果争议当事一方对 DAB 的管辖权提出异议（challenge），DAB 负有责任考虑管辖权异议并作出是否撤销还是继续的决定，即 DAB 决定是否对争议具有管辖权。

影响 DAB 管辖权的因素很多，可能包括：
（1）合同性质，是否是建筑工程合同，特别是在英国法定裁决的情况下。
（2）提交给 DAB 作出决定争议是否构成争议。
（3）当事方合同中的规定。
（4）是否根据 FIDIC 合同条款第 20.4 款［取得争议委员会的决定］提出争议申请。
（5）合同约定 DAB 只能一次解决一项争议，但是否可以对多起争议具有管辖权。
（6）DAB 任命无效。

在笔者处理的埃塞俄比亚公路局的某公路项目争议中，该项目使用的是 FIDIC 合同 2005 年多边开发银行协调版合同条款。在争议裁决申请书中第 3 节 "争议裁决协议书和争议委员会管辖权"（Agreement to Refer the Dispute for DB and DB's Jurisdiction），提及第 20.4 款并论述了第 20.4 款的前提条件，如下：

III AGREEMENT TO REFER THE DISPUTE FOR DB AND DB's JURISDICTION

12. Sub-Clause 20.2 [*Appointment of the Dispute Board*] and 20.3 [*Failure to Agree on the Composition of the Dispute Board*] of GCC provides that：

"*Disputes shall be referred to a DB for decision in accordance with Sub-Clause* 20.4 [*Obtaining Dispute Board's Decision*]. *The Parties shall appoint a DB by the date stated in the Contract Data.* "

" *If any of the following conditions applies, namely：*

(a) *the Parties fail to agree upon the appointment of the sole member of the DB by the date stated in the first paragraph of Sub-Clause* 20.2, [*Appointment of the Dispute Board*],

(b) *either Party fails to nominate a member (for approval by the other Party), or fails to approve a member nominated by the other Party, of a DB of three persons by such date,*

(c) *the Parties fail to agree upon the appointment of the third member (to act as chairman) of the DB by such date, or*

(d) *the Parties fail to agree upon the appointment of a replacement person within* 42 *days after the date on which the sole member or one of the three members de-*

clines to act or is unable to act as a result of death, disability, resignation or termination of appointment,

then the appointing entity or official named in the Contract Data shall, upon the request of either or both of the Parties and after due consultation with both Parties, appoint this member of the DB. This appointment shall be final and conclusive. Each Party shall be responsible for paying one-half of the remuneration of the appointing entity or official. "

13. When the disputes arose between the Contractor and the Employer, the Parties failed to reach agreement on the appointment of Sole Dispute Board Member for more than a year and half. On 24 October 2016, the Contractor addressed to the Chairman of International Court of Arbitration, International Chamber of Commerce ("ICC"), the appointing authority as set forth in Sub-Clause 20.3 of PCC, requesting ICC to recommend the Sole Dispute Board Member.

14. On 24 January 2017, ICC appointed Mr. _____ as the Sole Dispute Board Member and accordingly Mr. _____ was accepted as the Sole Dispute Board Member to settle the disputes arising from the captioned road project in Ethiopia.

15. On 4 May 2017, the Employer, the Contractor and Mr. _____ signed the Dispute Board Sole Member Contract including Annex 1: Procedural Rules, Annex 2: Dispute Board Sole Member Declaration of Acceptance ("Tripartite Agreement").

16. Thus, all prerequisites to initiating dispute referral to DB under Sub-Clause 20.4, GCC were satisfied. Either the Employer or the Contractor may refer any dispute in question to DB for his decision.

17. Subject to the Contract between the Parties being valid and the Tripartite Agreement, the disputed matter being referred to DB falls within the purview of both the General Conditions of Contract and the Tripartite Agreement referenced above, and accordingly the Sole Dispute Board Member, Mr. _____ has jurisdiction to make his decision as requested by either the Employer or the Contractor.

18. In terms of the meaning of dispute, the Referring Party cites the court verdict under case AMEC Civil Engineering Ltd. v The Secretary of State for Transport [2005] Adj. L. R. 03/17, which addresses:

    " From his review of the authorities, the judge derived the following propositions:

    (1) The word "dispute" which occurs in many arbitration clauses and also in Section 108 of the Housing Grants Act should be given its normal meaning. It does not have some special or unusual meaning conferred upon by lawyers.

    (2) Despite the simple meaning of the word " dispute", there has been much litigation over the years as to whether or not disputes existed in particular situations. This litigation has not generated any hard-edged legal rules as to what is or is not a dispute. However, the accumulating judicial decisions have produced helpful guidance.

    (3) The mere fact that one party (whom I shall call " the claimant") notifies the other

party (whom I shall call "the respondent") of a claim does not automatically and immediately give rise to a dispute. It is clear both as a matter of language and from judicial decisions, that a dispute does not arise unless and until it emerges that the claim is not admitted.

(4) The circumstances from which it may emerge that a claim is not admitted are protean. For example, there may be an express rejection of the claim. There may be discussions between the parties from which objectively it is to be inferred that the claim is not admitted. The respondent may prevaricate, thus giving rise to the inference that he does not admit the claim. The respondent may simply remain silent for a period of time, thus giving rise to the same inference.

(5) The period of time for which a respondent may remain silent before a dispute is to be inferred depends heavily upon the facts of the case and the contractual structure. Where the gist of the claim is well known and it is obviously controversial, a very short period of silence may suffice to give rise to this inference. Where the claim is notified to some agent of the respondent who has a legal duty to consider the claim independently and then give a considered response, a longer period of time may be required before it can be inferred that mere silence gives rise to a dispute.

(6) If the claimant imposes upon the respondent a deadline for responding to the claim, that deadline does not have the automatic effect of curtailing what would otherwise be a reasonable time for responding. On the other hand, a stated deadline and the reasons for its imposition may be relevant factors when the court comes to consider what is a reasonable time for responding.

(7) If the claim as presented by the claimant is so nebulous and ill-defined that the respondent cannot sensibly respond to it, neither silence by the respondent nor even an express non-admission is likely to give rise to a dispute for the purposes of arbitration or adjudication. "

19. Based on the learned judge's decision in the above case, it is obvious that a dispute does not arise unless and until it emerges that the claim is not admitted. However, the disputes as to Contractor's Additional Costs Claim, in this particular case of Construction Works, arise and exist between the Employer and the Contractor as to the Contractor's entitlement, quantum of additional costs as well as the level of substantiation presented by the Contractor in the course of the claim. The Contractor's Additional Costs claims under different heads were not primarily admitted and objected to by the Employer, and that thus the dispute arises.

业主认为，承包商没有在提交争议裁决的首封函中提及第 20.4 款，因此，争议委员会独任裁决员没有管辖权。DB 独任裁决员在第 1 号决定中指出：

"31　DB 首先就 2015 年 5 月 15 日承包商递交第 1 号争议申请书（Dispute Referral

No.1)中第3节'争议裁决协议书和争议委员会管辖权'提及的第20.4款[取得争议委员会的决定]作出决定。

32 DB认为,按照第1号争议申请书的题目可以看出,承包商清晰的意思表示就是根据合同和按照法律规定DB拥有提交争议的管辖权。承包商长篇叙述了适用的合同条款以及当事方未能就任命独任裁决员达成一致事宜,促使承包商不得不通过指定机构,即国际商会替代性争议解决中心于2017年1月24日任命独任裁决员。

33 在第1号争议申请书第12段中,承包商重申第20.2款规定,'本争议根据第20.4款提交DB作出决定'。在第16段中写道,'通用合同条款第20.4款规定的争议申请的前提条件成就。业主或承包商任何一方可将有关争议提交DB作出决定'。

……

44 如上所述,DB认为本争议申请符合第20.4款的程序要求,DB具有对第1号争议申请书的管辖权。"

如上所述,争议当事一方对DAB管辖权的异议理由多种多样,DAB应根据具体情况决定其是否具有管辖权。

14.5 争议裁决申请书的答辩

在当事一方递交了申请后,争议裁决申请书的当事另一方有权在DAB给出的时间内提出答辩(answer,reply或rejoinder),这是当事方的权利。当事方可以在答辩状中阐明事实、提出观点,提出主张和证据。当然,当事方也可以提出反请求(counter-claim),要求DAB作出决定。需要注意的是,与国际仲裁一样,当事方在庭审前不提出任何答辩意见不影响当事方的权利和在庭审上进行抗辩和主张的权利。

当事方在答辩时,应针对争议裁决申请书中提出的事实进行答辩,这与国际仲裁和诉讼中的要求没有什么差异。当事方需要针对事实、观点、主张进行答辩,并提供相应的证据支持自己主张的事实、观点和主张。

在国际工程争议中,答辩的基本内容如下:
(1)争议当事双方名称和地址。
(2)主要观点。
(3)每一项争议的事实、主张和证据。
(4)结论。

无论在国际仲裁还是在诉讼中,当事方在收到申请书后是否行使答辩权利,不影响当事方的任何权利,当事方可以递交答辩状,也可以不递交答辩状。在听证会或者庭审过程中,当事方可以当庭提出答辩意见。但是,一般而言,当事方均会递交答辩状,阐明事实、主张、观点和证据。

14.6 争议委员会听证会

在争议当事方提交争议裁决申请书和答辩状后,DAB将作出举行听证会(hearing)的指示，决定在哪个日期、地点举行听证会。DAB 通过程序令的方式向争议当事方发出指示。一般而言，国际工程争议的 DAB 听证会地点在工程所在国或地区的首都举行，也可能在现场举行。或者，争议当事双方按照合同约定的地点或发生争议时约定的任何其他地点举行听证会。

一般而言，听证会程序的安排如下：

(1) 申请人提出开庭陈述 (opening submission)。

(2) 被申请人提出开庭陈述。

(3) 申请人针对每一项争议提出事实、主张和证据；被申请人提出答辩，提出事实、主张和证据。

(4) DAB 可以在庭审过程中询问争议当事方有关事实和查证证据。

(5) 争议当事方庭后陈述。

(6) DAB 进行庭后安排并给出作出决定的预计时间。

(7) 庭审结束。

在国际工程项目中，由于 DAB 大多数情况下是第三国的工程专家和律师，DAB 会指示其中当事一方安排住宿和机场接送。一般而言，在争议的当事另一方是工程所在国政府部门时，DAB 会指示承包商安排住宿和机场接送。但在机场接送时，为了避免与任何当事一方单独接触，仅要求司机开车接送。承包商也应避免与 DAB 成员单独接触。

14.7 争议委员会决定和不满通知

FIDIC 合同条款规定 DAB 作出决定的期限为 84 天，自争议一方当事人提交争议裁决申请书之日起算，因此，DAB 在听取会的最后需要告知争议当事人作出决定的预期时间。

DAB 决定应清晰地表明其作出的决定，例如，在涉及付款时，当事一方向当事另一方支付应付款的具体日期。或者，在决定承包商的索赔金额时，应对具体金额作出决定。但在国际工程的 DAB 实践中，往往发生在承包商要求对索赔的具体金额作出决定时，DAB 未能在决定中作出具体金额的决定，而是作出希望承包商与业主协商具体金额。此类决定表明，DAB 未能履行其作出决定的职责。例如，在埃塞俄比亚公路局某公路项目中，在中国承包商提出增值税索赔时，虽然合同规定承包商应在合同中考虑所有的税和费，在工程量表（BOQ）中的总结页没有明确列明 15% 增值税的情况下，独任 DAB 成员仅作出了承包商对增值税没有义务纳入合同价格的义务。但是，在承包商在争议裁决申请书中要求业主返还或支付增值税具体金额的情况下，独任 DAB 成员仅作出了承包商没有义务在合同价格中考虑增值税的义务，但没有在决定中确定业主返还或支付给承包商的具体金额，不得不说，独任 DAB 成员未能尽到尽职义务。

在国际工程实践中，有的 DAB 在作出决定时，在涉及工期的情况下，仅对工期延长作出决定。但对于承包商的费用索赔，往往不作出具体金额的决定，而是要求业主和承包商进一步协商。这种裁决显然是避重就轻，DAB 成员未尽职责。不得不说，这种 DAB 决定丧失了 DAB 快速解决争议的功能。这种情况发生时，可能导致承包商或业主不得不通过仲裁方式解决争议。

DAB 决定不存在固定的格式，但在实践中，DAB 决定至少应包括如下内容：

（1）争议当事方的名称和地址。

（2）裁决形式和类型。

（3）DAB 成员的任命基础和条件。

（4）项目和争议的背景。

（5）争议范围和需要决定的问题，以及听取会期间新的请求项。

（6）申请人要求的救济措施。

（7）裁决员管辖权来源，以及存在异议时，DAB 对管辖权的决定。

（8）听取会情况。

（9）相关的合同条款。

（10）当事方的主张。

（11）对当事方每一项争议的决定。

（12）DAB 决定。

（13）决定或裁决总结。

此外，DAB 在作出决定时，每个裁决员应在决定上签字。DAB 决定中的每个段落应注明顺序号码。参考文件应可以相互参照并提供案卷号码。DAB 决定应分成各个部分表述。

根据 FIDIC 合同条款的规定，DAB 作出决定并发送给争议当事方后生效，除非争议当事方在收到 DAB 决定之后的 28 天内发出不满通知（Notice of Dissatisfaction）。也就是说，在争议当事方在规定的期限内发出不满通知后，DAB 裁决将不具有法律效力。如果争议当事方没有在规定的期限内发出不满通知，则 DAB 决定具有法律效力，当事方应当遵守和执行。

以某国际工程项目为例，承包商在争议委员会作出决定后发出不满通知示例如下：

Dear Sir,

Subject: Notice of Dissatisfaction

The Contractor, _____, for the captioned project hereby, pursuant to Sub-Clause 20.4 of General Conditions of Contract (GCC), issues the Notice of Dissatisfaction against DECISION NO. 2—CONTRACTOR's CLAIMS Nos. 1&2 released by Mr. _____, Sole Dispute Board Member (SDBM) on 14 September 2017.

1　Provisions of Sub-Clause 20.4 relating to Notice of Dissatisfaction

Sub-Clause 20.4 of GCC quotes:

"*If either Party is dissatisfied with the DB's decision, then either Party may, within 28 days after receiving the decision, give notice to the other Party of its dissatisfaction and intention to commence arbitration.*" and

"*In either event, this notice of dissatisfaction shall state that it is given under this Sub-Clause, and shall set out the matter in dispute and the reason(s) for dissatisfaction.*"

2　Compliance with Sub-Clause 20.4

The Contractor states that this Notice of Dissatisfaction is given and submitted on the date of 11 October 2017, which is within 28 days after receiving the decision by email of 14 September 2017.

> The Contractor also states that this Notice of Dissatisfaction is given under Sub-Clause 20.4 of General Condition of Contract.
>
> 3　Matter in Dispute and Reason(s) for Dissatisfaction
>
> Sub-Clause 20.4 addresses as well that this notice of dissatisfaction shall set out the matter in dispute and the reason(s) for dissatisfaction. In this particular regard, the matter in dispute in the Contractor Additional Costs Claims 1 & 2 which was decided by SDBM and is not satisfied by the Contractor includes in the Table 1 and Table 2 below:
>
> 　　Table 1　Summary of Additional Costs Claim No.1
>
> 　　Table 2　Summary of Incurred Additional Costs No.2
>
> 　　The Contractor, after scrutinizing the Decision No.2—Contractor's Claims Nos. 1&2 of 14 September 2017 (the "Decision"), holds that the Decision is unfair, without taking consideration of all particulars of the case, for the Contractor to judge the entitlement of claims and exhibits. The Contractor maintains as well that the Decision, with the cursory judgment of current delay for EOT No.1 and wrongful application of concurrent delay for EOT No.2, is not acceptable by the Contractor.
>
> Based on the foregoing, the Contractor issues this Notice of Dissatisfaction against the Decision No.2—Contractor's Claims Nos. 1&2 of 14 September 2017. Pursuant to the provisions of Sub-Clause 20.4 of GCC, the Contractor hereby informs the Employer of his intention to commence arbitration as set forth in Sub-Clause 20.6 of GCC.
>
> Sincerely,

FIDIC合同条款1999年第1版第20.7款［未能遵守争议裁决委员会的决定］规定，在以下情况下：①合同双方中的任一方在第20.4款［获得争议裁决委员会的决定］规定的期限内均未向争议裁决委员会发出表示不满的通知；②争议裁决委员会的有关决定（如果有）已成为最终决定、具有约束力的；③有一方未遵守上述决定，则另一方可以在不损害其可能拥有的其他权利的情况下，根据第20.6款［仲裁］的规定将上述未遵守决定的事项提交仲裁。在此情况下，第20.4款［获得争议裁决委员会的决定］和第20.5款［友好解决］的规定应不适用。

14.8　充分利用争议委员会机制解决争议

承包商在施工过程中应管理风险，及时解决小问题，避免小问题累积为大问题和大风险，而DRE和DAB争议解决机制为减少和避免争议提供了有效的解决机制。

尼泊尔某水电工程项目是当地为发展水电而兴建的第三期工程。在项目实施过程中，承包商遭受了下述不可预见的人为障碍或物质条件等困难：

（1）当地居民干扰施工。

（2）业主不能按时提供进场，导致工期延误和额外费用。

（3）业主延迟提供图纸，导致厂房施工停滞。

（4）业主不能提供2号支洞进场道路和现场占有权。

（5）业主对变更工程不予计量和付款。

（6）业主对4号IPC不予付款。

（7）电压过低导致无法进行隧道通风和施工进展缓慢。

承包商为此提出了大量的索赔，包括967天工期延长和约1000万美元额外费用索赔。工程师对此不予理睬。在业主的催促下，对承包商进行了索赔评估，仅给予67天工期延长和约2万美元的额外费用补偿。

本项目使用FIDIC合同条款1987年第4版，采用争议审议委员会（dispute review board, DRB）。承包商在工程师作出不公平决定后，将争议提交DRB进行裁决。

在听证过程中，承包商提出了自己的主张和证据，业主提出了反驳意见。DRB在听取了各方的陈述后，根据双方提交的证据，作出了有利于承包商的决定，即给予承包商867天工期延长，给予180万美元的额外费用补偿。对于承包商在施工过程中提出的争议，争议评审委员会作出的决定见表14-1。

表14-1 某国际工程项目争议委员会决定统计

序号	承包商提交DB作出决定		工程师决定	DB决定	
	提交事项			决定内容	
	事项	索赔工期和费用		EOT工期	Cost费用
1	因当地居民干扰导致工程停工	49.50天 +86,030,140.19NR	15.50天 +616,834.52NR	27天	16,180,534.60NR
2	2号和3号支洞延迟提供现场占有权	867.50天 +122,294,911.55NR	0天 +439,011.12NR	867.5天	44,417,685.42NR
3	因现场道路、当地居民干扰导致厂房施工延误	782.45天 +240,539,167.66NR	0天 +520,308.48NR	737天	50,909,976.42NR
4	4号支洞施工道路延误	273天 +22,713,285.75NR	0天 +0NR	84天	3,640,129.81NR
5	延迟提供取水口现场占有权	185天 +36,955,400.65NR	0天 +0NR	182天	9,216,765.31NR
6	上游水道（支洞-1A）不可预见的物质障碍	37,644,608.16NR	0 NR	143.5天	11,465,052.96NR
7	供电电压过低导致无法施工	31,917,077.40NR	0 NR		759,780.00NR
8	延长工期内的拖延费用	165,848,133.99NR	0 NR		0 NR

从表14-1可以看出，中国承包商提交给争议委员会作出的决定，争议委员会支持了承包商提出的大多数主张。

中国承包商应汲取的经验和教训是：

（1）承包商应坚持自己的主张。在工程师不能公平行使职权的情况下，应采用争议裁决机制，争取自己的权利。

（2）承包商的工期延长和额外费用索赔应有理有据，特别是在证据和证明力方面下足功夫，论证索赔权利的成立和额外费用的实际损失。

（3）无论是 DB、DAB 还是 DRB，均是合同规定的争议解决方式。承包商应充分利用这一机制，维护自己的合法权益。

乍得某公路项目是乍得政府为改善首都恩贾梅纳与喀麦隆边境交通基础设施建设的道路工程。根据国际工程专家为中国承包商所做的工期延长索赔报告和额外费用索赔报告，依据2013 年 9 月与业主谈判工期延长索赔的结果，在业主方提出将双方争议提交争议裁决的提议下，中国承包商接受业主的提议，将争议提交争议裁决专家解决。

按照通用合同条款第 6 条和专用合同条款第 6 条的规定，争议裁决将由一名来自法国的专家进行，即由独任裁决员裁决争议。

争议裁决内容包括：

（1）承包商的工期延长索赔要求。承包商提出 391 天工期延长，业主仅给予 164 天工期延长（实际为 10 个月工期延长），承包商认为业主给予的工期延长未能反映承包商所遭受的困难，承包商坚持 391 天工期延长要求，即要求业主将工期延长至 2014 年 7 月 26 日。

（2）额外费用索赔要求。承包商提出了 668 万美元额外费用要求，业主认为此项争议应由争议裁决专家进行裁决。

2014 年 6 月 18 日，争议裁决专家进行了现场考察，国际工程专家赴现场与承包商代表一同视察了现场。针对争议裁决专家提出的问题，国际工程专家给出了详细的解释和说明，并针对工期延长要求和额外费用索赔提出了看法。

中国承包商应汲取的经验是：

（1）争议裁决机制是快速和高效解决国际工程争议的最为有力的方式。实践证明，争议裁决机制是承包商维护自身权益的方式之一。

（2）争议裁决机制是有效制止业主或工程师不公平的一种方式。只要承包商提出的争议是有依据的、有证据，往往能够获得争议裁决的支持。

（3）争议裁决是有效平衡业主不作为、蛮横无理的一种方式。对承包商而言，利用争议裁决专家支持自身的主张，是对业主行为的一种制约。

从全球层面来看，争议委员会得到了业主和承包商的认可，当事方的满意度情况统计见表 14-2。

表 14-2　争议委员会解决国际工程争议时的当事人满意度

地　　区	项 目 总 数	当事人满意数量	当事人满意百分比
欧洲	64	43	67%
亚洲	28	21	75%
非洲	99	84	85%
美洲	35	31	89%
澳大利亚/新西兰	5	4	80%

（资料来源：James Perry. Dispute Board Advantage in Dispute Avoidance and Resolution. 2018.10.31）

从表 14-2 可以看出，争议委员会作为一种高效、快速和低成本的解决国际工程项目的替代性争议解决方式，获得了工程业界的认可。中国承包商也在国际工程项目中大量使用争议委员会机制解决国际工程争议，因此，对于中国企业而言，在国际工程项目中应积极使用争议委员会机制解决与业主之间产生的争议。针对中国承包商在使用争议委员会中存在的问题，建议应注意如下问题：

（1）承包商应仔细阅读和研究业主招标文件中的争议解决条款和争议委员会的安排是否合理和可行，如认为不合理和不可行，则应在招标阶段以答疑方式向业主提出，要求业主澄清。

（2）在合同规定了争议委员会解决争议机制的情况下，应在合同约定的期限内，例如开工日期之后28天内成立争议委员会，避免业主以资金紧张为由故意拖延任命争议委员会成员的情况发生，或者，承包商为了省钱，也不愿意更早地任命争议委员会成员的情况发生。

（3）在业主或承包商因争议委员会成员任命无法达成一致的情况下，应积极寻求向合同约定的指定机构要求任命争议委员会成员。

（4）如果承包商与业主/工程师之间因争议产生分歧，僵持不下，双方观点和立场对立时，应寻求采用争议委员会解决争议，避免与业主/工程师陷入毫无效率的、相互伤害的、旷日持久的争执之中。中国承包商应特别注意这个问题，应学会利用和使用法律手段解决国际工程项目发生的争议。

（5）在准备提交争议委员会争议解决过程中，承包商应仔细准备申请书（dispute referral）、答辩状（reply）和证据（exhibits），进行详细的事实陈述，明确诉求（relief）。

（6）在听证会环节，承包商应详细阐明事实、主张和诉求，有理有据，不卑不亢。如果承包商在听证会环节无法做到这一点，应积极寻求第三方帮助，包括律师、专家咨询顾问等。

（7）如果承包商对争议委员会的决定不满，则应在合同规定的期限内，例如FIDIC合同条款规定的28天内或者其他合同条款规定的更短的时间14天内，发出不满通知。

第 15 章 国际仲裁

> The advantages of arbitration are that, where the substantial
>   questions are matters of fact, a final and conclusive
> decision can be obtained in a manner which, theoretically,
>   is quicker and cheaper than the ordinary processes of law.
>
> 17-006, *Keating on Construction Contracts*. Eleventh Edition. 2020

15.1 仲裁条款和仲裁协议

15.1.1 仲裁条款和仲裁协议必备要素

仲裁条款或仲裁协议是合同当事双方在订立合同时同意的，把将来可能发生的争议提交仲裁解决的合同条款。这种仲裁条款是合同条款的一个组成部分，包含在合同之中。

目前，根据大多数国家的法律，只要合同中有仲裁条款，在发生争议需要提交仲裁时，合同当事方无须另行签订仲裁协议，凭合同中的仲裁条款即可将争议提交仲裁。但在没有仲裁条款的情况下，则要求合同当事方在提出仲裁之前达成仲裁协议，凭仲裁协议才可将争议提交仲裁。

在合同当事方订立了仲裁条款或仲裁协议后，仲裁条款和协议的效力如下：

(1) 合同当事方应受仲裁条款和协议的约束，如发生争议，应提交仲裁解决，而不能向法院提起诉讼。

(2) 仲裁机构取得对争议案件的管辖权。

(3) 取代了法院对争议案件的管辖权。

一项具有效力的仲裁条款或仲裁协议的主要内容应包括：

(1) 仲裁地点。仲裁地点（place of arbitration）是合同当事双方争论的焦点。业主、当地总包商都希望将仲裁地点确定在自己的国家，而外国承包商、外国分包商或外国总包商则不希望将仲裁地点确定在业主或当地总包商的国家，而希望选择在第三国进行仲裁。对于分包合同而言，为了避免选择在工程所在国的仲裁机构进行仲裁，一般而言，在第三国仲裁是一项总包商和分包商均可接受的选择。

(2) 仲裁机构。某些国家，特别是英美等发达国家，有全国性的仲裁机构（arbitration institute），如英国伦敦仲裁院，也有许多专业性的组织都设有仲裁机构，如伦敦油籽协会、伦敦谷物贸易协会等，可以从事仲裁业务。因此，合同当事人在选择了仲裁地点后，还需要进一步选定仲裁机构。

(3) 仲裁规则。仲裁规则（arbitration rule）是仲裁机构制定的如何进行仲裁的程序规则,包括如何提出仲裁申请、如何答辩、指定仲裁员、如何作出仲裁裁决和裁决的效力等内容。一般而言,合同当事方在选择了仲裁机构后,都会选择该仲裁机构自己制定的仲裁规则。当然,合同当事方也可以选择其他机构制定的仲裁规则。

(4) 仲裁的效力。合同当事方应在仲裁条款或仲裁协议中明确规定仲裁的法律效力 (legal binding),即仲裁裁决是终局的裁决,对当事双方都有约束力。

15.1.2 仲裁条款范例

在标准合同格式中,一般都明确规定了一项完整的仲裁条款的内容,但在分包合同中,在总包商自己起草分包合同时,应注意仲裁条款的有效性和完整性,以便发生争议时可以依据仲裁条款将争议提交仲裁解决。

中国国际经济贸易仲裁委员会提供的标准仲裁条款如下:

"凡因本合同引起的或与本合同有关的任何争议,均应提交中国国际经济贸易仲裁委员会,按照申请仲裁时该会现行有效的仲裁规则进行仲裁。仲裁裁决是终局的,对双方均有约束力。"

"Any dispute arising from or in connection with this Contract shall be submitted to China International Economic and Trade Arbitration Commission (CIETAC) for arbitration which shall be conducted in accordance with the CIETAC's arbitration rules in effect at the time of applying for arbitration. The arbitral award is final and binding upon both parties."

需要注意的是,在国际工程合同的仲裁条款中,上述仲裁条款中还应明确仲裁地点和仲裁语言,如下:

"Any dispute arising from or in connection with this Contract shall be submitted to China International Economic and Trade Arbitration Commission (CIETAC) for arbitration, which shall be conducted in accordance with the CIETAC's arbitration rules in effect at the time of applying for arbitration. The arbitration shall be held in _____. [place]. The arbitration shall be conducted in _____ [language]. The arbitral award is final and binding upon both parties."

在标准合同格式中,特别是工程施工合同格式中,如 FIDIC、ICE、JCT、AIA 等合同格式,一般均以争议裁决条款方式规定解决争议的方式。有关仲裁机构,如联合国国际贸易法委员会建议合同当事双方以下述方式订立仲裁条款:

"凡本合同引起的或与本合同有关的,或与违反、终止本合同伙合同无效有关的所有争议、争执或请求权,应按现行有效的联合国国际贸易法委员会仲裁规则以仲裁方式处理。
注:双方当事人可考虑增订:
(1) 指定仲裁员的机构应为……(机构或人员名称);
(2) 仲裁员的人数应为……(一人或三人);

(3) 仲裁地点应在……（城市或国家的名称）；

(4) 仲裁程序所使用的语言应为……"

"Any dispute, controversy or claim arising out of or relating to this contract, or the breach, termination or invalidity thereof, shall be settled by arbitration in accordance with the UNCITRAL Arbitration Rules.

Note. Parties should consider adding：

(a) The appointing authority shall be . . . ［name of institution or person］；

(b) The number of arbitrators shall be . . . ［one or three］；

(c) The place of arbitration shall be . . . ［town and country］；

(d) The language to be used in the arbitral proceedings shall be . . . "

国际商会（ICC）提供的标准仲裁条款如下：

"All disputes arising out of or in connection with the present contract shall be shall be finally settled under the Rules of Arbitration of the International Chamber of Commerce by one or more arbitrators appointed in accordance with the said Rules. "

同时，国际商会也提示，需要在仲裁条款中规定如下内容：

(1) 合同准据法（the law governing the contract）。

(2) 仲裁院人数（the number of arbitrators）。

(3) 仲裁地点（the place of arbitration）。

(4) 仲裁语言（the language of the arbitration）。

关于仲裁员人数的问题，建议不在仲裁条款中约定仲裁院人数，这是因为对于金额较小的争议，仲裁机构仲裁规则均规定了适用独任仲裁员（sole arbitrator）的制度。例如国际商会仲裁规则规定争议金额小于200万美元、贸仲委仲裁规则规定争议金额小于500万元人民币时，适用独任仲裁员审理案件。如果超过上述独任仲裁员审理的争议金额，则应适用三名仲裁员审理案件。在国际仲裁实践中，如果当事方约定了独任仲裁员，如果当事双方无法在仲裁开始时改变约定，则无论争议金额大小，均应适用独任仲裁员审理案件，这可能导致争议金额较大或巨大时，由独任仲裁员审理案件情况的发生，而当事方可能会产生怀疑，争议金额巨大适用独任仲裁员是否可以公正判断案件的是非曲直，是否会产生程序的瑕疵。如果当事方约定了三名仲裁员审理案件，则无论争议金额大小，均应适用三名仲裁员审理案件，这可能导致争议金额较小时，适用三名仲裁员审理案件，当事方将为此付出高额的仲裁员费用。

关于国际商会仲裁规则第6条的效力问题，根据俄罗斯最高法院2018年判决，在仅规定ICC仲裁规则的情况下，ICC仲裁规则第6条"选择了ICC仲裁规则就是选定国际商会管理案件"的规定并不意味着国际商会具有案件的管理权，即在其他的仲裁机构中也可以适用国际商会仲裁规则。因此，在使用国际商会仲裁规则时，应增加提交给国际商会的内容，如下。

"All disputes arising out of or in connection with the present contract shall be finally submitted to the International Chamber of Commerce under the Rules of Arbitration of the International Chamber of Commerce by one or more arbitrators appointed in accordance with the said Rules. "

在国际工程项目中,一份完整的仲裁协议可参考如下示范条款:

"(a) In the event of any differences or dispute arising from this Agreement or any other matters related thereto which cannot be settled amicably between the Parties within 60 (sixty) days as from the notification of such dispute by a Party to the other Party and/or Parties, such differences or dispute shall be finally referred to _____ ("_____") and settled in accordance with the existing Rules of Arbitration ("Rules") by a tribunal of three arbitrators appointed in accordance with the Rules. Each Party shall bear its own costs and expenses of arbitration. The arbitrators shall assess in their award the amount of the costs and expenses of arbitration and the arbitrators' fees. The prevailing Party/Parties shall be entitled to all costs, expenses and reasonable attorney fees.

(b) If each of the Parties has partly lost and partly won, the arbitrators shall apportion the costs, expenses and fees between the Parties.

(c) The arbitration shall be held in _____.

(d) The arbitration shall be conducted in the English language and the decision of the arbitrators shall be in writing and in English.

(e) The decision of the arbitration shall be final and binding on the Parties and may be enforced by any court of competent jurisdiction at the request of the prevailing Party in accordance with the applicable rules. "

或者:

"14. 3. 3 Arbitration

14. 3. 3. 1 Any Dispute that is not settled amicably by the Parties under Sub-Clause 19. 2. 1 [*Consultation and Amicable Settlement*] (including where the Management Committee does not reach an unanimous decision or is not properly convened in accordance with Sub-Clause £19. 2. 1(ii)), shall be referred to and finally settled by arbitration in accordance with this Sub-Clause 19. 2. 2.

14. 3. 3. 2 The arbitration shall be conducted according to the Arbitration Rules of the _____ ("Rules") for the time being in force, which rules are deemed to be incorporated by reference in this Sub-Clause 19. 2. 2, in _____, or another mutually agreed location. The seat of the arbitration shall be _____ In the case of conflict between the Rules and the provisions of this Sub-Clause 19. 2. 2, the provisions hereof shall prevail.

14. 3. 3. 3 Unless otherwise agreed between the Parties, three arbitrators shall be appointed. Each Party shall nominate an arbitrator, and the two Party-appointed arbitrators shall jointly nominate the third (who shall be the presiding arbitrator) within 30 days after

the confirmation of the second arbitrator, failing in which the third arbitrator shall be appointed by the LCIA in accordance with the Rules.

14.3.3.4 Any decision rendered by the arbitral tribunal, including the arbitral award, shall be treated in secrecy by the arbitral tribunal and as confidential information by the Parties, pursuant to Sub-Clause 1.9[*Confidentiality*].

14.3.3.5 The arbitrators shall have full power to open up, review and revise any certificate, determination, instruction, opinion or valuation of (or on behalf of) the Parties with respect to a Dispute. Neither Party shall be limited to the previous evidence or arguments on any matter whatsoever relevant to a Dispute in the proceedings before the arbitration.

14.3.3.6 The award rendered by the arbitrator(s) shall be final and binding and the Parties agree that neither of them may appeal to any court from any award or decision of the arbitrator(s). Judgments upon awards or orders for enforcement may be entered and shall be enforceable in any court of competent jurisdiction and execution may be carried out in accordance with the law of execution generally applied in the jurisdiction where enforcement is sought.

14.3.3.7 The Parties shall be obliged to continue the performance of their obligations in accordance with the Contract notwithstanding the existence of any Dispute, provided that the Employer shall be entitled to withhold any disputed portion of a payment claim until the Dispute is resolved."

承包商必须注意的是，各个仲裁机构的仲裁规则不同，世界上的大部分仲裁机构的仲裁规则均规定选择了该会的仲裁规则，就视为选择了该机构作为仲裁机构，例如国际商会2012仲裁规则第6.2条如此规定。中国国际经济贸易仲裁委员会仲裁规则第4.4条规定"当事人约定按照本规则进行仲裁但未约定仲裁机构的，视为同意将争议提交仲裁委员会仲裁"。但是，在适用联合国国际贸易法仲裁规则时，如果当事方在仲裁条款或仲裁协议中仅约定按照联合国国际贸易法仲裁规则仲裁，但没有约定仲裁机构，则根据该规则，在合同当事双方没有达成任何进一步协议的情况下，则应向位于海牙的国际常设仲裁院要求指定仲裁机构管理仲裁案件。这就意味着，合同当事方在约定使用联合国国际贸易法委员会仲裁规则时，应约定仲裁机构。

15.1.3 仲裁条款形式

仲裁条款或仲裁协议应当采用书面形式。书面形式包括合同书、信件、电报、电传、电子数据交换和电子邮件等可以有形地表现所载内容的形式。在仲裁申请书和仲裁答辩书的交换中，当事一方声称有仲裁协议而当事另一方不做否定表示的，视为存在书面仲裁协议。

在国际仲裁中，仲裁条款或仲裁协议的效力是争议当事方争议的焦点之一。在实践中，影响仲裁条款或仲裁协议效力的因素是：

（1）仲裁条款约定"仲裁和诉讼"或者"仲裁或诉讼"。

（2）仲裁条款或仲裁协议没有约定仲裁机构。

（3）仲裁条款或仲裁协议约定了两个或两个以上仲裁机构。

（4）仲裁条款或仲裁协议约定的仲裁机构名称错误，但又无法合理推断出仲裁机构。

（5）仲裁条款或仲裁协议指定了错误的仲裁机构。

（6）在中国仲裁法下选择了临时仲裁机构。

（7）合同当事双方都是中国企业时约定境外仲裁机构。

（8）其他影响仲裁条款或仲裁协议效力的事项。

在国际商事仲裁实践中，仲裁条款或仲裁协议效力认定的原则是：

第一、尊重当事方仲裁意愿的原则。由于仲裁是当事方之间约定的协议管辖，构成了仲裁能否进行的基础。仲裁条款受当事方的共同意愿支配，而没有必要依据某一特定国家的仲裁法。

第二、仲裁管辖权优先原则。自1958年《纽约公约》生效以来，支持仲裁的理论逐步在国际上得到确认。《纽约公约》规定"各缔约国承认仲裁协议的效力""对于当事人就诉讼事项订有仲裁协议的，法院受理诉讼时，应依当事一方请求，命当事人提交仲裁"。例如，在当事人既约定仲裁又约定诉讼的仲裁条款的效力问题，不同地区法院的普遍做法是仲裁管辖权优先的原则。例如中国香港高等法院在 William Company v. Chu Kong Agency 案中认定，提单中的仲裁条款"在中华人民共和国法院解决或在中华人民共和国仲裁解决"是有效的。而新加坡法院在 Da Yun Shan 案中，法院虽然认为"该案不是一个一定要通过仲裁解决的"争议，但最终还是通过运用自由裁量权中止了诉讼程序。

15.1.4　争议方式的选择

中国企业在选择仲裁还是诉讼上，存在两种不同的情况：

（1）中国企业之间在对内贸易、各种经济合同纠纷和在中国建筑市场的争议和纠纷，往往面临两种选择，一是在争议发生之后诉诸诉讼，二是诉诸仲裁。

（2）中国企业对外贸易和对外承包工程项目上，往往倾向于选择仲裁。这主要是对外贸易和对外承包工程的涉外性质决定的，国外当事方也往往倾向于采用国际仲裁方式解决争议，特别是对外承包工程，国外业主往往选择仲裁，或者业主选用的标准格式合同，如FIDIC合同条款第20条［索赔、争议和仲裁］规定了仲裁条款。

承包商需要牢记的是，在与业主签订的合同中应使用和选择国际仲裁方式解决争议，在与工程所在国当地分包商签订的分包合同中应选择国际仲裁方式解决争议，避免采用当地法院解决争议。

对于中国承包商与分包商之间的分包合同，影响中国企业选择仲裁方式的主要因素在于仲裁与诉讼的优劣比较。有些企业认为，仲裁一裁终局，在可能出现对己不利的裁决时，无法通过上诉的方式纠正。而法院诉讼在一审败诉后，仍然可通过二审程序得以翻盘。影响中国企业选择仲裁的第二个主要因素在于有些企业怀疑仲裁员的素质和公正性，担心出现错裁或误裁，以致企业合法权益无法得到保障。为此，需要通过多种手段强化仲裁在解决商事纠纷中的作用和地位：

（1）通过立法手段强化仲裁作用和地位，给予当事方法律上的保障。以英国为例，通过立法给予建筑合同的争议裁决机制（Dispute Adjudication）合法地位，使得这种适用于建筑工程的替代性争议解决方式合法化，从立法上推动争议解决机制的创新。

（2）修改仲裁法，使之适应国际上仲裁的趋势、惯例和最佳实践，使中国的仲裁国际化，取消仲裁法中一些限制或妨碍仲裁实施的规定。

（3）加强仲裁机构的建设，树立仲裁机构的权威，加强仲裁宣传，使企业了解仲裁的优点，了解仲裁裁决的公正性和权威性。

（4）加强仲裁员队伍建设，使仲裁员队伍保持纯洁，聘用优秀的仲裁员，使企业在发生争议时，可以从仲裁员名录中找到适合案件的仲裁员，给企业建立信心，使他们能够确信由优秀仲裁员组成的仲裁庭可以从事实、法律、证据等方面作出正确的判断，给予公正的裁决。

（5）加强仲裁裁决的执行力度，通过立法和司法手段，使仲裁裁决得到及时和快速的执行，维护权益受到保护的当事人的合法权益。

（6）加强国际仲裁机构之间的合作，运用《纽约公约》的效力，加强仲裁裁决的国外执行和效果，使国际仲裁裁决得以在域外有效执行。

15.2 使用 FIDIC 合同条款时常见的仲裁条款问题

在业主编制基于 FIDIC 合同条款的招标文件并且最终形成合同文件时，在业主与承包商之间发生争议诉诸仲裁方式解决时，经常发现合同文件仲裁条款中存在各种问题，给业主和承包商的仲裁程序带来困扰和麻烦，导致当事方需要首先解决合同约定的仲裁的条款中存在的各种程序问题。

15.2.1 FIDIC 合同条款 2005 年、2006 年和 2010 年多边开发银行协调版第 20.6 款〔仲裁〕

在多边开发银行协调版（MDB）FIDIC 合同条款 2005 年、2006 年版中，甚至 2010 年版第 20.6 款〔仲裁〕第（d）项的规定，均说明合同与本地承包商签订时按照业主所在国法律进行仲裁程序。这在主合同中应该不会产生歧义。

但是，FIDIC 分包合同条款 2011 版第 20.7 款〔分包合同仲裁〕规定："经分包合同 DAB 决定未能成为最终和有约束力的任何分包合同争议，除非友好协商，应根据国际商会仲裁规则最终解决，主合同第 20.6 款〔仲裁〕应适用。"

上述工程项目的承包商在使用 FIDIC 合同条款多边开发银行协调版（MDB）2005 年版、合同数据以及 FIDIC 分包合同条款 2009 年版时，承包商与分包商因终止合同事宜产生分歧。对于 FIDIC 分包合同规定的仲裁地点和管理机构，分包商提出异议，认为根据 FIDIC 分包合同第 20.7 款〔分包合同仲裁〕指引的使用 MDB2005 年版 FIDIC 合同条款第 20.6 款〔仲裁〕的规定，分包商作为当地承包商，应适用合同条款第 20.6 款〔仲裁〕(d）项的规定，通过当地的仲裁机构解决争议，应根据孟加拉仲裁法进行仲裁程序，并依此提出国际商会仲裁管辖权的异议。FIDIC 合同 MDB2006 年 3 月版第 20.6 款〔仲裁〕规定：

"20.6 Arbitration   Unless indicated otherwise in the Particular Conditions, any dispute not settled amicably and in respect of which the DB's decision (if any) has not become final and binding shall be finally settled by arbitration. Unless otherwise agreed by both Parties:

(a) for contracts with foreign contractors, international arbitration with proceedings administered by the institution appointed in the Contract Data conducted in accordance with the rules of arbitration of the appointed institution, if any, or in accordance with UNCITRAL arbitration rules, at the choice of the appointed institution,

(b) the place of arbitration shall be the city where the headquarters of the appointed arbitration institution is located,

(c) the arbitration shall be conducted in the language for communications defined in Sub-Clause 1.4 [*Law and Language*], and

(d) for contracts with domestic contractors, arbitration with proceedings conducted in accordance with the laws of the Employer's country.

The arbitrators shall have full power to open up, review and revise any certificate, determination, instruction, opinion or valuation of the Engineer, and any decision of the DB, relevant to the dispute. Nothing shall disqualify representatives of the Parties and the Engineer from being called as a witness and giving evidence before the arbitrators on any matter whatsoever relevant to the dispute.

Neither Party shall be limited in the proceedings before the arbitrators to the evidence or arguments previously put before the DB to obtain its decision, or to the reasons for dissatisfaction given in its notice of dissatisfaction. Any decision of the DB shall be admissible in evidence in the arbitration.

Arbitration may be commenced prior to or after completion of the Works. The obligations of the Parties, the Engineer and the DB shall not be altered by reason of any arbitration being conducted during the progress of the Works."

在签订合同之前业主和承包商签署的会议纪要对 FIDIC 合同条款第 20.6 款 [仲裁] 第 (a) 项进行了修改,将仲裁地点修改为法国巴黎,这是因为会议纪要在修改时将 (a) 项修改为:

"For contracts with foreign contractors, international arbitration with proceedings administered by the institution appointed in the Contract Data, conducted in accordance with the rules of arbitration of the appointed institution, if any, or in accordance with ICC arbitration rules, Paris, France."

在上述修改中，业主不是直接将文字表述为："the place of arbitration shall be Paris, France"，而是 "ICC Arbitration Rules, Paris, France"，使人产生困惑。

在孟加拉高等法院2016年6月14日判决中，法院驳回了孟加拉分包商的诉讼请求，认为在适用主合同第20.6款［仲裁］时，分包合同明确约定了国际商会管辖，根据第20.6款［仲裁］中的条款顺序，可以推断出国际商会具有仲裁管辖权。在分包合同明确约定国际商会管辖时，第20.6款［仲裁］第（d）项不能予以适用。法官在判决中写道：

"据此，法院认为仲裁程序应适用国际商会仲裁规则，但是实体法律应根据分包合同的规定适用孟加拉法律。法院无法接受申请人主张的第20.6款第（a）、（b）项全部无效的主张。实际上，根据会议纪要第15条达成的协议和分包合同通用条款第20.7款的规定，国际商会仲裁规则应予适用，并应按照国际商会仲裁规则第1.1条和第1.2条的规定成立仲裁庭解决争议。

鉴此，法院认为起诉书第12节提出的任命仲裁员的主张不能成立。法院还认为，此项主张与孟加拉仲裁法第7Ka条的规定相悖。

为此，驳回原告诉讼请求。"

因此，承包商在使用FIDIC合同条款时，特别是FIDIC MDB2005年、2006年和2010年版合同条款时，应特别注意第20.6款［仲裁］的规定是否完备，是否明示约定了仲裁规则、仲裁机构、仲裁语言和仲裁地点。

15.2.2 UNCITRAL仲裁规则中的仲裁机构

与国际上普遍设立的仲裁机构不同，由于联合体国际贸易法委员会为联合体机构之一，无法在联合国层面设立仲裁机构，在使用UNCITRAL仲裁规则时，应注意合同中第20.6款［仲裁］是否约定了仲裁机构。如果合同没有约定仲裁机构，则在发生争议时，当事方需要根据UNCITRAL仲裁规则的规定向位于海牙的国际常设仲裁院提出仲裁机构的选定事宜，这无疑增加了争议双方的争议成本和时间。

在某国际工程项目中，业主采用了FIDICMDB合同条款2005年版，其中第20.6款［仲裁］规定如下：

"20.6 Arbitration
Unless indicated otherwise in the Particular Conditions, any dispute not settled amicably and in respect of which the DB's decision (if any) has not become final and binding shall be finally settled by arbitration. Unless otherwise agreed by both Parties：
(a) For contracts with foreign contractors, international arbitration with proceedings ad-

ministered by the institution appointed in the Contract Data, conducted in accordance with the rules of arbitration of the appointed institution, if any, or in accordance with UNCITRAL arbitration rules, at the choice of the appointed institution,"

业主在编制合同时，在合同数据中将第 20.6 款第（a）项修改为：
"Rule of Arbitration: Sub-Clause 20.6 (a)　UNCITRAL"

但是，业主在编制合同数据时未能指定仲裁机构，这就导致了在发生争议时，承包商发现合同条款未能规定仲裁机构。如需要确定仲裁机构，则首先需要根据 UNCITRAL 仲裁规则的规定向位于海牙的国际常设仲裁院提出仲裁机构的选定事宜。

15.2.3　FIDIC 合同专用条款中未能约定仲裁地点

在某国际工程项目中，业主采用 FIDICMDB 合同条款 2010 年，其中第 20.6 款［仲裁］规定如下：

20.6　Arbitration	Any dispute between the Parties arising out of or in connection with the Contract not settled amicably in accordance with Sub-Clause 20.5 above and in respect of which the DB's decision (if any) has not become final and binding shall be finally settled by arbitration. Arbitration shall be conducted as follows: (a) if the contract is with foreign contractors, 　(1) for contracts financed by all participating Banks except under sub-paragraph (a)(2) below: international arbitration ①with proceedings administered by the arbitration institution designated in the Contract Data, and conducted under the rules of arbitration of such institution; or, if so specified in the Contract Data, ②international arbitration in accordance with the arbitration rules of the United Nations Commission on International Trade Law (UNCITRAL); or ③if neither an arbitration institution nor UNCITRAL arbitration rules are specified in the Contract Data, with proceedings administered by the International Chamber of Commerce (ICC) and conducted under the ICC Rules of Arbitration; by one or more arbitrators appointed in accordance with said arbitration rules. (b) if the Contract is with domestic contractors, arbitration with proceedings conducted in accordance with the laws of the mployer's country.

The place of arbitration shall be <u>the neutral location specified in the Contract Data</u>; and the arbitration shall be conducted in the language for communications defined in Sub-Clause

1.4 [Law and Language].

在施工过程中发生争议后，承包商发现合同条款第20.6款［仲裁］规定的仲裁地点为"合同数据规定的中立地点"，但承包商检查合同数据发现，合同数据仅规定了仲裁规则修改为国际商会仲裁规则，如下：

"Rules of arbitration：　　20.6(a)　　International Chamber of Commerce"

但上述合同数据没有明确规定具体的仲裁地点，而中立地点仅能理解为不属于业主所在地国家和承包商所在地国家，但中立地点到底是什么地点，无法从合同条款中得出结论。此时，承包商只能寻求与业主就仲裁地点达成一致。如果业主和承包商无法就仲裁地点达成一致，则只能诉请仲裁庭决定具体的仲裁地点，或者，根据某些国家的仲裁法，将仲裁地点的争议诉至法院，由法院作出仲裁地点的裁决。无疑，这将为争议当事双方带来时间金钱成本以及诉累，浪费司法资源。

15.2.4　仲裁条款中约定工程所在国仲裁法的效力

在某国际工程项目中，业主采用FIDIC合同条款1987年第4版。根据合同第67.3款［仲裁］(b)项的规定，适用巴基斯坦《1940年仲裁法》进行仲裁。虽然此项约定与国际商事仲裁约定某仲裁机构的仲裁规则大有不同，使用起来非常不方便，导致程序具有不确定性，但应视为是一项有效的仲裁约定，合同约定的仲裁条款有效。需要注意的是，此项约定可能产生没有仲裁机构负责管理仲裁程序，形成临时仲裁（ad hoc arbitration）。

根据巴基斯坦《1940年仲裁法》及其修正案，仲裁程序如下：

（1）仲裁申请，当事一方向另一方递交仲裁申请书。鉴于没有仲裁机构，仲裁申请书应向另一方递交。

（2）由当事双方各自指定一名仲裁员，首席仲裁员可由双方指定的仲裁员指定。如果双方或一方对指定仲裁员或者首席仲裁员提出异议，应向巴基斯坦有管辖权的法院提起诉讼，由巴基斯坦法院作出裁定，裁定仲裁员或首席仲裁员人选（现行法律为独任仲裁员，但根据案情，应可申请三人仲裁庭）。

（3）在双方就仲裁员、首席仲裁员达成一致的情况下，仲裁庭成立。在仲裁庭成立后，由仲裁庭主导和管理仲裁程序。

（4）仲裁庭可要求当事另一方即被申请人提交答辩状和证据。如有反请求，则应在规定的期限内提出反请求。

（5）仲裁庭制作《审理范围书》，明确争议焦点和庭审范围。

（6）仲裁庭审，由双方各自陈述和答辩，然后进入事实证人交叉盘问，在完成事实证人交叉盘问后，进行专家证人的交叉盘问，庭审结束。

（7）仲裁庭作出仲裁裁决。根据巴基斯坦《1940年仲裁法》及其第1号修正案，任何一方均可向法院提出诉讼，要求撤销仲裁庭作出的裁决。

（8）根据巴基斯坦《1940年仲裁法》及其修正案，任何一方均可对仲裁裁决提起上诉程序，最终通过上诉法院判决最终确定仲裁裁决。

15.3　仲裁机构

一般来说，大多数国家的相关组织和机构都设有各种类型的仲裁机构，有的是全国性的，有的是地区性的，有的则是专业性的仲裁机构。目前，在国际上比较有影响力的仲裁机构是：

（1）国际商会仲裁院。
（2）美国仲裁协会。
（3）中国国际经济贸易仲裁委员会。
（4）瑞典斯德哥尔摩仲裁院。
（5）伦敦国际仲裁院。
（6）新加坡国际仲裁中心。
（7）北京仲裁委员会/北京国际仲裁中心。
（8）香港国际仲裁中心。

15.4　仲裁规则

除了各个仲裁机构都制定了自己的仲裁规则外，为了统一世界各国的仲裁规则，一些国际机构也制定了仲裁规则，主要有联合国国际贸易法委员会仲裁规则（UNCITRAL Arbitration Rules）和国际商会仲裁院仲裁规则（ICC Arbitration Rules）。FIDIC 合同条款中推荐使用的是国际商会仲裁院仲裁规则，但业主和承包商也可约定使用其他机构的仲裁规则。

联合国国际贸易法委员会于 1973 年制订了供世界各国使用的仲裁规则，1976 年获联合国正式通过，并推荐给各国采用。根据该仲裁规则的规定，凡合同当事方达成书面协议采用这一规则时，他们之间发生的争议就应按照这一规则进行仲裁。

仲裁员的人数由合同当事双方事先约定。如双方未约定一名仲裁员，则应指定三名仲裁员。如指定一名仲裁员，则仲裁员的国籍应与合同当事双方的国籍不同。在指定三名仲裁员的情况下，合同当事双方指定两名仲裁员，然后由两名仲裁员指定第三名仲裁员，并由其担任首席仲裁员。

仲裁地点由合同当事双方在仲裁条款或仲裁协议中约定，如未约定，则由仲裁员根据具体情况决定仲裁地点。如合同规定了合同的准据法，则仲裁员应予适用。如合同未能规定准据法，则仲裁员可根据法律冲突原则确定合同的准据法。

在作出裁决前，如合同当事方同意和解，仲裁员可发出停止仲裁的命令，也可以裁决方式记录调解的内容。

仲裁裁决对合同当事双方具有约束力，裁决应采用书面形式，并应表明裁决理由。裁决中还应明确裁决费用。仲裁费用通常由败诉一方承担，但仲裁员也可以决定由合同当事双方分担。

15.5 仲裁程序

国际性的仲裁规则和各个仲裁机构制定的仲裁规则都规定了仲裁应该遵守的程序,这些程序基本相似,现以具有代表性国际商会仲裁院 2012 年仲裁规则为例加以说明。

15.5.1 仲裁申请

发生争议后,当事一方应根据仲裁条款或仲裁协议,向国际商会仲裁院秘书处递交仲裁申请书。秘书处收到申请之日即为仲裁程序开始的日期。秘书处在收到申请后,应将申请书副本和附件寄送给被诉人。被诉人应在收到文件后的 30 天内提出答辩。

仲裁申请书没有固定格式,但为了具有逻辑性和说服力,一份仲裁申请书应包括:

(1) 封面,表明申请人和被申请人,代理律师名称和地址。
(2) 前言,表明争议性质。
(3) 仲裁条款或仲裁协议,表明仲裁机构具有对案件的管辖权。
(4) 提交争议的主要内容。
(5) 事实。
(6) 相关的合同规定和法律规定。
(7) 申请人主张。
(8) 申请人申请任命仲裁员,如有,给出姓名和联系方式。
(9) 请求仲裁庭裁决的救济措施(Relief Sought)。
(10) 附件:证据(Exhibits)。

一般而言,仲裁申请书以说明所有事实和争议为基本要求,但也避免内容冗长、篇幅过多,这样容易使人无法把握重点。

以某国际工程仲裁为例,申请人提交的仲裁申请书(Request for Arbitration)摘录部分内容如下:

TABLE OF CONTENTS

Preamble _____
I Introduction _____
II Parties to these Counterclaims _____
III Agreement to Arbitration and Governing Law _____
IV Facts and Circumstances of Counterclaims _____
V The Claimant's Counterclaims against the Responden _____
VI Relief Sought _____

REQUEST FOR ARBITRATION

PREAMBLE

THIS REQUEST FOR ARBITRATION is put forward to the International Court of Arbitration of the International Chamber of Commerce against losses and damages suffered from the ignorance, and breach of Subcontract by the Respondent.

In this Request, _____ Co. , Ltd. , China ("Claimant") hereby requests counterclaims against _____ ("Respondent") pursuant to Article 5 (5) of Arbitration Rules of International Chamber of Commerce ("Rules"). The Claimant requests the claims on behalf of itself and in its capacity as the party of Subcontract Agreement contracted with the Respondent for _____ ("Project"). The Respondent is a sole Subcontractor employed by the Claimant for civil and installation works of the Project in _____ .

This Request arises out of a dispute over the Respondent's failure to complete the Subcontract Works within the contractual time of 780 days from 31 October 2011 to 19 December 2013 and an extended period of 4 months up to 10 April 2014. The Claimant issued the termination notice of the Subcontract on 10 April 2014, pursuant to Sub-Clause 15. 6 of General Conditions of FIDIC Subcontract 2011 Version which is applied between the Claimant and the Respondent.

This Request is put forward by the Claimant, based on the following founded facts:

(a) The Respondent is in breach of the Subcontract obligations which are established upon the founded facts and findings as described in the Counterclaims. The Respondent completed 26% of the Subcontract Works only within the contractual time and extended time period due to poor management, lack of manpower, material, machinery and equipment as well as the supporting fund. Meanwhile, the Respondent refused, before and after termination of Subcontract on 10 April 2014, to give the date of completion to _____ ("the Employer") and _____ ("the Engineer").

(b) The Respondent refused to leave the construction site until October 2014, failing to perform the obligations as set forth in Sub-Clause 15. 6 of Subcontract and Main Contract and impeding the Claimant to continue the works of the Project.

(c) The Respondent has taken several litigations in local courts as to validity of the termination notice of Subcontract, bank guarantees, place of arbitration, application for jurisdiction by the local court on the dispute, application for injunction against payments to the Claimant. The Claimant believes that these litigations are initiated by the Respondent arbitrarily in the Supreme Court and the local courts in Bangladesh, incurring not only the legal costs by the Claimant, but also the progress of the works of the Project, the cash flow to complete the Project.

(d) The Claimant has to execute, complete the Subcontract Works including civil and installation works by himself, and thus the Claimant suffers resultant loss and damage which Sub-Clause 15. 6 of Subcontract and Main Contract entitles him to claim the same.

(e) The Claimant is entitled to claim liquidated damages on delay caused by the Respondent pursuant to Sub-Clause 8. 7 of Subcontract and recover the resultant loss and damages incurred or to be incurred when the Claimant continues to execute and complete the Subcontract Works by himself pursuant to Sub-Clause 15. 6 of Subcontract.

I INTRODUCTION

1 The Main Contract titled _____ was signed between the Employer and the Contractor on 15 June 2011, through international competitive bid process. The Engineer is _____, whose Team Leader was Mr. _____ from commencement of the Main Contract Works to January 2015 and Mr. _____ has been assigned as Acting Team Leader since January 2015 up to date. The time of completion for the Main Contract is 900 days, i. e. the completion date is intended as 8 May 2014. The construction site is located in _____ The General Conditions of Main Contract is FIDIC MDB Harmonized Edition 2006.

2 The Claimant contracted with the Respondent to execute and complete civil and installation works for _____ under Subcontract No. _____ ("the Subcontract") on 31 October 2011. The Accepted Subcontract Amount excluding value added tax and income tax (equivalent to withholding tax, remarked by the Claimant) is _____ The time of completion of Subcontract Works is 780 days and the intended date for completion of Subcontract Works is determined as on 19 December 2013. The General Conditions of Subcontract is FIDIC Conditions of Subcontract for Construction 2011 Version.

3 The Subcontract Works includes all of civil works and installations of _____ as set forth in the Subcontract. The Respondent was a sole subcontractor for the Claimant.

4 As recorded in Termination Notice of Subcontract by the Claimant on 10 April 2014, the total completion percentage of the Subcontract Works, since commencement date of Subcontract Works up to 31 March 2014 (total days: 882 days), is only 26% of the Subcontract Works. It proves an undisputed and undeniable fact that the Respondent fails to perform his obligation within the Subcontract Time.

5 The statistics of the Respondent's progress in January, February and March 2014 illustrates that the Respondent has just achieved the progress of the Subcontract Works with 0.43% per month, with less input of resources on the Site. It can be concluded from these facts that the Respondent is in a weak desire and reluctant to execute the Subcontract Works and fails to perform his obligations under the Subcontract. The Respondent's failure to complete the Subcontract Works within the Subcontract Time constitutes the substantial and fundamental breach of the Subcontract.

6 The Severe delayed progress caused by the Respondent has resulted in the direct and consequential effects on the Claimant's trust and confidence by the Employer as well as the progress. The Claimant has to take over the Subcontract Works from the Respondent, execute, and complete the Subcontract Works by himself, incurring resultant costs and expenses.

7 The Claimant's construction works has been hampered by the Respondent's refusal to leave the site to allow the Claimant to execute the Subcontract Works. On the other hand, the Claimant has suffered loss and damages as a result of the Respondent's failure

to complete the Subcontract Works within the Subcontract Time since the Claimant has to execute, and complete the Subcontract Works by himself. The Claimant is entitled to recover the full measure of the loss and damage the Respondent caused pursuant to Sub-Clause 8.7 and Sub-Clause 15.6 of Subcontract.

II PARTIES TO THESE COUNTERCLAIMS

8 The Claimant is a limited liability company, registered and existing under the laws of _____, with its registered office at _____ The Business License is attached herewith for reference.

9 The Respondent is a company organized and existing under the laws of _____, with its principal office at place of business located at _____, with phone number _____

10 The Claimant is represented in this arbitral proceeding by _____ All correspondence related to this matter should be directed to the following:

_____

_____

Address: _____

III AGREEMENT TO ARBITRATION AND GOVERNING LAW

11 The arbitral jurisdiction of International Court of Arbitration of the International Chamber of Commerce is based on Sub-Clause 20.7 [*Subcontract Arbitration*] of General Conditions of Subcontract, which states:

"*Unless settled amicably, any Subcontract dispute in respect of which the Subcontract DAB's decision if any has not become final and binding shall be finally settled under the Rules of Arbitration of the International Chamber of Commerce and Main Contract Sub-Clause* 20.6 [*Arbitration*] *shall apply.*

12 Sub-Clause 20.7 of Subcontract introduces Main Contract *Sub*-Clause 20.6 to be applied, which Sub-Clause 20.6 [*Arbitration*] of Main Contract states:

"*Unless indicated otherwise in the Particular Conditions, any dispute not settled amicably and in respect of which the DB's decision (if any) has not become final and binding shall be finally settled by arbitration. Unless otherwise agreed by both Parties:*

(a) For contracts with foreign contractors, international arbitration with proceedings administered by the institution appointed in the Contract Data, conducted in accordance with the rules of arbitration of the appointed institution, if any, or in accordance with UNCITRAL arbitration rules, at the choice of the appointed institution;

(b) The place of arbitration shall be the city where the headquarters of the appointed arbitration institution is located;

(c) The arbitration shall be conducted in the language for communications defined

in Sub-Clause 1. 4 [Law and Language], and
(d) For contracts with domestic contractors, arbitration with proceedings conducted in accordance with the laws of the Employer's country.
   ..."

13　Clause 15 of Memorandum on Contract Negotiation for Contract No. KWSP-C-1 under the Main Contract states:
"*It is agreed by the Parties that the arbitration set forth in Sub-Clause* 20. 6 *of the General Conditions shall be under the rules of the arbitration of the International Chamber of Commerce in Paris* ".

14　These clauses such as Sub-Clause 20. 7 of Subcontract, Sub-Clause 20. 6 of Main Contract and Clause 15 of Memorandum on Contract Negotiation for Contract No. ··· under Main Contract provide expressly that:
" Any Subcontract dispute···shall be finally settled under the Rules of Arbitration of the International Chamber of Commerce ", and that " *the place of arbitration shall be the city where the headquarters of the appointed arbitration institution is located,*" and that "It is agreed by the Parties that the arbitration set forth in Sub-Clause 20. 6 *of the General Conditions shall be under the rules of the arbitration of the International Chamber of Commerce in Paris* ".

15　Therefore, the place of arbitration shall be in Paris, France as set forth in Sub-Clause 20. 6 (b) of Main Contract and Clause 15 of Memorandum on Contract Negotiation for Contract No. KWSP-C-1.

16　The governing law is provided in Sub-Clause 1. 8 of General Conditions of Subcontract, which states:
" *The law of the country (or other jurisdiction) which governs the Main Contract shall govern the Subcontract.* "

17　Part A-Subcontract Data of Particular Conditions of Subcontract provides:
" *Governing Law* 1. 8 ＿＿＿＿＿＿＿＿＿＿ "

18　The ruling language of the Subcontract is ascertained as English pursuant to Sub-Clause 1. 8 of General Conditions of Subcontract and Part A-Subcontract Data of Particular Conditions of Subcontract. Thus, the Claimant submits that the arbitration should be conducted in English as established in Sub-Clause 1. 8 of General Conditions of Subcontract and Part A—Subcontract Data of Particular Conditions of Subcontract.
...

被申请人有权对仲裁申请提出答辩意见（answer，reply，rejoinder），但是，如果被申请人没有提出答辩意见，不影响被申请人权利和案件的审理。

被申请人也可以提出反请求，此时，被申请人应递交反请求申请书，并提供证据。需要注意是，如果仅是对申请人提出请求的回应，例如，申请人主张应付100万元，而被申请人主张仅欠付80万元时，被申请人的主张不是反请求，而是对申请人请求的抗辩。在国际工程争议中，在申请人提出索赔 100 万元，而被申请人认为申请人工程延误应支付工期延误违约金时，被申请人索赔工期延误违约金构成反请求。或者，申请人提出被申请人提出的终止合同通知无效，而被申请人认为终止合同通知有效，此时，被申请人不应提出反请求，要求仲裁庭裁决终止合同通知有效，被申请人对申请人的请求提出抗辩即可。

15.5.2　组成仲裁庭

如仲裁庭由三人组成，则合同当事双方应各指定一名仲裁员，首席仲裁员由仲裁院指定。如是一人仲裁员，合同当事方可协商提名，并报仲裁院确认。

在仲裁案件争议金额低于某一额度时，根据仲裁规则，可以采用独任仲裁员审理仲裁案件。国际商会 2017 年仲裁规则设定的争议金额低于 200 万美元的仲裁案件，采用独任仲裁员审理仲裁案件。中国国际经济贸易仲裁委员会 2015 年仲裁规则规定低于 500 万人民币的争议，采用独任仲裁员审理仲裁案件，适用简易程序。但是，合同约定争议采用独任仲裁员时，无论争议金额大小，均应采用独任仲裁员审理仲裁案件。

在仲裁案件中，争议当事双方可以对仲裁员，包括首席仲裁员提出回避要求，回避要求应按照仲裁规则列明的事项提出。因此，争议当事双方应根据仲裁规则的有关规定，在规定的时间内提出回避要求。一般而言，在存在利益冲突的情况下，仲裁员应予回避。

15.5.3　审理范围书

仲裁庭在审理开始时，应起草"审理范围书"（Term of Reference，TOR）文件，并制定审理日程表。需要注意的是，在实践中，仲裁庭编制的审理范围书应得到仲裁院的审核和批准。一般而言，仲裁院不允许在实体审理过程中将程序问题带入，需要在庭审之前解决仲裁程序问题。在确认合同当事人已经交纳预付仲裁费后，仲裁庭开始审理案件。

一般而言，审理范围书应包括：

（1）当事人及其代理（The Parties and Their Representatives）。
（2）仲裁庭（The Arbitral Tribunal）。
（3）程序事项（Procedural Matters）。
（4）通知和联络（Notification and Communicationa）。
（5）当事人索赔和救济总结（Summary of the Parties Claims and Relief Sought）。
（6）争议焦点清单（List of Issues to Be Determined）。
（7）IBA 证据规则（IBA Rules on the Taking Evidence）。
（8）保密（Confidentiality）。
（9）责任和保证除外事项（Exclusion of Lability and Indemnity）。

在国际商会仲裁案件中，审理范围书是仲裁庭在庭审之前必须完成的一项工作，且需要由争议当事双方签字。在中国国际经济贸易仲裁委员会仲裁程序中，仲裁规则没有规定仲裁庭需要出具审理范围书，在国内仲裁案件中，不需要仲裁庭准备审理事项文件，但在国际仲裁案件中，仲裁庭均应被要求出具审理事项，以便指导仲裁庭审理仲裁案件。

15.5.4　仲裁庭审

在确定了庭审（hearing）日期之后，仲裁庭可以开始庭审。

在中国企业之间，中国的仲裁机构仲裁时，在仲裁案采用普通程序审理时，通常的审理程序如下：

（1）庭前评议，由三名仲裁员在开庭前一个小时进行评议，争取就案件审理思路和注意事项达成一致。

（2）开庭的程序审查包括：审核出庭人员签到表，核实当事方及其参加庭审人员的基本情况，核实当事方名称与营业执照，处理当事方主体变更情况，审核是否有特别授权，要求旁听人员出示身份证，征求对方是否同意旁听，交代旁听纪律，注意是否有缺席审理的情况和按照仲裁规则进行处理。

（3）介绍仲裁庭组成人员，询问对组成仲裁庭程序是否有异议，对仲裁庭组成人员是否申请回避。

（4）询问当事方对仲裁协议效力和仲裁庭管辖权的意见。

（5）核实材料递交情况。

（6）询问当事人对已经进行的仲裁程序是否有异议。

（7）询问当事人对自己权利和义务是否清楚，并告知庭审纪律。

庭审顺序：实体审理。

（1）当事方陈述和被申请人陈述反请求，双方答辩。仲裁庭需要注意请求、事实和理由的一致性。仲裁庭需要注意答辩书是否存在反请求事项。

（2）举证和质证阶段，对证据的真实性、关联性和合法性发表意见。

（3）庭审调查阶段，对本案的争议焦点进行调查，要求申请人和被申请人提出支持其主张的事实和证据，并确认无争议的事实。

（4）庭审辩论阶段：本案将就争议焦点问题进行辩论。

（5）调解阶段：询问申请人和被申请人调解意向，明确本案的调解条件。

（6）对后续程序的安排：询问是否有补充证据，要求在庭审7日内提交书面代理词。

（7）最后陈述：要求申请人和被申请人发表明确意见。

（8）宣布开庭结束。

仲裁员在庭审和评议时应本着"辨别事实，识别证据证明力，确定验证标准"发表意见，而不应以是否为当事一方聘任的仲裁员，或者对当事一方是否有利为标准发表意见。这是因为：

（1）虽然仲裁员多是当事方聘请的，但仲裁员不是任何一方当事方聘请的代理人，而是根据当事方选定的仲裁规则聘任的解决当事方争议的公正的第三方，应本着公平和公正原则处理当事方之间产生的争议或分歧。

（2）在庭审和评议过程中，仲裁员不应表现出倾向任何一方的看法或意见，另一方当事方可能会因此提出异议。

（3）仲裁规则和仲裁员守则要求仲裁员不应在庭审和评议中表现出倾向当事一方的意见。

仲裁员在庭审和评议过程中应遵守仲裁规则和仲裁员守则，客观、公正，以事实为依据，明辨证据证明力，作出公正的判断和裁决。

国际商会仲裁庭的庭审与国内企业之间的国内仲裁存在较大区别。一般而言，国际商会仲裁院的庭审分为三个阶段进行：

（1）开庭陈述（opening submission）。根据程序安排，每方可以使用两个小时进行陈述，或者根据案情，减少或增加争议当事双方的开庭陈述时间。

（2）事实证人的交叉盘问（cross-examination）。首先由申请人的证人出庭作证，由被申请人的代理律师进行盘问，核实事实。然后由被申请人的证人出庭作证，由申请人代理律师进行盘问。在国际商会仲裁案件中，证人交叉盘问是庭审的主要环节，在双方各有三个证人出庭时，交叉盘问时间可能达到3.5天或4天左右。

必须指出，对于中国承包商或者中国其他企业而言，在国际仲裁案件中，应事先对中国企业的证人进行作证培训，包括衣着、行为举止、如何回答问题、在使用中文翻译时如何与翻译配合等。中国企业的证人常出现的问题是不知道如何回答问题，或者长篇大论、大讲道理，或者缺乏耐心、不屑回答问题等。这些行为都必须在庭审中予以改正。国际仲裁证人作证的黄金原则：一是讲事实，二是回答问题简短和简明。牢记这两项准则，就可以在国际仲裁庭审中从容面对。

（3）专家证人作证。在国际工程争议中，专家证人主要作证的内容是工期延长的计算和判断，还有工程量和估价的鉴定。在国际仲裁中，申请人需要聘请一位专家证人，被申请人也需要自己聘请一位专家证人。专家证人之间需要沟通，在庭审之前递交双方达成协议的清单，称为：Scott Schedule（斯考特清单）。在斯考特清单中，双方聘请的专家证人应就清单中的每项争议达成协议。如果专家证人之间不能达成一致，则应在专家证人出庭作证时说明为什么不能达成一致，然后由仲裁庭作出判断。

在中国国内的仲裁中，当事双方对工程造价存在争议如要求鉴定时，应向仲裁庭提出书面申请。由仲裁庭决定是否进行工程造价鉴定，聘请有资质的工程造价鉴定公司作出鉴定报告，作为证据供仲裁庭使用。当事双方可以在开庭时或庭后对鉴定报告提出意见。对于工期延误的鉴定，目前中国没有此类资质的鉴定公司从事工期延误鉴定工作。因此，需要争议当事方自己聘请咨询公司进行工期延误鉴定，然后，咨询公司作为专家证人出庭作证，说明工期延误鉴定的有关事宜和结论，供仲裁庭采信。

15.5.5　作出仲裁裁决

根据国际商会2012年仲裁规则，在合同当事方签署"审理事项"文件后的6个月内，仲裁庭应作出仲裁裁决。秘书处应向合同当事双方宣告裁决文本。

需要指出，在仲裁庭作出裁决时，裁决不能超出仲裁请求要求作出裁决的范围，即不能超裁，否则，裁决无效，并有可能被当事方要求撤销。

15.5.6　仲裁裁决的执行

与法院判决的执行不同，由于仲裁机构属于民间组织，如果败诉一方拒不执行裁决，仲裁机构就无能为力，只能由胜诉一方向有关法院提出申请，要求法院强制执行。为了解决各国在承认和执行外国仲裁裁决上存在的分歧，国际上作出了积极的努力，在联合国的主持下，1958年在纽约缔结了《关于承认和执行外国仲裁裁决的公约》，简称《纽约公约》。目前，已有130多个国家加入了《纽约公约》，使得承认和执行外国仲裁裁决有了国际公约的支持，扫清了外国仲裁裁决执行的障碍。

《纽约公约》的主要规定如下：

（1）公约规定，缔约国应该相互承认和执行对方国家作出的仲裁裁决。

（2）公约规定，申请承认和执行裁决的一方当事人应提供经过适当证明的裁决的正本或副本。

（3）公约详细规定了拒绝承认和执行外国仲裁裁决的条件。

（4）公约允许各缔约国在参加该公约时可以发表声明，提出若干保留条件。

目前，在承认和执行外国仲裁裁决的公约时，各国均根据该公约承认和执行有关的外国仲裁裁决。在国际承包工程项目中，业主、承包商和分包商可以选择仲裁方式解决争议，而不必纠结于仲裁裁决的执行问题。

《纽约公约》第5条对执行外国仲裁裁决义务作出了例外的规定，如下：

在第1项中：

（a）第二条所称协定之当事人依对其适用之法律有某种无行为能力情形者，或该项协定依当事人作为协定准据之法律系属无效时，或未指明以何法律为准时，依裁决地所在国法律系属无效者；

（b）受裁决援用之一未接获关于指派仲裁员或仲裁程序之适当通知，或因他故，致未能申辩者；

（c）裁决所处理之争议非为交付仲裁之标的或不在其条款之列，或裁决载有关于交付仲裁范围以外事项之决定者，但交付仲裁事项之决定可与未交付仲裁之事项划分时，裁决中关于交付仲裁事项之决定部分得予承认及执行；

（d）仲裁机关之组成或仲裁程序与各国间之协议不符，或无协议而与仲裁地所在国法律不符者；

（e）裁决对各国尚无拘束力，或业经裁决地所在国或裁决所依据法律之国家之主管机关撤销或停止执行者。

在第2项中：

（a）依该国法律，争议事项系不能以仲裁解决者；

（b）承认或执行裁决有违该国公共政策者。

许多机构的仲裁规定都特别允许任何当事一方可以向法院提出临时救济决定。在没有该项条款时，当事方可以向仲裁员或仲裁庭申请采取救济措施。根据《纽约公约》，这些临时性的决定可在法院予以执行，但延误任命仲裁员，然后再获得临时救济决定将会导致当事方无法获得临时救济决定。

参 考 文 献

[1] 崔军. FIDIC 合同原理与实务 [M]. 北京：机械工业出版社，2011.

[2] 崔军. FIDIC 分包合同原理与实务 [M]. 2 版. 北京：机械工业出版社，2018.

[3] Furst S. Hudson's on Building and Engineering Contracts [M]. 13th Edition. London：Sweet & Maxwell,2015.

[4] Dennys N. Keating on Construction Contracts [M]. 8th Edition. London：Sweet & Maxwell,2006.

[5] Beale H. G. Chitty on Contracts [M]. 30th Edition. 北京：商务印书馆，2012.

[6] Bryan A. Garner. Legal Writing in Plain English [M]. Second Edition. Chicago：the University of Chicago Press,2013.

[7] Goodman A. Effective Written Advocacy [M]. Second Edition. London：Wildy, Simmons & Hill Publishing,2012.

[8] Rose W. Pleading Without Tears [M]. Oxford：Oxford University Press,2017.

[9] 托特蒂尔. FIDIC 用户指南 [M]. 崔军，译. 北京：机械工业出版社，2009.